Confronting
Child and Adolescent
Sexual

For Jamie who was with me throughout,
ever believing in his Mom.

Confronting
Child and Adolescent
Sexual Abuse

Cynthia Crosson-Tower

Professor Emerita
Fitchburg State University

Los Angeles | London | New Delhi
Singapore | Washington DC

Los Angeles | London | New Delhi
Singapore | Washington DC

FOR INFORMATION:

SAGE Publications, Inc.
2455 Teller Road
Thousand Oaks, California 91320
E-mail: order@sagepub.com

SAGE Publications Ltd.
1 Oliver's Yard
55 City Road
London, EC1Y 1SP
United Kingdom

SAGE Publications India Pvt. Ltd.
B 1/I 1 Mohan Cooperative Industrial Area
Mathura Road, New Delhi 110 044
India

SAGE Publications Asia-Pacific Pte. Ltd.
3 Church Street
#10-04 Samsung Hub
Singapore 048763

Printed in the United States of America

Library of Congress Cataloging-in-Publication Data

Crosson-Tower, Cynthia.
Confronting child and adolescent sexual abuse / Cynthia Crosson-Tower.

pages cm

Includes bibliographical references and index.
ISBN 978-1-4833-3311-3 (alk. paper)

1. Child sexual abuse. 2. Sexually abused children—Rehabilitation. I. Title.
HV6570.C756 2015

362.76—dc23

2013038717

This book is printed on acid-free paper.

Acquisitions Editor: Kassie Graves
Editorial Assistant: Elizabeth Luizzi
Production Editor: Jane Haenel
Copy Editor: Beth Hammond
Typesetter: Hurix Systems Pvt. Ltd.
Proofreader: Laura Webb
Indexer: Kathy Paparchontis
Cover Designer: Candice Harman
Marketing Manager: Shari Countryman

14 15 16 17 18 10 9 8 7 6 5 4 3 2 1

BRIEF CONTENTS

DETAILED CONTENTS

▶ # PART II

Victims, Perpetrators, and Nonoffending Parents   63

► PART III

Intervention 193

11. Initial Intervention in Child Sexual Abuse 195

12. Assessment and Treatment Planning for Children and Family Members 213

PREFACE

I didn't know what children did with their fathers. Mine told me that his nightly trips to my room for what he called "goodnight loves" were what every girl did with her father. I didn't want his groping touch, his hot breath that reeked of garlic and sometimes booze. I didn't want to keep those things that we did from my mother or brother. No, I didn't want to have my father tell me that I was special because I let him touch me. Let him? I didn't know that I had a choice. I just wanted him to protect me. I just wanted to be loved.

* * *

I wanted to live with you. You were such a good teacher, and I was sure that your home was happy and that I could be happy there. I knew that in your house I would not have to listen to my father and mother scream at each other or endure my father's whispers as he told me about their fights and caressed me. But after we had a program about abuse in your class, I learned that what my father and I did under the covers at night was wrong. I felt dirty and alone. I knew that it must be my fault. I knew then that I couldn't be like the other children. I had just wanted you to think I was special.

* * *

I thought that you were God when you stood up there on Sunday morning. Everyone spoke of you with such reverence. My parents told me that I must always be respectful. When you began to take an interest in me, I was overjoyed. When you asked me to join the youth program and began to give me special treats, I thought that I was so special. When you began to "counsel me" alone in your office, I loved the special attention. I told you all about what my father had done, and you comforted me. I didn't ask for you to fondle me. I believed you when you said that if I told anyone, I would go to hell. I didn't want that. I just wanted to feel comforted.

* * *

You really seemed to understand when I first saw you. You told me that you knew what my father had done to me. I wanted to tell you about our priest too, but I was too ashamed and didn't want to go to hell.

We hear the lament of abused children in many ways. We are not always aware of what we have heard, but their cries linger in the air—the cries of the children who just want to be loved, to feel special, to feel comforted. There are the constant echoes of the children who are ashamed of what they perceive were their wrongdoing and who are frightened that, because of it, some terrible ill will befall them. We must learn to listen to these children and protect others from the abuse that will add their voices to the echoes.

Every year, thousands of children are sexually abused by parents, caretakers, acquaintances, and strangers. The recent crisis in the Roman Catholic Church brought to our attention that even the most trusted in our society may be sexual offenders. Each time I teach a class in child sexual abuse, parents in the classes beg for answers about how to protect their children from sexual abuse. Survivors recount their stories, and we wonder where the abuse will end.

When I spoke at and attended conferences on child maltreatment in the 1980s, there was just a smattering of books addressing various aspects of child sexual abuse. In fact, the first books that raised this type of maltreatment as a current problem were not written until 1979. Today, when I attend conferences seeking to discover what is new on the subject, I find that the writings have multiplied from very few to so many that the space on my bookshelf or limitations of my pocketbook will not allow me to purchase them all. They address every aspect of the phenomenon of child sexual abuse possible. These writings alert us to the fact that over several decades, we have been painfully aware of child sexual abuse, have trained professionals in how to intervene, have established treatment programs, have instituted prevention programs, and have attempted to raise the consciousness of the general public. And although some experts report that the rate of child sexual abuse has diminished, it remains a national problem.

As I wrote this text striving to highlight the information that we have learned about sexual abuse, I found that much of our knowledge was based upon theories postulated years earlier. Therefore, many of the references outlining the important aspects of child sexual abuse appear to be several decades old. Only as new crises arose did the literature begin to reflect our renewed search for understanding. For example, the crisis of abuse by clergy gave rise to a myriad of texts that made a sincere attempt to analyze the culture of the Catholic Church (see specifically Cozzens, 2002; Crosson-Tower, 2014; Frawley-O'Dea, 2007; Hidalgo, 2007; Jenkins, 2001b; Sperry, 2003) as a way of explaining why priests and other clergy have been found to be abusive.

My search for the most current books in the area took me to British, Canadian, and Australian publications and helped me to recognize that Britain and much of Europe and Australia are in the throes of what the United States experienced in the 1980s and 1990s. In those parts of the world, sexual abuse is now a source of much concern and an increasingly researched problem. Although some of our classic writings on child sexual abuse are now a decade or two old, writers from Britain and Europe are taking a fresh look at this subject. I have made use of the writings from these countries when possible and applicable.

As I continue to teach about child sexual abuse to psychology, social work, and divinity students, as well as to practicing educators and clergy, and as I survey the voluminous writings on all different aspects of child sexual abuse from both the United States, Canada, and abroad, I feel the need for a comprehensive text that will begin the student on his or her journey toward understanding this societal problem. Yet I begin this book with some sadness. It is sad that such a text is necessary. But until we strive to understand the complexity of child sexual abuse, we cannot hope to stem the tide. We should not need another book addressing this heart-wrenching problem.

But the fact is that we do. And we also need to train future professionals so that they will understand how to deal with the victim, the perpetrator, the nonoffending parent, the systems that seek to intervene, and the society that provides the backdrop for the sexual abuse of children. And it is also my intent, through this book, to help the student gain an affective perspective as well as a cognitive one. Child sexual abuse is so far out of the frame of reference for most of us that learning about it can have a profound emotional impact. For those who have had personal experience with abuse, different issues arise, making the study of this type of maltreatment an emotional as well as an intellectual endeavor.

THE DESIGN OF THE BOOK

It is with all of the preceding discussion in mind that I sought to draw from the magnitude of writings available on the subject today and present a comprehensive overview of the subject of child sexual abuse. As I wrote this book, I asked myself the question that so many are asking today: How do we confront child sexual abuse? How can we protect our children? The answer lies deep within our culture. To fully understand how we must protect children from sexual abuse in the future, we must consider the past as well as the present. We must understand not only the concept of sexual maltreatment but probe the psychology of the abuser, the victim, and those who appear to be bystanders. We must dissect the complex network of helping to explore how we can improve the services to children and their families. Only by fully understanding can we hope to improve the way in which we protect children from sexual abuse.

This book is designed to give the reader an overview of child sexual abuse from the historical beginnings of our knowledge of the problem to delving into the personalities of those who are affected, both directly and indirectly, by abuse. And we will explore the existing services that are offered to abused children and their families.

Chapter 1 looks at child sexual abuse historically as it came to the attention of professionals and mandated that we determine ways to intervene. Chapter 2 discusses the definition and dynamics of child sexual abuse. Chapter 3 identifies some of the models that have developed to explain sexual abuse and sexual offending. These models are continuously evolving, and an introductory knowledge is crucial to understanding the field and its changes. The victimology of child sexual abuse is the subject of Chapter 4, including how abuse affects the victim's development and what types of symptoms a victim might exhibit. Chapter 5 looks at the offender against children and why someone might want to sexually abuse children. Chapter 6 delves more deeply into intrafamilial abuse or incest, looking at not only the offender but how the victims and nonoffending parents are influenced by him or her.

Child sexual abuse outside the family is considered in more detail in Chapter 7, exploring how pornography and the Internet influence sexual offending as well as child prostitution. It is not only adults who commit sexually abusive acts against children. Chapter 8 discusses how children and teens may act out sexually against other young people. Chapter 9 addresses how offenders against children may be those in such respected roles as educators, day care providers, and therapists, whereas Chapter 10 looks more closely at sexual abuse by clergy.

Chapter 11 looks at initial intervention into child sexual abuse by the helping systems and the roles of the various helpers involved. Chapter 12 progresses to the next steps of intervention, those of assessment of and treatment planning for abused children and their nonabusive family members. The treatment of victims and families is spelled out in Chapter 13, whereas the treatment of sexual offenders is the subject of Chapter

14. Chapter 15 addresses the treatment of adult survivors of child sexual abuse.

And finally, the book concludes with a look at what it might be like to work in the field of child sexual abuse by considering the individual worker's perspective and some thoughts about agencies (see Chapter 16) and an overview of prevention (see Chapter 17). Review questions at the end of each chapter aid you, the student, in assessing what you have learned and in preparing for tests and exams.

Any text on child sexual abuse should include a note of caution to the reader. Some sections of the book are particularly graphic—a necessity in seeking to explain this phenomenon.

At the same time, I am well aware that some readers will have personal experience with sexual abuse and may find this material particularly disturbing. It is important to monitor your own feelings and perceptions, taking time away from the material to process. If the subject matter triggers memories or becomes too disturbing, it is important to talk with someone about your concerns. Or it may be wise to seek professional counseling as a form of self-care.

It is my hope that, by the completion of this book, you, the reader, will be ready to consider how we might more effectively protect children from sexual abuse. It is also my hope that you will want to take up the challenge and be part of the solution.

ACKNOWLEDGMENTS

This book has been a long time coming, and there are many who have helped me along that journey. Thanks go to my family for putting up with me while I was in writing mode and not always available. Special thanks to my son, Chay, for his assistance in some of the editing, and to my friends and colleagues Stephanie Flynn and Pat Quinlin for cheering me on when it was much needed. And I am especially grateful to my dear friend Tony Rizzuto for his consultation and support. Thanks to my research assistant, Peggy Prasinos, who, despite her own illness, was always there to help. I would also like to extend a special thank you to Jeanne Braham who, through her editorial assistance and friendship, helped to bring this project to fruition. And I cannot express how appreciative I am to my editor Kassie Graves and the staff at SAGE who were enthusiastic about a book that needed to be published.

We would also like to thank the reviewers of this text:

Annalease M. Gibson, Albany State University

Barbara J. Nowak, Albany State University

Beth Walker, Western New Mexico University

Ed FitzGerald, Indiana University East

Katya V. Shkurkin, Saint Martin's University

Kimberley L. Wacaster, Idaho State University

Kniesha Primes, Clark Atlanta University

Nancy DeCesare, Chestnut Hill College

Yan Dominic Searcy, Chicago State University

PART I

Overview of Child Sexual Abuse

CHAPTER 1

Yesterday and Today

The History of Sexual Exploitation and Intervention as a Backdrop for Today's Understanding

I t is a lovely warm summer day at the playground. You watch the children laughing and running; their joy seems infectious. Just watching these happy children, you feel relaxed, hopeful, and carefree. If you were told that one in three of those adorable little girls and one in five, or possibly more, of the boys would be sexually abused or at least approached prior to her or his 18th birthday, you might suddenly find that your mood had changed dramatically. It is difficult to imagine as one watches children how anyone could want to do them harm, especially sexually. And yet, somewhere, possibly not far away, is someone who will at some time molest a child. A sobering thought. But why would an adult want to become sexually involved with a child?

To fully understand the dynamics of sexual abuse today, it is necessary to look at the phenomenon as our awareness of it first emerged and to trace our knowledge of abuse up until the present.

CHILDREN AND SEXUALITY IN EARLY HISTORY _____

Our perception of children and childhood has changed significantly over the last few centuries. In fact, there was no such state as "childhood" prior to the 20th century. Instead, people who were young in age and small in stature were seen as inferior and treated as property (Colon, 2001; Hilarski, 2008b).

The Fate of Little Girls

In ancient times, children were seen as the property of their fathers. Disrespect of one's father could result in dismemberment or even death. In early Greece, it was considered to be medically necessary for female children to engage in sexual intercourse at the commencement of menarche. The rationale for this practice was that the medical community at that time believed that the blood could not leave the body unless the hymen had been broken. If the menstrual blood was denied an egress, it would then accumulate around the heart of the virgin and threaten her life. A young female who experienced symptoms like bloating (supposedly from the buildup of toxic fluid) or madness (the result of the toxicity) could be cured by intercourse and marriage. It therefore became the duty of males to have sex with female children, the younger the better (Demand, 2004; Hilarski, 2008b).

In early Roman culture, marrying a close relative was not only legal but encouraged in order to preserve class structure. It was, in fact, illegal to marry outside of one's class or ancestry. Early Greeks too saw the preservation of their Hellenistic ancestry more important than incest laws (Colon, 2001; Hilarski, 2008b). Colon (2001) quotes an ancient wedding invitation that reads "Herais invites you to the marriage of her children, at home, the 5th, starting at the ninth hour" (p. 95).

Throughout early history, in many cultures, female children were betrothed to the men of their father's choosing. The legal age for marriage for young women was 12, whereas their male counterparts could not marry until 14 (Colon, 2001; Hilarski, 2008b; Rush, 1996). The fact that females were used as barter made them valuable, and it was not uncommon for girls to be married at a very early age. In some cases, betrothal was expected to be sealed by intercourse. The transaction was considered to be a business arrangement, and men were urged to examine their acquisition carefully as one would a horse or any other purchased beast (Hilarski, 2008b; Rush, 1996). In addition, it was often the custom to prepare young girls for marriage by breaking the hymen, an act that was no doubt for the child.

Dowries, the payment of money or goods by the girl's father, were often an additional benefit of marriage. But when a girl's father could not afford such a fee, she might be compelled to enter a convent. Such a future could be determined by her sixth birthday, and she would then live her days in the confinement of the convent. One assumes that this would also protect her from unwanted sexual duties. However, at the beginning of the 18th century, it became apparent that such girls were being used as "wives" by the monks. Their discretion on this matter was assured by the fact that the girls were threatened with excommunication if they were to resist or tell (Rush, 1996).

By the Victorian Era, attraction to female children had developed in adult men. The modern reader might find the seductive tone of William Blakes's poem "The Traveler" to be unsettling given today's standards.

The honey of her infant lips
The bread and wine of her sweet smile
The wild Game of her roving eye
Does him to Infancy beguile.

The result of the "cult of the little girl" was that, while adult women sought peace from their husbands' sexual attentions through protesting about their modesty, little girls became targets for prostitution, molestation, rape, and pornography. The stories of several well-known men of the time who preferred the company of young girls exemplify society's preoccupation with the image of the nubile nymphet. At 27, William Wordsworth became enamored of a 12-year-old girl whom he courted until she was 15, at which time, he proposed marriage. Her refusal did not appear to daunt him from his pursuit of underage love objects. But when the age of consent in England was raised from 13 to 16, he apparently concluded that his choices would remain within the legal limits (Rush, 1996).

Edgar Allen Poe's marriage to his 13-year-old cousin, Virginia, apparently did not blemish his career. And Charles Dickens left his wife and children to take up with an 18-year-old mistress. Although his choice was well within the confines of adulthood by the definition of the times, the 27 year age difference between the two lovers gave some pause (Rush, 1996). Interestingly enough, Dickens would later become known not only for his books lamenting the fate of children but also for his efforts to protect them from abuse.

Some biographers of Lewis Carroll feel that his interest in very young girls was far from innocent. This author reportedly sought out young girls to photograph and spend time with. Because his preference was to photograph his models nude, his practices were met with some questions. Florence Rush (1996), in her *The Best Kept Secret*, writes that Carroll argued that his propensity to choose young female friends did not categorize him as a child molester as some contended. Some might counter that, in today's cautious social climate, Carroll's preference for play with his child friends at their own level would cause concern.

In seeming contradiction to the stiff climate of the Victorian Era, child prostitution was very much available for men who were looking for a way to act out their fantasies about nubile young girls. Even into the 19th century, slave owners in the Southern regions of the United States found pleasure with the female children of their slaves. These girls, who might be as young as 11, 12, or 13, often produced offspring that could be sold or serve to increase the property of free labor for their masters (Colon, 2001; Hilarski, 2008b; Olafson, Corwin, & Summit, 1993; Rush, 1996).

One cannot conclude that the sexual abuse of children is an old phenomenon because the aforementioned use of girls and the sexual attentions to their male counterparts were not considered to be abusive. How could one be abusive to someone who has no rights? Thus, not only is the concept of childhood new but the definition of sexual abuse is relatively recent as well (Bolen, 2007).

A Little Boy's Lot

Boys fared better in some ways but were nonetheless used sexually in early times. Pederasty (the sexual use of boys by adult men) was especially common in early Greece. Boys were chosen for their vibrant beauty and their "bloom of youth," two concepts that the Greeks found to be synonymous. Young boys would be initiated into sexuality by mature males who hoped also to prepare them to be soldiers. Given our current ideas of masculinity, this connection seems incongruous, but the poetry of the day gives the image seen by men at that time:

In a young man all is beautiful when he possesses
The shining flower of youth
Alive he is adored by men and desired by women
And the finest to look at when he falls
In a forward clash

—Barnstone, 1972, p. 40,
as cited in Rush, 1996, p. 49

Because the Greeks needed a strong army and a healthy supply of young men to fight, militarism and pederasty were suited for one another. The close relationship of the pederast and his boy provided an excellent mentorship to train soldiers according to strict governmental standards. Thus, young boys from noble families found themselves required to acquiesce to an adult lover for training in both sexuality and soldiering (Hilarski, 2008b; Rush, 1996; Verstraete, 2004).

Unlike the Greeks, the Romans felt that sex was a way of humiliating rather than elevating inferiors. Mutilation of the genitals and castration were seen as particularly degrading forms of torture or retribution (Rush, 1996). Pederasty is documented again in Italy during the 15th and 16th centuries among such figures as Leonardo da Vinci and Michelangelo (Colon, 2001). The Roman Catholic Church attempted to suppress this behavior, described as sodomy, and some sources indicate that the guilty and the youth who were seen as "coconspirators" (the legal age of consent varied from 6 to 10 years) may have been subjected to flogging, torture, or even being burned at the stake (Hilarski, 2008b). It was not until 1548 that boys were afforded any type of protection from being sexually used. In that year, England passed a law protecting boys from being forced into sodomy (Conte & Shore, 1982).

Incest and Its Prohibition

The word *incest* refers to sexual relationships between family members. DeMause (1991) points out that, since ancient times, every culture has had a prohibition against incest. These prohibitions have been, on a society-wide basis, largely effective, and therefore the breaking of this taboo becomes societally unacceptable. The origin of this taboo is much debated in anthropological literature. Meiselman (1992) examined this literature and cited several explanations for the original taboo. Morgan, a nineteenth century theorist (Meiselman, 1992) traced the incest taboo to the fear that inbreeding among immediate family members might create deformed or damaged offspring. Westermark (Meiselman, 1992) supported this view and compared these results of inbreeding to the animal kingdom. Other theorists argued against this theory of inferior offspring. Some suggested that there had been no attempt to look at the original gene donors who might themselves have had defects. Thus, the original defects might have been strengthened by inbreeding, although the converse, combing closely related genes with superior characteristics, could also be true. Geneticists also pointed out that recessive genes would be more likely to combine when the two parents had similar gene pools, thus bringing out characteristics that might not be observable in either parent. Some of these recessive genes could produce beneficial characteristics.

Other researchers pointed out that primitive people would probably not have had the sophistication to recognize that inbreeding could combine unwanted genes and thus be deleterious to offspring. Further, animals may breed between mothers and sons and fathers and daughters as well as siblings, yet species do not die out due to defective offspring. Thus, these biological explanations ceased to be popular (deMause, 1991; Meiselman, 1992).

In 1922, Westermarck (as cited in Meiselman, 1992), although originally a proponent of the biological explanation for the incest taboo, also postulated that a natural aversion to sexual expression developed between people who lived together from childhood. He then suggested that, because it is families that raise these individuals in close proximity, there evolves a taboo against incest or sexual expression within the immediate family. Later in 1962, Fox pointed out that societies in which sexual expression between siblings is not prohibited still give rise to sexual aversion that is embodied in the incest taboo. Using the Israeli kibbutz, Fox also pointed out that brothers and sisters need not be related by blood to develop an aversion as children brought up in the kibbutz rarely sought out sex partners among those raised with them (Fox, 1980; Meiselman, 1992).

Critics of the aversion theories argued that there would be no need of a taboo if aversion naturally occurred. And yet most cultures have some manner of actively enforcing the incest taboo, from censor and shunning to prosecution (Meiselman, 1992).

Freud disagreed with both the biological and aversion theories and in his text *Totem and Taboo* (1946) came up with another explanation. He suggested that early humans existed in hordes that were controlled by a tyrannical father who kept all the females to himself and drove out all male children. When they revolted and, overtaking the father, cannibalized him, their resulting remorse and grief caused them to create a taboo against the women in the family. Critics decided that Freud had lost his senses, and the father of modern psychology eventually became dissatisfied with this largely allegorical explanation (Durkheim, 1963; Meiselman, 1992).

Malinowski (1927) proposed that incest would be disruptive to family relationships:

> Incest would mean the upsetting of age distinctions, the mixing up of generations, the disorganization of sentiments and a violent exchange of roles at a time when the family is the most important educational medium. No society could exist under such conditions. (p. 251)

It was White (1948) who suggested that the origin of the incest taboo was economic.

He explained that early humans, often existing in tribes or clans, had a need to seek out and cooperate with other such groups to expand their resources. This they did through barter, and their commodity to barter became their females whom they offered in marriage. Thus, to sexually use these females prior to offering them to another clan was to diminish their value. An incest taboo protected the integrity of the "commodity."

Although such an explanation may be difficult for us to imagine today, the fact is that there is little father-daughter incest in India, because in that society a young woman's marriage is often seen as a way of enhancing the social status of her birth family. Thus, the incest taboo is strong in an effort to preserve her innocence and virginity for her marriage partner. Such a modern representation of ancient custom attests to the believability of White's theory.

Murdock, a theorist writing in the late 1940s (Meiselman, 1992) drew from several earlier theories when he postulated that the origins of incest were several fold. Freud's contention that each individual had a strong repressed desire for incest that created a repression and aversion to that desire and therefore the condemnation of acting upon it was one explanation. Along with that, Murdock accepted Malinowski's family disruption explanation and also espoused White's idea that the incest taboo allowed cooperative ties and shared resources between groups. This multidisciplinary explanation became the most widely accepted view (deMause, 1991; Meiselman, 1992).

In the 1950s, social scientist Talcot Parsons further contributed to the understanding of the etiology of the incest taboo. Parsons (1954) believed that the incest taboo was vital to the development of the child. In fact, the prohibition of incest is "linked with the functioning of every society" (as cited in Justice & Justice, 1979, p. 37). Borrowing from Freud, Parsons spoke of the belief that a

very young child . . . is capable of diffuse erotic excitement, and the mother is the main source of stimulation that produces such excitement in early life. The child's yearning for this kind of stimulation provides the incentive to progress to higher, more difficult stages of development; such progress depends, however, on the mother's ability to frustrate the child at appropriate times and use the sexually tinged attachment to her to push and pull the child through developmental stages. (Meiselman, 1992, p. 12)

Later in their development, children begin to look outside of the nuclear family, often to the peer group, for their stimulation toward development. At this time, too close an attachment to the family, especially the mother, would impede their developmental progress. Although Parson's work did not speak to the original cause for the incest taboo, it did speak to its usefulness to the developing individual (deMause, 1991; Meiselman, 1992).

THE DISCOVERY OF CHILD SEXUAL ABUSE

It is difficult to determine the exact time when sexual abuse of children was fully recognized. Certainly victims were aware of their misuse, but little credence was given to any reports that children might have made about being used sexually by adults. It was adult survivors who eventually brought their abuse to the attention of the world.

In 1862 in France, forensic medical expert Ambroise Tardieu studied 515 sexual offenses, 420 of which had been perpetrated on children who were under 15. His study was from a medical perspective with only minor recognition of the trauma caused to victims. However, Tardieu was the first to identify the sexual misuse of children as a problem facing society (Bolen, 2007; Cunningham, 1988; Herman, 1997; Masson, 1984). Around the same time, Jean Martin Charcot, a noted neurologist, observed that sexual abuse was an issue that must be dealt with. Charcot was more interested in the designation of offenders as mentally ill rather than predators. In his estimation, a great number of the reports of sexual abuse were actually false (Cunningham, 1988; Herman, 1997). Alfred Binet, another researcher, considered the childhood of offenders, postulating that they had had some type of childhood trauma. In addition, he presented children as suggestible, feeling that they might well be talked into having had sexual abuse that never actually happened (Bolen, 2007; Cunningham, 1988).

Freud's Cover-Up

In 1885, while completing his medical studies in Paris, Sigmund Freud studied under Charcot, a man whom he admired. While in Paris, Freud had exposure not only to the work of Charcot but also to that of Tardieu and other Frenchmen who had begun to study the problem of child sexual abuse. Returning to his home in Vienna, Freud established a practice using the new "talking cure" and specializing in nervous disorders. A large number of his patients were women who were diagnosed with hysteria. His work took him into the realm of his patients' innermost thoughts (recognized and unrecognized), which eventually became referred to as the unconscious. By 1896, Freud had developed his own ideas about the etiology of hysteria and presented several papers outlining his theories. These papers suggested that his patients had been sexually abused as children by fathers, brothers, and other caretakers, both male and female. It was only to his friend William Fleiss, to whom he wrote numerous letters of significance, that he confided that he felt that most of the perpetrators were actually the women's fathers (Bolen, 2007; Masson, 1984; Rush, 1996).

The medical community met Freud's theories with raised eyebrows. As a young doctor,

Freud was actually presenting an idea that went against both beliefs of the German medical community and the moral sensibilities of the day. Charcot, who was known for his research on trauma, found it unbelievable that anyone would molest his own children (Bolen, 2007). Given this pressure, it may not be too surprising that Freud, in 1897, is said to have repudiated his own theory. In a now-famous letter to Fleiss, he wrote "I no longer believe in my *neurotica*" (as cited in Masson, 1984, p. 264). From this point, Freud developed his Oedipus complex, which some researchers (Bolen, 2007; Masson, 1984; Rush, 1992, 1996; Whetsell-Mitchell, 1995) contend was a significant setback to the development of effective interventions and treatment for child sexual abuse.

Freud's new theory got its name from an ancient legend that told of an infant prince who was exposed to die because of a prophesy that he would someday murder his father. Rescued by strangers, the young prince, Oedipus, is brought up in another court. But as an adult he becomes a warrior; he meets the King of Thebes along the road and kills him in a quarrel. What Oedipus does not know is that this man was his biological father. After successfully solving the riddle of the Sphinx, which in turn saved the Thebans from attack, Oedipus is elevated to their throne and given the dead king's wife as his own. It was not until much later that Oedipus Rex discovers that his wife, and now the mother of his children, is also his mother. The tragic end for both mother and son is her suicide and Oedipus's self-inflicted blindness and aimless wandering (Green, 2011, Greenberg, 1992).

Using the Oedipus legend as a very loose basis, Freud postulated that during the third or fourth year of life, a child develops fantasies of love for the parent of the opposite sex. Children of this age might actually express their love in desire to marry the idealized parent. Eventually, the boy realizes that his mother is "taken" by the father and strives to be more like his male parent in order to someday find a woman who will be like the "girl that married Dad." In the same manner, the girl gives up her fantasies about her father and seeks to identify with her mother (sometimes referred to as the "Electra complex" after another mythological character). Having developed such a theory, Freud went on to assume that the girl's descriptions of sexual interactions with her father are actually metaphorical and therefore part of her fantasies. Thus, reports of sexual abuse were rationalized away as part of psychosexual development.

What appeared to be Freud's turnaround is especially disturbing if one looks at some of his publicized cases with the lenses tinted by today's research. For example, in 1905, he included a very vivid description of 14-year-old Dora's seduction by her father. Freud went on to describe how she was "used as a pawn in [his] elaborate sex intrigues" (Herman, 1997, p. 14). The description is so ripe with the characteristics of known sexual abuse cases, that it is difficult to believe that Dora's memories could be dismissed as metaphorical fantasies.

Why did Freud, who seemed so convinced by his original hypothesis about hysteria and sexual abuse, change his opinion so dramatically? Bolen (2007) suggests a threefold explanation. First, Freud's initial seduction theory was developed early in his career. He was young, inexperienced, and perhaps impressionable. And undoubtedly this young doctor was anxious for acceptance by his older, more experienced peers. The unpopularity of his theory must have been difficult for him to take. He feared for his reputation as a serious professional when he was ridiculed for his ideas. Thus, young Freud may have taken the path of least resistance and rescinded his theory in favor of the Oedipal complex (Bolen, 2007; Masson, 1984).

Second, some biographers find that the hysteria that Freud made a career of studying may not have resided too far from home. Masson (1984) reports that in a small excerpt from a

letter to his friend Fleiss, Freud stated that it was the father who was the perpetrator of incest; in fact, he implied that he suspected that his own father was also guilty of this. Westerlund (1986) interprets this to mean that Freud's own father had been sexually abusive. In addition, Freud confessed to Fleiss that he had had a dream of a sexual nature about his own daughter. Westerlund concludes that the creation of the Oedipus complex and the denial of the seduction theory might have been based on Freud's own need to deny his personal experiences with incestuous material.

Bolen (2007) also discusses the fact that Freud found the abundance of the sexual stories reported to him to be unbelievable. How could so many fathers be abusive to their daughters? Perhaps it was more credible to believe that the abuse took place only within the confines of the woman's mind rather than behind the closed doors of her childhood home. We have also learned from Freud's writings and his biographers that his patients often did not return after their disclosures, making it difficult to corroborate their accusations (Bolen, 2007; Masson, 1984). However, the fact that Freud's patients left therapy after disclosing their abuse is also interesting in light of the fact that many survivors of trauma experience a great deal of anxiety when they have disclosed their secret. It is not uncommon for them to seek to avoid further opportunities to discuss the issue.

The fact remains that Freud's renunciation of the seduction theory in favor of the Oedipal complex changed the future of psychoanalytical thought. Along with these changes came the suppression of sexual abuse recognition and intervention. Victims who admitted their abuse were accused of seducing their abusers in order to fulfill their own fantasies (Bolen, 2007; Rush, 1996). It is not surprising that victims felt silenced and tended not to report their abuse. Summit (1989) comments that "with Freud's retraction of the seduction theory, he left behind at once the simple explanation of trauma, his endorsement of the intrinsic strengths of the post-traumatic patient, and his intrepid strategies for undoing the traumatic effects" (p. 423).

DeMause (1991), however, feels that the story of Freud's cover-up has been grossly distorted. This researcher explains that 18 of Frued's patients exhibited symptoms of hysteria and had conscious memories of sexual seductions by family members. Believing that only repressed memories could result in clinical hysteria, Freud determined that these remembered memories were not at the root of his patients' problems and that only an earlier repressed memory could be the underlying cause. He was puzzled, however, that these patients had "no feeling of remembering the scenes of their abuse" (as cited in deMause, 1991, p. 126). He then concluded that these nonfeeling-based memories were actual fantasies of seductions that were imagined but never occurred. It was this reasoning that provided the basis for his seduction theory.

Freud did report having patients who had clear memories of having been sexually abused with the resulting ability to explain the tactile elements of what they had experienced. This evidence suggests, says deMause, in contradiction of Masson (1984) and others, that Freud never denied there was such a problem as child sexual abuse. Rather, he took great pains to distinguish actual cases from those that were part of the patient's developmental striving toward understanding her or his identity. DeMause goes on to report that, for the remainder of his life, Freud "reiterated his belief that these clear memories of incestuous attacks were real" (p. 127). Freud would later write, "the sexual abuse of children is found with uncanny frequency among school teachers and child attendants . . . and phantasies [sic] of being seduced are of particular interest, because so often they are not phantasies but real memories" (from "Freud's Introductory Lectures on Psychoanalysis," vol. XVI, 1916–1917, p. 370 as cited in deMause, 1991, p. 127).

Later Phases of Sexual Abuse Exploration

Freud's debate about sexual abuse influenced his followers well into the 20th century. One of his colleagues felt strongly that the reports of abuse were real rather than imagined. In a 1932 paper, Sandor Ferenczi voiced his contention that children might be victims of sexual abuse and that the adult world may be denying that fact (Olafson et al., 1993). Interestingly enough, Freud joined the professional community that sought to censure Ferenczi and squelch the furthering of this theory (Masson, 1984; Summit, 1989). This brief upsurge of the idea of the prevalence of sexual abuse served to silence the psychiatric community for the next few decades.

Freud had opened the question of children and sexuality, and others would also have their say. In 1907, Karl Abraham, a student of Freud, published a paper titled "The Experiencing of Sexual Trauma as a Form of Sexual Activity" that suggested that children did not report their sexual interactions with adults because they had unconsciously desired such contact. He also postulated that children "allowed themselves to be seduced" because of these secret desires (Olafson, 2002, p. 87).

In 1937, two researchers, Loretta Bender and Abram Blau, studied 16 cases of children from ages 5 to 10 who had been sexually involved with adult men (and one woman). From this study, they concluded that not only were the children *not* traumatized by these contacts but they derived some pleasure from the experience (Finkelhor, 1986; Olafson, 2002; Salter, 1988). In fact, these researchers contested that children did not deserve the "cloak of innocence" in which they had been wrapped by the moralists of the time (Bender & Blau, 1937; Olafson, 2002).

Over the next few years, child sexual abuse was not without its researchers, but initially these researchers tended to pursue their studies independently and in various parts of the country. During the 1930s, 1940s, and 1950s, there were several studies that focused on the sexual abuse of children. Terman, in 1938, studied 752 married women, 32% of whom reported being abused prior to the age of 15. In 1940, Landis published his findings in two related studies, the first of 153 "normal" women and the second of 142 psychiatric patients, reporting that 24% of these subjects reported being sexually abused as children. Later in 1956, Landis expanded the study to 1,800 college students, discovering that 35% of the females and 30% of the males had been sexually abused at an early age (Finkelhor, 1986; Salter, 1988).

Alfred Kinsey and his research team would also contribute to information gleaned about child sexual abuse. In the 1950s, Kinsey, Pomeroy, Martin, and Gebhard (1953) examined the sexual behavior of the adult female discovering that 24% of their sample of 4,441 Caucasian women reported that they had been sexually abused by the adult men in their lives. These women who were between 16 and 50 years of age when interviewed were from upper to middle socioeconomic classes (Whetsell-Mitchell, 1995). The results of this study also pointed to extended family, intergenerational incest when the researchers pinpointed the fact that women had been abused slightly more often by their uncles than by their fathers (Courtois, 2010). Kinsey and his associates made little of these findings, however, in fact relegating them to an insignificant part of their report. Kinsey's comment "It is difficult to understand why a child, except for its cultural conditioning, should be disturbed at having its genitalia touched, or disturbed at seeing the genitalia of other persons, or disturbed at even more specific sexual contacts"

(as cited in Olafson, Corwin, & Summit, 1993) would certainly create a stir among many adults today. Instead, Kinsey et al. (1953) blamed the adults in the victims' lives for reacting to disclosures of sexual contacts in such a manner as to create trauma for the children (Bolen, 2007).

In a less-known study, Kinsey and his colleagues also interviewed a group of men to explore the nature of man-boy sexual relationships. These known pedophiles described, in graphic detail, their abuse of 604 underage boys, one of whom was as young as 5 months old. As his biographer James H. Jones (1997) explains, "Kinsey's deep-seated animosity to traditional morality led him to take a benign view of child molestation and incest" (p. 620). In fact, Kinsey seems to have believed that sexual outlets for children were both natural and advisable. Kinsey once received a letter from a man who reported that his wife was rubbing the penis of their 9-year-old nephew to orgasm on a nightly basis. He asked the renowned researcher if this was advisable. Kinsey's response, reports Jones, was:

> Apparently the small boy is erotically responsive and it looks as if he is already so conditioned to the sort of contact that he has had that the chances of getting along without a regular sexual outlet are now reduced. If he were forced to go without any outlet of any sort, it is probable that he would be nervously disturbed and might be difficult to handle socially. (p. 620)

Kinsey eventually concluded that sexual initiation of children by adults could cause some emotional upset, but only because of the taboos imposed upon them by Western society. Children themselves were inherently sexual, but the culture burdened them with repressive norms to limit their sexuality (Olafson, 2002).

Between the first of the Kinsey group surveys and the late 1970s, despite some scattered research, the public was relatively sheltered from concerns over child sexual abuse. Therapists were told that the instances of such abuse were rare or imagined (Olafson, 2002). Later reports of survivors alert us to the fact that such abuse was very much a part of the fabric of people's lives, but its existence was covered in secrecy.

The "Rediscovery" of Child Sexual Abuse as a Type of Child Maltreatment

Although sexuality and its effect on children were being debated by a variety of professionals, other types of child maltreatment were certainly being addressed. In the 1940s, John Caffey, a radiologist, had contributed to the knowledge of physical child abuse by making public his own research. Caffey had seen the x-rays of six infants whose injuries he suspected were inflicted by caretakers. Several physicians became interested in his findings including C. Henry Kempe who later coined the term *battered child syndrome* and encouraged the further study of physical abuse (Myers, 2011). During the 1960s, Polansky and his colleagues were undertaking the study of neglectful mothers in both rural and urban areas. The findings of these researchers contributed significantly to the understanding of child neglect.

As a result of the increased research on child physical abuse and neglect, the Child Abuse Prevention and Treatment Act (93–247) was passed on January 31, 1974, creating the National Center on Child Abuse and Neglect. But it was not until 1978 that the definition of child sexual abuse was included in this act. In that same year, researcher Diana Russell (1983) brought child sexual abuse to the attention of the public when she published the results of her rigorously conducted study of 930 San Francisco women. Of these, Russell found that 38% had been sexually abused as children (Myers, 2011). Such a startling percentage may have contributed to the publication of several writings within the next year.

In the late 1970s, three books uncovered the issue of child sexual abuse and brought it to the public's attention. The first two were based on first person accounts. Sandra Butler's aptly titled book *Conspiracy of Silence* (1978) chronicled the experiences of numerous women who had been forced to hide their childhood abuse throughout their lives, along with a similar book, Louise Armstrong's *Kiss Daddy Goodnight: A Speak-Out on Incest* (1978). The third book, Karen Meiselman's *Incest* (1992), was the first published research study on the subject. Susan Forward and Craig Buck's *Betrayal of Innocence* (1978) presented some more factual suggestions as to the effects and etiology of this newly uncovered form of abuse. Over the next decade child sexual abuse would become a well-discussed phenomenon both in print and in the press.

Some might ask why the study of this type of child maltreatment suddenly became so popular. Finkelhor (1984) suggested that the child protection movement, empowered by the knowledge provided by the research on physical abuse and neglect, had the resources to recognize a new challenge. In addition, the feminist movement had given strength to women to speak out especially about the injustices done to them due to the unequal power of men. Out of this movement would later came the publication of Herman's classic incest study in *Father-Daughter Incest* (1981 revised in 2000) and Rush's study of the history of the sexual violation of children in *The Best Kept Secret* (Rush, 1992, 1996). While agreeing with the influence of the feminist movement, Bolen (2007) speculates that the political and social environment, perhaps stimulated by the controversy over the Vietnam War, was now focused on moral dilemmas and raised consciousness about the impact of these issues.

No longer was the status quo taken for granted, but it was often the impetus for controversy and rebellion. Social consciousness-raising and revolution in thought were rampant. Within this sociocultural context it was probably far more difficult to suppress the "discovery" of child sexual abuse. (pp. 21–22)

One cannot explore the history of the rediscovery of child sexual abuse without becoming aware of the name Roland Summit. As a practicing psychiatrist, Summit was exposed to a variety of patients for whom sexual abuse was a grim reality. When he was approached by Jolly K., a young woman seeking to begin an organization that is now well known as Parents Anonymous, Summit became even more interested in the treatment of child sexual abuse. But when Jolly K. asked him to write a training manual, he recognized his need to learn more about the subject. After participating in several conferences and collaborations with other child abuse therapists and researchers, and testifying in numerous court cases, Summit wrote his now classic article "Child Abuse Accommodation Syndrome" (Corwin, 2002; Myers, 2011).

The sexual abuse accommodation syndrome describes in five points the effects of child sexual abuse on girls who have been abused by their fathers or other close relatives. Summit's theory contends that these victims *feel helpless* because their abuser has sworn them to *secrecy*, by threat or coercion. After the abuse, the girl feels trapped in the relationship to which she feels that she must accommodate (*entrapment and accommodation*), finding it difficult to tell anyone. If she does disclose, it often comes as a *delayed, unconvincing disclosure* and may not be believed. Disturbed that she is not believed, the girl may retract her disclosure (*retraction*) and continue to feel the effects of the abuse without benefit of support (Goodyear-Brown, Fath, & Myers, 2012; Kinnear, 2007; Summit, 1983). This simple theory (discussed in more detail in Chapter 3) created the basis for the early treatment of child sexual abuse.

Summit felt that the accommodation syndrome had its most significant usefulness in court testimony. He comments that

the legitimate argument for the accommodation syndrome. . . is simply to introduce as a rebuttal that if children have not immediately complained about sexual abuse, or if they give an inconsistent development of reporting, or even if they retract on prior statements, that's not inconsistent with the reality of sexual abuse. . . . The purpose of the article was to allow children their own normalcy in dealing with sexual assault. (Corwin, 2002, pp. 8, 16)

The writings and research of the 1980s brought child sexual abuse to the attention of the social service system that, although very much aware of the fact that sexual abuse had been happening to children, had not as yet developed the resources to deal specifically with this type of abuse. With recognition came funds for further study and the development of treatment programs. These programs sprung up in pockets across the country with very little connection to one another.

It is interesting to note that most of the early study of sexual abuse victims centered on female children. One can speculate that this was the result of several factors. First, it was the feminist movement that gave much of the momentum to the disclosures of adult survivors, and due to this fact, these survivors tended to be women. Second, men are enculturated (taught by the culture) to be strong and not to become victims. In fact, society taught men over the years to hide any abuse lest they bring upon themselves ridicule or doubts about their masculinity. And third, there are definite cultural messages about what constitutes the abuse of boys (see later discussion of the "Summer of '42" Syndrome), meaning that boys who are sexually abused by adult women may be made to feel that theirs is an enviable initiation into mature sexuality (Finkelhor, 1984).

During the 1980s, with the publication of several books on the victimization of males, the sexual abuse of boys began to come to the attention of the public as well. In addition, attention was drawn to the abuse of males by clergy. Jason Berry (2000) explains that

> between 1983 and 1987, more than two hundred priests or religious brothers were reported to the Vatican Embassy for sexually abusing youngsters, in the most case teenage boys—an average of nearly one accusation a week in those four years alone. In the decade of 1982 to 1992, approximately four hundred priests were reported to church or civil authorities for molesting youths. (p. ix)

Sipe (1995) suggests that the abuse of boys by priests dates back even further. While the Council of Trent (1545–1563) sought to reform the church of abuses, Pope Julius III, who presided over part of this council, was involved in a sexual relationship with a 15-year-old boy whom he later made a cardinal. There is speculation that the notorious Marquis de Sade was "introduced to whippings and sodomy by his Jesuit teachers when he studied with them between the ages of ten and thirteen" (p. 11). And it was between 1960 and 1972 that Father James Porter victimized 200 children while he was serving as an active priest and receiving accolades for his leadership. It was not until one of his victims, 42-year-old insurance investigator, Frank Fitzpatrick, remembered his abuse and searched out his perpetrator that these abuses were fully uncovered.

The Catholic Church was not alone in the scandal of clergy abuse of children, especially boys. In the book *Brother Tony's Boys*, author Mike Echols (1996) chronicles the case of Tony Leyva, a respected Pentecostal evangelist who sexually abused adolescent boys in 23 states. Examples of abuse by clergy fill the newspapers from almost every denomination (Park, 1996), stimulating the development of abuse-reporting protocol by every major denomination (see Chapter 10 for further discussion of clergy abuse).

"It has become quite obvious," remarked one clergyman, "that child sexual abuse has become the concern of our churches today." Reports of survivors of such abuse suggest that there have always been a small number of clergy who were abusive, but now the climate is right for these cases to come to light (see Chapter 10 for further discussion of sexual abuse by clergy).

New Areas for the Sexual Exploitation of Children

The new surge of interest in child sexual abuse in the 1980s greatly increased the number of treatment programs and prevention programs to deal with this problem. At the same time, another innovation made children more accessible to sexual predators and changed the complexion of their engagement process of their victims. Finkelhor, Mitchell, and Wolak (2000) in the National Center for Missing and Exploited Children report, *Online Victimization*, estimated that 24 million of U.S. children between ages 10 and 17 are on the Internet on a regular basis. As more and more households accessed the Internet and hundreds of children began to sprint beyond their parents in their knowledge of the use of this new technology, child abusers found themselves faced with a smorgasbord of new ways to engage children. No longer need the pedophile be watchful of police and security as he looked for children in local malls, video arcades, and playgrounds. Now he could engage any number of children from across the country or across the world, merely by sitting down at his computer. With the advent of the Internet, the incidence of child molestation took on different parameters, and law enforcement was faced with the need for larger nets to catch perpetrators.

Ironically, efforts to protect children from sexual abuse were in place long before the computer became the popular method of engaging victims. In 1977, the Sexual Exploitation of Children Act was enacted prohibiting the use of children in producing pornography as well as sexually explicit advertising or the transport of children across state lines. In 1986, the Child Abuse and Pornography Act made it illegal to produce or use advertisements for child pornography. The Child Protection and Obscenity Enforcement Act in 1988 made it unlawful to transmit advertisements for child pornography via computer, produce visual pornographic depictions of children online, or obtain custody of children for the production of pornography. More recent laws like the Children's Privacy Protection and Parental Empowerment Act in 1993 and the Child Pornography Prevention Act in 1996 sought to further tighten regulations to protect children (see Chapter 8 for more details). Currently, both the Federal Bureau of Investigation and the Postal Service are actively engaged in preventing and investigating the seduction of children through both the mail and the Internet (Baker, 2002).

And Then Came the Backlash . . .

After a decade of publicity, intensified research, and the uncovering of new pockets of deviance, it is not surprising that there would be some who would be critical of the effects of the heightened interest in sexual abuse. Bolen (2007) suggests that the best word to describe the 1990s was *backlash*. Even before the 1990s dawned, Hechler (1988) warned that a backlash was brewing:

> One thing is clear: there *is* a war. There are those who feel that the country is suffering from an epidemic of child sexual abuse and those who feel that there is an epidemic alright, but not of sex abuse—of "sex excuse," as some disparagingly called it. The pendulum has swung too far, they say, and what we see now is a blizzard of false accusations. In response, they are trying to winch the pendulum back. (p. 3)

Hechler (1988) traced the roots of this backlash to outrage over highly publicized cases that brought as many critics as accusers. One such case

in point was set against the backdrop of Jordan, Minnesota, a small town that was the center of incredible controversy. During the much publicized trials that rocked this unsuspecting hamlet, 24 adults and 1 juvenile were charged with the sexual abuse of children in two sex rings. After much controversy and investigation, the charges were dropped, and only James Rud, a previously twice-convicted child molester, was charged. But the events of that case brought to light a myriad of prejudices and mistakes that could result in the accusation of child molestation.

Cases like the one in Jordan, Minnesota, as well as the McMartin day care case at Manhattan Beach, California, stimulated criticism about the way that sexual abuse cases were investigated. Accusations of biased investigation, in turn, led to several eventual inconclusive trial outcomes (Conte, 2002; Eberle & Eberle, 2003). Out of these scandals was born a skepticism that would give rise to such groups as VOCAL (Victims of Child Abuse Laws). VOCAL contends that the problems of child sexual abuse are

> not as extensive as the "child savers" would have us believe. In a climate of "hysteria," social workers and police investigators are only too ready to believe the guilt of anyone accused, regardless of the facts. For this reason, VOCAL leaders say, it is impossible to get a fair investigation, much less a fair trial. (Hechler, 1988, p. 11)

Another vocal group about the injustices perpetrated by those who "see sexual abuse where it does not exist" is the False Memory Syndrome Foundation, established in 1992 in Philadelphia (see Chapter 15 for further discussion). This group found its roots when psychologist Jennifer Freyd, herself a researcher in the area of human memory, recovered memories of sexual abuse by her father. Her mother, Pamela Freyd, blamed these on her daughter's therapist. After going public with the allegations made against her husband, the elder Freyd, with her husband Peter, started the False Memory Syndrome Foundation, dedicating herself and her group to the debunking of the concept that long ago abuse could be "forgotten" or repressed and the memories could emerge at a later date. To support her beliefs, Freyd sought out a variety of experts on memory who supported her contentions. Still gaining momentum, the Philadelphia-based society continues to stimulate controversy (Courtois, 2010; Jenkins, 1998; Stanton, 1997).

Giving support to what she called the "myth of false memory" was Elizabeth Loftus, a noted researcher on human memory. Loftus stated that she did not believe that repressed memories exist explaining that there is "no scientific evidence [that] currently exists to support the idea that memories from trauma are routinely repressed and reliably recovered years later" (as cited in Kinnear, 2007, p. 67). She did, however, admit that memory is "not a black and white entity" and expressed concern about both survivors of childhood trauma and those accused on the basis of such memories.

Spurred on by organizations and critics like Loftus, VOCAL, and the False Memory Syndrome Foundation, the mass media quickly picked up the skepticism about the efficacy of child abuse recovered memories. In the early 1990s, programs such as *20/20*, *60 Minutes*, and *Prime Time* became arenas in which the public could witness the debate. Programs featured a similar scenario of a female survivor, who sought therapy for some nonsexual problem like an eating disorder. During the course of therapy, the woman would uncover memories that would convince her and her therapist that her real problems could be traced back to sexual abuse—often ritual abuse—when she was a child. The patient would then sever her ties with family members and often point a finger at those she felt had abused her. The question was raised, often quite convincingly, whether the therapist had planted these ideas in the mind of the unsuspecting victim. After such an airing,

the *New York Times* reported that the United States was now at the mercy of "an incest survivor machine" (Jenkins, 1998).

Although it is unclear to what extent the fervor over sexual abuse had generated false reports, the backlash certainly had the potential to force some victims, who had finally gained the courage to talk about their abuse, to feel further betrayed, isolated, and without hope of help. In addition, although some of the eyes of the average citizen were opened to the magnitude of the sexual misuse of children, others, once skeptical but beginning to believe, were provided with confirmation that child sexual abuse, at least to the degree that it was reported, was one more mass media hoax.

Bolen (2007) postulates that the backlash of the 1990s began as a result of several controversies over the knowledge base currently available. Two areas received particular attention. First was over the issue of women as perpetrators. A perusal of the research and practice literature in the 1980s makes it clear that emphasis was on men as perpetrators of child sexual abuse. Indeed, the public found it difficult to imagine that the gender responsible for giving birth to and protecting infants and children could possibly use them sexually. Yet research and an abundance of uncovered cases in the 1990s brought with them the assertion that women were underidentified as abusers. A second controversy centered on the fact that more and more mothers involved in divorce disputes were accusing their ex-spouses of sexually abusing their children. But as the backlash gained momentum, it was clinicians who were most severely attacked.

Clinicians, spurred on by their recognition that child sexual abuse did exist in the childhoods of many who might seek treatment, were accused of looking for these abuses sometimes where they did not exist. Perhaps, suggests Bolen (2007), these professionals were making "clinical judgments beyond the limits of the empirical research base available" (p. 23). When these judgments were questioned, there was not enough knowledge to support them.

Bolen (2007) cites several reasons why "the climate was ripe for a backlash" (p. 23). Although there had been a wide array of research done during the earlier decade, it had been descriptive and exploratory and had not provided a sufficient empirical base. Therefore, there was not, as yet, a knowledge base with enough depth to answer the myriad of questions that cases of sexual abuse were posing. Without this factual knowledge, clinicians were not sufficiently trained to deal with the types of cases that they were encountering. Also, the reality of sexual abuse was still so far out of the frame of reference of most individuals that the fact that it existed to the degree suggested by statistical reports was unsettling, causing even clinicians to minimize its impact.

ଔ _____

Simon was 15, a quiet, introspective boy. He was no trouble in class. In fact, I was surprised when I caught him passing a note to Justin, a troubled boy who seemed to have few friends. Had the note-passing not taken place during an exam, I might not have ever read the contents of the hastily scribbled missive. "Tell her that I'll sneak out during last period. You have to work after school, right?" Assuming only that I was interrupting a possible truancy, I questioned Simon after class. What I learned surprised me. Apparently, Simon was having a sexual relationship with Justin's Mom. I remembered the lovely blonde who had attended teacher's conferences and thought that I would have envied Simon during my own uninteresting youth. To learn about sex from such a gorgeous woman! A teenage boy's dream. But at the same time, the episode bothered me. I mentioned it to my wife that night, careful not to use names, and she was horrified. "That's abuse!" she insisted. And then I wondered too. What do you think? ଔଚ

CONCEPTUALIZING SEXUAL ABUSE TODAY _____

This situation came to me from a student in my graduate class on child sexual abuse. To me, the case was so clearly one of sexual abuse. As an experiment of sorts, I created a similar scenario where 15-year-old "Sonya" passed a note to her girlfriend intended for the girlfriend's father with whom Sonya was sexually involved. In the next class on abuse, I broke the class into small groups, distributing the two cases to different groups. No one knew that the genders differed. The lively discussion that followed confirmed my worst fears. Those who had the scenario of Simon either did not feel that it was abuse or were unsure. Those groups with Sonya concluded beyond a doubt that she was being sexually abused. This was but one of the many inconsistencies that we, as a culture, have in our attempts to define child sexual abuse.

Society's Permeable Boundaries

What is sexually appropriate in today's world? In the last decade, we have seen an overwhelming increase in couples who have become sexual partners, living together under the same roof, and yet there are many who question if this is entirely acceptable. Despite the frequency of such living arrangements, U.S. laws are just now beginning to give rights to the live-in partner in cases of death or relationship dissolution, suggesting that there still may be some hesitancy about recognizing such arrangements as the ideal or the norm. Usually, one's sexual behavior or the quality of relationships is thought to be an individual choice influenced perhaps by the cultural, contextual, or religious group of which one considers himself or herself to be a part. But we are adults and certainly sexuality is something about which adults can make their own decisions. It is different for children, we argue.

Do children have a right to be sexually active? At what age? How old should a child's partner be? These questions also differ from person to person and group to group. And yet as some circles suggest that young people learn to abide by the rule of abstinence until they are able to either marry or choose sexual partners with wisdom, we bombard them with a multitude of sexual messages. Advertising uses a variety of sexually provocative images to sell a variety of products. The self-help bookshelves of a multitude of bookstores feature manuals on how to develop sexual prowess. It is difficult to find a popular movie that is not ripe with sexual themes or explicit scenes. Television shows depend upon sexual innuendos and sexually driven plots for their ratings (see also Freeman-Longo & Blanchard, 1998). A friend of mine told me that she gave up daytime soap operas quite a few years ago when the most devoted and romanticized couple in popular series had begun their relationship when the hero raped the heroine.

It is clear to many of us that people in the United States are confused about how we feel about the human body and sexuality. And each culture represented has its own customs. Several years ago, a foreign exchange student whom we were sponsoring attempted to change into his bathing suit on a public beach. This is a customary practice in Europe, and he thought nothing of it. Fortunately, his American friends quickly dissuaded him. He was perplexed explaining that he had seen a variety of nearly naked images on television and in advertising. What was the difference? No one seemed able to answer him.

So, here we are in an atmosphere where nudity is both paraded and hidden and sexual acts are both controversial and underlie our entertainment. What messages are we giving to vulnerable children? And how are we contributing to the justification used by men and women who argue that their sexual misuse of children is acceptable? This is not meant to be a statement of any of my own personal moral beliefs, but rather an attempt to point out how difficult it is given society's confusion about sexuality, to adequately define what is acceptable and what is abusive.

The Issue of Consent

For years, those who would support the practice of sexual contact between adults and children would say, "What's wrong with it anyway?" Some argue in a benign way, suggesting that children are not really harmed by being exposed to sexuality early. Others, often part of groups like the North American Man-Boy Love Association (NAMBLA), the Rene Guyon Society, or the Childhood Sexuality Circle (see Chapter 8), contend with conviction that children, often early in their development, actually benefit from being introduced to sexual practices by adults. VOCAL (mentioned earlier), begun by those who contended that they were falsely accused of child sexual abuse, argues that the state has no right to interfere in families and that the family is autonomous (Freeman-Longo & Blanchard, 1998). Such beliefs, although they may appear lofty to some, may also shield offenders.

Perhaps the only value that most of us hold when it comes to the parameters of sexual relationships is that they should be between consenting individuals.

What is consent? Finkelhor (1979) was the first to suggest that consent was an issue in child sexual abuse cases. He theorized that to consent, an individual needs the knowledge and authority to do so. Children have neither the knowledge of the implication of sexual interactions nor the authority by virtue of age and status to exercise the right to consent (Faller, 2003; Kinnear, 2007).

Faller (2003) suggests that consent is not a simple matter and has wide-reaching variables.

First, gender influences consent even in children. She goes on to explain that

> sexual socialization of boys differs from that of girls. In simplified vernacular terms, boys are taught that they should like sex and should seek it—that is they should be the initiators. In contrast, girls are taught that they shouldn't like it too much and that they should wait to be asked. When girls are asked, they should say no. (p. 25)

In addition, boys may perceive the "invitations" they get differently than girls, and therefore be apt to respond differently. For example, in the case of Sonya and Simon discussed earlier, Simon saw his liaison with his friend's mother as an experience in which he was willingly participating, that is to which he had consented. Sonya, on the other hand, although now deeply involved in the relationship, had initially seen herself as forced into compliance. Despite the differing views of these children, the child protection community would argue that the children did not have the power to consent by virtue of their ages. They were, therefore, both being sexually abused.

Understanding and Intervention

Our understanding of child sexual abuse has come a long way over the years. And yet we still have a long way to go. Karson (2001) cautions that we must approach intervention in child maltreatment fully cognizant of the complex patterns that we will encounter. In his examination of child abuse and the child welfare system, this author explains that we must learn about the intricate patterns inherent in abuse in order to effectively intervene. Then we must operate from within the pattern, not from without.

Without fully understanding the complexity of victims, perpetrators, and other family members as they interact within systems, often influenced by their cultural origins, we cannot hope to successfully intervene. As we continue in our discussion of the sexual abuse of children, it will be necessary to look at not only individual characteristics of those involved but how families and even society are woven into a web of pathology. Only when we are able to look at this web of patterns can we fully understand the issue of child sexual abuse.

Summary

The perception of children has changed significantly over the years. Although at one time children were seen as property, now they are recognized as individuals with rights, even though these rights often need protection. In ancient cultures, little girls were used for barter and often married at an early age. Little boys, in some early cultures (e.g., Greece), were indoctrinated into sexuality as part of their training to be soldiers. Incest, or the sexual interaction between blood relations, has been taboo in most cultures since ancient times. There are numerous reasons for this taboo, such as the belief that offspring from an incestuous union would be defective. Eventually, the accepted explanation came down to the needs for cultures or tribes to intermingle for protection and the exchange of resources, and brides became one resource to be bartered.

It is unclear when the sexual abuse of children was "discovered" as a problem, but in the 1800s, several individuals in medical communities began to study the effects of early sexual indoctrination on children. Freud's involvement in the discovery that some of his patients had been sexually abused is well known, although he is criticized by discounting these experiences. Instead he called them fantasies in the development of his Oedipal theory. Kinsey too, in his studies of the sexual behavior of women and men, would uncover incidents of sexual abuse in his subjects' childhoods.

The study of sexual abuse as a form of child maltreatment came during the late 1970s through the efforts of both the child protection movement and the feminist movement. Initially, incest or intrafamilial abuses took the attention of researchers and clinicians. Later, reported abuse by such respected figures as teachers and clergy would enhance the efforts to understand and intervene in child abuse situations. More recently there has been concern about how the Internet gives abusers better access to children. The backlash arose in the 1990s when former victims' reports of sexual abuse to therapists gave rise to the false memory movement that suggested that people had gone overboard in their belief in the frequency of child sexual abuse. Yet there is no question that child sexual abuse is a problem today. Our sexualized society is not always clear about its boundaries, and the result is that children sometimes suffer.

Review Questions

1. How were children viewed in ancient times?

2. What risk was there to little girls in early history? To little boys?

3. What were the earliest explanations for the taboo against incest? What appears to have been the most logical one?

4. Explain the early research on trauma. What influence did Freud have on the study of trauma?

5. What is meant by the Freudian cover-up?

6. What impact did Kinsey have on the study of sexual trauma?

7. How and when did sexual abuse become a public issue?

8. What has been the most recent focus of research on sexual abuse?

9. What is the False Memory Syndrome Foundation, and how did it originate? What was the underlying debate that sparked it?

10. What factors contribute to the sexual abuse of children today?

CHAPTER 2

The Dynamics of Child Sexual Abuse

ღჳბი

My father never had sexual intercourse with me, so I assumed that what I experienced was not sexual abuse. It was so much a part of my childhood—first, him there watching me in the shower—that I never really thought too much about it at first. But as I got older, he'd make comments about how my body was developing. He started to make me nervous when he did that, and I asked him to stop. But he would laugh it off and make me feel like I was just being neurotic. While my mother worked nights, he would put me to bed by rubbing my private parts, which he said would help me sleep. It actually felt good, and I got so I would ask for him to come in just so he'd do it. I later learned that he'd put me to sleep and then masturbate because he got so excited. But I never would have called it abuse. It was just how things were. But now I realize how that all affected my life.

ღჳბი

WHAT IS CHILD SEXUAL ABUSE?

Often when we think of the sexual abuse of children, we assume that there is some type of penetration involved or that perpetrators use force. In fact, sexual abuse covers a wide range of behaviors that may have various degrees of impact on children depending upon the child. The term *sexual abuse* is often interchangeable with such phrases as *sexual assault, sexual molestation, sexual misuse, child rape*, and *sexual victimization* (Finkelhor, 1984; Whetsell-Mitchell, 1995). Kinnear (2007) points out that child sexual abuse is sometimes defined situationally, or by the situations in which it occurs. For example, in some cultures, parents regularly sleep with their children and children may witness sexual intercourse between their parents. In other cultures, adults kiss children on the mouth or have physical contact in a manner that would not be acceptable in others.

In the United States, the wide variety of cultural backgrounds requires that we have a definition of what is sexually unacceptable behavior between adults and children. Such a definition was provided from a legal perspective by the 1974 Child Abuse Prevention and Treatment Act (amended in 1992). This act defines child sexual abuse as

A. the employment, use, persuasion, inducement, enticement, or coercion of any child to engage in, or assist any other person to engage in, any sexually explicit conduct or simulation of such conduct for the purpose of producing a visual depiction of such conduct; or

B. the rape, molestation, prostitution, or other form of sexual exploitation of children, or incest with a child.

Although originally referring to *direct or contact sexual abuse* (touching the child in some manner), this law now includes *indirect or non-contact* sexual abuse, including sexual comments, exhibitionism, voyeurism, and watching or producing child pornography. However child sexual abuse is defined, it is clear that it involves several important components:

- The victim is a child or underage.
- The act is for the sexual gratification of an adult.
- Because of his or her status, the child has neither the knowledge nor the authority to consent; therefore, the act(s) involve(s) the following:
  o Some form of enticement, entrapment, coercion, or force in order to gain access to the child;
  o Some degree of secrecy that allows the abuse to happen and possibly to continue.

Child Sexual Abuse as Trauma

Much has been written in the last decade or so about trauma (see Berliner, 2011; Blaustein & Kinniburgh, 2010; Herman, 1997; Silva, 2004) and the impact of trauma on children. Is sexual contact between adults and children always traumatic? Studies indicate that this is not always the case. Whether or not a child is traumatized depends on several variables (Tower, 1988, pp. 14–15; see also Berliner, 2011):

- *Identity of the abuser.* The closer the relationship of the victim to the abuser and the greater the trust involved, the more risk there is for trauma when that trust is betrayed. However, this is not to categorically minimize trauma when there is not a close relationship.

- *Duration of the abuse.* The longer the duration of the abuse, the greater the risk of trauma to the victim, unless short-lived abuse is accompanied by significant violence.

- *Extent of the abuse.* As a general rule, the child who experiences less intrusive contact, like fondling, may be less traumatized than the child who is digitally or penile penetrated.

- *Age of the abused child.* A child's age has a bearing on how the experience will be viewed in later life. Feelings and tasks are mastered at different developmental stages; at certain ages a child's inability to complete a developmental task will have greater impact in the future.

- *First reactions of significant people to disclosure.* Intense reactions to disclosure, especially blaming the child, intensify guilt and isolation. How parents and other important people in the child's life respond at disclosure affects the child's ability to integrate and understand it.

- *When and how the abuse is disclosed.* A child tells an adult about being sexually abused for several reasons: because he or she realizes it is wrong, to protect other siblings from similar abuse, or because of a desire to get on with his or her life. If someone else recognizes the abuse and reports it, the power of disclosure is taken away from the child. In some cases, the abuse is not disclosed until adulthood.

- *The victim's personality.* So much depends on the individual personality of the victim. The same event happening to different children may be interpreted differently by each of them.

Children may not be traumatized if they have a support system that responds immediately and appropriately. Or some children may not perceive being touched sexually by an adult as traumatic. Unfortunately, it is often only when a child is traumatized that he or she reports the abuse or that the abuse is brought to the attention of anyone outside of the child's home.

Gender as an Impediment to an Inclusive Model

Another factor in identifying or recognizing sexual abuse is the gender of the child. In our culture, sexual contact between children and adults is not always interpreted as abusive. This is most often the case with male children. In Chapter 1, we discussed two scenarios of Sonya and Simon where both a female student and a male student were in sexual relationships with adults of the opposite sex. Most people identify sex between a young girl and an adult as abusive, but this is not so in the case of a boy. Our Western culture actually elevates the act of an adult female's sexual involvement with a male adolescent. This was no more obvious than in a movie some years ago called *Summer of '42*. This movie featured a young woman whose husband was fighting in World War II and several young male adolescents who saw her as the object of their budding sexual desire. When the woman discovers that her husband has been killed, she drowns her grief in sexual relations with one of the young boys amidst all the romantic lighting and beautiful music that Hollywood could muster. In all probability, there were many teenage boys watching the movie who wished that they were in the young boy's place. The acceptance of this film as a "sweet movie" made clear that the general public's view of sexual liaisons between teenage boys and older women was more of an initiation than sexual abuse. It is this attitude that, despite a barrage of information about abuse, continues to exist, that I refer to as the "Summer of '42 Syndrome."

This disparity between defining sexual behaviors as abusive to young girls and not so when perpetrated against boys leads to a distortion when assessing the incidence of sexual abuse among boys. Although current statistics about the incidence of abuse report that between 1 in 4 or 1 in 3 (depending upon the source) girls will be sexually abused or at least approached prior to the age of 18, the rate for boys is said to be 1 in 5 or 6. And yet, if one studies the victims reported by perpetrators whose primary victims are boys, the numbers are quite high, often in the hundreds. On the other hand, those who sexually abuse girls are likely to report fewer victims in a career of abuse. Therefore, the numbers of unreported abuse to boys are probably much greater than studies reflect.

What accounts for this discrepancy? Clearly the cultural attitudes embodied in the "Summer of '42 Syndrome" do have some influence on these statistics. If a boy has sexual contact with an adult female, he may consider it to be an initiation rather than abusive. Further, he may believe that to label the situation as abusive somehow casts doubts about his masculinity (Dorias, 2009; Finkelhor, 1984; Gartner, 2001; Lew, 2004). In addition, the boy who is molested by an adult male also wonders if he was chosen because he is homosexual and might not disclose the abuse.

In general, boys report their abuse less often, even if they perceive it to be abusive. The reasons for this, in addition to the aforementioned, are also cultural. It is not "cool" for a boy to admit that he has been a victim. In fact, he may be labeled a sissy and teased or ostracized among his peers as a result of being in a victim role. And finally, our culture allows male children much more freedom than their female counterparts. It does not take much for a boy to realize that if he tells his parents that someone at the public playground abused him, he is probably going to be prohibited from spending much time there alone. The abuse may actually be less problematic for him than the loss of his freedom (Dorias, 2009; Finkelhor, 1984, 1990; Gartner, 2001; Lew, 2004).

Thus, the inclusiveness of the definition of sexual abuse may be hampered by societal attitudes.

Ethnicity and the Definition of Child Sexual Abuse

There is some disagreement among experts as to how culture impacts the definition of child sexual abuse. In addition, although some researchers have sought to study the differences in definition, perception of abuse, and outcomes across the major ethnic categories (Caucasian, African American, Hispanic, Asian, Native American), it is important to reiterate that within these classifications, there are major variations in cultures and values.

One might assume that there would be differences in how sexual abuse is defined by different cultural groups. Variables such as values about family, relationships with the community, roles of males and females, views of self, and concepts of group cohesiveness all impact the way that individuals define deviance—especially sexual deviance. In addition, the reporting of sexual abuse is likewise influenced by values as well as collective and individual experiences of oppression and interactions with law enforcement and social agencies. Not only are some ethnic groups less likely to report child sexual abuse but also when they do, it is likely that the abuse has been of an extremely serious nature (Lowe, Pavkov, Casanova, & Wetchler, 2005; Russell, 1999).

In one study of 179 college freshmen (72.1% females and 27.9% males) representing three ethnic groups (63.1% Caucasian, 17.3% African American, and 19% Hispanic), Lowe et al. (2005) concluded that there were major differences among these groups as to how child sexual abuse was defined. On the other hand, Ullman and Filipas (2005), basing their sample on 461 female college students, found that more African American and Hispanic students reported abuse than did their Asian or white peers. These authors then wondered if this is based on differences in definition.

It is clear that there is a need for more extensive research on ethnicity and child sexual abuse especially with other ethnic groups.

Myths About Child Sexual Abuse

When the average person thinks of sexual abuse, he or she is often influenced by a variety of myths surrounding this phenomenon—myths that often protect the offender, keep survivors and victims quiet, and prevent professionals from becoming involved in helping (Whetsell-Mitchell, 1995, p. 106). The following are the most common myths (see Whetsell-Mitchell, 1995, for variations of these as well as other myths):

- *Children lie about being sexually abused.* In reality, most children, especially young ones, would not have the vocabulary or knowledge to lie about sexual abuse. Summit (1983) believes that abused children are actually more likely to understate the frequency and duration of their abusive experiences rather than to make up experiences that never happened.

- *Boys are rarely victimized.* As mentioned earlier, boys are victimized but are less likely to report their abuse. Gartner (2001) points to numerous studies that document the abuse of boys and concludes that *"one in six men reported direct inappropriate sexual contact by age sixteen"* (p. 24, italics are Gartner's). This author then suggests that an additional 1 in 10 men has experienced inappropriate noncontact sexual activity. He therefore concludes that one in four men has had some sexual abuse in his history.

- *When children behave in a seductive manner, they are asking for sex.* Young children do not have the knowledge of what constitutes adult sexual activity unless they have observed it or until they reach a higher developmental level. However, children may behave in ways that appear to adults to be sexual. For example, a 3-year-old girl who sidles onto her father's lap and attempts to cajole him into some special favor may seem to some to be seductive beyond her years. But such behavior may be mimicking her mother's coquettishness or be part of her own developmental exploration about what it means to be female in this culture. Provided she has not already experienced sexual abuse, her actions are in no way asking for the adult to respond in a sexual manner. She is likely seeking attention in a manner that is normal for 3-year-olds. It is the adult who interprets this behavior as sexual. The healthy adult would respond appropriately, but the adult with a predisposition to being abusive would rationalize this behavior as looking for sexual contact.

- *One can always tell a sex offender by his or her appearance. The offender looks strange.* In fact, sexual offenders come in all shapes, sizes, ages, genders, and professions. Experts insist that there is no classic profile and that sexual offenders are not easily recognizable by appearance. Sexual abuse is often perpetrated by those—both men and women—who would seem to be the most trusted and the least likely to be abusive.

- *Children who have special needs are not as vulnerable as other children.* In fact, children with special needs are *more* vulnerable to sexual abuse for several reasons: First, those with disabilities must depend on others for their care or help. Thus, they become more trusting as their very survival may depend upon it. The care that they need may place them in positions that offenders have access to them. For example, a nonverbal child in a group home is at the mercy of the staff and may not be able to tell someone when a staff member becomes abusive. And some people assume that those with disabilities may be less sexually attractive. But sexual abuse is not about attractiveness but rather vulnerability and control. And finally, children with special needs, whether these disabilities are physical or emotional, may not be able to resist being abused or to tell someone if they are. Or, in many cases, they may not be believed.

- *Offenders who abuse their own children will not seek children to abuse outside the home.* Although this was originally thought to be correct, experts now realize that an offender may take any opportunity to abuse depending upon the nature of his or her pathology and what types of victims meet his or her needs (see Chapter 5). The offender must then have access to those victims. These children might be his or her own or might come from the community. Only when one begins to understand the pathology of the individual offender does his or her victim of choice become clear.

- *Sexual offenders are sick or mentally ill.* Although pedophilia has now been included in the diagnostic indexes, those who sexually abuse are not necessarily physically or mentally ill. Instead, sexual offending must be understood within the framework specific to this pathology (see Chapters 4, 5, and 6).

- *Sexual abuse happens more in lower socioeconomic groups.* Sexual abuse crosses all socioeconomic strata and can as easily be seen among the wealthy as among the poor. The social service system may be less likely to become involved with those with more resources, but perpetrators and victims alike come from all walks of life.

INCIDENCE OF CHILD SEXUAL ABUSE

How many children are actually sexually abused? We can see the tip of the iceberg by looking at the reports of sexual abuse. One source of incidence reports is the National Child Abuse and Neglect Data System (NCANDS) of the U.S. Department of Health and Human Services. This system was established as part of the Child Abuse Prevention and Treatment Act as amended in 1988, at which time, the secretary of the Department of Health and Human Services was directed to establish a system to collect and analyze data on child maltreatment from each of the 50 states. In 1992, the first report was published based on the voluntary reports of the states. Since that time, the NCANDS has collected data on a yearly basis, distributing them in a comprehensive report (NCANDS, 2002).

According to the Children's Bureau of the U.S. Department of Health and Human Services, in the year 2011, 61,472 children were reported as victims of child sexual abuse (Children's Bureau, 2012). Although sexual abuse statistics have diminished very slightly since the 1990s, there is still cause for concern.

Older statistics may be available from studies undertaken in the 1990s. For example, according to the Commonwealth Fund Study (Schoen, Davis, DesRoches, & Shekhder, 2004), boys as well as girls in grades 5 through 12 reported being victims of sexual assault. This study included both girls and boys in these grades and focused on their health and safety. From December 1996 to June 1997, questionnaires were distributed to 6,748 students, 3,586 of whom were girls and 3,162 were boys. It was the findings on boys that were the most interesting. Thirteen percent of the high school boys reported being physically or sexually abused. One third of the boys who were sexually abused reported that the abuse happened at home, leaving two thirds of the abuse of boys happening outside the home. Asian American boys were 3 times as likely as Caucasian boys to report sexual abuse, whereas Hispanic boys also had a higher incidence of abuse than white boys. Rates of sexual abuse among African American and Caucasian boys were similar (Schoen et al., 2004).

Boys, according to this study, were also much less likely (48%) to tell anyone that they had been abused, whereas only 29% of girls kept silent. Boys who had been sexually abused were more likely to escape their feelings about the abuse through drugs, alcohol, or risky behaviors (Schoen et al., 2004).

Because sexual abuse is often kept secret, it is difficult to know how accurate these statistics might be. Often victims do not disclose their abuse until their adulthood. Survivor organizations attest to the fact that the statistics may be much higher than we realize. Estimates by those who have researched survivors are that 1 in 3 women and 1 in 5 men were sexually abused or approached prior to the age of 18 (Russell & Bolen, 2000).

In addition to secrecy, many of the behavioral indicators of sexual abuse are also indicative of other types of trauma or nontrauma. For example, sudden emotional or behavioral changes, fears, clinginess, school problems, encopresis or enuresis, anxiety, withdrawal, eating disorders, and sexual behaviors may all find their root in other life experiences as well as sexual abuse (Berliner, 2011; Goodyear-Brown, Fath, & Myers, 2012). Often it is the problem that is first noticed or becomes the most problematic that brings the child to the attention of adults. Children who are sexually abused often suffer from a variety of types of violence, which can obscure the diagnosis (Saunders, 2012).

Therefore, assessment must consider a wide range of possibilities, only one of which is sexual abuse.

TYPES OF CHILD SEXUAL ABUSE

To categorize child sexual abuse is, in some ways, an intellectual exercise as the trauma that sexually abused children may experience cuts across all types of sexual abuse. But it is helpful to conceptualize the ways in which abuse happens to children. Sexual abuse falls, albeit not neatly, into several categories:

- *Incest* or abuse occurs between family or surrogate family members in the home setting.
- *Nonfamilial sexual abuse* occurs outside the home at the hands of nonfamily members.
- *Exploitation* is in the form of prostituting or trafficking children or using children in the production of pornography.

Some authors break sexual abuse down further into contact and noncontact abuse. *Noncontact abuse* involves the following:

- *Sexual comments* and remarks that are of a sexual nature. As one survivor put it:

My father used to talk about how much my breasts were growing—but these were not just casual comments. He would go into great detail about their size and what they reminded him of. I would feel like he was undressing me with his words. It used to make me feel so dirty.

These sexual comments are usually arousing to the offender who fantasizes through them and may also masturbate after or during the comments. Some offenders will not progress beyond the verbal abuse, but for others, this behavior represents a progression to more tactile forms of offending. Such talk may also be designed to lower the victim's resistance to later contact abuse. This type of abuse also includes obscene phone calls (Bolen, 2007; Faller, 2003; Sgroi, 1982; van Dam, 2001; Whetsell-Mitchell, 1995).

- *Exhibitionism* refers to the act of the adult exposing his or her genitals to the child. This exposure is intentional, and the adult derives pleasure from the reactions of the victim. Samantha spoke of her uncle's exposure of himself:

છ ───────────────────

My uncle wore boxer shorts that had a very large opening. I think that he must have made it larger than it was. He used to parade around the house like that when my aunt was not home. It made me uncomfortable, but I didn't dare say anything. Once he was at the kitchen sink and I walked in. He turned around, and his whole penis was protruding from his shorts. I could not help but react, and he started laughing and saying "what's wrong kitten? You'll get to like men someday."

───────────────────── ઇ

- *Voyeurism* refers to the adult watching the child undressing, using the bathroom, or bathing. Although such actions may be couched in normal everyday activities, the offender will often go to great lengths to observe and will find these activities sexually stimulating.

છ ───────────────────

I used to wonder why Daddy was always the one to give me my baths. I later learned that he told Mom that he would do it and insisted that she had better things to do. While I was in the tub, he would sit there and watch me in a way that made me uncomfortable. Sometimes he would tell me to wash myself and that he would watch to see if I did it right. He got this look in his eye that was weird. Once I saw him touching himself. I never realized until I was older that after he got me out of the tub, he would stay in the bathroom for a while and masturbate.

───────────────────── ઇ

Encouraging children to watch pornographic videos or look at explicitly sexual pictures is another form of noncontact abuse. All types of noncontact abuse may be an end within themselves with the offender gaining sexual satisfaction from these activities. More often, however, this type of abuse is part of a progression of sexual activity that is designed

to desensitize the victim to more intrusive sexual behaviors (Sgroi, 1982; Whetsell-Mitchell, 1995).

Contact abuse refers to the types of behaviors when a child is actually touched or physically manipulated. These may include activities like kissing, fondling, oral-genital contact, vaginal or anal penetration, frottage, or the use of children to produce pornography. Table 2.1 outlines some of the types of sexual abuse.

PHASES OF CHILD SEXUAL ABUSE

The sexual abuse of a child can often be seen in a somewhat predictable pattern. Some theorists refer to this pattern as the phases of abuse (Burgess, Groth, Holstrom, & Sgroi, 1978; Freeman-Longo & Blanchard, 1998; Sgroi, 1982; Whetsell-Mitchell, 1995). It should be noted that these are more phases than stages as they do not necessarily have definite parameters but rather flow into one another. For example, while a perpetrator is engaging a child, he or she is also beginning the sexual behaviors and is compelling the child to keep these behaviors secret. But looking at the sexual abuse through the lens of a pattern helps us to understand the dynamics as well as the motivation of the perpetrator and the effects on the victim.

Engagement Phase

It is during the engagement phase that the perpetrator gains access to the victim and begins the process of enlisting some degree of cooperation or compliance. The words *cooperation* and *compliance* in no way suggest that children are openly complicit in their abuse. Rather, perpetrators use their advanced knowledge and experience to trick children to comply. In addition, children are taught to obey and respect adults, giving the perpetrator even more leverage as he or she seeks to draw the child into the deception of abuse. Most children do not fully realize that they have the option of resisting or refusing when it is an adult

Table 2.1   Types of Sexual Behaviors Defined

Noncontact or Indirect Sexual Abuse	
Sexual comments	Statements made to the child of a sexual nature. *Example: A father comments on the firmness and roundness of a 12-year-old daughter's budding breasts and indicates that he would love to suck them.*
Voyeurism	When an adult observes a child bathing, undressing, or using the bathroom, often becoming aroused by doing so. *Example: A father insists that his daughter leave the door of the bathroom open at all times. While taking a bath, he insists that she part her legs and show him so that "he is sure that she is clean."*
Exposure to pornography	Compelling a child to watch or knowingly allowing a young child to watch pornographic acts either in magazines or on videos or be in the room while adults engage in sexual acts. *Example: A perpetrator convinces a child to watch a pornographic movie while he looks on and masturbates.*
Contact or Direct Sexual Abuse	
Kissing	Intimately kissing a child on the mouth or sticking the tongue in a child's mouth or kisses a child in other areas such as the genitals or breasts. *Example: An adult gives a child an openmouthed "French" kiss using the tongue.*
Fondling	The adult massages, caresses, or handles a child's genitals or breasts. *Example: An adult rubs a child's genital area in the bath in a manner beyond simple washing and to the point that the adult is aroused.*
Oral sexual contact	An adult puts his or her mouth on the child's genitals, sucking, biting, or licking. Or an adult compels a child to put his or her mouth on the genitals of the offender. *Fellatio* refers to stimulation of the penis by the mouth. *Cunnilingus* refers to stimulation of the vagina by the mouth. *Example: An offender sucks on a little girl's labia and places his tongue in her vagina. An offender sucks on a little boy's penis. Or an adult compels a child to suck on his penis.*
Digital penetration	An offender uses a finger to penetrate a girl's vagina or anus or a little boy's anus. An object like a hairbrush handle or a vibrator might also be used. Or an adult compels a child to put his or her fingers in the vagina or anus of the adult. *Example: An aunt uses a vibrator to stimulate her nephew's anus, or a father inserts his fingers into his daughter's vagina.*

Table 2.1 (Continued)

Contact or Direct Sexual Abuse	
Penile penetration	An adult male inserts his penis into the anus or vagina of a child. *Example: A father inserts his penis into his daughter's vagina telling her that this is what big people do.*
Frottage	The adult rubs himself or herself against the child in a sexual manner. Often this leads to arousal and sometimes orgasm on the part of the adult. *Example: A grandfather rubs his penis between his grandson's buttocks to the point of climax.*

SOURCE: Sgroi (1982), Whetsell-Mitchell (1995), Jones (1997), and Faller (2003).

who has asked them to do something—especially an adult with whom they have developed a relationship. Some perpetrators are so skillful in their ability to engage a child that, by the time the abuse has become intrusive, the child feels that he or she has agreed to it if not asked for it. Certainly the child feels equally to blame as the perpetrator.

Engagement Strategies

Different types of offenders use various types of strategies to engage their victims. These may be broken down into four types: enticement, entrapment, threat, and force (Crosson-Tower, 2014; Freeman-Longo & Blanchard, 1998; Preble & Groth, 2002; Sgroi, 1982; van Dam, 2001). For each of these strategies, there is a component of "or else"—that is what does the child believe will be the consequences if he or she does not comply with the perpetrator's wishes or requests.

Enticement refers to the actions of the perpetrator who attempts to bribe or tempt the child into compliance through the offer of some type of reward (Preble & Groth, 2002). Such a reward might be something tangible such as money, a gift, or a promised toy, or the abuser may let the child

know that cooperation will mean that he or she will spend more time with the child. Because abusers often target children who are in need of adult attention, this can be a powerful incentive. For the victim, this exchange often seems just. He or she receives something that may be much wanted while he or she in turn gives something to the offender. It also provides leverage for the offender when it is time to compel the child to keep the secret. "After all," the offender points out to the child, "you agreed to do this for me. Look what you got." Thus, the victim feels complicit and becomes as interested in keeping the secret of the interaction as the offender.

Entrapment is another type of engagement strategy in which the abuser uses guilt at the onset. The leverage is that the child is already involved or has already done something that the offender can hold over her or his head. An incestuous father may say, "After all I do for you, this is the least you can do for me." Or he may say, "You are all that is holding my marriage to your mother together. If you do this for me, we can continue to remain a family." For most of us, the logic is obviously faulty, but children do not have the experience to understand that they are being used or manipulated.

Sometimes the perpetrator entraps the child in another manner. Perhaps he or she has discovered the child smoking marijuana, stealing something, or guilty of some other misbehavior. The perpetrator then uses his or her knowledge of this to compel the child to engage in sexual activity. Or the abuser may have already noticed the child's interest in sexuality.

ॐ _____

My father caught me masturbating when I was 7. I am not sure that I even knew what it really was, but I knew that it felt good. I also knew that it was strictly forbidden by my mother. She caught my sister once, and all hell broke loose. According to Ma, all the saints and angels would come down to strike us if we ever did that. When my father caught me defying the saints and angels, he pretended he was angry. Then he laughed and said that he wouldn't tell Ma if I'd play this "little game" with him. I felt so guilty that I'd been caught and so afraid that he'd tell Ma, so I agreed. That began 8 years of sexual abuse at his hands. I didn't dare say no. I figured it was all my fault because of what he'd seen me doing.   ॐ

_____

The child who is engaged by entrapment is made to feel incredibly guilty. Although most adults have learned to come to terms with guilt, children feel it profoundly and it can permeate their thinking. The shame that is closely tied with this guilt is the obvious "or else" perceived by the child. For some cultural groups, shame has an even stronger message. Children in these cultures may go to great lengths to avoid feeling shame (Fontes, 2008). Because the child does not want to feel like a "bad person," he or she is manipulated into compliance with the offender's wishes.

The offenders who use enticement or entrapment—strategies that Preble and Groth (2002) refer to as persuasion techniques—tend to be the most common in child sexual abuse. An engagement strategy should not be confused with the method by which offenders compel children to keep the secret of the abuse. For example, an offender who entices the child to comply with the abuse might later threaten the child that if he or she tells anyone, the offender will leave or hurt the child or someone the child loves. The engagement strategy is what he or she has used *initially* to hook the child.

There is an advantage for the offender of using a persuasion strategy as opposed to coercion. Many offenders see themselves as people who are sincerely interested in children. "I would never *hurt* a child!" is not an uncommon exclamation. Certainly we might like to further define the term *hurt*, but in the offender's mind, persuasive techniques do not hurt the child. In addition, children who are persuaded can be kept in the dark longer as to the fact that they are being abused. Yet, if they are threatened or hurt, victims easily recognize that there is something wrong with the behavior. Thus, they might be more likely to tell someone what has happened. But the "gentle" abuser who plays with them, gives them treats, and who may even demand something for something is not the boogie man (or woman) against whom they have been warned. And they may actually feel they are getting something emotionally from the relationship.

Might an offender change the type of engagement strategy he or she uses? Offenders usually have a strategy of choice but might adopt another if that one does not work in a particular situation. Other offenders will just abandon the victim who will not comply with the offender's preferred strategy and move on to another potential victim. Offenders are less likely to move from the more benign persuasion strategies of enticement or entrapment to the more coercive strategies of threat or force, but it is possible if they feel sufficiently unable to use preferred strategies.

There are some offenders who do coerce their victims through either threat or actual force. They may adopt this strategy either because they do not have the luxury of time to groom the victim, because of their own poor impulse control, or because their pathology is more geared to taking the power and control in this manner. *Threat* may be implied by virtue of the adult's authority over the child or verbal by threatening him or her with harm. Threat may also be through the use of the brandishing of a weapon or another tool that lets the child know that he or she must comply (Preble & Groth, 2002). Obviously, the "or else" for the child here is the fear of being harmed.

Few child sexual abusers use actual *physical force* to carry about their abuse, but there is a small number who do. These offenders are less likely to spend time grooming their victims as they use force to overpower them. Or they may not have the luxury of time in which to groom the victim. Again the use of force often frightens the child and makes him or her more likely to disclose unless there is fear that there will be retaliation for disclosure. Even then the fearful affect of the child might alert adults to the fact that there is something wrong. For all these reasons, most child sexual abusers will take time to groom their victims.

Grooming the Child Victims Through Progression

Child sexual abusers may be quite skilled in engaging their victims and in preparing them for sexual relationships. Van Dam (2001) outlines a 5-step process through which offenders ready their victims. They first (a) identify a likely victim (see further discussion under Risk); (b) engage the child often through peer-like involvement; (c) desensitize the child to being touched; (d) isolate the child from other adults or those who might protect him or her; and (e) make the child feel responsible for the abuse. This intricate process of preparation is referred to as *grooming*. Perhaps the most crucial part of grooming for the offender is his or her desensitization of the child through a progression of behaviors from less intrusive to more sexually intrusive.

Leberg (1997) points out that there is not only a physiological component to this grooming but also a psychological one. By beginning with noncontact forms of abuse, the offender can gauge the children's reaction to his or her actions while participating in activities that could probably be explained away. The father who practices voyeurism while he bathes his child could easily deny that he was doing any more than was necessity to ensure that she washes properly. In the meantime, the child is getting a message—that is it acceptable for the perpetrator to see her or him naked and to observe closely. Later, the offender may touch the child, but by that time, the child is used to being observed and may not be as likely to resist.

Offenders are keen observers of children's reactions when they are in the process of grooming. A slight hesitation on the child's part will usually be met with coaxing or reassurance. Sometimes there is more definite pressure. But if the child refuses outright, many offenders will retreat and wait awhile before they try again to lower the child's resistance.

ᐤᔉ ━━━━━━━━━━━━━━━━━━━━

Pop used to take showers with us when we were little. No one thought much about it. It was just a guy thing. After a while, he would tell us that we weren't washing well enough and he had to do it for us. I remember the first time he soaped up my penis. It felt weird to me, and I objected. He said "okay, do it yourself, but you better do it right!" My little brother let him, and he seemed to pay more attention to him from then on. After a while, I figured "what the heck!" and told him he could wash me too. I began to realize that it felt really good. But it didn't stop there. By the time he was sodomizing us, it didn't seem like that big a deal. We'd been carefully prepared. ᔉᐤ

━━━━━━━━━━━━━━━━━━━━

A typical progression might include the following (Adapted from Sgroi, 1982, p. 72):

- Nudity on the part of the adult (e.g., Dad runs from the shower forgetting his towel)
- Disrobing in front of the child
- Exposing genitals to the child (e.g., Grandpa's robe gapes open to expose his penis)
- Observation of the child bathing, undressing, or excreting (often passes for normal child care)
- Kissing the child on the lips especially in a lingering sexualized manner

- Fondling the child's breasts, genitals, thighs, or buttocks
- Masturbation (mutual or solitary)
- Fellatio—oral stimulation of the penis (to the perpetrator or the child)
- Cunnilingus—oral stimulation of the vulva or vaginal area (to the child or the perpetrator)
- Digital penetration of the anus or rectum
- Penile penetration of the anus or rectum
- Digital penetration of the vagina
- Penile penetration of the vagina
- Dry intercourse or frottage (rubbing the perpetrator's penis on the genital area or rectal area, inner thighs, or buttocks of the child often to ejaculation)

If the child resists at any point, the abuser will often back off and normalize the behavior until the child feels comfortable in proceeding.

Not every abuser grooms his or her victim in the same exact manner, but unless the assault is an actual rape, some form of grooming will be necessary for the abuse. Often when the abuser has ventured into more forbidden behavior, he will convince the child that it was the child's idea and thus make the child feel like a cocontributor to the activity.

Perpetrators will usually seek opportunities where they can be alone with a child unobserved. Sometimes they can be quite creative in how they gain access to children.

Nonabusive adults sometimes wonder how perpetrators of sexual abuse could possibly engage a child. But children are prime candidates for abuse due to their inherent characteristics. Children are taught to trust and depend upon adults, respecting their elders and their wisdom. When an adult tells a child to do something, the child usually assumes that he or she must comply. Children are facing new experiences each day. They are curious, willing to try new things, and often enjoy risk taking. Thus, when an adult approaches them with "something new" they might be ready to try it (Sax, 2009a).

Children naturally crave attention and affection. Offenders are expert at finding the children who have been deprived of this basic need and are the most in need of it. Children with disabilities are especially vulnerable because not only are they more dependent on adults but they may feel more in need of adult affection and attention. Having already discussed noncontact forms of abuse like exposure and observation, let us now consider the forms of contact abuse through which a perpetrator grooms a child.

Kissing as a form of grooming must be distinguished from the affectionate and pleasant kisses that parents and other adults give children. Kissing used by perpetrators has sexual overtones: kissing on the mouth, open-mouthed kissing using the tongue (soul kissing or French kissing), or kissing that is lengthy. Kisses may also be on other parts of the body that are suggestive of sexual activity such as the thighs, genitals or breasts. As the offender administers these kisses, he or she gauges the child's reaction.

Fondling refers to the adult rubbing the child in a suggestive or sexual manner especially in areas such as on the upper thigh or the upper arm near the breast. Fondling may also involve handling the breasts or genitals. Some offenders manage to fondle their victims in ways that may not even be clear to the child to be sexual abuse.

ଔ ⸻

When I was going to sleep at night, my Mom would rub me all over. She said that it would relax me. She would begin with my face and head and move down my body. She'd stop various places like my chest and tell me that someday I would have hair there and my arms saying that I'd grow big muscles. She'd rub my belly, and I would hardly even realize it when she got to my penis. I used to get an erection, and she'd laugh and say that she could tell that her rubbing felt good. It seemed like a natural part of our nightly ritual, and it didn't even occur to me that it was abusive until later when she wanted me to do things to her—sexual things. ଔ

What begins as fondling may become *masturbation* when the perpetrator rubs the child's genitals with the clear intent to excite him or her.

The abuser may then suggest that the child do the same to him or her, deriving pleasure from the activity. The same victim continues his story:

ॐ

One day when Mom was rubbing me she told me that she was tired and she needed to relax too. She asked if I'd be willing to help her to relax. When I said "sure," she showed me how to rub her genitals in a way that made her really feel good. I wasn't sure I liked it, but what could I say? She always was so great about helping me relax and go to sleep. The least I could do was help her out.

ॐ

The sexual activity may then progress to oral-genital contact. *Fellatio* refers to oral stimulation of the penis, and *cunnilingus*, the oral stimulation of the vulva or vaginal area. Perpetrators may lick or suck the child's genitals or request or demand that the child stimulate them in the same manner.

ॐ

Pops used to call the game "lollypops." I never realized that there was a touch of irony in his title for it. He told me that his penis was a lollypop and if I'd suck on it, he'd get me the kind of lollypop I was used to—the candy kind. Later, when I began to resist, he would promise me bigger and better prizes. I learned that I could get a lot of special things by just doing that for him. Now, the whole idea makes me sick, but then, it was all part of keeping Dad happy. His anger was terrible and everyone wanted him to be happy.

ॐ

The abuse may progress to *digital penetration of the victim's anus or vagina.* By the time this occurs, the child may be very used to being touched in a variety of ways and may not see this as that different. Digital penetration in very young children may be the offender's attempt to stretch the anal or vaginal opening for later penile penetration. Gradual stretching will be less painful for the child, and thus, he or she may be less apt to resist as the abuser escalates his abuse. Some perpetrators against little girls will gradually stretch the hymen

rather than breaking it abruptly. One professional describes her experience.

ॐ

When I worked as an investigator, we were taught to ask physicians examining young female victims about the condition of the hymen. This membrane can be broken when a little girl falls on something, but a hymen that has been carefully stretched can be a tell-tale clue to the fact that she was being abused.

ॐ

Sgroi (1982) speaks of *dry intercourse*, an act that is also referred to as *frottage.* Frottage occurs when the adult rubs himself or herself against the child, usually to the point of orgasm. The adult may be clothed, partially dressed, or nude, and the child may not even realize what is happening.

ॐ

My cousin used to play hide and seek with me and my other cousins. He always used to want to hide with me. We'd go in a closet a lot of times where we were really close. He'd often turn me away from him and rub up against me. I thought it was funny at first especially when he breathed heavily. But he'd hug me too and that felt good. And it seemed like part of the game. After awhile he'd just relax. When it first started, I was only 6 or 7 and he was 15. Then one time, when it was summer and we just had on bathing suits, he pulled mine aside and I realized that his was pulled down. When I got out of the closet later, I was wet between my bum. I remember wondering why that was. I supposed we were just sweating a lot. I now realize that he had probably ejaculated while he was rubbing up against me.

ॐ

Frottage may occur at any point in the progression.

Perpetrators may not reach the point of *penile penetration* due to lack of opportunity or fear of pregnancy in an older female child. In order to accomplish penile penetration with the child, the offender will require the physical setting where he and the child can be alone for a period of time. In addition, he will have had to engage the child's cooperation to the point that he or she does not object or the perpetrator can overcome the object. To anally or vaginally rape a child using force is certainly possible, but most child abusers prefer to enlist the child's compliance. A frightened child who has just been raped might be more likely to tell someone what has happened to him or her, despite the offender's insistence that the secret be kept.

CR _____

My uncle came to live with us after he got divorced. I think my mother was relieved because she'd just left my father and it meant that she could have some time away from us four kids. My uncle used to babysit. He liked me a lot, and he used to take me on his lap and rub my back and stuff. One night he came into my room after I was asleep. I now know that he'd been drinking, but at the time, I didn't realize that. He got into bed with me and suddenly he took off my pajamas and turned me over and just raped me. I started to scream, and he held his hand over my mouth. When he was finished, he started crying and I was crying too. He begged me not to tell my mother and helped to wash me up. I was afraid of him then, but he was really sweet and crying and I kept the secret. And then it happened again about 6 months later. The next day, I couldn't eat, and I was so sore that I had trouble sitting. My mother asked me what was wrong and kept badgering me until finally I started crying and just blurted it out to her. She was really mad, and that is the last time I ever saw my uncle. But I remember him—and what he did.   ৪১

_____

Although some perpetrators will use force, this is often the exception rather than the rule.

Grooming the Adult Community

While an offender is carefully grooming the victim in preparation for abuse, he or she is also aware that there will have to be opportunities of closeness to the child and time with the child in order to engage in sexual behaviors. Van Dam (2001) contends that offenders also groom the adult community much as they do the child (see also van Dam, 2006). In incestuous situations, the abusive parent needs to only gain opportunities when the child's other parent is not aware or watchful. Many incestuous fathers do this through volunteering to perform child care, especially in the area of toileting or putting the child to bed. Some parents are alone with children either because they are single parents or due to the work schedule of their spouse.

It is the nonparental abuser who may need to be more skilled in his or her grooming of the adults in the child's life. Van Dam (2001) suggests several means through which the offender gains the trust of the adults and, as a result, opportunities to abuse the child. Choosing families that are more *socially isolated* may be the first step. Single parents with children to care for may welcome the offer of another adult to help out. Or patriarchal or authoritarian families where children are taught not to question are also prime targets. Families with limited support systems or shaky marriages between parents may also put children at risk for attention from outside adults.

Offenders quickly get to know families by name (*name recognition*), making them feel like the offender is a trusted friend. Many of the Catholic priests who were found to be sexually abusive to children were seen as valued family friends before the abuse was disclosed (see Berry, 2000; Boston Globe, 2002; Bruni & Burkett, 2002; Frawley-O'Dea, 2007; Frawley-O'Dea & Goldner, 2007). Offenders used other ways of securing adult confidence as well. They may offer to do something for the adults, especially when it comes to caring for or entertaining children. When an offender presents himself or herself as someone who enjoys working with children, adults begin to see him or her as someone who does this well—someone who can be trusted.

Once this reputation has been established and accepted in the community, it is difficult to dispute (van Dam, 2001, 2006).

ଔ

Mr. Bigby was everyone's friend in our neighborhood. He had said that he was a widower, and I think everyone felt sorry for him . . . a guy alone. He used to encourage the kids to visit him. He'd have cookies for us and play games with us. It all started when he happened to drop in when my sister was having a kids' birthday party at our house. He said that he'd just come to borrow some sugar. My Mom was frazzled, and when Mr. Bigby saw this, he came in and started leading the games for her. After that, he'd come and ask to take us for ice cream or to the zoo. After a while, he'd have kids at his house all the time. He told our parents that he missed his grandkids and it helped to have all of us around. He became everybody's babysitter too. Once one family on the street started asking him to watch their kids, everyone did.

It was Kevin who started the whole scandal. He said that Mr. B. had pulled down his pants and done things to him. His mother told him that he should be ashamed to talk that way. There were rumblings amongst some of the other kids too. But none of the parents would believe it. He never touched me, but I was a pretty assertive kid. Finally he just moved away, and everyone gave him a big party. Kevin swears to this day that he molested kids. I think he was probably right, but no one could have convinced our parents.

ଔ

Like Mr. Bigby, a child abuser who can enlist the support of the adult community often has many more opportunities to abuse children.

Sexual Interaction and Secrecy Phase

Once the offender has fully engaged the child and manipulated the adults around him or her so that there are opportunities to have access to the child, the sexual abuse progresses. When the behaviors become more obviously sexual, the offender will mostly likely request that the child keep their relationship or at least their specific activity secret. In fact, it is rare for an offender not to ask that their secret be kept. Having the child keep the secret is probably the only guarantee that the abuse can continue.

Offenders use a variety of inducements to see that the child tells no one. These may be divided into categories: (a) a simple request for secrecy, (b) request for secrecy that plays upon the relationship, (c) request for secrecy using guilt, and (d) request or demand for secrecy using threat or force (Berliner, 2011; Flora, 2001; Leberg, 1997; Preble & Groth, 2002; Seto, 2008; Sgroi, 1982).

A *simple request for secrecy* is not that common given what the offender has at stake if the child tells. Such a request, if made, would just ask the child to keep their activities between the two of them and not to tell anyone else. Most offenders feel the need to add some contingency that ensures that the child will not tell. To simply ask a child not to disclose the activities without using threat or playing on the child's need for the relationship often suggests a greater degree of pathology and denial on the part of the abuser. Is the abuser so unaware of the fact that these acts are against societal conventions that he or she does not see the importance of secret keeping? The case of Jacob is an example of such an abuser:

ଔ

Jacob was mildly mentally retarded and lived in a residential community for people with mild psychiatric disabilities. Prior to placement, he had been abandoned by his mother and siblings and sexually abused by his father with whom he then lived. His father made it clear to Jacob that he had done him a favor by keeping him and the sexual favors were his payment for that care. When Jacob was 17, his father died and the boy was placed in what became a series of community residences. Jacob did not feel he was abused by his father but was aware that when the other adults in his life found out about the abuse years later, they told him that it had been wrong.

Due to his high functioning as well as the lax policies of the residence, Jacob had a good deal of autonomy when he was not at work. He began spending time at the playground and talking to some of the young boys. One particular boy, Eric, was nice to him, and Jacob took a special liking to him. Eric was from an alcoholic home and frequently spent the nights in the park when his parents had been drinking and were abusive. Jacob would bring the boy food and help him elude the police officers who patrolled the park during evening hours. Feeling attracted to the boy, Jacob initiated sexual activities, which Eric did not seem to reject. However, remembering the reaction of his social workers to his relationship with his father, Jacob suggested that they should keep their special time together a secret. ❧

Some offenders will request *secrecy in a manner that plays on the relationship* or makes the relationship the leverage point. For example, an offender may say, "We have such a special thing between us. If you tell anyone, they will break us up." Here the child sees that the benefit for keeping the secret is that the relationship will be allowed to continue. Because the child may be basking in the attention given to him or her by this adult, the price of secrecy may seem like an insignificant one in the face of the loss of the attention. Or an offender may tell the child that either the child or the offender will be "sent way" if the abuse becomes known.

Requesting secrecy through the use of guilt is one of the more common methods that offenders ensure that the child does not disclose the abuse. By the time the secrecy is required, the offender has skillfully made the child feel complicit in the abuse. During grooming, the offender will often retreat slightly if a child shows any resistance. When the child is desensitized to the point that he

or she no longer resists, the offender may even ask if it is alright to continue. One victim describes her abuse.

❦

When I was little, Grandpa used to rub my back and later other parts of my body. One night he started to rub me with his penis instead of just his hand, and it felt weird so I pulled away. He was very understanding and said that we did not need to do that now. But when he seemed a little distant for the next few weeks, I was afraid he didn't think I was special anymore. I remember that I really tried to get his attention, climbing in his lap. I think I even asked him to play the rubbing game with me. Then one night when we were alone, he suggested that he could rub me in a "special way" like he did before. He asked me if that was okay. I said that it was because it didn't matter. I just wanted him to like me. Later he told me that I had better not tell anyone because I had asked him to do it and they'd think that I was a bad girl. I felt so guilty that I knew I could never tell anyone. ❧

Offenders who use guilt may also tell the child or imply that their complicity will hurt someone else. For example, an offender might say, "You can't tell your mother. Think how jealous and hurt she would be that you are more important to me than she is." As a child, the victim is unable to see the manipulation being used on him or her. Instead, the child's guilt keeps him or her silent.

Sexual abusers who *request or demand secrecy through the use of threat* will often threaten either the child or someone or something that is important to the child. Such offenders have made statements that disclosure on the child's part will result in the offender harming or even killing loved animals, other family members, friends, or the child himself or herself. And *using force*, the offender could apply some type of physical pressure or do harm to the child, insisting that there would be more to come if the child told anyone.

Disclosure Phase

Disclosure of abuse may or may not happen in childhood. Some victims carry the secret of their abuse into adulthood or even to death. For these individuals, the repressions of the information may actually intensify the trauma (see Chapter 15, "Treatment for Adult Survivors" for more information). When disclosure does occur in childhood, it may be either accidental or intentional.

Accidental disclosure comes about in several ways:

- *Behavioral acting out.* A child may act out a piece of sexual behavior that is then observed by an adult or another child who tells an adult. Usually this happens when the child is young and mimics behavior that he or she has seen or experienced, often in an attempt to make sense of it. This behavior may also be connected with questions or a narrative.

Joey was a 3-year-old in my day care class. He enjoyed playing with the dolls we had at the center and would act out elaborate stories with them. We were not always aware of the exact content until one day he asked me why the dolls didn't have "weenies," his word for penis. I asked him why he couldn't just pretend. Because, he told me, he wanted to put one doll's "weenie" in another dolls "bum" and play the game that Uncle Harvey and he played. After talking with Joey more, it became clear to us that Uncle Harvey was sexually abusing him.

- *Reports from other children.* A child may tell a peer about sexual abuse and that peer may tell an adult. Sometimes it is unclear whether the child expected his or her peer, either on a conscious or unconscious level, to tell an adult. Or it may be obvious that the child expected that his or her confidence would be respected.

It is not uncommon for middle-school-age girls to share secrets. When Shannon told Melinda that her father was abusing her, I think that Shannon believed that it would be kept in confidence. But Melinda and I have always had a close mother-daughter relationship, and I know that she was really concerned about Shannon. Melinda begged me not to tell anyone until I helped her to realize that secrecy would not enable Shannon to get the help she needed.

- *Medical symptoms.* Children may develop some type of medical problem that, once investigated, leads to the disclosure of the abuse. Younger children with venereal diseases, for example, must be carefully evaluated as to their origin. Tearing to the rectum or vaginal area can also be suspect of abuse. Genital rashes or infections, although possible through the introduction of substances that are foreign to the body or that create an imbalance in bodily chemistry, may also be the result of sexual abuse (Adams, 2010). For example, some bubble baths upset the ratio of natural bacteria in the vaginal areas of some little girls and can cause a rash. But if a rash is discovered, it is important to find the cause.

- *Observation by a third person.* Sometimes sexual abuse is discovered when an adult or another child sees the sexual interaction between the victim and the perpetrator (Sgroi, 1982).

I remember how shocked I was when I walked into my sister's bedroom one night to find my stepfather in bed with her. At first, I thought he was comforting her or something, but he had the sheet drawn back and I could see what he was doing to her. I started crying and hitting him, and Mama heard us and came to see what was happening. She was so angry and threw him out that very night!

- *Pregnancy* is another possibility for older girls who are being sexually abused. Given the risk involved, the perpetrator will usually guard against the victim becoming pregnant, but there are always accidental occurrences. Sgroi (1982) also mentions that some perpetrators may withhold contraceptives from the child as "punishment." Or, some offenders believe that the child is too young to become pregnant.

Intentional disclosure occurs when the victim intentionally tells someone outside of the abuse relationship. Why might a child disclose an abusive relationship at one point when he or she has probably been caught up in secret keeping until that point? The reasons are myriad but tend to fall within the following (Sgroi, 1982):

- The child's own development has reached the point where he or she knows that the sexual relationship is wrong.
- The child has been exposed to prevention materials that describe the relationship as wrong.
- The child has reached the point where he or she wants to have more access to opposite sex peers or dating, and the offender is preventing it. Or the child just wants more freedom.
- The child fears becoming pregnant.
- The child seeks to protect younger siblings from the offender's abuse.
- The child sees the offender's interest in younger siblings and is jealous of that attention.
- The child feels too much pressure in the incestuous family situation and hopes to modify it.
- The child may become angry with the perpetrator and tell in retaliation.
- The child may have found an ally who he or she believes will listen and help.
- The child just wants the abuse to stop.

Children who intentionally disclose the secret of the abuse may initially feel relieved by their act. However, as the social service system begins to get into gear, the child is often distressed at how others react. He or she may then feel guilty, frightened, and horrified that the disclosure has caused such a range of emotions. For this reason, children who have just disclosed need a great deal of support (see also Chapter 10).

When children tell someone of their abuse, the immediate reaction of the perpetrator, and sometimes the nonabusive parent, will be to get the child to recant. If the rabbit (abuse) can just be stuffed back in the hat (secrecy), all will be well, they believe. Certainly, the offender has a great deal at stake, and if he or she can discredit the child, the picture may look brighter for the offender.

Even after disclosure and even if the child is not convinced to recant, there may be a desire on everyone's part to forget the disclosure was ever made.

Suppression Phase

Suppression takes place when an abuse case has been disclosed as well as when it has not. No matter how the abuse is disclosed, the child's family and those close to the child may try to suppress publicity, information, intervention, and even the memory that the abuse has occurred (Sgroi, 1982). The rationale is often articulated that "it is better for the child." Adults and related children may sincerely believe this, but the fact is that abuse affects everyone close to the situation, casting over them a net of embarrassment, fear, suspicion, anger, disgust, and a variety of other unwanted emotions. Putting the knowledge of the abuse in the back of a dark symbolic closet may relieve some of these feelings.

☙

My father was a minister with an important position in the community. My mother, too, was well known. When I was sexually abused by a member of the church, it was difficult for everyone. I felt like everyone was looking at me and thinking that I was dirty. The police were involved when I told my mother what had happened, and everyone in the church was buzzing about it. My Dad found it especially difficult given that the man was a member of the church. And I know my Mom was upset. She couldn't eat or sleep. She was too overprotective, and that made me feel worse. Then, it was like a curtain came down. Suddenly, no one wanted to talk about it. It was like, if we didn't think about it, we could pretend that it never happened. We never discussed it. The subject was taboo. Then the nightmares came. I would wake up at night reliving the experience. Knowing what I know now, I think my parents should have gotten me help, but they didn't. They would just soothe me and tell me to go back to sleep and forget about it. ✆

Even in situations where there has been no disclosure, there is suppression for the victim and often the perpetrator. Once the abuse has stopped, neither may want to think of it. They may pretend that it never happened. For the victim, this intense suppression with no outlet may become repression where the psyche relegates the information and feelings to the darkest corner of the mind. Sometimes the victim can recall the information consciously or given certain stimuli. In other cases, the facts and feelings associated with the abuse remain unavailable although the victim may well send out tentacles that become symptoms. These unexplained feelings, behaviors, and images distress the victim who has no knowledge of their origin.

RISK FACTORS ASSOCIATED WITH CHILD SEXUAL ABUSE

When considering the victim of child sexual abuse, a much-researched question always arises: "Is there a 'typical victim profile'?"

After consulting a number of research studies, Bolen (2007) concludes, in relation to the race and ethnicity of victims, that the findings are too diverse to form a conclusion. The victims studied, and therefore the representation of ethnic groups, may depend on how and where the sample was gathered. "Female children are more at risk than male children," report the experts (Bolen, 2007; Finkelhor, 1990; Kinnear, 2007). However, this finding is in jeopardy when one looks at the number of victims to the type of offender. Those who sexually abuse boys are likely to have more victims in a lifetime than many of the offenders who abuse girls (Abel & Osborn, 1992; Finkelhor, 1984; Gartner, 2001; van Dam, 2001). Therefore, are fewer boys coming forward and therefore skewing the statistics? The pathology of the offender seems to have a direct bearing on the gender of his or her victim (Dorias, 2009; Stevens, 2001; van Dam, 2001).

As far as the age of victims, boys seem to be abused at younger ages than girls (Bolen, 2007; Dorias, 2009; Finkelhor, 1984; Whetsell-Mitchell, 1995). Bolen (2007) concluded that the most vulnerable age for girls was between 11 and 13 but did note that abuse can occur when the child is very young. It may be distorted memories or the child's inability to recognize the episode as abuse that keeps it from being reported. The most vulnerable age for boys seems to be between 7 and 9 perhaps due to the fact that boys in this culture are seen as more powerful at an earlier age than girls (Finkelhor, 1984; Gartner, 2001). Plus, the typical offender against boys is looking for a child who has not yet developed secondary sexual characteristics.

It becomes clear as one peruses the research that a dysfunctional family puts a child at much more risk for child sexual abuse than one that is functioning well (Bolen, 2007; Finkelhor, 1984; Kinnear, 2007; Saunders, 2012; van Dam, 2001; Whetsell-Mitchell, 1995). Girls with stepfathers, for example, are at greater risk for being abused than their counterparts in other families (Faller, 1988a; Finkelhor, 1984, 1990; van Dam, 2001).

Bolen (2007) felt that the impact of both religion and family income was unclear when one considered the various studies available. Once again, this may also be dependent upon how and from where the sample was drawn.

There seems to be a bit more of a consensus on the psychological characteristics that might make a child vulnerable to being abused. Ferrara (2002) explains that it is the cycle of unmet needs that makes a child unable to meet the challenge of normal developmental tasks and also renders a child more vulnerable to being sexually abused.

When a child does not receive adequate nurturing, he or she searches for attention elsewhere. Children whose everyday life has been peppered with messages that demean do not develop healthy self-esteem and are therefore at risk for manipulation and possibly abuse. Paradoxical messages or behaviors from parents confuse the child and can also make him or her unable to discern what is safe and what is unsafe.

&

Helen's mother, Letty, was totally overwhelmed by her role as a single parent to four children. Pregnant at 15, Letty moved in with her boyfriend who beat her. When she had her first child, Helen, social services told her that the baby would be removed unless she left her abusive boyfriend. Letty returned to her own mother's and got a job that kept her away from the house for long hours. When she was not working, she was using a variety of drugs. Helen was cared for by her grandmother who told her from the onset what a burden she was. This woman tied Helen to her crib and deprived her of food. When Letty did come home, she showered affection on little Helen, but her intervention was sporadic. Finally, after a feud with her mother, Letty took Helen and moved in with another boyfriend. With him she had three more children. These years were somewhat stable for Helen despite the frequent violent arguments between Letty and her boyfriend. But the boyfriend was killed in a motorcycle accident, and Letty was again on her own. Now she turned on Helen who she saw as the beginning of all her problems. Helen was no longer a cute baby and, as a child of seven, had a mind of her own. Letty could not deal with the child's oppositional behavior and often tried to beat her into compliance. When she learned that a new boyfriend had started to sexually abuse Helen, Letty was furious insisting that Helen had "taken him away." Helen had enjoyed being with this new man. He gave her the attention that she so desperately craved.

&

Interviewed offenders reported that they targeted children with low self-esteem. This child was one who had significant stress in his or her life, usually due to family problems. This child also tended to be alone and was naïve, needy, and trusting (Elliot, 1993; van Dam, 2001, 2006). When children acquiesce to adults readily, they can more easily be targeted. The child who is more verbal, confident, and assertive has a significantly lower risk for victimization.

Children who lack friends or do not socialize well with peers may also look to adults for attention. Because many offenders will break down the child's defenses by becoming an ally and acting like a peer, vulnerable children can be easily fooled into believing that the adult merely wants to be a friend (Gartner, 2001; Leberg, 1997; van Dam, 2001, 2006).

Although any child could be the target of a sexual offender, these abusers tend to look for the characteristics that make the child the most pliable.

Summary

What is child sexual abuse? Child sexual abuse refers to an underage child being touched or exploited sexually by an adult or older child for the gratification of that abuser. This abuse usually involves some type of enticement, entrapment, coercion, or force, and the abuser often requests or leads the child to believe that secrecy is necessary.

Child sexual abuse is usually traumatic although this may be influenced by such factors as the identity of the abuser as well as dynamics related to the child and his or her environment. Gender may also play a role in how the child is abused and how he or she reacts. Society often sees the sexual abuse of boys as "training" rather than abusive.

There are numerous myths surrounding child sexual abuse related to whether the child invited the abuse, who is abused more often, and the behavior of the offender.

Although child sexual abuse has decreased somewhat in the last few years, it is still a problem.

There are several types of child sexual abuse including incest, abuse outside the family, and sexual exploitation, which refers to prostituting or using children in the production of pornography. There are phases of sexual abuse beginning with the engagement of children through a progression of behaviors that desensitize them to the abuse referred to as *grooming*. In addition, offenders often groom the adult community by gaining the trust of the adults who might otherwise protect these children.

The sexual interaction and secrecy phases follow engagement. Sometimes there is disclosure of the abuse, but in other situations, there is not. Disclosure may be accidental or intentional. In addition, there is often suppression when either the child tries to deny or recant that anything has happened or the adults around the child—sometimes trying to protect the child—try to deny the abuse or encourage the victim to forget. Some experts believe that there are risk factors for certain children to be abused, whereas others do not.

Review Questions

1. How is sexual abuse defined?

2. What influences the degree of trauma that children experience from sexual abuse?

3. How does gender figure in the definition of child sexual abuse?

4. What are the prevailing myths about child sexual abuse?

5. What are the types of child sexual abuse?

6. Name the phases of child sexual abuse. What happens during each one?

7. How are children groomed for sexual abuse? Who else is groomed?

8. How might abuse be disclosed?

9. What puts children at risk for sexual abuse?

CHAPTER 3

Theories, Models, and Context of Child Sexual Abuse

To better understand the personal impact of child sexual abuse on victims, perpetrators, and families, it is first necessary to consider some of the theoretical efforts to explain the phenomenon in terms that we can comprehend and then address. This chapter looks at some of the theories that have been developed and the assumptions that have been made about the dynamics of child sexual abuse.

EARLY THEORIES AND MODELS

Early theories tended to center around the incestuous family and the perpetrator. The former was stimulated by the work of the child protection movement, whereas the characteristics of the nonfamilial perpetrator often originated in the criminal justice camp. Later, there was more cross-fertilization as a variety of professionals sought to understand the complex nature of child sexual abuse.

Father-Daughter Incest and Systems Theory

During the 1960s and 1970s, when child sexual abuse attracted scrutiny from professionals as well as the lay public, systems theory had become prominent. This theory, gleaned originally from biology, was applied to social work and especially to incestuous family situations. The general theory suggested that organisms were a complex system of parts that were interconnected and interdependent. Change in one area would necessarily affect the other parts of the system. One of the first to apply systems theory to incest was physician Judith Herman in her well-known book, *Father-Daughter Incest* (1981). This early attempt to provide a systematic picture of the incestuous family as an interconnected system where each of the members influences the behaviors of others and the system as a whole met with enthusiastic endorsement.

Herman and Hirschman (2000) characterized the father/offender as someone whose own impaired development has left him with a "capacity to nurture [that] is severely impaired" (p. 56). He also learns that he, by virtue of his gender, inherits a variety of societal rights, including the rights to subordinate women and children. This patriarchy, as well as his pathology due to his own unmet needs, impacts his family in an intricate network of relationships, spelling out discord with his wife and the sexual abuse of his daughter.

Although Herman and Hirschman wrote largely from a feminist perspective, other authors added their voices to the description of families where every member had a contribution to the incestuous dynamics (Forward & Buck, 1978; Giaretto, 1982; James & Nasjleti, 1983; Justice & Justice, 1980; Meiselman, 1992). Justice and Justice (1980) broadened the profile of the incestuous and *tyrant* father to the *introvert* who keeps himself shut away from the world and turns to his child for nurture and the *rationalizer* who explains away his behaviors by saying that he is teaching his daughter about sex, protecting her from others, and loving her, or sees nothing wrong with in-house expression of sexuality (pp. 59–77). Despite this more inclusive typology, these theorists also saw the entire system as dysfunctional and interdependent in its pathology. Bolen (2007) points out that these early systems theory approaches "(a) applied primarily to father-daughter incest and (b) continued to remove blame from the offender" (p. 27) by crediting the entire family with the dysfunction.

Theories of Victim Dynamics

Bolen (2007) also postulates that several early theories of child sexual abuse suggested that the victim was in some way responsible. Had she perhaps seduced the offender (Bender & Blau, 1937; Kreiger, Rosenfeld, Gordon, & Bennett, 1980)? Some theorists fell back on Freud's seduction theory (discussed in Chapter 1) that entertained the possibility that abused girls had mistaken fantasies for actual abuse. Others theorized that the child might have encouraged or initiated the abuse (Kreiger et al., 1980). Another suggestion was that the victim initiated the abuse due to her attempts to maintain the family as a unit or due to rejection from her mother (Alexander, 1985; Cohen, 1983). Currently, clinicians lean away from the assumption of victim culpability,

believing that any apparent seductiveness on the part of the victim is either misinterpreted or learned behavior from previous abuse.

Child Sexual Abuse Accommodation Syndrome

It was Roland Summit's Child Sexual Abuse Accommodation Syndrome that most significantly influenced the response to and treatment of victims. As mentioned briefly in Chapter 1, Summit postulated that the abused child developed a set of survival mechanisms that enable her (or him, although Summit's emphasis was on females) to survive in the face of the abuse, the family's denial of it, and society's tendency to "look the other way" or question the disclosing child's credibility. The theory suggests five categories, the first two of which, secrecy and helplessness, are already woven into the tapestry of family and victim interaction. According to Summit (1983), the remaining three categories "are sequential contingencies which take on increasing variability and complexity" (p. 83). The categories of the Child Sexual Abuse Accommodation Syndrome are (a) secrecy; (b) helplessness; (c) entrapment and accommodation; (d) delayed, conflicted, and unconvincing disclosure; and (e) retraction.

Secrecy is often a part of the family's makeup before the onset of the abuse. "What happens in the family stays in the family" is the classic family motto. Thus, children are also hesitant to go outside the family to seek help when they are being abused. To compound this and allow an atmosphere perfect for the incubation of the abuse, the family members are also not effective in communicating with one another. It is quite common for siblings to be enduring abuse in the same household and never talk to one another about the fact. This lack of communication is accompanied by an insistence that the children in the family respect and acquiesce to adults. Even if children are taught that it is acceptable to ignore strangers, they must be compliant to the adults they know. Adults have the only power, placing the children in positions of powerlessness and encouraging feelings of *helplessness*.

When the sexual abuse occurs, the child may not feel that disclosure is an option. Instead she or he feels trapped into coping with what a more powerful adult is subjecting her or him to (*entrapment*). The only way to cope with the abuse, therefore, is to live with it, or accommodate (*accommodation*), sometimes even coming to assume that it is the norm for families. But the violated child may not be able to totally contain her or his emotions. Instead, the repressed feelings leak out in self-punishment, self-mutilation, eating disorders, and behavioral problems. These behaviors may actually be cries for help—unrecognized and addressed often by a response to the behavior rather than the cause. These *conflicted, delayed, and unconvincing disclosures*, when not recognized by adults, convince the child that "no one cares," believes, or will help. Even when the child does make an outright disclosure, she or he feels compelled to retract the accusations (*retraction*) so convinced that no one will believe what is happening.

Summit's theory was the first to look seriously at the impact on the victim and make a major contribution to the treatment of abused children (see also Corwin, 2002).

Theories of Nonoffending Parent Responsibility

The nonabusive parent too was assigned blame in the early years of child sexual abuse research. Mothers, as partners of abusive fathers, were said to have colluded in some manner. Krane (2003) suggests that the term *dysfunctional families* as used in reference to incest could more likely be described in the mind of early practitioners as "dysfunctional mothers." The author describes early views of incestuous families in light of the relationship between the abuser and his wife. She explains that the etiology of the problem was explained in the following manner:

> The incest served to reduce the father's sexual tension that stemmed from an impaired sexual and emotional relationship with his wife. . . . By assuming material roles, the daughter [victim] became the central figure and satisfied the father's needs. These needs were assumed to be denied by the man's wife, who was seen as inadequate on many fronts. . . . [T]he mother was identified as the "cornerstone" in the "pathological family system." She consciously or unconsciously orchestrated or sanctioned the incest. (pp. 65–66, based on Lustig, Spellman, Dresser, & Murray, 1966)

Mothers in incest situations were described as cold, rejecting, withdrawn, infantile, and dependent (Bolen, 2007; Krane, 2003; Sgroi, 1982).

Many researchers believed that the mothers were aware on some level that incest was taking place. These women, it was believed, had difficulty with their roles as wives due to their ambivalence about their own sexuality and the resulting inability to tolerate intimacy. As a result, she abandoned her role as mother, placing their daughters in the position of assuming the wife role and with it sexual partnership with their fathers (Bolen, 2007; Cohen, 1983; Greenspun, 1994; James & McKinnon, 1990).

Bolen (2007) believes that early theories about the nonabusive mother can be organized into three categories: (a) that she was collusive and withdrawn, (b) that she had distinct personality defects that complemented the father in a manner that stimulated his incestuous behavior, and finally (c) that she was herself a helpless victim who was unable to protect her daughter (see also Johnson, 1992a). This author goes on to postulate that if there was any truth to these characterizations of the mother, there were also reasons for any similarities she might have to the beliefs about her.

Withdrawal and collusion may have been based on patterns that the mother had learned if she was sexually abused as a child. Some authors point to the possibility and even probability of abuse in the mother's own background (Finkelhor, 1984; Oates, Tebbutt, Swanson, Lynch, & O'Toole, 1998; Sgroi, 1982). In addition, incestuous families are characterized by an extreme number of stressors: financial concerns, unemployment, a higher number of children, emotional isolation, rigid roles, alcoholism, rigidly followed division of labor, and others that might tax even a higher-functioning mother (Bolen, 2007; Carter, 1999; Herman & Hirschman, 2000; Johnson, 1992a; Strand, 2000). Strand (2000) concludes that blaming the mother in an incest situation is an offshoot of the fact that society frequently holds mothers responsible for the problems of their children.

The view that these mothers were weak, helpless, needy, and dependent upon their husbands is in essence elevating the offender (Bolen, 2007; Cohen, 1983). Later theorists argue that this view is also to dilute his responsibility for the offense. Similarly, labeling the mother as a victim who would sacrifice her child's needs is to deny her own possible traumatization that may prevent her from conceptualizing her role in a manner that allows her to protect her child (Bolen, 2007). In a comparison of studies of nonoffending mothers, Tamraz (1996) found that no consistent conclusions could be drawn about the pathology of these mothers due to the variability of the data.

Although current research does not support the theory that mothers necessarily collude in the abuse of their children, early beliefs continue to echo through the helping system. The stigma of "failure to protect" is still often the tag given to nonoffending mothers (Krane, 2003). In reality, the nonoffending parent, given the right amount of support and attention, can provide an important role in the child's healing (Bratton, Ceballos, Landreth, & Costos, 2012).

Early Theories Around Sexual Offending

When one explores the early years of research on sexual offending, there are sexual theorists who immediately come to mind. The first is A. Nicholas Groth, a psychologist who practiced with incarcerated male offenders in both the Massachusetts and Connecticut correctional systems. From his work, he devised the much used, copied, and adapted typology of pedophilia. Groth postulated that most offenders fell into one of two categories: fixated and regressed (Burgess, Groth, Holstrom, & Sgroi, 1978).

Typology of Pedophilia

The *fixated offender* was one whose primary orientation was toward children, and predominantly male children. Emotionally and developmentally he became fixated in adolescence, and his maladaptive resolution of life issues created an individual who rationalized his abusive behavior in such a manner that he felt little guilt, shame, or remorse. His choice of male victims was a way of undoing or redoing his own victimization as a child in a compulsive, premeditated manner, while identifying closely with his victims and seeing himself as a fellow child. This offender, Groth believed, had little or no interest in age-mates unless he had children who might become his targets. Nor did he have many social skills with which to forge relationships with age-mates. He had no history of alcohol or drug abuse (Groth, 2001; Preble & Groth, 2002; Sgroi, 1982).

The *regressed offender* presented somewhat differently. He seemed to have achieved a tenuous developmental level in adulthood, but the crises and conflicts of his life cause him to regress to a sexual interest in children. He may have relationships with women but finds these relationships conflictual, seeking a female child as a substitute.

In doing so, he treats her as a miniadult, showering her with attention, gifts, and so on, that he might an adult partner. His initial abuse of her is impulsive, episodic, and precipitated by stress although he may then get into a pattern of abuse. His abuse of the child may coexist with his sexual relationship with an adult partner. This offender often needs bolstering by drugs or alcohol to commit his offense or more often excuse his behavior. He does feel shame and guilt although these may not be sufficient deterrents to future offending (Groth, 2001; Preble & Groth, 2002; Sgroi, 1982).

Groth's theory, popular in the helping community, was adapted in numerous ways. However, the theory was developed based on incarcerated males, and practitioners felt that it did not fully address all types of offenders. Despite this shortcoming, echoes of Groth's thinking can still be seen in the field of child sexual abuse assessment and treatment.

Sexual Addiction Theory

Another camp adopted the *addiction theory* as a way to explain sexual offending against children. Initially suggested by Patrick Carnes, this theory compared sexual offending to other types of addictions that had a specific cycle. An addict, said Carnes, develops a delusional thought process that is supported by a distorted belief system. He uses denial and rationalization, and eventually he begins to believe his own lies. His addiction becomes part of a 4-step cycle. First he becomes preoccupied with sex and his fantasies about being sexual with children. These ideas actually become obsessive, and he begins a ritualized set of behaviors that will eventually lead to the offending behavior. For example, he might engage a child in a specific manner, in a specific place—all part of a choreographed behavioral dance. He feels unable to stop or control his behavior. Despair may follow his offending, but when

the cycle begins again, he falls into the pattern once more (Carnes, 2001; Marshall & Marshall, 2006).

In short, a sexual addiction is characterized by several factors (Schwartz, 1995, pp. 2/16–2/17):

- A pattern of out-of-control behavior
- Significant consequences that result from this behavior
- Inability to stop the behavior despite these consequences
- Persistent pursuit of high-risk or self-destructive behavior
- An ongoing desire to limit the behavior
- Presence of sexual obsession and/or fantasy used as a coping strategy
- Escalation of type of sexual activity as current level is not enough
- Severe mood changes around the sexual activity
- Preoccupation with and excessive time devoted to sexual interests and pursuits
- Neglect of normal daily activities in favor of sexual fantasy and pursuits

Critics of the addiction theory being used to explain child sexual abusers argue that it is not entirely applicable as it might be in the case of chemical addiction such as alcohol. Carnes and his colleagues refute this argument by saying that there is a chemical component to sexual addiction, but an internal one. This physiological dependence results from "a bio-chemical connection based on the relationship between the endorphins, a peptide known as phenylethylamine (PEA) and monoamine oxidase (MAO)" (Schwartz, 1995, p. 2/17; see also Carnes, 1992).

Even those who may still borrow many of the tenets of the addiction theory without seeing the theory as an adequate explanation to describe all child sexual abusers will agree that presenting this type of deviance as an addiction has served to bring the treatment of the condition to the mainstream of therapy through connecting it with more commonly treated addictions like alcoholism (Schwartz, 1995).

Preconditions Model

Perhaps the most influential early theory about sexual offending against children was Finkelhor's preconditions model. This model postulated that in order for the sexual abuse of a child to take place, there must be four preconditions in place: (a) motivation to sexually abuse on the part of the perpetrator, (b) overcoming the perpetrator's internal inhibitors, (c) overcoming external inhibitors, and (d) overcoming the child's resistance (Finkelhor, 1984).

The offender's *motivation to sexually abuse* has three components, which are not in and of themselves preconditions. First, the offender must feel some *emotional congruence* to the child in that the child or children fulfill some emotional need in him. Such emotional congruence may be the result of his own arrested emotional development or may be a reenactment of his own childhood trauma. Some offenders have a need to be powerful and controlling and turn to a child to meet this need. Next, he must feel *sexually aroused* by the child or by children in general, a possible result of the offender's own traumatic childhood experience or his modeling of the sexual interest of someone in his childhood. It is not surprising that offenders would be attracted to child pornography, which serves for them, among other things, to normalize their sexual interest. Further, there is *blockage*, meaning that the offender's other sources of sexual gratification are either unavailable to him or less satisfying. Many sexual offenders do not have the social skills to forge healthy and satisfying adult to adult relationships (Finkelhor, 1984).

A second precondition for offending is that the offender *must overcome his own internal inhibitors*. Internal inhibitors can be explained simplistically as the small voice that tells a person that a thought or action is "not okay." But certain factors like the influence of substances or the influence of abnormal family rearing can drown out that voice to the extent that some offenders are able to ignore it or in fact never hear it. The tolerance of acts when one is under the influence of alcohol, the weak criminal sanctions against offenders, and a social tolerance for sexualizing children in advertising further mask the inhibiting voice in the offender's mind.

A third precondition relates to *overcoming external inhibitors* that might otherwise protect the child. The primary caretaker, usually the mother, is in the pivotal role to protect the child. When that caretaker is absent or unable to protect the child for some other reason, the offender has more opportunity to abuse. The lack of support given to parenting in today's society means that parents sometimes unwittingly may place their children at risk. In addition, U.S. culture still believes in the sanctity of the family—a value that may be beneficial unless it is within the family that the child is being abused (Finkelhor, 1984).

Finally, the fourth precondition involves *overcoming the child's resistance*. When children are insecure, are deprived, or lack knowledge of sexual abuse, they are more vulnerable to sexual abuse. In addition, the inherent social powerlessness of children who are often taught to follow the directions of adults without question adds to their risk (Finkelhor, 1984).

Finkelhor's model has been widely accepted and is still used as a way to understand not only the motivation of offenders but also why children might be abused.

Cognitive Distortions Theory

Other significant work was done by Gene Abel and associates as they sought to explain what motivates offenders toward sexual abuse. Although not a well-defined theory per se and not articulated fully in any single publication, the work of Abel et al. (see Abel et al., 1989; Abel, Mittelman, & Becker, 1985; Abel, Rouleau, & Cunningham-Rathner,

1986) brought to light the concept of cognitive distortions to aid in understanding the psychopathology of offenders. Although other theorists had suggested that faulty thinking was inherent in some forms of pathology, Abel's work was the first to frame these cognitive distortions as part of antisocial behavior and sexual offending (Ward, Polaschek, & Beech, 2006).

Abel and his colleagues propose that boys learn in childhood what arousal patterns are appropriate and which are not, inhibiting the latter. In some boys, these deviant patterns of sexual arousal are not successfully extinguished, and when, in his early 20s, the existence of these patterns begins to be disturbing to a young man, he compensates by developing idiosyncratic beliefs that rationalize his deviant sexual interests, for example, in children. In the case of a child molester, Abel et al. (1989) explain that the cognitive distortions "appear to allow the offender to justify his ongoing sexual abuse of children without anxiety, guilt and loss of self-esteem that would usually result from an individual committing behaviors contrary to the norms of his society" (p. 137).

In short, the cognitive distortions protect the offender's self-concept and allow him to continue to perpetrate the behavior. Over time, these thinking distortions become more and more embedded in the personality of the offender (Abel et al., 1986).

Ward and Keenan (1999) later identified five areas in which they believed that sexual offenders hold distorted views. First, sexual offenders see the child as a sexual being able to and wanting to engage in sexuality. Second, they do not believe that the sexual activity will harm the child in any way. Some even rationalize that it will be of some benefit (e.g., experience or undoing past harm). Third, they may believe that on some level they are superior and therefore entitled to engage in sex with whomever they choose. Fourth, the offenders see the world as dangerous and others out to reject or hurt them, meaning that they

must fight back to regain control. And finally, because they perceive the world as uncontrollable, the offenders believe that circumstances in their environment are out of their control (see also Marziano, Ward, Beech, & Pattison, 2006).

Although Abel's initial work was further developed by others and has done much to enhance the understanding of offending behavior, some critics argued that cognitive distortions are only the tip of the psychological iceberg that explains the motivation and pathology of offenders.

CURRENT THEORETICAL UNDERSTANDING OF SEXUAL OFFENDING AGAINST CHILDREN _____

The purpose of postulating theories in a field such as the abuse of children is to enable practitioners to better address the problem, treat the participants, and prevent the abuse from occurring in the future. Although there has been much attention given to the symptomology of the victim and the involvement of the nonabusing parents, it seems clear that theorists need to understand why offenders behave as they do in order to fully address the problem. Ward et al. (2006) suggest that theories about sexual offending can be broken down into three categories: (a) multifactorial theories, (b) single-factor theories, and (c) descriptive models.

Multifactorial Theories

A *multifactorial theory*, as applied to child sexual abuse, is one that suggests that there are several important variables that result in the offending behavior occurring. Perhaps the best known of these theories is the precondition model mentioned earlier. As explained earlier, Finkelhor

(1990) suggested that several factors needed to be in place in order for the abuse to take place.

A second multifactorial model is Marshall and Barbaree's (1990) integrated theory. This theory was developed to explain sexual offending in general but can also be used to address child sexual abuse specifically.

The integrated theory suggests that an important task for adolescent males is to learn how to discriminate between their aggressive and sexual impulses, learning also to control aggression during sexual experiences. Individuals who have attachment difficulties, low self-esteem, poor coping skills, and inadequate coping skills—referred to as vulnerability factors—will find this task much more difficult to accomplish. These vulnerability factors combined with the surge of male hormones inherent in adolescent development increase the chances of a teen behaving in a sexually aggressive manner (Marshall & Marshall, 2000; Ward et al., 2006).

This theory also looks at the etiology of the vulnerability factors. Inadequate child rearing (abuse, neglect, etc.) results in a child who has difficulty attaching to the caretaker, which then results in difficulty trusting. At the same time, the individual feels unworthy of being loved. The impaired development and its consequences result in poor emotional coping, a feeling of personal ineffectiveness, low self-esteem, hampered judgment, poor self-regulation, and impulsivity. Feeling that those who were supposed to be there for him (parents and other significant people) have not been, he feels rejected and interprets the world as an unsatisfying and threatening place. This individual will often meet his psychological needs through sexual activity. His interest in sex is enhanced by his use of pornography, which he eventually plays out through his abuse of children (Marshall, 1997; Marshall & Barbaree, 1990; Marshall & Marshall, 2000; Ward et al., 2006).

One criticism of the integrated theory is that it identifies the lack of self-regulation as an important factor. Critics argue that some offenders are quite able to plan, which involves a good deal of self-regulation (Ward et al., 2006).

Hall and Hirschman's *quadripartite theory* is another multifactorial model. These authors hypothesized that the most significant contributor to child sexual abuse is physiological sexual arousal. A second factor, cognitive distortions, allows the offender to explain his behavior and enables his continued abuse of children. In addition, a third factor was related to the offender's inability to identify and manage his own emotions (known as *affective dyscontrol* by Hall and Hirschman and *emotional regulation* by others). In other words, an offender who feels lonely or sad, rather than acknowledging these feelings, may try to escape this discomfort by the use of alcohol, by masturbation, or through pornography, which may in turn lead him to sexually acting out. Or he may feel aggression as a result of his perceived helplessness, and not having clear differentiation between aggression and sexuality, he may act out sexually (Hall & Hirschman, 1992; Ward et al., 2006).

The final factor in this model is that of personality problems, which have emerged from adverse circumstances during his developmental years (e.g., abuse, neglect, alcoholism). These experiences have shaped his attitudes and inhibited normal skill development especially in the social and emotional realm.

A significant criticism of Hall and Hirschman's model is that the authors fail to clarify in any detail how the four factors are developed as well as how they interact with each other to explain the causes of child sexual abuse (Ward et al., 2006).

In a knitting together of the aforementioned three multifactorial theories, Ward and Siegert proposed the *pathways model*. The key assumption of this model is that all human actions are the result of the interaction between psychological and physiological systems. To explain why someone offends against children, Ward and

Siegert (2002) identified four psychological mechanisms that interact: (a) emotional dysregulation, (b) intimacy and social skills deficits, (c) cognitive distortions, and (d) distorted sexual scripts (Ward et al., 2006).

To understand how individuals who sexually offend experience *emotional dysregulation*, one must identify emotional competence. Ward et al. (2006) explain that there are skills that, when present, suggest emotional competence. In the estimation of these authors, an individual must not only be able to discern his or her own emotional state but must also be sensitive to the emotions of others. Further, he or she must be able to respond to them with empathy, recognizing that relationships are built upon understanding and regulating emotions in a variety of situations. This individual must also have the ability to adapt when emotions are unpleasant. And finally, culture plays a role in what emotions are considered to be appropriate, how they are expressed, and how one responds. It is in many of these emotional areas that sexual offenders have a great deal of difficulty.

Ward and Siegert (2002) also believe that the difficulty with intimacy and social skills experienced by offenders results from issues in childhood that have hampered their ability to forge healthy attachment relationships. The difficulty in building fundamental relationships inhibits trusting, self-regulation, problem solving, and so on.

These authors point to cognitive distortions but outline them more fully than other theorists. They suggest that offenders against children believe that their victims are sexual in nature and have sexual needs themselves. Therefore, offenders believe that any sexual interaction with children may actually be beneficial for these children rather than harmful. In addition to beliefs about their victims, offenders also have preconceptions about the world in which they live, seeing it as uncontrollable and dangerous. As a result, some people, themselves included, are entitled to assert their rights and replicate the rejection and abuse they may have experienced or perceived that they have experienced (Ward et al., 2006).

Finally, these authors explain the deviant arousal of sexual offenders by suggesting that they have developed sexual scripts through the faulty and abusive experiences they have had during development. The culture and their own experiences have also contributed to this script. A sexual script is basically an assumption about when sex will take place, where, how, and with whom as well as how it should be interpreted. Distortions in a sexual script might relate to inappropriate partners, maladaptive practices (e.g., sadism), or inappropriate contexts (e.g., impersonal sex, having sex only when angry) (Ward et al., 2006).

The pathways model also describes that there are different pathways through which each offender might abuse (see Figure 3.1). In other words, there is always a primary causal mechanism or area in which the offender has the most difficulty. Ward et al. (2006) use the example of a sexual offender who lacks emotional regulation skills and turns sex into a way of coping with his feelings of inadequacy. When he is feeling stressed or despondent, abusing a child may elevate his mood temporarily. Another offender might have such significant deficits in intimacy that his only way of feeling at all intimate or satisfied is through sexually abusing a child.

Ward and Siegert explain that their model is an emerging one and subject to further change (for more details, see Ward et al., 2006).

Single-Factor Theories

Single-factor theories refer to models that examine individual factors that are implicated in sexual offending. The most widely known of these is the use of cognitive distortions to explain sexual offending. According to this

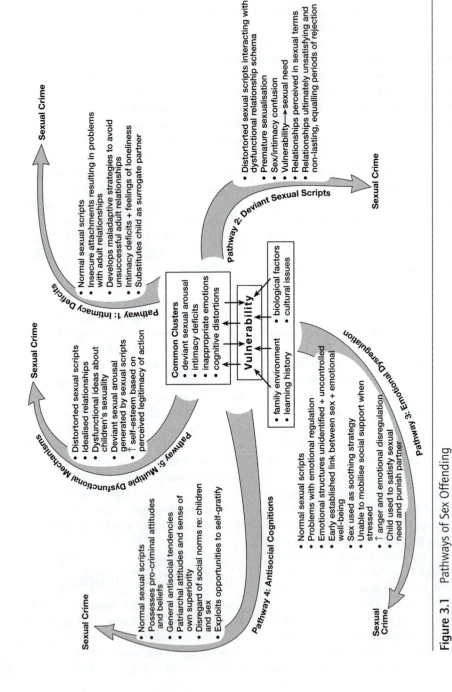

Figure 3.1 Pathways of Sex Offending

SOURCE: Connolly, M. (2004). Developmental trajectories and sexual offending. *Qualitative Social Work*, 3, 39–59. © SAGE Publications, 2004.

theory, sexual offenders use rationalizations and justifications to normalize their behaviors. Their impaired view of reality has often resulted from their own early experiences. Abel and his colleagues (1989) first used the concept of cognitive distortions to explain the faulty thinking of those who sexually offend. As these researchers explained,

> Clinically, a child molester's cognitive distortions appear to allow the offender to justify his ongoing sexual abuse of children without the anxiety, guilt and loss of self-esteem that would usually result from an individual committing behaviors contrary to the norms of his society. (pp. 137–138)

Offenders exhibit a variety of types of distorted thinking. They may believe that everything is black or white, that they are entitled to do something because they want to, and that they are themselves victims, or make other excuses for their behaviors (Flora et al., 2008; Ward et al., 2006).

Another popular idea was that offenders were deficient in empathy and could not relate to the impact that their abuse was having on children. Thus, one part of treatment must be to aid them in developing empathy (Seto, 2008). Several other single-factor theories emerged over the years including those that suggested that offenders have deviant sexual preferences and that they have intimacy deficits and are unable to achieve healthy adult intimacy (Ward et al., 2006). These theories all have merit but have tended to be replaced by more complex multifactorial theories (for more detailed explanation of such theories, see Ward et al., 2006).

Descriptive Theories

Descriptive theories is a term used by Ward et al. (2006) to refer to models that consider the offender's chain or process of offending. Addiction cycles and relapse prevention models fall into this category. All of these models outline specific steps that lead up to offending. For example, Salter's deviant cycle model is one such descriptive theory. In this model, Salter (1995) suggests that the offender begins in a negative affective state and feels deviant sexual arousal. He then makes seemingly unimportant decisions that nonetheless lead him toward abusing. For example, his route for his evening walk takes him, seemingly coincidentally, past the park where children are playing. The cycle continues when he spies a child that attracts him and begins his sexual fantasies about that child. He may then begin to groom the child by meeting him or her and engaging that child. This leads to his offense and his efforts to maintain secrecy. What follows may be his remorse or fear of getting caught. Theories such as this one that describe the offender's cycle can also be used in treatment to help him to interrupt that cycle (for more detailed explanation of such theories, see Ward et al., 2006).

Built upon the concept that an offender can understand his cycle of offense and interrupt it before the abuse occurs is what gave rise to the treatment model that, until recently, has been the primary model used in the treatment of offenders.

The relapse prevention (RP) model uses some of the principles of cognitive-behavioral therapies and is actually educational in nature, focusing on helping the offender to recognize his own pattern of abusing and learning to monitor and interrupt it himself. With roots in the treatment of substance abuse, the original RP model was developed by G. Alan Marlatt and his colleague, who also suggested (see Marlatt, 1985) that such treatment designed to deter relapse could also be used with sexual offenders. After some revision, D. Richard Laws later tailored this technique to the sex offender population and published the technique in his volume *Relapse Prevention With Sex Offenders* (1989) with the warning of sorts that this might not be the perfect treatment for sex offenders. Despite this remark, many clinicians began to use this model as the best method to treat sex offenders (Laws, Hudson, & Ward, 2000). Certainly with a motivated offender, the idea of self-regulation can be an asset.

The theories mentioned so far were designed primarily to describe male perpetrators. But women also abuse children. How are these offenders addressed theoretically?

Women Who Sexually Abuse Children

Compared to what the literature has to offer on males who sexually offend against children, there has been less research done on their female counterparts. Yet victim disclosures tell clinicians that women do abuse children. Despite the fact that only 1% to 2% of convicted sexual abusers are women, adult survivors report that between 6% and 60% (depending upon the particular study) of their abusers were women (Davin, Hislop, & Dunbar, 1999; Ford, 2006; Hislop, 2001). What accounts for society's apparent failure to recognize women as sexual offenders and therefore generate data on the etiology of their offending behavior? The consensus among researchers is that the reasons are based on the societal perception of women (Bunting, 2007). As early as 1984, Finkelhor proposed that women were not as likely to perpetrate and/or be recognized as perpetrators for several cultural reasons. The reasons that seemed to underlie the presumption of the lower rate of abuse for women compared to men might be summarized as follows (Finkelhor, 1984):

- Women prefer older and larger sexual partners, whereas men prefer younger and smaller partners.
- Women are less likely to initiate sexual relationships.
- Women are less likely to sexualize emotional or affectional behavior.

- Women react differently from men to the availability of sexual opportunities.
- Women are culturally trained to look at the well-being of the whole child.
- Women are well aware of the feelings of being victimized and therefore less likely to victimize children.

As mentioned in Chapter 1, these assumptions about women are further compounded by the fact that the victims of women are less likely to report the abuse. Boys who are victimized fear that they will be seen as sissies if they report their abuse or worry about their own homosexuality. Daughters who are abused by mothers are frequently sufficiently traumatized that they tend to question their own mental health before they would disclose the abuse.

In addition, sexual abuse by women is out of the frame of reference of most people. Women are seen as mothers, nurturers, and protectors of children. How, for some reason, could a woman abuse a child? The presupposition is that women who sexually abuse must be either overpowered or coerced into the behavior by men who are the primary abusers or, in the case of adolescent boys, somehow dominated by this developing male. The few women who abuse as sole perpetrators are assumed to be mentally ill. Although not the whole picture, these beliefs are in fact supported to some extent by some of the earliest theories about female sexual offenders (FSOs).

The theories about women began with a study of 26 women in a Dallas Incest Treatment program. Much like later theories, McCarty (1986) suggested that the women fell into three categories: the independent offender, the co-offender who abused with a male abuser, and the accomplice who had a less active role in either the abuse or the failure to intervene.

In 1987, Faller added that women offenders could be seen as part of a polyincestuous group involving multiple offenders and multiple victims, as a single parent who uses her child as a surrogate for a mate, as adolescents whose hormonal changes stimulate their pathology, as mentally ill (psychotic) offenders, or as noncustodial parents who either substitute the child for their lost spouse or take their anger at that spouse out on the child through sexual abuse (Faller, 1987).

Matthews, Matthews, and Speltz (1989) devised three categories similar to their predecessors. The teacher–lover is a woman who abuses adolescents relating to them as if they are peers. She sees herself as teaching them about sexuality, as a sexual partner with them, or a combination of the two. The predisposed sexual abuser is one who has had a history of severe sexual abuse and has learned to equate sexuality with nurturing and intimacy. She sees her sexual relationship with her own children as intimacy with them. The male-coerced offender is one who is needy and dependent upon a male in her life. Initially she may be coerced into the abusive acts by him, but later some women will continue to abuse children on their own.

Similarly, Saradjian (1996) separated 50 female abusers in her study into three more groups to study motivation and offending cycle rather than to design specific categories. Women who abused young children did so not only for physical gratification but also to gain feelings of power and control. This may also be their only way of feeling connected to the child (Ford, 2006). Women who abuse adolescents may also be seeking power and control but they tend to idealize their relationships with their victims. Many attribute this to the immature adolescent characteristics normally associated with adults. The woman sees the victim as able to raise her self-esteem and listen to her problems, skills that she does not feel that her adult partners have had. This category is quite similar to Matthews et al.'s teacher–lover group. Once again there is a category of women who are coerced by the men in their lives to become abusive to children (Ford, 2006; Saradjian, 1996).

Some theorists argue that the theories about female offenders have been based on samples that are too small to develop accurate criteria. Further, Vandiver and Kercher (2004) suggest that these categories can be distorted by the sample studies. For example, when a sample comes from a clinical perspective, the results imply that female offenders suffer from severe psychological problems. Samples derived from prison populations are also skewed as few women who offend actually serve prison time. Acknowledging these problems, Vandiver and Kercher (2004) studied 471 female offenders who were registered as such in the state of Texas. They categorized female offenders somewhat differently. The largest category these authors identified was the *heterosexual nurturer* ($n = 146$). These women, who averaged around 30 years of age, victimized male children at an average age of 12 years. Their motivation appeared to fall within the teacher–lover category of the earlier Matthews et al. study. The next group was the *noncriminal homosexual offenders* ($n = 114$), whose victims were females around the age of 13, whereas the offender was usually around 32. These offenders may have been acting with male accomplices, but this information was unclear. The women in both of these categories tended to have only one arrest, and it was projected that they were the least likely to commit sexual offenses in the future (p. 131).

The *female sexual predators* ($n = 112$) were slightly younger, at an average age of 29 years, and abused male children at an average age of 11. This offender's sexual offending was part of a criminal history that involved other offenses. The adult child exploiters ($n = 50$) averaged around age 28 at the time of arrest and their victims averaged at 7 years old. Half of these offenders were related to the victim and included mothers molesting their own children. Again, it was inconclusive as to how often these women abused with a male co-offender. The *homosexual criminals* ($n = 22$) whose average age was 32 years had the highest number of arrests and victims averaged around 11 years of age. This group was more likely to force their victims into sexual acts or prostitution (Vandiver & Kercher, 2004, p. 132). The last cluster, *aggressive homosexual offenders*, abused adults rather than children and therefore are not explained more fully here.

Although these researchers did have a significant sample, they admit that there were some limitations with this study. Future studies should have a more random geographically based sample and employ broader sampling methods. Variables such as co-offending should also be considered.

In a small study (*n* = 15) of incarcerated FSOs, Beech, Parrett, Ward, and Fisher (2009) compared patterns seen in male offenders with those seen in female offenders. Instead of calling these cognitive distortions, these authors explained that people develop deeper level cognitions or groups of cognitions (sometimes referred to as schema or implicit theories [ITs]) that they then use to assess, screen, and interpret the stimuli coming to them from their world. These researchers sought to discover if the five ITs postulated to be present in male offenders could also be attributed to women who abuse children. The ITs present in male offenders were the belief that children are sexual objects, a sense of entitlement, belief in a dangerous world, the concept of uncontrollability, and beliefs related to the nature of harm done to the child. In this study of women offenders, Beech et al. found that, like the men, 87% of these women believed that the *world was dangerous* to them, 53% believed that *they could not control* what happened, 47% saw *children as sexual objects*, and 20% felt that the *sexual activity was not of harm to the children*. The final IT found in men, entitlement, was not identified in any of this sample. There was some indication that these women demonstrated the themes of subjugation and self-sacrifice, but these researchers did not feel that the results of this particular study were sufficient to make a definitive judgment on this factor.

Gannon, Rose, and Ward (2010) developed what they termed the *descriptive model of female sexual offending (DMFSO)* that looks at three main sections of the offender's life: background factors, the preoffense period, and the postoffense period. The life of each offender studied is examined to determine what she experienced in her early family environment, what abuse she may have suffered, what deviant peer influences she had, and what social supports were present. Further, these researchers considered the maladaptive coping styles she may have developed and what mental health problems may have resulted. After examining these factors, Gannon et al. divided their FSOs into three categories according to the pathway to abuse that they adopted.

Explicit approach (Pathway 1) FSOs made up the largest group of the sample. These women explicitly planned their interaction with their victims, showing some similarity to male offenders. Their intent was to sexually abuse their child victims, and they achieved sexual gratification and intimacy through these encounters. Their desire to offend seemed related to their distorted cognitions and values that in turn resulted in problematic goals and coping styles. *Directed avoidant* (Pathway 2) FSOs intended to avoid sexual offending but were groomed and/or coerced to do so by a co-offender (usually male). This type of FSO pattern bears no resemblance to her male offender counterparts. Her feelings of intimacy come from pleasing the coercive male for whom she will do anything, including abuse her own children. She sees him as all powerful and all knowing. She lacks assertiveness, is easily influenced, and rationalizes that the offending behavior is acceptable as she assumes that her male partner sees it so.

The implicit disorganized (Pathway 3) FSO represented the smallest number in the Gannon et al. study. This woman has self-regulatory issues and exhibits sudden and impulsive offense-related behaviors. She does not plan the abuse but does so as a lack of control over her impulses. Although it is not clear whether or not this offender had any sexual fixations, some of the FSOs demonstrated the need for revenge or sexual intimacy through the abuse. In general, she will need help with her ability to cope effectively with major life stresses in a functional manner (Gannon et al., 2010).

Although additional study is needed on female offenders, the research to date demonstrates that they have some characteristics in common with men but still must be seen as a different type of offender with unique needs and perspectives.

RECENT THEORIES TO ADDRESS SEXUAL OFFENDING

Although initially the formulation of theories about sexual offending was as much to understand why people abuse children as it was to treat them, the emphasis is now clearly on treatment. Several models have recently emerged in the field of sexual offending that have been well received in the treatment community.

The risk–needs–responsivity (RNR) model, first outlined by Andrews, Bonta, and Hoge (1990) and later elaborated upon by Andrews and Bonta (2010), has become widely accepted throughout Canada and the United States as a model to inform treatment. As its name implies, the model is based upon three principles: *risk principle* that asserts that criminal behavior can be predicted and the offenders at greatest risk should be treated first; *needs principle* that emphasizes the importance of focusing in treatment on those factors that will reduce recidivism or reoffending; and the *responsivity principle* that suggests that treatment programs should be matched to the specific offender characteristics such as motivation, learning style, individual personality, and interpersonal circumstances (Andrews & Bonta, 2010; Andrews & Dowden, 2007; Laws & Ward, 2011; Ward, Melser, & Yates, 2007). The model builds on the research done on offender characteristics and treatment

outcomes over the last few decades. Theorists know that certain characteristics put someone at a higher risk for offending. Among these are

- antisocial personalities;
- procriminal attitudes combined with social supports (friends, family, peers) that encourage these beliefs;
- substance abuse;
- poor family and peer relationships; and
- failure to excel in school, work, and other pursuits, combined with a lack of acceptable pleasurable outlets (e.g., hobbies).

Theorists also know that offenders whose needs have not been met—resulting in poor self-esteem, anxiety, depression, mental health issues, and health problems—will often seek criminal outlets to feel better. Research has also suggested that offenders do not fit neatly into a mold but rather have individual limitations and circumstances—for example, culture, language, personality style, cognitive abilities, motivation—that must be addressed if there is any hope for change. Considering all these factors allows the clinician to address the specific treatment needs of the offender to promote individual change (Andrews & Bonta, 2010; Ward et al., 2007; Ward & Maruna, 2007; Yates, Prescott, & Ward, 2010).

Critics of the RNR model suggest that, although it can be effectively used as a model to inform treatment practice, it remains a deficit-based approach. These critics argue that strength-based orientations are now meeting with more success with offenders.

One popular strength-based treatment framework is the good lives model (GLM), which offers therapists insight into the assumptions that cause sexual offending, suggests effective aims of therapy, and provides guidelines to aid in treatment. The basic premise of GLM is that people commit sexual offenses because they have not had the ability or opportunity to acquire specific things (goods) in their lives. Instead, various psychological or social influences have led these individuals to take the path of offending to get their needs met. Treatment then uses a cognitive-behavioral approach to helping the offender to find acceptable ways to meet his or her needs while reducing the risk of reoffending. A key component of the GLM is the emphasis on the therapeutic relationship to promote offender motivation and to achieve the goals of treatment (Laws & Ward, 2011; Yates et al., 2010).

How these two models are applied is discussed further in Chapter 14.

OTHER FACTORS INFLUENCING OFFENDING AGAINST CHILDREN _____

The recent theories about sexual abusers have emphasized that it is crucial to look at the variables influencing sexual offending. One interesting clinical finding associated with sexual offending in males is the fact that the use of pornography plays a significant role in their fantasy life and precursor to offending. Investigation into the lives of male sexual offenders indicates that many have other paraphilias in addition to pedophilia (Ball & Seghorn, 1999; Kingston, Federoff, Firestone, Curry, & Bradford, 2008; Nelson, Soutullo, DelBello, & McElroy, 2002; van Dam, 2001).

Paraphilias

James McLaughlin, a New Hampshire detective responsible for the investigation and prosecution of numerous sexual offenders against children, comments, "I have always felt that the sexual urge involved in child sexual abuse had been dismissed too easily. Although the power issue is alive and well, it seems like only one of the pieces behind the behavior." (McLaughlin, 2003)

The term *paraphilia* was first coined in the 1800s by Richard von Krafft-Ebing, a German psychiatrist who studied sexual deviance. Identification of the condition led to extensive research to determine how to treat affected individuals. The term *paraphilia* itself is derived from the Greek *para* (deviation, altered, or the side of) and *philia* (attraction or love) (Flora, 2001; Hickey, 2005; Kaplan & Sadock, 1998). Those exhibiting a paraphilia demonstrate an obsession with some type of unusual sexual response or practice. Fantasy is a fundamental component of the behavior as the individual responds or acts out sexually. There is often a ritualistic aspect to the act as well. Paraphilias usually depend upon this specialized fantasy to achieve arousal. For example, an individual may find it necessary to dress in woman's clothing in order to become sexually aroused. He may or may not act upon his sexual urges.

Although usually found in males, paraphilias have been seen in some women. The onset is usually at the end of puberty (around 20 years old), and by definition, the condition causes extreme distress for the individual. Distress may be a result of the addictive nature of the paraphilia as well as the fear of others learning of the problem (Flora, 2001; Flora et al., 2008; Hickey, 2005).

Some types of paraphilias may be

- *pedophilia* or sexual attraction to children;
- *exhibitionism* or exposing one's genitals;
- *fetishism* or an obsessive sexual attraction to objects;
- *frotteurism* or intense sexual pleasure from rubbing up against or touching strangers or nonconsenting individuals;
- *sexual sadism* or deriving sexual satisfaction from the pain or humiliation of others;
- *sexual masochism* or sexual arousal from having one's self beaten, bound, or humiliated;
- *transvestic festishism* or having intense sexual urges or fantasies as a result of dressing in the clothes of the opposite sex; and
- *voyeurism* or observing unsuspecting people who are naked, disrobing or dressing, or engaging in sexual activity.

Other paraphilias involve intense interest in something by which the individual is aroused sexually including (adapted from http://www.psychdirect.com/forensic/Criminology/para/paraphilia.html)

- *telephone scatalogia:* obscene phone calls;
- *necrophilia:* corpses;
- *partialism:* a focus on specific parts of the body;
- *zoophilia:* animals;
- *coprophilia:* feces;
- *klismaphilia:* enemas; and
- *urophilia:* urine.

Paraphilias: Children and Adolescents

There are several paraphilias that refer specifically to a sexual attraction toward children or adolescents. The most common is *pedophilia* from the Greek *paidos* (child) and *philia* (love). Technically, a pedophile is an individual who is attracted to young or prepubescent children, who may be either male or female. This does not necessarily mean that he or she will act on that attraction. Nor are all those who sexually abuse children classic pedophiles (see Chapter 5). The pedophile fantasizes about prepubescent children and obtains erotic arousal and is often dependent upon this fantasy for any sexual gratification. Fantasies often lead to masturbation or may even be played out in sexual activity with an adult partner. Some pedophiles will also sexually abuse children.

Nepiophilia (from the Greek *nepion* [infant] and *philia* [love]) is the technical term for those who are attracted to children under 3. In common parlance, however, this term is rarely used. Instead, pedophilia often is employed to refer to an interest in children of any age.

More recently, the term *ephebophilia* (from *ephebos* [a postpubescent young person] and *philia*) has come into vogue. Referring to an interest in adolescent boys or girls, the term gained popularity during the clergy abuse scandals as many of the victims were teens. Shortened to *hebophilia* by some sources, this attraction to teens is not as fully understood and is subject to much controversy (Cimbolic & Cartor, 2006). Is it in fact abusive for an adult to have an interest in an adolescent, some question? Others argue that the age of the adolescent as well as his or her knowledge and experience also play a part in the decision.

Several other terms are useful for discussion although rarely used in general references. *Chronophilia* is a rarely used term coined by John Money, which refers to a pedophile sexual interest being discordant with his or her age but more consistent with the age of the victim. For example, a man of 45 might see himself more like a boy of 10 and therefore closer to the age of the boy in whom he is interested. Some researchers attribute this type of interest to the abuser's own victimization around the age of his or her interest: in the earlier situation, around age 10. A *Lolita complex* refers to the attraction of an adult male to female adolescents and was coined based on Vladimir Nabokov's novel *Lolita*. A *Shota complex* is derived from a Japanese word that describes an attraction on the part of an adult (male or female) to a male adolescent.

Although theories that describe offenders discuss their sexual interest in children, not everyone who finds children or adolescents sexually stimulating will act upon those desires. A pederast or an individual engaged in *pederasty* is an adult male who has a sexual relationship with an underage boy. Pederasty was widely practiced in ancient Greece (see Chapter 1). The intent was rationalized as educating the young boy in sexuality rather than just for the pleasure of the adult male.

The motivation and pathology of sexual offenders are complex. Throughout the text, we will begin to look at more individualized pictures of the nature of sexual abuse and those who are impacted by it.

Summary

Numerous theories and models have been developed to aid in the understanding of child sexual abuse and sexual offending. Early models surrounded incest and suggested that such intrafamilial abuse was a result of a dysfunctional family system. There was even a taint of victim culpability as well as the accusation that the nonoffending parent may have enabled the offender to abuse.

Victim dynamics were also studied, and one of the leading theories was that of Roland Summit and his Child Abuse Accommodation Syndrome. This theory suggested that the secrecy of the abuse and the feelings of helplessness in the victim subjected him or her to accommodating to what was being done by the abuser. Thus, victims often did not report abuse or retracted their disclosures. There was much debate over the role of the nonoffending parent, some believing that she or he knew of the abuse while others believed that she or he was unaware of it.

The predominant early theories around sexual offenders were Groth's Typology of Pedophilia, dividing offenders into fixated and regressed categories; Carnes's (and others) sexual addiction theory, suggesting that offenders showed signs of addictive behavior; and Finkelhor's preconditions model, postulating that certain conditions must be in place in order for abuse to occur. Another prominent theory spoke of the influence of cognitive distortions (thinking errors) on the offender's pattern of abuse.

More recently, Ward et al. have categorized many of the more popular theories about offending into the category of *multifactorial theories* (such as the preconditions model and integrated theory). One of these theories, the pathways model, suggests that offenders adopt different pathways based on their individual manner of functioning and view of the world.

Single-factor theories refer to those models that point to a specific factor as an entry into explaining sexual offending. Some popular theories have addressed cognitive distortions, deviant sexual arousal, and issues with developing empathy. Descriptive theories refer to those models that look at an offender's chain or cycle of behavior that leads to his offending behaviors.

Women who abuse children have not been studied as extensively as their male counterparts. The general public does not expect women to abuse as frequently, and in fact, experts believe that some of the abuse by women is couched within caretaking tasks. Those who have studied women believe that their dynamics differ from that of male offenders. Although some women abused as solo offenders, others do so in conjunction and reportedly feeling compelled to do so by male companions.

Several models are impacting the current view of sexual offending and treatment. The Risk–Needs–Responsivity (RNR) Model and the Good Lives Model (GLM) of treatment have been given particular attention. The RNR model focuses services on moderate- and higher-risk offenders, targets for change those characteristics of offenders that are directly linked to reoffending and are responsive to offenders' learning styles, and focuses on social learning and cognitive-behavioral treatment approaches. The GLM focuses on helping individuals achieve in socially acceptable ways the primary human needs sought by all humans. The goal is to help the individual develop a good life that is inconsistent with nonoffending. The GLM de-emphasizes a focus on traditional risk management and avoidance strategies.

There is a high correlation between sexual abuse and other paraphilias or sexual deviations. These are discussed at some length.

1. What was one of the first models that made people aware of child sexual abuse?

2. What is meant by the Child Abuse Accommodation Syndrome?

3. How were nonoffending parents viewed when sexual abuse was initially studied? How are they viewed today?

4. What is Groth's theory of pedophilia?

5. Is sexual offending an addiction? What do experts say?

6. Explain Finkelhor's preconditions model.

7. What are multifactorial theories? Give some examples.

8. What are some explanations about why women are not more often reported as sexual abusers?

9. What theories about sexual offenders are favored today?

10. What are paraphilias? How do they fit in with the explanation of child sexual abuse?

PART II

Victims, Perpetrators, and Nonoffending Parents

CHAPTER 4

Child Victims of Sexual Abuse

Development and Symptomatology

As we consider the child who is being sexually abused, we must look first at what is normal sexual development throughout childhood and then at how sexual abuse affects children of different ages.

HEALTHY SEXUAL DEVELOPMENT

The healthy sexual development of children differs based on a variety of variables, including societal expectations and the culture in which a child is raised. For example, several generations ago, children were not expected to be sexually active as early as they are today. But exposure to sexually explicit information through the media and other factors has increased the knowledge of youth today at earlier ages. In addition, some cultures expect that young children should be shielded from sexual information until later in childhood or adolescence. Still other cultures expose their young people to sexual relations and birth as normal parts of life.

Recently, a number of organizations in collaboration produced the *National Sexuality Education Standards* (Future of Sex Education Initiative, 2012) that outlined what these organizations believe are the current needs of children in grades K–12 for sexuality education. From this document, as well as other contemporary sources, it is possible to put together a very generalized picture of the sexual development of children (see Table 4.1).

These assumptions about children's sexual development give us some perspective as we continue the discussion of how children are impacted at specific ages by being sexually abused. But again this must be tempered by the recognition of an individual child's life construct and culture.

AGE AND THE IMPACT ON DEVELOPMENT

Age as a Factor in Symptomology

The age of the child at the onset of the abuse will have a significant effect on his or her symptomology. A common myth is that very young children, especially those who are preverbal, will not be as affected by the abuse. In fact, this is not the case. The difference is that children who are abused before they are verbal may not have the words to explain what has happened to them. However, memories are often

Table 4.1 Healthy Sexual Development

Age	Phase or Task
Birth to 1 year	Primary center of stimulation is mouth Becoming aware of body Touching genitals just as another part of body Touching mother's breasts, especially when nursing May have erections or vaginal lubrication
1–4 years	Touching or rubbing genitals may feel soothing (beginning masturbation) Early recognition of gender differences Curious about bodies Showing genitals to others is common Removing clothes and wanting to be naked Attempting to view others when dressing or naked Asking questions about bodies and bodily functions Talking about poop and pee especially with peers
4–6 years	Purposefully touching genitals, masturbating, sometimes in front of others Attempting to see others (especially adults) naked or using the bathroom Very curious about bodies Imitating dating behaviors as seen (e.g., holding hands, kissing) Talking about genitals and sexual actions as "dirty" (no comprehension of meaning) "Playing doctor" (sexual play) or exploring sexual parts with same-age peers Might ask questions about reproduction ("Where did I come from?") Learning words related to sex and using them, not always appropriately Mimicking adult sexual behaviors if seen on TV or in person
6–9 years	Developing definite ideas about male and female roles Gender identity becoming more clear Beginning to understand sexual orientation Developing strong friendships with children of same gender May masturbate May continue sexual play or exploration with others Beginning to be modest about nudity and bathroom time May begin to use sexual terms to insult peers Talking about sexuality with friends, comparing notes on what they have heard
9–12 years	Masturbation may continue but in private and secretively Playing games with peers that involve sexual behaviors (e.g., boyfriend–girlfriend, truth or dare) May experiment with dating behaviors (e.g., kissing, petting, masturbating to orgasm) Having romantic feelings toward same and/or opposite sex Attempting to see others naked or dressing Attempting to view or listen to media, books, and so on with sexual content Very interested in details of reproduction and sexual behaviors and seek information Expressing concerns about being normal socially or sexually Having strong sexual feelings

Age	Phase or Task
	May be beginning puberty (more likely for girls) Developing secondary sexual characteristics (e.g., pubic hair, enlargement of breasts) and feeling embarrassed about these changes
13–18 years	Experiencing bodily changes of puberty Emotional responses to growth and hormones Exploring and developing independence Having increased sexual feelings Wanting physical closeness with chosen peers, "falling in love" Sexual and romantic fantasies Developing preference for romantic relationships over friendships May face peer pressure to be sexually active May become sexually active Facing decisions about contraception May be exposed to violence in relationships (e.g., date rape, sexual harassment)

held in the psyche and are manifested though nonverbal behaviors.

CҀ ─────────

Misty does not remember much of her early childhood. She remembers little of her mother who committed suicide when Misty was 3. Nor does she remember that her father's alcoholism became so problematic that he was no longer able to care for his children. When Misty was 5 and her brother Gray was 12, they were removed from the home and placed in a foster home by children's protective services. Misty did well in her new home initially, but for Gray, the adjustment was more difficult. He was frequently in trouble and after 18 months, Gray was placed in residential treatment after he molested another foster child in the home. Misty missed her brother whom she saw as her protector. She began having nightmares about his being taken away. In her nightmares, she frequently felt that she could not breathe. Soon this feeling punctuated her daytime hours as well. The child gasped for breath and had difficulty being calmed. A medical evaluation uncovered no organic cause. It was Gray's therapist who finally was able to shed light on the changes in this little girl who had become fearful and sickly almost overnight. In therapy, Gray disclosed memories of watching his father sexual molest infant Misty.

"He'd put his [penis] in her mouth and get her to suck on it," the boy told his therapist. "I tried to stop it, but he'd beat me and shut me out of the room." **ҀD**

─────────

It seemed while big brother Gray had been near Misty, safely holding the memory of her abuse in his own consciousness, she was free of symptoms. Once he was no longer there, the symptoms emerged behaviorally as she had no words with which to remember. It is not uncommon for such traumatic memories to be repressed and be manifested in behaviors (Fredrickson, 1992; Johnson, 2010). Children who have verbal skills at the onset of the abuse may have the tools to discuss it at some point. However, children of any age may repress the fact that they have been abused and the feelings around the abuse.

Beyond the usual inability of preverbal children to express their trauma in words, it is difficult to attach specific symptoms to abuse at certain ages. When abuse begins at a particularly young age, there are certain factors that must be considered. The less control the child perceives that he or she has, the greater the trauma that may occur. If force is used, the trauma can be intensified. If the abuse began when the child is young and is not discovered until the child is older, the opportunity for multiple incidents over time and even for multiple perpetrators is greater (Finkelhor, 1984; Herman & Hirschman, 2000; Whetsell-Mitchell, 1995).

Developmental Considerations

Child development is influenced not only by the genetic makeup of the child but also by environmental influences, both positive and negative. Development can be broken down into three categories: physical, cognitive, and social or emotional. In addition, there is a moral component to development that can be affected by sexual abuse. And when related to sexual abuse, theorists often look at sexual development to help them recognize symptomatic behavior that falls outside the normal range. In turn, each developmental stage can be impacted by sexual abuse.

The onset of sexual abuse will vary. Most clinical studies found children who were sexually abused to be between the ages of 7 and 12 (Ferrara, 2002; Finkelhor, 1984; Scannapieco & Connell-Carrick, 2005). However, some experts suggest that younger children are more at risk because of their inability to report the abuse or their failure to recognize the touch as abusive (Hewitt, 1999). It is useful to think of sexual abuse within a developmental context and how the child may be impacted if he or she is abused during each developmental stage.

Infancy and Toddlerhood

In infancy, healthy development is dependent upon an environment that fosters this development. The child must be sufficiently stimulated, nurtured, fed, and protected. In abusive homes, parents are sometimes unable to provide such environment. For example,

CR ————————————————————

Henry was born to a teen whose family had responded to her pregnancy by telling her to "find another place to live." At 15, Annette had few friends and no place to go. Living in one shelter after another, Annette spent her evenings in bars where she met Jerome, a 34-year-old man who agreed to let the obviously pregnant girl move in with him. Jerome was an alcoholic who had lost his own wife and family years earlier. He was on disability and assured Annette that he would help with the baby. But soon after Henry's birth he demanded that Annette keep house while he spent all his time with the baby. This resulted in numerous fights, some of which became physical. During these, Henry's cries often went unheeded. In addition, Jerome's attention to the baby included fondling his genitals. Thus, when his cries were attended to, the baby was often soothed by sexual abuse.

Sometimes the fights between Annette and Jerome sent him out on a drinking binge and the mother and baby were left alone in an uncomfortable relationship that met the needs of neither. Annette was ill equipped and unwilling to care for a baby while Henry, who had never fully bonded with her, met her inept attempts with frustrated cries which further alienated her from him. This neglect, interspersed with Jerome's returns and sexual abuse, continued until children's protective services learned of the situation and intervened.

———————————————————— ℰℐ

The result of this early environment for Henry was that he was slow to reach any of the typical developmental milestones—rolling over, sitting up, crawling, developing a differentiated cry—which are the tasks of the first year of life.

Children who are sexually abused during infancy or during the toddler years may fail to master the physical tasks of the stage. For example, crying is the first mode of communication that the infant uses with his or her world. Infants develop a different cry for each need that they have. If you have ever been in the presence of a mother or father who is in tune with her or his infant, you may have heard her or him respond to a cry by "Oh, he's hungry" or "She's just tired." When the connection with the outside world is distressing or unfulfilling to an infant, that differentiated cry may not develop as in Henry's case. Some abused infants become passive, having learned that those in their environment will not meet their needs. The far end of the continuum of passivity is nonorganic failure to thrive, when an infant turns inward, often refusing to eat to the point that he or she might actually die.

Abused infants also fail to develop the motor skills appropriate for their age. Eating difficulties, hyperactivity, anxiety, frequent crying, and head banging may also be manifestations of some type of distress or disturbance and could be associated with sexual abuse (Berk, 2012; Scannapieco & Connell-Carrick, 2005; Woody, 2003). The brain is also impacted by traumatic events such as sexual abuse. Memories of the abuse may alter the child's perception of his or her environment and therefore the way in which he or she interacts with it (Hilarski, 2008a; Perry, 2003; Scannapieco & Connell-Carrick, 2005).

Scannapieco and Connell-Carrick (2005) suggest that very young infants may not suffer effects from sexual abuse. However, as stated earlier, some may be traumatized but not have access to the verbal memory of this trauma. Perry (2003) postulates that

the earlier in life, the less "specific" and more pervasive the resulting problems appear to be. For example, when traumatized as an adult, there is a specific increase in sympathetic nervous system reactivity when exposed to cues associated with the traumatic event. With young children, following traumatic stress, there appears to be a generalized increase in autonomic nervous system reactivity in addition to the cue-specific reactivity. Due to the sequential and functionally interdependent nature of development, traumatic

disruption of the organization and functioning of neural system can result in a cascade of related disrupted development and dysfunction. (p. 1)

This may account for disturbances in the motor and language development in young children as well as behaviors (e.g., hypervigilance), which requires the child's energy and may prohibit him or her from the natural exploration necessary to develop in a healthy manner (Berk, 2012; Gaskill & Perry, 2012; Hilarski, 2008a; Perry, 2003, 2009; Johnson, 2010). The way in which information about the abuse is encoded also means that later retrieval will tend to be based on nonverbal behaviors rather than verbal skills.

Infants and toddlers who are sexually abused may associate genital touch with that abuse, inhibiting normal developmental processes such as normal masturbation (Perry, 2003). The child may also not develop trust in the caretaker's ability to nurture and keep him or her safe. Earlier in this chapter, we discussed the impact of the failure to bond with and therefore to trust the caretaker, disrupted attachment, and its effect on the child's later life.

There is increased emphasis in the field of child maltreatment on the assessment of not only the risk for and the effects of child abuse but also the *protective factors* that reduce the risk of the abuse or at least the trauma resulting from it. For sexually abused infants, the most significant protective factor would be to have a healthy relationship with one of the parents.

CҨ
_____

Eugene was determined that he would be a better father than his father had been to him. When Michael was born, it was in the middle of tax season and as an accountant, Eugene had little time to spend at home. His wife, Georgia, had always been a moody person subject to changeable behavior and moods. He also knew that she was very insecure and hoped that a child would help her to feel more needed.

Once tax season was over, Eugene was home more. He encouraged Georgia to get out more. But she was so attached to the baby that she resisted. She didn't want him to care for the baby either and that really upset him. It was the fodder for many a fight. Baby Michael was not a secure child. He cried a great deal, and Eugene worried about him. He asked Georgia if she took him for his regular doctor visits which she insisted that she had.

The more Eugene tried to involve himself with the baby, the more Georgia pushed him away. She even closed the door on him when she changed Michael on the changing table in the bathroom. One day, Eugene came home from work early and pushed open the partially closed door, about to insist that he be the one to change the baby. What he saw was his wife fondling their infant son and putting his small penis in her mouth. Horrified, he grabbed the baby and left the house with him. At his mother's house, Eugene discovered that the baby's genitals were red and his anus showed signs of having been torn. Michael shrank from his touch when his father or grandmother tried to put ointment on him. Distressed, Eugene called the pediatrician who, after examining the baby, reported the situation to child protection. An investigation uncovered that the unstable mother had been abusing her baby almost since the time of his birth.

ઙ

The intervention and later the nurturing of baby Michael by his father gave Michael the chance for a healthier life after his mother's abuse. Other protective factors might include the child's own temperament or a social or cultural support system for the family (Fontes, 2008; Fontes & Plummer, 2012; Scannapieco & Connell-Carrick, 2005).

Preschool-Age Children

During the preschool years (3 to 6) children are expanding their language and understanding of their world. They are often engaging with peers and developing socially. They are also beginning to understand issues of gender and the beginnings of sexuality.

Most well-nurtured children at this age have a fairly optimistic opinion of themselves believing that they can "win" in most situations (Scannapieco & Connell-Carrick, 2005). In addition, they have developed a rudimentary understanding of how the body works and may have an inkling that boys and girls are different. Abused children may not feel as good about themselves. But perhaps the most obvious sign that preschool children are being sexually abused is precocious sexual knowledge. These children may be aware of sexual practices that are far beyond their developmental age. Some children simulate behavior that they have seen such as "humping." Their play with other children may become sexualized, mimicking what they have experienced. These children might also become preoccupied with sexual behaviors, masturbate to excess, and appear overly seductive. A note of explanation is necessary here. The years between 3 and 6 are a time when some children, especially females, can appear to some as especially coquettish. But if this behavior is looked at for what it is, the beginning of the children's recognition of their gender and what that means, the usual conclusion is that it is not seductive. Sexually abused children, on the other hand, have learned that sexual behavior is a way to relate to others, especially adults. Therefore, their behavior takes on a recognizably seductive tone.

Young children who have been abused may manifest their stress in other ways as well. Anxiety, nightmares, hyperactivity, depressions, excessive guilt, aggressions, tantrums, and difficulty separating from caretakers can be other indicators of abuse at this age.

Physically and sexually abused children may have genital tears (from insertion of a penis, an object, or fingers); may bleed from the genital area; have difficulty moving, walking, or sitting; wet the bed (enuresis); or soil themselves (encopresis). Genital itching, pain, or odor may be indicative of some type of infection or even venereal disease (Faller, 2003; Ferrara, 2002; Hewitt, 1999; Sgroi, 1982; Johnson, 2010). Children of preschool age and school age may also somatize their anxiety through developing headaches, stomachaches, and asthma.

Sexually abused children may also not relate to their peers in a comfortable manner. In addition to the antisocial or sexual behaviors that they might exhibit, they may also isolate themselves feeling somehow that forming relationships with others will uncover the secret of their abuse. Abused children have internalized a sense of shame and badness that makes them hesitant to engage in interactions with others (Berliner, 2011; Scannapieco & Connell-Carrick, 2005).

There are also similar protective factors that impact the child between 3 and 6 years such as the child's temperament, the presence of one or more nurturing caretakers, secure attachment, and cultural or environmental support systems. In addition, the preschool child can be somewhat protected from additional trauma from sexual abuse if he or she has had a positive experience in nurturing prior to this age (Scannapieco & Connell-Carrick, 2005).

School-Aged Children

Children between the ages of 7 and 11 years are involved in school life and the acquisition of new cognitive as well as physical and social skills. This is a time when children who are not abused will think little of sexuality and will devote their time toward learning and making new friends. The failure to accomplish these tasks or difficulty doing so may be the first clue to an interruption in development that may have sexual abuse at its core.

When sexually abused children reach school age, their distress over being abused is often seen in school-related activities. Poor school performance or conversely obsession with "getting things right" may exist along with poor peer relations. Learning difficulties are often how such children come to the attention of school personnel. They may have difficulty with concentration and fail to attend to what is being taught. Low self-esteem and self-degradation enhance this already-negative picture. And children trying to cope will often exhibit regression or immaturity. Or children may act out through exhibiting conduct disorders: lying or stealing (Berliner, 2011; Crosson-Tower, 2002; Scannapieco & Connell-Carrick, 2005).

The symptoms relating to sexual disturbance mentioned earlier may also be present, such as precocious sexual knowledge, sexualized behaviors or preoccupation, excessive masturbation, genital exposure, and seductive behavior. Children who exhibit these symptoms may have begun to act out sexually against others (Erooga & Masson, 2006; Faller, 2003; Lundrigan, 2001).

In addition, this age group may also experience the genital distress at being abused complete with the enuresis, encopresis, and risk of infection or venereal disease. This is also an age when fears, nightmares, obsessions, undue anxiety, and phobias are most likely to be seen (Silva, 2004). These may lead to tics, or children may turn inward or outward in hostility, anger, and rage. Suicidality may also be observed. The guilt and shame that they feel at their own perceived culpability is often an underlying cause (Sgroi, 1982; Silva, 2004).

In addition to the protective factors mentioned for earlier age groups, these children may develop a peer group to whom they might go for support. They might also develop social networks through which they might get help. They are more mobile and have access to more community supports even though all children might not feel able to use them. And again, healthy development in the previous stages will be important as a factor in minimizing trauma.

Adolescence

Adolescence is a bridge between childhood and adulthood with a myriad of resulting tasks. As a period of transition and transformation, it represents a time when it may be somewhat difficult to discern if some behaviors are the result of sexual trauma or are peculiar to the adolescent's attempts to forge his or her way through this developmental stage. Developmental delays may have been present for some time but become more obvious when the adolescent is expected to begin to assume adult responsibilities. It may be difficult as well, in an age when sexual mores are diverse and often unclear, to determine if a sexually acting out teen is behaving in an age-appropriate manner or has been exposed to sexual abuse.

Adolescents who are being sexually abused often assume that they are transparent and that everyone knows their secret. They also reason that if people know, they are doing nothing to stop the abuse. The typical response for the sexually abused adolescent is to withdraw or act out in disillusionment, anger, and rage. Adolescents often become seductive, having learned that sexuality is one form of barter to get their needs met. This seductiveness may be acted out through promiscuity or other sexualized behaviors. It is difficult to determine in a highly sexualized culture like the United States how adolescents learn sexual behaviors. Sexually abused teens may have learned them through experience (Berliner, 2011; McGee & Holmes, 2012; Scannapieco & Connell-Carrick, 2005; Silva, 2004).

Sexually abused adolescents often act out their anxiety either passively through somatic complaints, eating disorders, or sleep problems or aggressively through delinquent acts, aggressive behaviors, running away, truancy, leaving school, early marriage, early pregnancy, or prostitution (Crosson-Tower, 2014; Scannapieco & Connell-Carrick, 2005; Sgroi, 1982). There is a high correlation between the incidence of self-mutilation and eating disorders with sexual abuse in adolescents. The purpose of self-mutilation—cutting, scratching, branding, and picking—is to reduce both the psychological and physiological pain (McGee & Holmes, 2012; Scannapieco & Connell-Carrick, 2005). Abused adolescents feel helpless and out of control, and eating disorders give them a sense that they are controlling, to some small extent, what is being done to their bodies. Eating disorders either surround the teen with a protective layer of flesh (obesity) or are an attempt to purge the badness (bulimia). Not eating (anorexia) also exerts a form of control (though ironically the teen becomes out of control) and may be a wish to "fade away" and therefore not be available to be abused (Jaffa & McDermott, 2006; McGee & Holmes, 2012; Scannapieco & Connell-Carrick, 2005).

Protective factors for adolescents include those mentioned earlier, as well as an increased mobility and the ability to move within the community offer the possibility of more protective allies.

Attachment

Although mentioned earlier, attachment deserves a special section given the fact that it has become clear that the impact it has on abused children is significant. The role of attachment and how it is affected by sexual abuse has been widely studied especially in the last decade. *Bonding* refers to the initial connection between parent and child and begins at birth or even in utero. *Attachment* is a life-long process that an individual experiences, which is often based upon the initial bonding experience (Hewitt, 1999). Caretakers who are dependable, nurturing, and responsive and meet the child's needs in a prompt and caring manner help the child to develop a *secure attachment* style that prepares that child for healthy relationships built on trust, positive belief systems, and the ability to become independent and to cope with most situations (Anderson & Alexander, 2005; Bacon, 2001; Brisch, 2012; Hewitt, 1999; Levy & Orlans, 1998).

Children who are sexually abused may not have the parent-child relationships that foster secure attachment. If the abuse takes place in the home, dysfunctional family patterns have already developed. The child's primary attachment figure may be the one who is sexually inappropriate. Or the correlation between domestic violence and sexual abuse suggests that a mother might be fearful for her own safety and not fully emotionally available for her child. Other family issues or the fact that a parent is sexually abusive and perhaps attempting to hide the fact creates an atmosphere that may not allow the child to develop secure attachment.

There are three other patterns of attachment in addition to secure attachment: anxious resistant attachment, anxious avoidant attachment, and disorganized or disoriented attachment. *Anxious resistant attachment* develops when caretakers are not consistent in their relationship with the child, not meeting the child's needs, not able to adequately soothe the child who is in need of calming, and perhaps even stimulating him or her. Although these children continue to seek comfort from their caretaker, they do not see her or him as a secure base. Somewhat paradoxically they may also cling to that caretaker in the fervent of hope of their needs finally being met. They may exaggerate their style of demanding, appearing fussy, difficult, or demanding, which may further alienate the caretaker. These children appear insecure and hesitant to explore the world around them. Later in childhood, these children will appear babyish, be angry, and see themselves as unworthy of the attention of others. Thus, they may seek attention in a variety of needy and sometimes irritating ways (Anderson & Alexander, 2005; Bacon, 2001; Brisch, 2012; Hewitt, 1999; Levy & Orlans, 1998).

ନ୍ଦ

Malcolm was the third child born to Tasha and was fathered by her new boyfriend, Zak. While Zak was thrilled with the birth of a son, Tasha was not as sure. Her girls, products of a previous relationship, had been little trouble and at 8 and 10, she saw them as fairly self-sufficient. She did not want to be pregnant again but had done little to prevent it. Zak's enthusiasm about having a son did not curb

his staying out late after work, however. Alone during the day with baby Malcolm, Tasha found him cranky and annoying. It was easier to leave him in his crib or play pen. Sure he cried, but he got over it. When the girls and Zak got home, the baby got plenty of attention anyway. Then Tasha would pretend that she had tended to Malcolm all day. Since he was everybody's pet, anything less would not be tolerated. And when there were other people around to pick up some of the responsibilities, she figured that Malcolm wasn't that bad.

Malcolm was a clingy baby as he got into his toddler years. He cried a lot and was sometimes difficult to soothe. When the child was 2, Tasha discovered that Zak was having an affair. They fought, and Zak would leave for days at a time. At night, Tasha found that if she brought Malcolm into her bed, he would quiet down. She sometimes stroked him, fascinated at his small body. She was surprised that boys so young got erections and she started playing with his penis to see how it would respond. A few nights later, Zak would return and Malcolm would be left to cry in his own crib until the pattern of his parents' relationship repeated itself. Eventually, Zak left altogether and Tasha has a string of boyfriends in his place. When she was alone, she kept Malcolm in bed with her, evicting him only when there was another male to take his place.

Malcolm grew to be a moody child who clung to Tasha and isolated himself when she had no time for him. He frequently complained of a variety of ailments and was prone to severe temper tantrums. Tasha described him as a "tough kid who could be nice sometimes, but a real pain at others."

ନ୍ଦ

Some children exhibit *anxious avoidant attachment* when their parents are emotionally unavailable or rejecting when they seek contact. They blunt their negative emotions and avoid the parent during times of emotional distress. These children are not likely to protest when the caretaker leaves them, seeming indifferent and later relatively self-reliant. They often turn to toys rather than people giving an impression of isolation, which may appear hostile or antisocial (Anderson & Alexander, 2005; Bacon, 2001; Brisch, 2012; Hewitt, 1999; Levy & Orlans, 1998).

❧

Barbie was a quiet, serious child. Her mother, Irene, described her as being "little trouble." It was a good thing, Irene explained, as when Barbie was a baby, life was total chaos. Irene's husband was abusive, she explained tearfully.

"He used to beat me up at least once a week! I was afraid for Barbie but she just sat in a corner and never got in the way. But when I found out he was messing with her and my other girls too, that was it. He was gone!" Irene talked about how she had always worked two jobs to make ends meet and thought that it might have been Barbie who got the worst of it between witnessing the abuse and Irene's emotional and physical unavailability.

Barbie had little affect. In fact, although Irene spoke of her fondly, the child seemed to have little attachment to her mother. During the interview, 7-year-old Barbie sat quietly in the floor apparently intent upon whatever toy she had brought with her. Once she fell and hit her chin on the table. There were no tears despite the bleeding cut that resulted. Barbie found tissue to put on it and went stoically back to her isolated play, quiet and eerily self-sufficient.

❧

Disorganized or *disoriented attachment* occurs when there have been more blatant interruptions in parent-child relationships. When parents are physically abusive or overtly or indirectly threatening resulting from their own unresolved abuse or trauma, they may not enable their children to attach properly (Hewitt, 1999).

Levy and Orlans (1998) explain that

> disorganized infant attachment is transmitted intergenerationally: Parents raised in violent, frightening, and maltreating families transmit their fear and unresolved losses to their children through insensitive or abusive care, depression,

and lack of love and affection. The infant is placed in an unresolvable paradox: Closeness to the parent both increases the infant's fear and, simultaneously, need for soothing contact. (p. 62)

When children exhibit a disorganized or disoriented attachment style, they lack the organization to respond consistently to their environment and demonstrate confused, unpredictable, and contradictory behaviors. For example, a child might reach for the parent in a demanding angry manner that appears to indicate attachment, but suddenly retreat or freeze. Or the child might be extremely fearful of the parent or display confused reactions when reunited with a parent.

❧

Polly was a 2-year-old child who had been hospitalized with a broken leg. There was also some question of sexual abuse in the home. Her mother had taken out a restraining order against Polly's father, and the father was prohibited from hospital visitation. Polly spent her time rocking or banging her head in her hospital crib. When mother came to visit, she was at first anxious and reached out her arms for her. Then Polly would shrink away and move as best she could to one side of her crib. Her interactions with her mother seemed to be characterized by this push–pull behavior.

❧

Not all sexually abused children demonstrate attachment disorders, but a significant number do. Because the ability to develop a positive and safe relationship is so much a part of healing for sexually abused children, the presence of a disrupted attachment style compounds the trauma. Each attachment style brings with it different types of behaviors.

The style of attachment that a child develops may also be influenced by culture. Northern European cultures demonstrate higher incidences of insecure avoidant attachment, whereas Asian cultures that attempt to minimize anxiety for their children produce fewer children with disrupted attachment patterns. Societies that stress community and provide close relationship for children with multiple adults (e.g., Hispanic cultures) tend to produce more emotionally enmeshed relationship patterns (Bacon, 2001; Hewitt, 1999).

THE WORLD OF THE SEXUALLY ABUSED CHILD

It may be hard to imagine what it is like to live in the world of a child who is sexually abused. The ideal is for children to grow up in families where they are nurtured and protected from harm. This develops in them a sense that the world is benevolent and predictable and that they have some worth. According to researcher Ronnie Janoff-Bulman (1992), trauma develops when children are exposed to an environment that does not allow them to develop these important assumptions.

CR

The most striking thing as I look back on my childhood is the unpredictability of our home. You never knew what would happen. There weren't any real rules—at least rules we knew about in advance. The rules seemed to emerge after we had been punished for something that we "knew we weren't supposed to do" according to our mother. My sister Dinah and I just tried to keep out of everyone's way. My father's temper was legendary. He never hit us, but he broke things a lot. We never knew when he'd be home, and I never knew when he would come into my room and start stroking me. He used to tell me that my mother "never gave him any lovin'" and it was up to me to do so. I never knew until we were adults and Dinah tried to commit suicide that he did the same to my sister.

Dinah and I weren't even sure what my mother did, but she would go out of the house for some reason each day—but not at predictable hours. The only thing we could count on was school when we went. Sometimes mother would keep us out to do chores until someone visited

from the school and we had to start going again. When I was 10 and Dinah was 8, my father just stopped coming home. I remember being kind of relieved. But then my mother started having her "gentlemen friends" come to the house. They were no gentlemen and more than one of them came into my room after they'd been drinking and my mother passed out. But I was used to it by then. They just wanted what Daddy had wanted. I knew all those rules.

℠

Although not every home is as chaotic as Dinah and her sister's, the unpredictability is apparent. One woman remembered that during her childhood her father was the nurturer. When he came into her room and forcibly raped her one night, she was not sure that she had not imagined it. For many years, she denied that her loving father could have done this to her. Only in adulthood when she learned from her sister that the same thing had happened to her did this woman believe in her memories of childhood.

Symptoms and Indicators of Child Sexual Abuse

It is not uncommon for children to be sexually abused through several developmental stages. Therefore, it is important to become familiar with generalized symptoms associated with child sexual abuse.

Physical Indicators

The physical indicators of child sexual abuse may be more obvious than behavioral ones. Some of these symptoms might include (Adams, 2010; Berkoff et al., 2008; Berliner, 2011; Muram & Simmons, 2008; Saunders, 2012; Sgroi, 1982)

- bleeding, bruising, or tears around the anus or vagina;
- labial adhesions;
- hymnal perforation;

- difficulty walking or sitting;
- semen in the vagina or anus of a young child;
- injury to the penis or scrotum;
- vulvovaginitis or yeast infection;
- chronic urinary tract infections or painful urination;
- frequent urination;
- evidence of enuresis or encopresis;
- evidence of venereal disease symptoms (e.g., from syphilis, gonorrhea, trichomoniasis, chlamydia) such as vaginal or penile pain or discharge, genital or oral sores, genital warts;
- gonorrhea of the throat as a result of oral sex;
- presence of HIV/AIDS virus;
- evidence of excessive masturbation;
- pregnancy at a very early age;
- frequent psychosomatic illnesses; and
- symptoms associated with post-traumatic stress disorder (PTSD).

Although such symptoms should raise concern about sexual abuse, others could be attributed to other causes (Adams, 2010). For example, urinary tract infections and vaginitis may be caused by bubble bath, antibiotics, or other factors upsetting the natural balance of the body. Excessive masturbation may be indicative of other types of anxiety. Likewise, bruising of the scrotum, labia, or rectum might be contracted through injury. The HIV virus can be transmitted through contact with other bodily fluids or in utero. However, without clear knowledge of the cause, sexual abuse should not be ruled out when the aforementioned symptoms are present.

Behavioral Indicators

Children may respond to being sexually abused in a variety of ways: some obvious as to their origin and others that might be attributed to a variety of causes. The following are a few such indicators:

- Exceptionally secretive
- Demonstrating sexual knowledge that is beyond the child years

- Preoccupation with sexual talk or body parts
- In-depth sexual play with peers that appears to go beyond mutual exploration
- Sexually acting out against other children or animals
- Sexually explicit drawings
- Appearing much older and more seductive than appropriate
- An inordinate fear of males (or females)
- A sudden drop in school grades or sudden desire not to participate in peer-related activities
- Sudden phobic behavior
- Gagging or difficulty breathing with no apparent organic reason
- Crying without provocation
- Regressive behavior
- Sleep disturbances including nightmares
- Eating problems or disorders
- Depression
- General social withdrawal
- Feeling damaged
- Fear of being alone
- Cruelty to animals (especially those that would normally be pets)
- Setting fires and enjoying watching them burn
- Self-mutilation (cutting, scratching, burning self)
- Obsessive-compulsive behavior
- Desire to or act of running away excessively
- Substance abuse
- Suicidal ideation or attempts

Many of these indicators are obviously connected with abuse, but others may not seem as obvious. Sexual acting out against other children, adults, or animals may be the victim's attempt to put into perspective what has happened to him or her. It is also a way to gain control over what seemed like an out-of-control situation. There are victims and victimizers. The victim feels out of control, whereas the victimizer takes control.

Because sexual abuse is very much about control, other behaviors in victim symptomology that are about controlling are evident. For example, when children set fires they feel in control as they watch the adults around them strive to gain control, often without success, of the fire. Eating disorders are about taking control, in a negative manner, of one's own body. As one teen victim put it, "If I did not eat and got really thin, maybe I would just disappear and he could not find me to sexually abuse me!"

Victims of sexual abuse feel intrinsically damaged. Sgroi (1982) uses the term *damaged-goods syndrome* to describe how victims perceive themselves. Suicide is the ultimate control of one's own destiny. It also feels to some victims like the only way to end what seems to them to be an inescapable situation.

Victims of sexual abuse may also demonstrate symptoms that might not seem related to what has happened to them unless the deeper psychological significance is understood. Obsessive-compulsive behavior may be another attempt to control the environment. Ten-year-old Renee could not control the fact that her stepfather was abusing her, but she took control of other aspects of her life. Rigid routine became her escape. Every toy and piece of clothing must be in a specific place in order for Renee to feel at all secure. These were parts of her life that she could predict. When her stepfather came to her room to molest her, his behavior was out of her control.

Some victims experience physiological responses to their abuse. Enuresis, or wetting the bed or one's pants, and encopresis, or soiling, are behaviors that may not be entirely voluntary. They are instead psychological reactions to being violated in those bodily areas. There may also be an unconscious recognition that to wet or soil may make one undesirable, and the wish is that the abuse would cease.

Some children and many more adult survivors complain of difficulty in breathing or swallowing. Difficulty breathing may be related to a body memory of having an adult on top of them when their small bodies feel crushed. This response becomes embedded in the sensual memory and may plague them for years to come. Gagging or difficulty swallowing is often related to being orally violated. The presence of an adult

penis in a child's mouth may make the child feel like he or she cannot swallow or must gag. This response too may continue after the penis has been removed.

Learning may be difficult for children who are being sexually abused. Trying to deal with the conflict of what is happening to them that they may not understand saps the psychic energy necessary to concentrate and conceptualize. Schoolwork may suffer, and grades may drop. On the other hand, there are children who use school and learning as an escape in order to cope with what they are experiencing. It is often even more difficult for teachers to recognize trauma when children excel at school. And yet, these children are often obsessive and are perfectionists, falling apart if they do not achieve.

The behavioral symptoms of child sexual abuse can also point to other types of problems as well, especially when emotional upset is at the root. It will be important for parents and helpers to screen out the possibility of sexual abuse before assuming that these behaviors are indicative of other disturbances.

EFFECTS OF CHILD SEXUAL ABUSE ON VICTIMS_____

Finkelhor and Browne (1985) postulate that the effects of child sexual abuse can be divided into four main categories: trust and betrayal, traumatic sexualization, stigmatization, and powerlessness.

Trust and Betrayal

Developing trust is the first task for a child. As early as infancy, children must learn to trust the predictability of their caretakers in order to develop in a healthy manner. Trust is the foundation on which children build the future of their relationships and their approach to the future. That trust is twofold. As children begin to trust caretakers and therefore their environment, they in turn learn that they can trust themselves and their responses. When the trust of others is undermined, the betrayal for the child can feel profound. As a child begins to lose trust in the environment, trust in the self and in his or her own perceptions may also be shattered.

ℭ ──────────

"I was alone a lot," Darren explained. "I thought that I was pretty self-sufficient. My Mom was an okay mom I guess, but she raised me and my brothers alone and had to work long hours. We'd spend a lot of time at the ball field. There was one coach I really liked. He spent a lot of time with me, and I began to feel like he was almost like a dad. And then one day he asked me to do some things to him—some sex stuff. I wasn't really into that, and I said 'no.' The next thing I know he had pinned me down and was raping me. I was crying, and I couldn't believe what was happening. I trusted him. Afterward, he told me that after all we'd meant to each other, letting him do me was the least I could do. I left the ball field that day, and I didn't want to go back. But I did, because it was the only place that I had to go. And he made me do it again—touch him and he'd touch me. After a while, I didn't even care. I began to hate him and yet want to spend time with him. I began to wonder who I could trust. Could I even trust myself?" ℭ

──────────

Victims become unsure of whom to trust, and this may carry into their adult life. In addition, they wonder about their own judgment in discerning who is worthy of trust. This creates an isolation and feeling of vulnerability that further intensifies their problems and makes them vulnerable for future victimization (Finkelhor & Browne, 1985; Russell, 1999; Sonkin, 1998). For racial minorities this sense of betrayal is often intensified when the system that they may look toward to help them further victimizes them through racially biased attitudes (Fontes & Plummer, 2012).

Traumatic Sexualization

The realm of adult sexuality is one that most children enter only when they become teens or adults. Sex is usually something one learns about gradually, in age-appropriate increments. But sexually abused children are thrust prematurely into a sexual world that they may not fully understand. Often the perpetrator equates sex with affection and rewards the child for sexualized behavior. The child learns to barter for such favors through using sexuality. The result is that the victims become confused between sex and affection and see sex as a tool to get their needs met. They may develop a distorted perception of sexual norms assuming that what they have been taught is normal. They often compensate through promiscuity or survive through prostitution.

In addition to being learned behavior, promiscuity is also a form of self-destructive repetition compulsion—something that victims do over and over in an attempt to make sense of it. The original pain of betrayal combined with bodily sexual pleasure makes them repeat the sexual act again and again for recognition or attention (Maltz, 2012).

Although survivors of child sexual abuse do not necessarily become professional prostitutes, they do often use sexuality as a way of getting their emotional needs met. It may not be surprising given this fact that an extremely high percentage of professional prostitutes were victims of sexual abuse in childhood. Some theorists suggest that both promiscuity and prostitution are a combination of anger, feelings of worthlessness and futility, and the mind–body split that allows sexual abuse victims to separate themselves from what is happening to their bodies (Courtois, 2010; Maltz, 2012; Russell, 1999).

Some victims of child sexual abuse develop an aversion to sex, and as adults, they seek out therapy for such issues as arousal dysfunction, desire dysfunction, or difficulty achieving orgasm (Courtois, 2010; Maltz, 2012). Still others grow up confused about their sexuality or when adults choose partners of the same sex because they have learned in childhood that those of the opposite sex cannot be trusted (Courtois, 2010; Maltz, 2012; Sonkin, 1998).

Stigmatization

Children who are sexually abused feel that they have been damaged. In fact, society lets them know this at almost every turn. They are spoken about in hushed tones, and adults are unsure how to deal with children who have prematurely entered the world of adult sexuality. This sense of being different or damaged heightens the feelings of isolation inherent in being abused. They do not feel like their peers and may isolate themselves socially.

∝ ⎯⎯⎯⎯⎯⎯⎯⎯⎯⎯⎯⎯⎯⎯⎯⎯⎯⎯

When we read the *Scarlet Letter* in high school English class, I began to identify with the character. That's what I felt like knowing that my Dad had abused me since I was 10. I felt like I had this big red letter on me, telling everyone what an evil, dirty person I was.

⎯⎯⎯⎯⎯⎯⎯⎯⎯⎯⎯⎯⎯⎯⎯⎯⎯⎯ **ଛ**

Children who have been sexually abused often believe that their bodies are evil, unclean, or distorted. Those who recognize what is being done to them become confused by the physiological pleasure that they feel. As a result, they may feel anger toward their bodies and punish them through eating disorders or self-mutilation. Some children somatize their conflicts through developing headaches, nausea, menstrual or vaginal problems, or even asthma (Maltz, 2012; Russell, 1999; Sgroi, 1982).

Powerlessness

Children recognize that they have no power, but children raised in healthy environments begin to develop a sense of power over themselves and eventually their environment. But being sexually abused can rob children of this ability. Continued powerlessness becomes a major problem for victims of sexual abuse, and these feelings follow them into adulthood. This feeling of being powerless in almost any situation actually puts the victim at risk for future victimization.

These feelings of powerlessness may also have gender-specific variations in the way these feelings are manifested. Women have been socialized to accept powerlessness. Even though many women today strive to be in control of their lives, social messages that they have little power usually feel familiar. Men, on the other hand, are expected by society to have some power. Thus, when a boy grows up feeling powerless, the guilt over this powerlessness compounds his feelings of inadequacy. He may therefore withdraw, become a victim again, or have sexual adequacy issues. Some boys as they develop overcompensate by becoming overly aggressive, violent, or even abusive (Dorias, 2009; Hunter, 1990; Lew, 2004; Sonkin, 1998).

Once again, cultural identity plays a part in how a child is affected. The sense of powerlessness may become intensified for minority children who already struggle with feelings of being robbed of their power.

∝ ⎯⎯⎯⎯⎯⎯⎯⎯⎯⎯⎯⎯⎯⎯⎯⎯⎯⎯

Krystal's family was the only African American family in their neighborhood. She was raised by her grandmother who cooked for one of the wealthier families. Her mother had died when she was an infant, and her father also worked for the family.

"I went to the neighborhood school, but there was no question about who I was," she explained. "I was the hired help's kid, and everyone let me know it. When an older white man who used to come to the house started abusing me, no one seemed to know what to do, so no one did anything. And I was so caught up with the way everyone saw me—a nobody who didn't dare criticize the 'white folks'—that I just figured that was the way things were. But the anger grew into rage at how powerless I felt."

രാ

Post-Traumatic Stress Disorder

PTSD is common in both children and adults who have been sexually abused. This condition is described in the *Diagnostic and Statistical Manual of Mental Disorders* as characteristics of individuals who have experienced extreme traumatic stressors through direct personal experience. PTSD has recognizable characteristics: problematic behaviors including fear or horror, feelings of helplessness, agitation, or general disorganized behavior. Often the individual reexperiences the trauma, suffering from flashbacks, anxiety, and a sense of increased arousal. Any people or situations that might remind one of the traumatic events are avoided. These symptoms persist over time and impede the individual's functioning (Briere, Kaltman, & Green, 2008; Courtois, 2010; Saunders, 2012; discussed more fully in Chapter 13).

രാ

Eight-year-old Edgar's school recommended that he be seen for evaluation. For the last several months, he had been exhibiting behavior that concerned his teachers. When approached by the teaching aide, Edgar began crying uncontrollably and hid under a table. The teacher's aide, Joel, a very gentle but large man, at first tried to talk with him, but Edgar's behavior intensified. Once the aide left the room and Edgar could be coaxed out from under the table, he remained agitated and unable to return to his work. He whimpered softly, but if anyone approached him, Edgar would begin to cry again in earnest. Eventually, he was calmed, but when Joel returned to the classroom, Edgar began to cry once more. His teacher finally realized that the child's agitated behavior occurred only when Joel was in the classroom. Knowing that the aide had in no way harmed Edgar, the teacher asked the parents if there was another cause. His parents admitted that he had been having nightmares lately. It was finally discovered that while at a friend's house, Edgar had been raped by an older boy in the neighborhood—a large boy who resembled Joel.

രാ

The intensity of trying to push aside the memory of the rape and his inability to tell anyone what had happened had caused Edgar the intense emotional distress. Fortunately for this child, a competent therapist was able to gain his trust and eventually help Edgar to face the abuse and heal.

Summary

Child sexual abuse affects victims in a variety of ways. Developmentally, being abused during a particular stage puts the child at risk for symptoms related to the tasks of that developmental period. There may also be factors that serve to protect the child from experiencing these reactions (protective factors). One of the most significant risks for children who are abused at home is that there may be an interruption in their attachment to caretakers. Anxious resistant attachment, anxious avoidant attachment, and disorganized attachment can create problems for children in their later lives.

There are a variety of symptoms that are often indicative of childhood sexual abuse, although some of these may also denote other problems. These symptoms fall into the categories of physical indicators and behavioral indicators.

The effects of child sexual abuse are myriad. Finkehor and Brown (1985) suggest that these can be categorized into four main categories: betrayal, traumatic sexualization, stigmatization, and powerlessness. Victims may also suffer from post-traumatic stress disorder. In addition, children may act out their trauma either behaviorally or sexually, or exhibit somatic symptoms. It will be important to rule out sexual abuse if these symptoms are observed.

Review Questions

1. What influence does age have in the study of child sexual abuse?

2. What impact does sexual abuse have on infants and toddlers?

3. What influence does sexual abuse have on school-age children?

4. What impact does sexual abuse have on teens?

5. What influence does the study of attachment have on understanding child sexual abuse?

6. What are some physical indicators of child sexual abuse?

7. What are some behavioral indicators of child sexual abuse?

8. What are the four main categories of the residual effects of child sexual abuse?

9. What is the meaning of the phrase post-traumatic stress disorder?

CHAPTER 5

Sexual Offending Against Children

〇℥⣊〇

Marshall was one of the most popular teachers at the preschool where he worked. Everyone knew that Marshall loved the kids and would do anything for them. When several little boys reported that Marshall played "secret games" with them, some of the mothers discounted it. But one mother, an abuse survivor herself, was worried. She took her small son to an expert in child sexual abuse and what she learned both confirmed her suspicions and horrified her. This mother alerted other mothers, and soon it became obvious that Marshall was sexually abusing a small group of boys. The parents joined together and reported what was happening to their children. Even after Marshall was arrested, these shocked parents kept asking themselves, "How could such a gifted teacher have betrayed us so?"

〇℥⣊〇

W hy would someone sexually abuse children? For many people, child sexual abuse is so far out of their frame of reference that when it touches our immediate environment, it is difficult to believe.

The general public often asks what a sexual abuser of children looks like. Although sexual offenders may be from any ethnic or socioeconomic background, Sax (2009a), a former deputy district attorney who has prosecuted numerous sexual offenders, suggests some observations that might be made based on her cases.

Sexual offenders tend to *abuse children with whom they have existing relationships*, using the trust that they have gained with both the child and his or her parents to provide access and opportunity. As mentioned in Chapter 2, some child molesters are *experts at grooming the community* surrounding the child as well as the child (van Dam, 2006).

〇℥⣊〇

Lon came into Harriet's life when she was feeling at her lowest. Her husband had left her with three boys to raise, and she had no idea how she would hold down her job as the manager of the school cafeteria and raise her kids alone. Lon delivered the bread to the school and always had a kind word for her. He complimented her on any number of things, and she looked forward to his deliveries as did her staff. Lon was a charmer. When Lon told her that he was single and did not enjoy eating alone, she invited him to join her for dinner at her home. Her boys 4, 5, and 7 loved him. He insisted that she needed help with them and would often come over and assume their care while she relaxed in the evening. He often brought them gifts that Harriet could never have afforded. She was so grateful to Lon that he was able to give her children some of the material things that she could not.

Harriet introduced Lon to her large extended family and her friends. They loved him. At family gatherings, Lon would often organize games for the many children so that the parents had time to chat. Relatives and friends told Harriet how lucky she had been to find someone like Lon. She felt very lucky until she learned that he was sexually abusing her youngest son. What followed was a nightmare. No one seemed to want to believe that Lon could do such a thing. They wondered if Harriet could be mistaken until she began to doubt her own sanity.

ŝɔ

It is common for sexual abusers like Lon to prefer the company of children and to often seem quite good with them. The jobs that attract them also put them in proximity with children, giving them opportunity to gain trust and later offend. Part of their grooming process involves them doing favors for children or bringing them gifts. By gaining the trust of the community, offenders set up a situation in which they may be believed over the victim (Sax, 2009a; van Dam, 2006). When offenders pay special attention to children or give them gifts, parents may be flattered by their attention or in some cases relieved to have a break from child care. Sexual abusers of children can be adept at finding ways to engage children and the community and opportunities to carry out their abuse. Yet underlying the external facade are some deep-seated issues that give rise to their behaviors.

In Chapter 3, we discussed the various models that describe offending behavior, but how do these translate into real life? How might we recognize an offender? The bad news is that, although theories have emerged about the characteristics of offenders, they are varied and often based on a retrospective view of offending behavior. In fact, obtaining accurate statistics and information on sexual offending in general is problematic for several reasons. Sax (2009b) explains that because the legal definitions of sexual abuse differ from state to state, what is reported in one state may not be in another. Even if police departments and the Department of Justice had accurate counts of sexual offenders, these offenders' self-reports of what actually happened, their motivation, and other facts are traditionally unreliable. Victims too are reluctant to report the details of their abuse. Thus, a great deal of information that might lead to a picture of the typical child sexual abuser is lost.

Some experts argue that there is no such thing as an adequate profile of an offender against children (Bradford, 2001; Hanson & Harris, 2001; Quackenbush, 2003). There are undoubtedly more cases of child sexual abuse than those that are reported. Therefore, studies on offender characteristics are based upon apprehended and often convicted sexual offenders. And studies are reported in different ways, which make them difficult to compare (Bolen, 2007). Other authors believe that theorists know enough to create at least some rudimentary pictures of offender characteristics and behaviors (Carnes, 2001; Groth, 2001; Hilarski, 2008c; Sax, 2009a; van Dam, 2001).

Prendergast (2004) suggests that sexual offenders as a group have some distinctive characteristics, including what can be termed *basic inadequate personality*. Offenders tend to measure themselves in ways that will always find them lacking. Their exaggerated negative self-image, pervasive feelings of guilt, identity confusion, and fear of exposure cause them to suppress or displace their emotions and to avoid peer interactions and personal relationships in general, despite an exaggerated need for acceptance. They have a keen desire to control, but at the same time feel very much out of control, which may cause them to be unassertive. This characteristic does not stop them from trying to manipulate others and control anyone that they can—thus the choice of children to victimize. This extreme need to hide their perceived inferiority can give rise to seeming cleverness in dealing with others.

Sexually, offenders also see themselves as inferior. They believe that their penises are too small, yet have strong sexual performance needs. They exhibit deviant sexual arousal patterns and distorted sexual values to compensate (Prendergast, 2004).

Robin Sax (2009a), the former Los Angeles deputy district attorney who specialized in sex crimes, suggests possible traits that, in her experience, have been associated with sex offenders. Many offenders, though not all, experienced some form of maltreatment as children. Most have been subjected to other childhood stressors, which may include family substance abuse or being isolated from other children at an early age. For some offenders, rigid family religious values or practices in childhood have created repression that can feel overwhelming. As adults, these offenders exhibit depression, poor impulse control, poor social skills, a sense of entitlement, and an obsessive need for control. Some offenders may use alcohol or drugs. Unable to relate appropriately to other adults, they also have difficulty empathizing with their victims. Whatever the root, they have developed unusual sexual arousal patterns that in turn lead to distorted thinking, making them believe that the abuse is justified and should continue.

Van Dam (2006) postulates that, although most profiles characterize child sexual abusers as socially inept, there are also those who cover their feelings of inadequacy by learning to groom the community around the child and often seeming like a likeable or dependable person in whose care adults would have no difficulty placing their children.

Despite the contention by some theorists that there is no adequate profile of a sexual offender against children, there remain enough similarities in the descriptions of offenders to discuss some of the characteristics mentioned. For our purposes, we will consider first offender development, motivational factors, the progression of the pathology, cultural variation, and the differences between male and female offenders.

DEVELOPMENT AND SEXUAL OFFENDING

Retrospective studies on sexual offenders are unable to point to any specific developmental recipe that results in an offender. Although it is believed that many who offend against children had difficulty in their own childhoods, this dysfunction may take various forms. For example, some offenders are repeating a pattern of sexual abuse that began in their own childhoods.

ɷ

Wally was 5 when his uncle first violated him. He remembers vividly being anally raped at a beach house that his grandparents owned. He and his uncle were swimming, and he thought nothing about it when his uncle suggested they remove their suits. He had gone skinny dipping with his brothers in the secluded bay that was part of the cottage's charm. What Wally did not expect was his uncle's grabbing him and after beginning to penetrate him underwater, dragging him to the sand to finish. Wally would later say that that day changed his life.

Two years later, Wally was molested by a priest—the only one he had ever told of his uncle's assault. The priest told Wally that he would make things better, that he would make him forget. He fondled the boy gently and told him that this was therapy for what his uncle had done to him. Father Bart told Wally that God had ordered him to cleanse Wally's hurt in this manner.

As a teen camp counselor, Wally befriended a 7-year-old boy who had also been raped. Like Father Bart, he introduced the child into sex play gently, telling him that this would be a balm for his past hurt.

⁂

In research that compared 17 studies involving 1,037 sexual offenders and 1,762 non-sex offenders, Jespersen, Lalmiere, and Seto (2009) found that there was a higher prevalence of sexual abuse in the histories of the sexual offenders with the highest incidence among those who went on to molest children. In a comparison of childhoods of 137 rapists and 132 child molesters, Simons, Wurtele, and Durham (2008) discovered that the child molesters were more likely to have been sexually abused (73%) as children.

Not every offender was sexually abused in childhood. Some witness the abuse of their siblings but are never themselves molested.

⁂

Manuel knew that something was happening behind the curtains at night. He knew when Angelina went to bed that their father would soon join her. His sister was only 11, and he was 9 when it began. At first he could not identify the cause of the sounds that his father made. But later he knew. He knew too what was happening—that his father was doing to his sister what he had once seen his parents do. He wanted to tell someone, but whom? Certainly not his mother who worked nights and slept a good part of the day. Nor could he tell his oldest brothers who were both so involved in their gangs that they probably wouldn't care or they might question his own machismo.

As Manuel grew older, it continued to happen despite the fact that Angelina would often threaten to leave home. Once he saw that the curtain was slightly parted and he positioned himself so that he could watch their moving bodies. He began to fantasize what it would be like to have sex with his sister. One night after his father had left the house, Manuel crept between the curtains.

Angelina was crying, and he put his arms around her to comfort her. She took him into her bed, and he stroked her hair and began to feel like it had been he who had just had sex with her.

Years later, Manuel remembered that night with tenderness as he climbed into bed with his own daughter and began to stroke her. The molestation that followed would eventually result in his arrest.

⁂

Physical abuse, witnessing domestic violence, or living with alcoholic or drug-addicted parents may also be part of the offender's childhood experience (Seto, 2008), although Simons et al. (2008) postulated that violence in childhood was more characteristic of rapists than of child molesters.

Brain Development and the Role of Attachment

Over the last few decades, an abundance of studies have been done on the effects of trauma, especially as a result of child maltreatment, on the developing brain (see Bremner, 2002; DeBellis, 2001; Gaskill & Perry, 2012; Teicher, Andersen, Polcari, & Navalta, 2002; Twardosz, 2010; Zeanah, 2009). These studies have shown that traumatized children have difficulty with processing tasks, verbal memory, spatial memory, learning, and memory. The ability to problem-solve and develop new ways of coping may also be affected. Studies of the characteristics of child molesters often point to individuals who feel inferior due to a variety of functional inabilities, who use their deviance to cope (see later discussion), and who have often experienced trauma in their own childhoods. The origins of sexual offending are often linked to this early brain development as well as attachment issues.

Attachment refers to the bond that an infant develops with his or her caretaker early in the infant's life. Originally studied by John Bowlby

(1979), attachment is believed to be a fundamental developmental milestone toward healthy development. Through their attachment to their caregivers, children learn that the world is a friendly place and that they are loveable. With this thought under their emotional belt, children can then reach out to experience other aspects of this world with the confidence that they will be well received. As discussed in Chapter 4, the development of this positive attachment, referred to as secure attachment, gives children a secure base from which to operate. This secure attachment necessitates that the caregiver has been sensitive to the infant's signals, accepting of the infant, accessible when she or he is needed, attentive, and able to adjust his or her responses to the needs of the infant (Ainsworth, 1969; Bowlby, 1979; Levy & Orlans, 1998; Rich, 2006). Because the relationship with a caregiver is the first and primary interaction for an infant, the quality of that bond will influence his or her ability to connect with others in future relationships while choosing appropriate partners (ability to achieve intimacy), discern the feelings of others (empathy), navigate within society (social connectedness and social competence), and feel good about himself or herself (self-concept). Having a secure base also allows the individual in later life to adapt to his to her environment and regain stability if he or she is temporarily thrown off course. These individuals are usually seen by others as responsive, dependable, and reliable.

For those who do not have a positive attachment in infancy, life may present more significant obstacles.

☞

Clarence was the third child of an alcoholic mother, Lila. He had no knowledge of his father, but neither did his brothers, so it didn't matter. When his mother was sober, she was loving and attentive, taking her three boys with her whenever she could. She worked nights cleaning office buildings and would see that the boys were safely in bed before she left for work. Those were the good times. They never knew when their mother would not be there the next morning and would come in later in the day, smelling of booze and sometimes bringing a man with her. During those times, she would yell at them because the dishes hadn't been done or the place was a mess. And then she would lock herself in her bedroom with her latest man and they would be forced to fend for themselves. Bart, four years older than Sam and five years older than Clarence, would get them dinner and see that they got to bed. If it was a school day, Bart also got them all off to school. And then Lila would be back for them again, swearing off booze and promising that she would always be there for them.

☞ ──────────

For children like Clarence, life brought uncertainty. When their mother was there for them, life felt secure and safe, but they never knew when that would end. As an adult, Clarence was possessive and demanding, needing to control when those he cared about would be there for him.

His older brother Bart handled the insecure attachment that he developed in a different manner. Faced with loss, Bart would become indifferent, asserting that "People come and go! Big deal!" Both brothers demonstrated insecure attachment styles as children.

Infants and children who see their parents as frightening, as in abusive situations, may develop what is referred to as disorganized attachment, demonstrating behaviors that can be bizarre, incoherent, or unpredictable.

Marshall and Marshall (2000) suggest that the origins of sexual offending can be found in the poor attachment relationships that offenders have experienced with parents or early caretakers (see also Creeden, 2005). These authors believe that poor relationships left sexual abusers more vulnerable to being abused as children, leading them to be more sexually preoccupied and often using sex to cope with the stress in their lives. Theories related to sexual offending routinely mention the lack of social competence, which in turn affects empathy and the ability to achieve intimacy. In addition, feeling good about one's self tends to promote socially acceptable behavior, whereas a poor self-concept leads a person to see ways to overcompensate for what he or she does not feel good about. Sexual offenders have been described as using deviant behaviors to compensate for poor self-concepts.

CR _____

When Clarence (mentioned earlier) met Sylvie, she reminded him of Lila during her good times. While he had dropped out of school, Sylvie had finished and had an excellent job with prospects for promotion. She didn't seem to mind that Clarence moved from job to job, often saying that his last employer had been "out to get him." When she became pregnant, they moved in together. At first, Sylvie was understanding when he was in between jobs, but as her pregnancy progressed, she would often confront him with "Can't you do anything? If I work, the least you could do is clean up around here!" When the baby was born, Clarence suggested that he be the one to stay home with their daughter, baby Roseanne. But Sylvie even found fault with his fathering. Her shrill criticisms reminded him of Lila after her nights of drinking. She made him feel so useless. He began telling Roseanne how he felt about things. He could just tell that the baby appreciated him and what he did as her dad. Clarence and Sylvie continued this arrangement for the next several years. As Roseanne grew and developed a personality of her own, Clarence began to feel that she understood him, while his wife did not. On later reports of his sexual abuse of his child, the comment was made that "he treated his daughter more like a wife than a child." **СЭ**

Rich (2006) suggests that "attachment is one highly significant component in the development of sexual aggression, combined with many other elements that are found so frequently in the lives of juvenile and adult sexual offenders" (p. 180).

However, this author goes on to caution that although insecure attachment may be instrumental in the tendency toward sexual offending, it should not be seen as being the only causal factor. Instead, attachment issues may offer one pathway (see Chapter 3, pathways model) that may lead to the perpetration of child sexual abuse.

PROGRESSION OF PATHOLOGY _____

Not every individual who experiences abuse or neglect as a child or who does not benefit from a healthy attachment relationship becomes a sexual offender, especially against children. What then influences a person to act out his or her own developmental deficits by abusing children? Gilgun (1990) postulates that there are factors that can be associated with those men who go on to molest children after their own childhood abuse and those who do not. The first of these factors is the differences between their *confidant relationships* growing up. Having someone to confide in as a child and youth seems to limit the risk for offending in adulthood. The nonabusive males (the control group) in Gilgun's study had had intimate relationships with peers who enabled them to process their life experiences, whereas those who later became offenders did not. In the area of *sexuality and sexual development*, Gilgun found that sexual offenders used sexual behaviors to maintain their equilibrium; masturbated regularly prior to the age of 12; and had repetitive, coercive sexual fantasies as they masturbated. Controls, on the other hand, were more likely to have begun masturbation in later adolescence, had noncoercive sexual fantasies, and released sexual tension as appropriate to their peer group.

The *peer relationships* for sexual offenders, unlike those of their nonabusive peers, tended to center around antisocial activities, supporting the findings of some researchers that juvenile sexual offenders are also involved in delinquent behavior.

For sexual offenders, the need to prove their masculinity through violence; the degradation of others, especially women; and sexual conquests is common. Controls, on the other hand, equated masculinity with the respect for women and participated in more socially appropriate behaviors. And finally, the *families of origin* of sexual offenders tended to be dysfunctional, filled with maltreatment and domestic violence.

Sherman exemplified the characteristics identified by Gilgun's research.

ଔ ─────────────

Sherman would have been described as a loner. The oldest of two children and the son of two alcoholic parents, Sherman spent his time looking after his baby sister, Rikki. He wasn't particularly close to his sister, nor did he enjoy looking out for her, but his mother had made it clear that older brothers took care of their sisters. Sherman sometimes wondered if it was wishful thinking as he doubted that his mother's older brother had given her anything but grief. He had overheard his grandmother say once that his Uncle Hal used to beat up his mother as a child, but he had no idea if it was true. Maybe that was how she married his father who beat her up with regularity. Sometimes he wished that he had someone to talk to, but he wouldn't talk to Rikki, and who else was there?

Sherman actually enjoyed using Rikki as his personal slave. At an early age, he taught her to pick people's pockets and got a charge out of the fact that she did it so willingly to please him. When she didn't get anything, he would punish her by making her sit alone in a dark closet, something that frightened her. When he was 10 and Rikki was 8, Sherman walked in on his father sexually abusing his sister. They didn't see him as he ducked out of the room without making any noise. He thought of it a lot and started masturbating to the fantasy. Sometimes he masturbated so intensely that he actually made himself sore. One day when he was masturbating, Rikki walked in. She seemed curious, so he showed her how to do it and started doing it

to her too. Sherman was later arrested after sexually abusing another girl on the school grounds.

──────────────── ଔ

Some sexual offenders against children may also equate power with sexuality or the inverse. Just as Sherman found satisfaction in having power over his sister, studies have found the need for power as a possible motivator toward sexual offending (Groth, 2001; Herman & Hirschman, 2000; Kamphuis, DeRuiter, Janssen, & Spiering, 2005; Ward, Polaschek, & Beech, 2006; Wright & Schneider, 1997).

As mentioned throughout this chapter, offenders learn as children the abusive behavior they exhibit in later life. They learn as they watch parents and other adults interact that relationships are not always satisfying. They learn from abuse and from distorted models that sexuality equals exploitation (Garrett, 2010; Prendergast, 2004).

Prendergast (2004) outlines how an idea or learned behavior becomes the compulsion to sexually abuse. Initially, some traumatic event or events or patterns developed in childhood create the idea of a fantasy, which usually is sexual or aggressive in nature. The offender cannot escape the fantasy, and it becomes obsessive. At some point, he or she begins to masturbate to the fantasy, which in turn becomes habitual and often obsessive. Eventually, masturbation no longer satisfies his or her needs. In the meantime, the offender may have found ways to view or interact with children. His or her fantasy becomes centered on them if it was not already. At some point the offender steps over the line and abuses a child.

Dom's pattern was typical of many offenders.

ଔ ──────────────

As a really little kid, I remember lying in my bed and listening to my mother and her boyfriends go at it in her room. I used to get magazines from the bigger kids on the block and think about what it would be like—to have sex with someone. I had this one fantasy that involved my mother and me having sex, but I was still a little kid. I don't know if it ever really happened or if it was just my fantasy. It used to get me aroused, and sometimes I'd masturbate when I thought of it. But when one of the boyfriends sexually abused me, I decided that it wasn't that great to have sex. He [sodomized] me and it really hurt. Then I got really angry that he had hurt me like that. I stayed away from the apartment as much as I could, and I'd watch little kids and hope that no one ever hurt them like that. I started taking pictures of the ones I really liked. And I'd get home and I'd print out the pictures and think about how I'd do something to these kids that we'd both like. My fantasy turned to me being with a kid sexually.

One day, I was wandering around the park, and this little kid's ball rolled to me. I was sure it was a sign—like he'd chosen me. He came to get it, and we started talking. I went home that night, and all I could think about was him. The next time I saw him, I took his picture, and I began seeing him almost every day. At night, I'd masturbate when I looked at his picture and fantasize about being with him sexually. When I saw him, I felt less anxious, especially after I jerked off at home. But then that wasn't enough. I wanted to touch him. One thing just led to another, and pretty soon I was giving him money to do what I wanted. He liked it too, I think. I didn't hurt him.

_____ ᔕᗅ

Prendergast (2004, pp. 9–10) also suggests that, although sexually abusing has compulsive elements to it, there are points in the offending cycle where all offenders could have made a choice not to abuse. He or she usually fails to make that choice because of distorted thinking. Such thought processes include the following:

- Well, you've gone this far; you may as well finish it.
- It's no worse to finish than to stop. The punishment will be the same.
- I've already committed the sin, so I may as well get the pleasure.
- If I finish and make them feel good, maybe they won't report me.

- You know you're a pervert (rapist, child molester, etc.), so you may as well act like one.

This element of choice gave rise to relapse prevention as a treatment modality, wherein an offender is taught to interrupt his or her cycle of abuse at specific junctures (see Chapter 14 for more information on treatment).

Opportunity and grooming also play a part in whether the abuse will be carried out and how it progresses. The Internet now plays a significant part in the lives of offenders. It is easier than ever before to access child pornography and engage in conversation with children without leaving home or risking been observed (see Chapter 7 for more information on the Internet and sexual abuse). No matter the access to the child, the progression for the offender usually goes from fantasy to more and more intrusive abuse (Carnes, 2001; Groth, 2001; Prendergast, 2004; van Dam, 2001).

Some sexual offenders do not groom their victims. These offenders usually use threat or force to compel the victim instead of building a relationship. They often hurt their victims and, in fact, may derive pleasure from hurting them. They may also be the offenders who abduct and murder children (Cooper, Estes, Giardino, Kellogg, & Vieth, 2007; Groth, 2001; Sax, 2009a).

Much of the literature still refers to men when discussing offenders because the majority of reported offenders are male and there have not been as many studies about females. Let us consider each of these categories more closely.

CHARACTERISTICS ASSOCIATED WITH MALE SEXUAL OFFENDERS _____

Although, as mentioned earlier, many theorists argue that there is no such thing as an adequate profile of the typical sexual offender against children. There are, however, some characteristics that are often mentioned in case studies of sexual abusers. These are most commonly associated with males as their motivations and psychological makeup differ from those of female sexual abusers. However, some of the characteristics associated with males are also true of females. More research must be done on the differences between the two.

Some theorists describe the male sexual offender in terms of an inadequate personality—an individual who may exhibit some of the following: inadaptability to life; social incompatibility with others; inadequate responses to intellectual, emotional, social, and physical demands. These individuals harbor a sense of perfectionism that causes them to measure themselves against their peers in a way that always makes them feel that they fall short. As a self-fulfilling prophecy perhaps, they set themselves up to fail. They are constantly seeking acceptance and feel unable to forge relationships with others. For this reason, they choose those whom they feel superior to, like children. In addition, they feel out of control of their environments. Adults, especially those who are critical, intensify these feelings of being out of control. Once again, with children, they can feel more in control (Groth, 2001; Prendergast, 2004).

How this inadequate personality will manifest itself differs from offender to offender. Some wear their insecurities in every situation, feeling inadequate and playing a subservient role in all that they do. They often handle insults and abuse better than they do compliments or positive strokes. At the same time, the rage that they feel over being in this position translates into acting out sexually. Some of these offenders identify with children as peers (because they feel child-like), and others target children because they feel they are superior to them (Groth, 2001; Prendergast, 2004; Sgroi, 1982; van Dam, 2006; Yates, Prescott, & Ward, 2010).

Another offender will overcompensate for his feelings of inadequacy and being out of control by exerting unreasonable control on those around him. One manifestation of this is the overbearing and sexually abusive father described in early writings on child sexual abuse. This man rules his family with an iron fist and expects that he is entitled to respect and acquiescence from his family (Bolen, 2007; Groth, 2001; Herman & Hirschman, 2000).

And finally, some theorists suggest that another offender will overcompensate through developing a persona that looks "normal" and is respected. These offenders often look for positions of power or places where they are least likely to be questioned about their activities. Under close scrutiny, one would find this a superficial facade and that the offender lacks intimates or close alliances with others. An example might be the high school principal, the priest or minister, or the public official who uses his position to isolate himself from others in the community except for surface interactions (Prendergast, 2004; van Dam, 2006) although it should be noted that not all offenders in these professions necessarily fit this profile.

To better understand the male offender, let us consider several areas in which he has difficulties.

Issues of Self-Esteem and Social Competence

The sexual offender against children can be characterized by poor self-esteem that develops from a variety of, perceived and otherwise, assaults on the psyche. In Chapter 3, it was mentioned that offenders harbor a variety of key thinking distortions, two of which are that the world is a dangerous place and that they have little or no control over what happens in their lives. Their own development has often taught them to harbor these beliefs. Offenders who are raised in dysfunctional homes where their needs are unmet may well believe that the world is not a safe place.

Hector did not remember a time when he was not beaten. To quiet him as a baby, his mother would add vodka to his bottle. He and his brother were removed from the home by Child Protective Services on more than one occasion and then—for reasons he did not understand—returned home again to be abused and neglected once again. When he was 8, his father told him that he had to become a man and took him to a woman who told him she would "teach him." He was frightened despite this obvious opportunity to "grow into manhood," although he was not even sure exactly what was expected of him. The woman derided him on what a baby he was because he "couldn't even get it up" and began to slap him. When his father discovered that the meeting had been unsuccessful, he beat the boy and left him at home with his alcoholic mother.

Hector began to fantasize about the encounter with the woman and convinced himself that he had been very macho. Yet inside brewed a rage at what he knew had happened and his shame.

For Hector, there was little of a positive nature about his early life, except that he learned to survive. By 12, he was involved with a gang, and his main concern became protecting their turf. At least being a part of the gang and using force in whatever way they had to protect their territory from other gangs gave him a feeling of having some control. Secretly, though, he believed that he had little control and that the world would "get him" if he did not protect himself. Hector, like many sex offenders, had difficulty with one-to-one relationships (Flora, 2001; Groth, 2001; Hilarski, 2008c; Laws, Hudson, & Ward, 2000; Prendergast, 2004; Seto, 2008). His relationship with Rosa began purely as sex, and he would often beat her. He later taught their children that they only had each other. When he beat them, he told them that he was toughening them for the world

and the prejudice that they would face. His sexual abuse of his daughter, he rationalized, was teaching her to really love.

Because of the tapes that play from the offender's developing years that give him an innate sense of inferiority, failure, and powerlessness, he develops *selective perception*, or the ability to hear only the messages that fit with his view of the world and block out those that might be more positive (Flora et al., 2008; Prendergast, 2004). This constant reminder in the offender's mind, that he can do nothing to change, promotes feelings of anger and rage. To ward off the feelings of shame, rage, and betrayal, the sexual offender overcompensates through developing a sense of entitlement especially in relation to sex. In his own mind, the offender wants to believe, as a defense against feeling inferior, that he is better than everyone else in some way. If he can convince himself that he is better than others, then he feels that he is entitled to have sex with anyone. But he tends to choose those of lesser status (e.g., children) in order to keep his feelings of superiority intact (Beech & Mann, 2002; Marziano, Ward, Beech, & Pattison, 2006; Pemberton & Wakeling, 2009; Ward & Keenan, 1999).

In situations of father-daughter incest, this entitlement is exemplified by the father seeing his daughter as his property to do with as he sees fit (Herman & Hirschman, 2000; Pemberton & Wakeling, 2009).

Issues of Sexuality

It might be natural to believe that sexual offenders enjoy sex. In fact, the use of sex as their arena of deviance attests to their discomfort with it.

Sexual Experiences

Work with sexual offenders has taught researchers that offenders may have been sexually violated themselves or have grown up in homes where the view of sexuality was skewed. For example, when a boy grows up knowing on some level that his father is molesting his sister, his own view of sexuality may become distorted. On one hand, he may be aroused and yet he also feels guilty and may have a wish to protect his sibling. On the other hand, in later life, he has the potential for acting out this conflict in his own dealings with children.

Another offender may grow up in a home where sex is condemned to such a degree that he both develops an interest in it and feels terribly guilty about that interest.

ℭℜ _____

The first time his mother caught Angelo masturbating, she dragged him by the ear to the statue of the Virgin Mary and made him kneel there for an hour all the while telling him how evil he was and how he should "ask the Blessed Mother for her forgiveness." Angelo wasn't even entirely sure what he had done except that he knew that his mother considered bodies to be dirty and the genitals an area that was never touched except for cleaning oneself. What followed were regular lectures by his mother about how she knew he was having "evil thoughts" and must pray not to be taken to hell. Increasingly he was turned on by the fact that—if he did touch himself—it felt so evil. He began masturbating compulsively until his penis was sore, hoping that his mother did not know what he was doing or feeling.

_____ ℘

Still other offenders are raised in households where the sexual rules are so fluid, that they are not sure what is expected of them.

Prendergast (2004) contends that sexual offenders

for the most part, have never had sex just for fun and enjoyment. All of their sexual behavior, whether masturbatory or with another person, serves a purpose, and that purpose, most of the time, is to make them feel better about themselves by either proving something or denying something. (p. 85)

Masturbation itself from its onset in the offender's life is not a pleasurable experience, but rather one of release—often a way of feeling better after being rejected, punished, or humiliated. It is sometimes a release from depression (Gilgun, 1990; Laws et al., 2000; Prendergast, 2004). Chronic compulsive masturbation often continues throughout adulthood when often developmentally appropriate adult sexual activities should have decreased the habit. Some sexual offenders will even masturbate after having had another age-appropriate sexual experience like intercourse with a partner (Flora et al., 2008; Prendergast, 2004).

Most sexual offenders have some distorted sex value that affects their sexual life. Prendergast (2004) also suggests that offenders are *imprinted* by their early sexual experiences in ways that may inhibit their later sexual enjoyment or expression. Often an early sexual experience will have such a profound effect on the abuser that he replicates it in his own sexual life and abuse (Flora et al., 2008; Glasser et al., 2001; Prendergast, 2004). For example, the male child who is sodomized at an early age may be imprinted in a way that he is unable to achieve orgasm in later life unless he is anally stimulated.

As mentioned in Chapter 3, most also have some other type of paraphilia (Flora, 2001; Laws et al., 2000; Prendergast, 2004; Ward et al., 2006). Their feelings of inferiority, distorted thinking around sex, and paraphilias may inhibit the expression of their sexuality as normal adults. They may be sexually active but may not find fulfillment through sex. For example, a sexually abusive father may still be having sexual relations with his wife while he sexually abuses his daughter, but he would see his activity with his wife as superficial and unrewarding.

There has long been discussion as to whether sexual offenders had been sex abuse victims themselves. In a study of 747 males and 96 females at risk for being perpetrators, Glasser et al. (2001) looked at the link between sexual victimization and sexual offending. Of the women who had been victims of sexual abuse in childhood, only one became a perpetrator, whereas 225 of the men (30%) became abusers. Of these, 51% had been victims of incest and 61% victims of pedophiles outside the home, and 75% reported being victims of both incest and abuse by pedophiles (p. 17). Other theorists have argued that sexual abuse as a child is not the only factor that may translate into later sexual offending (Groth, 2001; Laws et al., 2000; Seto, 2008).

Few studies have focused on the conventional sexual development of sexual offenders. In addition to the above-mentioned studies and due to the fact that many child sexual abusers lack the social skills necessary for mature adult relationships, one might suspect that the number of their consensual sexual experiences would be fewer than those of nonoffenders. However, Cortoni and Marshall (2001) discovered that in a population of 59 sex offenders against both children and adults, the experiences of these offenders did not differ significantly from those of non–sexual offenders on the age at first intercourse, number of sexual partners, or types of sexual activity in which they had engaged. Kafka and Hennen (2003) came to a similar conclusion when the sexual offenders in their study also demonstrated comparable levels of sexual activity (masturbation and intercourse) to nonoffenders.

Fantasy and Sexual Offending

As mentioned earlier, a significant number of sexual offenders engage in some type of fantasy often through the use of child pornography (sexually explicit materials) (Flora, 2001; Flora et al., 2008; Groth, 2001; Prendergast, 2004; Seto, 2008). Not only is the use of pornography a precursor to sexual offending but a study of 341 child molesters that connected pornography with sexual aggression found pornography to be a significant risk factor for reoffending (Kingston, Federoff, Firestone, Curry, & Bradford, 2008). Pornography serves several functions in the offense cycle. It gives the offender a visual picture through which he can stimulate himself and may connect him with other offenders as there is often trading or buying involved. Viewing pornography desensitizes the novice offender and normalizes viewing children sexually. And the offender may also use pornographic pictures to show his victims to normalize the sexual images for them and also to desensitize them in preparation for the abuse (Groth, 2001; Kingston et al., 2008).

The use of the Internet has made child pornography infinitely more available than ever before in history. This creates an interesting dilemma. If the viewing of pornography has been found to be a risk factor in sexual aggression and the age of downloaders of Internet pornography is decreasing (see Reijen, Bulten, & Nijman, 2009), what does the future hold in the incidence of sexual offending?

Sexual offenders, in their tendency to measure themselves against others as inadequate, also feel sexually inferior. In this society where self-help is popular, there are many books and articles that talk about improving your sexual performance. Sexual offenders may feel that these books were written for them. Their poor social skills, feelings of inadequacy, and distorted sexual views may mean that they have not done well with women. Old tapes from childhood may also make them believe that women are not nurturing but punitive and even dangerous. Some theorists also suggested that sexual offenders have fears about having a too small penis, fears that may be unrealistic compared to other men. Always comparing themselves upward, abusers have used as their model the pornography they have seen or glimpses of other men furtively collected in public restrooms. Using his selective perception, he may not have noticed those that made him look superior or at least average. And the size of a penis cannot be fully observed by a flaccid penis, and this is probably what they have seen in restrooms. Again, lack of education and communication in the years when their caregivers should have been giving them healthy explanations may be absent (Flora et al., 2008; Prendergast, 2004).

Earlier, it was mentioned that offenders have distorted sexual values. These involve not only the *how*s of sexual relationships but also the *why*s. Most pedophiles and hebophiles believe, or at least rationalize, that what they are doing to their victims is "showing love" and reject any suggestion of harm to them. Still others argue that what they are doing to the child sexually is preparing or educating him or her for later life (Groth, 2001; Prendergast, 2004; van Dam, 2006). This is but another part of their distorted thinking.

Issues of Relationship

The relationships of a sexual offender have usually not been positive from his early childhood on. He may have been abused, rejected, or discounted at home. With peers, he usually feels left out and inadequate. His tendency to measure himself against others leaves him feeling that everyone else has peer relationships except him. Some of these individuals will deny that this feeling is important to them and will continue to take a victim role. Others will overcompensate by the use of aggression or the development of an overly assertive posture (Flora et al., 2008; Groth, 2001; Prendergast, 2004; Yates et al., 2010).

Control is a major issue for offenders. In their eyes, you either have the control or do not.

Each offender will find his own way of exerting some control. One may appear to be a wimp and yet seek out young children who see him as someone larger and more in control than they are. Or he may choose the expression of aggression in some manner.

In addition to his problems in the area of control, he lacks the ability to trust others, a vital component for healthy relationships. Unable to develop intimacy, he tends to relate at a very superficial level.

ॐ ────────────────────────

Mack had acquaintances but no real friends. If pressed, he would have called those with whom he drank in the evening at the local bar as his friends, but to them, he was "just some guy who comes into the bar." Mack trusted no one and was known to pick fights over the smallest implied insult.

As a child, he had had a stutter and was regularly teased by schoolmates. He spoke as little as possible. Discovering that he was not likely to tell, some of the older boys began using him as their sexual patsy. Anyone who wanted quick oral sex would get it from Mack. He began to see himself as accepted because of what he did for the older boys. But once when he was caught with one of them, the boy insisted that Mack had compelled him into performing sex on him, and it was Mack who was expelled. His anger intensified, and he became convinced that he could trust no one— certainly not his alcoholic father or the mother who had left them and not his peers.

As an adult, Mack's life consisted of drinking and going home alone to his rented room. It was when he met the son of a neighbor that he decided that his life began. Mack rationalized that because this boy was lonely too, he too wanted a sexual relationship. When the boy told his mother and Mack was arrested, his rage intensified. Now he knew that there was absolutely no one in life who could be trusted.

ॐ

Offenders who do become involved in relationships with other adults usually do so either because it is expected of them or because they see some gain from the relationship. Some offenders are looking for the love that they never got as children but later find that the responsibility of an adult-to-adult relationship is too great a price. Other offenders see a relationship as a means to an end. For example, Patrick met June at the dairy bar where she worked as a waitress. She often brought her two little girls to work with her on days that her sitter was unavailable. Patrick's attraction to the girls led to his forging a relationship with their mother. Moving in with her gave him unlimited access to them, and her long hours gave him opportunity for the abuse that followed.

Sexual offenders tend to avoid deep emotions as well as the responsibility for their actions in relationships. The other person will always be to blame in their eyes for any problems with the union.

The Influence of Substances on Sexual Offending

Alcohol, known to be a depressant to the central nervous system that produces impaired judgment, euphoria, disinhibition, and increased aggression, has long been thought to be associated with sexual acting out (Valliere, 1997). A number of sexual assaults on children are attributed to the fact that the offender was drinking or using drugs. Often the substance abuse will be treated to the exclusion of the sexual deviance. In fact, the depressant properties of alcohol and the variety of effects of other drugs may break down the offender's inhibitions about acting out his sexual fantasies, but the substances are not the cause for abuse. The fact that numerous alcoholics and drug users never abuse children attests to the fact that a tendency toward sexual deviance is required for someone

to act this out sexually (Bolen, 2007; Herman & Hirschman, 2000; Plante, 2004; van Dam, 2006; Yates et al., 2010). At the same time, anything that reduces the likelihood of the abuse happening must be addressed in the treatment of the offender (Laws et al., 2000). In some treatment programs, any ingestion of a substance is considered to be a relapse due to the impairment of the offender's judgment (Ward et al., 2006).

CHARACTERISTICS ASSOCIATED WITH FEMALE SEXUAL OFFENDERS

Although many of the issues discussed earlier might also apply to female sexual offenders, the fact is that there are differences in the genders. As mentioned earlier, our U.S. culture has a great deal of difficulty accepting that women might sexually abuse children (Bunting, 2007). In Chapter 3, the culturally expected characteristics of women, based on the research of David Finkelhor (1984), were discussed. To review, Finklehor suggested that women are less likely to sexually abuse children because of the ways they are enculturated (taught by the culture) and how they are viewed in these ways:

- Women tend to be the nurturers of children, seeing the total child.
- Because of that nurturing role, women are more likely to have empathy for the child.
- They have traditionally been the one to clean up the child before presenting him or her to Dad.
- They have been trained to prefer stronger and larger sexual partners, whereas men are enculturated to prefer younger and weaker partners.
- They have not been trained to equate affection with sex as their male counterparts have.

Although the fact that men have become more involved in the care of their offspring may have outdated these views somewhat, the trend remains that women are viewed as more in tune with children and therefore less likely to abuse. Once again, culture plays a part in defining the caretaking roles of men and women. In addition, there may be less reports of abuse by women due to the nature of their victims. Men are not as likely to report abuse by women. Women abused by other women are often caught up in the stigma of the taboo and also are not as likely to report.

Perhaps in keeping with this societal reluctance to see women as abusive and the fact that most reported sexual offenders are men, there has been little written about adult female sexual offenders of children in comparison to the literature depicting male abusers. More has been written of late about juvenile female offenders.

Theorists have suggested a few differences between women who sexually abuse and their male counterparts. Women *do not appear to have the sense of entitlement* demonstrated by male offenders (Beech, Parrett, Ward, & Fisher, 2009). They are more likely to give other reasons for the abuse than it is their due. Some researchers also suggest that there are *more psychiatric disorders* among female abusers (Ford, 2006; Hislop, 2001; Johansson-Love & Fremouw, 2009). There is also some evidence that women who sexually abuse children come from *lower socioeconomic families where poverty and neglect were common* (Ford, 2006; Nathan & Ward, 2002). There is some possibility that this may be related to the fact that statistically women who sexually abuse have been *pregnant at earlier ages* and therefore may not have had the opportunity to elevate themselves financially (Saradjian, 1996). Almost all the studies of women who sexually abuse have found that a high percentage of them *were sexually abused and many were physically abused or neglected* as children. Women offenders also *tended to be younger than males* who sexually abuse (Ford, 2006; Hislop, 2001; Johansson-Love &

Fremouw, 2009; Matthews, Matthews, & Speltz, 1989; Saradjian, 1996).

It is also useful to note the comparison between recidivism rates of male and female offenders. A study of 780 male and female sexual offenders in New York State found that males were more likely than females to be rearrested for sexual offenses (Freeman & Sandler, 2008). Women are also less likely to deny that they committed the crime in the first place (Faller, 2003).

Women offenders are often grouped in terms of their motivation and choice of victims. Ford (2006) divides female offenders into women who abuse young children, women who abuse adolescents, and women who are initially coerced by men.

Women Who Abuse Young Children

When women abuse young children, it is often a need for power and control or to seek physical gratification (Ford, 2006; Hislop, 2001; Saradjian, 1996). They may also have a distorted need of bonding and feel that the abuse bonds them more fully to the child (Ford, 2006; Saradjian, 1996).

ℭℛ
_____

Petra had grown up in a household where her parents had little time for her. Both were wine merchants and traveled extensively, leaving Petra with a series of nannies. It was a lonely existence. Most of the nannies retired to their own rooms after supper, and Petra was left alone to amuse herself. She tried the contents of her parent's well-stocked liquor cabinet, and after getting sick several times, decided that it was not worth it. She developed a habit of cutting when she was alone just because it helped her to feel something. She amused herself by talking with the gardener who spoke little English. One night when she went to his quarters, he began to sexually molest her. When she resisted, he raped her.

Petra was afraid to tell her parents when they returned but tried to avoid the gardener when she could. Not wanting to see him, she kept to her room, except when she was at school. She had frequent flashbacks of the rape and bought some drugs at school, which kept her mind off it. For hours she chatted on the computer with men who offered to meet her. At 17, she ran away with one of these men and lived with him until her parents found her and brought her back. Now pregnant, Petra convinced them to let her have her own apartment when the baby was born. After her son was born, her parents, secretly relieved at her flight into independence, bid Petra good-bye to attend a wine convention in Europe.

Petra adored her baby whom she named Wilhelm because it sounded unique to her. Her parents had hired a woman to look in on her in their absence, but Petra told her she could care for the baby herself. She knew nothing about caring for babies, but she got a book to read about it. Will was a good baby, and all Petra wanted was to be with him. She loved to undress him and just fondle his small body. She dreamed of having him back inside her so that they would be one again. 🔊

Petra's obsession with her baby later was found to be sexually abusive. In therapy, she explained that she wanted to be one with her baby again so that she too could feel cared for.

Women abusers with older children have an inadequate knowledge of child development and child care. They have difficulty with discipline and may use sexual abuse as a method of controlling their children (Ford, 2006; Hislop, 2001; Saradjian, 1996).

Women Who Abuse Adolescents

Women who abuse adolescents are not as concerned with power and control. Instead, they have idealized the victim into seeing him as a lover. The abuser seeks closeness, affection, and support in a relationship that she hopes will make up for those she has not had with age-mates. Matthews et al. (1989) characterized this abuser as the teacher–lover.

🔊

Cleo worked as a teacher's aide in the high school. She loved her job and wished that she could have been a teacher. But her chaotic home life and early marriage had spoiled all her plans to go to college, even if she could have found the money to do so. Her husband, Ben, was a mechanic who worked long hours. She rarely saw him, which was fine with her. Benji was his father's son, preferring to spend his time at the gas station. When business got slow, Cleo had taken the job at the school.

Jared was a 14-year-old boy who struggled with schoolwork. But he was talented at woodcarving and would sometimes bring his creations to school. Cleo, who was helping him with his schoolwork, loved the beautiful little animals that he made of wood. His hands were so gentle and delicate, not like Ben's big hands, always covered with grease. She found that the days she saw Jared became special to her. She fantasized about how they could be together outside of school. When summer came, Cleo began inviting him to the house and then they would go on picnics in the woods. She was later not sure how the sex had started. Whose idea was it? She did know that it felt good, and once it started, she delighted in teaching Jared things he did not know about sex. It was 9-year-old Benji who found them in the woods behind the house and told his father what he had seen. 🔊

Cleo was angry when her relationship with Jared was broken up. She saw nothing wrong with the fact that they were together. It is not uncommon for these women to feel wronged when others are upset with the abuse that has been perpetrated.

Women Who Are Initially Coerced by Men

Women who are coerced by men are often afraid of their partners. Initially, these women agree to sexually abuse out of the fear of what will happen if they do not help their abusive partners. Later, the women begin to have their own sense of power and control over the perpetration of the abuse. Because they have felt powerless, feeling powerful over someone weaker and younger has its appeal, and they may continue the abuse or go on to abuse other children (Ford, 2006; Hislop, 2001; Saradjian, 1996).

Other Types of Women Offenders

Matthews and her colleagues (1989) in their classic study suggested that there was another type of female offender who was motivated by her own abusive background to abuse children. Some abusers want to hurt children as they have been hurt or "get back" at someone who has abused them. An abuser may be so angered at the man who abused her in her childhood that she abuses her own sons "in retaliation." There may be a great deal of rage about her own childhood, and this can also be taken out on the children in more aggressive ways. These women may experience sexual fantasies like their male counterparts, often finding that the fantasies no longer satisfy them and they need to act them out (Ford, 2006; Saradjian, 1996).

Abuse by women can be particularly traumatic for victims. Boys who recognize that the behavior toward them is abusive may be concerned about their own sexuality. Daughters abused by mothers have a great deal of difficulty sorting out their own identities in later life. The role of women as nurturers in our society may serve to confuse the victim and impede his or her healthy differentiation between sex and affection (Hislop, 2001).

Need for More Research on Female Offenders

There is a great deal more that must be learned about women who abuse children and adolescents. Sexual arousal and fantasy, so well studied in men, have received little attention in regard to women who offend. Do women make use of pornography in the same manner as men? At this point, this seems somewhat unlikely as women are aroused by different stimuli (Finkelhor, 1984). However, some women may still use pornography to lure their victims or desensitize them to the sexual activity (Ford, 2006).

Other questions beg for answers. What causes a woman who is coerced into abusing children by a male to become an abuser in her own right? Would this same woman eventually become an abuser without the coercion? The link between childhood sexual abuse and later abuse by women must also be further understood (Ford, 2006). And finally, there is little known about the abuse by women from different cultural groups.

Summary

The general public often has a difficult time understanding how someone might abuse a child. There are no simple answers. Many experts suggest that there is no typical profile of a sexual offender. Others point to such characteristics as an inadequate personality, a need for acceptance, distorted perceptions, poor social and relationship skills, distorted sexual values, identity confusion, and other similar issues.

Offenders may have experienced problems in their development. Some have been abused sexually, whereas others have been victims of physical abuse, neglect, domestic violence, or other types of family dysfunction. Recent studies have indicated that most offenders have had problems with attachment with caretakers in their early lives, which may then lead to aggression. Offenders may also have had difficulty with peer relationships.

Theorists believe that offending is a learned behavior that originates in some trauma or phase of development. There are some compulsive elements to the behavior with opportunity and grooming playing a part. Currently, the Internet plays a significant role in the way that offenders are able to engage children.

Male offenders demonstrate problems with self-esteem and social competence, often using distorted thinking and selective perception to compensate. Many have sexual problems, using masturbation and sexual abuse to meet the needs that they are unable to fill with healthy adult-to-adult relationships. The use of pornography plays a significant role in their offending pattern. They use pornographic images to fantasize about children and sometimes as a way of engaging them.

Sexual offenders have difficulties with relationships, often measuring themselves and their ability to relate in a way that makes them feel inferior. Some also use alcohol, perhaps rationalizing that it causes their abuse.

The characteristics of female sexual offenders differ from those of male offenders. Part of this difference may be related to how women are viewed by society and how they are shaped by gender-specific cultural expectations. Research has shown that female offenders differ from male offenders in that they feel less entitled, have more psychiatric disorders, and were more often sexually abused as children.

Women who abuse young children, often when in nurturing roles, seem to do so for power and control or out of a distorted idea of bonding. Women who abuse adolescents are more likely to see them as a substitute for an adult lover. Some women are coerced into sexually abusing children because the men in their lives either coerce or threaten them to participate. Additional research is necessary to fully understand female offenders.

Review Questions

1. What are some of the characteristics thought to be associated with sexual offenders against children?

2. How might the early development of an offender predispose him to be abusive?

3. What are the influences of brain development and attachment on abusing?

4. What is Gilgun's theory about why some men abuse and others do not?

5. Some say that there are compulsive elements to sexual offending. How would you explain this?

6. In what ways does poor self-esteem contribute to the offender's abuse of children?

7. How does development in the area of sexuality affect sexual offending?

8. What role does fantasy play?

9. What are some of the characteristics of female offenders?

10. What is the difference between women who abuse young children and those who abuse teens?

CHAPTER 6

Intrafamilial Abuse or Incest

Intrafamilial abuse in the context of child sexual abuse refers to abuse of the child by a relative or family member. Sometimes termed *incest,* this type of abuse was the subject of much study and speculation when child sexual abuse became a household word in the 1980s (see Chapter 1). The study of incest was aided by such books as Judith Herman's *Father-Daughter Incest* (1981), postulating that the phenomenon should be looked at in the context of the whole family. Although uncles, grandfathers, brothers, sisters, and other relatives may abuse children, the most statistically significant type of incest has been found to be father-daughter; some sources also include stepfathers in this statistic (Bolen, 2007; Herman, 1981; Kinnear, 2007; Meiselman, 1992; O'Neil & Brown, 2010; Russell, 1983). Although initially, theorists believed that incest was the most prevalent type of child sexual abuse, studies uncovered that it accounts for only between 11% and 40% of the total number of cases (Bolen, 2007). In fact, rather than abuse by fathers, abuse by uncles was found to be the most prevalent by several studies (Bolen, 2007; Russell, 1983). One exception to this finding was Wyatt's (1985) study of African Americans that concluded that fathers (and cousins) were the second most common abusers; stepfathers were the most prevalent. All studies found that female relatives were the least likely to be sexually abusive (Bolen, 2007; Russell, 1983; Wyatt, 1985).

FRAMEWORKS TO EXPLAIN INCEST

Early understandings of incest were based on the incest avoidance work of researchers like Westermarck, Malinowski, and White (Meiselman, 1992) (see Chapter 1) who talked about children who were in close proximity with family members developing an avoidance to sexual contact with them (Bolen, 2007). This sociobiological explanation was later replaced by a family systems theory approach.

Family Systems Theory

Family systems theory (also discussed in Chapter 3) examines the family in which incest occurs. Incest was seen as a symptom of the family pathology that the family used to maintain its equilibrium. Each family member contributed to the dysfunction in some manner. Although the perpetrator, usually the father, used the excuse of not being understood or having the right to paternal authority, the mother was thought to have colluded in some manner. Her collusion was the result of her fear of the perpetrator; her desire to please him; or her sacrifice of her daughter to satisfy the needs that she chose, by abdicating her role as her husband's sexual partner, not to meet (Cohen, 1983; Hoorwitz, 1983; Sgroi, 1982). Some theorists believed that the incest was the glue that held the family together. Without it, there was a fear of family annihilation (Cohen, 1983; Hoorwitz, 1983).

Perhaps the family systems theory and its application to incest is best clarified by Kadushin and Martin (1988) who explain that

> [f]ather-daughter incest is a manifestation of disturbed family equilibrium and occurs in response to an effort to establish an adaptation that is functional. . . . The family in which incest occurs is likely to be an enmeshed, socially isolated, one in which intergenerational and parent-child role boundaries are vaguely defined and permeable. . . . A family experiencing marital conflict is maintained in tact by the reallocation of sexual-affectional role in incest. The female child is sacrificed . . . on the altar of family stability. . . . Participants share the feeling that incest is preferable to breakdown . . . [and] all participants have a vested interest in guarding against disclosure. . . . Secondary gains experienced by the daughter reinforce any reluctance to discontinue the relationship. . . . She has a special status. . . . And, there is a secondary gain in sexual pleasure. . . . A further secondary gain is considerable enhancement of her power. . . . Positive satisfactions in secondary gains increases [sic] the incentives to continue the relationship. (pp. 298–302 as cited in Bolen, 2007, pp. 31–32)

Kempe and Kempe (1984) characterized two different types of families where incest could be seen. The first they called the "chaotic family," and the second, the "normal-appearing family." The chaotic family tends to be dysfunctional with a lower socioeconomic status. There may be histories of substance abuse, incarceration, delinquent behavior, and general sociopathic tendencies. Most family members have little education, are often dependent upon financial assistance, and exhibit unstable and changing relationships. When children in these families become victims of abuse, their parental abusers are often separated from the family and incarcerated as the families do not have the monetary resources to seek treatment.

The normal-appearing families, according to Kempe and Kempe (1984), can project an image to the community that all is well. Parents may appear to have stable marriages, be financially comfortable, and even have significant roles within the community.

ଔ ─────────────────────────

Tucker Kramer was mayor of a small city. He, his wife, and three daughters had lived in the community for years and were well known. Tucker was everybody's friend, ingratiating himself with young and old. His wife, Florence, involved herself in a variety of community activities, and everyone marveled at how well Tucker could care for his daughters and still be an active mayor. He seemed like such a devoted father, and when the news that he had been abusing his daughters for some time was uncovered, the community was shocked. **ଚ**

────────────────────────────

Parents of this type may appear to be good caretakers, but it is often the children who are meeting the needs of their immature and emotionally needy parents.

Incest, according to the family systems perspective, is an attempt to maintain a family equilibrium. Families demonstrate specific characteristics. The family tends to isolate itself from the community in an effort to maintain its secret, a secret that all would deny. Individual members take their cues from the total family and believe about the family the scenario that rationalizes and protects the secret of the abuse. All other problems as well as the abuse are denied, and there is little or no acceptance of emotions such as anger, conflict, or deviations from the family ideal. There is a blurring of generational boundaries that leaves children unsure of their exact roles. They often feel that it is up to them to maintain the family and care for their parents emotionally. Children are further confused by the fact that physical contact tends to be sexual, and there is a lack of any other type of nurturance. Parents are either immature or emotionally unavailable, and children's emotional needs go unmet. Children are often encouraged to isolate themselves so that the paths to help are cut off and the abuser alone can gain their trust (Bolen, 2007; Courtois, 2010; Gannon, Gilchrist, & Wade, 2008; Mayer, 1983, 1985; Whetsell-Mitchell, 1995).

Because most of the focus in the family systems camp was on father-daughter incest, the explanations centered around this type of familial abuse. In time, there were attempts to shed light on the family dynamics with other perpetrators and victims (e.g., mother-son incest and father-son incest discussed later in the chapter; see Forward & Buck, 1978).

Feminist Theory Influence

Just as family systems theory had a significant voice in the early explanations of incest, so too did feminist camps. It was actually feminists who produced many of the early writings about survivors of child sexual abuse. As women felt more powerful, they began to speak out about what had been done to them in childhood. Writers like Herman (1981) and Rush (1992) spoke of the influence of the social environment on children and postulated that child sexual abuse was a symptom of a patriarchal society where males dominated females, making sexual abuse of women and children an extension of socially normative behavior (Bolen, 2007; Ward, 1985; Whetsell-Mitchell, 1995). Feminists disputed the blame placed on the nonabusing mother and proclaimed the message in nondisputable terms that the offender was solely responsible for the abusive behavior (Faller, 2007b; Krane, 2003). Feminists said that Freud's seduction theory muddied the waters (Bolen, 2007; Herman, 1981; Herman & Hirschman, 2000; Rush, 1992).

The feminist contention that the offender was the only one on whom the abuse could be blamed had an impact on the study of child sexual abuse, but those working in mental health did not always agree so readily. By the 1990s, clinicians surveyed in several studies attributed between 65%

and 84% of the blame to the offender (Johnson, Owens, Dewey, & Eisenberg, 1990; Kelley, 1990; Reidy & Hochstadt, 1993), suggesting that a fair number of mental health professionals still considered the viability of the family systems approach that suggested that the mother also had culpability. Particularly concerning, however, was the fact that clinicians were less likely to attribute blame to offenders who were of higher economic status (Kelly, 1994).

INCIDENCE OF FAMILIAL ABUSE

The only measure that researchers have to determine the number of familial abuse cases in the United States today is based on those that have been reported either to Child Protective Services (CPS), other agencies, or through research studies. Some young victims do not even recognize that there is anything wrong with the relationship with the perpetrator, as the abuse may have been explained as normal or otherwise purposeful (e.g., teaching) by the abuser. Many victims of incest are hesitant to report the abuse to anyone outside the family because of the impact on the family. Those within the family who know of the abuse may be reluctant to report as well (Atwood, 2007). The multicultural nature of American society also influences the number of reports; many cultures are less likely than others to make these reports (Fontes, 2008; Fontes & Plummer, 2012). For these reasons, it is difficult to determine the exact number of families in which incest has taken place. Past surveys of the general population have suggested that familial abuse represents between 11% and 40% of all sexual abuse cases (Bolen, 2007).

One study used a chat room to determine the incidence of incest. The researcher chatted with 2,345 individuals and discovered that, by their report, 36% of the females interviewed had engaged in incestuous acts including sexual intercourse, oral sex, or other genital contact. Of the 2,345 people interviewed, 138 identified themselves as males and reported incestuous experiences with younger female relatives (Atwood, 2007). Of the females that had engaged in incestuous acts, about 70% under 10 years old were involved with fathers, uncles, brothers, stepfathers, grandfathers, mother's boyfriends, stepbrothers, or babysitters. Of all of the children involved in incest, the highest percentage were abused by fathers (36%) and uncles (23%) (Atwood, 2007, p. 301). Of the 610 female victims, most had incestuous relationships with only one family member, whereas 223 were involved with multiple abusers, one family member and others in or outside of the family (p. 301). One finding was that 28 of the mothers, all of whose children were under 10 years old, also participated in the incestuous relationships, sometimes facilitating the interaction between father and child.

DYNAMICS WITHIN SEXUALLY ABUSIVE FAMILIES

Although there may be differences in family dynamics dependent upon the identity of the perpetrator, there are also similarities among incestuous families. These families provide an environment for incest because they are already dysfunctional. In fact, the incest itself compensates or meets a family need that has not been met in other ways. There are several dynamics that must be considered when looking at intrafamilial abuse. It should also be noted that much of the research on intrafamilial abuse per se was done in the 1980s and 1990s. Newer research has focused on both the aftermath of abuse and smaller samples.

Boundary Issues

Boundaries are the often unspoken conventions that people follow when engaged in relationships. They may be related to emotional, physical, cultural, and sexual attitudes and behaviors and will be influenced by such factors as age, cultural background,

upbringing, and religion. When it comes to boundaries related to sexual practices, families may differ. For example, one family with a hot tub may sanction bathing together in it naked regardless of the age or gender of the family members. Other families might expect that anyone using the hot tub with other family members will be wearing bathing attire. Friedrich, Fisher, Broughton, Houston, and Shafran (1998) compared the prevalence of certain family behaviors to increased sexual behaviors in children. When families had more relaxed approaches to co-sleeping, co-bathing, family nudity, witnessing adult sexual activities, and seeing adult movies, there was an increase in the sexual behaviors of their children, although these researchers did not necessarily frame these behaviors as more disturbed. From this study evolved the safety checklist (see Friedrich, 2002) that assesses family boundaries around such practices as co-bathing, co-sleeping, and family nudity. Gil and Johnson (1993) postulated that children being exposed to an increase in sexual behaviors usually designated to be adult did demonstrate problematic sexual behaviors (see also Johnson, 1999). Johnson (1999) pointed to extensive boundary violations in the homes of children who are demonstrating problematic sexual behaviors. This boundary violation, suggests this researcher, may be as influential as direct sexual abuse in causing sexual confusion, problematic sexual behaviors, and anxiety in children. Some theorists refer to this as "emotional incest" (Kaplan, 2010).

Boundary violations and distortions are also apparent in overt intrafamilial abuse (Berliner, 2011; Bolen, 2007; Johnson & Hooper, 2003; Sgroi, 1982). For example, although the family does not openly condone parental nudity, a father "forgets" his towel from shower to bedroom, thus exposing himself to his young daughters as a part of his grooming of them for sexual abuse. Or behaviors that are usually reserved for adult-to-adult relationships become part of child-adult interactions. In some incestuous families, there is a role reversal that not only violates normally prescribed boundaries but is part of the sexual abuse.

CR ─────────────────

When her mother returned to work as a nurse, Margie was 8. She did not mind having her father put her to bed. He had always been more approachable than her mother anyway. They began a ritual of using the hot tub (to help her to sleep better, Dad told her) before bed. While Mom insisted that everyone wear a suit, Dad assured her that he and Mom used the hot tub without them so it was all right for Margie and Dad to do so too. Dad began to rub her back during these times and then moved down to her legs. The warm relaxing water and her trust of Dad helped Margie feel that this was an acceptable part of their relationship. During these times, Dad also confided in his daughter about how difficult Mom had become since she returned to work. He told her that Mom never wanted to be close to him or to cuddle as Margie did. He made the child feel special. Sometimes he would encourage her to come into the bedroom that he shared with Mom and to try on her negligees. He told Margie that Mom never wore them anymore and Margie could have some of them. But maybe they should keep it a secret from Mom. Before long, Margie began to feel that she was more of a wife to her father than Mom was. After all, Margie was giving him all the things that Mom had refused to do for him. **CR**

─────────────────

When Margie happened to overhear sounds of her parents having intercourse sometime later, her bubble popped. When she told a friend about the relationship she had been having with her father and the friend told her parents, the friend's parents reported the situation. Eventually, Margie's family agreed to treatment. It became clear that the fragmentation of generational boundaries would be one treatment issue. Sgroi (1982) identifies the realignment of generational boundaries as one important piece of any treatment plan in families where there has been incest.

Family Stress and Dysfunction

Families where there is incest are often characterized by a good deal of stress and dysfunction. Early studies found that children were often the product unwanted pregnancies, roles were rigid, financial concerns were frequent, and marital stress was usually a given (Bolen, 2007; Hartley, 2001; Herman & Hirschman, 2000; James & Nasjleti, 1983; Justice & Justice, 1980). Offenders also report medical problems, alcohol abuse, and employment stresses (Hartley, 2001). The isolation present in these families makes it difficult for them to receive help from the outside, compounding their disconnectedness from the communities in which they live.

Today, the effects of the economic downturn that began in 2008 and led to greater rates of unemployment and financial instability among many families intensify the feelings of instability felt by all families but often more acute within families touched by sexual abuse. Marital discord, often with an accompanying lack of sexual interaction, is apparent in most of these families as well.

Cultural Implications

Not every family where there is intrafamilial abuse will have the same dynamics. One important variable is related to the culture with which the family identifies. Fontes (2008) points to the issue of shame as being central to understanding the implications of child sexual abuse for minority cultural groups.

Shame reaches into the core of the individual's self-concept. It is not about harm that has been done to one by others but rather the internal feeling that one is a defective human being (Fontes, 2008). In many minority cultures, shame is the opposite of honor, which is held high when conceptualizing personal worth. Shame undermines that worth and can be projected so that the shameful individual feels that everyone looks at him or her as an unworthy person. This feeling can undermine later relationships, relations with family and friends, and the person's ability to work and feel successful.

Feiring, Taska, and Lewis (2002) studied 147 children and adolescents at the discovery of their abuse and a year later to assess the impact of shame and attributional style on functioning. They found that the reduction of shame had a major influence on the child's healing and was, in fact, more important in his or her future adjustment than the severity of the abuse he or she suffered.

Shame is part of most victims of child sexual abuse. Victims recognize on some level that the sexual activities are taboo and feel shame over being involved. Perpetrators usually play on this shame to compel the child to keep the secret of the abuse. They may suggest that the child had initiated or lured the offender into the abuse, that the child has betrayed a relationship (e.g., with the nonoffending parent), and that the child would be considered to be "bad" if anyone knew of the sexual relationship—all designed to impair the victim's self-concept, make him or her more dependent upon the abuser, and isolate him or her from others (Fontes, 2008; Fontes & Plummer, 2012). This further intensifies a child's worldview that sees him or herself at the center and therefore seemingly responsible for much of what goes on. Even nonoffending parents who have cautioned the victim that the family's "dirty laundry should not be aired in public" add, sometimes unintentionally, to the victim's sense of shame. In intrafamilial abuse, the shame serves to isolate not only the victim but the whole family.

In addition to the shame imposed upon any victim of child sexual abuse, those from minority cultures grapple with additional mores and attitudes. Fontes (2008) identifies five specific areas that must be considered when working with these groups: responsibility for the abuse, failure to protect, the idea of fate, the influence of being damaged, and the importance of virginity.

In families where there is abuse, all parties look for someone on whom to rest the blame. In many traditional cultures, sexual relations are seen as a struggle between males and females; females must avoid them, whereas males seek them out and base their masculinity on their number of conquests. When a female is known to have had sexual encounters outside of marriage, it is assumed that she has made herself accessible or at least has not done enough to ward them off. This is true even for young girls. This sense that the victim has not lived up to the expectations imposed by the culture intensifies her shame. There is a strong mandate to protect children in most cultures, and when a child is abused, adults feel the shame of what they perceive as their failure to protect. Fontes (2008) points out that assigning blame to the child ("she was seductive") may actually protect the adults in the situation from their own feelings of shame. For example, if a Latino father's child is victimized, he may feel that he is a failure as a man based on his culture's ideas of machismo. When the abuse is discovered, he may well be at risk for suicide or he may decide to take matters into his own hands by physically going after the offender. So strong is this cultural value that some Latino fathers would prefer to spend time in jail rather than feel like they did not protect their child. Often such fathers must be helped to recognize that becoming entangled with the criminal justice system themselves will further intensify their children's distress (Fontes, 2008; Fontes, Cruz, & Tabachnick, 2001; Fontes & Plummer, 2012).

Where people see the locus of control in their lives is also cultural. The dominant culture in the United States bases ideas of individual control on the concept of rugged individualism that says that the individual must determine his or her own future through hard work and standing alone. Some minority cultures believe in an external locus of control, feeling that luck, fate, God's will, or other external forces dictate what will happen in their lives (Sue & Sue, 2013).

ை _____

Desiree had fled from Haiti and, with her 5-year-old son and 3-year-old daughter, Monique, settled in a poor section of a northern city. Desperately wanting to work, she was nonetheless unable to find a job or suitable day care for her children that she could rely upon once she got a job. When Desiree was feeling that life could not get worse, she met Thomas who promised to take care of her and her family. He had a good job, and things began to look up. Soon Thomas had moved in with the family, and the fights began. His tumultuous relationship with

Desiree lasted for several months until she found him molesting her daughter. In a rage, she kicked him out but was almost inconsolable afterward. "We are cursed!" she wailed. To her concerned neighbor with whom she had become friends, she confessed that her father in a fit of rage at her leaving had put a curse on her and her children. She was convinced that their luck would never improve, so total was her belief in the curse.

                                        ෨

The concept of "God's will" plays such significant role in the lives of some minority cultures; Latinos, for example, will often interject when speaking of future events the phrase "*Si Dios quiere*," translated "if God is willing." Some Southeast Asian parents may be misunderstood as having little sympathy for their sexually abused child. They attribute what has happened to the child's karma, his or her punishment for wrongdoings in a previous lifetime. Parents from other cultures, especially those with strong Roman Catholic roots, may feel that they are "being tested" by God or that God is somehow sending them a message by punishing them (Fontes, 2008).

When children are sexually abused, they usually feel damaged. And the adults around them often perceive them that way as well. In many minority cultures, preserving the beauty and innocence of the girl child for her future husband is paramount. Being "spoiled" or "soiled" by sexual abuse may seem life altering to families who espouse this value.

෧

"After the neighbor abused me, I knew that I could tell no one if I ever hoped to marry," admitted one woman whose family had immigrated from India when she was a child. "I never told anyone, but when I came to my husband on that first night, I felt so ashamed. My shame consumed me, affecting my health and bringing anger from my husband as well as my father."

                                        ෨

When her husband was killed unexpectedly, this young woman was so consumed with guilt that she stopped eating and was eventually hospitalized and later referred to a therapist. Her story came out as her therapist endeavored to discover why this beautiful young woman had no desire to live but was, at the same time, afraid to die lest her karma follow her into another lifetime.

The emphasis on virginity is strong in many minority cultures. Losing one's virginity means that the female child will be less valuable for marriage, an arrangement that could potentially elevate her status and her family's as well. Young girls are often checked for their virginal status (by determining if the hymen is broken) on a regular basis. Digital checking is done by the child's mother by inserting a finger in the child's vagina to determine if it will go in; CPS and courts often consider this method itself as a form of sexual abuse (Fontes, 2008).

Fears about loss of status and an impaired future as a result of being sexually abused may also deter a child from reporting it when she is sexually abused. And families who discover such abuse may not want to cooperate with CPS or the criminal justice system as they know that their own reputation could also be ruined were this abuse to become public. The entire family could potentially suffer (Baker & Dwairy, 2003; Fontes, 2008; Fontes & Plummer, 2012).

Boys, too, face cultural stigma when they are abused. The myth is that a boy who is sexually abused will either become homosexual or abuse others sexually. Fathers, especially, worry about the masculinity and sexual orientation of their sons. Boys who are abused within the family encounter another layer of stigma and conflict. When a boy abused by a male has an erection during the abuse, a natural physiological response to being touched, he may fear that he has enjoyed the experience and therefore that he is not masculine (Cassese, 2001; Fontes, 2008; Lew, 2004).

For both male and female victims of intrafamilial abuse, it is important for helpers to understand the cultural ramifications of this experience and how the victim can be helped to heal.

TYPES OF INTRAFAMILIAL ABUSE _____

Father-Daughter Incest

Father-daughter incest is said to be the classical type of incest that comes to mind in any discussion of the subject. In fact, according to most statistics, abuse of daughters by the father or surrogate father (e.g., stepfather) is the most common. It was also one of the first to be addressed by writers and clinicians (see Faller, 2003; Herman, 1981). The family pattern is well known—an "isolated, enmeshed system, balancing precariously in what they perceive as a hostile environment" (Crosson-Tower, 2014, p. 141).

Stern and Mayer (1980) suggested that there were three interactional patterns by which such incestuous families could be characterized: the possessive-passive, the dependent-domineering, and the dependent-dependent.

Possessive-Passive Pattern

The possessive-passive pattern is one that was first characterized in feminist literature as the patriarchal family. Herman and Hirschman (2000) commented of these men that

> their authority with the family was absolute, often asserted by force. They were also arbiters of the family's social life and frequently succeeded in virtually secluding the women in the family. But while they were often feared within their families, they impressed outsiders as sympathetic, even admirable men. (p. 71)

Power and control is what these fathers use to keep their families subservient and compliant to their wishes. There may be physical force, taking the form of domestic violence, or the father may be so feared that no actual violence is needed.

Gilgun and Connor (1990) highlight the concept of isolation as central to the perpetration of incest. Not only does isolation act as a contributor to the incest but it also is a result of the incest. The incest perpetrator learns about isolation through his own family of origin, which tends to be dysfunctional, often involved with substance abuse, mental illness, domestic violence, separation or divorce, child abuse, or severe financial stressors. As a child, the perpetrator has often seen his parents isolated from each other as well as from their children. He therefore feels discounted, unloved, and rejected. He develops a view of himself as unlovable, and this view influences his ability to relate to peers as he develops. He may well avoid girls or find his relationships with them extremely stressful (Bolen, 2007; Crosson-Tower, 2014).

Mothers in this family are often passive or unavailable emotionally. The daughter's vulnerability is increased by her father's dominance and her mother's inability or unwillingness to intervene (Bolen, 2007).

ॐ _____

Katrina could not blame her mother for being sick. She knew that her mother's physical pain was excessive at times, and she did her best to keep the household running when her mother took to her bed. She knew too that her father, recently retired from the Navy, demanded that things be shipshape and expected everyone to remember this. His anger when anything was out of place was frightening. As an only child, Katrina felt that it was up to her to compensate for what her mother was unable to do. Her feelings of responsibility were so great that when her father let her know that he was missing "a woman's company," she felt obliged to do what she could to be with him. The sexual touching began slowly, but at no time did Katrina perceive that she had a choice. And she appreciated the side of her father that she saw when he was touching her. He was not as gruff, and Katrina found that she enjoyed their time together. ॐ

_____

Although fathers in this type of family pattern were often presented as domineering and dictatorial, they might also have had a nurturing side as Katrina's father appeared to.

Despite the prevalence of this type of family and family pattern in much of the early literature, it is but one type of family dynamic.

Dependent-Domineering Pattern

This family pattern is characterized by a domineering wife and her weak ineffective partner. The wife often sees him almost like one of the children with whom he may align himself. Thus, the sexual interaction becomes—in his mind almost like peer play, so enmeshed is he with his daughter. At the same time, this mother may feel her own needs not being met, and she may withdraw from the family altogether. Children often see their fathers as warm and loving, whereas they feel rejection and coldness from their mothers.

❧ _____

Maddie and Billie Jean loved being with their father. As a disabled roofer, his disability allowed him to be at home with them. Their mother, Madge, resented the fact that she had to work outside the home. She had always been the dominant spouse, making decisions and ruling the household. Then Madge had developed a thriving real estate business and was often away from the home. When she was at home, she complained that the house was not cleaned to her standards and berated her husband, Will, and her daughters. In her absence, Will mocked his wife to his children, and they all laughed about her reactions. This developed into a feeling of "us against her" that all enjoyed. The sexual abuse began by Will joking and tickling the girls. Later, neither girl could have pinpointed when the touching became sexual. Each was afraid to let the other know what was happening and equally afraid to lose the closeness with their father by resisting.   ❧

Dependent-Dependent Pattern

When two extremely needy individuals marry, it is often because each hopes that his or her needs will be met by the other. Both have usually come from deprived or dysfunctional childhoods, and they are desperately seeking the nurturing that they lacked. Not recognizing initially that they have actually found another individual with like needs and incapacities, they constantly hope that they will find solace in the relationship (Hanson, Lipovsky, & Saunders, 1994). Often the disillusionment that eventually comes finds them looking for other sources of nurture, which some find in their children.

Because the parents are so needy, the daughter finds herself thrust into the role of *parentified child*, making decisions and taking the emotional lead in the family. She may feel responsible for one or both of her parents, assuming that it is her job to care for them. Her father may then see her as taking the role that he expected from his wife and is attracted to her sexually. The daughter may be resented by her younger siblings for her status, while she, in turn, resents her mother for not protecting her from the abuse.

❧ _____

No one in the community was sure how Martina had survived her early years. Both her father, Winn, and mother, Fran, had difficulty making decisions; tasks were often left undone because no one could decide how or by whom they would be accomplished. The family of five children had come to the attention of CPS numerous times. Social workers found the parents to be likeable but both extremely needy. But they always managed to rally just before CPS made the decision to remove the children because the parents were not able to follow through on court-ordered treatment. When 10-year-old Joan came to the attention of CPS as a runaway, the worker again visited. She found that 12-year-old Martina had cleaned up the usually dirty apartment and seemed to have things well under control. Joan's obvious resentment of her older sister was unexpected. Further investigation uncovered that Martina had virtually been cast in the role of mother and wife, including in her father's bed.   ❧

Although these categories may be somewhat outdated and every family does not fit neatly within one or the other of them, they can be useful in analyzing family dynamics.

The Incestuous Father

The parents in an incestuous family may differ according to the family dynamics. In general, *the father* experiences a poor self-concept, feelings of helplessness and dependency, a sense of failure, and an overwhelming sense of vulnerability. How these characteristics manifest themselves will depend upon the man and his circumstances (Bolen, 2007; Flora, 2001; Hanson et al., 1994; Hartley, 2001). Fontes (2008) points out that newly immigrated fathers who have difficulty acclimating to U.S. culture may experience a sense of failure, inadequacy, and helplessness. Although most immigrant fathers find other ways to cope with these feelings, the sexually abusive father may be influenced by these feelings. As mentioned earlier, some fathers will manifest these feelings by being tyrannical, whereas others become more retiring and even dependent.

One type of father will respond through power and control. This man may have witnessed his own father rule his family in just such a manner. Never having learned adequate social skills, this offender sees power in the fear that his family feels. This type of parent may also be the one who physically abuses his wife and/or his children (Bancroft & Sullivan, 2002; Bolen, 2007; Flora, 2001; Herman & Hirschman, 2000).

Another father may be more dependent, either submissive to his wife or equally as needy. Both of these fathers tend to demonstrate poor impulse control, low frustration tolerance, and the need for immediate gratification. Whereas the tyrannical father bullies his way into getting what he needs, the submissive father will tend to be more manipulative, sometimes using guilt to meet his needs.

What motivates these men to abuse their children? Hartley (2001) examined the motivators of a small group of incestuous fathers and found that the most common reasons for sexual abuse were (a) the need for sexual gratification, (b) seeking an outlet for the dissatisfaction in their lives, (c) contact as an expression of anger toward their wives, and (d) contact as an inappropriate show of affection or love toward their daughters (p. 464).

Rice and Harris (2002) suggested four similar reasons why a man might initiate contact with his sexually immature daughter, whether genetic

offspring or stepchild. First, these authors felt that incestuous fathers were not pedophilic and therefore not oriented sexually to children and usually did not offend outside the family. Rather their sexual preferences are related to intrafamilial links. Second, the incest avoidance mechanism present in most fathers has failed. Other researchers have suggested that a lack of involvement in early child care can prevent this inhibition from developing in some men (Finkelhor, 1984). Third, Rice and Harris suggest that there has been deprivation of sexual outlets with their partners—their preferred age and gender sexual interest—and these men have therefore substituted a surrogate sexual partner. And finally, there is some psychopathology present in the incest offender although the exact type and degree of this pathology is still the subject of research.

Although some researchers may disagree with these findings, Seto (2008) supports them saying,

> Incest offenders typically score lower on measures of anti-sociality than do other sex offenders against children, but no studies have found that incest offenders show greater sexual arousal to children. . . . These studies indicate that as a group, incest offenders are less likely to be pedophiles than other sexual offenders against children. (p. 123)

Although these findings would imply that incest offenders would be less likely to offend when their own children are no longer of an age that interests them, researchers have identified that some of these men will reoffend with other families (Courtois, 2010).

There may be additional issues where abuse by stepfathers is involved. Some men seek out their partners because of the women's children who may be at an age that interests them. Resentments both on the part of these children and the stepfather may add an element to the abuse. As one survivor explained,

℞ ————————————————

I was so angry with my mother for marrying this man and upsetting what I felt was a pretty good life after our father left us that my anger spilled out on everything. When my stepfather started coming on to me, I didn't do much to resist. I guess deep down I thought "that will serve my mother right!" ‰

In addition, stepfathers have often not been involved in the child's early rearing and do not have the same established taboo against sexual contact as a biological father might (Courtois, 2010; Finkelhor, 1984; Seto, 2008).

The families of origin of most abusive fathers have usually been fraught with dysfunction, trauma, and abuse. They have often grown up in patriarchal families where alcoholism, marital discord, and other problems are the norm. All the respondents in Hartley's study (2001) described parental unavailability, especially having little or no relationship with their fathers. Their relationship with their mothers lacked intimacy as the mothers seemed more preoccupied with their own problems. A majority of these men actually felt rejected by their parents. They emerge from childhood with the feeling that their needs have not been met, and they search for attention and fulfillment throughout their lives. When there has been sexual abuse, these offenders have often modeled their behavior, possibly unconsciously, on what they have experienced or witnessed. Although not all offenders have been sexually abused, physical abuse, neglect, and domestic violence are also common (Courtois, 2010; Freeman & Sandler, 2008; Groth, 2001; Hartley, 2001; Pelto, 1981; Seto, 2008).

The lives of these abusers just prior to the abuse have also been described by them as fraught with stressors. These issues included marital discord, alcohol abuse, medical problems, work stress, and the cessation of sexual relations with their wives. All felt dissatisfied with their lives. The marital conflicts took different courses but had often been long term. There appeared to be little communication between partners, and problems remained unaddressed and never solved (Bumby & Hansen, 1997; Courtois, 2010; Gilgun & Connor, 1990; Hartley, 2001; Trepper, Niedner, Mika, & Barrett, 1996; Williams & Finkelhor, 1992).

The Nonoffending Mother

The *mother* in a father-daughter incestuous family may also fit several different profiles. One of the primary debates about the nonoffending mother in father-daughter incest situations was whether or not she was to blame for the abuse. Although most current theorists—as recently as 2006—contend that the mother cannot be held responsible for the abuse, Lev-Wiesel (2006) suggested that there were four types of mothers in these families: the *unaware mother*, who does not know what is occurring in her home; the *unwitting accomplice*, who is characterized by latent cooperation with her husband; the *enabler*, who overtly or covertly encourages her spouse to rape her daughter; and the *common fate mother*, who shares a common fate of abuse with her daughter.

The categorization of nonoffending mothers in this manner prompted a commentary from well-renowned child sexual abuse expert, Kathleen Coulborn Faller:

> I thought that theories that blame mothers for their children's incest had lost currency and credence. It is not accidental that the author had to reach far back into the history of clinical sexual abuse literature to find an article to support the theory of the instrumental role of mothers in the sexual abuse of their daughters. (Faller, 2007a, p. 129)

Faller (2007a) goes on to point out that "mother-blaming" theories have been discounted throughout the more recent literature (see Bolen & Lamb, 2004; Elliot & Carnes, 2001; Plummer, 2006). She also suggests that Lev-Wiesel's small sample (19 mothers) actually broke down as follows: Nine were unaware of the abuse, eight were unwilling accomplices, and four were also victims of abuse, leaving only two mothers who could be called enablers. Faller contends that these descriptions indicate that most of the mothers could not be seen as responsible for their daughters' abuse (p. 133). The strength of Faller's criticism is supported by the current belief that mothers in incest situations have long been held responsible when the responsibility rests on the shoulders of the perpetrator. This is not to say that there is not significant family dysfunction, which, although not the "fault" of any one member, does point to poor communication and other problematic issues that require intervention.

In another study undertaken by Plummer (2006) at three different clinical sites, 125 mothers of children who were being sexually abused by another family member were interviewed to determine what knowledge they had of the abuse. This researcher found that 42% of the mothers first learned of the abuse from a verbal report by their child and 10% from observing the behavior of that child. Almost half of the mothers did admit to a sense that something was "not quite right" prior to the abuse. Mothers tried to determine the root of this feeling by various means: talking to the child about it (66%) and watching things more closely (39%) being the most frequent means of investigation. Mothers were most likely to be convinced that the abuse was occurring by their child's disclosure (74%), their child's behavior (66%), and their child's obvious emotions (60%). When the offender denied the abuse, 21% became uncertain in their belief. Plummer concluded that better education of mothers would have an impact on their ability to protect their children.

Thus, the question remains: Who is the mother whose daughter is being abused by her father? Some researchers felt that she had more than likely been sexually abused herself, and on some psychic level, this was her norm (Finkelhor, 1984). Even if she was not abused, her family background, similar to her husband's, is characterized by instability and emotional deprivation. Her childhood left her with attachment issues, low self-esteem, extreme dependency, and separation anxiety (Courtois, 2010). She feels powerless and incomplete and ends up often sublimating her needs by giving birth, raising children, and trying to meet the needs of her husband. Because her own models were inadequate, she may fall short. Studies of domestic violence have also shown that a disproportionate number of battered wives are incest survivors and now their husbands are physically abusing them and sexually abusing their daughters (Noll, 2005).

 CR _____

Nessa suspected that things were not entirely right with her oldest daughter, Janna, and her father, Nolan, but taking care of her other four children kept her busy. Plus she always tried to have the apartment clean when Nolan came home. His wrath if she had left anything undone was frightening to all. Then there were times when Nessa was sure he'd be pleased, but he found some small thing that displeased him. His angry insults would be followed by his fists, and more than once she had the bruises to show for whatever she had done. But what could she expect? Her father had beaten her mother when she was not good enough, too. It was probably what they both deserved.

When she found Janna's bloody underwear one day, she questioned the girl. Surely she could not be starting her period at 8. Janna finally admitted that her father had been especially violent in his abuse the night before, and the child thought that she was somehow damaged.   _____ ₰

It took Nessa several incidents like this before she was able to gain the courage to take her children and seek a battered women's shelter. Only when she saw the harm that was being inflicted on her own child was she able to seek help for her own abuse.

It is clear that strengthening the mother in a father-daughter incest triangle is the way to provide the victim with support. Some mothers, so afraid of or enamored of the offender, cannot support their children, and in these situations, removal of the child may be necessary.

The Daughter

There is no agreed-upon profile of a daughter in father-daughter incest. No personality traits or physical characteristics make her any more vulnerable. Instead, she is caught up in the dynamics of the dysfunctional family and becomes the pawn of sorts. It is usually the oldest daughter who becomes the first victim, but her younger sisters may follow. The oldest daughter is groomed by the perpetrator both as a sexual partner and often as a parentified child, supplanting her mother's role. She ends up feeling guilt, shame, and responsibility not only for the incest but also for the well-being of the family unit. She may also feel forced into silence lest her disclosure blow the family apart (Courtois, 2010; Herman & Hirschman, 2001). Daughters may find ways of stopping the incest through running away or getting out of the home at an early age. However, she usually carries with her the scars of feeling helpless and at the same time angry.

The Siblings

Little has been written about the siblings of the victim in father-daughter incest. Available studies attest to the emotional risk, on both a conscious and unconscious level, to the nonabused siblings in an incestuous family (Hollingsworth, Glass, & Heisler, 2007; Wilson, 2004). Brothers are at greater risk of acting out abuse against others in the future, whereas sisters, even though not abused themselves, may exhibit their own dysfunction in later life. Siblings may feel guilt that they are unable to protect their sister and develop their own sense of helplessness, shame, and fear. Other siblings wonder why they were not "chosen" for the special attention accompanying the abuse and resent the victim. And a final pattern may be that these siblings identify with the abuser, covering up what is happening in the family and sometimes even perpetrating abuse themselves (Courtois, 2010; Hollingsworth et al., 2007).

Father-Son Incest

Father-son incest is both underreported and not well addressed in the research literature. The largest study of father-son incest to date was the 1981 American Humane Association (AHA) National Reporting Study of Child Abuse and Neglect that reported on 199 cases of father-son incest, finding

that the median age of the sons at the time of reporting was 9.36 years, and that 49% of the sons were oldest children and 14% were only children. In this study, most of the abusers were biological fathers (as reported in Finkelhor, 1984). More information has actually been gleaned from the adult male survivors of father-son incest than from reported cases to CPS.

Family Dynamics

The father in this type of intrafamilial abuse is often experiencing some type of intrapsychic conflict or emotional breakdown. He may be plagued by feelings of inadequacy, latent homosexuality, self-hatred, anger, feelings of wanting revenge, and confusion in his sexuality. Many of these men were involved in some way sexually with their own mothers, whether it was actual abuse, ambiguous or covert sexual overtones, and/or intense fantasies about their mother (Courtois, 2010; Gartner, 2001; Hunter, 1990; Lew, 2004).

ॐ

Jerome remembers the heated fights between his parents inevitably ending in his father storming out of the house. His mother would find her small son who was frequently hiding in her closet and take him onto her bed with her. Lovingly she would explain the whole fight to him, presenting his father as "the mean giant" and herself as "a damsel in distress." Her tone was somehow sexual as she coquettishly rubbed his arm and spoke in a husky voice. Jerome would often feel overwhelmed with feelings of wanting to protect her, which aroused him. At the same time, the fact that she was his mother inspired in him acute guilt at these feelings. After years of his mother making him feel this way, he harbored resentment that built into intense anger.

In later years, his own marriage would replicate that of his father and mother in the degree of discord. Determined that his wife would not do to his son what his mother did to him, he would take the boy with him when he sought to get away from his wife. Memories of his childhood at his mother's side both aroused him and angered him. When he began to sexually abuse his young son, his memories, his anger, and his feelings about his son were difficult to separate.

&

Often marital distress is at the root of father-son incest, but certainly the seeds of pathology are already there. The abuser's problems with his own mother have hampered his ability to forge healthy relationships with female age-mates.

The mother in this triad may or may not be aware of the abuse. Her husband's sexual interest in her son may relieve her of the sexual obligations that she does not welcome for whatever reason. If she does recognize the abuse, she may fear the homosexual consequences, both from the perspective of her husband preferring a male partner and what this abuse might mean for her son's development. It may be easier for her to deny what is occurring than find ways to address the issues.

The son who is abused by his father suffers a variety of consequences. Often feeling quite powerless to stop the relationship given the power differential between him and his father, the son may develop anger that sometimes becomes rage. This rage may become self-directed as self-injurious behaviors, risk taking, substance abuse, or suicidal ideation or attempts. Or the son's anger may be directed toward his father in homicidal fantasies or even attempts. Still other survivors will strive mightily to not be like their fathers, turning them into compulsive "good guys" (Courtois, 2010; Crosson-Tower, 2014; Gartner, 2001; Lew, 2004).

Sexual confusion and identity issues are not uncommon among sons who have been abused by fathers. The son may wonder about his role in the abuse and his sexual orientation. He may also be hampered in his adult relationships by his confusion (Cassese, 2000; Courtois, 2010). It is also possible for him to reenact his abuse with his own children.

Mother-Daughter Incest

Mother-daughter incest is said to be one of the most difficult for victims. In her study of 930 women,

Russell found only 10 women who reported incest with their mothers (Russell & Bolen, 2000). It is possible that the intense double taboo may account for this type of abuse being underreported. First, there is a difficulty in believing that mothers would be abusive, and same-sex incest is also heavy with stigma. Studies have found that the women who were sexually abused by their mothers were prone to self-abusive behaviors, depression, and suicidal attempts (Mitchell & Morse, 1997; Ogilvie, 2004; Rosencrans, 1997). Bolen (2007) suggests that the degree of trauma perpetrated is dependent upon three variables: (a) the overall quality of the relationship between the mother and her daughter, (b) how much the daughter internalizes her mother's pathological attitudes and would therefore not be traumatized by them, and (c) whether the sexual abuse is masked within other mothering activities such as prolonged breast feeding or bathing. Many feel that mother-child incest in general is well hidden within society due to a mother's latitude in her caretaking activities (Bolen, 2007; Ogilvie, 2004; Rosencrans, 1997).

Interestingly, the tormented poet Anne Sexton abused both of her daughters—one of whom, Linda, has just written a memoire about it. Anne Sexton's biographer, Diane Wood Middlebrook (1991), described the pattern of the abuse. Linda was nearing puberty when the abuse began. She found that her mother would climb into bed with her, which then led to the molestation. Linda was sickened and humiliated by the sexual advances of her mother but, at the same time, had a desire to be close to her. The result of this confusion was severe depression, which she would fight well into adulthood.

In her own book, *Half in Love: Surviving a Legacy of Suicide* (2011), Linda Sexton recounts her struggle to cope with the scars of her childhood—the abuse, her mother's mental illness, and eventual suicide when Linda was 21. Linda's own life became a struggle with depression, hospitalizations, a resulting divorce, and a rash of therapists until she too felt driven to suicide. Surviving, she finally found a therapist who helped her to understand the legacy of her childhood abuse.

Family Dynamics

Clinicians and researchers working with abusive mothers often remark on her *differentness* from other perpetrators. These mothers usually come from highly dysfunctional families themselves where they have experienced a good deal of deprivation and have developed a severe psychological disturbance or psychoses. They are usually estranged in some way from their age-appropriate sexual partners and often isolated. There has often been confusion in their own sexual identities and/or substance abuse (Courtois, 2010).

Like Linda Sexton, the victim-daughter often becomes her mother's caretaker, whereas the needy dependent mother views her daughter as a sexual extension of herself in an almost masturbatory way. The abuse may begin as nurturing but progresses as the mother becomes more dependent. The daughter may enjoy the closeness with her mother, perhaps recognizing her own importance in the nurturing relationship. At some point, depending upon her own health, the daughter may feel smothered but often stay in the relationship recognizing her mother's need. She may not even recognize the incestuous nature of the relationship (Courtois, 2010; Mitchell & Morse, 1997; Ogilvie, 2004; Rosencrans, 1997; Sexton, 2011).

The effects for the victim later in life often include her own issues around sexual identity and overwhelming feelings of shame, betrayal, and grief. She may struggle even into adulthood with her mother's attempts to control and manipulate her and may be conflicted between wanting to continue to take care of this parent and wanting to totally break away.

In Rosencrans's study of women abused by their mothers, 47% felt so damaged by the abuse that they wondered if they would recover, 27% reported that the abuse was damaging but they would recover, and 29% vacillated between these two positions (1997, p. 124). Of these women, 90% had difficulty with trust as adults, and 85% continued to feel isolated (pp. 161–163). In the area of sexuality, 59% felt that they had problems with sexual identity with 48% having generalized sexual concerns (p. 130).

If she becomes a mother herself, the past victim may struggle with ambivalence about this role, a fear that she lacks the ability to carry out her mothering role and a lack of self-confidence along with anxiety, which may lead to a variety of symptoms and cause her to seek professional help (Reckling, 2004).

There have been few, if any, large-scale studies of late that would shed additional light on this population. However, the first-person account of the Sextons does shed some anecdotal light on this type of abuse.

Mother-Son Incest

Despite the romanticized view of an older woman initiating a young boy into sexuality, the fact is that mothers are not as likely to molest their sons, and when they do, the effect is more injurious than one might suppose. Perhaps the dearth of reported mother-son incest is a result of the statistical paucity of cases, the previously mentioned tendency of mothers to couch their abuse in nurturing activities, and the fact that boys are not as likely to report abuse by women (Crosson-Tower, 2014). In addition, most boys brought up in a society where motherhood is often idealized would not want to admit that their mother had been abusive.

Mother-son incest is not always overt but can also take the form of the mother's overly sexualized behavior toward her son, which can confuse this sexually developing child almost as much as overt touching (Dorias, 2009; Gartner, 2001; Lew, 2004). The variations may go from seductiveness to seemingly innocent bathing and sleeping together to overt sexual activity including oral sexual gratification and sexual intercourse.

Family Dynamics

It is rare for there to be a father or another adult man in a mother-son incestuous family. Even if the mother is married or has a partner, he is usually either regularly absent or somehow estranged. Feeling alone, the mother molds her son into her caretaker role, and influenced by his own oedipal desires, he moves into the role. Some researchers feel that the mother's previous indiscriminate relations with other men might have stimulated her son sexually. He may even fantasize or indicate in his immaturity his willingness to be another of her suitors, and she may be flattered by his interest, which a healthier mother would recognize for what it was. This mother, plagued with her own insecurities and pathology, may take her son's interest at face value and initiate sexual activity with him.

The son, with his heightened desire to protect and nurture his lonely mother and, in addition, keep her to himself, may feel at the same time victorious and guilty, angry, mistrustful, and fearful. In later life, he may feel anger and find himself confused about and unable to be successful at age-appropriate sexual relationships.

There are some situations when the son initiates the openly incestuous activity. In these situations, the son usually has psychological problems, and the incestuous activity may result from his overstimulation by other familial sexual activities—for example, having seen a father's abuse of other siblings (Ward, 1985). There is little indication in the literature of how son-initiated incest affects either mother or son. In the rare instance of son-mother rape—often more likely in the abuse of an older adult—the pathology of the son is obvious (Ward, 1985).

Sexual Abuse by Siblings

Some theorists believe that sibling incest exceeds all other types of intrafamilial abuse, but due to the fact that it is not often reported, this incest is generally not known. Why is it less likely to be reported? Often parents who discover sexual activity between their children rationalize that it is "just playing doctor." However, there exists no universally accepted definition of exactly what constitutes sibling incest and what differentiates it from sexual exploration (Caffaro & Conn-Caffaro, 1998). When considering how to differentiate between normal exploration and sexual abuse, most theorists suggest looking at (a) the age difference between the siblings; (b) the nature of the sexual behavior (e.g., is penetration involved), along with the frequency and duration compared to the children's developmental understanding of sex; (c) the motivation (e.g., curiosity vs. one child being gratified at the expense of the other); and (d) the mutuality or voluntariness of the activity (Caffaro & Conn-Caffaro, 1998; Carlson, Maciol, & Schneider, 2006). Sexual acts that lack consent on the part of one sibling, involve coercion or force, and involve a difference in power and resources are usually considered to be abuse.

Further, parents who discover sibling abuse and do recognize it as problematic often will not report what they have seen to any agency that might generate a report. Instead, these parents will either deny what they have witnessed or try to handle the abuse within the home. A few seek therapeutic help, but therapists also do not always report what has happened as abuse. Yet unaddressed sibling abuse often leaves the victims with later residual effects like depression, anger, and sexual issues (Bass, Taylor, Knudson-Martin, & Huenergardt, 2006; Caffaro & Conn-Caffaro, 1998; Carlson et al., 2006; Courtois, 2010; Hardy, 2001).

Studies have been done on the age differential between siblings when abuse was considered. Wiehe and Herring (1991), in their study of 100 individuals who experienced sibling abuse, found that the victims were between 5 and 7 years of age, whereas the perpetrators tended to be between 3 and 10 years older. A more recent study (see Cyr, Wright, McDuff, & Perron, 2002) recounted that the average age difference was about 5.3 years.

Sometimes siblings begin engaging in sexual behaviors on a consensual basis, and then the sibling with more power insists that the sexual relationship continue (Wiehe, 1997). This sexual relationship may last until disclosure, or for months, years, or even until adulthood (Bass et al., 2006; Caffaro & Conn-Caffaro, 1998; Carlson et al., 2006; Courtois, 2010; Hardy, 2001; Wiehe, 1997; Wiehe & Herring, 1991).

Incest between siblings may occur for a variety of reasons. Exploration is the most common initiator of sexual activity, often beginning as a game but being taken further by one of the siblings (Wiehe, 1997, 2002). Retribution is another common motivator when one sibling seeks to humiliate the other for some past injustice. Some perpetrators are seeking power and control for the purpose of dominance rather than retribution. Younger sisters may become involved in the incest initially because they look up to or are afraid of their older brothers or sisters (Cyr et al., 2002; Fontes, 2008; Wiehe, 1997).

Culture also plays a part when incest is considered. Bass et al. (2006) looked at how two Latino families responded to sibling incest and concluded that these responses are influenced by the level of family cohesion, the role that secrecy plays, and how the family views outside systems. In the Hernandez family, the abuse was viewed as normal when 15-year-old Antonio violated his brothers, Beto, 12, and Cesar, 10. The family relationships in general were distant, and secrecy was used to maintain the abuse and promote personal gain. Outside systems were seen as intrusive.

The Gonzales family, on the other hand, responded differently when Saul, 11, and Ernesto, 8, were abused by an older brother. The family relationships here were more connected, secrecy was used to protect the victims, and outside systems were seen as legitimate. The family did not see the incest as in keeping with their hoped-for environment, but rather as a mistake (Bass et al., 2006). These authors suggest that cultural variations must be considered in light of family dynamics around cohesion, secrecy, and community connection in order to understand the impact of sibling incest on a given family.

Older Brother–Younger Sister Incest

Most researchers believe that older brother–younger sister incest has similar dynamics to father-daughter incest but without the parent-child triangle of the latter (Courtois, 2010; Cyr et al., 2002). These siblings tend to come from large families where the supervision by adults is minimal. Parents may have provided inadequate nurturing or faulty sexual models that cause these siblings to seek out each other.

Courtois (2010) suggests that three variations on the nature of the relationship have emerged from the literature. First, there may be the older brother who sees his younger, more naive sister as a guinea pig for his own sexual experimentation and learning. Or the pre- or postpubertal brother does not have adequate social skills and uses his sister as a substitute for the peers that he is unable to engage and the parents who have neglected to nurture him. And finally, when a postpubertal brother, considerably older than his sister, was himself sexually abused, physically abused, or neglected, he may force his sister into a sexual relationship through coercion or violence in a pattern that most resembles that of an incestuous father. In a study of 75 girls of 5 to 16 years of age who had been abused incestuously by brothers, Cyr et al. (2002) found that penetration is more likely than in abuse by fathers or stepfathers. Another difference was that brother-sister incest tended to take place in families where there was more alcohol. Otherwise, characteristics did not differ significantly. Some of these brothers may have developed a pattern that will lead them to later abuse their own daughters.

Fontes (2008) comments that in Latino families this type of incest may be denied. Boys are held in such high regard that the girl may be blamed. At the same time, older males are supposed to take care of younger sisters, so the family might prefer not to acknowledge when this abuse happens.

How traumatic or injurious is brother-sister incest to the victim? Many victims describe guilt and complicity particularly if the abuse began as mutually agreed-upon touching and then moved into abuse when the brother would not allow it to stop. Some siblings come from families that teach them that it is the female's responsibility to regulate the level of sexual activity. Thus, when the sexual activity continues, these girls feel responsible.

Older Sister–Younger Brother Incest

There may be some similarities between older sister–younger brother incest and mother-son incest depending upon who had initiated the incest. When the older sister initiates the incest, it may be similar to affection-based brother-sister incest in that she may not feel comfortable with her peers and turns to her brother for reassurance, affection, and security. There may be an element of protecting each other from what may seem like an unnurturing world. Another sister may be aggressive, manipulative, possessive, and sexually demanding, possibly as a result of being abused herself and harboring resentment. In both situations, the effect on the brother may be to feel confusion, shame, guilt, resentment, and remorse. He may also feel a great deal of ambivalence toward his sister (Courtois, 2010; Crosson-Tower, 2014).

Same-Sex Sibling Incest

The fact that there are few reports of same-sex sibling abuse in the literature makes it difficult to characterize. Such abuse often occurs in families where there is already sexual activity between family members—most frequently father-son incest. Sexual interaction between brothers is often initiated for experimentation and exploration but becomes abusive when coercion enters in. Sometimes there is a possibility of homosexuality or bisexuality when the brothers are older. With so few cases reported, it is difficult to come to any conclusions about this type of incest (Dorias, 2009; Lew, 2004; Wiehe, 1997).

Sister-sister incest is even less studied. In Russell's (1999) study, there was none of this type of incest reported. This researcher concluded

that this may be because this type of incest is less upsetting than other types.

Sexual Abuse by Extended Family Members

Children are abused, not only by in-house family members but also by those in their extended families—uncles, grandfathers, and cousins. Russell (1999) found that this type of incest was most frequently perpetrated between uncles and their nieces. Abuse by an uncle who is not an immediate family member may not be as significant in terms of trauma as an uncle who is a close member of the family or lives in the child's household. In the Russell study, 96% of the female victims reported that the abuse by the uncle was unwanted, and 48% felt that it has a significant impact on their lives.

Russell (1999) also reported that, in her study, the majority of the nieces abused by uncles were being raised in a surrogate household—by grandparents or uncles and aunts. Courtois (2010) pointed out that most of the cases, in her research, have been part of multiple victimizations. The victim is abused by uncles and also by other family members. The degree of trauma varies depending upon the depth of the niece's relationship with her uncle, how often he has an opportunity to see the victim to abuse her, and what other types of abuse she may be enduring.

Uncle-nephew sexual abuse is often perpetrated either by men who are pedophiles and have access to their nephews or by men with similar characteristics to fathers who abuse their sons. Few cases have been reported, so it is difficult to determine what the characteristics may be.

Grandfathers may abuse either their granddaughters or their grandsons. Russell (1999) documented that between 6% and 10% of cases are grandfathers abusing their granddaughters, yet there has been a limited amount of research on this type of abuse. Abuse perpetrated against grandsons is rarely mentioned, and it is difficult to determine if this abuse is underreported or does not happen often.

Some grandfathers have molested their daughters, and the abuse of granddaughters is but a continuation of this pattern. Some are pedophiles who have abused other children outside the family. And often, those who are abused by grandfathers may have been victims of other forms of abuse by other family members (Bolen, 2007; Courtois, 2010; Crosson-Tower, 2014; Russell, 1999). There is also some speculation that this older man may be responding to the reality of his aging and the view that society has of older people as losing their competency. Although most studies do not report senility as part of the grandfather's issues, he may well feel lonely, depressed, pushed aside, and in need of reassurance about his worth and abilities (Bolen, 2007; Courtois, 2010; Crosson-Tower, 2014). Younger grandfathers may not be experiencing old age, and their abuse tends to more closely resemble father-daughter incest, especially if the grandfather has caretaking responsibilities for the victim.

Most victims describe the abuse by grandfathers as being gentle and progressive, but because of the gentleness, there may be less trauma to the child. Although one cannot assume that any type of abuse is benign, Russell (1999) did find that victims may not be as severely traumatized.

Abuse by grandmothers, although seemingly rare, is beginning to be reported more, especially as grandparents are more often in caretaker roles. Elliot (1993) mentioned cases of grandmothers who abused, some in conjunction with their daughters. More current research is required, however, to determine if this abuse mirrors other forms of abuse.

Abuse by cousins is the least addressed abuse in the literature. It may be that it takes on similar characteristics to sibling incest. Russell (1999) found similarities but also that abuse by cousins is often shorter in duration and less severe. Despite this finding, about one third of those victimized by cousins report long-term effects (Bolen, 2007; Courtois, 2010).

Any type of incest has the possibility of leaving scars and lasting effects on victims. Additional research is called for to better understand all the dynamics of intrafamilial abuse.

Summary

Intrafamilial abuse, sometimes referred to as incest, is the term used to describe sexual abuse between family members. The study of incest was popularized in the 1980s after the publication of several books by survivors and the scholarly text *Father-Daughter Incest*, by Harvard professor, Judith Herman. Early researchers and clinicians saw intrafamilial abuse through the lens of systems theory that postulated that the dysfunctional family where sexual abuse takes place is the responsibility of both parents. The incest actually is an attempt to achieve family equilibrium. The feminist movement also looked at intrafamilial abuse and argued that it was solely the responsibility of the offender and the nonabusing mother was in no way to blame.

It is difficult to know how many cases of incest there are today as families often keep it hidden and victims may be afraid to tell anyone. The dynamics involve blurred generational boundaries where the children often become emotional caretakers. The family is characterized by stress. There may be variations according to culture as various cultures have different views of family roles and responsibilities. The stressors on new immigrants trying to raise children in an unfamiliar culture can put such families at risk.

Intrafamilial abuse falls into several categories depending upon the identity of the abuser and the victim. Father-daughter incest is probably the most common and more widely researched. These families may exhibit one of three patterns: possessive-passive, dependent-domineering, and dependent-dependent. The father who abuses his daughter may be a tyrant who needs to keep close control of and power over the family or may treat his daughter more as a peer. These fathers often come from dysfunctional families themselves and do not know how to achieve healthy intimacy.

The nonoffending mother in father-daughter incest has been much discussed in the literature. The current feeling is that she may or may not know what is happening on some level, but her response when the abuse is disclosed is the important piece. The daughter often takes the role of her mother as far as nurturing her father or catering to him.

Father-son incest is both underreported and underresearched possibly because males are not as likely to report abuse. The father often battles with feelings of inadequacy, self-hatred, and anger as well as confusion about his sexuality. The mother is often absent either physically or emotionally or does not know of the abuse. The son grapples with confusion about his sexuality and often anger over not being protected.

Mother-daughter incest is often carried out by a parent with significant pathology. As a result of this and the stigma of abuse by women, the daughter struggles with a myriad of residual effects often throughout adulthood. Mother-son incest is often characterized by a dependent mother who places her son in the role of a surrogate for her male partner. The son suffers from confusion about this relationship, often wanting to care for his mother but feeling anger over what is occurring.

Several other types of abuse were discussed including abuse by siblings and abuse by extended family members such as grandfathers, uncles, and cousins. Whoever is the abuser, victims of intrafamilial abuse have a difficult time coming to terms with the betrayal of having been abused by a family member.

Review Questions

1. How does family systems theory explain incest?

2. What influence did feminist theory have on the study of child sexual abuse?

3. What are some of the dynamics associated with an incestuous family?

4. What are some of the cultural implications inherent in understanding intrafamilial abuse?

5. What are the types of intrafamilial abuse?

6. What are the patterns in father-daughter incest?

7. Describe the characteristics of the incestuous father in father-daughter incest.

8. Describe the nonoffending mother. What might be the relationship between this mother and her daughter?

9. What are the dynamics of mother-daughter incest and mother-son incest?

10. What are the dynamics of father-son incest, and what influence does this incest have on the victim?

11. What impact does sibling incest have on victims?

CHAPTER 7

Pornography, Prostitution, and the Internet

The world of child pornography and, to some extent, child prostitution has changed considerably over the last few decades. The Internet and its use not only by children but also by those who seek to sexually abuse children have put children at higher risk for abuse outside their families. Now, within the child's own home is a tool through which the pedophile can gain access to his or her victim.

CHILD PORNOGRAPHY

What Is the Problem With Child Pornography?

Even asking the question "What is the problem with child pornography?" may cause some readers to respond with horror, so conditioned are people to view child pornography as well as child abuse as an assault on children. Yet there are those who would disagree that there is a problem with either. Several organizations see themselves as decidedly pro adult-child sexual relations.

The North American Man-Boy Love Association (NAMBLA) promotes men having sexual relations with young boys. Despite the confusion in the minds of some about this organization's connection with gay rights organizations, both NAMBLA and most gay rights groups insist that there is little or no connection. In fact, those with a sexual interest in young boys do not see themselves as homosexual, and they lead heterosexual lives (Freeman-Longo & Blanchard, 1998; Hughes, 2007).

NAMBLA had its origins in Revere, near seemingly conservative Boston, where the backlash after the breakup of a sex ring caused like-minded individuals to band together in a society, promoting their sexual interests in boys (Crosson-Tower, 2014; Rush, 1992). NAMBLA continues to exist somewhat covertly given the illegality of its practices but publishes a newsletter, hosts a web site, and provides a network for pederasts.

The René Guyon Society originating in Beverly Hills, California, believes that sexual relations between adults and children provide a natural form of education. With a slogan that is reported to be "Sex by 8, or else it's too late!" this organization, like others of its type, may still exist, but prohibitions against its practices make membership statistics difficult to pinpoint. Similar organizations such as the Pedophile Alert Network (PAN) and the Pedophile Information Exchange (PIE) continue to provide contacts and the distribution of child pornography throughout the United States and abroad (Freeman-Longo & Blanchard, 1998; Hughes, 2007; Wells, Finkelhor, Wolak, & Mitchell, 2007).

What all of these organizations, past and present, have in common is that they promote communication between like-minded individuals who believe that children can be sexuality stimulating. Not all members act upon their interest in children and, despite pedophilic interests, may not technically be termed pedophiles (sexual interest in young boys is called pederasty). But the fact remains that one common method of communicating interest in sexuality and children is the distribution and sharing of sexually explicit pictures of children or child pornography.

Child pornography can be defined as depictions (real children or computer generated), images, or photographs of those under 18 (16 in Britain) nude (exposure of the genitals) in sexually suggestive poses or acts or performing sexual acts with other children, animals, or adults (Hughes, 1998; Jenkins, 2001a; Ost, 2002; Wells et al., 2007). There has been some controversy over whether photos of children that are naked and not in intentionally suggestive poses are considered to be pornographic. For example, witness the controversy over the pictures of nude children by American artist Robert Mapplethorpe in the 1980s. Although there is still some disagreement between artistic circles and religious moralist groups, most courts would consider carefully the suggestive nature of a depiction before labeling it pornographic.

So, if some people condone child pornography and others dispute what falls into the category, what can be the problem with the wide availability of child pornography, especially over the Internet? Law lecturer, Suzanne Ost (University of Manchester), expresses her concerns about Britain's child pornography problem that can be compared to that of the United States. Ost (2002) believes that there are three specific areas in which child pornography is problematic:

> First, it is recognized that child pornography poses a clear danger to children who are involved in the production of child pornography, whose physical and sexual abuse is often the very subject matter of the material created. Secondly, in recent years, a new consensus has emerged that children are placed at risk simply as a consequence of an individual being in possession of child pornography. Finally, there appears to be an acceptance of the possibility that the availability of child pornography is harmful to

society because it has a corrupting effect upon the general morality. (p. 437)

Expanding upon Ost's points requires considering how child pornography is used. Child pornography is obviously viewed habitually by those who find children sexually appealing. Not all of those who view such images act upon this interest, but the literature about sexual offenders indicates that many who sexually offend have initially developed an interest in pornography and continue that interest throughout their offending years. Not only do they find the images of children sexually stimulating, often masturbating to these pictures, but when self-stimulating activities no longer suffice, they are often moved to act on these fantasies. Continued interest in pornography then serves as reinforcement, allowing them to rationalize that their behavior is not unique to them (Flood, 2009; Jenkins, 2001b; McGee & Holmes, 2012; Ost, 2002; Taylor & Quayle, 2003; van Dam, 2006).

Child pornography not only uses children in its production, thus subjecting them to sexual abuse, but it is also used by perpetrators to seduce children.

ℭℛ ━━━━━━━━━━━━━━━━━━━━━━━━━

Nine-year-old Amber met Joe at a video arcade. When forced to watch her on his days off, Amber's older brother gave her some change and told her to go to the arcade and "give him some space." The product of an alcoholic home and sandwiched between too many brothers and sisters, Amber relished the attention that Joe gave her. He seemed like the father she had never had but not as old as her friends' fathers. When he suggested that she come for walks with him, she was glad to oblige. He began taking pictures of her and telling her that she could be a star. Bespectacled Amber, whom her siblings often called "ugly Amber," wasn't sure she believed him, but it didn't matter. She reveled in the attention anyway. Before long, their side trips ended up in a deserted apartment building where Joe posed the child against fallen masonry and half-removed doors, telling her that the settings made her look exotic. He urged her to remove more and more of her clothing. When she had removed all but her under-clothing, Amber resisted. Joe pulled out his camera phone and showed her pictures of other naked children. When she finally agreed to remove her clothes, Joe began to fondle her, showing her pictures of children in various sexual poses. One day, he brought a camera that allowed him to be in the picture as well and photographed Amber performing oral sex on him. Amber began to worry that she should not be doing "these things," but Joe told her that other kids did it too, but this secret was theirs. Furthermore, he threatened that if she told anyone, he had pictures to prove that she was a willing participant. He had showed them to others, he told her, and it was only a matter of time before she would be a star. 🔊

Convinced that other children too participated in such sexual activities, it did not take much to convince needy Amber to succumb to Joe's sexual abuse. He also used her pictures to trade with other pedophiles online.

Child pornography, say some critics, affects the status of children. Not unlike feminists who argue that sexual depictions of women in pornography demean them and create an image of them as objects, critics of child pornography contend that its effect on children is similar. However, with children, this opinion is compounded by the fact that society generally sees childhood as a time of innocence. Ost (2002) comments that

> innocence has become an essential representation of childhood, to such an extent that those "children" whose characters serve to challenge conceptions of childhood innocence are considered to be monsters, nefarious beings who have merely taken on the semblance of children. (p. 456)

Although some might believe that this statement is a bit strong, the reactions that many people have to children who are sexualized beyond their years or who commit particularly heinous crimes suggest that Ost might have a point.

Flood (2009) suggests that children's exposure to pornography perpetuates adherence to sexest and unhealthy norms, provides a dangerous sex educator, can negatively influence sexual behaviors, and can promote sexual violence.

In the face of the perceived innocence of children, the desire to protect them has become one of society's most fervently articulated endeavors. Therefore, the elimination of child pornography as something harmful to children becomes one of the by-products of society's quest. Ost (2002) suggests that the consumer, even the curious searcher with no intention of going out and committing child abuse, is responsible for supporting the production of this form of child abuse. Although difficult to monitor, viewing child pornography is illegal. This serves as a deterrent for some, but not all, casual viewers.

Although printed child pornography was something that could be moderately controlled by postal regulations and law enforcement stings, the advent of the Internet has made this control even more difficult. Despite the undisputable advantages provided by today's technology including the Internet, there are also many more risks not only for the distribution of child pornography but also for the access to and sexual abuse of children.

Youth, the Internet, and Child Abuse

A survey of 1,501 households in 2000 sponsored by the Crimes Against Children Research Center reported that 74% of children have access to the Internet and use it regularly. This statistic represented approximately 24 million youth between the ages of 10 and 17. Of these young regular Internet users, 1 in 5 reported sexual solicitation, 1 in 4 was exposed involuntarily to online pictures of people having sexual relations, 1 in 33 received aggressive solicitation to meet a perpetrator somewhere, and 1 in 17 was threatened or harassed sexually (Finkelhor, Mitchell, & Wolak, 2000). This survey does not encompass the numerous youth who do not report sexual activity on the Internet or seek it out. This study found that only 10% of the episodes experienced online were reported to an official outside the home and only 17% of the children and 10% of the parents had any idea where such a report should be made (Finkelhor et al., 2000). The minimal control over what appears online puts children in increased risk for sexual solicitation and exposure to sexual subjects that may be beyond their years.

The survey was repeated in 2005 and later in 2010 with interesting results. An increased number of youth were exposed to sexual materials* and sexual harassment on the Internet, but a decreased number were actually receiving unwanted sexual solicitation (Jones, Mitchell, & Finkelhor, 2012).

- Although 19% of youth received unwanted sexual solicitations in 2000, and 13% in 2005, only 9% received them in 2010.
- Although 25% of the youth surveyed reported being exposed to unwanted pornography in 2005, with a slight increase to 34% in 2005, only 23% of youth reported such exposure in 2010.
- However, there was an increase in online harassment from 6% in 2000, to 9% in 2005, and to 11% in 2010.

Jones et al. (2012) suggest that their findings might contradict the general public's common belief that there is increasing threat to children. These authors speculate that the decrease in threat to children is due to the fact that we are improving in our ability to protect children and teens who are online. The downside of these statistics is that acquaintances played a larger role in unwanted solicitations of youth. Despite the

fact that youth are more wary of strangers given media and parental cautioning, it may be that they are not as concerned (and therefore not as cautious) about people they already know.

Even though there is unarguably worthwhile access to vast quantities of information on the Internet, it has also opened homes to child molesters. Part of the access that pedophiles have to children lies in the very nature of Internet use in our culture today. Today's generation of computer-based children and youth look to the Internet for their information about a variety of topics as well as for their socialization. One CBS news story discussed the dangers of social media sites that become popular locations for young people to communicate. Newswriter Larry Magid reported that he launched an experiment on a popular web site. He said that he was looking for a 16- to 17-year-old "woman" who attended a high school near where he lives. Within seconds, a list of the names of 198 girls registered with the service appeared, and if the list included the boys as well, there were 577 listings of "current students," which represented about a third of the school's student body (Magid, 2006).

Magid goes on to explain:

One of the girls, who is 16, has a sexually suggestive word as part of her user name. Thanks to [social media site] . . . , I have a pretty complete picture of her life. I know the day she was born, the hospital she was born in, her full name, where she goes to school, what she likes to eat, what time she goes to bed at night and her favorite fast-food restaurant. She gets along with her parents "sometimes." In the past month she says she has consumed alcohol, eaten sushi, been to a mall, and gone "skinny dipping." She says she has shoplifted at least once, wants to be a lawyer and would like to visit Egypt. . . . Thanks to several pictures on her site, I also

---

* The Youth Internet Safety Survey defines *exposure to unwanted materials* as without asking or expecting it; the youth see people who are nude or having sex when using various programs on the Internet. *Harassment* refers to threats or other offensive behavior sent online or posted for others to see. *Sexual solicitation* encompasses unwanted requests to engage in sexual activity or talk or give personal sexual information to an adult. And *aggressive solicitation* refers to the adult soliciting offline contact by mail, by phone, or in person, or making attempts for offline contact (Jones, Mitchell, & Finkelhor, 2012, p. 3).

know exactly what she looks like and have seen pictures of many of her friends and am able to access her friends' profiles as well. This girl lives within a few miles of my house. Some of the pictures were clearly taken at the local high school.... Information such as this, which used to take predators months to extract from a child, can be skillfully used to help win a child's confidence. (Magid, 2006)

It goes without saying that the Internet is a popular pastime among youth—the "in thing" of today, which also becomes part of its allure. In addition to "*everybody is doing it*," there are other factors that make the Internet attractive to youth.

For most families, a computer and therefore the Internet are *affordable*. Even if a family either cannot afford a computer or chooses not to have one in their home, outside computer sites like cybercafes, bookstores, and schools make the Internet *available*. In addition, smart phones and iPads enable access to the same material. The *apparent anonymity* with which one can access Internet sites can also be appealing for youth who seek independence (Burrow-Sanchez, Call, Zheng, & Drew, 2011; Cooper, 2002; Mitchell, Finkelhor, & Becker-Blease, 2007; Wells et al., 2007). At the same time, the Internet *seems safe* to children who know that their parents are in the next room. While talking to people—especially those they do not know—may seem exciting, young people believe that no harm can come to them when they begin what seems like a harmless relationship while they are in the safety of their homes.

Although communication is easy on the Internet, some child development experts worry that the ease of "getting to know someone" online is deceptive. The fear is that youth who are not learning to develop well-rounded face-to-face relationships with peers can also not see through the advances of adults who may mean them harm. In addition, texting truncates conversations in a manner that changes communication patterns.

To the public concern about children being lured into sexual abuse over the Internet, Wolak, Finkelhor, Mitchell, and Ybarra (2008) suggest that the research be considered more carefully.

Although there is some validity to the fact that predators have easier access to victims, these authors feel that the issues are more complex. Extrapolating from the Youth Internet Safety Survey-1 (YISS-1) and the two follow-up surveys in 2005 and 2010 as well as the National Juvenile Online Victimization Study (N-JOV), which looked at Internet-initiated sex crimes that came to the attention of law enforcement (Wolak, Finkelhor, & Mitchell, 2008, 2012), researchers have found some facts that shed a different light on the controversy over online victimization. First, they suggest that sexual encounters initiated over the Internet are more in the line of statutory rape than any other crime. In other words, most of the victims who actually have sexual relations with so-called predators have done so voluntarily. The problem arises initially because as young teens (the predominant ages involved), these youth do not have the right of consent (Finkelhor, 1984).

Wolak, Finkelhor, Mitchell, and Ybarra (2008) go on to say that the majority of the youth who do meet and have sex with adults they met on the Internet are lonely, feel isolated and misunderstood, and may already have had some sexual experience. For example, youth who have been sexually abused in childhood or who are troubled are often searching for a loving, understanding adult and have a greater risk of agreeing to meet would-be perpetrators who they may perceive to be these idealized adults (Chiara, Wolak, & Finkelhor, 2008). Wolak, Finkelhor, Mitchell, and Ybarra also found that most of the youth who entered into these discussions online that led to meetings knew that the person they were talking to was an adult. Girls or boys who are questioning if they are gay are the most likely to enter into online relationships that lead to meetings.

Teens and Sexting

The use of technology, combined with the sexualization of society, has given rise to a disturbing practice among some of the nation's teens—sexting. *Sexting* refers to the use of a camera cell phone to take and send sexual images (e.g., nude pictures, sexual acts) to others. Not only does this practice blur the definitions of producing pornography but it can have problematic legal, social, and emotional implications for those who participate (Chalfen, 2009; Wolak & Finkelhor, 2011).

The Pew Research Center recently conducted a study to determine how many teens are taking part in the practice of sexting. As part of its Internet and American Life Project, the Pew research team (see Lenhart, 2009) surveyed a national sample of American teens between the ages of 12 and 17. On the self-report survey, 4% of teens reported that they had sent sexually suggestive, nude, or near-nude images of themselves to someone else via text messaging. Another 15% of teens who own cell phones said that they had received sexually suggestive, nude, or near-nude photos of someone they know. In the older age group (17-year-olds), 8% had sent sexted messages and 30% had received them. Teens who pay for their own phones are more likely to sext than those who do not.

There appear to be three main scenarios for sexting: (a) between romantic partners, (b) between partners who then share texts with others outside the relationship, and (c) between people not yet in a relationship but where one desires a relationship (Lenhart, 2009).

Despite the low percentage of teens who admit to sexting today, the concern among experts is that this number will increase among the 75% of teens who have cell phones and unlimited texting. Those who have text capability make an average of 125 texts per day (Brimer & Rose, 2012). Sexting itself can lead to or become a form of cyberbullying, sexual harassment, as well as inflicting psychological and legal harm. Brimer (Brimer & Rose, 2012) also contends that sexting blurs the lines between who perpetrates sexual crimes. For example, Phillip Alpert, an 18-year-old Florida youth, sent nude pictures of his 16-year-old girlfriend (which she had sent to him earlier) to numerous friends and family after an argument with the girlfriend. Alpert was arrested and charged with the felony of sending child pornography. The youth was later convicted and registered as a sexual offender and will remain so until he is 43 years old. He now speaks on his experience, cautioning other youth not to learn the hard way as he did (Brimer & Rose, 2012; Maybrey & Perozzi, 2010).

Because sending out photos of nude underage children and youth falls under pornography, consequences for the sender can be legally dire. For victims, anxiety, shame, guilt, rape-related post-traumatic stress disorder (PTSD), depression, and even suicide can be the result (Brimer & Rose, 2012; Chalfen, 2009; Walker, Sanci, & Temple-Smith, 2011; Weiss & Samenow, 2010).

The Lure of Cybersex for Adults

The same appeals of the Internet are true for those who perpetrate or may be inclined to perpetrate against children. Not only is the Internet affordable, available, and anonymous, but there is a certain excitement that some adults feel that they do not experience from adult life (Bowker & Gray, 2005; Crosson-Tower, 2006; McLaughlin, 2000). Those who have difficulty with social skills or relationships can fantasize about a kind of virtual love as they talk to others online. Some who might not know that they have an interest in children find a solace in the Internet that puts them at risk. As one man explained,

☙

My wife had just left me. My life was a mess. I used to come home from work and the computer seemed like my only friend. I'd go online for hours. I was curious about the obviously pornographic sites that were constantly in my Inbox. I used to read a lot of porno books when I was a teen. I loved the really young girls. So, I figured, what the heck. No one will know. I started accessing the sites and then got into some chat rooms. It opened a new world to me. I met a teenage girl online and she and I would talk about all the sexual stuff we wanted to do with each other. She really seemed to know about some stuff that I wouldn't have thought a kid her age would. It was a real turn-on. After awhile, I'd rush home just to get online for sexual stimulation. (Crosson-Tower, 2006, pp. 151–152)

ॐ

The fact that many adults use the Internet regularly for their work adds to the risk of misuse and possible addiction to cybersex. One man who worked from his home on the computer confessed that he would take some time every day to access kiddie porn (child pornography) sites.

ॐ

Before long, I discovered that I was spending more and more time with kiddie porn and less and less doing my job. I began to fantasize about what it would be like to have a sexual relationship with a child. I found a group online that offered to set me up with a child. Unknown to me it was a "sting," and I found myself meeting an undercover police officer who arrested me for what had originally seemed like a harmless pastime.

ॐ

According to one study of almost 40,000 adults who responded to a 76-question survey about their use of the Internet for sexual pursuits, 20% admitted going online at work for sexual activities. And 48% of those respondents reported that their workplace took no steps to block access to sexual sites (Cooper, Scherer, & Mathy, 2001, as cited in Cooper, 2002, pp. 110–111). Crosson-Tower (2006) discussed how addiction to cybersex can even become a problem for the clergy (see Chapter 10).

Although just accessing pornographic sites may not seem as problematic as meeting and molesting children, the fact is that frequent exposure to child pornography can desensitize one to any taboo related to acting upon the fantasies that child pornography may generate (Hughes, 1998). And research confirms that those who sexually offend against children often began their abuse careers through viewing and fantasizing about

pornography, intensifying the concern about such behavior (Crosson-Tower, 2006; Taylor & Quayle, 2003; van Dam, 2006).

Types of Pedophilic Pornographers

McLaughlin (2000) identifies several categories of perpetrators divided according to how the Internet was used to access or distribute pornography. *Collectors* begin by pulling up pornographic pictures of children and collecting them initially for their own use. At some point they may decide to act upon their fantasies and try to lure children via the Internet, or they may already be involved with children, using pornographic stimuli.

Travelers chat with children through chat rooms with the expectation that they will eventually encourage children to meet them. When talking to children, they will usually present themselves as peers and engage them in that manner. Their intent is to use children sexually. In addition, they collect pornographic pictures of children (McLaughlin, 2000).

Manufacturers produce their own pornography and upload it for others to access on the Internet. They photograph children—often those who are unsuspecting—in bathrooms or other places or may lure the children to be photographed. In addition, they may molest children themselves (Crosson-Tower, 2014; McLaughlin, 2000).

Chatters have the goal of chatting with children. They are not involved with pornography and may actually warn children against the evils of pornography, presenting themselves as the only adults on the Internet who can be trusted. Although they are presenting themselves as teachers, encouraging children to ask questions about sex, they are getting their own stimulation from this activity. They may then escalate the sexual talk even to the point of having phone sex with children. Their method of luring children, once they find one that works, becomes ritualized, and they will use it again and again (Crosson-Tower, 2014; McLaughlin, 2000; Marcum, 2007). Although perpetrators do not fit neatly into categories, McLaughlin feels that this general framework provides a useful tool for understanding pornographers and this type of pedophile.

Bowker and Gray (2005) suggest similar but slightly different categories of offenders who access pornography on the Internet. The first is the *dabbler* who has access to child pornography and a dealer. The *preferential offender* is one who has a deviant interest in children or adolescents and who uses the Internet to make contact, possibly through the lure of pornography. And the *miscellaneous offender* tends to be a prankster or "'misguided individual' who posses[es] these materials as a result of their own investigations" (p. 14).

Although some research suggests that accessing child pornography may lead some individuals to escalate to hands-on abuse of children, Bourke and Hernandez (2009), in their study of incarcerated offenders, found that the majority of offenders had committed acts of hands-on abuse prior to seeking pornography online. More research is needed in this important area.

Ways in which pornographers can access children multiply as technology advances. Despite this and a variety of problems in detection, arrests for the possession of child pornography have increased. In 2009, there were 4,901 arrests for possession of child pornography compared to 1,713 such arrests in 2000 (Wolak, Finkelhor, & Mitchell, 2012).

Children, Youth, and Pornography

Generating official statistics about child pornography is extremely difficult. High-profile cases like that of Gary Glitter, a 1970s rock star who was arrested in 1997 after a computer repair shop found pictures of nude children on his personal computer, may be recorded in the media, but there is little information available to the average citizen about the magnitude of the child pornography problem (Jenkins, 2001a). In addition, child pornographers are often not apprehended unless they act upon their interests by meeting children or engaging them in the production of pornography. Police who arrest child molesters routinely discover pornography on their computers, but had they not been arrested, their leanings might not have been known. The fact remains that viewing as well as producing child pornography is a legal offense.

Possession of child pornography in the computer age involves not only the storing of pornographic images on a hard drive but even downloading them (Jenkins, 2001a). But it is not just possession by pedophiles that becomes problematic. In addition to the effects of child pornography on the children used to produce it, there is an impact on children who might be inadvertently exposed to pornography over the Internet.

The Effect of Internet Sexuality on Children and Youth

Concerned parents and other adults involved with children want for them an opportunity to develop both physically and emotionally in a healthy and normal manner. Healthy development requires an integration of age-appropriate material that becomes part of the building blocks for the next stage. Researchers know from working with sexually abused children that premature introduction to sexuality and sexual stimuli creates confusion and can hamper the progression of healthy development.

Some theorists contend that stimulation through the viewing of child pornography promotes at best confusion in the minds of immature viewers but can also sexually stimulate and reduce inhibitions, leading to premature involvement in sexual behaviors (Cooper, 2002; Gallagher, 2005; Hughes, 1998; Taylor & Quayle, 2003). Pedophiles also have in child pornography a convincing tool that can be used to promote the idea that "everyone is doing it and therefore you should too."

Some adolescents who view sexually explicit material on the Internet at a time when they are involved in exploring their own identities may be prompted to explore more sexually dangerous, self-destructive behaviors just to act what they perceive as grown-up (Cooper, 2002).

ଔ _____

Vivienne originally encountered a pornographic site somewhat accidentally by typing in an incorrect URL. What she saw so stimulated her that she showed the site to several of her friends. The site showed young teens in various sexual behaviors with adults. It was not long before a pedophile began to converse with Vivienne in a chat room presenting himself as someone only slightly older than she but with much more experience. When his flirtation took on overtly sexual overtones, Vivienne remembered what she had seen and wondered if they might do that together. The man suggested that they meet, and Vivienne decided that this would be exciting. They had talked about sexual involvement so naturally that she was eager to see if the reality was as exciting. Fortunately for this 14-year-old, the pedophile was apprehended by a law enforcement sting only days before Vivienne was to meet him. Police discovered that he was responsible for the abduction of several other girls whom he had then sold into prostitution.

_____ **ଔ**

For teens who have feelings of loneliness and emptiness and poor self-concepts, the adults they meet through Internet sites can seem to provide the understanding they are seeking (Wolak, Finkelhor, Mitchell, & Ybarra, 2008). It is not just access to pedophiles that is problematic for teens. Studies have shown that the Internet has the potential to expose children to more types of sexuality than they would otherwise encounter. Ironically, excessive use of the Internet also has been found to promote isolation in children. Prior to the computer, youth were interacting with peers in ways that allowed sexual exploration between individuals with similar sexual knowledge. With the advent of the Internet and the possibility of isolation, vulnerable teens may not be learning relationship skills in healthy ways but rather through premature stimulation (Cooper, 2002;

Hughes, 1998; Subrahmanyam, Kraut, Greenfield, & Gross, 2000). For adolescents who already have sexual behavior problems, accessing pornographic sites and acting out what they see can be perceived to help them deal with negative-feeling states (Saakvitne, Gamble, Pearlman, & Lev, 2000; Wolak, Finkelhor, Mitchell, & Ybarra, 2008).

Researcher Janis Wolak (2007) of the University of New Hampshire's Crimes Against Children Research Center summarizes the concerns of a recent study of the effects of sexually explicit material on the Internet on children and teens by saying that it promotes earlier and more promiscuous sex, sexual deviancy, sexual offending, and sexually compulsive behavior.

Intervention Into Child Pornography

There is recognition of the dangers of sexually explicit material on the Internet and how children can be put at risk, but what can be done about this problem? In efforts to police the Internet, some critics worry about individual rights and privacy being jeopardized. Jenkins (2001a) comments,

> While admitting that privacy issues potentially pose an enormous threat to rights and liberties, we must ask why, in such an environment, the authorities cannot succeed in thwarting a [sic] electronic traffic that permits individuals to build up libraries of five or ten thousand wholly illegal images. Assuredly, it is not because law enforcement agencies in the United States or elsewhere are timid about proactively policing or launching stings; nor do they fear a backlash of public sympathy in favor of the pedophiles. Yes, obviously, the trade survives, with its network of boards and newsgroups. Why? (p. 142)

At one time, pornography was in printed form—either in print or in videos—and, although usually safe when viewed privately, was prohibited from being exchanged or mailed. It was often through the transfer of these materials that pedophiles were apprehended. Initially, the

Internet gave law enforcement similar opportunities to intervene. Suspect sites could be accessed by undercover detectives, and pedophiles or pornographers were prosecuted. Another easy form of detection was when a pedophile saved illegal materials on his or her hard drive. Police have also gone online posing as young people and luring pedophiles to meetings at which point they were arrested. For example, after a 3-year-long study of sexual exploitation of children and teens over the Internet funded by the Office of Juvenile Justice and Delinquency Prevention, New Hampshire police detective Jim McLaughlin and his colleagues apprehended over 200 perpetrators of sexual solicitation and abuse via the Internet in 40 states and 12 other countries (McLaughlin, 1998, 2000).

Since 1998, the federal government has offered training for those interested in intervention in the area of child pornography. The Office of Juvenile Justice and Delinquency Prevention has funded law enforcement cyber units to investigate the sexual exploitation of children. The Internet Crimes Against Children (ICAC) Task Force is responsible for seeing that state and local law enforcement personnel receive the proper training, knowledge, and equipment to investigate Internet sex cases (Jenkins, 2001a).

Internet service providers (ISPs) are also made responsible for being aware of how their gateways are used. As mentioned earlier, if an ISP becomes aware that pornographic material is available through one of its sites, it is expected by the federal government to respond with censure. Failure to do so can result in seized equipment and assets (Jenkins, 2001a). Unfortunately, this intervention may not be as easy as it sounds. As technology has become more sophisticated, so have the pornographers in plying their trade.

Prevention Strategies to Help Youth Use the Internet Safely

Although it is difficult to apprehend some of the more clever Internet pornographers, efforts are being made to educate consumers not to become victims or to place themselves at risk. A variety of resources are available for both parents and youth to raise consciousness and hopefully prevent child victimization. Some of the more common suggestions to youth are as follows (adapted from Baker, 2011; Cooper, 2002; Hughes, 1998; Lenhart, 2009; Magid, 2006):

- Avoid posting information like your name, address, affiliations (e.g., sports teams or clubs), and other identifying data that would allow a perpetrator to find you.
- If you "blog," see if the service has a "friends" list that allows you to control who can blog with you. Be careful about adding strangers to the site, and add only those whom you know and trust.
- Do not agree to meet someone whom you have met over the Internet unless you know his or her identity. Even then make sure that you meet in a public place with friends and/or family along.
- Avoid posting photos of yourself on the Internet. These make it too easy for someone to recognize you. Definitely do not post photos that are suggestive or sexual as these can be downloaded by others and used in any way they choose.
- Avoid postings that might embarrass you, your friends, or family. These can be downloaded and can come back to haunt you years later.
- If others are allowed to post on your blog, check the comments regularly and make sure that they are appropriate. If they are not, delete them.
- Do not lie about your age when you sign up for a blog.

In addition to educating their children, parents are encouraged to be vigilant about their children's Internet use. Experts recommend that parents regularly question children as to what they have seen on the Internet and if anyone has gleaned personal information or asked to meet. Blocks can be placed on more objectionable sites, chat rooms, or instant messaging. If the child wants to set up a home page (e.g., Facebook or Twitter), parents are urged to discuss what information can be posted. Experts also caution parents to watch children's behavior for extreme secretiveness, inappropriate sexual knowledge, and sleeping problems (Baker, 2011; Cooper, 2002; Hughes, 1998).

CHILD PROSTITUTION ⎯⎯⎯⎯

It is estimated that there are at least 1 million teen prostitutes in the United States, whereas others suggest that this number could be double. Of these about a half to two thirds (depending upon the source) are girls, many of whom are runaways; more than two thirds of runaways end up as prostitutes (Curtis, Terry, Dank, Dombrowski, & Khan, 2008; Flowers, 2001, 2005; Tattersall, 1999). Some, like Sari, began their activities through the Internet.

℃℞ ⎯⎯⎯⎯⎯⎯⎯⎯⎯⎯⎯⎯⎯⎯⎯

Sari, at 15, was the oldest of five children. Her mother's drug addiction meant that Sari was frequently the designated caretaker. She much preferred surfing the net on a computer left by one of her mother's most recent boyfriends who had been arrested. In fact, he had initiated her interest in some of his favorite sites featuring sexually explicit pictures. He also showed her chat rooms where she could talk with a variety of men who flattered her and made her feel older than her years. One man, Josh, wanted to meet her, and they arranged a meeting at an address that Sari realized was a motel. At first they talked, and he took pictures of her, which was kind of fun. Then, he told her that if she had sex with him he would give her money. Sex was nothing new to Sari. She had been sexually abused by her biological father and one of her mother's boyfriends. She decided that if she could get something for it, she might as well. Josh also gave her a smartphone for easier communication and began to set her up with his friends whom he said would also give her money. By the time Sari began to think better of her choice, Josh had taken pictures and told her that he could send them to her mother and then she'd

be in trouble and that she could also be arrested. Having endured numerous beatings at her mother's hands and having watched her mother's boyfriend be arrested, Sari decided that it was easier to go along with what Josh wanted. But before long, Josh had hooked her on drugs and began to beat her when she did not "turn enough tricks" or give him the money she earned. Josh's arrest as a result of a police sting uncovered that Sari was not the only teen prostitute who now worked for him. ℘

Juvenile prostitution has been of concern since the 1970s when researcher Robin Lloyd (1976) conducted a study of boys in prostitution that led him to estimate that 3 million young boys under 16 were prostitutes in the United States. The studies of Densen-Gerber and her colleagues (see Densen-Garber, 1980; Densen-Garber & Hutchinson, 1978) found that equally as many, if not more, underage girls were also involved in prostitution. And in a nationwide survey of 596 police department files, Campagna (1985) and his associate Poffenberger conservatively estimated that between 100,000 and 200,000 juveniles, with an average age of 15, were engaged in full-time prostitution in the United States.

Many believe that it was the hippie culture of the 1960s that brought this type of exploitation to the attention of most Americans. In the mid-1960s, the Haight-Ashbury district of San Francisco was home to over 7,000 young people who espoused the concept of "doing their own thing," which usually referred to a life of instant gratification and sexual permissiveness. Their transient lifestyle, in addition to their immediate need for food, shelter, and money to live, lent itself to the use of prostitution for barter (Weisberg, 1985).

Many of those who were known as hippies were actually runaways who came under scrutiny with Ambrosino's popular book *Runaways* (1971). The attention given to the issue of runaways culminated in the Runaway and Homeless Youth Act, enacted in 1978 and amended in 1980, which among other services provided assistance to organizations that offered temporary shelter to such runaways (Flowers, 2001, 2010). The act also recognizes the problems associated with running away, especially teen prostitution.

Runaways, mostly teens, tend to run from negative home environments such as substance abuse, domestic violence, or maltreatment. Some run because of their own emotional problems, substance issues, sexual issues, or peer pressure. The likelihood that runways will be sexually exploited is high, and each year several hundred thousand of these teens are lured into prostitution (Flowers, 2001, 2005, 2010).

Some prostitutes, often girls, are lured into the activity while still living at home. Like Sari, mentioned above, these girls may be contacted through the Internet or in other ways and offered money, excitement, or the promise of love to become sexually involved. Often the original john shares them with others and may shame them or coerce them into compliance. Or these girls may find the activity exciting or profitable.

Still other teens are throwaways, that is, those who are pushed out of their home environment by caretakers who no longer want the responsibility or who are so involved with alcohol, drugs, crime, or sex that they find a child is a liability. Some juveniles are abandoned, and some intending to run away for a short time are never allowed to return home by their parents (Flowers, 2001, 2010).

Definition and Incidence of Juvenile Prostitution Today

Prostitution refers to the solicitation of sex for which money or some type of barter is accepted (Flowers, 2001, 2005). *Child or juvenile prostitution* refers to the involvement of minors in "sexual acts with adults or other minors where no force is present, including intercourse, oral sex, anal sex, and sadomasochistic activities where payment is involved" (Flowers, 2005, p. 82). The average age at which teens enter prostitution is 14 with the average age being about 15 ½ (Flowers, 2001; Tattersall, 1999). *White slavery* and *commercial sexual exploitation of children* are terms that are sometimes used to refer to teen sexual exploitation. Unlike prostitution, which is considered to be consensual, white slavery refers to the trafficking of girls and women for sexual use against their will (Cooper, Estes, Giardino, Kellogg, & Vieth, 2007; Flowers, 2001; Johnson, 1992b). Although occurring more often in Southeast Asia, white slavery also exists in the United States (Flowers, 2001). *Trafficking* is the transportation of children (and adults) across state or more often international borders for the purpose of placing them in situations of forced labor—in this case, sexual prostitution. These children are kidnapped, deceived, or coerced so that they might be transported (Cooper et al., 2007). Although these children may be used as prostitutes, it is the so-called consensual prostitution that we will address here.

It is difficult to determine how extensive the problem of juvenile prostitution is in the United States. Efforts to gather statistics are complicated by the transience of some prostitutes as well as their covert nature. A 2008 study (Curtis, Terry, Dank, Dombrowski, & Khan, 2008), conducted through John Jay College of Criminal Justice, looked at teen prostitution in the New York City area to gain insight into the problem. The findings of this study contradicted some of the earlier beliefs about young prostitutes and their lifestyles. In a sample of 249 youth, 48% were female and 45% were male with 8% described as transgender, whereas previously most teen prostitutes were expected to be female (Cooper et al., 2007; Flowers, 2001, 2005). Nearly half (48%) of these teens were African American or of "mixed race." The majority of the youth prostitutes (56%) reported being born in New York City, and less than 8% said that they were born out of the United States, dispelling the myth that most youth prostitutes are trafficked. Many of those interviewed were homeless (32%) or living with "friends" (Curtis et al., 2008).

Almost all of the youth in the New York study serviced male customers, predominantly white men between 25 and 55 years of age. Although 11% of the girls and 40% of the boys reported having at least one female client, only 13% of the boys serviced exclusively women. Contrary to earlier beliefs that teen prostitutes found customers through managers, 70% of those in the study met their clients on the streets with only 37% admitting to having a particular area of operation or "tracks." Youth might make use of cell phones or the Internet to make some contacts. Once they connected with their clients, 51% went back to the clients' apartments and 45% were taken to hotels around the city (Curtis et al., 2008).

One statistic that greatly differed from past beliefs about young prostitutes involved their use of managers or pimps (referred to in the study as "market facilitators"). Although earlier studies reported that girls usually have managers or pimps who keep track of their activities and demand a cut or sometimes their entire take (Flowers, 2001, 2005; Weisberg, 1985), Curtis et al. (2008) found that only 6% of boys and 14% of girls reported having pimps (p. 4, summary). Of those who did have managers, 90% of the managers were males, and 76% of the total market facilitators had other youth working for them.

Almost all of the youth (95%) in the study were prostituting to support themselves and believed that they could not find legal employment that would net them what they made in the trade. Only 10% had a parent that they could go to if they needed to do so; 7% said there were other family members who would help them out with 17% feeling that they had no one to whom they could go (Curtis et al., 2008).

Encounters with the police were frequent, but the youth in the study said that they were rarely arrested. However, the study also found that in reality 60% had been arrested at least once and 37% in the year prior to the study with drug possession as the most common offense (Curtis et al., 2008).

A large percentage of youth (46% of girls, 44% of boys, and 68% of transgendered) reported that they had been influenced to enter the trade by "friends" although it was suspected that some of these "friends" were working on behalf of pimps. Although many described this peer pressure, the researchers believe that curiosity, economic lure, and fascination/risk might also have entered into their choices. Once in the trade, their choice began to be normalized. Although those in the field (e.g., pimps) posed a threat of violence, youth prostitutes were more afraid of violence at the hands of customers. Fears were of being kidnapped, threatened, or held hostage. About 87% of youth prostitutes wished that they could leave the life but were afraid to do so (Curtis et al., 2008).

Tildy was typical of some of the young people who fall into prostitution:

℞ _____

Tildy learned from several friends about Mrs. K., a woman who would give you a "job" for a night or two. All you had to do was go to some guy's hotel room, have sex, and you'd make $100 for just an evening's work. "At least they pay for it," Tildy commented to one of her friends after she had worked one evening. "My stepfather didn't even do that!" Sex was "no big deal" as Tildy put it. Her stepfather had been abusing her since she was small. When he moved out, she was relieved but also missed the excitement of keeping the sex secret from her mother. At 15, Tildy had also been sexually active with several boys. But after several weeks of working for Mrs. K., Tildy grew bored. Plus, the last guy had wanted her to do things she didn't want to do and had told her that she was obligated because he paid her. She decided that she'd rather pick her own sexual partners and told Mrs. K. she was no longer interested.

Tildy became one of the many girls who worked on her own, finding customers on the streets or through the Internet and supporting herself through this lifestyle.

_____ ℅

There is an increasing number of homeless prostitutes who may be runaways or throwaways and who seek money, food, and shelter through prostitution as a form of survival. Some prostitutes are drug addicted and support their habit through turning tricks. Some of these were addicted to drugs or alcohol before they became prostitutes, and others developed the habit either by being hooked by a pimp or through finding drugs easily accessible on the streets. Streetwalkers, those who pick up their customers (johns) on the street, are the lowest form of prostitutes.

Girls in Prostitution

It is estimated that over 1 million girls are engaged in prostitution in the United States with one half to two thirds of the total number who prostitute being girls (Curtis et al., 2008; Dean & Thompson, 1997; Flowers, 2001, 2005; NCMEC, 2002; Tattersall, 1999). Although some of these girls sell their services through escort services, nightclubs, massage parlors, and brothels, most are streetwalkers.

Although many teen girls enter prostitution voluntarily, it is not uncommon for younger children to be prostituted by their parents or caretakers.

CR _____

Ginger was 5 when Uncle Matt began including her in his "parties." Ginger, abandoned by her mother who did not know the identity of the girl's father, was raised by her grandmother until she became too ill to do so. Then, the task of child rearing fell to Uncle Matt who also lived with them. When Ginger's grandmother died, Matt assured her that he would take good care of her. He began selling her small body to his friends when they had seen her at the parties. When she resisted, Matt used drugs to quiet her. Ginger was in high demand among his customers. There were other young girls who came to the parties and went off with the adult men. But one night they were raided by the police, and Ginger was placed in a foster home. She was also given medical attention as the foster mother discovered how badly she had been used sexually.

At 10, Ginger, who had been in several foster homes, ran away and started to hang out with some other young girls who told her that Rudy would give her a place to stay. Rudy, a pimp who had 10 girls in his "stable," was glad to take Ginger on as one more. Ginger had no trouble falling back into the life of prostitution. Rudy was not bad as pimps went, and she grew fond of him. Sure he beat her sometimes but only when she tried to hold out on him. It wasn't a bad life, Ginger decided. ❧

Other girls enter prostitution after being propositioned by a john (customer), often through the Internet. Most girls who enter prostitution voluntarily do so initially on a part-time basis to earn money for cigarettes, food, alcohol, drugs, or shelter. Johnson (1992a) postulated that most girls will be turning tricks on a full-time basis within 8 months to a year after their initial experience.

Streetwalkers ply their trade by wearing seductive outfits and standing on or strolling along streets where johns are likely to cruise by. Their services will range anywhere from masturbating and oral sex to intercourse. Because many work in the johns' cars, oral sex is often the service that is most practical. Others give "full service" in apartments or hotel rooms.

Although most studies place young female prostitutes in the lower socioeconomic class, some studies have also suggested that prostitutes may also come from the middle or upper-middle income groups.

CR _____

Hilary was the daughter of two attorneys and the youngest of three children. Her brother and sister, both considerably older than Hilary, were in college where they aspired to professional careers. Hilary had a severe learning disability and never felt that she was part of the rest of her family—all high achievers and obvious intellectuals. With both of her siblings in college and her parents working long hours, 14-year-old Hilary felt increasingly isolated. When a group of kids at school befriended her, she basked in what she saw as her new popularity. She did not recognize that her new friends were impressed only by her clothes and the amount of money she had at school. She attributed their desire to "borrow" things, which were frequently not returned, and their insistence that she pay for their snacks to the price for having friends. Hilary began hanging out with them after school and in the evenings. Later, she could not remember when they turned her on to drugs nor when the get-togethers began to include sex. One of the guys, whom everyone called Horse, convinced her that they could have some fun by seeing how many guys she could have sex with in one evening. Wanting to please Horse and possibly high on drugs at the time, Hilary agreed. She did not realize that Horse was extracting a fee from everyone who availed themselves of Hilary's services, nor did she know at the time that his buddies were taking pictures. After that evening, Horse convinced her that she was "a natural" at turning men on and suggested that she "work for him." He threatened that if she refused, her parents would be shown the pictures of her having sex with a variety of men. Hilary agreed to become a part-time prostitute, trading her services for Horse's attention and protection. ℰℴ

More often, girl prostitutes, regardless of their class, come from families where there is divorce, violence, abuse, or other dysfunction. Parent-child relationships are usually fraught with conflict. Substance abuse is often a factor in the home on the part of either the parents or the child or both (Flowers, 2001, 2005, 2010).

The Role of the Pimp

If the New York City study can be seen as representative of a greater population, it would seem that the trend is now for girls to work independently rather than having pimps. Other experts report that some girls still rely on pimps or managers who provide them with some protection and

structure (Flowers, 2005, 2010). Homeless girls are particularly vulnerable to being picked up by pimps once their money or ability to make it on the streets is exhausted. Substance abusers too are an obvious target for pimps who then take over the provision of drugs. Some pimps also act as recruiters or hire "runners" to do this job for them. The recruiter scours bus and train stations, video arcades, malls, coffee shops, and anywhere else where runaway, homeless, or lost teens might hang out. Once spotted, these teens are easily engaged by the recruiter who befriends them and offers money, shelter, or resources in addition to a "friendly" face. Some recruiters come on to the girls who may be feeling alone, unattractive, and unwanted, making them gullible for the attentions of a seemingly interested male (Barry, 1995; Flowers, 2001, 2010; Johnson, 1992a).

Pimps (and their runners) recruit through kindness, gifts, money, and attention. They will choose girls who are particularly vulnerable like those who may be a bit on the chubby side, have few social skills, or do not feel attractive to boys their own age. Once a pimp has hooked a girl, he will take control of all aspects of her life, eventually making the girl totally dependent upon him. He will probably be having sex with her by this time and will convince her that—if she really loves him—she will have sex with his friends to prove it. This becomes her pathway into prostitution as she continues to try to please her pimp-lover (Flowers, 2001, 2010).

Although the focus here is teens involved in prostitution, it is an interesting sidebar to look at how pimps begin in this role. The National Center on Missing and Exploited Children study on female teen prostitution considered this topic. This study suggested that pimps begin their careers after their own dysfunctional childhoods. Many witnessed domestic violence or were physically or sexually abused as boys. Some spent time in reform schools or prisons where they may have learned from others the lucrative nature of prostituting others (NCMEC, 2002). For other pimps, the idea is planted by their own experiences.

CR _____

Derik was 12 when his father took him to a neighborhood prostitute, suggesting that he was old enough to "become a man." Derik admits that he was so intimidated that the woman took pity on him, and they played cards together instead of sex. Afraid that his father would once again beat him and belittle him, Derik begged the woman not to tell what they had actually done. Her story to Derik's father about how he had the potential to be a "real stud" won his devotion, and he began offering to do errands for her in his spare time. In time, she did indoctrinate him sexually but also told him about how lucrative her business had become. Once she had a pimp but was now independent working out of a local bar. She suggested to Derik that there was money to be made by creating his own "stable" of girls.

At 18, Derik became involved with a younger girl who adored him. Both from impoverished families, Derik and his girlfriend dreamed of making money. He convinced her that they could make quite a bit if she agreed to provide sex for his friends for money and talked some of her girlfriends into doing the same for a cut. They developed a small business until they had a falling out. Derik threatened several of the girls into continuing with him and moved his "business" to another area. He developed his skills at recruiting other girls with whom he was not as democratic. He learned that keeping all of the proceeds and threatening them into compliance increased his financial gains. His girls knew that it was not wise to incur Derik's anger. He also managed to pay off the local police so he was rarely ever bothered by raids or arrests. By 20, Derik had developed a sizable "stable" and was making a steady income. But a new police chief changed all that. By 23, Derik found himself incarcerated and wondering where it all had gone.

SO

Although some do not use violence, the number of teen girl prostitutes who experience violence at the hands of their pimps is significant. Usually this violence occurs not as much

to force them into prostitution but to control them once they are part of the pimp's stable. The physical, emotional, and sexual abuse that these girls experience from pimps serves not only to assert the pimp's authority and control but also reinforce the girls' low self-esteem, dependence, and loyalty (Curtis et al., 2008; Flowers, 2001).

Pimps find other ways to keep their girls connected with them, including selling drugs for them, involvement in child pornography, changing their identity, cutting off the girls' ties to family and friends, using jealousy to imply caring, and humiliating them and letting them know that no one else would have them (Flowers, 2001, 2010).

Boys in Prostitution

According to the New York City study (Curtis et al., 2008), boys are almost equally represented in prostitution as are girls. The number of boys who run away is similar, and many of these boys become "hustlers"—selling their bodies—in order to survive. Boy prostitutes are usually referred to as *chickens* and the men who avail their services as *chicken hawks* or *chicken queens*.

Flowers (2005) characterizes a typical chicken hawk as a middle-aged man, usually a white-collar professional or worker, who related to children better than he does to adults, and who may be either single or married. He sees the boy as the aggressor and tends to be nonviolent himself. He tends to associate with like-minded individuals who also like chickens. The man comes onto the boy by pretending to be his friend (p. 87). A typical scenario of meeting might be for a chicken hawk to see a boy waiting in a spot known to be a meeting place—for example, a particular bench at a mall or on the steps of a building. The man eyes the boy and makes eye contact. He continues to make eye contact until the boy nods, and he returns the nod. They may use hand signals to begin the deal, or they approach and talk about the details in a roundabout manner. Boys sometimes work in twos as some men are interested in two boys (Flowers, 2001). Some men are now also finding boys via the Internet.

Boys who prostitute tend to be on average 15 years old and probably either a runaway or a throwaway (pushed out by parents). Money is the factor that motivates them, whereas girls, although working for money, may also be seeking acceptance or love. Boys too tend to be from dysfunctional families where domestic violence, abuse, and substance abuse are the norm. Most have been victimized by some type of abuse themselves and have dropped out of school. Many hustlers also commit other delinquent acts like stealing. Boys work in pairs or solo and do not use pimps (Curtis et al., 2008; Dean & Thompson, 1997; Flowers, 2001, 2010; Tattersall, 1999).

Consequences for Juvenile Prostitutes

For both male and female teen prostitutes, the price of their trade can be dear. Brutality by both customers and pimps may mean injuries. Girls may be subject to gynecological problems, and both boys and girls may contract sexually transmitted diseases (STDs). HIV in particular presents a significant risk for young prostitutes today (Flowers, 2001, 2005; NCMEC, 2002; Walker, 2002). Flowers (2001) comments that boys might have a slightly greater risk of contracting HIV/AIDS due to the homosexual and bisexual relations as well as the high use of intravenous drugs in their culture. Yet girls too with their abundance of sexual partners, often with unprotected sex, are vulnerable to HIV infection.

The high rate of substance abuse among both male and female teen prostitutes also takes its toll. Studies have estimated that marijuana, alcohol,

crack cocaine, and other street drugs are very much a part of the lifestyles of young prostitutes (Curtis et al., 2008; Flowers, 2001, 2010).

It is not just physical disorders that plague young prostitutes. Their lifestyle subjects them to pressures that often cause depression, personality disorders, thought disorders, and suicide. Some come to the trade with preexisting mental health issues that are aggravated by their experiences in prostitution. Dissociate disorders may actually provide teen prostitutes with a survival mechanism that protects them against even worse disorders (Barry, 1995; Flowers, 2001). Some teens also suffer from PTSD as a result of the experiences to which they are exposed (NCMEC, 2002).

There is a high risk for suicide among juveniles who prostitute. One estimate is that 7 in 10 girls and 4 in 10 boys who ply the trade try to commit suicide due to depression and the realities of their lifestyle (Flowers, 2001, 2010; Tattersall, 1999).

Exiting Prostitution

Although some young people die or commit suicide while they are still prostituting, some do leave the lifestyle. The National Center for Missing and Exploited Children study suggested that there are several primary reasons that cause teen prostitutes to abandon their trade. First, they may develop an aversion to the customers, perhaps resenting the ill treatment or the nature of the interaction. Some gain sufficient financial security to seek other pursuits. Those who suffer from ill health may be forced to give up prostitution. When some prostitutes become adults, they have the power and resources to find other means of support. Others are incarcerated and when released choose not to return to prostitution. And the outreach of programs catering to young prostitutes can provide the incentive for some to leave the lifestyle (Curtis et al., 2008; NCMEC, 2002).

Summary

Child pornography is an age-old problem. Several organizations still advocate for the involvement of boys with adult men, often promoting themselves through exchanging child pornography. The North American Man-Boy Love Association, the René Guyon Society, the Pedophile Alert Network, and the Pedophile Information Exchange are a few of such groups.

Child pornography is defined as images or photographs of those under 18 years of age in suggestive poses or performing sexual acts with adults, other children, or animals. There has been some controversy about whether artistic representations fall into the category of pornography. Pornographers also use children for the production of pornography, which is considered child exploitation and is a form of child sexual abuse.

Recently the practice of sexting—when youth send nude or sexual pictures of themselves or others over cell phones—has become an issue. Although at this time only a small number of young people have been documented as engaging in sexting, there are significant legal and emotional ramifications for participants.

The Internet has altered the production, use, and exchange of pornography greatly, making it more available to even casual users. In addition, the Internet, despite its contribution to worthwhile educational and healthy leisure activities, provides greater opportunity for a variety of perpetrators to contact youth. Recent studies on Internet use in households across the United States found that at least 1 in 5 young people was exposed to unwanted sexual solicitation and sexual materials. In the last few years, there has been a decrease in sexual solicitation, which experts believe is a result of increased efforts to protect children online.

The Internet has become a popular way for all types of offenders to access children and youth. Computers have become affordable, and perpetrators also enjoy anonymity as they talk with youth. Young people can form relationships quickly without knowing accurately the identity of the individual with whom they are communicating. Research indicates that the youth who meet offenders offline usually do so voluntarily; it is often because they are feeling isolated and needy.

Adults who access child pornography on the Internet often do so at work as well as at home, attesting to the addictive quality of the activity. Several theorists have categorized men who access the Internet. McLaughlin (2000) identifies collectors, travelers, manufacturers, and chatters, whereas Bowker and Gray (2005) suggest the categories of dabbler, preferential offender, and miscellaneous offender. Additional research has found that those who access child pornography on the Internet may have already sexually abused children offline.

Being exposed to pornography on the Internet confuses children at best. Adolescents, in the throes of exploring their own sexuality, may be prompted to explore sexually dangerous and risky behaviors, some of which may end in choosing to meet an offender. Continued efforts are being made by various organizations to protect children and teens from inappropriate exposure to pornography.

Experts estimate that more than 1 million teen prostitutes live in the United States currently. Most are runaways; some are what are referred to as "throwaways." An upsurge in teens in prostitution was seen in the 1960s with the hippy generation. Youth from dysfunctional homes sought excitement, understanding, and money and drifted into prostitution. It is estimated that teens often enter prostitution as young as 14; some continue into adulthood; some lose their lives through violence, drugs, or ill health; and some are able to exit as they grow older. Young prostitutes may ply the trade on the streets full-time or only on a part-time basis.

Both boys and girls tend to operate independently though some girls deal with pimps who act like managers, often finding their customers, taking the money, and supporting the girls. Some pimps use violence to keep their "stable" in line, whereas others use psychology or special attention. Boys in prostitution are more likely to act without pimps but also have a shorter life expectancy.

Life for young prostitutes is fraught with dangers between violence, HIV/AIDS, and drugs. In the last few years, there have been increased arrests in an attempt to intervene with these young people.

Review Questions

1. Why is child pornography a problem?

2. What have recent surveys said about youth being exposed to unwanted sexual material and solicitation on the Internet?

3. What are some issues for youth on the Internet?

4. Why might adults be attracted to using the Internet to access children?

5. What are some types of adults that are attracted to pornography?

6. What is being done to protect children from Internet solicitation?

7. What era influenced the upsurge in youth prostitution today?

8. Describe the life for girls in prostitution.

9. What is prostitution like for boys?

10. What roles do pimps play?

CHAPTER 8

Children and Adolescents Who Sexually Abuse

⋐෴⋑

I remember going to my grandmother's on holidays when I was a kid and playing with my cousins in the basement of the house. There were four of us girl cousins about the same age, a boy several years younger, and my oldest cousin, Gene, who was about 6 years older than I was. Apparently no one thought it was strange that he always wanted to spend time with us even when he was in his later adolescence. His favorite game was hide-and-seek. There were lots of rooms and closets down in the basement and stuff piled to make crannies—great places to hide. What I remember most though was how Gene would want to hide with me, and while we were hiding, he'd try to feel me up. It must have started when I was only 8 or 9 and was always the same when we got together at Gran's. I hated his hands on me, and I used to try avoid having him hide with me, but then I felt jealous when he would make a big deal about one of my cousins. In later years, I learned from my other girl cousins that he used to do the same thing to them. He'd threatened to tell if we said anything, and we were afraid that if we told, we wouldn't get to come to Gran's, and that would be awful. Sometimes he'd threaten to hurt us too if we told. We finally told each other, but no one ever said anything to the adults even when he tried to have intercourse with one of my cousins. She got scared and started to cry, and we found them before anything else happened. We never thought of it as sexual abuse. It was just our cousin, Gene, "being weird."

⋐෴⋑

Over the last few decades, there has been a great deal of interest in and research on the issue of juveniles who sexually abuse other children. Often referred to in the literature as *adolescent sexual offenders*, these youths usually target younger children or those over whom they have some power. This population has come to the notice of professionals largely due to retrospective studies of adult offenders who often began their abusive careers in adolescence (Lane, 1991; Prescott & Longo, 2006). But various authors have questioned the appropriateness of the term sexual offender to describe all children who are found to engage in such sexual acts. Araji (1997) points out that children as young as 2 ½ years old have been referred to clinicians for acting out sexually against other children. Referring to them as *sexually aggressive children*, Araji joins other researchers (Cantwell, 1995; Gil & Johnson, 1993; Johnson

& Doonan, 2006; Schmidt, Bonner, & Chaffin, 2012) in attempting to understand these young abusers. Eliana Gil and Toni Cavanaugh Johnson, in their classic work *Sexualized Children* (1993), proposed that there is a continuum of children's sexual behaviors, ranging from normal to abusive. Children who have experienced abuse in their own lives and demonstrate specific characteristics (to be discussed later in this chapter) can be seen as sexually reactive (Johnson, 2009).

In the literature on young abusers, terms like *juvenile sexual offenders* and *youthful sexual offenders* are also noted. But the word *offend* brings to mind more forethought and sophistication that is often seen in youth who act out sexually. Rather than using this term, I have chosen to call youth, both children and adolescents who act out against others sexually, *juvenile sexual abusers* as the behaviors described here are abusive to the victims whether the youth perpetrating them intend them to be or not.

DEFINING AND MEASURING SEXUAL ABUSE BY JUVENILES ____

Historically, society's view of what constitutes sexual abuse by children and adolescents has not always been clear, nor was it always taken seriously. For example, in the chapter-opening vignette, none of the cousins saw what was happening to them as sexually abusive. If they had told their parents—prior to the attempt at intercourse—the parents may have passed it off as sexual exploration. Even if the adults had recognized that Gene, 6 years older than his female cousins, had a definite problem in that he tried to force his female cousins into sexual activity, these adults would probably have responded within the family in some manner by keeping Gene either upstairs or away from his cousins. It is also possible that some of the adults might have seen the four girls as "leading their male cousin on." In short,

in the past, children and adolescents who acted out sexually were assumed by many adults to be "just going through a stage" or, because most of those who abuse are males, as "boys being boys." It was often expected that a word to the adolescent was sufficient to halt the behavior. However, after studying adult offenders who began their abusive behaviors in childhood or adolescence, researchers now recognize that the problem can be more serious than first assumed.

Despite this recognition, it is still difficult to determine the exact magnitude of sexual abuse by juveniles for several reasons. First, societal attitudes prevent reporting of many cases in which juveniles are abusive. Because the victims of juvenile sexual abusers are most likely to be relatives and friends (Barbaree & Marshall, 2008; Becker, 1998; Righthand & Welch, 2004; Ryan, Leversee, & Lane, 2010; Ryan, Miyoshi, Metzner, Krugman, & Fryer, 1996), the abuse is less likely to be reported beyond the family or friends (Araji, 1997; Righthand & Welch, 2004; Ryan et al., 2010). In fact, it is estimated that 3 out of 4 incidents of abuse by juveniles are not reported to any civil or legal agency (Finkelhor, Ormrod, & Chaffin, 2009; U.S. Department of Justice, 2004). Yet it has also been proposed that by the time a juvenile offender reaches the criminal justice system at approximately 14 years, he will have averaged between two and seven victims for which he was never reported (Ryan & Lane, 1997). And yet, of those reported, over 35% of those known by police to have committed sexual offenses against minors are juveniles themselves. There is a marked jump in the numbers of youth who sexually abuse after the age of 12 (Finkelhor et al., 2009).

Most of the juvenile sexual assaults are committed by males and directed toward females regardless of the age. The majority of these assaults are against children below the age of 6 or 7. And juveniles are more likely to use threats, force, and violence than adult offenders (Finkelhor et al., 2009; Rich, 2003). Despite these accumulated facts and estimates, Rich (2011) cautions that there is no accurate statistical picture of a juvenile abuser; the reasons and degree of pathology of the abuse are varied, which is another reason why determination of the magnitude of the problem is difficult.

Friedrich (1990) postulates that there was, until more recently, a paucity of information on preadolescents who abuse for four reasons. First, clinicians had a difficult time accepting children as sexual beings and therefore as capable of committing sexual offences. Second, there is a difference in the recognition and triggering of sexual behaviors between male and female therapists. Friedrich comments that

> male therapists are aware of more sexual behaviors in children because they represent a different stimulus to children—that is, male therapists may cue sexual behaviors in children who have been victimized by males, who make up the largest percentage of known offenders. (p. 243)

Third, according to Friedrich, is that parents of sexually acting out children—possibly feeling some self-blame—may screen out the existence of deviant behaviors. And finally, the field divides itself into victim therapists and offender therapists, and the understanding of the etiology and consequences of children's sexual behaviors differs depending upon the therapist's orientation. Victim therapists may not want to look at sexually acting out by their juvenile clients as anything other than reactive (pp. 242–243).

In addition to the failure of identification by parents and some professionals, young abusers may fall between the cracks in that agencies addressing offenders do not accept those who are very young. Now many programs address the preadolescent abusers, but these programs are still not numerous (Araji, 1997; Johnson & Doonan, 2006; Lundrigan, 2001). In addition, young children tend to fall within the jurisdiction of the child protection system as they are usually victims of abuse or family dysfunction. In many instances, they do not become designated as sexual abusers but rather are treated as dependent children with other issues (Araji, 1997).

Even adolescent abusers may not be labeled as such. Juvenile sexual abusers, both preadolescent and adolescent, tend to exhibit other delinquent behaviors, possibly coming to the attention of the juvenile justice system for other delinquency-related matters and therefore not labeled as a sexual offender per se (Barbaree & Marshall, 2008; Rich, 2011; Ryan et al., 2010).

Offenses perpetrated by juveniles, whether preadolescent or adolescent, vary. Some authors divide offenses into two categories: hands-off, no-touch offenses and hands-on, assaultive, or touch offenses. Hands-off offenses involve, but may not be excluded to, the following: obscene phone calls, voyeurism, stealing clothing for sexual purposes (e.g., masturbation), exhibitionism or exposure, public masturbation, or public display of obscene materials (Araji, 1997; Erooga & Masson, 2006; Rich, 2003, 2011; Righthand & Welch, 2004; Ryan et al., 2010). Hands-on assaults include fondling or molestation, frottage (rubbing up against another for sexual purposes), oral sexual contact, digital penetration of the vagina or anus, penetration of the vagina or anus with an object, penile penetration, or sexual torture (Araji, 1997; Erooga & Masson, 2006; Rich, 2003; Righthand & Welch, 2004). Juveniles may also be involved in such indirect sexual acts as the creation, possession, or distribution of pornography or bestiality (sexual interactions with animals) (Rich, 2011).

DIFFERENTIATING JUVENILE ABUSERS FROM ADULT SEXUAL OFFENDERS

Research tells us that many adult sexual offenders begin their sexual acting out in adolescence or even childhood. These retrospective studies of adult offenders alert researchers that juveniles who abuse have the potential for becoming adult offenders, although not all do so. As yet, researchers are just beginning to understand why some youth who are sexually abused go on to offend in adulthood and why some do not.

Although adults and juveniles who sexually abuse do share some characteristics and behaviors, theorists should be cautious not to assume that the two groups are identical (Calder, 2001; Rich, 2003). According to the Association for the Treatment of Sexual Abusers (ATSA) (2001),

> the significantly lower frequency of more extreme forms of sexual aggression, fantasy,

and compulsivity among juveniles than among adults suggests that many juveniles have sexual behavior problems that may be more amenable to intervention. (p. 1)

In addition, recent studies have suggested that if provided with specialized treatment, many juveniles will cease their sexually abusive behavior by the time they reach adulthood (ATSA, 2001).

Keeping the need to distinguish between adults and juveniles who sexually abuse, Table 8.1 outlines some of the distinctions.

Table 8.1 Differences in Youthful and Adult Abusers

Youthful Abusers	Adult Abusers
Patterns of sexual interest, arousal, and deviance just developing	Have usually developed fixed interest and arousal patterns
Perpetration behaviors less consistent and sophisticated	Have usually developed consistent cycle of offending
More likely to abuse according to the situation or opportunity	Tend to have fixed, cognitive patterns and distortions
Closer in age to own abuse experience, closer to feelings generated	Have usually developed set responses to remembered abuse that play out in offense
Less developed sexual knowledge	More developed sexual knowledge based on age and experience
Live in world of adolescent values, beliefs, and expectations that may be more fluid	Live in a world of adult expectation to which they probably feel unable to live up to
Role of the family more critical	May have little contact with family of origin. Often isolated or may not have established own family
Developmentally resisting external controls	Expect and anticipate more external controls
Used to using education to develop new skills	May be distanced from or disillusioned with education. Adults also learn differently
Less research on juvenile offenders to inform treatment	Larger body of knowledge about characteristics and treatment developed over time

SOURCE: Based on Becker & Johnson (2001), Calder (2001), Rich (2003), Righthand & Welch (2004), Ryan et al. (2010).

Differentiating between adult and juvenile abusers is also significant when considering treatment. Prescott and Longo (2006) suggest that the trickle-down phenomenon—importing strategies for adult treatment into the world of juvenile abusers—has influenced treatment models for juveniles until quite recently. The contamination by adult treatment models can mean that juvenile abusers are often erroneously considered to be of more danger to the community than they actually are and have a poorer prognosis than is probable. By recognizing that treatment models for juveniles must be differentiated from those of adults, it becomes apparent that the fluidity of the development, attitudes, and behaviors of youth—especially those in the younger groups—provides more hope for change and a better prognosis for most juveniles than for many adult offenders.

SEPARATING SEXUALIZED BEHAVIORS FROM SEXUAL ABUSE IN YOUNG CHILDREN

How does one separate sexual experimentation between children from sexual abuse? Gail Ryan (1999), noted expert on juvenile offending, comments that "it is not sexual behavior that defines sexual abuse, but rather, it is the nature of the interaction and the relationship that give an accurate definition" (p. 424). She goes on to define abusive behavior as being against the victim's will, without consent, and as being aggressive, exploitive, and manipulative, or involving threat (1997, p. 3). Children often learn about sexuality through experimentation, but this experimentation with others needs to be mutual and the participants of a similar age and developmental level. Sexual activity becomes abusive when the situation is unbalanced, for example, when one of the youth is older, has more resources, and uses exploitation, manipulation, or threat.

Johnson and Doonan (2006) also suggest that the term *sexual behaviors* in children can also be misleading. In young children, behaviors that appear sexual may not be motivated by the same urges as they are in adults or teens. Young children mimic the behaviors of adults without seeking emotional connections or intimate relationships. Instead the "sexual" behaviors of children, rather than being motivated by sexual arousal, personal gratification, or orgasm—all of which are possible for young children—are more likely related to sex through mimicking. For example, children may "hump" one another not for gratification but rather mimicking behavior that they might have seen and are trying to replicate.

Johnson (Gil & Johnson, 1993; Johnson, 1999, 2000, 2009; Johnson & Doonan, 2006) explains that children's sexual behavior can be seen along a continuum from normal and healthy to abusive. She divides this continuum into four subsections: normal sexual exploration, sexually reactive behavior, extensive mutual sexual behavior, and children who molest. *Normal sexual exploration* is children's way of gathering information about sexuality. It tends to be age appropriate (see Johnson, 1999, 2009) and involves exploring others' bodies visually and tactilely ("playing doctor"), and the participants—although possibly of different genders—are usually of similar ages and developmental levels. These children tend to get along with one another and are mutual participants ("You show me yours, and I'll show you mine"). The behavior results from curiosity, and although they may feel, on some level, that they are doing something that may not be acceptable, there are no deep feelings of shame or guilt. These feelings may arise if the adult's reaction at disclosure leads them to believe that what they have done by way of exploration is "sinful" or abnormal (Gil & Johnson, 1993; Johnson, 1999, 2000, 2009).

Sexually reactive children exhibit a sexual interest that is out of balance with that of their peer group. Usually these children have been sexually abused or at least exposed to sexual stimulation (e.g., pornography) beyond their level of comprehension. In some manner, they have been overstimulated sexually, and their sexual acting out is an attempt to make sense of what they are developmentally not able to understand. Sexually reactive children may be plagued by extreme guilt and anxiety about their behavior. This behavior may not always be directed toward others but may involve their own bodies such as excessive or compulsive masturbation, exposing themselves, or inserting objects into themselves. If their behavior is directed toward other children, their intent is not to coerce, victimize, or frighten them. Some of these children are said to be suffering from post-traumatic stress disorder (PTSD) as a result of their own victimization (Gil & Johnson, 1993; Johnson, 1999, 2000, 2009). Riley is an example of such a child.

CR ──────────────────────

Riley was an attractive 6-year-old whom his parents brought in for counseling because of his "disturbing behavior." They first became aware of it when their usually good-natured dog snapped at Riley. Another child in the room reported that Riley had been trying to play with the dog's penis. The parents scolded Riley and assumed that he was just curious. Subsequently, Riley attempted to insert a toy in his 3-year-old sister's rectum when the two were playing in a backyard pool. They had also noticed that he was masturbating frequently and in almost a frantic and compulsive manner. A report was made to child protection services as the therapist believed that Riley himself had been victimized. It was later learned that Riley had been molested on several occasions by an older boy, the son of Riley's day care provider who watched Riley after his half-day kindergarten.

──────────────────────── SO

It soon became clear that Riley was trying desperately to understand the sexual abuse to which he had been subjected.

Children who exhibit *extensive mutual sexual behaviors* frequently have their own past histories

and, being thrown together in some manner, practice these behaviors on one another. For example, Arlin and Jed, half brothers a year apart, had both been sexually abused and had been placed in the same foster home. The extent of their sexual abuse had not been shared with the foster mother as there were numerous family problems as well. Assuming that they would enjoy sharing a room, the foster mother gave them one together. After she walked in on the boys engaged in oral sex, the foster mother questioned the worker more closely and realized that these boys should not room together.

The sexual behavior of children in this category is much more pervasive and focused on sexuality. They are usually of similar ages or developmental levels and participate in the full range of normally adult behaviors including oral genital contact, sodomy, and intercourse. The participation is usually mutual; however, some of these children may resort to force or coercion (falling into Johnson's fourth category) if their partner hesitates. Gil and Johnson (1993) point out that the marked difference between these children and those exhibiting normal sexual exploitation is a difference in affect. In fact, there is a lack of affect instead of the spontaneity of normal children or the aggression of molesters. These children have probably learned the use of sexual behaviors as a manner of relating (Gil & Johnson, 1993; Johnson, 1999, 2000, 2009). For example, it was later learned that sexuality was very much a part of the household from which Arlin and Jed were removed. From an early age when they watched their mother entertain a variety of johns to the sexual abuse at the hand of her latest boyfriend, the boys were well aware of what it meant to be sexual. But at ages 7 and 8, they were not able to fully integrate with their environment, and being placed in a new and strange home, they replicated the familiar by sexually interacting with one another.

Children who molest demonstrate minds and actions pervaded with sexuality. These children exhibit a wide range of sexual behaviors from oral sex to all types of penetration. Their behavior is impulsive, compulsive, and aggressive, and they employ bribery, force, and threats to compel their victims. In some cases, there can appear to be an almost sadistic quality to their abuse, linking sexuality with anger, rage, loneliness, and fear. Victims are usually younger and often chosen either because they are available (such as younger siblings) or because they are particularly vulnerable by virtue not only of age but emotional neediness, intellectual impairment, depression, or isolation. Perpetrators use threats to keep the victims quiet and may even resort to force (Gil & Johnson, 1993; Johnson, 1999, 2000, 2009; Rich, 2003, 2011; Righthand & Welch, 2004; Vizard, 2013).

Juvenile molesters tend to have other behavior problems at home as well. Their coping skills are problematic, their problem-solving abilities are lacking, and they demonstrate poor impulse control. Early inadequate attachment and bonding are often blamed for these young abusers' inability to form healthy relationships with others. For the victims, they show little empathy, and about their abuse, they do not appear particularly remorseful (Araji, 1997; Gil & Johnson, 1993; Johnson, 1999, 2000, 2009; Rich, 2003, 2011; Ryan et. al, 2010). (The full range of these characteristics will be addressed more fully later in this chapter.)

The typology discussed earlier was primarily addressed to young children—under 12. Rich (2003, 2011) points out that adolescents must be seen somewhat differently. Just as younger children, adolescents engage in sexual behaviors as a way of developing, and this exposure has changed over the last few decades. In contemporary Western society, teens are exposed to many more explicit sexual messages than during their grandparents' time. Familiarity with oral sex and intercourse at a younger age has become the modern norm, making it difficult to determine when adolescents are engaging in offending or abusive behavior. Rich (2003) explains that adolescents

are considered to be engaging in abusive sexual behaviors only when there is an unwilling other party (through either clear force or significant coercion), a clear imbalance of power, or a distinct age difference. Even so, there are times when the line between force, coercion, and mutual consent can be blurry. Nevertheless, for an adolescent to be considered an offender, there must be a victim, defined lack of consent, a power differential, age, or other clear circumstances. (p. 35)

STRIVING TO UNDERSTAND THE JUVENILE SEXUAL ABUSER

Even though researchers have not developed a totally accurate profile of juveniles who abuse others, there are numerous attempts to do so. In addition, researchers are able to isolate some factors that appear to describe many juvenile sexual abusers. The difficulty is that all such abusers do not fit neatly into any one category or another. Nonetheless, let us look at what research tells us.

In addition to Johnson's continuum of sexual acting out, there have been several attempts at empirically derived typologies.

Developed Typologies

Sponsored by the National Center on Child Abuse and Neglect, Pithers, Gray, Busconi, and Houchens (1998) looked at 127 children between 6 and 12 years of age—83 boys and 44 girls—who had been referred for child protection and mental health services for sexually problematic behaviors covering a full spectrum from fondling and masturbation to more intrusive behaviors like vaginal or anal penetration. Through analysis of demographic variables and data compiled from a battery of tests given to the children and their parents, the researchers identified three profiles of children: conduct disordered, highly maltreated and traumatized, and nondisordered. The conduct-disordered group was further broken down into sexually aggressive and rule breakers. The sexually aggressive group was made up of almost entirely males (94%), whereas rule breakers consisted of 58% of males with 42% females (Rasmussen, 2004).

The second subtype was divided into highly traumatized children and abuse-reactive children. About two thirds of the highly traumatized children were males, whereas 96% of the abuse-reactive children were males. Those in the third group—nondisordered—tended to be predominantly females who were young (mean 8.6 years of age) and who did not have as extensive histories of maltreatment although they had been in some way exposed to a sexualized environment. These children tended not to use coercion in their sexual acting out (Pithers et al., 1998, pp. 400–404).

Bonner, Walker, and Berliner (1999) studied 201 children (126 males and 75 females) between the ages of 6 and 12 who had been referred to various agencies for sexualized behaviors. After administering a series of inventories, these researchers categorized the children into the subgroups of sexually inappropriate, sexually intrusive, and sexually aggressive. The sexually aggressive group tended to be male, older, and generally aggressive (Rasmussen, 2004).

Hall, Mathews, and Pearce (2002) looked at the case records of 100 children between the ages of 4 and 7 who had been referred for sexual behavior problems. These researchers developed three categories: developmentally expected, sexualized self-focused (without any interpersonal contact), and interpersonally focused (engaging in problematic sexual contact or touch). They then grouped their findings based upon variables relating to childhood development, family background, and caregiving environments. From this grouping, they clustered their findings into categories that described the underlying intent of the sexual behaviors: interpersonal, unplanned; interpersonal, planned (noncoercive); and interpersonal, planned (coercive). A subsequent analysis allowed Hall and colleagues to conclude that the three sexual profiles could be best differentiated by (a) elements of the child's abusive experience; (b) opportunities to learn and/or practice problematic sexual behavior; and (c) family variables (including sexual attitudes, interaction styles, family violence and criminality, maltreatment histories, appropriateness of parent-child roles) (Rasmussen, 2004, p. 65).

Hunter (2006) identified three groups of adolescents who molest young children. The adolescent onset–nonparaphilic were youth with psychosocial inadequacies who expected ridicule and rejection from their peers and gravitated toward younger children, especially females. Their behaviors tended to be opportunistic rather than well planned. The lifestyle persistent group tended to be aggressive and oppositional and committed their abuse against young adolescent girls. They were also the group with the most nonsexual arrests. And finally, the early adolescent onset–paraphilic group had begun to develop pedophilic interests, targeting young males. They also had the highest rate of recidivism.

When describing youthful abusers, most theorists look at specific factors within the children's or adolescents' lives and evaluate the facts they know about a majority of those who act out sexually. We will consider each of the most often cited areas.

Maltreatment Histories

The literature on juvenile sexual abusers attests to the fact that there is a high correlation between dysfunctional childhoods and sexual acting out for children and adolescents. Childhood sexual abuse is often cited as a precursor to juvenile sexual offending and pedophilia (Barbaree & Marshall, 2008; Burton, 2000; Lee, Jackson, Pattison, & Ward, 2002; Rich, 2003, 2011; Righthand & Welch, 2004; Ryan et al., 2010; Schmidt et al., 2012; Vizard, 2013). Becker and Hunter (1997) estimated that between 40% and 80% of juvenile offenders have experienced sexual abuse. In addition, children who experience physical abuse and neglect and who witness domestic violence are also represented among juveniles who sexually abuse (Rich, 2011; Righthand & Welch, 2004; Ryan et al., 1996). Considering sexually aggressive children under 12, Araji (1997) found that although sexual abuse is often in the backgrounds of these children, it tended to be more intrusive, involving genital contact and penetration or both. This author also noted the presence of physical abuse and neglect in many of the homes of these children. Johnson and Aoki (1993), looking at the same young population, discovered that of the 158 children between 6 and 11 years of age that they studied, physical abuse was a significant contributor to the sexual behavior problems that the children exhibited (p. 15).

Aggression was a major factor in the homes of young acting-out children. There was frequently conflict in addition to exposure to adult sexual activity, pornography, and poor sexual boundaries (Araji, 1997; Friedrich, 1990; Gil & Johnson, 1993; Ryan et al., 2010). Araji (1997) summarizes her findings about the families of sexually aggressive young children by identifying five variables that act as contributors: These children

(a) are recipients of multiple types of abuse that include physical violence and in some cases sexual abuse; (b) experience abuse that is extreme and of longer duration in percentages that exceed those reported in large samples of sexually abused children; (c) are victims of sexual abuse experiences that involve genital contact and various types of intercourse; (d) are exposed to sexualized adult behaviors in some format; (e) exist in families characterized by aggression, anger, conflict, and little parent support, and in which the child may be the family scapegoat. (p. 86)

Not all children or teens from such environments become sexually aggressive, however.

Burton (2000) postulated that several factors—including victim–offender relationship; the frequency, type, and physical invasiveness of the child's abuse; and the developmental stage at which the abuse occurred—may be linked to the correlation between childhood abuse and the child's sexual offending (see also Rich, 2003; Wyre, 2000). Children who witnessed domestic violence were also found to be at risk for possible sexual offending (Lee et al., 2002; Rich, 2003, 2011; Ryan, 1999; Ryan et al., 2010).

Some would disagree with the assertion that there is a decided connection between a history of child abuse and neglect and sexual offending. Some theorists question whether or not there is enough conclusive evidence to connect these two variables (Craissati, McClurg, & Browne, 2002; Glasser et al., 2001). The fact remains that a history of abuse appears to be present in the histories of both children and adolescents who sexually abuse (Araji, 1997; Friedrich, 1990; Gil & Johnson, 1993; Rich, 2003; Righthand & Welch, 2004; Ryan, 1999; Ryan et al., 1996).

Family Dynamics

As mentioned earlier, the families of sexually aggressive children often have their share of dysfunction. In addition to domestic violence, such factors as parental conflict, criminality, substance abuse, family instability, and psychopathology were often present within families whose children sexually acted out (Rich, 2003; Righthand & Welch, 2004; Ryan, 1999; Zankman & Bonomo, 2004). The Richters are an example of just such a family.

&

Twelve-year-old Simon Richter came to the attention of the Department of Youth Services when it was reported that he had sexually molested a 6-year-old neighborhood girl. Investigation uncovered that Simon had molested several other children in his neighborhood and also his 6-year-old sister, but the situations had never been reported to an agency before. The agency assigned a worker to investigate the home.

Simon was the oldest of seven children, including two sets of twins. Several of the children had been fathered by different men as Mr. Richter, an alcoholic who had had numerous jobs, appeared to come and go from the home. When he was there, the family had often come to the attention of police for domestic violence. Neighbors also believed that he had sexually abused Simon and several of the younger children. Mrs. Richter was known to have a history of mental illness, having been diagnosed as bipolar. While in her severe depressive moods, Mrs. Richter had been reported to children's protective services for the neglect of her children. Cybil, the oldest daughter and a year younger than Simon, was the apparent caretaker of the younger children. Belligerent and self-protective, Cybil told the investigating worker that she could never trust Simon who had on numerous occasions "tried to feel up the little kids."

&

Exposure of violent models at home places youth at high risk for acting out what they see. Domestic violence is often in the background of juvenile sexual abusers (Carter & Matson, 1999). There is also research that points to community violence as a factor, which desensitizes juveniles to the point that they are at risk for acting out in violent and sexual ways (Johnson-Reid, 1998).

Relationships, Attachment Issues, and Social Skills

Not surprisingly, given the family dysfunction often present in the homes of children and teens who act out sexually, these youth often have difficulty with relationships. The ability to connect in relationships is developed early in life with the child's opportunity, or lack thereof, to bond— or attach—with primary caretakers. Levy and Orlans (1998) define attachment as "[t]he deep and enduring connection established between a child and caregiver in the first several years of life. It profoundly influences every component of the human condition—mind, body, emotions, relationships and values" (p. 1).

To adequately attach, a child must be provided with a consistent and reciprocated relationship with his or her caretaker. Family dysfunction, substance abuse, mental illness, and other such factors may hamper the caretaker's ability to attend to the child in a manner that allows the child to develop this important bond (Brisch, 2012; Friedrich & Sim, 2006; Rich, 2006). Rich (2006) explains that the experience of becoming attached to another human being is what allows a child to develop a pattern through which he or she can form social connections with others and the strategies to maintain those relationships. He suggests that "attachment is a process, an organized set of procedures *and* a state of being" (p. 6).

Becoming socially competent enough to make healthy connections with others, therefore, requires the ability to feel safe, feel connected to another, and derive a sense of well-being from experiencing this relationship (Friedrich & Sim, 2006; Rich, 2003; Schmidt et al., 2012). Children who have not had the opportunity either to feel safe or connected or to be involved in true reciprocity with an adult will not have the tools necessary to engage in healthy relationships with others. Ryan (1999) noted that youth who sexually abuse others have had a high incidence of parental loss and difficulty with attachment as a result of the breakdown of early parent-child relationships. Pithers et al. (1998) theorized that insecure attachments between children and their parents may put the children at risk for the development of later sexual offending as well as delinquency and other adult criminal behaviors (Friedrich & Sim, 2006; Rich, 2003, 2009; Ryan et al., 2010).

Attachment is also required in order to develop empathy for others—something that juvenile sexual offenders lack. Empathy is built on having experienced early reciprocity from adults that models caring for one another.

ଔ ————————————————————

Wes, a 16-year-old who had sexually molested his younger sister, could not understand why she did not want to see him at the residential treatment center to which he had been sent. "What's the big deal?" he asked irritably. "I didn't hurt her or nothing. Why is everyone so freaked?" Told by his angry mother that the little girl was having nightmares, Wes shrugged impassively. "She'll get over it. She always was really dramatic." He seemed to have no concept of what the little girl was feeling—despite his own abuse at about her age by his stepfather.

———————————————————— ଛ

Like many other young abusers, Wes was not able to understand the impact of his behavior on his victim or care about the pain he had caused her.

The inability to connect with others, the failure to generate empathy in the face of the pain of others, and the fact that they cannot trust enough to become intimate robs young sexual abusers of the capacity to engage in meaningful peer relationships. Juvenile abusers lack the social skills to form these relationships, leading to feelings of rejection, isolation, and loneliness, which then further compound their withdrawal, anger, and mistrust of others (Friedrich & Sim, 2006; Rich, 2003, 2009; Righthand & Welch, 2004; Ryan et al., 2010).

When youth have effective social skills, they are able to form reciprocal relationships, demonstrate effective problem solving, exercise decision making, and experience a sense of control over their environment. Sexually abusive youth, on the other hand, have not mastered these tasks effectively and are characterized as having inadequate social skills (Becker, 1998; Becker & Hunter, 1997; Becker & Johnson, 2001; Rich, 2003, 2011; Righthand & Welch, 2004).

Cognitive and Academic Functioning

Research on juvenile sexual abusers indicates that a high percentage experience difficulty in school performance and learning (Barbaree, Marshall, & McCormick, 1998; Erooga & Masson, 2006; Miner, Siekert, & Ackland, 1997; O'Reilly & Carr, 2006; Rich, 2003; Righthand & Welch, 2004; Ryan et al., 2010). Many who act out sexually also exhibit learning disabilities, truancy, poor academic performance, and disruptive behaviors. Often they are placed in special classes. There are other youth, however, who do well in school, using this setting as their only safe and consistent environment (Righthand & Welch, 2004).

When juvenile abusers have difficulty in school, it may be for a variety of reasons. Some have cognitive impairments. In their study, Ferrara and McDonald (1996) estimated that between one fourth and one third of juvenile sexual offenders have some form of neurological impairment. These researchers further determined that many juveniles who act out sexually had particular difficulty in two areas: (a) executive functions such as planning, thinking in the abstract, inhibition of inappropriate impulses, and cognitive flexibility and (b) difficulties with expressive and receptive language (Righthand & Welch, 2004). Frustration over these difficulties may intensify these youth's feelings of isolation and anger putting them at further risk for acting out.

Behavioral Disorders, Delinquency, and Mental Health Issues

Other types of behavioral problems are often seen in youth who act out sexually. And many such youth have been diagnosed with recognizable mental disorders (Carter & Matson, 1999). Perhaps the most common documented diagnosis is conduct disorder, which refers to an individual consistently or repeatedly violating societal norms and rules expected for that age group. Those with conduct disorders may be aggressive toward people or animals, willfully destroy property, practice deceitfulness or commit theft, or be guilty of serious violation of rules set down by caretakers, their school, or society (Johnson, 2006; Miner et al., 1997; O'Reilly & Carr, 2006; Rich, 2003; Righthand & Welch, 2004; Ryan, 1999; Ryan et al., 2010; Ryan & Lane, 1997; Seto & Lalumiere, 2006).

☙

Tony, 13, who had been frequently truant from school, came to the attention of school officials who reported the situation to children's protection. When he was in school, Tony was belligerent, often initiating fights with other students and with teachers. He seemed to enjoy destroying other children's lunchboxes and had been ordered to pay for the last flattened lunchbox. Despite the fact that his destruction was witnessed, Tony fervently denied that he had either taken the lunch box or smashed it. He was also suspected of stealing other items from classmates but never admitted to the thefts. He had attempted to beat up smaller children on the playground on two separate occasions. Tony boasted that he had cut the ears off the family dog, but no one was sure if this was true. His mother did report that he was especially cruel to both the family dog and stray cats in the neighborhood.

☙

After an investigation by children's services, it was also discovered that Tony had sexually abused his younger sister.

Rich (2003) contends that a diagnosis of conduct disorder or oppositional defiant disorder "is almost a given because the diagnoses are virtually a description of the very behaviors that underpin much juvenile sexual offending" (p. 49). Attention deficit disorder and PTSD are also frequent diagnoses seen in the files of juveniles who act out sexually. These labels—though appearing in the *Diagnostic and Statistical Manual of Mental Disorders*—are not in the same category as more severe mental illnesses. Even in the face of more severe diagnoses, Rich (2003) cautions that professionals should be careful to assess the behavior fully. For example, shallow or superficial affect, lack of empathy, risk-taking behaviors, and egocentrism to the exclusion of others can also be seen as normal adolescent behaviors, which may be developmentally appropriate. And because a significant population of juvenile abusers have experienced sexual or physical abuse in their own lives or witnessed domestic violence or severe family dysfunction, sexually acting out teens may be modeling what they have seen rather than exhibiting true mental illness. In addition, it is difficult to determine what role substance abuse plays in juvenile behaviors. Some researchers have identified drugs and alcohol as playing a major part in the lives of young sexual abusers (Miner et al., 1999; Righthand & Welch, 2004; Smallbone, 2006).

Another diagnosis frequently seen in the histories of juvenile abusers is that of attention deficit disorder (ADD) or attention deficit/hyperactivity disorder (ADHD). Symptoms of ADD or ADHD may include an inability to concentrate or organize, impulsivity, easy distraction by stimuli, and failing to pay close attention to details. Adding hyperactivity creates symptoms like fidgeting, constant activity, excessive talking, and increased impulsivity. Research has uncovered that adolescents with ADD have sexual intercourse at an earlier age than their peers and that those with ADHD have more history of promiscuity (Barkley, 1998, 2002; Johnson, 2006). Johnson (2006) recounts that research points to the fact that socialization skills are problematic for both adolescents with ADHD and adolescent sexual abusers. Having found a significant number of those with ADHD in his own practice, Johnson concludes that this is important and often overlooked assessment criteria.

As previously mentioned, a significant amount of research has identified other antisocial and delinquent acts in the histories of juvenile sexual offenders (Rich, 2003; Righthand & Welch, 2004; Ryan, 1999; Ryan et al., 2010; Smallbone, 2006). The same individual factors that are precursors to delinquency—low intelligence, impulsivity, poor concentration, risk taking, and sensation seeking—combined with the family dynamics of divorce, abandonment, poor parental monitoring/supervision, abuse or neglect of children, parental conflict, and substance abuse, put children at risk for delinquency as well as being seen in juvenile sexual offenders (Almond, Canter, & Salfati, 2006; Ronis & Borduin, 2007; Rutter, 2003; Ryan, 1999; Smallbone, 2006).

In an effort to determine how juvenile sexual offenders and nonsexual offenders differ in characteristics, Ronis and Borduin (2007) studied 115 males, who they divided into five equal-sized groups: (a) sexual offenders against peers or adults, (b) sexual offenders against younger child victims, (c) violent nonsexual offenders, (d) nonviolent nonsexual offenders, and (e) nondelinquents (p. 154). The mean age of their sample was between 13.8 and 14.3 years. The race was predominantly Caucasian (61%–78%) with 21%–39% African American. Whereas none of the nondelinquents had a history of physical or sexual abuse, 35% of those offending against peers or adults and 48% of those abusing younger children had been abused physically or sexually (p. 155). Based on interviews and a series of assessment tools, these researchers determined that juvenile sexual offenders and other types of delinquents share the same problems, including poor bonding with family and school as well as high involvement with deviant peers. These authors did acknowledge that 94% of offenders against peers and adults and 89% of offenders against child victims had also been adjudicated for nonsexual offenses (p. 161). They also determined that the causal factors in the offenders' background did not differ according to those who chose older victims and those who victimized younger children.

Sexual Knowledge and Experience

Most researchers believe that youth who sexually abuse others have had prior sexual experience, often to a degree that exceeds other nonsexually abusive juveniles (Brown & Schwartz, 2006; Erooga & Masson, 2006; Righthand & Welch, 2004; Ryan et al., 2010). Certainly some juveniles who sexually abuse have their own histories of abuse. And some have been exposed to sexuality in their home environment or exposed to pornography. Wieckowski, Hartsoe, Mayer, & Shortz (1998) found that exposure to pornographic material at a young age was especially prevalent among juveniles who sexually abuse. Because youth are sexually active earlier now than in the past, the likelihood of preadolescents and adolescents to have experienced some type of sexual interaction with peers is greater. The American Academy of Pediatrics (2001) reports that the juveniles most likely to engage in early sexual activity are those with social, behavioral, or emotional problems; low intelligence; learning problems or low academic performance; family dysfunction; and poor parental supervision. Given the fact that many of these characteristics also pertain to juveniles who sexually abuse, it stands to reason that they may have had other types of sexual experiences. On the other hand, some theorists would argue that those who sexually abuse do so because they lack the social skills to engage in sexual behaviors with peers.

Even when youth do have early sexual experiences, the understanding and interpretation of sexual behaviors may be problematic. In a study of 1,600 juvenile sexual offenders, Ryan et al. (1996) found that only one third of those studied saw sex as a way to demonstrate caring or love to another. Rather, many saw sex as a way to feel powerful and in control, to relieve anger, or to hurt, degrade, or punish (Righthand & Welch, 2004).

Healthy sexual education therefore becomes an important part of treating juveniles who sexually abuse. Although sexual education has been recognized since programs for abusive youth were initially developed, Brown and Schwartz (2006) suggest that there is a paradigm shift in the way that treatment is recommended for youth. Initially, juvenile treatment in the area of sexuality mirrored adult treatment programs that also include such material. Brown and Schwartz trace the move away from the traditional adult-based model to a more holistic model specifically for juveniles.

Further, these authors believe that a paradigm shift is based on significant changes in the beliefs in the field about sexuality. Sexuality is now seen from a more health-based perspective instead of as the basis for problematic behavior.

Girls Who Sexually Abuse

Much of the existing literature mentioned so far refers to sexual abuses by male juveniles because it is estimated that between 92% and 98% of youth offenders are males, leaving a small percentage of females who are known to be abusers (Finkelhor et al., 2009; Frey, 2006; Hunter, Becker, & Lexier, 2006; Rich, 2003; Righthand & Welch, 2004; Vandiver & Teske, 2006). There is some speculation that there may be more girls who abuse others, but they manage to hide their abusive behavior in seemingly acceptable behaviors (e.g., helping with toileting, bathing) that involve childcare situations. Studies conducted on juvenile female offenders are therefore frequently based on small samples, and therefore, accurate results are difficult. Only one study (see Vandiver & Kercher, 2004) was able to generate a sample of over 100 female juveniles.

Studies of female offenders found that they were more likely than their male counterparts to have been victims of sexual abuse. They have also

been victims of physical and emotional abuse. In general, the abuse histories of girls who abuse are more severe than boys (Gil & Johnson, 1993; Hunter et al., 2006; Righthand & Welch, 2004; Vandiver & Teske, 2006). Young female offenders also tend to come from homes where there are high levels of family dysfunction and little parental support or nurture, often impeding their ability to attach effectively and develop healthy self-esteem (Frey, 2006; Righthand & Welch, 2004).

Like youthful male offenders, girls who sexually abuse have often been involved in other delinquent acts. They have also been found to be sexually promiscuous, have significant peer relationship problems, and have problems with school performance. These girls have often been involved with the mental health system with significant degrees of psychopathology (Hunter et al., 2006; Righthand & Welch, 2004; Robinson, 2006; Ryan et al., 2010; Vandiver & Teske, 2006). Typically, females tend to internalize their abuse backgrounds, resulting in such self-abusive behaviors as substance abuse, suicidal ideation or behaviors, self-mutilation, and unprotected and risky sex.

The age at which girls begin to sexually abuse differs according to the research study. Earlier studies, based upon the histories of adult females as well as small samples of juvenile females who were known to have sexually abused, reported that girls began abusing at slightly older ages than boys (Elliott, 1993; Ryan & Lane, 1997). However, Gil and Johnson (1993), suggesting that girls are reacting to their own victimization, report that they may begin abusing other children at young ages. In their study of both male and female juveniles who came to the attention of the justice system in Texas, Vandiver and Teske (2006) report that the average age of the female offender was 14.16 years and the male was 14.82 years. However, the distribution differed with over half of the females falling between the ages of 11 and 13, whereas more than half of the males fell between 14 and 16.

Victim selection shows some variation between young females and males who are abusive. The selected victim gender for both females and males is thought by most researchers to be girls (Elliot, 1993; Gil & Johnson, 1993; Vandiver & Teske, 2006), whereas others (Vandiver & Teske, 2006) believe that female abusers are more likely to depend upon opportunity and availability of potential victims rather than having a specific gender preference.

The average age of the victims of both female and male abusers also differs slightly. Whereas the abusers in Vandiver and Teske's (2006) study had an average age of victim of 7.6 years for female abusers and 8.4 years for male abusers (p. 161), the females were more likely to victimize children between infancy and 5 years.

LEGAL AND ETHICAL ISSUES IN WORKING WITH JUVENILE SEXUAL ABUSERS

Working with children and adolescents brings up ethical dilemmas that must be carefully considered. In many cases, these are also connected with legal decisions. There are several significant questions that must be addressed before continuing on to a discussion of treatment for juvenile abusers.

Latham and Kinscherff (2006) believe that a first issue to be addressed is based on who has custody of the child or adolescent. Because youth are by definition underage, proper informed consent must be obtained from the legal guardian(s), whether this is the parents or an agency, before treatment can proceed. If there are two legal parents involved and they disagree about what professional services should be provided to the child, a court decision may become necessary. State and federal laws differ about when persons under the age of 18 can authorize their own treatment, so those working with such youth will need to be fully cognizant of the laws of their particular state. Some states allow "emancipated minors" to authorize their own treatment, but this again will vary.

Confidentiality rights can also come into question when working with young abusers. Latham and Kinscherff (2006) point out that some confusion can be lessened if professionals understand the difference between confidentiality and privilege when dealing with legal matters. *Confidentiality* refers to "the general duty to keep private information that is received while providing services" (p. 227). There are several limitations to professionals' obligation to keep client information confidential; these include if clients are threats to themselves or to others or if they are abusing children. Once again, when working with children, privilege "is an exception to the general duty to testify about matters of which they have personal knowledge when called upon to do so in court" (Latham & Kinscherff, 2006, p. 227). Once again, the exact interpretation of each of these is determined by state law. These authors conclude that

> if clinicians do not keep the distinction between confidentiality and privilege clear, it will be difficult to decide how to protect professional communications. Testamentary privilege applies *only* when the content of those communications may be offered into evidence in a legal proceeding. (p. 228)

Thus, when a parent with legal custody of a juvenile abuser signs a release to allow information about a son or daughter to be shared with another information agency, it is confidentiality and not privilege that is involved.

TREATMENT ISSUES FOR JUVENILES

Although Chapter 13 addresses treatment issues for adult offenders, a discussion of treatment for juvenile offenders might imply that they are the same or similar to adults in their treatment needs. However, that is not necessarily the case for several reasons. First, not all children and adolescents who abuse others can be classified as sexual offenders. As mentioned earlier, some fall within the category of children who are reacting to their own abuse and respond well to treatment. For others, it is not as clear. Are they reactive with more serious pathology, or are they budding sexual offenders? Treatment programs too grapple with this question. Any child who acts out sexually should receive some type of assessment and possibly treatment, but the needs of these juveniles may differ according to their diagnosis.

Second, juveniles are different from adults in that they are at different developmental stages. Their offending patterns are often influenced by their development at the time of the abuse, and some attention must be given to the distinction between sex play and experimentation gone astray and the actual development of sex-offending patterns. Further, developing patterns may not be as well established as those of adult offenders and are therefore more conducive to positive treatment outcomes.

Third, although the family may or may not figure in the treatment of adult offenders, it is not as significant as when one is treating juvenile abusers. The dependent status of juveniles in most cases requires that some family—natural, foster, or adopted—be involved in treatment. Fourth, the fact that juveniles are required to receive an education until a certain age means that the educational system also comes into play when treatment is under discussion. Thus, the complex issues inherent in the treatment of juveniles who sexually abuse require that the discussion of these techniques be kept separate from the discussion of the treatment of adult sexual offenders.

Rich (2003) suggests that the current models for treatment of juveniles who sexually abuse are

often too simplistic, or unintegrated, focusing on either (a) a forensic and correctional approach assuming that the clinical treatment of juvenile sexual offenders is dealt with elsewhere (in specialized treatment program), or (b) a mental health approach that fails to recognize and

incorporate a forensic mind-set and assumes that criminal issues either are not present or have been dealt with elsewhere (presumably in a prior correctional program). . . . The task, then, is to develop practitioners who understand the complexities of the juvenile sexual offender, are trained in both forensics and mental health, and understand the world and behavior of the adolescent. . . . "Our work with juvenile sexual offenders requires the mental health approach be informed and guided by a forensic mind-set that seeks to understand offending and related behaviors as meeting criminogenic needs (factors that contribute to criminal behavior), as well as needs related to personal identity, social attachment, and emotional satisfaction." (pp. 5–6)

Early work with juvenile offenders (see the National Adolescent Perpetrator Network, pp. 126–127, as cited in Becker, 1990; Efta-Breitbach & Freeman, 2004a) outlined significant issues that must be addressed with juvenile sexual abusers. These included

- accepting responsibility for the abuse without externalizing the blame;
- identifying their cycle of offending behavior;
- developing the ability to interrupt the cycle before an offense occurs;
- understanding their own victimization;
- developing empathy for victims;
- coming to terms with their own power and control issues;
- reducing deviant arousal;
- developing a positive sexual identity;
- understanding the consequences of the abusive behavior for the family, the victim, and the victim's family;
- understanding their own family dysfunction and how it triggers the juvenile's abusive behaviors;
- understanding their own cognitive distortions;
- learning to recognize and express feelings;
- learning appropriate skills for improved relationships with peers and developing such relationships;
- developing trusting relationships with adults;

- overcoming addictions or other delinquent acts;
- learning to identify skill deficits that prevent healthy functioning and developing these skills; and
- considering how to make restitution to victims and the community.

The similarity to the treatment goals with adult offenders does not go without notice. Although these goals are still used within the treatment framework of juveniles, those involved in such treatment caution that work with youths necessitates attention to the needs of this population as well.

What does the treatment of juvenile abusers entail, and how is it currently carried out? In a survey of 800 programs for male and female sexual offenders, Burton and Smith-Darden (2001) included 357 programs for juvenile offenders that served 6,422 children and adolescents of which 69% treated boys and 31% treated girls. Despite these statistics, the population in facilities for girls was much smaller, and only about 7% of the juvenile offenders were female compared to 93% male (as cited in Rich, 2011, p. 221). Another deceptive aspect of these data is that after considering all the aspects of these programs, it became apparent that 41% of the total care was provided in residential settings, whereas 59% on an outpatient basis (Burton & Smith-Darden, 2001, as cited in Rich, 2003, p. 222).

The average length of treatment for both male and female adolescents was about 18 months, whereas for younger children the length of care averaged 13 months for outpatient services and 10 months for residential. In outpatient care, juveniles attended an average of one 55-minute therapy session, 80 to 90 minutes of group therapy, and an average of a 60-minute family session. In a residential setting, the juveniles attended one or two sessions of 50 to 55 minutes of individual therapy, three or four 70- to 85-minute group sessions, and one 60- to 70-minute family session (Burton & Smith-Darden, 2001,

as cited in Rich, 2003, p. 222). Within these sessions, the most widely discussed topic was sexual assault and the dysfunctional behavioral cycle (83%), art therapy (30%), experiential therapy (18%), and sex education (13%) (Burton & Smith-Darden, 2001, as cited in Rich, 2003, p. 222).

Lundrigan (2001) suggests that there are a variety of different types of care available for juveniles who sexually abuse. Level A facilities are either holding facilities or treatment centers. Holding facilities (e.g., detention centers, locked psychiatric units) keep juveniles temporarily until they are either stabilized and/or other long-term programs can be located. There is little or no intensive treatment available in holding facilities. Secure treatment facilities, on the other hand, provide an atmosphere of high staff-to-client ratio and high structure in a locked environment where intensive treatment can be conducted. Some of these are just residential (correctional) in nature, whereas others are psychiatric. The youth within these settings require the most intensive treatment (Lundrigan, 2001).

Level B settings provide intensive treatment for the individual as well as group and family but are less physically restrictive. Some treat sexual offenders specifically, whereas others are generic, addressing a variety of juvenile problems. Although the approaches may differ from institution to institution, most are based on a milieu delivery system including the three components: residential, clinical, and educational services.

Level C includes other living arrangements such as specialized foster care, small group homes, or independent living programs. Specialized foster parents are specially trained to work with a specific population—in this case, juvenile sexual offenders—and are an integral part of the treatment team. The juvenile will attend some type of treatment provided by a local agency and may attend public or private (agency-based) school. This is a transition into the community for the juvenile who needs less supervision.

Independent living is the last out-of-home setting usually for older juveniles who are about ready to live on their own. They will probably still attend group and individual therapy and may also access other community resources (e.g., tracking programs).

Some juveniles are able to participate in community-based treatment and live within the community—at home or with relatives. Some attend specialized school programs, whereas others go to public schools.

Treatment for juveniles who sexually abuse—whether residential or community based—follows a relatively characteristic set of steps. Initially there is an *intake*, which gathers information necessary for a diagnosis. *Assessment* involves an exploration of psychosocial factors including the juvenile's offending patterns, his or her other delinquent behaviors, family demographics, supports available to him or her, and an evaluation of the level of cooperation expected from the juvenile and the family. Part of this assessment will also be an evaluation of the risk to reoffend. This assessment culminates in the formulation of a treatment plan (Lundrigan, 2001; Rich, 2003; Schmidt et al., 2012).

Treatment planning involves working with the juvenile to develop an anticipated procedure for treatment. Having the juvenile "buy into" such a plan is crucial to the success of treatment. Some programs use treatment contracts where the worker and the juvenile outline the steps of treatment together and each signs off on the plan.

ଓଃ

Ty was a 15-year-old African American boy who had been left with a withered arm by a congenital abnormality. He was self-conscious about it and often kept it under his shirt in an almost Napoleonic manner. His small stature completed the image. Because of his deformity and perceived helplessness, Ty had not been invited into one of the gangs that populated his neighborhood, a fact that was obviously seen as a disgrace. It became evident in the assessment at the residential treatment center in which he had been placed that Ty's feelings of inferiority and his desperate need for recognition and superiority combined with the scars of his own

sexual abuse by his father motivated him to target younger boys whom he abused sexually. At first, Ty was not only unable to admit that he had offended against young boys but denied his own abuse as well. He was belligerent and uncooperative with an attitude that caused the other boys in his unit to both taunt him and fear his rage. The first step in his treatment was to gain enough trust in his therapist to allow treatment to progress. John, his therapist, who, also small in stature, had developed himself physically through weight lifting, engaged Ty by suggesting that he could help Ty to "develop his muscles" without referring to the arm specifically. Once trust had been developed, Ty and John designed a treatment plan that included not only Ty admitting to his offenses and outlining them step by step but also exploring his own victimization, learning the social skills he would need to develop healthy relationships with peers, and working within his family to develop more functional and satisfying relationships. Built into the treatment plan as an incentive were regular workouts in the gym under John's direction. The hope was that Ty's development of a more powerful body combined with addressing such treatment issues as understanding his offense cycle, his own abuse, his family issues, and his ways of coping would help him to develop the confidence to not need to sexually offend. Fortunately for all, the plan was successful.

ଃଓ

The process of treatment involves enhancing the youth's understanding of himself or herself and the world and giving him or her the skills to navigate in that world. The family and the home environment do not always make this easy, and many youth struggle with these issues. The approach favored by most treatment facilities seeing youthful abusers is group-based cognitive-behavioral interventions that allow youth to focus on changing their attitudes and then behavior (Schmidt et al., 2012).

The hoped-for outcome of treatment is that the juvenile will have an awareness of the offense cycle as well as develop skills that allow him or her to form healthy relationships with peers and others. *Relapse prevention planning* is based on knowing his or her offense cycle and how to prevent abusive behavior in the future. Hopefully there will be the availability of some type of *treatment follow-up* in the form of an outpatient program or group in the community. This all-too-often-missing resource will allow youth to maintain the progress they have made in intensive treatment.

Risk for Recidivism

Treatment programs are especially interested in research regarding what factors are associated with juveniles' reoffending and base their programs on these factors. Research has identified several variables that appear to correlate with recidivism in young abusers.

• *Failure to complete (sexual offender–specific) treatment* is cited by numerous sources as a contributor to reoffending (Efta-Breitbach & Freeman, 2004b; Rasmussen, 2004; Rich, 2003; Worling & Langstrom, 2006). When juveniles do not complete treatment, it may be because they have not initially engaged or because they do not see the inherent benefits in change.

• *Family history and dysfunction* is another risk factor for reoffending (Efta-Breitbach & Freeman, 2004b; Rasmussen, 2004). Sometimes juveniles are motivated in treatment to change, but lack of support of these changes from the family sabotages treatment efforts. Or some youth cannot see themselves getting beyond historical family limitations. As one young sex offender commented, "My old man was a sex offender and so was his. What chance do I have?"

• *Prior abuse/maltreatment* in a juvenile's own background can put him or her at risk for continued offending (Efta-Breitbach & Freeman, 2004b; Rasmussen, 2004; Rich, 2003; Schmidt et al., 2012; Worling & Langstrom, 2006). The link between one's own abuse and acting it out is a complex one. Many researchers believe that failure to understand their own histories leaves some

youth with a compulsion to act the abuse out. Others may not agree. In her sample of 170 juvenile offenders, Rasmussen (2004) found that sexual abuse in juveniles' histories was only weakly linked with recidivism. Langstrom and Grann (2000) also found that historical factors like abuse did not necessarily predict relapse. However, if the abuse has created a *deviant sexual interest* in the juvenile that does not respond to treatment, the prognosis for relapse may be different (Efta-Breitbach & Freeman, 2004b; Worling & Langstrom, 2006).

<hr>

Dwayne was sexually abused by his father and two older brothers when he was quite young. As a 10-year old, he was then sexually abused by a priest. All of the abuse involved sodomy, and Dwayne, as a teen, soon found that he could not become sexually aroused unless sodomy was involved. He recognized that homosexuality was not accepted within his peer group, nor paradoxically was it condoned at home. Dwayne soon found that he could become aroused by molesting and sodomizing young boys. Even after being arrested and undergoing treatment, his deviant sexual arousal patterns did not change. Soon after he was released from a residential program for young offenders, Dwayne began molesting again.

<hr>

Another factor that supports the possibility of reoffending relates to the nature of the offense. For example, juveniles who have *multiple victims* are more likely to offend again (Efta-Breitbach & Freeman, 2004b; Rasmussen, 2004; Worling & Langstrom, 2006). Those who select *strangers as victims* may also be at higher risk to reoffend (Langstrom & Grann, 2000; Worling & Langstrom, 2006). And those juveniles who demonstrate impulsivity that cannot be curbed are also at higher risk (Worling & Langstrom, 2006).

Researchers who study juvenile offenders also point to *social isolation* as a risk factor to relapse (Hanson, 2000; Langstrom & Grann, 2000; Rich, 2003; Worling & Langstrom, 2006). When youth who have abused are unable to form interesting and fulfilling peer relationships, their feelings of rejection and exclusion may direct them to abuse younger children.

The relationship between mental health problems and the likelihood of a juvenile to reoffend is also complex. Some types of mental illness present more of a risk than others. Surprisingly, it was found that it is often the healthier youth who are more prone to relapse. One exception is that of a diagnosis of antisocial personality disorder, which may correlate with reoffending (Efta-Breitbach & Freeman, 2004b). The presence of substance abuse in the juvenile's profile can also be positively connected with recidivism.

The aforementioned risk factors can also be offset by what are known as resiliency factors. These are factors that promote successful coping in the face of difficult or risk situations. For juvenile offenders, there are several of these that could contribute to their ability to keep from reoffending. Higher intellectual or cognitive abilities, for example, enable juveniles to develop better coping mechanisms that may prevent reoffending. Better command of the language may allow juveniles to get their needs met more effectively and negotiate more satisfying relationships with others (Efta-Breitbach & Freeman, 2004b; Langstrom & Grann, 2000; Worling & Langstrom, 2006). Some theorists have also argued that higher intellectual capacity can also work as a risk factor, allowing more clever manipulation of victims (Luthar, 1991).

Another resiliency factor is that youth who are able to develop higher self-esteem leading to higher levels of self-efficacy are better able to make choices that do not involve reoffending. Those juveniles capable of self-regulation, enabling them to regulate their emotional reactivity and react positively in the face of stressful events, are also less likely to reoffend (Efta-Breitbach & Freeman, 2004b; Worling & Langstrom, 2006).

Through self-regulation, individuals can also develop the attitude that they can control their own life course. For these people, the locus of control is not seen as something outside themselves but something that comes from within. They feel more in control with more power over their lives and environment. When juveniles are helped to develop these attitudes, their risk for reoffending decreases (Efta-Breitbach & Freeman, 2004b).

And finally, some authors (see Henry, 1999) found that those who espoused some type of faith had a better sense of purpose, better self-esteem, and more ability to make better choices than to reoffend.

Treatment programs with juvenile offenders seek to enhance the resiliency factors to lessen the risk of reoffending.

WORKING WITH JUVENILE SEXUAL ABUSERS

Addressing specifically adolescent sexual offenders, Lundrigan (2001) suggests that those seeking to work with this population face several challenges that fall into four categories: (a) clients, (b) intra- and interpersonal struggles inherent in this work, (c) limitations of the system, and (d) a society that contributes to and promotes sexual misconduct.

Clients themselves can be complex and demanding. On one hand, they represent a fragile population beset with their own emotional issues resulting from their personal trauma. On the other hand, their way of coping with these feelings of vulnerability is to manipulate others and sometimes become aggressive as they seek to fill their unmet needs. The victim constantly wars with the perpetrator in one sometimes small body. Clinicians and child care personnel working with juvenile abusers must be able to cope with the overt behaviors connecting with the offending patterns, while helping them to understand and confront their own thoughts, feelings, and maladaptive behaviors. At the same time, a worker must recognize the pain and trauma from which the client suffers, and although this pain is not an excuse for the offending behavior, it has certainly contributed to the behavior.

Intrapersonally, workers often find that they have preconceived ideas about sexual abusers—even those in smaller packages—that must be faced and overcome. Then, juvenile abusers have learned to survive through manipulation. Their behaviors or attitudes may replicate aspects of difficult relationships in the workers' lives and, as a result, bring up a variety of negative feelings. Not only do abusers "push buttons" for many of those who work with them but their families can also be challenging and may also push emotional buttons. The sexually stimulating material that is very much at the forefront of this work might also cause issues for workers. Workers who have themselves been victimized in the past may have responses to this population that must be attended to. And workers must guard against falling into the clients' typical stance of minimizing their abusive behaviors (Lundrigan, 2001).

Working with such a difficult population can also spill over into conflicts with coworkers. Consistency is paramount when working with troubled youth, and disagreements over policies or different styles not only create issues for staff but can be detrimental for clients.

In any system, stresses can arise. However, systems that address problematic behaviors in youth can be especially fraught with problems. And not only are staff working within the treatment program but they must interface with other agencies such as the juvenile justice system, the child protection system, the court system, the mental health system, and the police, all of whom may be pulling in different directions with contradictory results (Lundrigan, 2001; Rich, 2003).

And finally, frustration arises when those who work with juvenile sexual offenders interact with the world that seems intent upon sabotaging the efforts of treatment. In U.S. society, sexuality is rampant with openly displayed sexual materials, sexual themes in mass media entertainment, and an attitude that prizes sexual conquests. The Internet is easily accessible to meet a variety of sexual appetites. As one worker put it:

ॐ

I spend my working days trying to help young offenders to extinguish sexual messages from their every thought and action and then return home to be barraged by a myriad of sexual messages. ৪০

Despite these challenges, working with juvenile sexual abusers, for many of whom the prognosis is positive, can be a rewarding experience.

Summary

Over the last few decades, there has been increased interest in understanding juveniles who sexually offend and designing treatment for them. Some sources estimate that approximately 1 in 6 of those arrested for sexual assaults are juveniles. Adults are not always ready to recognize a child or teen's sexual behavior as an offense. Yet given the fact that studies also show that effective early intervention usually prevents the juvenile from becoming an adult sex offender, recognition and intervention are important.

There are some distinct differences between adult and juvenile offenders. In fact, not all children who act out sexually can be considered to be sexual offenders. Some children are trying to make sense of the abuse that they experienced and are termed *sexually reactive*, whereas others have a more serious pattern of sexual offenses. Several researchers have developed typologies to characterize the different levels of juveniles who act out sexually (Bonner et al., 1999; Hall et al., 2002; Johnson, 2009; Pithers et al., 1998).

Most of those who act out sexually as juveniles have maltreatment histories. A large percentage is also from dysfunctional families. They may have faulty attachment with early caretakers and have difficulties with peer relationships, leaving them feeling isolated. Many juvenile sexual offenders have also committed other nonsexual offenses. The typical youth who sexually offends has difficulty in school and may have mental health issues. Given that their own early sexual experiences were abusive, these youth also have deviant ideas of sexuality and sexual relationships. Girls who sexually abuse others are even more likely than their male counterparts to have been sexually abused themselves.

There are specific legal and ethical issues inherent in working with juvenile offenders. First, they are underage, and therefore, treatment will necessitate permission from their parents. Confidentiality may require more careful interpretation than that with adult offenders.

Treatment for juvenile offenders is also more complex as these youth are at different developmental stages, requiring approaches that take this fact into consideration. Cognitive-behavioral techniques seem to be the most successful. Goals of treatment are getting the youth to accept responsibility for the offense, identifying the cycle of offending behavior, helping him or her to interrupt that offending cycle, and working with the family to support the offender's progress. The average length of treatment for a juvenile is approximately 18 months although it may vary according to the needs of the young offender. Some youth are treated on an outpatient basis, whereas others receive treatment through institutional treatment centers. Whether or not a juvenile reoffends sexually will depend on a variety of risk and resilience factors.

Working with juvenile sexual offenders can be complex and demanding. Consistency is vital to helping these youth develop the trust that motivates change.

Review Questions

1. Are all children who act out against others sexually considered to be juvenile offenders? Please explain.

2. How do juvenile offenders differ from adult offenders?

3. What are some typologies of youth who act out sexually?

4. What are some family dynamics for juvenile offenders?

5. In what areas might juvenile offenders have difficulties?

6. What are some common diagnoses for youth who sexually abuse?

7. What are some differences between girls and boys who sexually abuse?

8. What are some legal and ethical issues inherent in working with juveniles who sexually offend?

9. What are some treatment issues that are peculiar to juvenile offenders?

10. What should one consider when working with this population?

CHAPTER 9

Offenders in Roles of Authority

Teachers, Coaches, Day Care Providers, and Therapists

Over the last decade, there has been an increasing amount of publicity about child sexual abuse at the hands of those who are in positions of authority, allowing them special access to victims. Although formerly almost above suspicion, teachers, coaches, therapists, and even clergy joined the ranks of perpetrators. Many have wondered why such trusted professions should have come under scrutiny. The answer is to be found not in the profession itself but in the fact that such professions may attract individuals who seek—either consciously or unconsciously—opportunities for access to children.

CONTRIBUTORS TO ABUSE BY HELPING PROFESSIONALS

What factors contribute to child sexual abuse by professionals who work with children? The most obvious factor is opportunity—having proximity to children that may be unsupervised due to the trust given the profession.

———— ⊗ ————

I went to school in a very small, very rural town where there was only one school. In fact, there was only one teacher. When Mr. Moe, a large, handsome man who was rumored to be a former football player, came to our school, we were all in awe of him. He was like a Pied Piper—an attraction for all of us. The girls especially used to ask for special help after school just so that we could stay there with him. He'd give it to us cheerfully enough and even seemed to enjoy our crushes on him. But it was the boys, he said, who really needed his help. He'd single out a boy who he said was far behind, and after we'd gotten whatever help he felt we needed, Mr. Moe would send the rest of us home and keep this one boy even later. I'm not sure how it all came out, but suddenly there were whispers of scandal, and Mr. Moe just disappeared one day. Years later, I would learn that he had been molesting many of the boys and even a few girls. We were all available to him. He could have molested any of us, and those who were "chosen" would never have said a word because Mr. Moe was such a trusted, respected person in the town.

———— ⊗ ————

Professionals who work with children are often regarded with a great deal of respect by both parents and their children. Parents who are seeking help may not want to admit that there is anything amiss.

> "We were having such a hard time with Emmy," explained one mother, "that when we found a therapist who could deal with her outrageous behavior, we were so thankful. I gave this man an inordinate amount of power over my daughter—over my whole family. When my other daughter told me that Emmy had confided that she was being abused by the therapist, I did not want to believe it. She was such a difficult kid. She'd say anything, I reasoned. It took Emmy's attempt at suicide and subsequent hospitalization for me to wake up and recognize that she had been telling the truth."

Abuse by some professionals is so far out of our frame of reference that it is hard to imagine. At one time, abuse by clergy, for example, was met with total disbelief. How could a "man [or woman] of God" be capable of sexually molesting a child? Unfortunately, the clergy abuse scandals across the United States have made Americans recognize that clergy too may be among the abusers of children (see Chapter 10).

ABUSE GOES TO SCHOOL: EDUCATORS AND COACHES AS ABUSERS

Abuse by Teachers

Teachers, those professionals who have the most influence on and proximity to children after their parents, have also been among those who abuse children. In 1989, Wishnietsky (1991) surveyed high school graduates in North Carolina and discovered that 17.5% reported that they had been touched sexually by a teacher with 13.5% having had intercourse with a teacher. In 1993, a study done by Wellesley Centers for Women uncovered that 4,200 girls in grades 2 through 12 reported being sexually abused or sexually harassed in a school setting. Of these girls, 3.7% accused a teacher, school administrator, or other school staff member of the abuse (Stein, Marshall, & Tropp, 1993). Shakeshaft and Cohan's (1995) study surveyed 778 superintendents in New York State in an effort to identify the incidence of sexual misconduct of educators against students, uncovering 225 cases of sexual abuse by teachers over a 4-year period. Perhaps some of the most extensive work was done under the auspices of the American Association of University Women (AAUW). A 1993 study of 1,632 field surveys looked at 79 U.S. public schools, concentrating on students in grades 8 through 11, and found that 25% of the females and 10% of the males said that they had been sexually harassed by a member of the faculty or school staff (AAUW, 1993). The later replication of that study, consisting of 2,063 field surveys, found that a total of 9.6% students reported teacher sexual abuse with 56% of these being females and 44% males (AAUW, 2001).

Of the students reporting that they were targeted sexually by teachers, 51.5% were Caucasian, 25.3% were of African descent, 15.7% were Latino/a, and less than 1% (0.5%) were Asian (Shakeshaft, 2004). As recently as 2007, a nationwide Associated Press investigation published a report disclosing that 2,570 educators lost credentials or were sanctioned for alleged sexual misconduct between 2001 and 2005 (Associated Press, 2008, as cited in Morgenbesser, 2010).

The roles of the abusive school personnel varied depending upon the study. The AAUW (2001) and Shakeshaft (2003) estimated that about 18% of these were teachers, 15% coaches, 13% substitute teachers, 12% bus drivers, 11% teacher's aids, 6% principals, 5% counselors, and the remainder falling into the categories of security guards or other school staff (Shakeshaft, 2004).

Abuse by male teachers far outweighed abuse by female teachers. A 1998 examination of newspaper stories on sexual abuse by teachers reported that 80% of the offenders were male teachers as opposed to 20% female teachers (Hendrie, 1998). In a Texas-based study of 606 abusive teachers, Jennings and Tharp (2003) reported that over 83% were males and not quite 13% were females.

The AAUW (2001) analysis found that 57.2% of the offenders were males, whereas 42.8% were females, uncovering a much higher rate of females as abusers than in other studies. Kinnear (2007) also points out that no matter the statistical rate of prevalence, male teachers receive stiffer sentences when they are apprehended. This author also criticizes the fact that there is no central registry that keeps track of teachers who have been found guilty or convicted of child sexual abuse, thus allowing the possibility of teachers to be quietly transferred to other states where they may continue to teach and possibly abuse.

Ironically, perhaps one of the best-known cases of sexual involvement between a student and a teacher involved a female rather than a male educator. In 1997 in Burien, Washington, 36-year-old Mary Kay LeTourneau, a wife and mother with four children, admitted having sexual relations with Vili Fualaau, a 6th grader. They had met when Vili was in the teacher's second grade class and had continued a friendship over the years. As the relationship became more involved, LeTourneau blamed her own marital problems for the eventual sexual involvement. LeTourneau was convicted of child rape and sentenced to 7 ½ years in prison. But pleas from the defendant and even the boy's mother saw the sentence reduced to 6 months plus a suspended sentence for the remainder of the time with the provision that she not see Vili (Cloud, 1998; Courtois, 2010; Kinnear, 2007; Knoll, 2010). When she was again found with the boy, her prison sentence was reimposed. During her prison stay, her husband divorced her. When released from prison, LeTourneau married Vili Fualaau, then 22 (Becker, 2005; Knoll, 2010).

The LeTourneau case was controversial, to say the least. Some even argued that perhaps there was more to the relationship than child abuse, but the ages of the adult and the child required that it be treated as such. Some critics suggest that this view is one more example of the dual standard of society, for had the gender of the victim been female and the gender of the offender male, there might have been criticism.

One advantage that teachers have as perpetrators is the time that they are able to spend with children. One former teacher perpetrator serving time for multiple offenses admitted the following:

ᘒ _____

It was easy to find things that I could do with the kids that did not create suspicion. From helping me to clean up the classroom and feeding the gerbils to giving them remedial help, all explanations seemed plausible. No one really questioned me. ᘒ

Van Dam (2006) suggests that the more socially skilled molesters like teachers groom the community as well as the child. The offender in the previous example explained that he made himself an integral part of the educational community, and this gave him more opportunities.

ᘒ _____

I found that if I volunteered for anything the administration was looking for help with, I got the reputation for being a really dedicated teacher. The principal actually offered me chances to be with kids from doing special projects with them to chaperoning field trips. And once the abuse came out, no one believed it at first. The principal brought me into his office and almost apologized for having to report me. ᘒ

Although there is a significant amount of research on the effects of child sexual abuse on children, there is a lesser amount on the effects of abuse by teachers. There is some indication that there may be a risk of suicidality among victims, but there is certainly depression and low self-esteem (Knoll, 2010). Courtois (2010) likens the effects of abuse by educators to those from incest, given the betrayal of trust present in both situations. Most experts feel that, given the profound effect that teachers especially have on the lives of children, this betrayal creates significant emotional problems for the young victims (Courtois, 2010; Knoll, 2010).

Abuse by Coaches

Coaches, too, often ingratiate themselves with administrators. One high school was so desperate for a girls' softball coach that the administration recruited a man whose questionable references in relation to his boundaries almost denied him being hired in the first place. Van Dam (2006) recounts that coaches may be in such demand that their schools and leagues become apologists for their difficult behaviors.

☙ ─────────────────────

Over the years, parents complained: [Coach] Carl was gruff. His manner was offensive. He yelled at the players and belittled the children and parents alike. He brazenly pulled on children's ears, slapped their bottoms, told them they were useless, and on occasion, would grab at clothing to pull it off. Sometimes the shirt tore off, sometimes the pants. Parents would usually watch in amazement but never knew what to do or say. . . . Parents who complained also found their children benched or kicked off the team. As a result, children begged their parents to say nothing. (p. 26)

☙

Coaches with personalities like Carl have less difficulty explaining their behaviors if they become suspect. "That's just who they are," supporters argue.

Fasting and Brackenridge (2009) suggest that abuse by coaches is made possible by several qualities of the coach-athlete relationship. First, the relationship between the athlete and the coach is based on power with the coach in the position of extreme power. Knowledge, wisdom, and authority are the basis of the coach's power, and the athlete knows that his or her future in sports rests in the hands of the coach. In fact, this power goes beyond just the athlete's performance on the field of his or her sport and extends into his or her personal life. The coach has power over the athlete's eating habits, sleeping habits, recreation, and school career. But perhaps the coach's greatest power is the ability to enhance or diminish the athlete's self-esteem (p. 24).

Coaches are in an excellent position to nurture and groom their players. Often unscreened and volunteers themselves, they are nonetheless given complete control over their child athletes (Courtois, 2010; Parent, 2011; Parent & Demers, 2011; Peterson, 2004). They have often already won the trust of the children and youth, and the approval of one's coach is often a much sought-after commodity (Fibkins, 2006; Peterson, 2004), thus increasing the vulnerability of his or her victims. Coaches have opportunities to be around children who are dressing and taking showers—times that make children vulnerable to sexual advances. In addition, many coaches do not receive any training in boundaries and other types of training that some professions do. Like teachers, there is no central registry for coaches, allowing those who are offenders to move freely from state to state, sometimes without detection (Fibkins, 2006; Kinnear, 2007).

In a study of female athletes who reported sexual harassment by their coaches, Fasting and Brackenridge (2009) grouped these coaches into three categories. The *flirting-charming coach* was known to joke, flirt, and try to touch in a variety of ways. One of the girls in the study reported that her coach was concerned about the girl's weight and would attempt to poke or pinch her to "discover if she had put on weight." The *seductive coach* was described as "trying to hit on everyone." He often jokes sexually and was described as a "ladies man." The *authoritarian coach* was one who used his power to degrade. He expected his players to do what they were told by him (pp. 27–28).

Some coaches complain that the increased scrutiny they have come under, as a result of the coaches who do abuse athletes, hampers their ability to perform their roles (Bringer, Brackenridge, & Johnston, 2006; Parent & Demers, 2011).

The causes and characteristics for abusers within educational and sports settings run the gamut of those for sexual offenders (see Chapter 5). Some are classic pedophiles who prey on children as a sexual object of choice. Others are more likely to have adult relationships but turn to children in times of stress. Some see themselves as natural teachers, and in their distorted thinking, they see the sexual abuse as an extension of that teaching.

Parent and Demers (2011) suggest that a few steps might be taken to protect young athletes. First, coaches must be screened more diligently. Parents and athletes should receive sexual abuse prevention training. Boundaries between coaches and players should be firmly established and adhered to. And finally, when situations of abuse are suspected, they should be taken seriously, and administrators should develop and implement intervention policies. Through these simple steps, children might be at less risk.

DAY CARE PROVIDERS AS ABUSERS

One factor that increases the vulnerability of child victims in day care is their ages and the fact that they might not be developmentally able to discuss what is happening to them. Day care may be provided at home, bringing in a caretaker, but here we are focusing on day care professionals who care for children either as licensed providers in their own home or as staff members of a day care center. Finkelhor, Williams, Burns, and Kalinowski (1988) did determine that a child had a greater chance of being sexually abused in his or her own home than in a day care center, but the fact remains that there have been a number of well-publicized cases of abuse in day care settings.

The McMartin Preschool

In the late 1980s, the McMartin preschool abuse case rocked the California coast. The case began in 1983 when the mother of a 2½-year-old boy accused teacher Raymond Buckley, son of the school's administrator Peggy McMartin Buckley and grandson of founder Virginia McMartin, of sexually abusing her son. Buckley was arrested but subsequently released when insufficient evidence

was found to support the abuse. But the accusing mother, Judy Johnson, persisted, claiming that her son and other children had been the victims of bizarre satanic abuse rituals by Buckley, his sister Peggy Ann Buckley, and other staff. Police sent letters to other parents whose children attended the school in an attempt to discover if there were other allegations. Children questioned by their parents began to describe being forced into engaging in anal and oral sex by school staff. Accusations included reports of mutilated animals and ritualized abuse, which may have taken place in underground passageways or rooms at the McMartin school (Besharov, 1990; Eberle & Eberle, 2003; Linder, 2003; Summit, 1994). However, Nathan (1993) suggests that the lack of the presence of such hidden areas only serves to further debunk the reports of the abuse. Summit (1994), on the other hand, attests to seeing such tunnels when he was invited to view an archaeological project, which, in 1990, uncovered the rooms that the children had mentioned.

After one of the longest and most expensive trials in history, no convictions stuck against the numerous defendants. Criticism was leveled at the interviewing techniques with the children, which were said to have planted ideas in their minds. The medical tests that attested to the abuse were felt to be viable at the time but were later determined to be of no use. Several trials beginning in April 1987 and ending in April 1989 resulted in acquittals on some of the counts and a deadlocked jury on others. Owing to the outcry from parents and child welfare advocates and professionals, Ray Buckley was tried a second time in 1990, resulting in another deadlocked jury. By this time, he had spent 5 years in jail, and his mother, Peggy, spent 2 years (Besharov, 1990; Eberle & Eberle, 2003; Linder, 2003; Rabinowitz, 2004; Summit, 1994; Whetsell-Mitchell, 1995).

To date, there are some who insist that the McMartin case was a well-publicized hoax that affected the lives of numerous families and ruined the careers of many of the McMartin staff (Eberle & Eberle, 2003). At the same time, others wonder how totally unfounded accusations by so many children and parents could have had little or no substance. Former New York City Family Court prosecutor Douglas Besharov (1990) suggests that there are lessons to be learned from the McMartin case. Although parents and other adults must be alert to the possibility of child sexual abuse in day care settings and children are encouraged to tell adults when they are concerned or confused about the behavior of their day care providers, we must also continue to improve impartial investigative interviewing when children do disclose. Child abuse in day care settings can be extremely hard to prove, owing to the age and abilities of the children, but that does not negate the need to abandon the due process of the law. Nor does it mean that the courts should jettison the concept of innocence until proven guilty for the defendants in order to protect children. This author believes that the jury system is the best protection against overzealous law enforcement.

The Fells Acres Day Care Center

The McMartin case, despite being one of the best known, was not the only publicized case where day care providers were accused of sexually molesting children. In 1984, the Fells Acres Day Care Center in Malden, Massachusetts, also made the news when a 5-year-old boy accused Gerald Amirault, handyman and son of the owner Violet Amirault, of "touching his private parts." Amirault defended his behavior saying that he was helping the child change his wet pants. When the child subsequently began displaying unusual behavior, his mother reported to the authorities, and Amirault was arrested. Police urged parents to question their children who were also enrolled in the center, and reports began to emerge of abuse in a "magic room" by a clown or robot. Other children reported being photographed naked and raped. Finally, 41 children between the ages of 3 and 6 had disclosed varying degrees of abuse. Gerald Amirault was then accused of abusing 19

of these children, his mother Violet and his sister Cheryl of abusing another 10. Physical evidence in some children supported the conviction of Gerald to 30 to 40 years in prison, and each of the women a sentence of 8 to 20 years. In 1995, a state Supreme Court judge overturned the conviction of Violet and Cheryl due to the fact that the seating in the trial did not allow the children to face their accusers. A new trial saw the two women released on bail, whereas Gerald continued to serve his sentence. He was released in 2004 (Public Broadcasting System, 1993; Rabinowitz, 2004).

Subsequent Day Care Abuse Scandals

In April 1985, another day care setting came to light. At the Wee Care Nursery School in Maplewood, New Jersey, a 4-year-old boy being examined at a physician's office commented, as he had his temperature taken rectally, that this was what his teacher did to him at naptime. The physician's nurse reported the incident, and an investigation ensued. After extensive interviews of the children at Wee Care Nursery School, authorities concluded that 23-year-old Kelly Michaels had abused all of the 41 children in her care (Crowley, 1989). After an 11-month trial, Michaels was convicted of 115 counts of sexual abuse and was sentenced to 45 years in prison. Her attorney appealed, and 5 years later, she was released when the New Jersey Supreme Court concluded that there was again question about how the children had been interviewed. In addition, the judge had questioned the children in his chambers while the jury watched via closed circuit television. His interviews were criticized as well (Public Broadcasting System, 1993).

Another day care center came under fire in 1989 when Bob Kelly, the co-owner with his wife Betsy of the Little Rascals Day Care Center, was accused of sexually abusing children at the center. The case had significant implications for Edenton, North Carolina, and ended up involving not only the Kellys but other staff at the center and other town officials such as the sheriff and the mayor of the town. In another long and costly trial, over 90 children accused 20 adults of sexual abuse, including ritual acts and even murder. Bob Kelly was convicted of 99 counts of abuse and was sentenced to twelve consecutive life sentences in prison. After serving 6 years in jail, his sentence was overturned. On May 23, 1997, the prosecution dropped all allegations against Kelly, his wife Betsy, their staff, and others in the Little Rascals case (Abbott, 1994; Geltz, 1994; Lamb, 1994).

Day care centers were not the only sites of well-publicized scandals. In 1984, the upscale neighborhood of Country Walk in Miami, Florida, became known for the case of Frank and Ileana Fuster, who were accused of sexually abusing the children they cared for in their suburban home. Frank Fuster, a 36-year-old Cuban immigrant, came under suspicion partially because of his past record of manslaughter and the fondling of a 9-year-old child. The day care license had been taken out by his 17-year-old wife, Ileana, and in so doing, Fuster's previous record was not uncovered until the scandal broke. The case came to the attention of authorities when a mother of a child at the center became concerned about what the child reported was happening at day care. After investigation, the children accused the Fusters of anal and oral sex, the production of pornography, forcing them to take drugs, the mutilation of animals, and satanic rituals (Hollingsworth, 1986).

The Country Walk case was handled quite differently from earlier day care cases due mainly to the intervention of then District Attorney Janet Reno. Reno brought in Joseph and Laurie Braga, child development specialists, to evaluate the three dozen children involved. The use of experienced child development interviewers was also designed to minimize trauma to the children and provide guidance for their concerned parents. Reno's office built a case not only on the testimony of the children but on the confession of Ileana who insisted that she was not guilty but did not wish to put the children through any

more scrutiny (Hollingsworth, 1986; Summit, 1994). Despite the good intentions of looking out for the children's best interests, the videotapes of the interviews were later evaluated by authorities as demonstrating interview techniques that were "leading, suggestive and unreliable" (Public Broadcasting System, 1993, p. 8). Nonetheless, Frank Fuster was convicted of life in prison without parole. Ileana served 3 years of her 10-year sentence and was then deported to her native Honduras (Hollingsworth, 1986; Public Broadcasting System, 1993).

Nathan (1993), a noted skeptic about day care abuse, suggests that the Country Walk case has become legendary as the case that based conviction on hard proof and the conviction of one of the perpetrators. However, this author questions the authenticity of this case based upon the way in which it was handled by investigating authorities.

Authenticity of Reports of Sexual Abuse in Day Care

Given the overturned cases in quite a few of the well-publicized cases, one might question how often children are abused in day care settings. Before considering this question, it should be noted that most of the above-mentioned cases involved the use of ritualized abuse. Therefore, the argument about the authenticity of reports in day care settings often becomes confused with opinions as to whether ritual abuse was present. In addition, the publicized cases have been termed by some to be situations where mass hysteria superseded the rights of the accused (Eberle & Eberle, 2003; Lamb, 1994; Nathan, 1993). Faller (2003) argues that although during the height of the scandals mentioned above, people were eager to point fingers and see convictions, the climate has now changed. Today, there is more of a tendency to come to the defense of the accused for several reasons. First, those who have been accused have been vigorous in their defenses, sometimes aided in their efforts at self-protection by funds from their insurance carriers. Second, the literature on the suggestibility of children, especially as related to sexual abuse, has grown considerably, and there are now expert witnesses who will testify as to the vulnerability of children as witnesses (Bruck, Ceci, & Hembrooke, 1998; Faller, 2003). Third, the skepticism is related to the reports themselves, often involving multiple perpetrators, significant numbers of victims, and bizarre acts of abuse that are often termed *ritualistic* or *satanic*. These factors are compounded by the overturned convictions of the 1980s and 1990s. And finally, Faller (2003) contends that "the media, evidently having exhausted the potential of portraying the horrors of sexual victimization in day care, now have turned to exposes of allegedly false accusations involving day care" (pp. 215–216).

This author goes on to say that she still considers sexual abuse in day care settings to be a "genuine phenomenon" that must be seriously investigated (p. 216).

Lindblad and Kaldal (2005) suggest that there are several factors that contribute to the problem of validation in day care cases. First, the children's developmental skills mean that their cognitive prerequisites are more limited (e.g., language skills and memory functions) than those of older children, which influences their abilities to communicate about abuse that they may have experienced. Second, some experts (see Ceci & Bruck, 1993) contend that younger children are more easily misled by the methods of or suggestions by interviewers and parents. In addition, a psychological group process may emerge when accusations have been made, which can lead to "group contagion"; that is, false allegations can spread among the children involved. It may be difficult to distinguish between this group contagion and the reality of similar abuse being perpetrated on more than one child. Yet, paradoxically, in day care cases, it has often been children reporting on abuse being perpetrated to others that has uncovered seemingly legitimate instances.

There is a similar psychological interplay that also takes place among the adults involved. The impact of the exposure of their children to sexual abuse, for example, may create in parents a hypersensitivity to anything that could be indicative of abuse in their own children. After outlining the dangers and difficulties in the investigation of day care abuse, Lindblad and Kaldal (2005) make a case for the need for recognizing these problems while going forward in the thorough investigation of such cases.

Efforts to Study Day Care Abuse

One of the most extensive studies of day care abuse to date was undertaken by Finkelhor, Williams, Burns, and Kalinowski in 1988; when using data from 1985, the researchers projected that approximately 1,300 children in 267 day care centers (of the 229,000 in the United States) had been abused that year (Faller, 2003; Finkelhor et al., 1988). This study plus subsequent studies by Faller (1988a, 1988b); Kelley, Brant, and Waterman (1993); and Waterman, Kelley, Oliveri, and McCord (1993) considered the type of abuse being perpetrated in day care settings (Kelley, 1994). Fondling was the most common act perpetrated against children, whereas penetration of the anus or vagina with an object was also commonly reported. A significant number of children in these studies also reported sexual exploitation that involved pornography—either being photographed nude or in pornographic poses or engaging with other children in sexual behavior. Although the children's descriptions were convincing, law enforcement frequently found no evidence of this pornography. The question then centered around whether perpetrators destroyed such evidence or telling the children that they were being photographed was a way to engage them in "the game." For example, the children in several cases talked of a "naked movie star game" (Kelley, 1994).

It was also necessary for perpetrators to not only engage children but also prevent them from disclosing that they had been abused. Gallagher (1998), in a study of the abuse of children in institutionalized settings, postulates that children are most often entrapped by their abusers through a variety of ways of drawing them in and even the use of guilt. In some instances, children were used to entrap other children. In most instances, the children's silence in day care settings was induced through threatening to harm them, their parents, or family. Some perpetrators mutilated animals or threatened to do so to ensure secrecy. Threats of demons, monsters, or other scary creatures were also used (Kelley, 1994; Kelley et al., 1993; Waterman et al., 1993).

Motivation of the Day Care Offender

Although theorists might like to believe that perpetrators can be characterized in a manner that would give insight into the prevention of future such abuse, this is not the case. Like the general population of sexual offenders, there is no profile of a typical offender. Many theorists contend that perpetrators who abuse in their professional capacity deliberately seek out positions that put them in contact with children of an age that interest them (Faller, 1988b; Kelley, 1994; Sullivan & Beech, 2002). Due to the fact that there are often multiple perpetrators in day care settings (Finkelhor, et al., 1988 reports 17%), these abusers may support one another. This leads Sullivan and Beech (2002) to question the level of sophistication of this type of offender compared to those who engage children and abuse alone. The institutional perpetrators must also disguise their behavior move cleverly or be in a position where they are not likely to be questioned or challenged (Sullivan & Beech, 2002).

Although there is no accurate profile of a day care abuser, Faller (2003) identified patterns that have emerged as to the type of scenarios present in day care abuse. She suggests that these variations can be divided into the following categories: (a) single offender/single victim, (b) single offender/multiple victims, and (c) multiple offenders/multiple victims.

The *single offender abusing a single child* may be detected before he or she has moved on to other children or other incidences of abuse have not been detected as yet. Another possibility is that the abuser is a serial offender who develops a relationship with a particular child, molests the child, and when that child is no longer accessible for some reason, he or she moves on to another victim. Faller (2003) states that in her research, most of these offenders have been female and the victims were male. In addition, the offender was often not a direct employee of the day care center but rather in a position to come into contact with day care children because of his or her relationship with the day care center—for example, a bus driver, custodian, or relative of an employee (Schumacher & Carlson, 1999). Faller terms these offenders *circumstantial offenders* (2003, p. 220).

The *single offender who abuses multiple children* is one that has been widely publicized in the media—despite cases with multiple offenders that have been more sensationalized. These offenders usually have a definite role at the day care center serving as teachers, aides, or even directors. They operate alone, managing to keep their behavior secret from the rest of the staff as they find opportunities at nap time or during bathroom trips to molest children. They convince the child to keep the abuse secret through the strength of their relationship, bribes, or threats that disclosure will mean that the child cannot return to day care or the offender will get into trouble. Offenders may be either male or female and may abuse children of either gender depending upon the preference of the abuser (Faller, 2003; Schumacher & Carlson, 1999).

Multiple offenders/multiple victims are by far the most widely publicized cases of day care abuse. McMartin, Fells Acres, and Country Walk are the most notorious of these cases. In most cases, the abuse takes place in day care centers, although the Country Walk case was more of a babysitting service. These offenders tended to find secluded areas of the centers where the abuse could not be detected were an outsider to happen to visit. The children abused were both male and female, and who was abused was less dependent upon the tastes of any one offender. Offenders tended to be of both sexes as well. Children were often coerced or threatened into sexual acts often by using one child to have sex with others, which further intensified the children's guilt and served to strengthen their hesitation about disclosing (Faller, 2003; Hollingsworth, 1986; Kelley et al., 1993; Waterman et al., 1993).

In multiple offender cases, the abuse is usually planned and premeditated often with complexity. It is in these types of settings where children are more likely to be ritually and often sadistically abused. Not surprisingly, children who are the victims of this type of abuse are more severely traumatized (Faller, 2003; Hollingsworth, 1986; Kelley et al., 1993; Schumacher & Carlson, 1999; Waterman et al., 1993).

Impact of Day Care Abuse on Children

Children abused in day care settings may be significantly traumatized. Although abuse in a home setting is usually the most traumatic abuse for children, abuse in day care has an impact that is peculiar to that setting. Because, for many children, this is the first experience they have had of being separated from parents, these young victims may also be processing their fears about separation and be even more vulnerable. In addition, although these are not the parents, the day care providers are people whom the parents have trusted and may have communicated this fact to their children. Thus, the child may begin to believe that the parent has also sanctioned the abuse (Faller, 2003; Kelley et al., 1993; Schumacher & Carlson, 1999).

Beyond the aforementioned factors, the impact of the abuse on the victim is dependent on the nature of the abuse that is perpetrated. Certainly ritualized or sadistic abuse creates a particularly disturbing degree of trauma. When the perpetrator was not someone who was instrumental in running the day care center or if the abuser was a woman, the victims seemed to be less impacted. The ability of the parents, especially the mother, to respond effectively to the child upon disclosure also minimized symptoms (Finkelhor et al., 1988).

Symptoms demonstrated by victims in day care settings tended to involve sleep disturbances, nightmares, sexualized behaviors, phobias, depression, bed wetting, temper tantrums, anxiety, fears, and other problems with social functioning (Faller, 2003; Finkelhor et al., 1988; Kelley et al., 1993; Waterman et al., 1993). Friedrich and Reams (1987) suggest that how children are affected by the trauma is also influenced by their family environment, the degree of support the child feels at home, and the atmosphere at home that follows the disclosure of the abuse.

Many researchers discovered that the parents often had as intense a reaction as their children to the fact of the abuse, and their response had a significant influence on their children. Parents whose children were ritually abused displayed the greatest difficulty in responding in a manner that was beneficial to their children. Mothers who were themselves victimized as children also had greater difficulty in supporting their children effectively. When investigators and clinicians neglect to consider the needs of the parents in abuse situations outside the home, the children may suffer (Hollingsworth, 1986; Kelley et al., 1993). Parents of abused children may feel disbelief, guilt, anger at perpetrators, and concerns about how to handle their children's reactions, and for parents with victimization in their own childhoods, the abuse may cause post-traumatic stress reactions (Faller, 2003).

It behooves professionals to be aware not only of the possibility of such abuse but about the necessity of giving support and offering treatment to parents as well as their children.

THERAPISTS AND OTHER TREATMENT STAFF AS ABUSERS

There has been media coverage in the past about therapists who sexually abuse those in treatment, but most of these victims have been adults. Kenneth Pope (2001), in his research about exploitation at the hands of mental health professionals, found that 4.4% of psychiatrists, psychologists, and social workers have sexually exploited clients at some time in their careers. Of these, 7% were male therapists and 1.5% were female. However, in these self-report surveys, none of these reported that their client was a minor at the time of the abuse. Yet a previous study with Pope and Vetter (1991) discovered that of the 958 adults they studied who had reported sexual contact with their therapists, 5% were children at the time of the abuse. In a separate study with Bajt (Bajt & Pope, 1989), the researchers determined that of the cases of minors abused by therapists, 56% were female with an average age of 13.7 years (with a range of 3–17 years), and 44% were males with an average age of 12.5 years (with a range of 7–16 years) (p. 455). Looking at the Pope studies, Hidalgo (2007) estimates that no more than 0.2% of therapists with 0.5% males and 0.1% females have sexually abused their child clients.

Although the incidence of child abuse by outpatient therapists may not be that significant, children are more likely to be abused by treatment professionals and other staff within institutions. Residential facilities may provide an opportunity for abusers to have access to children without the scrutiny of their parents or other adults.

Insufficient supervision, inadequate structure, and accessibility of young victims make such abuse possible. In addition, individuals who are predisposed to abuse children will seek out roles or positions through which they have access to children. Courtois (2010) suggests that abuse in residential settings can create similar symptoms to incest as the child is betrayed in a setting where he or she should have been able to feel safe and by people who were caretakers.

The sexual abuse victim who is also vulnerable to being abused by a therapist is the survivor of child sexual abuse. The sex abuse survivor may have difficulty recognizing when she or he is falling into an abusive relationship. The intensity of the transference and countertransference that is part of a long-term relationship between therapist and patient requires that the therapist have appropriate training to work with sexually abused clients and receive ongoing supervision. The sexual abuse survivor has often learned to get her or his needs met through being seductive, cajoling, and manipulative. Therapists whose own needs have not been sufficiently met or who have not resolved their own issues may be vulnerable to misconduct (Dryden, 1991). At the same time, open discussion of sexuality over time can lead to the sexualizing of the relationship. Courtois (2010) also suggests that incestuous dynamics can develop in the relationship that can simulate a parent-child interaction.

Professionals of all types have an obligation to maintain appropriate boundaries with their clients and to seek out supervision to ensure that their own needs do not supersede those of their clients.

Summary

Over the last few decades, there has been increased new coverage and speculation on sexual abuse by authority figures who work with children. Teachers, who may have the closest contact with children of any adults other than parents, have been documented as abusers by a variety of sources. Male teachers are more frequent abusers than their female counterparts. The well-publicized case of Mary Kay LeTourneau surrounded a teacher who became involved with her sixth-grade student, was imprisoned for abuse, and later, upon release, married him.

Coaches too have been known to abuse the athletes with whom they work. This betrayal of trust is made possible by the fact that coaches have inordinate power over the lives of their young charges. They are in positions of respect and are in an excellent position to groom and nurture their players. Several types of coach abusers have been identified, each with a different method of engaging his or her victims.

There have been several much publicized cases of sexual abuse in day care settings. The McMartin preschool in California, the Fells Acres Day Care Center, the Wee Care Nursery, and the Little Rascals Day Care Center are but a few. There is some controversy about whether the incidence of such abuse was as significant as many reporters suggested. Children in day care present excellent opportunities for such abuse given their age and developmental skills that may make it difficult for them to explain what happened. On the other hand, some researchers suggest that the principle of "group contagion" means that some children may report abuse that they did not themselves experience.

Offenders within day care settings may be single offenders of a single child or a single offender of multiple children. There have also been alleged cases of multiple offenders who have abused multiple children. Children who have been abused in day care centers exhibit a variety of symptoms, and parents may not know how to best respond.

Therapists may also be abusers; fortunately there have been only a few reports of therapists abusing children. It is difficult to determine if such abuse has not occurred or is underreported. However, there have been reports of adult survivors who have been abused by their therapists. Patients are especially vulnerable if they have been abused as children, and being abused by someone to whom they have come for help revictimizes them.

Review Questions

1. What contributes to the sexual abuse of children by authority figures?

2. How often are children and youth abused by teachers?

3. Why can abuse by coaches have such an impact on young athletes?

4. Describe some recent cases of day care abuse.

5. Why were the day care abuse cases mentioned in text controversial?

6. What are the inherent problems in the reporting of abuse in day care settings?

7. What might be the motivation of an offender in day care settings?

8. How high is the incidence of the abuse of children by therapists?

9. What population is more often targeted by therapists? What problem does this cause?

CHAPTER 10

Sexual Abuse by Clergy

A Unique Offender

Over the last few decades, society has become increasingly aware of the abuse of children by priests, ministers, and others associated with the church. The scandal in the Roman Catholic Church stimulated speculation and study of this type of abuse. But clergy abuse is not exclusive to the Catholic Church. Although very few cases have been uncovered among rabbis, Protestant clergy have also abused children. However, because it was the scandal in the Catholic Church that brought about the intense scrutiny of the problem, it is worth considering these events.

SEXUAL ABUSE AND THE CATHOLIC CHURCH

Perhaps the best known and most pervasive scandals involving child sexual abuse and the Roman Catholic Church took place in the archdioceses of Chicago and Boston, but many who have chronicled the crisis have pointed to Henry, Louisiana, in 1983 as the site of one of the first allegations of clergy sexual abuse (Berry, 2000; Bruni & Burkett, 2002; Frawley-O'Dea, 2007; Jenkins, 2001b). Father Gilbert Gauthe was the pastor of St. John's in the small bayou country town of Henry, where he was known for his availability to and his involvement with the youth of the parish, even taking them on Friday night sleepovers at an island camp house. When 9-year-old Craig Sagrera reported being molested by Father Gauthe, the boy's father questioned his two older sons, who admitted that they too had had a similar experience with the popular priest. The senior Sagrera then contacted an attorney who in turn notified the diocese only to learn that Henry was Gauthe's sixth parish and his frequent moves had followed his molesting children since 1973, 10 years before. Under pressure from the attorney, the diocese finally removed Gauthe, but at the same time, the Sagreras were urged not to cause trouble by making too much of a fuss about what had happened in order to prevent publicity. But the word spread, and others of Gauthe's victims came forward, launching civil lawsuits. The civil suits stimulated criminal charges, and in 1985, Gauthe was finally sentenced to 20 years in prison for child rape

---

Note: It should be noted that the term clergy in the Roman Catholic Church also includes deacons, but this chapter refers only to those serving as priests as well as to non-Catholic clergy.

and the possession of pornography. After 10 years of incarceration, Gauthe was released and subsequently molested a 3-year-old boy. He was returned to prison but later released again (Berry, 2000; *Boston Globe*, 2002; Bruni & Burkett, 2002; Frawley-O'Dea, 2007).

Getting wind of the scandal, the press erupted in a flurry of interest that led reporter Jason Berry to write the first book about the scandal, *Lead Us Not Into Temptation*, in 1992. Part of the intense conflict about this and the later scandals that emerged resulted from Catholics' hesitancy to criticize the church that they had loved and often grown up with. But these same feelings would later explain the webs of secrecy that had been allowed to exist in one of the oldest institutions in the world.

Further scandals came to light, and a pattern emerged. Between the 1950s and 1990s, a typical scenario was for a young priest to enter a church filled with enthusiasm and charisma. He would quickly become involved with the parish youth, developing close relationships with predominantly boys who often came from troubled or poor families and reveled in the attention of their priest. Having been taught by devout parents to respect and honor priests in addition to often being pushed into the path of the Father's attentions by parents who were flattered by these attentions, the children were not only confused but hesitant to disclose their abuse. When the attention became sexual, the children were already so caught up in the relationships and all that it meant to their families that they usually kept their secret buried. Who would believe them anyway if they were to accuse Father of abuse (Frawley-O'Dea, 2007)?

So, the pattern continued throughout the United States until later in life young men began to come forward to tell their stories. The *Boston Globe* (2002) reported that over 130 individuals had reported being raped or fondled by former priest John J. Goeghan while they were in grammar school. These reports covered a period of 30 years and half a dozen Greater Boston parishes.

An Epidemic of Abuse

The archdiocese of Chicago was the scene of one of the most "vigorous debates" over abuse by clergy perhaps because of the attention of noted sociologist, writer and Roman Catholic priest, Father Andrew Greeley, who termed it *the pedophile crisis* (Jenkins, 2001b). The cases of reported sexual abuse of minors by priests within that archdiocese rose at an alarming rate between the mid-1980s to the early 1990s. Nineteen cases of such abuse were reported in the years 1990 to 1991 (Bruni & Burkett, 2002; Jenkins, 2001b). The problem of clergy abuse was so significant as to lead Chicago Cardinal Joseph Bernardian to apologize for the church's handling of the situations and to appoint an investigative commission to look into the allegations over the previous 40 years. In June 1992, this commission implicated 59 priests who had outstanding allegations of sexual misconduct made against them. The media attention brought forward newly formed activist groups like SNAP (Survivors Network of those Abused by Priests) and VOCAL (Victims of Clergy Abuse Laws), who demanded that the church be held accountable and discuss reform (Jenkins, 2001b).

Ironically, this was not the first church group dedicated to the study of clergy abuse nor the first criticism that the Catholic Church was not responding as it should. In 1985, a confidential report titled "The Problem of Sexual Molestation by Roman Catholic Clergy: Meeting the Problem in a Comprehensive and Responsible Manner" came before Catholic officials. The report, generated by the attorney on the Gauthe case (mentioned earlier) as well as several Catholic priests, stimulated the (then) National Conference of Catholic Bishops (NCCB) to conduct several confidential discussions on the matter. For several years thereafter, the NCCB met and continued the discussion while outwardly failing to take a stand, which elicited media criticism that the bishops were ignoring the problem (Berry, 2000; Bruni & Burkett, 2002; Jenkins, 2001b). In the meantime, the instances of abuse and disclosure continued.

One name that stands out in the roll call of offenders is that of Father James Porter, who was assigned to parishes in Fall River, North Attleboro, and New Bedford, Massachusetts. When it was learned that he was continuing to molest children of both sexes within his various parishes, despite being relieved of his duties at least eight times over a 6-year period, Porter was sent to a treatment facility in New Mexico. Following his treatment, he was reassigned to a parish in Bemidji, Minnesota, where he continued his molestation activities. In 1974, Porter left the priesthood, married, and fathered his own children and was later convicted of abusing their babysitter. It was not until one of his former victims, Frank Fitzpatrick, an insurance investigator by profession, found Porter and tape-recorded their phone conversation during which Porter admitted that he had abused up to 100 children that the former priest would be brought to trial. After finding Porter, Fitzpatrick sought out other victims, and together they approached the Bristol County district attorney and urged him to investigate their allegations. During this investigation, it was also determined that the actual number of Porter's victims was greater than originally assumed. Porter was eventually tried in both Massachusetts and Minnesota and was sentenced to 18 to 20 years in prison (Bruni & Burkett, 2002; Jenkins, 2001b).

The abuse scandal in the archdiocese of Boston became one of the best-known exposés of clerical abuse not only because of the amount of media attention, including the book *Betrayal* written by the investigative staff of the *Boston Globe*, but also because of the clearly documented evidence of cover-up through the years by Catholic authorities.

In 2002, reports of the extensive abuse of children perpetrated by Father John Geoghan became front-page news. Investigations uncovered multiple incidents of abuse by other Boston area priests, and Catholics demanded a response from Cardinal Bernard Law, who apologized for the Geoghan affair and assured the public that the church would take a tougher stand on abusive priests in the future. But when other clerics were found to be abusive, the scandal intensified (*Boston Globe*, 2002; Frawley-O'Dea, 2007; Frawley-O'Dea & Goldner, 2007). In December 2002, the archbishop, "whose credibility as a moral and spiritual leader was damaged beyond repair by the central role he played in the church's mismanagement of the problem" (Kline, McMackin, & Lezotte, 2008, p. 291), resigned his position.

Studying Abuse by Priests

In 2004, New York City–based John Jay College of Criminal Justice, commissioned by the United States Conference of Catholic Bishops (formerly the National Conference of Catholic Bishops), came out with the most definitive study to date on abuse by Roman Catholic priests. This study, titled "The Nature and Scope of the Problem of Sexual Abuse of Minors by Catholic Priests and Deacons in the United States: A Research Study Conducted by John Jay College of Criminal Justice," attempts to capture the nature and scope of the abuse of children within the Roman Catholic Church from 1950 to 2002. A later updated study, "The Report on the Implementation of the Charter of Children and Young People (2005)," covered up to the year 2004.

The John Jay study (2004) found that between 1950 and 2002, there were 4,392 priests abusing minors. And in 2004, the follow-up report (USCCB, 2005) documented another 311 abusive priests. Frawley-O'Dea (2007) suggests that these numbers might actually be low given the fact that 2% of diocesan priests and 20% of religious priests are not included in the John Jay study. This author also blames "sloppy record keeping" in some chanceries and provincial offices for the loss of some statistics (p. 174).

Based on the John Jay study, Frawley-O'Dea (2007) computed the exact percentages of offender priests who were ordained each year from 1960 to 2000. The highest number of offenders seems to have been ordained prior to 1980 with the years 1973 and 1975 yielding 9% of priests for each of these years as sexual abusers of children (p. 175, based on John Jay College, 2004). It is also noteworthy that many seminaries began to require psychological evaluations of candidates in the 1980s, which may have screened out or at least deterred some potential abusers (Frawley-O'Dea, 2007).

Miles (2012) has an interesting take on why the highest percentage of clergy offenders were in seminary during the 1950–1970s, suggesting that reform in the Catholic Church may have had an unwitting contribution. Prior to the reforms initiated by Vatican II (1962–1965), seminary education emphasized strict discipline and absolute obedience. Yet with the advent of the more permissive 1960s and the second Vatican council, the emphasis changed to the encouragement of personal growth. Standards were relaxed and with this, inhibitions were reduced, which may well have led to confusion among priests trained in the more conservative period. At the same time, those trained in the late 1960s and 1970s were influenced by the permissiveness and fluidity of the times and some may never have developed the inhibitions demanded of earlier trained clergy.

Compared to other explanations of the background of abusive priests (see Sperry, 2003), it is interesting that only 6.8% of offenders in the John Jay study (2004) reported having been abused in childhood and only 4% claimed sexual abuse. Statistically, priests tended to begin their abuse of minors later than one might expect with the average age between 38 and 48. Many of the priests who offended (55.7%) reported having only one victim. Of the others, 26.7% had two to three victims, 13.9% had four to nine victims, and 3.5% had ten or more. Most of the victims were between ages 10 and 14 at the onset of the abuse. The study does suggest, however, that there was a shift over the years, and more victims of abuse in later decades reported being first abused between ages 15 and 17 (John Jay, 2004). One explanation for this phenomenon might be related to a perpetrator choosing a victim around the age of the arrest in his own development. As males began to enter the priesthood later, it may have been older boys who felt like their psychological peers (Cartor, Cimbolic, & Tallon, 2008; Cozzens, 2002; Frawley-O'Dea, 2007; Hidalgo, 2007; Miles, 2012; Sperry, 2003).

As one peruses these studies and observes the numbers of abusive priests, it is no wonder that the incidence of clergy abuse was not carefully documented within the Catholic Church.

Anatomy of the Cover-Up

Some critics suggest that there were two issues for the Catholic Church: the sexual abuse by priests and the cover-up by Catholic hierarchy. Initially, when Gauthe and the other early priest scandals were being uncovered, disclosure would begin when some parent, neighbor, victim, or fellow priest complained to a diocesan representative that Father X was abusing a child. In the early days, the reporter might well have been chastised for considering bringing scandal to the church, insisting that too many other clergy would be harmed if Father X's indiscretions were to come out. The parishioner was then sent home with the assurance that "the matter will be attended to" and he or she "need not mention it again" (Bruni & Burkett, 2002; Frawley-O'Dea, 2007; Jenkins, 2001b).

In the meantime, the diocese might actually have confronted Father X about his behavior, and often he would admit what he had done. Having promised that he would not "sin" again, Father X would be moved to another parish where he would often go on to abuse again. In later cases, Father X might be sent off for some type of psychological evaluation—often by those not schooled in abuse issues or at least clergy abuse issues—and possibly to some type of treatment. It should be noted, however, that treatment of child sexual abuse was then in its infancy and often not that effective. After treatment, Father X would again be returned to the parish ministry or, if his sins were too widely known, relegated to administrative ministry that theoretically did not put him in contact with children. However, more than once, when there was a shortage of priests, the vacancy was at least temporarily filled by someone from an administrative position. And if the priest was either reassigned or brought in temporarily, often neither fellow clergy nor parishioners were aware of his background (*Boston Globe*, 2002; Frawley-O'Dea, 2007; Jenkins, 2001b; Miles, 2012).

Finally, as the scandals unfolded in the 1990s, if the original complaint was taken seriously, the reporter was assured that Father X would be dealt with appropriately. The church offered to pay for counseling for the victim in exchange for his or her silence about the matter. Evidence of numerous of these secret settlements came out when the Boston archdiocese situation was fully examined (*Boston Globe*, 2000; Bruni & Burkett, 2002; Frawley-O'Dea, 2007).

One wonders how and why such a major cover-up could have been perpetrated. Frawley-O'Dea (2007) cites two contributors to the cover-up by Catholic bishops and hierarchy: Victorian sexuality and "the Irish Factor." This author points out that 80% of the Catholic bishops of leading dioceses between 1983 and 2003 were born before 1940 and almost 50% before 1930 (p. 12). Looking at these statistics, it becomes evident that these men were raised in an era when sex was little discussed and sexual abuse had not been widely "discovered," let alone discussed. These were individuals still influenced by Victorian morality where it was the social custom to maintain respectability, virtue, and good conduct while satisfying one's sexual needs covertly and discretely. Catholic teachings resisted the shedding of these Victorian values in the 1970s' sexual revolution and continued to accept a very narrow range of sexual behaviors. Thus, to a man, even one who had been elevated to bishop, his early development punctuated by acceptance of a Catholic moral code, the obvious solution was to overlook that which was not acceptable.

At the same time, Frawley-O'Dea (2007) points out that in 1900, 75% of American bishops were Irish or of Irish decent, and in the 1990s, still a significant number of bishops were of Irish heritage (see also *Boston Globe*, 2000). The Irish had come to the United States—like many other immigrants—craving respectability but having to fight mightily for this. One road to such respectability for many Irish families, especially in the eyes of mothers, was to have their sons study for the priesthood. When the son finally became a bishop, the benefit to the family and the culture felt immense and in some manner made up for the discrimination the family had borne in the past. As a result, acknowledging and confronting a blemish like sexual abuse on the priesthood was unthinkable for many bishops of Irish decent. Frawley-O'Dea goes on to suggest that the harsh life in Ireland and as immigrants had taught the Irish to use a "creative imagination to cope with and escape from the realities of life" (McGoldrick & Pearce, 1981, as cited in Frawley-O'Dea, 2007, p. 13). Thus, the Irish achieved a high tolerance for suffering and were able to gloss over it in seeming indifference. Both of these factors contributed to the years of cover-up at the hands of Catholic bishops.

A Uniquely Catholic Problem?

When the topic of clergy sexual abuse is raised, many wonder why the media attention seemed to focus on abuse by priests. Is this uniquely a Roman Catholic problem?

Hidalgo (2007) suggests that, unlike the rate of abuse by Catholic priests (documented in the John Jay College report, 2004), there are no reliable statistics on abuse by Protestant clergy or rabbis. The only study known by this author is by the Presbyterian Church in eight states over a 6-year period that yielded 17 cases of sexual misconduct by clergy. All of the 31 victims were female, and only one was a minor (p. 30). G. Lloyd Rediger (2003), author of *Beyond the Scandals* (2003), estimates that between 2% and 3% of Protestant clergy sexually offend (p. 57) although he admits that this is based upon conjecture rather than hard research (Hidalgo, 2007). In addition, most of these offenses are against adult women.

Hidalgo (2007) used statistics from the John Jay study (2004) and compared these findings with figures gleaned from the U.S. Department of Justice and the Census Bureau about the number of men and women who report sexual offenses against minors and came up with some estimates to compare the rates of abuse by Catholic and Protestant clergy. Based upon victim and perpetrator surveys, Hidalgo estimates that the rate of abuse of minors by Catholic priests is 8.4%, and the abuse of minors by Protestant clergy was not statistically significant enough to be measured. On the other hand, 12.7% to 37.2% (depending upon the source) of Protestant male clergy may have been guilty of sexual misconduct with adults, whereas the figure for priests is 30.5% (p. 25). Does this mean that Protestant clergy do not abuse children? There have certainly been cases of the abuse of minors, but statistically the Protestant minister who acts out sexually is more likely to do so with adults.

Given the previous statistical findings, why are Catholic priests at greater risk to abuse children? Several theorists have emerged in the crisis of the Catholic Church, each presenting a theory as to the cause. A. W. Richard Sipe (1995, 2003), an ordained priest himself and now a psychotherapist, blames the long passed-down belief in the fallacy of a celibate priesthood that leads to a distortion between sex and power within the clerical culture. In addition, he cites the seminary structure that has traditionally taken boys in adolescence, delaying their sexual and emotional maturity and protecting this delay through an all-male clerical culture (Hidalgo, 2007).

Eugene Kennedy (2002), also a former priest and now psychologist, postulates that it is the Catholic Church's unresolved and still unaddressed conflicts around sexuality that produce "sexually wounded priests" who "prey upon the weakest in their flocks for temporary relief of their own pain" (Hidalgo, 2007, p. 3). Stephen Rossetti (1996, 2003), the former Director of St. Luke's Institute, a private Catholic treatment center, also supports the idea that abusive priests are psychosexually immature (Hidalgo, 2007). Len Sperry (2003) further develops this concept through a series of rating scales that assess emotional and sexual development. And Donald Cozzens (2002), priest and professor at John Carroll University, also supports the church's difficulty with sexual issues and the fact that church leaders have become "dependent on collective denial to manage their overwhelming feelings of anxiety related to post-modern sexual issues" (Hidalgo, 2007, p. 3).

Mary Gail Frawley-O'Dea, a clinical psychologist who was the only mental health professional to address the U.S. Conference of Catholic Bishops (USCCB) during its 2002 meeting at the height of the sexual abuse crisis, offers some interesting clinical observations on the problem of abuse by priests as well as for the cover-up that ensued (discussed later). Frawley-O'Dea (2007) postulates that one issue that contributes to the predominance of Catholic priests as abusers is that of male supremacy within the church. She explains that Catholicism favors males as religious leaders, yet the church gives inconsistent messages on maleness as it pertains to clergy by prescribing behavior for its priests that contradicts culturally accepted male characteristics and roles. Unlike the expectations placed on most males, priests are prohibited from sexual outlets as well as from marrying, fathering children, and assuming the duties of family support.

This author goes on to say that conditioning these male priests to play more traditionally feminine roles—nurturing, submitting, obeying—while making it clear that they should not be competitive, aggressive, or ambitious—traditionally male attributes—creates dissonance with the societal expectation of their gender. Add to this the fact that although this gender-dissonant lifestyle was supported in seminary, once a priest entered a parish, he no longer had such support. There he was expected to mingle with parishioners who might have very different expectations of maleness. For some, the cloak of priesthood protected them from feeling totally out of sync with the environment, but for those priests who may have been plucked from adolescence before they had time to resolve issues around their male identity, the result may have been an immaturity and insecurity, which led them to seek out dysfunctional ways in which to alleviate their anxiety—sometimes leading to abusing children (Frawley-O'Dea, 2007; Saffiotti, 2011).

In responding to the question of sex abuse scandals being unique to the Catholic Church, there has been much speculation on how priest sexual abusers might differ not only from the general population of abusers but also, in some areas, from those within the Protestant faiths. This is discussed below.

CLERGY AS PERPETRATORS

Clergy who sexually abuse fit into all types of categories developed to explain offending behaviors against children (see Chapter 5). Rather than attempt a categorization of clergy abusers alone, it is important to look at some of the antecedents, motivators, and similarities in clergy who abuse.

Some clergy are motivated to abuse by stressors inherent in clergy life. We have already discussed the fact that being a member of the clergy can set one apart from the rest of the population. Ministry is based on relationships, and being set apart can make forging these relationships even more challenging. For less secure clergy, relationships with youth who do not challenge them and their competency can seem to be more fulfilling. In addition, clergy are assumed to have close connections with God, which can be both a stress and an invitation to abuse power. On one hand, some clergy feel unworthy of their exalted status of what the Catholic faith refers to as *Alter Christus* or "another Christ" (Frawley-O'Dea, 2007; McGlone, 2003; Saffiotti, 2011). Various faiths interpret the pastor's role in relation to God differently. From Catholicism to congregationally based denominations that see the pastor as partially leader and partially church member, the fit for an individual cleric may not always feel right.

Some clergy see their perceived connection with God as a source of power in the face of their own feelings of powerlessness. It was just this misinterpretation of power that allowed many of the clergy who abused children to both rationalize their own behaviors and present the rationale to children (Firestone, Moulden, & Wexler, 2009; Hidalgo, 2007; McGlone, 2003; Saffiotti, 2011; Sperry, 2003).

A study of the various backgrounds of abusing clergy uncovers childhood issues that give rise to adult dysfunction and in some cases abusive behavior. A history of childhood abuse or family dysfunction is represented in a high percentage of clergy who abuse. Family alcoholism, exposure to sexual deviance as children, loose family sexual boundaries, or conversely overly repressive family sexual norms are seen in abusers' backgrounds (Rossetti, 1996; Sperry, 2003). Inadequate social and sexual development also punctuates the lives of some abusers, especially those who are priests. This arrested development may be a result of trauma or, as discussed earlier, being isolated through seminary training at an early age. The lack of peer relationships inherent in ministry, resulting in forced or chosen isolation, can add to an inhibited ability to lead a healthy adult life. Some clergy abusers have developed passive, dependent, or narcissistic personalities that promote a sense of entitlement and an increased likelihood of sexually acting out (Rossetti, 1996; Sperry, 2003). In fact, early ecclesiastical training for priests may instill in them a grandiose sense of entitlement that appeals to some of the more insecure (Frawley-O'Dea, 2007).

Healthy sexuality plays an important part in the adjustment of an individual, and failure to achieve it often leads to deviance. The backgrounds of clergy perpetrators showed evidence of confusion about sexual orientation, severe guilt and shame around sexuality, repressed sexuality, or, conversely, an overwhelming interest in and preoccupation with sexuality (Cartor et al., 2008; Firestone, Moulden, & Wexler, 2009; Hidalgo, 2007; Miles, 2012; Rossetti, 1996; Saffiotti, 2011; Sipe, 1995; Sperry, 2003).

Attempts to categorize clergy offenders have been made by describing them through preexisting terms. For example, whereas some clergy are classic pedophiles, others do not fall into this category. A pedophile, as explained earlier, is an individual whose primary sexual interest is in prepubescent children (Jenkins, 2001b; Lothstein, 1994; Sperry, 2003). The pedophile is interested in children—usually male—before they begin to develop secondary sexual characteristics (pubic and facial hair, voice change, etc.) and is attracted to them due to their softness and innocence. The pedophile has little interest sexually either in age-mates of both sexes or in adolescents. The pedophile is often immature and has childish interests. Some clergy exhibit these characteristics and target young children, but a significant number of priests, especially, have been termed *ephebophiles.*

Ephebophilia refers to the sexual preference for boys who have entered puberty—usually 14 to 17 years of age (Cartor et al., 2008). Although girls may also be abused, the ephebophile is attracted to them for their virginity, whereas in a boy he sees a psychological age-mate. Ironically, Catholic clerics who are attracted to girls are also deterred from having sex with a virgin due to the church's idealization of virginity (Frawley-O'Dea, 2007; Lothstein, 1994).

Jenkins (2001b) suggests that the fact that many of the priests found to be abusive were involved with teenage boys muddied the waters in several ways. First, although pedophilia—the abuse of children—is considered to be a heinous act by most, involvement with teens—although against the laws of celibacy—does not hold the same stigma. It is also not surprising, given the age of the victims, that some confused the abuse of minors with homosexuality. Jenkins further points out that the age of consent within Catholic law is 16 rather than 18 as in many U.S. jurisdictions (see also Sperry, 2003).

Although the distinction between pedophilia and ephebophilia may seem academic to some, the characteristics are somewhat different and are necessary to distinguish in treatment. To deny an ephebophile access to young children while allowing him to come in contact with teens, for example, is to ignore the problem (Cartor et al., 2008; Jenkins, 2001b; Lothstein, 1994; Sperry, 2003).

Both pedophiles and ephebophiles have been stunted in their emotional growth but at different ages. They become fixated at a particular stage and are attracted to children who fall within that developmental age range. Some theorists stick to the classic definitions of these terms (Jenkins, 2001b), whereas others suggest a distinction between a fixated pedophile or ephebophile and a regressed pedophile or ephebophile (Frawley-O'Dea, 2007; Lothstein, 1994; Sperry, 2003). The regressed offender's primary sexual preference is for adults, but his development is immature, and under stressful circumstances, he may regress back to an interest in children.

As discussed in Chapter 5, it becomes evident here that most of the existing theories of offending relate to male perpetrators. With clergy especially, the incidence of female offenders is so insignificant as to discourage any type of categorization.

It is clear that those factors that are associated with clergy abusers could be attributed to non-clergy abusers. Therefore, the question arises: Do clergy become abusive, or are those who have the predisposition toward being abusers seek out the role as clergy person? Comparing the needs of someone who is predisposed to perpetration, with the benefits provided by clergy life, Crosson-Tower (2014) notes that much of what the church, especially the Catholic Church, offers a priest would be attractive to perpetrators. These are outlined in Table 10.1.

Table 10.1 Comparison of the Needs of Sex Offenders and What the Church Offers Clergy

Characteristics and Needs of Offenders	Offered to Clergy
Acceptance by others (often feel rejected)	Community-wide sanction by virtue of role
Respect (as opposed to rejection)	Respect for the role/assumed connection with God
Feeling inadequate/like a "nobody"/inferior	Elevated in esteem by virtue of role
Pervasive feelings of guilt (for some)	Guilt transformed into faith-related concepts
Feeling out of control, but desire control	Role gives illusion of control; others look up to him
Opportunity to be alone with children	Role offers unlimited access to children and trust by parents*
Protection from detection	Role offers trust from community and ability to come and go freely†
Searching for unconditional love	Love emphasized along with forgiveness
Desire to make up for feeling unloved in childhood	Surrounded by the "Mother Church" and all-loving Father-God
Feeling abandoned/uncared for as child	Parishioners often care for clergy through meals, attention, and so on.
Poor social skills	Can be slightly aloof, not making close friendships due to expected boundaries
Not comfortable sexually with peers	Some faiths expect celibacy; others may sanction diminished sexual interest

NOTE: It should be noted that in the Roman Catholic Church, clergy also encompasses those who serve as deacons. Deacons, unlike priests, are free to marry and do not necessarily enjoy the same privileges listed here.

*Admittedly the sex abuse crisis among clergy has caused some caution among the adults caring for children.

†Denominations vary according to what they offer.

In addition to these factors, the Internet can play a role in sexual abuse by clergy. It is well established in the current study of offenders that many are involved with or have an interest in pornography. One of the roles of pornography in their offending cycle is to desensitize them to acting out their fantasies. Clergy might find that cybersex—sexual sites accessed over the Internet—are problematic for them and lead to acting out sexually. Crosson-Tower (2006) suggests the threat to clergy for several reasons: First, clergy spend time on the Internet, creating bulletins, accessing sermon ideas, and reading newsletters. An accidental or intentional side trip to a pornographic site would be free, easy, and anonymous. Priests and Protestant clergy would not suffer the shame of detection, as they usually work alone. They might also rationalize that just looking does not go against any ethical standard that they agreed to in their ordination. It can be exciting and taboo and gives them a respite from the sometimes stressful need to negotiate relationships. But viewing pornography lowers their psychological inhibitions, and research shows that their risk of acting out sexually, given other mitigating factors, can become greater.

Although they may become desensitized through pornography, clergy gain access to their victims usually through their relationship with them. These are children of parishioners whose parents trust the pastor and willingly place their children in his care. Often, these clerics play the role of substitute parent (Hidalgo, 2007; John Jay College, 2004). Many abusive priests, for example, targeted single mothers to whom they offered themselves as surrogate parent. Often poor and saddled with numerous offspring, these mothers welcomed the support offered, therefore unwittingly putting their children in the hands of the perpetrator. The victims were then groomed carefully through providing rewards, isolating them, offering spiritual justifications, and finally encouraging them to share the shame and secrecy for the sexual behaviors. The abuse usually took on spiritual overtones, like praying together as the initial intimate contact. Isolation too was accomplished through elevating the victims spiritually in the eyes of their peers. For example, being made a special altar boy to whom Father gives special privileges serves to separate a victim from his peers (Hidalgo, 2007). At one time, adults too might have been hesitant to question such a relationship setting the scene for later cover-up.

Impact of Abuse by Clergy

Many have wondered and voiced the question—"If child sexual abuse is so prevalent in our society today, why does sexual abuse by clergy attract so much attention?" Frawley-O'Dea (2007) comments, in relation to the Catholic Church:

> I think a partial answer is in the hypocrisy it bespeaks. The Catholic Church tells us that it knows the truth and lives the truth of moral principles deriving directly from Jesus Christ. The Church is particularly certain and stringent about what is morally correct in the area of human sexuality. At the same time that popes and other officials spoke with convictions about how human beings should lead their moral lives, however, they were and still are presiding over a moral scandal of the worst kind—the sexual abuse of children and young people by priests and the ecclesiastical cover-up of those crimes. The juxtaposition of manifest moral rectitude offset by evidence of underlying moral corruption capture the human imagination. (p. 7)

Although this author speaks of the Catholic Church, all churches teach the importance of moral integrity. Therefore, the impact of abuse by clergy is significant and has been threefold. First and foremost, it has had an *effect on individual victims*. Victims have experienced what others who have been sexually abused have grappled with—fears, nightmares, flashbacks, poor self-esteem, and other indicators of post-traumatic stress. Survivors often experience a sense of powerlessness, anger, difficulty trusting, addiction to drugs or alcohol, relationship difficulties, dissociation, and somatic complaints (Crosson-Tower, 2006). But abuse by clergy is further compounded by an assault to the faith and beliefs of the individual in a most intimate way. The fact that someone who is so closely associated with God has betrayed the victim's trust leads to deep feelings of betrayal as well as questions about the compassion and power of God. Would a benevolent God let such a thing happen? As one survivor put it,

ೞ ————————————————————

When I was a kid and our minister was sexually abusing me, I figured God knew and thought it was okay. After all, God was everywhere and knew all, and here was his spokesman doing these things to me. God must know. It drove me away from the church and God for many years afterward. ☙

Thus, the victim may develop a mistrust of God that turns him or her away from any faith. Even in later life, survivors discover that the scars are still there.

ೞ ————————————————————

I went back to church after being gone for many years. My wife told me that the church had changed a great deal, and it wouldn't bother me to go. But this was a church that still used incense, and suddenly the smell brought back the memories . . . the images of being a timid little boy abused by our parish priest in the back of the altar where the faint smell of incense still lingered. I could feel my skin tingling with fear as I tried to concentrate on the worship. ☙

In addition, the victim may feel abandoned by God and devoid of anywhere to turn in his or her need.

ೞ ————————————————————

I always wondered why God had not intervened when the priest fondled my privates in the dark recesses of the rectory. He would take me to this room that seemed not to be used too often. At first I used to pray that God would lead someone to find us or that God would send down a lightning bolt to crush Father John right there. At night I would pray that it would never happen again. But God did not seem to hear, and it would happen again and again. Finally I decided that he just wasn't listening and eventually I concluded that it was my fault that he had abandoned me. I just wasn't important enough for him to hear my prayers. ☙

Because God is often characterized in traditional theology as a male, victims of male clerics may suffer this confusion between God and their abuser. However, even those abused by females may have faith issues.

ೞ ————————————————————

I was abused by a nun, Sister Mary. I wasn't even sure it was abuse at the time. She taught at my school and used to invite me over for cookies after school. We got really friendly. She had a little house near the school. There were other nuns who lived with her, but they never seemed to be there. I think they had other jobs.

One day, when I was pretty young, I had fallen at school and was really dirty. I had on new uniform pants, and they were full of mud. I knew my Mom would be furious, and I was crying about it. Sister told me to take them off, and she'd wash them. I should get into the bathtub. I thought it was kind of neat, taking a bath at a nun's house. I wondered if the water they used was holy. When I got out, she started to help me get dried, and then she began rubbing my genitals without the towel. I remember how good it felt. My mother had told me that touching myself was a sin, but I figured that if a holy person like her did it, it was okay. I started going over there a lot, and she would find other excuses to touch me. I liked it for a while. But then she started getting weird and demanding, insisting that I should do things to her. I didn't like that as well and tried to resist. She also told me I had to keep our relationship a secret, and I began to realize that we weren't supposed to be doing what we were.

One day another nun came home and found us touching each other. She didn't say anything to us, but she slammed the door really hard and then came back in and sent me home. Sister Mary was gone from school the next day and never returned. They said she'd gotten sick. I felt awful. I was sure that I made her sick, or then I decided that I had killed her. My mother said that some sexual things were mortal sins, and I figured that meant God killed you for them. Maybe Sister Mary had been killed because of what we were doing. And then I had trouble facing anyone. I was sure that everyone knew that I'd killed her. I felt God's recrimination on me too. As a teenager, I began to look at the Virgin Mary and somehow see Sister Mary. It made me want to avoid her, too. I realized that, when I was in church, I felt dirty and shameful. I left the church, trying to put it out of my mind. ◈

In addition to having an impact on the victim, abuse by clergy *affects those close to the victims.* Parents too find that they are confused about their faith. How could they have blindly believed that all was well and not have seen the signs. Parents who have encouraged their children's relationships with the parish priest feel guilt and even anger at themselves. Concerned parents watch helplessly as their children suffer from the effects of clergy abuse. One mother, whose adolescent son committed suicide after it was discovered that their parish priest had been abusing boys for years, speaks of her own anguish.

◈

I kept going over and over the few weeks before Neil died, trying to figure out what I could have done—how I could have helped him not to take such a horrible and permanent action. It will haunt me. ◈

Friends of victims wonder what they could have done to help; why did they not realize what

had been happening. Those who had been abused think about how a disclosure on their part might have helped others. Those who were not targeted by a particular priest ruminate over why their friend was abused and not them.

It is not only the family and friends of the victim who are impacted but abuse by clergy has *an effect on those close to the abuser.* The family of the abuser who may have been proud of the abuser's choice of profession finds that pride now tarnished. Family members look back, wondering if they could have detected some difference in the abuser—something that might have alerted them of his future misdeeds (Crosson-Tower, 2006). If the abuser is a deacon or minister with a wife and family, they feel the impact. A wife (or husband) must recognize that she (he) is not the abuser and that she (he) is also a victim.

◈

I could not believe how I felt right after George was arrested, explained Penny, the wife of a Protestant minister who was abusing young girls in the church. Not only did I wonder if I could have seen what was happening before it got to that point but I wondered if I could have stopped it. I felt tainted somehow—like it was partially my fault. Could I have been a better wife? I was afraid to go anywhere. Would people point the finger at me? ◈

A partner and children need the ability to talk to someone, receive support, and grieve over the losses that they have suffered—the betrayal by the abuser, their perceived loss of respectability, and often the loss of a livelihood and lifestyle (Crosson-Tower, 2006).

One of the most obvious effects of abuse by clergy *is on the churchgoer,* whether within an affected church or just of the same faith (Kline et al., 2008; McGlone, 2003). Seeking to make changes within the church that would prevent such wide scale abuse from happening again, a group of laypeople within the Catholic Church initiated the group Voice of the Faithful, soon after the outbreak of the Boston scandal. This group has been vocal in calling for greater transparency and accountability in all dioceses. Even those who have not joined such groups speak of how their faith in the church has been shaken. Elder members of the Catholic Church lament about how the foundation of their lives now seems no longer reliable.

And finally, abuse by some clergy *affects other clergy*, some of whom feel that their once honorable profession has become tarnished by the scandals.

⊗

I used to enjoy the trust that I had from my congregations, explained one priest. I enjoyed having them come to me, helping them through a myriad of everyday struggles. Today, it is different. I wonder about that little bit of mistrust that might be in the minds of each of my parishioners—always wondering—will I step out of line and be abusive? I never have, and I don't believe that I will. I resent the way these scandals have affected me and others like me who are not abusers and have never knowingly met one for whom we are covering. ∞

LESSONS FROM THE CRISIS OF CLERGY ABUSE

Those who have studied the abuse scandals, especially within the Catholic Church, strive to come up with answers as to the cause—answers that will inform the future of the modern church. Critics of the crisis in the Catholic Church observe the changes that have already resulted from the scandals and project future changes. Certainly lay voices have taken on greater strength and initiative. Much like a family impacted by incestuous sexual abuse, church members—like nonabusive family members—have been forced to consider their own roles (Courtois, 2010). Those within churches that have experienced clergy abuse may learn that the congregation helped to enable the abuser (Crosson-Tower, 2006). As more denominations begin to realize this fact, there is an increased need for scrutiny of church practices and policies on both a local and wider level. Many churches are now developing safe church policies that aid them in recognizing abusive behavior and reporting it. As more churches seek to build in such safeguards, they may be less attractive to those with abusive tendencies.

Initiatives have also been taken to prevent sexual abuse before it happens. For example, in the wake of the sexual abuse crisis in Boston, the Office of Child Advocacy of the Archdiocese of Boston undertook to train anyone in its parishes who came in contact with children. In addition, all children in Catholic schools in the archdiocese as well as those in religious education in individual parishes are required to attend prevention training offered by the archdiocese. The prevention efforts have been extensive.

On a national level, the USCCB addressed the problem of sexual abuse by priests in its 2002 meeting, taking a stance on the problem and offering some solutions. This included the establishment of a National Review Board, the publication of the national Charter for the Protection of Children and Young People, and ongoing national audits of dioceses and archdioceses to ensure that they are addressing prevention (see http://www.usccb.org/issues-and-action/child-and-youth-protection/charter.cfm). Given the current crisis among Catholic churches in Ireland and other locations in Europe, there is increased collaboration between Catholics on what can be done to address the problem of abuse by clerics. Protestant churches and Jewish synagogues too have paid more attention not only to safe church protocol but also to opportunities for prevention training for staff and parishioners.

In addition to prevention with parishioners and churches, seminaries are beginning to recognize not only the need for screening applicants but also the necessity for adding to the curriculum material that will train future clergy around appropriate boundaries and sexual health. Andover Newton Theological School, a leading Protestant seminary, has two courses addressing child abuse: "Ministering to Abused and Neglected Children and Their Families" and "When the Shepherd Strays: An Overview of Abuse by Clergy." These two courses serve to acquaint future clergy with the problem of child maltreatment and how they might encounter it in parishes but also include affective components that help seminarians assess their own risk of becoming abusive.

Summary

Over the last few decades, abuse by clergy, especially priests, has been a hot topic for the media and the subject of research by others. The interest peaked as a result of the scandal of abuse by priests in the Catholic Church. One of the first cases was uncovered in Louisiana in 1983 when Father Gilbert Gauthe was found to be molesting boys. This and other scandals prompted the writing of Jason Berry's book, *Lead Us Not Into Temptation*, which exposed a variety of other instances of abuse by priests.

The archdioceses of Chicago and Boston both struggled with addressing the problem when some priests within their churches were found to be abusive. One name that became a household word was Father James Porter, who molested boys within the Boston and Fall River dioceses. He later left the priesthood but continued his molestations until he was found by one of his former victims and brought to trial.

The Boston scandal became one of the best known not only because of the massive cover-up involved but also through the efforts of the *Boston Globe* investigative staff who chronicled the abuses and cover-up in their book, *Betrayal*.

Responding to the numerous reports across the United States, the John Jay College of Criminal Justice studied the phenomenon of abuse by priests and published a 2004 report that documented that between 1950 and 2002, there were 4,392 priests in the United States who had abused minors. Experts who have studied the abuse, especially in Boston, relate that there were two issues in the scandal: First, there was the abuse by priests and then the fact that the church covered it up. But was this a uniquely Roman Catholic problem? Most theorists believe that, although there are factors within Roman Catholicism like celibacy and the training and role of priests that put them at risk, sexual abuse is a problem for Protestant and Jewish faiths as well.

Clergy who abuse have tended to target males in their young teens rather than younger children, giving rise to the distinction that they are considered to be ephebophiles rather than pedophiles. These offenders have often had difficult family backgrounds and feel isolated, which is compounded through seminary training. They are then attracted by what the church can offer them: respect, opportunities to be with children, being cared for, and so on.

The impact of clergy abuse on both victims and churchgoers is significant. Being betrayed by a respected representative of God damages faith and has driven the faithful from church attendance. Clergy abuse has also traumatized victims beyond the usual effects of child sexual abuse. In addition, abuse by some members of the clergy impacts nonoffending clergy, giving them concern about any cleric's ability to be trusted by parishioners.

The positives that have come from the clergy abuse scandals are the attention to the development of policies that keep children safe in churches and the development and offering of sexual abuse prevention training in religious settings.

Review Questions

1. Where were the most widely publicized cases of child sexual abuse in the Catholic Church?

2. How did the problem of abuse by clergy first come to light on a national level?

3. What was the first major study on priest abuse, and what did that study indicate was the problem?

4. What was meant by the Catholic cover-up?

5. Is abuse by clergy uniquely a Roman Catholic problem? Why or why not?

6. What are some of the characteristics associated with clergy perpetrators?

7. What is the impact of abuse by clergy on victims?

8. What is the impact of clergy abuse on the community at large?

9. What lessons may have been learned from the clergy abuse scandals?

10. What steps are currently being taken to protect children from abuse by clergy?

PART III

Intervention

CHAPTER 11

Initial Intervention in Child Sexual Abuse

The dynamics of child sexual abuse are complex and call for careful intervention and assessment. First, intervening authorities deal with children who may not be able to express themselves in a clear or concise manner. In addition, the public's emotional reaction often implies that offenders are not suitable for rehabilitation, and one need only confine them in prison and throw away the key. Sensitive intervention is required in light of the impact of disclosure not only on the victim but also on the family members of the victim and the offender. And finally, there may be cultural implications that influence intervention, assessment, and later treatment. The language, values, and customs of ethnic groups will play a part in how child sexual abuse is handled within their environment.

HOW DOES CHILD SEXUAL ABUSE COME TO THE ATTENTION OF THE "SYSTEM"?

Child sexual abuse exists in an atmosphere of secrets and therefore may not always be easily uncovered. Disclosure may occur in a variety of ways and may be either purposeful or accidental (see Sgroi, 1982).

Purposeful Disclosure

Children do not always recognize that sexual abuse is wrong. If they tell someone about it, it is usually because they are either trying to make sense of what is happening to them or they just want the abuse to stop.

———————————————————— ‎⛬ ————————————————————

When Danny was sexually abused by a neighborhood boy, he wasn't sure what was happening. He knew that what the older boy was doing to him felt kind of good, but he worried that meant that he was gay. He knew that the kids in his neighborhood who were gay didn't have it easy. Sometimes they got beaten up, and at the very least, they got harassed. Trying to sort out his feelings, Danny confided in his older brother who said that there was nothing wrong with Danny, but that he had to tell their mom. Reluctantly, he did so.

———————————————————— ‎⛬ ————————————————————

A *child may disclose to a trusted adult* that he or she is being sexually abused. In some cases, children tell their peers who recognize the need for them to tell an adult. Some disclosures are outright admissions, but others may come in the form of metaphor to which the adult must be sensitive.

Sylvia Beecher began her career as the counselor for a middle school. During her tenure there, quite a few children had reported to her that they had problems at home. Many told her that Dad or Mom hit them or were never home. She also had complaints that "my uncle is messing with me" or similar stories. Sometimes the middle schooler would ask if she could talk to her about a "friend" whose father was touching her in ways that made her feel funny. It would become fairly obvious as the story progressed that her student was actually the "friend" in question. But in her new role in the elementary school, it took her a few minutes to realize that 7-year-old Pundy's concerns about his beloved stuffed bear were cries for help with sexual abuse. Pundy's family was newly immigrated from Calcutta, India. His teacher asked Sylvia to see him because he was talking about how his bear hurt "behind his legs," and the teacher did not at first know what he meant. After observing a recent prevention training with her class on sexual abuse, Pundy's teacher wondered if there might be a connection. After talking to Pundy about his bear, which he clutched tightly to him, Sylvia began to recognize that the bear's "hurt" was Pundy's own. Further investigation uncovered sexual abuse by a family "friend" who had sodomized the boy, causing physical injuries.

In addition to being harmed physically by the abuse, children may want it to stop because they have recognized that it is wrong. When a school or other organization working with children provides prevention training, it is not uncommon for children to disclose that they are being abused. Often the prevention training has given them the comfort of a trusted adult to whom they can reach out to disclose.

Some children disclose to protect younger siblings whom they recognize could be the perpetrator's next targets. Ironically, when the abuser does go on to abuse a younger sibling, the original victim may experience an element of jealousy.

This may sound strange unless one recognizes that the abuse has often been surrounded by a good deal of attention from the perpetrator that may include such benefits as time, gifts, special outings, or being made to feel special.

Other reasons for purposeful disclosure may be fear of becoming pregnant or a desire to participate in age-appropriate activities. In order to ensure that the child keeps the secret of the abuse, many perpetrators are possessive, limiting the contact the child has with others. When a child grows older, she or he may see peers with more freedom to go places and date, whereas the victim feels restricted by the abuser. Thus, by disclosing the abuse, the victim hopes that it will stop and she or he will have more freedom.

Most children hope that when they tell an adult about the abuse, it will stop. They do not realize the turmoil that will be generated when the abuse is disclosed. What adults also forget sometimes is that some children may have relationships with abusers that they value. Some are upset when they are told, after disclosure, that they can have little or no contact with the abuser.

Sexual offenders control the possibility that a child will disclose the abuse by suggesting that there will be dire consequences if the child tells anyone. Perpetrators may threaten any of the following:

- "No one will believe you if you tell."
- "We will be separated and not be able to see each other again."
- "I will be put in jail."
- "You will break up our marriage [when the offender is married] if you tell anyone."
- "Everyone will think you are a slut."
- "You will be sent away."
- "Everyone will be really angry and upset ['with you' is implied]."

In fact, when a child does disclose the abuse, some of these threats may become real. The perpetrator and the child will probably be separated with the offender possibly going to jail or prison. In some cases, marital relationships do dissolve, and the adults impacted may blame the child and erroneously accuse him or her of leading the abuser on. If the perpetrator is in the child's home and the nonabusing parent will not or cannot protect the child from further abuse, the child's removal to a foster home is always possible. And the child's world may feel a good deal worse before he or she can see any benefits from intervention. Even though he or she cannot know all the implications, a child who considers disclosing will weigh the consequences of that disclosure against the continuation of the abuse.

When a child discloses voluntarily, it is important to discern his or her motivation in order to be of the most help. The child may be looking for magical solutions, assuming perhaps that once the secret is out, all will be well. Sgroi (1982) suggests that the child be provided with what she refers to as *anticipatory guidance*—that is, an explanation of what might happen next. The child should also be helped to recognize that there might be a wide variety of reactions from his or her family to the disclosure. Children who tell are sometimes blamed for disrupting the family. The reactions of family members will be discussed later in this chapter.

When a child reports being abused, it may be difficult for adults to hear. Adults prefer not to believe that another adult would sexually molest a child. Sax recommends the following (adapted from 2009a, p. 90):

- The child should be taken seriously, assuring him or her that he or she is believed.
- A report should be made to child protective services (CPS) or the police.
- Adults close to the child may be asked to participate in or support the child during an investigation.
- The child should be assured that sexual abuse is never his or her fault.
- The child should be told that he or she has made the right decision by telling an adult.

Can a child who reports abuse be believed? In fact, it is difficult for a child to talk about a subject as sensitive as abuse. Therefore, it often takes courage for the child to come forward. Obvious disbelief on the part of a trusted adult may cause the child to doubt his or her own perception, recant the allegation, and not get the help that is needed. Young children, especially, do not have the words or information to talk about sexual behavior that they have not seen or experienced. Even older children who might be more sexually knowledgeable may not have the sexual sophistication to fabricate an abuse report. Thus, it is important to seek help for the child and allow the experts to determine the validity of the abuse.

Sgroi, one of the first theorists to write about validation in child sexual abuse, notes that the presence of the following enhances the child's credibility (1982, pp. 69–73):

- If the child describes multiple incidents over time. When a child has the courage to disclose, the abuse has usually gone on for a period of time.
- When there is a progression of sexual activity from less to more intrusive.
- If there are elements of secrecy, for example, the perpetrator has told the child to keep the secret.
- When there are elements of pressure and coercion on the part of the perpetrator. The perpetrator may use bribes, misinterpretations, pressure, or other forms of coercion to enlist the child's "cooperation."
- If the child has explicit details of the sexual behavior (especially if these are beyond the expected knowledge of the child's age group).

Accidental Disclosure

Accidental disclosure occurs when another person recognizes the child displaying symptoms of sexual abuse or someone witnesses the abuse.

The most obvious way that the abuse comes to the attention of adults is through recognition of physical indicators. Unfortunately, physical signs may not always be present or may be observable only by a select group of adults, like parents, other caretakers, and medical personnel. Such injuries may be (Adams, 2010; Berkoff et al., 2008; Cooper, Estes, Giardino, Kellogg, & Vieth, 2007; Faller, 1990; Muram & Simmons, 2008; Sgroi, 1982)

- trauma to the genital area including lacerations, bleeding, or burns either internal or external;
- foreign bodies in the genital, rectal, or urethral openings;
- abnormal dilation of the urethral, vaginal, or rectal openings;
- trauma to the breasts, buttocks, lower abdomen, or thighs;
- the presence of sexually transmitted diseases;
- sperm in or around the vagina, especially in a prepubescent child;
- pregnancy; and
- HIV/AIDS (although children may contract the disease in other ways).

It is also possible for a child to cause physical harm to himself or herself in reaction to the abuse. Compulsive masturbation that becomes excessive may be the child's way of reacting to the abuse and may result in discomfort that is observed by parents and professionals.

Sexual abuse may also be observed by others.

ଔ ─────────────────────────────

Summer hated the games of hide-and-seek that her teenage cousin liked to play with her sister Reba and her. She tried to hide, because when she was "it," what happened was always the same. Sixteen-year-old Derrick would get into the hiding place with her and touch her all over before he would call out that he had found her. She wondered if he did the same thing to Reba. Then one day when he "found" Summer, Derrick showed her how to put her mouth on his penis. When she resisted, he told her that if she didn't do it, he'd tell her father about how she had stolen some candy out of the penny candy bin at the country store. Knowing how angry her father would be, Summer did as Derrick directed. Suddenly the door of the closet where they were hiding flew open, and Reba was standing there.

"What are you two . . . ?" the words froze on her lips. Suddenly she burst out, "I see what you are doing! Ugh! I'm gonna tell Ma! Ma . . . !" and she ran off to disclose their secret.

───────────────────────────── ଔ

Sometimes a child's sexualized behavior is noticed by an adult who becomes concerned about abuse. In young children, sexualized behavior may indicate a knowledge that is beyond what is typical for their age. For example, when 4-year-old Eric was "humping" another child in preschool, his teacher suspected that it was behavior that he had either observed or experienced. It was disclosed that an 18-year-old stepbrother was forcing the child to watch pornographic videos and then sexually molesting him. Any young child who knows of or demonstrates oral-genital contact, especially if he or she knows that ejaculation can occur, has mostly likely been asked to perform or has experienced fellatio.

AMBER Alerts

Children may also be abducted by those who intend to sexually abuse them. An AMBER alert is used to notify drivers, communities, and cell phone users that an abduction has taken place. The alert is used only when (a) law enforcement has established that a child has in fact been abducted and (b) it believes that the child is in danger of serious bodily harm (Sax, 2009b). Through this program, law enforcement cooperates with broadcasters and transportation agencies in the interest of bringing the child home safely. Often television programming is interrupted so that viewers can be given a physical description of both the child and the abductor, as well as information about the site of the abduction, the vehicle involved, and other information necessary to find the child. Some freeways in larger urban areas have signage capable of electronically displaying information about the vehicle and its license number so that drivers might help in the search (Sax, 2009b).

Mandated Reporting

As of the 1974 Child Abuse Prevention and Treatment Act, every state has designated individuals who are *mandated reporters*: that is, individuals required by law to report all forms of child abuse and neglect, including child sexual abuse. Mandated reporters are identified by some state statutes by a laundry list of professionals (e.g., police, school personnel, medical professionals). Other states indicate that any person is responsible for making a report when he or she suspects child sexual abuse is occurring. These state laws also spell out a variety of other scenarios regarding how and to whom child abuse must be reported (Crosson-Tower, 2002, 2014).

- *To whom must a report be made?* In some states, the first agency to receive a report is the police or the district attorney (DA), whereas in others, reports are made directly to public CPS, child welfare, or social and human services. There may also be stipulation as to when reports should be made to what agency. For example, some states require that sexual abuse by a caretaker be reported to child protection whereas non-caretaker cases should be brought to the attention of law enforcement.

- *When must a report be made?* State laws usually give one of three scenarios: suspicion of abuse, reasonable cause to believe there is abuse, or reasonable cause to suspect that there is abuse. Those not designated as mandated reporters are also encouraged to report abuse.

- *What is the time period in which the report will be investigated by the appropriate agency?* Time periods range from 2 hours to 30 days depending upon who receives the report.

- *What if mandated reporters fail to report?* Failure to report on the part of a mandated reporter is punishable by anywhere from a fine to imprisonment.

- *What immunity is there for mandated reporters who do report?* All states provide some type of immunity if a report is made in good faith.

Anyone may make an anonymous report of abuse, but generally agencies like CPS encourage reporters to identify themselves for several reasons. First, intake workers from CPS agencies are required to investigate a report if it comes from a mandated reporter but can use their own judgment on anonymous calls. If the caller is in fact a mandated reporter who could be fined or imprisoned for not reporting, anonymity does not protect him or her from consequences of not making a report. Plus, perpetrators and families often expend a good deal of energy trying to determine who made an anonymous report. Disclosing that information up front allows them to process their feelings and get on with addressing the important issues.

Influence of Culture on Intervention

It is vital to recognize the importance of cultural sensitivity when intervening in child sexual abuse cases. Jones, Loredo, Johnson, and McFarlane-Nathan (1999) cite several barriers to the effective management of sexual abuse from a cultural perspective. One barrier is what these authors refer to as *institutional racism*: that is, most institutional systems—such as educational, mental health, child protection, and criminal justice systems—look at problems from a monocultural perspective. Institutional racism supports the marginalizing of minority and lower socioeconomic populations, which adds to the overrepresentation of minorities in the client population. This may also serve to increase prejudice against those deemed "difficult and unworthy" and thus influence the resources available for addressing the services provided.

Ethnocentrism also comes into play. This can be defined as using one's own values or standards from one's cultural background to make judgments about those from other cultures (Jones et al., 1999). Ethnocentrism may be system wide or within a particular profession or may be the problem of an individual worker. Thus, when intervening with child sexual abuse, workers are encouraged to examine their values and prejudices as well as be aware of those of the profession or wider system in which they are employed (DePanfilis & Salus, 2003; Fontes, 2008; Fontes & Plummer, 2012; Rothman, 2007). Agencies are now recognizing the need to train workers in cultural sensitivity, but if this training is not available on an agency level, it is important for workers to find ways to learn about the cultures that they serve.

Lewis (1999) points to several areas that may create problems when working with minorities: biculturality, family tradition and structure, degree of acculturation, language, eye contact, help-seeking behavior, social tolerance for deviance, and spirituality. *Biculturality* becomes problematic in that families from diverse racial and cultural groups, especially the newly immigrated, are often striving to function in two different environments: their culture of origin and that of their new environment. Often their children adapt more easily than their parents and other relatives, a fact that can bring with it a myriad of relationship problems. *Family structures and traditions*, including roles, rules, and values that differ from those of the wider environment, create tension that may be reflected in family disharmony or put the family out of sync with those around them. Some individuals and families find it easier to move from the family culture to the mainstream culture (termed *acculturation*) than others. *Language* too presents a stumbling block. Certainly those who either speak English or learn it easily feel more at home in public places unless those places accommodate cultural minorities through multilingual signs and resources. For those who are not English speaking, interpreters must be provided. Having an interpreter, however skilled, places one more barrier and chance of misunderstanding between the client and the provider.

Something as seemingly subtle to an Anglo culture as *eye contact* can create problems for those from other cultures. Although the mainstream culture sees looking someone in the eye as a sign of honesty and respect, other cultures see this behavior as rude and disrespectful. In communication between men and women, eye contact can have serious implications. Not every ethnic group sanctions asking for help with problems from outside the family or ethnic group as something one should do. *Help-seeking behaviors*—that is, the way in which one is able to ask for help—vary widely among cultures and individuals. Some cultural groups believe that to be involved with the "system"—even as a victim—is shameful and unwise. This belief may play out through client resistance, missing appointments, or withdrawal. Such client behaviors can be interpreted by culturally insensitive agencies as uncooperative and uncaring for the children (Fontes, 2008).

In addition, some ethnic groups have more *tolerance for social deviance*. For example, Lewis (1999) relates that

[m]uch of the sexual abuse in Native American families involves father-daughter and stepfather-stepdaughter incest. Frequently, the offender is not convicted of a sexual crime and does not receive treatment for a psychosocial disturbance. Instead, he is treated for alcoholism or other substance abuse problems. The offender's spouse and the community then accept that the "problem" has been addressed. (p. 54)

And finally, *spirituality* differs from cultural group to cultural group. For example, for many African Americans, spirituality is central to their lives. A prominent cultural view is that this group survived slavery through a strong spiritual foundation (Fontes, 2008; Fontes & Plummer, 2012; Lewis, 1999). But religion and spirituality should not be seen as the same. Therefore, it will be important for a worker to become familiar with what spirituality and religion mean to a client from a diverse ethnic group not only to work with the client but also to determine if need be whether the individual client's view is culturally specific or deviant. While learning about the values of a specific culture, it is also important not to generalize completely. Some workers have reported that what they assumed was a cultural variation was, in fact, not a part of the client's culture but rather indicative of the client's own pathology. Workers must learn to use knowledge of culture as a backdrop against which to attempt to understand the individual.

True and False Allegations

Do children falsely report that they have been sexually abused? What if an angry spouse accuses another of sexual abuse during a divorce? Can symptoms observed in a child lead to the incorrect assumption that the child is being sexually abused? Although all of these are possible, experts find that false allegations are less likely than one might guess. And because child protection agencies do not take reports lightly, workers are also trained to weed out false reports.

As mentioned earlier, reports may originate from purposeful disclosure by the victim or a report from another individual. It was also explained that children, especially young children, rarely have the necessary details to confirm a report of sexual abuse that they have not experienced. A carefully orchestrated interview by a trained protective worker or trained police officer will usually determine if the child's report is accurate. But what of older children in a society where peer-to-peer sexual activity is occurring at younger and younger ages? What if a youth with more experience wants to strike out at an adult and accuses him or her of sexual abuse? Even though older children and teens may have the knowledge to make a seemingly convincing report, there are details that will not support the abuse report.

ൠ _____

Thirteen-year-old Dee, who was extremely jealous of her mother's new boyfriend, Marty, told a neighbor that he was sexually abusing her. The neighbor reported this to CPS. After interviewing Dee, her mother, and Marty, all individually, the intake worker suspected that the allegation was false but did not let on to the alleged victim. Dee's story seemed plausible until she recounted the details of the abuse. Although Dee stated that Marty had invited her to view his penis, masturbate him, and bring him to ejaculation, the girl had very little information about the mechanics of this act. Nor did she know that Marty was being treated for erectile dysfunction and had also lost all of his pubic hair due to another medical issue. Pointing out some of these discrepancies to Dee resulted in her admission that Marty had never touched her sexually.   ൠ

Despite this particular case, most experts believe that erroneous reports of abuse by children are few. One study done by the Kempe Center found that false allegations comprised only 1% of all reports made (Jones & McGraw, 1987). In a follow-up study by the same center, only 2.5% of the cases were false reports. These cases fell into three categories: The child was compelled by an adult to allege abuse (three cases, or 0.5%), the child was confused or mistaken (three cases, or 0.5%), and the child himself or herself fabricated the report (eight cases, or 1.5%) (Oates et al., 2000, as reported in Faller, 2007a, p. 203).

Although reports of sexual abuse have sometimes been alleged during divorce proceedings, some experts point out that divorces may occur as a result of sexual abuse being discovered. In addition, the nature of divorce proceedings may uncover previous abuse or the stress of family disharmony may precipitate abuse. In a relatively few instances are allegations of abuse that does not exist used successfully in divorce cases (Faller, 2007a; Sax, 2010).

REACTIONS OF PARTICIPANTS UPON DISCLOSURE _____

Child sexual abuse involves a variety of individuals— victims, abusers, and family members, all of whom may be experiencing a myriad of different reactions at the time of disclosure.

The Child Victim

The child victim of sexual abuse may have a myriad of emotions at the time when the abuse is uncovered. If the child has disclosed the abuse himself or herself or when the disclosure has been accidental (i.e., suspected, reported, or observed by another), the child may have a fleeting feeling of relief. Abuse is a heavy burden for a child to carry, and when the child can share that burden with another, he or she may feel better. And yet children are rarely prepared for the results of disclosure. They may not anticipate the chaos that a report sets into motion. "What have I done?" the child who has disclosed may wonder. She or he probably just wanted the abuse to stop without throwing the world into turmoil. The offender is often angry, and even if he or she is denied access to the child, the victim may be very much aware of that anger. Plus, the victim may have an attachment to the abuser and feel the loss of his or her proximity. As an inducement for secrecy, the offender may have told the child that if the abuse were disclosed, they would be separated, and now the child feels guilt at having precipitated the predicted outcome.

Abusers also try to make children believe that they have invited or actively participated in the sexual activity. As a result, children feel guilt and shame and wonder what will happen to them. Shame may be intensified that the secret is out. Children often feel dirty and damaged as bystanders react to what they perceive is an awful situation. Careful counseling by family members and professionals must let children know that the abuse is not their fault. In fact, when they learn that children have been abused, adults often do treat them like they have been damaged, thus intensifying the children's shameful feelings. In addition, if parents or others close to the victim believe the perpetrator rather than the child, trauma to the child is intensified.

Young victims who have disclosed may feel alone and isolated. It is crucial therefore that parents be helped to support their children emotionally and that intervention by those trained to understand the needs of victims be immediate.

One young adult who was abused as a child remembers clearly how she felt when, at 12, she told her mother of her abuse.

ॐ _____

When I told my mom that my stepfather sexually molested me, she didn't believe me at first. She put me in my room away from my sister while she talked to her husband. I was so afraid. I was sure that they would both come in and do—I don't know what—to me. I was so sorry that I had told her. I had just hoped that he would not start doing it to Ginny [younger sister]. I wanted to disappear. I even checked the windows to see if I could get out and run away, but they were painted shut. I looked in the bathroom for razor blades, thinking that I could kill myself, although I was not exactly sure how. I was shaking, and I even threw up at one point. I wondered if they'd send me away because I was too much trouble.

And then the door opened, and my mom came in. She was sobbing, and I flinched, thinking she would hit me or something. But she grabbed me roughly and hugged me and told me that she believed me. I remember this feeling washing over me—this relief. But immediately I thought of him—my stepfather. Where was he? Would he hurt me? And at the same time, I remembered the good stuff—the time he spent with me when my mom worked nights and the gifts he bought me. And I felt a terrible sense of loss.

"I told him to leave," my mother said, probably sensing some of what I was wondering. "He's gone." And then she started sobbing really hard, and I felt so guilty. What had I done to her? He was a good provider, and we had struggled for so many years before she married him. Maybe I should have just sucked it up and let him do what he wanted. ॐ

Faced with a myriad of conflicting feelings plus possible pressure from the abuser, children often are moved to recant and deny that the abuse happened. This is another reason why initial intervention by caring adults who believe and support the child is so crucial.

The Perpetrator

It is not always easy for professionals to consider the feelings of a perpetrator at disclosure. But the needs of this individual—no matter what he or she has done—must be addressed. Usually an abuser's first response is denial. Some individuals deny only to exonerate themselves; others really believe their own rationalizations and thinking errors (see Chapter 5) so they believe they have done nothing wrong.

ைை _____

"I really love Amy," one abuser of a 7-year-old girl told the worker. "Her mother is always on her case, and when she is not nagging her, she neglects her. Amy and me do things together. I'm good for her." ைை

Some abusers are capable at some point of feeling shame and guilt for what they have done to the child, but others are not. Even if they do feel any remorse, many will strive to make their case at the onset. One social worker, who dealt exclusively with sexual abuse, remarked that he had enough contacts from senators, congressmen, and influential people for a lifetime.

ைை _____

"Perpetrators go into 'circle the wagons and bring in the big guns' mode when a case comes to light," he commented. "They bring in anyone they know who they feel can influence their situation by intimidating the worker." ைை

Certainly underlying the offender's need to intimidate is an incredible sense of fear. Some offenders seek ways to escape. Suicidal thoughts are typical, and often offenders must be supervised closely to prevent them from carrying out these thoughts.

Offenders often project blame onto others. "If my wife had paid more attention to me, I wouldn't have abused our daughter" and "Those boys came on to me. I was just doing what they wanted" are not uncommon types of statements.

A therapist who treats offenders believes that the predominant sentiment among them at the point of disclosure is anger.

ைை _____

Some guys are angry that they have been caught. One of my clients kept talking about how burned he was by the police officer who caught him in a bathroom with a boy. He blamed the officer for not just walking on by! Some of my guys are angry with spouses or their victims for blowing the whistle on them. And sometimes, I'll get someone who is angry with himself for what he did. For the most part, my clients feel very much alone. On some level, they know that they don't "fit" with everyone else. Some tell me that they are angry at the cards that life dealt them. It's rationalization, but a lot of them figure they would never have been what they are if they had not had such lousy lives. ைை

Family Members of the Victim

Nonabusive family members also have a myriad of reactions at the time of disclosure. Often responses depend upon the identity of the perpetrator.

When the perpetrator does not reside with the child or is not a parent or immediate caretaker, parents are usually expected to support the child. And yet therapists sometimes forget that these parents have issues of their own.

ைை _____

My first response when I learned that Jenny had been molested by the husband of her math tutor was disbelief. Our daughter had been taking lessons in the Hobart home for several months. I knew that Mr. Hobart was at home on disability, but I never thought that his being there would be an issue. We had found Agnes Hobart through the school when Jenny was having difficulty with math. When we learned that Mr. Hobart had also been a math teacher before his auto accident and that he sometimes helped his wife, I remember thinking, "Great! Two for the price of one!" But Jenny's story seemed too real. She had details that horrified me. I felt a sick feeling in the pit of my stomach and knew I had to call someone and report it. But I worried for Jenny, too. At 9, she hardly needed this. But she hadn't needed the abuse either. After I called the police, Jenny started sobbing; she was so scared. I tried to comfort her, but there were all these thoughts in my head. I was angry—angry at both the Hobarts. How could this have happened? I was angry at myself for choosing them and putting Jenny in harm's way. Fleetingly, I wondered if Jenny had done anything to provoke the inappropriate touch, and then I was horrified at myself. What could a 9-year-old possibly do! No, the fault was mine for sending her there. My husband, Stan, had been against it. He thought that we should just help her ourselves and that she did not need outside instruction. Stan! I had to call him. I was as afraid of his reaction as anything. Would he blame me for hiring a tutor?

"Mommy? Will they take me away?" I heard my daughter ask.

"No honey, you did nothing wrong," I assured her. And then my mind flashed back to the time when our neighbor had molested me. I had put it out of my mind until this happened to Jenny. Having my parents call the police had been a nightmare for me. Surely they were better trained now. Then I wondered, had I somehow jinxed us? Was there some kind of curse that had predestined Jenny to be abused? Was Jenny somehow damaged as I had always felt damaged? So many thoughts and feelings and what I should have been doing was just comforting my daughter!

                                                                           ഇ

Parents whose children are abused outside the home may experience disbelief, anger, guilt, and need to comfort the child along with their own conflicts. For those who have been abused themselves, old mental tapes, bringing up possibly repressed feelings, may make it especially difficult for them. Those who believe that the abuse happened may want to overprotect the child in the future. Or some parents fault the child if he or she was somewhere that he or she should not have been. For example, Sam had been told not to go to the park without another child or adult with him. When he was abducted for several hours by a stranger who sexually molested him, his father was angry at Sam. "He was told not to go there!" the father bellowed. There had been previous molestation incidents that he had not told the boy about, thinking that his instruction to avoid the park alone would be sufficient. His anger with Sam for what this father felt had been a result of his son's disobeying made it difficult for him to see his son's need to be helped through the process of reporting.

Some parents feel shame that something as "unmentionable" as sexual abuse has happened to their child. In some instances, this shame may be enough to make them not want to report that anything has happened. Nor do they want others to know what has happened to their child or in their family. Public exposure feels as shaming as the abuse itself. Even well-meaning parents often tell the child to forget about the abuse and that it is over. Such intentional repression of an event as traumatic as sexual abuse can actually add to the child's own shame and trauma. There are also parents who do not believe their child's report of being abused. When pressuring children to keep the secret about being abused, perpetrators will often tell children that no one will believe them should they tell. The self-fulfilling prophecy of parents not believing them can lead to a feeling that the abuser is all powerful and/or that the child is at fault.

In Chapter 6, we discussed the feelings of nonabusing parents when they discover that their child has been abused by a family member within the home. The issue of conflicting loyalties when the perpetrator is close to or well liked by the parent may come into play even when the abuser is not a family member.

We had known Myrna and her family even before she had children. When John was born, I remember how excited I was. But when her husband was transferred to Germany, we didn't see them for years. By the time they returned, John was 15, and I had Gabrielle, who just turned 4. John seemed like a nice kid—quiet and into his computers—but aren't all kids today? I was pleased when he said that he would babysit for Gabby. But after several times of him watching her, Gabby seemed afraid of him. I finally got from her that John had been touching her in ways that confused her and sometimes hurt. I took her to a therapist to figure out why she'd say such things. The therapist told me that John was sexually abusing her and that she (therapist) would need to report it. I couldn't believe it. Surely it must not be true. We knew Myrna and Frank. How could their son whom I had loved as a baby ever be hurting my daughter?

When parents are dependent upon the abuser as one might be on a day care provider, physician, teacher, and so on, there is also a sense of disbelief. Abuse at the hands of someone who should be caring for a child is out of the frame of reference of most parents.

Siblings of a child who has been abused sexually often feel victimized by being overlooked. When the abuse is extrafamilial, there is often an attempt to keep it from the siblings. But children know when there is something wrong in their homes and pick up the shame associated with "whatever has happened." Families must be encouraged to talk with siblings to help them to cope with this family disruption.

Siblings of children exposed to intrafamilial abuse also experience a disruption of family life in a much more fundamental way. They may feel anger toward the perpetrator but also may resent the victim whom they see as the cause of the family crisis. They, too, suffer from shame after the disclosure that brings exposure and publicity. They often feel that they must choose between the victim and the perpetrator (Sgroi, 1982).

The period immediately following disclosure is difficult for all the individuals involved. It is so important that they receive competent care by well-trained professionals who understand the dynamics of child sexual abuse.

GOALS AND ROLES IN INTERVENTION

The process through which a child sexual abuse case is investigated will differ from state to state. Whether the case is reported through law enforcement or through CPS, there will be a protocol that will eventually be followed during which members of specific agencies assume their pre–agreed-upon roles. In some states, the police in specially trained units will be the first point of contact. In other areas, CPS assumes that role. In other instances, CPS will intervene and investigate if the child is abused by a caretaker, whereas law enforcement investigates in cases when the perpetrator is not caring for the child. *Caretakers* can also be loosely defined as those who at a given time are in that role. For example, day care providers or babysitters may, in some states, be investigated by CPS if the abuse is perpetrated while the child is in their care. The good news is that whatever agency receives a report of child sexual abuse, the prescribed protocol should help the case be directed to the proper agency. Ideally there should be a multidisciplinary team to improve communication.

The Multidisciplinary Team

The multidisciplinary team is a group of professionals from CPS, law enforcement, mental health, child advocacy, medical, and legal agencies who work together on behalf of a child sexual abuse victim. The coordination of this team streamlines the process and better serves victims and their families. For example, the use of such a team means that interviews will not have to be repeated, thus retraumatizing the child (Sax, 2009b). Another strength of a multidisciplinary team is that members have different areas of expertise and are able to collect the two types of information that is required: forensic, which pertains to court or legal proceedings, and clinical, which pertains to therapeutic, usually mental health, intervention (Faller, 2007a). Team members represent both of these perspectives and by working together will be able to glean information both for possible court intervention and for treatment planning for the healing of those involved.

Sax (adapted from Sax, 2009a, p. 119) summarizes the role of the various professionals as follows:*

Law Enforcement

- Responds to and stabilizes crime scenes
- Collects and preserves physical evidence
- May be involved in interviewing witness, especially the perpetrator
- Runs criminal history checks and gathers other information on the perpetrator

Children's Protective Services

- May take and respond to initial report (or report may be channeled through law enforcement)
- Determines immediate safety of children and whether they should remain in the home
- Determines what type of contact (or not) children should have with the perpetrator and parents
- May be involved in initial and/or assessment interviews
- Negotiates visitation (for children) with lawyers
- Presents state's case in family or juvenile court
- May coordinate the team

DA's Office/Prosecutor

- Assesses evidence for provability in a criminal case
- Determines what (if any) criminal charges should be filed
- Negotiates bail, plea agreements, and any other criminal actions
- Presents state's case at trial

Medical Professionals

- Interpret medical findings to the team
- Perform forensic medical exams
- Preserve physical evidence found during medical exam
- Testify in court as to medical findings

Child Advocate or Advocacy Agency

- May coordinate team or act as contact person
- Provides guidance in interviewing based on child's age, developmental abilities, gender, and emotional state
- Makes treatment recommendations and gives referral to child's caretaker
- May accompany the child to court if the case is filed

In some states, it is CPS that takes on the coordination and interviewing role, whereas the child advocate, if there is one, deals only with guarding the children's rights and preparing them for court.

The Child Protection Agency

CPS is a division within the state or county government that addresses the needs of abused and neglected children and their families. In most areas, CPS is the agency mandated through the Child Protection and Treatment Act of 1994 to investigate and assess maltreatment reports. In recent years, CPS is more likely to work as part of a team of community professionals who meet the needs of abused children and their families; although it is usually this agency that has the primary responsibility for service, contracting out when needed.

The philosophy of CPS is that parents love their children and with appropriate support can care for them and keep them safe. Some families need assistance to achieve adequate parenting, and it is CPS's role to provide that assistance, recognizing the impact of culture, race, economic status, and alternative lifestyles. At the same time,

---

*With some adaptation for other states.

families must be held responsible for the safety and well-being of their children. CPS workers also recognize that helping parents succeed is more likely to be accomplished when these parents are involved and actively participate in the helping relationship. When parents are unable to fulfill their obligations to their children, CPS must make reasonable efforts to develop safety plans, appreciating that children should be with their parents whenever possible, but ready to find alternative care to protect the children's well-being. Permanency planning—that is the best and most permanent setting for the child, as early as possible—is the CPS orientation (DePanfilis & Salus, 2003; Knight, Chew, & Gonzalez, 2005). Summarized, the CPS agency is responsible to (National Association of Public Child Welfare Administrators, 1999, as cited in DePanfilis & Salus, 2003, p. 25)

- assess the safety of the children,
- intervene to protect children from harm,
- strengthen the ability of families to protect their children, and
- provide either a reunification or an alternative, safe family for the child.

The CPS social worker (sometimes known as the protective services worker) is committed to the idea that each child has the right to a permanent family, that parents have untapped strengths that may help them to parent more effectively, and that each child and parent must be empowered to work toward clear goals. Workers are trained to understand family systems, human development, cultural diversity, child abuse and neglect dynamics, community resources, and conflict resolution (Crosson-Tower, 2014; DePanfilis & Salus, 2003; Knight et al., 2005).

Child Protection Process. Initial reports of child sexual abuse made to CPS are received by *intake*, which may be a specific unit or a section of a specialized unit (e.g., some agencies have a unit that handles sexual abuse specifically). Reports to CPS may come from the police, other professionals (e.g., teachers, physicians), private citizens, other social workers, therapists, and so on. Intake (referred to, by Knight et al., 2005, as *emergency response*) determines whether the report is a viable one and should be screened in or screened out. In many states, intake is obligated to screen a report in (i.e., move it on to assessment) if it came from someone who is designated by state law as being a mandated reporter. At this point, the case may also be referred to the DA's office if the referral has not already been done. Once screened in, the case goes into an initial investigation or assessment. States differ in how this is accomplished. In some states, police detectives have already commenced an initial investigation, which may then be ongoing (Sax, 2010). In other states or situations in which the report comes directly to CPS, it may be this agency that does the initial investigation (DePanfilis & Salus, 2003). And the DA's office may also do an investigation. These various investigations will have similar but different goals. The goals of CPS are to determine what is in the best interests of the child and how a family might be helped to provide a safe environment for that child. In working with perpetrators, CPS will be primarily concerned with not only the safety of the child but also the rehabilitation of the perpetrator. Criminal justice goals will be discussed in a later section.

The words *assessment* and *investigation* may be used interchangeably in many states, but they are not synonymous. An investigation, as done by CPS, is designed to determine if sexual abuse has occurred while assessment strives to evaluate the child's safety risk and determine what services will be needed to meet the child's and family's needs (DePanfilis & Salus, 2003). Assessment will be based on (DePanfilis & Salus, 2003, p. 26)

- identifying family strengths,
- identifying and addressing factors that place the child at risk and determining how these might be reduced, and
- helping the child (children) to cope with the effects of the sexual abuse.

One aspect that differs slightly from the way in which other agencies (e.g., criminal justice, legal) undertake investigations and assessment is that the CPS worker develops a relationship with the victim and family and often the perpetrator as well. This rapport building is vital to learning more about the situation as well as to determining the client strengths so that the principles can be engaged in later case management and treatment.

The fear expressed by most parents when they become involved with CPS is "will they take my child away from me?" In reality, this is the last resort. It is the CPS worker's role to try to enhance the family's ability to properly care for and support the child within the family and the community. Separation usually does not benefit a child unless he or she is in acute danger. When the perpetrator is a family member, CPS will usually seek to have the abuser removed from the home rather than the child.

Case planning follows assessment. It is during this phase that the CPS worker joins with the family in determining how the victim and family can be helped. Many agencies now draw up a *service provision plan* that outlines the goals of treatment and gives specific direction as to how these goals may be achieved. Service provision is part of case management when the CPS worker empowers the victim and family to access the services that they need. If the family is not able to support the victim and/or follow through, the work of the CPS worker may be primarily with the victim. The majority of CPS agencies provide only case management and do not have the resources to actually treat clients. Treatment is usually contracted out to agencies specializing in these services. The problem is that there are often few treatment resources or funds available for families seen by CPS to access.

Ideally, case closure would happen when a victim and family had been helped. The reality is that this is not always the case. Sexual abuse is extremely disruptive to most families and requires a great deal of time and effort for them to heal. Some are unable to follow through. Even when the victim and family are well motivated, the services they need may not be available, usually as a result of funding.

Criminal Justice and Child Sexual Abuse

The criminal justice system is usually involved in some manner in child sexual abuse cases; although in some states, other types of maltreatment may or may not involve police and the courts.

In some areas, it may be the patrol officer or "street cop" who receives a report of child sexual abuse. He or she may then do an initial investigation determining the who, what, where, when, and why of the situation. Then the case will usually be assigned to a detective. Detectives, unlike patrol officers, specialize in specific types of crime. Increasingly, there are detective units that address child-related crimes or more often sex crimes (Flora, 2001; Sax, 2010). This means that these detectives have been trained in their specific area, which is especially important when working with children and child sexual abuse. Detectives, determining that a sexual crime has occurred, will arrest the suspect and then refer the case to the DA—also called the prosecutor. It is the role of these two professionals to investigate the sexual crime that has been committed and determine how legal intervention will proceed.

Sax (2009b, p. 52) points out that the criminal justice system divides child sexual abuse into three categories—sexual assault, sexual molestation, and sexual exploitation—and uses specific definitions for each. *Sexual assault* that refers specifically to sexual contact is further divided into

- lewd and lascivious acts—any sexually motivated touching regardless of whether it is done in the child's private areas;
- rape—penile penetration of a child's vagina;
- sodomy—penile penetration of the child's anus (no matter how slight);

- digital penetration by a foreign object—the vagina or anus is penetrated by something other than the penis;
- oral copulation—when a person puts his or her mouth on a child's sexual organs; and
- incest—the perpetrator has a blood relation to the child.

Sexual molestation refers to the intent of the perpetrator to cause some type of sexually inappropriate behavior. An example might be indecent exposure in front of a child or peeking at a child for sexual purposes. Sax (2010) further identifies sexual molesters as preferential, or those fixated on children, and situational, or those who engage in some sexual behavior related to children although children are not their primary orientation. *Sexual exploitation* refers to the use of children by an adult for the adult's personal advancement, sexual gratification, or financial gain. An example would be the use of children in prostitution, human sex trafficking, or pornography, or the exposure of children to pornography or sexually explicit material.

The criminal justice system sees sexual abuse as a crime, subject to the same investigation procedures as any other crime. The fact that a child is involved, however, usually alerts the professionals involved that care must be taken to protect the child, whenever possible, from further trauma through intervention techniques and procedures. As the case is investigated, the prosecutor's responsibility will be to prove beyond reasonable doubt that a crime has been committed. When dealing with an issue like sexual abuse and with children as witnesses, this task is not always an easy or straightforward one. The investigative team will be looking for corroboration that supports the initial evidence and/or the child's story of what happened. Specifically the team will be looking at (Sax, 2009a)

- the defendant or alleged perpetrator's prior record (e.g., has he or she been convicted of similar charges?);

- medical evidence (e.g., genital injuries, other injuries, sexually transmitted diseases);
- physical evidence (e.g., bodily fluids, collection of pornography items in a car);
- scientific evidence (evidence leading to the assumption of the crime, e.g., pubic hair in a victim's mouth can corroborate oral sex); and
- defendant's statements (admissions or stories that do not support innocence).

Many cases of child sexual abuse lack the medical or physical evidence to prove conclusively that a crime was committed. One reason for this is that many sex abuse reports are not made immediately and the passage of time obscured evidence. When samples are not collected immediately, they may fail to produce evidence. For example, when a child bathes, there may no longer be any evidence of sexual contact. Further, although sexual acts may have been committed, there may be no injury. And even if injury occurred, the genital area heals remarkably quickly (Sax, 2009a; Sgroi, 1982).

If there is sufficient evidence to corroborate that sexual abuse has been committed, the case may go to court (see Chapter 12).

DIVORCE OR CUSTODY BATTLES AND CHILD SEXUAL ABUSE

In the last few decades, it has not been unusual to hear of allegations of child sexual abuse during nasty divorce proceedings. Although many who hear such accusations would assume that it was just another ploy to besmirch the character of one or other of the parents, former assistant DA Robin Sax (2010) believes that divorce cases actually "open the door" for the disclosure of legitimate cases of sexual abuse against children. Other experts agree. DeVoe's study of 169 cases of child sexual abuse in the mid-1990s (see Faller & DeVoe, 1995) concluded that 67% of the abuse reports that were uncovered at the time of divorce proceedings were substantiated. Faller (1991) identified four scenarios in which child abuse might become an issue during divorce. In some instances, the *abuse can lead to divorce.* In other situations, preexisting abuse that is not known to the nonoffending parent *comes to light during divorce proceedings.* The stress of the marital discord leading to the divorce *may also precipitate the abuse.* And finally, *some of the allegations of abuse may actually be false.*

Sax (2010) also points out that the process of divorce makes children vulnerable, and vulnerable children are the primary targets of sexual perpetrators. Thus, it is important to see that children whose parents are divorcing have support and outlets for their stress so that they are not put at risk for abuse outside the home as well.

From initial investigation, child sexual abuse cases that are screened in will then be assessed to determine what services are needed and can be offered. This will be the subject of Chapters 12 and 13.

Summary

Child sexual abuse comes to the attention of child protection agencies or law enforcement through either purposeful or accidental disclosure. Children often tell someone they are being abused to get it to stop because they find someone whom they feel they can trust or to prevent an abuser from targeting others. Offenders warn victims that they will not be believed or held accountable as a way of getting children to keep the secret. Such warning may deter children from telling; when the offender's predictions come true after disclosure, children may also be negatively impacted.

Accidental disclosure occurs when the abuse is observed by others or when the child exhibits physical or behavioral symptoms that point to abuse. Amber alerts have been established by law enforcement as a way to intervene when it is suspected that a child may have been abducted.

The Child Abuse Intervention and Treatment Law of 1974 designated certain people as mandated reporters who are required to report suspected child abuse. Each state defines these mandated reporters differently—some naming particular professionals whereas others including any person who suspects abuse. State laws also outline when and to whom reports of child maltreatment must be made.

When intervening in child sexual abuse, it is important to take into consideration that other cultures differ in their definition of and response to child abuse. It is also true that the behaviors practiced in some cultures may be considered abusive in the United States, but investigators must be trained to assess and deal with these variations. In addition, although young children especially do not have the information to make false reports, investigators assess the validity of a report carefully.

Each person impacted by child sexual abuse will have a different set of responses. Child victims may be confused about the chaos that follows the report of child sexual abuse. They may also experience fear, guilt, shame, and wonder what will happen to them. Children's relationships with abusers may have had positive aspects, and children feel the loss when they are separated. They may feel alone and isolated.

Perpetrators, too, have an array of feelings at disclosure. Some feel guilt, whereas others do not, believing instead that they are themselves victims of misunderstanding. Abusers often deny or blame others. It is not unusual for an abuser who has access to a victim to pressure the victim to recant.

Nonabusing family members also have a myriad of reactions. Some feel guilt at not protecting the child. Some feel anger at the abuser, whereas others believe the abuser over the child. Siblings, too, must be considered and are often the forgotten victims of child sexual abuse.

The goals of intervention are to stop the abuse and provide help for all involved. This is often best accomplished by multidisciplinary teams that include a variety of professionals trained to help in child sexual abuse case. The role of the child protection agency (CPS) is to investigate the abuse in an effort to determine what is best for the children. When a report is made to CPS, it will investigate, assess the treatment needs of the victim and family, and determine what plan should be developed. In the meantime, a referral is made to the office of the district attorney (DA), where a determination is made about the guilt or innocence of the alleged perpetrator and what course of action should be taken.

In some cases, sexual abuse is also uncovered or alleged in the process of divorce or custody battles.

Following initial intervention, a case will be referred for further assessment and treatment planning, the subjects of Chapters 12 and 13.

Review Questions

1. What are the ways that child sexual abuse might come to the attention of the "system"?

2. What is purposeful disclosure, and what steps should one take when receiving such a report?

3. How might accidental disclosure occur?

4. What is an Amber alert?

5. What is meant by "mandated reporting"? Who are mandated reporters?

6. What must one know when making a report?

7. What influence does culture have on intervention in child sexual abuse?

8. What are some of the typical reactions of the victim when abuse is disclosed? The perpetrator? Family members?

9. What is meant by *multidisciplinary team*?

10. What is the role of the child protection agency?

11. How does child protection interface with the criminal justice system?

CHAPTER 12

Assessment and Treatment Planning for Children and Family Members

Once a case involving child sexual abuse has been screened in and determined to require services, it is time to plan for the type of intervention or treatment that will be needed.

MODELS FOR ASSESSMENT

Over the last two decades, several models have emerged in the assessment of child sexual abuse, which have been summarized by Faller (2007a) as the child interview model, the joint investigation model, the parent-child interaction model, and the comprehensive assessment model.

The Child Interview Model

The child interview model is based on the interview of the alleged victim of the sexual abuse. It has its origins in the work of child protective services (CPS) that used interviews (or one interview) with the child as the primary method of investigation. Child advocacy centers adopted this approach, and some law enforcement agencies did as well. The problem was created when different agencies required input from the child, resulting in multiple interviews by different interviewers (Carnes & LeDuc, 1998; Faller, 2007a; Merchant & Toth, 2001).

The child interview model is based on the assumption that children are usually reliable in their reports of an issue like sexual abuse, whereas offenders and nonabusing parents may have vested interests in concealing information about any possible abuse (Faller, 2007a).

The Joint Investigation Model

The joint investigation model recognized that different agencies—child protection, law enforcement, legal—required information that would be best obtained by collaboration with a minimum of stress to the child. In the mid-1980s, many states amended their child protective statutes so that such collaboration was mandated (Faller, 2007a; National Center for the Prosecution of Child Abuse,

1997). This shift in philosophy also increased the emphasis on the fact that child sexual abuse is seen as a crime.

In this model, the data gathering is not just limited to the child but to any of the parties who may be involved. One problem when CPS and law enforcement first sought to collaborate was the differences in style and philosophy. Whereas CPS tends to see the child as its primary client and treatment as its goal, law enforcement sought to investigate a crime with the child as the victim and witness. Although these two viewpoints may still cause some friction, agencies have come a long way toward effective collaboration to meet both the needs of the child and the societal needs to protect other children.

The Parent-Child Interaction Model

The parent-child interaction model has its roots in mental health practice. During the 1970s and 1980s, some clinicians sought to explain child abuse as rooted in bonding distortions between parents and children. They felt that observing parents and children together might provide insight into their needs in treatment. When applied to sexual abuse, usually intrafamilial abuse, it was assumed that the sexualized interaction between parent and child, or conversely the child's avoidance and fear of the abusing parent, would be useful in determining which allegations were true and which were not when assessed by a trained mental health professional (Faller, 2007a). More recent research on a clinician's ability to determine what behavior points conclusively to sexual abuse has tended not to support this model. In addition, those working regularly with children in sexual abuse situations question the effect on the child when he or she is interviewed with the offending parent (Conte, Sorenson, Fogarty, & Dalla Rosa, 1991; Madonna, Van Scoyk, & Jones, 1991).

The Comprehensive Assessment Model

The comprehensive assessment model arose not only because of the criticisms of other models but also based upon the practice of comprehensive family evaluations used by CPS and mental health agencies. Pertinent information is gathered by either a single investigator or a team including social workers, physicians, lawyers, psychologists, and possibly other concerned professionals. Some team members have expertise in interviewing children, whereas others may be skilled with offenders or other family members. Referrals are made to teams by courts and law enforcement who then collaborate in order to provide the best assessment and recommend the most effective treatment for the child and family. Siblings may be included and interviewed, which has not always been a part of sexual abuse treatment (Faller, 2003, 2007a).

The emphasis on family evaluation makes it obvious that this model is appropriate for cases of intrafamilial abuse but not for extrafamilial allegations. The model's hallmark is the extent of data gathering and history taking that informs professionals as to how best to proceed with family intervention (Faller, 2007a).

In reality, CPS, law enforcement, and legal agencies within specific states and counties often develop procedures that work the best for them. Hopefully, it is a collaborative effort. Recognizing that there are several models and that individual practices may combine a variety of techniques, let us consider the assessment and treatment planning for children and their families.

ASSESSING AND PLANNING FOR THE NEEDS OF THE CHILD

Working with children who have been sexually abused requires knowledge, skill, and patience. Whatever type of professional assesses the child's needs, he or she should be trained specifically for work with abused children. In cases of sexual abuse, children are usually interviewed and may also receive a forensic medical examination to determine if the allegation of abuse can be supported medically (Adams, 2010).

Interviewing the Child

Interviews of children may be conducted from several perspectives. The *forensic interview* is usually undertaken by an investigator from law enforcement or the district attorney's (DA) office to determine if a crime has been committed. *Forensic* means "belonging to the courts" and describes procedures that have legal implications. The interviewer searches for facts to support an allegation of abuse and uses nonleading techniques in order to solicit the child's story. The interview is carefully documented and may even be videotaped. The result will be a report that may be presented to the court as part of legal proceedings (Faller, 2007a; Sax, 2009b).

The *clinical interview* is conducted by a member of the therapeutic team, a clinician skilled in working with children. It is designed to uncover first what the child says happened and then to determine what types of therapeutic intervention will be necessary. This child-centered interview is supportive and strives to assess the child's subjective experience. Data gathering may include some seemingly leading questions to help the child to open up. Documentation in the form of note taking is less extensive with the end result being a possible short report or suggested treatment plan (Faller, 2007a; Morgan, 1995; Sgroi, 1982).

The role of the CPS differs depending upon the state and its procedures. In some states, a CPS investigator, whose role is to determine the facts for the DA's office, investigates a child sexual abuse case. This investigator may be responsible for generating a report that will be used in court. Another CPS worker may then assess the therapeutic needs of the child to determine what

treatment is needed (Crosson-Tower, 2014; Hirschy & Wilkinson, 2010; Knight, Chew, & Gonzalez, 2005).

There is some concern about how many interviews the child will be subjected to as retelling the story in and of itself can further traumatize the child. Although it would be ideal to have the child interviewed by only one professional, the reality is that there may well be multiple interviews. Some experts have cautioned against blurring the roles of clinical and forensic interviewers because of the distinct differences in the approaches (Faller, 2007a; Kuehnle & Connell, 2010; Poole & Lamb, 1998). The forensic interview seeks to gather information to prosecute the victim's perpetrator, whereas the clinical interview is geared more toward helping the child. There is another school of thought, however, that suggests that the same clinician should move from clinical to forensic mode as the "forensic questioning techniques . . . [are] triggered by the child's disclosure of sexual abuse for which the clinician is providing treatment" (Faller, 2007a, p. 5). There are certainly some problems with joining these two types of techniques.

One method of interviewing children that seems to be effective is the use of a team and a one-way mirror. One social worker explained how this method has been useful in her agency.

☙ ▬▬▬▬▬▬▬▬▬▬▬▬▬▬▬▬▬

We have a team of social workers in our sexual abuse unit who are really tuned in to kids and are skilled in interviewing them. Our agency has a large interview room, one whole side of which is a one-way mirror. A child is interviewed by one social worker, and the other professionals on the team, an investigator from the district attorney's office, as well as other social workers observe through the one-way window. The interviewer has an earpiece through which the rest of the team can ask her to add specific types of questions. Sometimes during the interview, the interviewer may tell the child that she needs to step out for a moment, which gives her an opportunity to discuss briefly with the team how they should proceed. When the child is alone in the room she or he is also observed. Sometimes children will behave in ways that are particularly telling when the interviewer is out of the room.

ଈ

This worker went on to describe such a case.

ଔ

Our interviewer had been talking with the little girl about what her abuser had done to her. They were using anatomically correct dolls and had undressed them. The interviewer, frustrated that she had not elicited from the child any indication of the perpetrator's actions, left the room to speak with the team. No sooner had she left than the child began to narrate her own story of what happened using the dolls. She had the doll that they had designated as her stepfather telling the child doll that he just wanted her to suck on "the lollypop" at which point she placed the penis of the father doll in the mouth of the child doll. Through this small segment of playacting, the interviewer was able to conduct the remainder of the interview in a manner that allowed the child to tell her story with facts that were later used to prosecute the abuser.

ଈ

Extended Assessments

Currently, in most areas of the United States, victims of suspected child sexual abuse are interviewed once or twice by a forensic interviewer who is, hopefully, skilled with children. When a child victim is from a diverse culture, it is also possible for the worker most familiar with the child's culture to be the one to complete the interview. During these interviews, the information that is gleaned will provide the basis for an assessment of the child's safety as well as the decision about the prosecution of the sexual offender. Faller, Cordisco-Steele, and Nelson-Gardell (2010) argue that one or two interviews are not enough and suggest rationale for using

extended assessments in some situations of child sexual abuse.

Concerned that too many interviews by multiple professionals would further traumatize children, the National Children's Advocacy Center (NCAC) developed a model whereby children would be interviewed fewer times (usually once or twice), and a team would work together to use what was disclosed in the interviews to develop an assessment, a criminal prosecution plan, and a treatment plan. The single-interview model was supported for several reasons. First, fewer resources were necessary for the investigation. High caseloads for both CPS and criminal justice investigators require streamlining whenever possible. Second, the above-mentioned trauma to the child was considered. And finally, there was the fear that multiple interviews might program the child to falsely accuse an adult of sexual abuse (Cross, Jones, Walsh, Simone, & Kolko, 2007; Faller et al., 2010; Jones, Cross, Walsh, & Simone, 2007; LaRoy, Lamb, & Pipe, 2008).

Despite concerns about victims' well-being, several studies demonstrated that this plan was not successful in gaining full disclosure. For example, the NCAC discovered that even though 78% of the victims had disclosed the sexual abuse to someone prior to being interviewed, 9% denied the abuse during the first interview and 73% were reluctant to discuss it at all (Faller et al., 2010). In fact, some experts feel that the disclosure of sexual abuse by a child is not an event but a process, which takes time (Faller, 2003; Faller et al., 2010; Olafson & Lederman, 2006; Saunders, 2012).

Videotaping

Often these interviews are also videotaped. Tapes may or may not be used in court but can be useful in a manner of different ways. Having a taped recording is certainly preferable to and more accurate than notes that an interviewer might take after an interview. And when a perpetrator is shown a tape of a child disclosing the abuse in some detail, he or she might stop denying that the abuse happened. Or a nonabusive parent may be helped to believe and support his or her child after seeing such a taped interview. Showing a victim the tape of a previous interview might also refresh his or her recollection of what happened during the abuse and lessen the chances of recantation. In addition, even when tapes are not admissible as evidence in court proceedings, such tapes provide a verbatim audio and visual record of the interview that can help prosecutors and investigators to build a case against the abuser (Faller, 2007a).

Although videotaping would seem to be an important tool, there has been a controversy over the use of such techniques. In the mid-1980s, videotaping was highly favored as a manner of preserving information for litigation in sexual abuse cases. Not only did this practice lesson the number of interviews to which a child was subjected but it was thought that tapes could be used in place of the child's testimony in court (National Center for the Prosecution of Child Abuse, 1997). In recent years, there have been suggestions that videotaping can also have disadvantages. For example, the defense may use such a tape to attack the victim for minor inconsistencies or discredit the interviewer. And some legal organizations argued that a defendant has the right to face his or her accuser even if that accuser is a child. Some clinicians feared that if videotaping forensic interviews became the norm, they might be expected in clinical and treatment interviews where the client's right to confidentiality would then be jeopardized (Berliner, 2011; Faller, 2007a; Myers, 1998). Parents and professionals alike have also worried about the child's privacy in the making and distribution of such tapes. Therefore, when such a videotape is made, prosecutors usually seek orders from the court that the tape not be viewed or distributed beyond the scope of the investigation or trial (Sax, 2009b).

Experts suggest that there may be other disadvantages involved in videotaping interviews with children. First, the recognition that taping is being done may inhibit the child from disclosing or speaking freely. Or the child may behave differently (e.g., acting silly or hamming for the camera) if he or she knows that there is taping. A poor quality tape may obscure important data, or the fact that a camera will record only what is in range may mean that significant information is missed. Those viewing the tape may also be focused more on, and therefore distracted by, the interviewer's technique rather than what the child has disclosed. And finally, some courts may feel that a taped record of a child's testimony is not as persuasive as the child himself or herself when used as testimony (Berliner, 2011; Faller, 1996, 2003, 2007a).

Medical Examinations

Medical exams are undertaken with sexually victimized children for several reasons. First, the hope is to uncover physical evidence that will substantiate the abuse. Unfortunately, there may not always be obvious physical evidence or forensic specimens (e.g., semen, vaginal or rectal tearing), especially if the child was not penetrated either vaginally or anally. Further, a forensic medical exam determines if there are any sexually transmitted diseases or injuries that must be treated; the prevention of a possible pregnancy may also be necessary (Rosas, 2005). Adams (1995) suggests that there are additional reasons to complete a medical exam. These include the following:

- To document the child's description of what happened
- As a way of reassuring the victim that he or she is "OK" and has not been physically injured to any serious degree
- To identify any physical changes that may have resulted from previous injuries
- To provide prophylaxis for pregnancy or disease as needed
- To provide documentation for court testimony if such becomes necessary

Exams may be completed on an acute basis—that is, they are being conducted within 72 hours of the last sexual contact—or on a nonacute basis—that is, as much as 7 days after the abuse (Adams, 1995; Rosas, 2005). Because it is part of an investigation of a crime, parental consent is not required to give a child a medical exam (Sax, 2009b).

As part of the medical exam, a description of what happened is also obtained from the child's caretaker before the exam is undertaken. And a detailed medical history enables the examiner to be more accurate in his or her assessment (Adams, 1995). It may also help to determine if symptoms sometimes related to sexual abuse (e.g., blood in the diaper or panties, redness in the genital area, warts, scars in the genital area) are indicative of problems other than abuse (e.g., urinary tract infections, abrasions, lichen sclerosus, a skin condition) (Adams, 1995).

Although a medical exam may produce findings that support that the child has been sexually abused, this is not always the case. When a child is not penetrated or physically hurt, the evidence of abuse may not be obvious. In addition, the hymen, often thought to be indicative of virginity, can actually stretch to allow partial penetration without tearing. Or it may have become torn through other child-appropriate activities. The anus is even more expandable, and even if tears do occur, they usually heal rapidly, leaving no trace of an injury. Nor can a physical exam tell how often a child may have been violated sexually. The usefulness of a medical exam is only in conjunction with other types of evidence and testimony (Adams, 1995).

Cultural Considerations

Child sexual abuse cuts across all races and cultures, and a child's race and ethnic background must be considered when interviewing for alleged child sexual abuse. Fontes and Faller (2007) suggest that interviewers are not as diverse a population as the clients they serve, necessitating that interviewers be schooled in and pay attention to cultural differences and how these affect interviews. Despite the abundance of resources now available for interviewing, there is little that addresses cultural competence in interviews with children around sexual abuse (Fontes & Faller, 2007; Fontes & Plummer, 2012).

Children who have been sexually abused come to an investigative or assessment interview with preexisting barriers to communication built around their hesitancy to discuss the actual sexual abuse. Combine this hesitancy with language difficulties and attitudinal perspectives based on cultural differences, the interviewer may be challenged to overcome those barriers. Fontes (2008, p. 85) suggests that prior to the interview, certain facts be ascertained.

- What language does the child speak generally?
- What language does the child speak with siblings or friends?
- Is the child an immigrant or a child of an immigrant, and if so, from where?
- Who lives at home? Who stays at home?
- What do the adults do for a living?
- What is the child's religion, and how observant is the family of this religion?

It will be especially important to know about the culture of the child's family of origin. Not only might the child's culture have prohibitions against talking about sexual matters but there may also be differences in the definitions of appropriate sexual activities. Sometimes seemingly abusive practices may also have cultural routes; for example, "a Latino mother or father grabbing briefly at her/his toddler or preschool son's crotch in public and commenting on how he is going to 'get the girls' when he grows up" (Fontes & Faller, 2007, p. 169). Cultural practices like the digital penetration of a girl's vagina by a parent as a "virginity check" are illegal in the United States but should be handled with the knowledge of the cultural origins (Fontes, 2008; Fontes & Faller, 2007; Fontes & Plummer, 2012).

In addition to knowing the child's ethnic background and some of the practices of that culture, it is important to know when an interpreter would be useful. However, it is also important to be aware of the possible bias of a particular interpreter. For example, family members as interpreters might have vested interest in the story coming out in a certain way. If the interpreter is a professional, he or she should be knowledgeable of the issues involved in sexual abuse so that the responses are translated accurately (Fontes, 2008; Fontes & Faller, 2007; Fontes & Plummer, 2012).

Some cultures are more insistent on having the child accompanied by a family member. However, this can also be problematic. Having a family member present in an interview is usually not advisable because even knowing that his or her relative is waiting outside may impede the child's disclosure (Fontes, 2008).

Techniques that are part of any interview become more complex when there are cultural differences between the child and the interviewer. For example, the use of body language, including certain gestures and nonverbal cues, is impacted by culture. Fontes (2008) explains that an interviewer asking a Latin American teen a question might be greeted with a shrug, which is often interpreted as "I don't know." However, Latinos may use this gesture to indicate "I don't care" or "I don't want to talk about it," which may be a different message. And although being face-to-face and making eye contact are appropriate in middle-class Anglo American circles, it could be disrespectful in some other cultures. Thus, the untrained interviewer may assume that the child was avoiding the truth rather than looking away to be respectful. Voice tone, the use of touch, the use of silence, and the arrangement of seating are other issues that may have different significance in different cultures. It will be extremely important to the success of the interview that cultural variation be considered (Fontes, 2008; Fontes & Faller, 2007; Fontes & Plummer, 2012).

Children With Disabilities

There are numerous misconceptions about children with disabilities and sexual abuse. First, there is the belief that children who are disabled in some manner are at low risk for sexual abuse because people would feel pity for them and not take advantage of their special needs. On the contrary, the very fact that they are disabled may put these children at higher risk for abuse. Cognitive limitations and mobility issues as well as communication difficulties may cause perpetrators to view them as safe risks. Disabled children may also be dependent upon caretakers, heightening the risk of abuse by those same adults. And the large number of caretakers over time in the life of a disabled child makes the percentage of risk greater. Although it is true that children with disabilities are less likely to interact with strangers, statistics indicate that abuse is more likely to be at the hands of those known to the child (Davies & Faller, 2007; Horton & Kochurka, 1995).

Faller (2007) points out that there may be both professional and child-related barriers when interviewing children with special needs. Professionals may be biased that the identified symptoms of sexual abuse are caused by the child's developmental disability. For example, self-injurious behaviors in developmentally delayed children may be attributed to their disability although such behavior can also be symptomatic of child sexual abuse (Davies & Faller, 2007; Mansell, Sobsey, & Moskal, 1998). A study out of Sweden (see Cederborg & Lamb, 2006) brought to light the fact that those interviewing children with disabilities may lack the expertise in evaluating children with such disabilities (Davies & Faller, 2007).

Children with disabilities also present barriers to accurate interviewing. First, their disability may present challenges to accurate communication. In addition, children with special needs are not always provided with the information about sexuality given to other children, resulting in a deficit in their knowledge about their private parts, sexual acts, or the fact that they may have been sexually abused at all (Burke, 2008; Davies & Faller, 2007; Mansell et al., 1998). Because some abuse is disguised as child care, the problem of recognition that an act is abusive is compounded. Children with disabilities may also be dependent upon the perpetrator and/or socially isolated. Speaking about any possible abuse may be too difficult for them and may trigger abandonment fears (Davies & Faller, 2007; Horton & Kochurka, 1995).

Prior to interviewing, the interviewer should take care to familiarize himself or herself with the specifics of the child's disability. Initial interviewing involves getting to know the child's capabilities and understanding of sexuality and abuse. Data gathering must also take into consideration the child's limitations around communication. (For more detailed information, see Davies and Faller, 2007.)

Assessing Truthfulness

When interviewing children about sexual abuse and especially when they may be testifying in court, the question arises, "How does one know when a child is telling the truth?" Bernet (1993), after a review of numerous writings on false reporting, identifies possible reasons for false reports. These include indoctrination of the child by others, suggestion, fantasy or delusion, misinterpretation, miscommunication, lying (both innocent and intentional group contagion when others have reported similar events), and perpetrator substitution (when the abuse did happen but not at the hands of the perpetrator reported). Other authors have suggested that false reports might arise out of custody battles or other forms of manipulation of a child (Faller, 2007a; Friedrich, 2002; Lyon, 2005; Sgroi, 1982).

Early in the study of the assessment and treatment of sexual abuse, Sgroi (1982) postulated that an abuse report was more likely to be true if the child reported that there were multiple incidents of abuse over time; there was a request, demand, or implication of secrecy expected by the perpetrator; there were elements of pressure or coercion involved in the abuser's technique; and if the child could give explicit details of the abuse including tactile details of sexual activity. Later attempts to determine truthfulness outlined specifics in content. Lyon (2005, p. 165) outlines some of the content criteria originally developed over time through the work of Raskin and Steller (1989) and Steller and Boychuck (1992). These content criteria include

- the characteristics of the content—is it logical and detailed?
- the specific contents—are there descriptions of interactions, conversation, unexpected complications, and the context in which the abuse occurred?
- peculiarities noted—unusual or superfluous details, related external associations, and indications of the child and perpetrator's mental states;
- Motivation-related contents—spontaneous corrections, admissions of not being able to remember or self-doubts, pardoning, or forgiving the offender; and
- the specifics of the offense.

In using content criteria, these authors suggest the importance of also assessing the abilities of the child, the nature of the abuse, and the skill and strategies of the interviewer.

Assessment of Ritual Abuse

During the 1980–1990s, there were numerous reports by child victims and adult survivors of bizarre acts of abuse, often perpetrated in groups with ritualized overtones; these were soon labeled as ritual or cult abuse (Charles, 1995; Cook, 1991; Hudson, 1991; Noblitt & Noblitt, 2008; Noblitt & Perskin, 2000). Law enforcement, child protective agencies, and clinicians struggled to sort out fact from fiction in what seemed like unbelievable accounts. Public's mistrust of reported incidents fostered the development of the False Memory Syndrome Foundation (see Chapter 15 for more detail) and other efforts to discredit those reports. However, there was enough similarity in the events depicted that the criminal justice and child protection fields were compelled to devise methods to assess and treat those who reported ritualized abuse.

Ritual abuse is defined by Noblitt and Perskin as "abuse or maltreatment that occurs in a ceremonial or circumscribed manner and where the abuse causes traumagenic dissociation and/or establishes or reinforces control over dissociated states already in existence" (as cited in Noblitt & Noblitt, 2008, p. 25).

The reports appeared to reference specific indicators including unusual and often sadistic sexual behaviors, torture, death/murder, being tied up or otherwise restrained, the use of supernatural symbols, bestiality, consumption of bodily fluids, cannibalism, harming animals, dressing in ritual apparel, and the encouragement of strange beliefs (Charles, 1995; Noblitt & Perskin, 2000; Sinason, Galton, & Leevers, 2008).

When a report is made that suggests ritual abuse, criminal justice and child protection investigators gather evidence that they hope will suggest some type of pattern. To date, no diagnostic tool effectively diagnoses ritual abuse (Charles, 1995; Faller, 2007a). Some experts suggest that ritualized abuse should be at least ruled out in any case where children report multiple perpetrators or being abused in a group (Charles, 1995; Noblitt & Noblitt, 2008). One key to diagnosis seems to be related to a child having extreme dissociative symptoms. The likelihood of a child's purposeful disclosure is rare given the fears instilled in the victims by perpetrators. In addition, the bizarre nature of the abuse makes it difficult for the victims to frame a way of describing it. When children recount confused descriptions of seemingly unbelievable events, they are less likely to be believed. Thus, cases more frequently come to the attention of law enforcement and CPS through reports of tangential events such as animal abuse. Once ritual abuse is suspected, careful listening, an open mind, and trained interviewers are key.

ASSISTING FAMILY MEMBERS IN SUPPORT OF THE CHILD

The impact of child sexual abuse is sometimes forgotten on those family members who are not the abusers. They may have their own reactions and conflicts that hamper their ability to support the child as they process their own emotions. We discussed in Chapter 11 the difficulty that family members may have in believing the initial allegations of child sexual abuse, as well as their reactions and feelings as they hear the child's story. Some nonabusing parents will be able to support the child, believing him or her, and will protect the child against future harm from the perpetrator. Other parents' own needs are so great that they cannot stand by the child. When the latter is the case, removal of the child from the home is often necessary.

Even when a nonabusive parent believes the child's allegations, supporting the child will require courage and, often, additional professional support. This parent, too, feels like a victim. She or he is embarrassed and questions why she or he did not know earlier. As one mother put it,

❧ ─────────────────────────

Did I have suspicions? The amount of time my husband spent with our daughter, taking her on outings that it seemed clear I was not invited to be a part of, tucking her in at night, stealing out of bed in the wee hours of the morning. Weren't these actions just part of being a father? Maybe I should have realized how secretive they both had become. But he was always out of work and I was always trying to make ends meet. Maybe I thought that it was the least he could do, taking care of our daughter. How could I have been so blind? ❧

Some nonabusive parents blame themselves, heaping on the guilt about what they should have seen or what they should have done (Stone, 2005). Sometimes the abuse had been out of their frame of reference; it never occurs to them that their mate might abuse a child. Other parents have their own agendas and chastise themselves for not protecting their children.

❧

I knew that Isabella was a needy person. Before our son was born, I used to feel smothered sometimes. She wanted so much from me—things I couldn't give emotionally. Then when our son was born, I thought she'd have something to keep her busy. But still she demanded. I was glad when I got the sales job. It gave me time to be away from home for long stretches. Now I wonder if it's my fault that she started sexually abusing our son. He was only a baby! ❧

Other parents are unable to see the child's needs over their own and the importance of the offender in their lives.

❧

Gertie could not believe it when it was reported to her that her boyfriend Emmett was sexually abusing her daughter Lissie.

"Lissie been a liar her whole life!" the mother protested. "Who gonna believe her! Emmett treat me good and pays the bills. No way I gonna kick him out because of that girl's lies." ❧

Gertie's inability to believe and protect her daughter necessitated the placement of Lissie in foster care.

Disclosure of sexual abuse is often so traumatic an event for the victim's family that they respond out of a crisis-survival mode. Suddenly, their whole world feels at risk. Their child has been compromised, which in turn may influence their marriage, their other children, their privacy, their economic welfare, their self-sufficiency, and their self-concept. Although the ideal goal of case management and treatment would be to keep the family together, this can be accomplished only by giving a great deal of support to those supporting the child emotionally (Crosson-Tower, 2014; Faller, 2003).

Assessment of nonabusive parents requires that professionals answer several questions:

- Does the parent believe the child?
- Did that parent set up, condone, or cover up the sexual abuse of the child?
- Is the parent able to achieve emotional independence from the offender in order to support the child?
- Can the parent, with support, be consistent in standing by the child?

Denial is a classic response when confronted with the news that one's child has been sexually abused. There may be a great deal of stake especially if the offender is a parent or a close family member. Thus, those who intervene must help the family members sort out their feelings, including their attitude toward the child and what has happened to him or her.

❧

When Fawn first learned that her husband, Bud, had abused their daughter, Heather, she could not believe it. She wanted to talk to Bud and confront Heather, but the police allowed her to do neither. When the CPS investigator interviewed her, Fawn sobbed bitterly, saying that she could not go on because it was so terrible. At first, she felt that there must be a mistake and that the teacher had misunderstood Heather's report that her father was abusing her. Finally, this mother was able to hear how upset her daughter was; she then realized that the allegations must be true. Fawn worried about how she and Heather would live without Bud. Could they make it financially? After voicing her own concerns, Fawn knew that she could keep Heather safe. She knew too that she must support her daughter through further investigation and later as they went to court.

ᴂ

Several studies found that nonoffending mothers were more likely to believe their children when they bore their first child in adulthood, the offender was not the mother's current partner, the mother did not have knowledge of the abuse before disclosure, and the child was not displaying any sexualized behaviors (Elliot & Carnes, 2001; Joyce, 2007; Pintello & Zuravin, 2001). Nonsupportive mothers in another study had difficult relationships with their own mothers (Leifer, Kilbane, & Grossman, 2001).

Some family members feel such anger toward the perpetrator that it diverts the energy that they might have had to help the child. One task of CPS will be to help these family members to channel their anger into positive action.

The goal for CPS, once it is determined that the family members are able to support the victim emotionally, will be to provide resources, both tangible and psychological, to help these individuals to support the child as intervention proceeds and treatment is begun. To do this, CPS will carefully assess the strengths of and challenges for these family members.

COURT INVOLVEMENT IN CHILD SEXUAL ABUSE

Types of Courts

Victims, families, and perpetrators of sexual abuse might become involved with the court system in a variety of ways, and the process in which they are involved with different types of courts might

differ. *Juvenile or family court* hears dependency cases, including protective petitions on behalf of children who have been abused as well as delinquency matters and status offenses (those acts, like running away or truancy, that if committed by adults would not come to the attention of the court). Juvenile courts are not criminal courts, and decisions are made on behalf of the children (Faller, 2003; Noel, 2013). They do not have the power to punish, rather they determine how the child can best be cared for.

ᘒ

Sally was sexually abused by her mother's boyfriend who is sometimes a tenant in the home. Sally's mother, Lona, had approached CPS for services a year earlier when she needed the placement of her children to undergo an operation. Finding no relatives who could give the children care, CPS placed 5-year-old Sally and 2-year-old Frankie in a temporary foster home and worked with the mother during her recuperation from surgery. Unfortunately, Lona became addicted to pain killers, and CPS remained involved while she tried to detox and for subsequent months monitored her progress. During this time, Lona met Ira, a violent man who also had a drug problem. The CPS worker suspected that Ira beat Lona but was unable to prove this. When the school reported that Sally was being sexually abused by her "stepfather," CPS intervened. But Lona denied these allegations and was clearly ready to protect Ira at all costs. CPS then determined that a petition must be filed in juvenile court in order to protect Sally's safety.

ᴂ

Because Sally is no longer safe at home given her mother's decision to protect Ira, it will be the role of the juvenile court to decide what is best for the child.

In some states, domestic relations are handled by *probate court* where custody rights, child support payments, and child guardianship are determined (Faller, 2003; Sagatun & Edwards, 1995). Other states use the term *family court* to describe the civil court that oversees custody disputes, visitation, family support payments, and mandated counseling. Only family members can avail themselves of the services of family court (Sax, 2009b).

Offenders usually come to the attention of *criminal court* as child sexual abuse is a crime subject to the appropriate punishment. The objective of the criminal court is to determine the guilt or innocence of the accused and, if found guilty, levy some type of consequence. Criminal courts are responsible when the crime is considered to be "against society" (Sagatun & Edwards, 1995; Sax, 2009b; Walsh, Jones, Cross, & Lippert, 2010).

Civil courts settle disputes between two or more parties related to negligent behavior, property rights, or contracts. Here the offense is committed against another individual rather than society. Sometimes, an offender may be found not guilty in criminal court but will be taken to civil court. For example, the husband of a small day care provider was accused of sexually abusing the children in his wife's care. She was also charged as an accomplice. The case was dismissed from criminal court for insufficient evidence. Soon after, the parents of several of the children involved sued the couple in civil court for negligence on behalf of their children in failing to provide a wholesome atmosphere while they were in day care. These parents sought financial damages in order to pay for the therapy for their abused children.

Court Process

How these courts are used, at what point in the case process they are brought in, and how they influence the case will differ from state to state. In Massachusetts, for example, a case of child sexual abuse perpetrated by a family member is most often reported to the Department of Family and Children's Services (the CPS agency). Once the case is screened in, an intake worker will begin collecting and sorting out the facts. At the same time, the case is referred to the office of the DA, which also does an investigation. CPS may or may not involve juvenile court depending upon whether or not the nonabusing parent is able to protect the child and will cooperate. If the child is in danger because this parent is not supportive and/or the abuser still has access to the child, a care and protection petition (seeking the court's aid in protecting the child) might be filed in juvenile court.

In the meantime, the abuser usually would have been arrested and/or removed from the home through criminal court. A forensic investigation will seek to find medical evidence, the defendant's criminal record, possible other victims of the same abuser, other witnesses, and so on, to determine if a crime was committed by the accused. It may be that the DA's office does not find enough evidence to go forward in criminal court, but CPS is convinced that the child needs protection and that the parents need help in protecting the child in the future. If this happens, CPS will continue to work with the family.

When an offender is reported to law enforcement for another alleged crime, abuse of children may also be discovered.

ᙣ ———————————————————

Willie prided himself on his collection of pictures that he had taken of the children whom he had sexually abused. All boys between the ages of 7 and 9, Willie had met them through his job as a school janitor. He enjoyed going to a gym after work where he met several other men who shared his interests in young boys. It was here that he was observed with his pictures and arrested by an undercover police officer who had been investigating a pornography ring in the town. After interrogating Willie, the police discovered that not only did he have pornography but the pictures were taken when he was abusing young boys. Subsequently they learned the names of Willie's numerous victims and began the arduous process of talking with their parents. Willie was arrested for child assault.

ᙢ

Sax (2009b) outlines the steps that might be taken in her state with an offender like Willie.* An arrest is made when the police report is filed. A determination is made about how recently the sexual assault occurred, how much proof is available, and whether the accused confesses to the crime. Bail is set depending on what charges the prosecutor chooses to file. An arraignment is scheduled where the abuser is officially charged and asked if he or she chooses to plead guilty or not guilty. Pleading guilty to a sexual assault case will have long-term implications, including that the accused will be registered as a sex offender. The judge will then set bail and schedule future proceedings (pp. 142–143).

The preliminary hearing or grand jury indictment is like a minitrial where the prosecution strives to prove that the accused is guilty of the abuse. Witnesses may be called upon with the goal of determining if there is sufficient evidence for the accused to stand trial. If trial is scheduled, there will be a series of pretrial motions while the prosecutor and the defense both argue to determine what evidence will be admitted at trial, a determination made by the judge (pp. 143–144).

Trials have become the fodder for numerous TV shows and so are familiar to most. Few are as dramatic as often portrayed on TV, but it is always possible with such a controversial issue as the sexual abuse of children. It is also possible for attorneys to plea bargain—or settle a case by agreeing on mutually acceptable terms. This means that the case will no longer be heard in a courtroom. A plea bargain is usually offered by the prosecutor after he or she determines the strength of the case. Going to court presents not only a risk to the accused but also exposure through media. Thus, a plea bargain is often presented in a way to present further exposure as well as expense, inconvenience to witnesses, and the time involved. If the accused goes to trial and is found guilty, he or she has the right to appeal to a higher court (Sax, 2009b).

Attorneys Involved in Child Sexual Abuse Cases

Sexual abuse will most likely come to the attention of one or both of two courts: juvenile court for child protection or criminal court for the prosecution of the offender.

Attorneys in Juvenile Court Procedures

There are three different attorney roles in juvenile court: attorney for CPS, attorney for the child, and attorney for the parents.

The attorney for CPS is often the initiator of the court proceedings on behalf of a child. This lawyer may be on the staff of CPS or borrowed from the prosecutor's office. This attorney and the worker from CPS work together closely as the case is prepared for court. The social worker, with his or her expertise on the welfare of children, makes recommendations about the child's well-being and suggests witnesses, who are then subpoenaed by the attorney (Faller, 2003; Sax, 2009b).

The Child Abuse Prevention and Treatment Act (CAPTA) of 1974 mandated that each state through CPS provide a child being seen in juvenile court with a *guardian ad litem*, usually an attorney, who is given the task of representing the child's best interests. Because CAPTA was not clear as to how children's interests should be represented by this guardian ad litem (sometimes referred to as *GAL*), states interpreted the law

---

*Robin Sax is the former deputy district attorney for Los Angeles County, California.

differently. Some states now provide an attorney, who is the child's advocate, throughout the process. Others use this attorney to determine the child's best interests but pay the attorney only for court appearances. Faller (2003) suggests that such a system does not provide adequate investigation and, therefore, sufficient advocacy for the child, especially if this guardian ad litem uses the CPS records as his or her only guide and does not actually meet with the child. Still other states offer both an attorney for the child throughout the process of hearings and a guardian ad litem who is assigned to interview and advocate for the child on a more individual basis.

Court-Appointed Special Advocate (CASA) agencies may also provide a specially trained volunteer to assist the juvenile court by advocating for children. CASA was started in Seattle, Washington, in 1977 by David Soukup, a juvenile court judge, in the interest of seeing that the voices of children are heard when their welfare is being considered. Today there are CASA agencies in every state (Faller, 2003; Sagatun & Edwards, 1995; Sax, 2009b).

Parents in juvenile hearings are also given legal representation. It is possible in cases of sexual abuse that the mother and father have different interests in the outcome of the proceedings especially if one of them is the sexual abuser. In these cases, parents may elect to have separate attorneys. The parents' right to an attorney is not a federal mandate as it is for the child, but if a parent cannot afford an attorney, a court-appointed attorney can be provided. These attorneys come either from law firms who do predominantly child welfare work or from those firms that do some pro bono work. In the latter situation, these attorneys may know little of child welfare law.

Attorneys in Criminal Court Procedures

In criminal court cases, there are usually only two roles for attorneys: the prosecutor and the defense attorney. The victim does not have an attorney, except in very rare cases where a guardian ad litem advocates for the child's interests. More often, someone from the victim-witness assistance program, associated with the prosecutor's office, provides support for the victim.

The prosecutor represents "the people" or society in a criminal case. The police bring their investigative findings to the prosecutor who makes the decision, based on the amount of evidence available, about whether or not to pursue criminal prosecution of the abuser. The prosecutor also assesses his or her likelihood of convincing a judge and jury of the guilt of the defendant before deciding whether to go to trial. Crucial in this decision is the believability of the child as a witness. Because the accused has the right to face his or her accuser, children usually are required to testify if at all possible. Rather than subject a child to scrutiny in court, the prosecutor may instead try to obtain a plea from the offender (see under the section "Court Process"). When an offender pleads, it may not be to the sexual crime he or she has committed, but to a lesser offense, and jail time may not be an issue (Faller, 2003; Faller & Henry, 2000; Sagatun & Edwards, 1995).

The defense attorney hopes to win an acquittal for his or her client. If this attorney does not feel that the case for acquittal is substantial enough, he or she may seek to negotiate with the prosecutor to reduce the terms of the punishment. As mentioned earlier, he or she may be appointed by the court and, although less costly for the client, may not have the same vested interest in them as an attorney who has been hired by the client.

Children Going to Court

In both juvenile and criminal court proceedings, it may be necessary for the victim to appear in court. In both situations, it is vital that the child be prepared about the process and what might happen.

Most juvenile courts strive to make the environment as child friendly as possible. The arrangement of a juvenile court is less likely to be intimidating as the larger criminal courtrooms. Admittedly, some juvenile courts do use courtrooms in which other proceedings take place, but this is the exception rather than the rule.

It is helpful if the child can see the courtroom, know where he or she will be seated, and who else will be in attendance. The more information a child has about who will be in court and what will happen, the better witness he or she will make (Sax, 2010). The supportive adults in the child's life should also be briefed on what to expect in court. Court appearances can be intimidating even for adults, and if the adults are as comfortable as possible, they are more able to support the children appearing as well.

Children should be alerted to the fact that there may be specific people present. In juvenile court, these people may be at the least

- judge;
- court clerk;
- attorneys for CPS, the child, and the parents;
- witnesses;
- police or investigators; and
- parents.

Depending upon the age of the child, he or she may need only to be identified or may remain for part or all of the proceedings. Courts usually try to spare children from hearing difficult testimony.

In criminal court, those present will include

- judge,
- prosecuting attorney,
- defense attorney,
- bailiff,
- court clerk,

- defendant,
- court reporter,
- investigating officer or detective, and
- jury (jurors).

When preparing children for criminal court, it is necessary to let them know that the abuser or defendant will not have physical access to them but will be present; this presence in and of itself may be intimidating depending on the child's relationship with the abuser. Children must also be advised as to how much time they may be on the stand, that they must tell the truth, that they should stop answering a question when an attorney says "objection!" and then continue only when told to do so, and about other timing issues and procedures that might add to his or her comfort (Sax, 2009a).

When children must appear in criminal court, attempts are made to account for children's shorter attention spans, their comfort (to some degree), their privacy as much as possible (e.g., limiting media coverage), and any court accommodations that can make them more comfortable. For example, judges may not wear robes or not sit behind a high bench or regular rules of evidence may be relaxed slightly for the child's comfort (Sax, 2009a).

Children should also be made aware of typical defense that attorneys may use to discredit them. Sax (2009a, p. 155) suggests several: The defense attorney may say that the child is lying because

- of the delay in reporting;
- the victim has disclosed more and more over time;
- the child minimized, denied, or recanted the allegations;
- he or she was coached or bullied by parents or prosecutors; or
- he or she wants attention or because the rules at home are too strict.

Or the defense attorney may say

- the child misunderstood the defendant's behavior or actions,
- the defendant is an upstanding member of the community who never could have done this,
- the child has a history of bad behavior and lying and cannot be believed, or
- the child is caught up in a custody battle and is confused.

Although good prosecutors often foresee such discrediting tactics and know how to refute them, children may be upset by them, assuming that they are not believed or are somehow at fault. Thus, the prosecutor or victim-witness advocate must prepare the child carefully to minimize the effect of such an approach.

WHAT HAPPENS NEXT?

Following the investigation and assessment of treatment needs, as well as possible court appearances, child sexual abuse cases may then be referred for treatment. Treatment for victims and family members is discussed in Chapter 13, whereas further assessment and treatment of offenders is the subject of Chapter 14.

Summary

Several different models are used for the overall assessment of child sexual abuse. The child interview model is based on the assumption that children are truthful in their reports of child sexual abuse; this model seeks to interview children as a way of gathering data on the case. The joint investigation model joins personnel from several agencies who have an interest in the case and through cooperation uses fewer interviews with children to obtain the information needed. The parent-child interaction model looks at the interplay between parents and children to determine if clues to the likelihood of sexual abuse exist in the relationship. And the comprehensive assessment model combines a team of professionals intent upon determining if there was abuse and assessing the needs of the clients. The emphasis here is on a more complete family evaluation to assess strengths and challenges that might be addressed.

Child victims of sexual abuse may be interviewed with several different goals. A forensic interview seeks facts that could be used in legal proceeding against the perpetrator. A clinical interview is designed to uncover the child's version of the abuse and to determine what therapeutic intervention will be needed. There is some concern about subjecting children to multiple investigative interviews; as a result, several means are suggested to prevent multiple interviewing. One is that a child be interviewed in a room with a one-way mirror with other professionals observing behind the mirror. Videotaped interviews are also used in some states. There are several advantages to videotaping. These include using tapes to confront offender denial, helping the nonabusing parent recognize the validity of the abuse, and refreshing the child's memory at a later time. Disadvantages often center around the offender's right to face the accuser.

Medical examinations, too, serve several purposes, including the collection of evidence, assessment of the need for prophylactic treatment, and the ability to assure the child that he or she is not damaged physically.

During assessments, it is vital that professionals are aware of cultural variations as well as any special characteristics present in the child, such as a disability. Children with special needs can be especially vulnerable to being sexually abused.

Professionals take care to assess the truthfulness of children who report sexual abuse. Looking at the content and details of the report and possible motivations may assist in this assessment. It can be especially difficult to assess validity when the report concerns ritualized or cult abuse.

Family members whose children have been sexually abused may require special consideration if they are expected to be of support to these children. Family members may have their own reactions to the abuse and may need to sort these out first. Investigators will assess the ability of these family members to support children as a way of determining whether placement will be necessary.

Sexual abuse cases may be seen in several courts: juvenile or family court, criminal court, or sometimes probate court. Each type of court uses a different approach. There are a variety of professionals who work in these court settings, including attorneys, court staff, and victims' advocates. The court process is also outlined in this chapter. It is important that children be prepared to go to court in order to protect them from undue anxiety.

Review Questions

1. Name the typical models for assessment. What model is favored today?

2. What types of interviews must a child go though?

3. What are some of the concerns about interviewing children?

4. How are these concerns addressed?

5. What are some of the cultural considerations involved?

6. How is truthfulness in children assessed?

7. How must family members be helped in order for them to support the child?

8. What are the types of courts involved in child sexual abuse? What role does each play?

9. What do attorneys do with child sexual abuse cases?

10. How should children be prepared for going to court?

CHAPTER 13

Treatment for Victims and Families

A lot must be accomplished to bring the child sexual abuse victim and his or her family from disclosure to treatment. Throughout this process, the efforts of the child protective services (CPS) and medical, mental health, and legal systems will all converge. Such issues as recognition or denial, separation or removal, conflicting loyalties of the family toward the offender, anger, and shared familial distortions will need to be addressed (Hewitt, 2012; Pipe, Lamb, Orbach, & Cederborg, 2007; van Eys & Truss, 2012).

BARRIERS TO TREATMENT

Before discussing the barriers to treatment, it is important to look at who may need treatment. Child sexual abuse can have a significant impact on its victims, altering their ability to grow and develop normally. It is always recommended that a child victim at least be screened for possible treatment services. Some children may need time before they are ready to process what has happened to them. Some would benefit from long-term treatment, whereas others from brief therapy. More often than the child refusing or not needing therapy is the parents' well-intentioned argument that the child just needs to forget what happened and move on. In fact, children do not forget the abuse, and internalizing the conflict of abuse without having processed it can lead to increased trauma in later life. On the other hand, some children do find ways to make sense of what has happened and move on without extensive therapeutic services. Knowing which child needs help and which does not may be determined with the help of a competent clinician schooled in sexual abuse (Berliner, 2011; Saunders, 2012).

Sexual abuse may not be the only trauma that a particular child has experienced. Therefore, it is important for the professionals doing the assessment to glean the full trauma history. For example, has the child experienced other types of abuse at the hands of caretakers? Has he or she witnessed domestic violence, substance abuse, or violence within the school or community? Has the child been abused or witnessed abuse by peers? Saunders (2012) also recommends that children who have newly immigrated be assessed for violence that they may have witnessed in their homeland or during transport to the United States.

Families of victims may also need treatment, especially if another family member perpetrated the abuse. However, even when a stranger or someone not intimately known by the family abuses a child, the parents and siblings may need help coping with their own conflicts and questions about the abuse. For example, one father described his feelings when his young daughter was abused by a neighbor.

My first reaction was that I wanted to kill the guy even though I didn't really know him—he lives a couple of doors down. I couldn't even imagine how he had seen Hayley enough to do anything to her, but she told me that he had new puppies and had invited her in on her way home from school. I think I would have killed him if my wife hadn't convinced me that I'd be hurting Hayley more. I knew that my wife's father had sexually abused her as a kid, and it was as if I had failed at protecting both of them. I felt like a real wimp. It began to affect everything I did. I couldn't make decisions, I started drinking, and I almost got fired because I was such a bear at work. How could I have let this happen? What was wrong with me as a father?

Feelings of guilt and rage and the beginnings of a substance abuse problem made it necessary for this man to seek treatment. Because his wife supported him in it and their insurance covered the sessions, the outcome was successful. It is common for parents whose child is abused by someone outside the home to also have feelings that require processing.

When the abuser is a family member, the members of that family are especially in need of treatment services. Despite what workers in the field of child protection and mental health have learned over the years about the treatment needs of sexual abuse victims and their families, effective treatment does not always take place. There are several reasons for this.

First, resources may not be available for treatment. Sexual abuse cases are time and resource intensive. Most of the attention is given to intervention after disclosure to ensure that the child is protected from further abuse and society is protected from the perpetrator. After the dust of this crisis-ridden process clears, the family and victim may or may not be offered services toward their healing. Although there will be services for intervention and case management within a community, it is possible that little will be available for ongoing treatment services. Sexual abuse

treatment requires a specific body of knowledge that not all social work and mental health professionals are trained in. Years of guarding the family secret would have created families who may still be secretive and manipulative and who require a definite knowledge of sexual abuse issues on the part of the clinician to really help them.

Some social work agencies and mental health clinics have made it a point to train staff in sexual abuse protocol, but these are not always available. Sexual abuse cases should be assessed and treated by those who have been specifically trained in dealing with such material. In recent years, numerous studies have sought to identify and fine-tune the most comprehensive and effective types of treatment approaches with child sexual abuse. Saunders (2012) cautions that clinicians should employ the best evidence-based practice methods that have been tested to determine their efficacy. Lists of such evidence-supported interventions can be found at various web sites, including the National Registry of Evidence-Based Programs and Practices (http://www.nrepp.samhsa.gov), the California Evidence-Based Clearinghouse for Child Welfare (http://www.cebc4cw.org), the National Child Traumatic Stress Network (http://nctsn.org/nccts/nav.do?pid-ctr_top_trmnt), and Child Physical and Sexual Abuse: Guidelines for Treatment (http://musc.edu/ncvc/resources_prof/OVC_guidelines04–26–04.pdf).

Funding also becomes an issue in planning for treatment. Society wants abuse to stop and therefore will support intervention. But funds are often not always available for treatment, especially when the offender is seen as part of the treatment.

Even if resources are accessible, families may not be willing to commit to long-term treatment. Sometimes who will pay for such services becomes the issue. Treatment services can begin using a family's health insurance if they have it. But health insurance rarely covers more than the initial stages of treatment so that even the motivated family may find it necessary to discontinue treatment. Many of the families seen by CPS do not have private insurance. Agencies have used grants to help fund these services to families, but in these difficult economic times, financial resources are scarce.

Even if funds are available for treatment, not every family is willing to undergo treatment. Sexual abuse within the family is a complex family problem that requires significant changes in family attitudes, rituals, and goals. Not every family is able to commit to treatment as such difficult emotional work can shake the entire structure on which the family members have built their lives.

As one mother put it,

◌⃝ _____

After learning that my husband was sexually abusing our two sons, I wanted to deny that anything had really happened. But once I accepted that my sons were indeed telling the truth, I was so ashamed. I wanted to hide—taking them with me—and never show my face again. I knew that this was not possible and endured all the investigations, the court procedures to convict my husband, and what seemed like the scorn of all our neighbors. It took a year before my husband was convicted and sent to prison, and we stopped having to see a variety of professionals and testify. It was then that we were offered therapy to cope with what we had just been through. Our insurance would pay for the sessions. But at that point, I just wanted to forget that part of our lives. I wasn't convinced that anything would ever repair what had been done to my little boys, and I wanted to put it all out of my mind. I canceled the first couple of appointments at the mental health center for the boys and me. And then I just told them that I didn't want any help.

_____ ◌⃝

TREATING CHILD AND ADOLESCENT VICTIMS _____

Assumptions and Theories Surrounding Treatment

The assumption based on emerging research is that early treatment can mitigate the negative effects of child sexual abuse (Bratton, Ceballos, Landreth, & Costos, 2012; Olafson & Boat, 2000; Saunders, 2012). In addition, research indicates that for children who have been sexually abused, the nonoffending parent-child attachment bond can be crucial to their healing (Bratton et al., 2012). But what constitutes effective therapy?

Several factors must be taken into consideration when planning for the treatment of child victims. First, *paramount to the treatment of victims is parental support* (Bolen, 2007; Bratton et al., 2012; Olafson & Boat, 2000; Saunders, 2012). If a mother in an incest situation is financially dependent upon the abusive father, for example, she may have difficulty fully believing her child's disclosure and committing to subsequent treatment. Even if a parent has agreed to protect the child and the child has therefore remained with her or him, this parent may have conflicts about the child's therapy. In these situations, the parent must be helped to understand her or his own feelings so that she or he can be of support to the child (Bratton et al., 2012; Crosson-Tower, 2014; Olafson & Boat, 2000).

Second, *where does the child reside?* Treatment may be carried out somewhat differently if the child is at home as opposed to being in a foster home. In the latter case, the child will also be grappling with abandonment issues as separation from his or her parents probably means that parental support was lacking and the child may worry that he or she is the one who is at fault.

Next, *the identity of the perpetrator* is an important factor. Abuse by a family member may add issues like feeling betrayed to the child's need to process. Plus, he or she may need to understand why there are conflicting feelings about the abuser.

What *involvement the child had or still has with the criminal justice system* may also inform treatment. What has been said in court may make the child feel more guilt about not only the abuse but the end result for the perpetrator.

◌⃝ _____

Eight-year-old Nancy's father had been incarcerated, and her mother took her to visit him in prison every few weeks. Seeing her father in that setting always intensified her feelings of guilt for the testimony she had given, which she felt had put him there. Therapy sessions after these visits were often dedicated to reality testing about the fact that it was the abuse perpetrated on Nancy, a child, that ended her father in prison and nothing that she had done. ⭊

And finally, treatment must take into consideration *the cultural background* of the child and his or her family (Fontes, 2008; Fontes & Plummer, 2012). While some workers may be trained to work with specific cultural populations, they may not also be trained in treating sexual abuse.

Treatment Issues for Children

Early work by Sgroi (1982), supported by later findings (Cattanach, 2008; Faller, 2007a; Gil & Johnson, 1993; Hunter, 1990; Nurcombe, 2008; Olafson & Boat, 2000), suggests that children who have been sexually abused come to therapy trying to make sense of 10 specific issues:

- Feeling like "damaged goods"
- Guilt
- Fear
- Depression
- Low self-esteem, leading to poor social skills
- Repressed anger and hostility
- Difficulty trusting
- Blurred generational boundaries and role confusion
- Pseudomaturity, masking failure to have completed certain developmental tasks
- Control and mastery over self

Finkelhor and Browne (1985) had earlier identified four categories that encompass the traumagenic dynamics of child sexual abuse:

- Traumatic sexualization
- Stigmatization
- Betrayal
- Powerlessness

Later, Briere (1996a) would devise the trauma symptom checklist for children to include the following:

- Anxiety
- Depression
- Anger
- Sexual concerns
- Dissociation
- Post-traumatic stress

Children who have been abused internalize a variety of messages that can result in residual effects. Perhaps these were best addressed by Finkelhor and Browne's (1985) early model mentioned previously.

Traumatic Sexualization

Sexuality is not a concept that is forefront in the mind of most children. Although Freud would indicate that children are basically sexual beings, people see sexual matters as being in the realm of the adult. Therefore, when a child is introduced to sex prematurely and by trickery, coercion, or force, the result can be traumatic.

Sexualized trauma may manifest itself in abused children through chronic and overt masturbation, sometimes to the point of injury; sexually acting out against other children or adults; or sexualized talk or play. Sexual self-stimulation may be used regularly as a way of trying to make sense of the trauma that the sexual abuse has created. Abused children may also feel damaged and worry that they will not be able to function as adults.

⭘

Isabella was abused by an older boy in her neighborhood. As he stroked her genitals, he asked with apparent malice if she was going to grow up and "be a little mama." Following the abuse, the 6-year-old was convinced that the perpetrator had damaged her so that she could never have children. This was one of her main fears in her subsequent therapy. ⭊

Ironically, when children have been exposed to sexual activity—seen by most to be the realm of adults—teachers, adults around them, and even parents sometimes treat them as if they have been somehow damaged, intensifying their own assumption that the sexual abuse has left them as damaged goods.

Adolescents who have been traumatized by sexual abuse may avoid sexual contact, have flashbacks, or conversely use sex as a bargaining tool or engage in sex as an indicator of poor self-esteem issues ("I'm damaged anyway, so who cares!"). Studies have also found that there is some correlation between early teen pregnancy and sexual abuse (Boyer & Fine, 1992; Kellner, 2013; Logan, Holcombe, Ryan, Manlove, & Moore, 2007; Olafson & Boat, 2000).

Treatment for abused children and teens trying to make sense of premature traumatic introduction to sexuality will require a combination of therapeutic processing of the abuse as well as age-appropriate education around healthy sexual knowledge.

Stigmatization

Child sexual abuse differs from other types of maltreatment in that there is stigma attached to not only the abuser but the victim as well. Mentioned earlier was the tendency for the adults in the victims' lives to sometimes treat them differently—as if they have treaded on ground only open to adults. In addition, children sometimes feel that the very fact that they were abused says something about them. "I probably asked for it," says a 12-year-old girl, "my mom says I dress like a slut." The boy who is convinced that he must have looked homosexual to be abused by a pedophile needs help to recognize that not only are homosexuality and pedophilia usually different but the choice of him as a victim had to do with the perpetrator's own pathology rather than the victim's orientation.

Victims feel they are to blame for the abuse and feel guilt over the havoc it caused in the lives of those around them. Victims' self-esteem may already have been low, and such stigmatization intensifies these feelings. The concern that they cannot trust anyone and that everyone feels that they are to blame can promote isolation and regression back to a time where they felt safe (Nurcombe, 2008). Often when children are sexually abused, their development is interrupted because it seems too much of a risk to progress to a level of greater maturity. The skillful therapist helps these children learn to trust and place the responsibility of the abuse on the shoulders of the abuser.

Betrayal and Powerlessness

Betrayal and powerlessness often go hand in hand when children are abused. Therapy helps these children to recognize that betrayal was not about them but the responsibility of the adults in their lives. As trust develops between the therapist and the young client, the child begins to regain some control over what he or she can appropriately control. Family treatment may also be necessary to realign the generational boundaries that have become blurred or skewed in the abuse. For example, in intrafamilial abuse, the nonabusing mother may have intentionally or even unknowingly abdicated her role as partner and parent, whereas the abused daughter takes her place in the father's bed and life. Unraveling the complex patterns of family relationships will uncover the etiology of the problem, and the child can be helped to not only process the betrayal that she feels but also gain a sense of mastery over her life.

A great deal of the success of therapy depends upon the child's ability to form a trusting relationship with the therapist, an adult who can then help the child to navigate the complex channels that lead to healing after sexual abuse. This therapist will be in the role of helping the child to understand why the adults in his or her life acted as they did, as well as encouraging the child to process feelings about the abuse and develop strategies for subsequent relationship with those adults. In addition, education is a crucial part of therapy as the child tries to understand his or her world.

Treatment for Sexually Abused Children

When considering treatment for abused children, it is important to do so after making several assumptions. Child sexual abuse was an event in the child's life and is not in and of itself a disorder that requires treatment. However, exposure to sexual abuse can put a child at risk for developing a wide array of behavioral and mental health issues. Saying that a child has been sexually abused also suggests a wide variety of possibilities in terms of the acts committed against the child, the amount of risk, the identity of the perpetrator, and so on, all of which affect the response that the child will manifest. The child may also have been the victim of other types of abuse, violence, or trauma, and this too must be considered. The family may not have been functional prior to the abuse of the child, which will also have an impact. Not all abused children will need mental health intervention, but assessment to determine this need is nonetheless warranted (Berliner, 2011; Saunders, 2012).

It is common knowledge in the field of child welfare that children are affected by child sexual abuse in various ways, and some theorists would contend that that there is no evidence of a single cohesive syndrome resulting from child sexual abuse (Saywitz, Mannarino, Berliner, & Cohen, 2000). Different types of symptoms will require different types of treatment techniques. It is known that over 50% of children who are abused sexually suffer from post-traumatic stress disorder (PTSD), which, according to the American Academy of Child and Adolescent Psychiatry, is underdiagnosed in children (King et al., 2003; Saywitz et al.,

2000). Untreated PTSD may lead to the development of psychiatric disorders and distress in adulthood (Finkelhor, 1990; Finkelhor & Browne, 1985; King et al., 2003; Nurcombe, 2008; Saywitz et al., 2000).

Screening for Post-Traumatic Stress Disorder

In recent years, there has been increased recognition that sexually abused children often suffer from PTSD. PTSD is a medically recognized diagnosis that was originally formulated in response to the symptoms exhibited by veterans returning from the Vietnam War. These symptoms had been noticed earlier in soldiers and given such names as battle fatigue and shell shock. Further study into PTSD brought to mind the symptoms that Freud and later clinicians and researchers had associated with other types of trauma, like childhood abuse (Herman, 1997; Saunders, 2012).

PTSD can be divided into three symptom categories: reexperiencing symptoms, avoidance, and hypervigilance or increased arousal. *Reexperiencing* the abuse may subject victims to flashbacks, memories of different kinds involving the abuse, nightmares or night terrors, or other forms of anxiety. Victims may be triggered to reexperience the sensations and emotions they felt during the abuse when something reminds them of it (e.g., a smell or sound).

Victims go to great lengths to *avoid the memories* of the traumatic event or events that have brought on their PTSD. They may isolate themselves from certain people or situations, keeping so busy that they have no time to think. They may try not to feel, often effectively numbing themselves. They may withdraw from normal activities and sometimes from families and friends.

At the same time that victims are attempting to avoid the feelings associated with the trauma, they remain *hypervigilant*—a state of constant arousal. These victims are always alert for danger. This may prevent them from being able to concentrate or from falling asleep and staying asleep. They feel unsafe and are easily startled. The tension of having to be always on guard can also make them angry and irritable.

Screening for symptoms of PTSD in child victims is a crucial part of the preparation for treatment. Van Eys and Truss (2012) also point out that although the abuse may have perpetrated symptoms of PTSD in varying degrees in victims, the experience of navigating the social service and criminal justice systems may also evoke trauma. Thus, it will be important for a comprehensive assessment and treatment approach that strives to keep the focus on the child's well-being.

Treatment Techniques

There are a variety of treatment techniques that work well with sexually abused children. Bratton et al. (2012) suggest child-parent relationship therapy (CPRT), which is a play therapy–based technique that uses parental support and education in order to facilitate a better parent-child relationship. As the parent learns to understand the child and his or her needs more fully, the relationship becomes the vehicle for promoting the child's healing. CPRT is based on two concepts: first the importance of the parent-child relationship as a curative factor toward the child's well-being and second that the parent has the ability to learn new skills and to apply them as therapeutic agents in his or her child's healing (Bratton et al., 2012).

Some clinicians prefer to use individual therapy initially, especially those based on play or expressive therapies. Individual therapy with an abused child allows him or her to develop a trusting relationship with an adult (therapist), especially in a world where adults may not have seemed particularly trustworthy in the past. Because sexual abuse can be difficult for children to discuss, given not only the stigma placed upon it by adults but also the child's lack of healthy knowledge in the area, play or expressive therapies help the child act out conflicts. Because play is the natural arena of children, this type of therapy can be particularly effective (Cattanach, 2008; Crosson-Tower, 2014; Ellsworth, 2007; Malchiodi, 2012). Drawing and the use of figures in a sand tray or doll house can help enable victims to act out and make sense of what is bothering them. Talking through puppets or toys helps them to gain a bit of distance from discussing difficult topics directly.

Sexually abused children experience a myriad of feelings that cause them to wonder if they are different from their peers (Lowenstein & Freeman, 2012). Group therapy can be especially helpful as it gives children support from peers who have also been abused. Being in a group of peers allows children to recognize that they are not alone, to vent anger, and to take risks in developing socialization skills (Lowenstein & Freeman, 2012; Nurcombe, 2008). It is often particularly effective to use a male and female as cotherapists as this allows the victims to not only develop trusting relationships with both genders but also process the feelings they may have about the males and females in their lives.

How should children who have been sexually abused be treated? There are as many different answers to this question as there are types of treatment. Some experts feel that abuse-specific cognitive-behavioral therapy (CBT) can be particularly effective. CBT is designed to change negative patterns of thoughts and behaviors by teaching the client the relationships between thoughts, feelings, and actions and how to use specific behavioral interventions to address specific problems (Deblinger & Heflin, 1996; Olafson & Boat, 2000; Saywitz et al., 2000). Recent studies (Fitzgerald & Cohen, 2012; Hirshfeld-Becker et al., 2008; Hirshfeld-Becker et al., 2010; Kendall, Hudson, Gosch, Flannery-Schroeder, & Suveg, 2008; Monga, Young, & Owens, 2009; Rapee, Schniering, & Hudson, 2009; Silverman, Pina, & Viswesvaran, 2008) continue to find CBT to be effective, especially with children and families when the young children are exhibiting anxiety and depression, two frequent symptoms of child sexual abuse.

In their classic text on CBT, Deblinger and Heflin (1996) suggested that this approach was particularly suited to children who have been abused because of the wide range of intervention that might be used, matching a wide range of symptoms observed in these children (see also Fitzgerald & Cohen, 2012). In addition, this approach is flexible, can be short term, and teaches parents coping skills that can be used at different developmental stages and by those of a variety of cultural backgrounds (Olafson & Boat, 2000). The abuse has created a sense of helplessness in both the victims and their nonoffending parents. CBT also gives them a mechanism through which to regain a sense of control over their lives.

Alternative therapies have also found favor in some areas. For example, Powell and Cheshire (2010) studied the efficacy of massage offered by a London-based program for the treatment of abused children and their nonabusing mothers. These researchers found that not only did the massage lessen the child's anxiety, transform the child's negative feelings about touch into more positive ones, and invite the child to feel safe and relaxed, but there were significant benefits to the mother-child relationship, an important component in helping the family to reconnect in a positive manner. The mothers were taught how to give therapeutic massage to their children, which then heightened the bonding between mother and child, improving what is often a complex, problematic relationship between the child and the parent that can feature mistrust and fear. Through the tactile connection of massage, mothers became more empathetic and more invested in their children and their safety.

The particular techniques used with children are also subject to debate. Although resources for child therapy may not always be easily identifiable or accessed in some geographic areas, it is important for child victims to have an opportunity to work out their issues around the abuse and the future. Parents should be helped to recognize this necessity and support the therapy for their children.

Efficacy of Treatment With Sexually Abused Children

The evaluation of the efficacy of treatment for sexually abused children can be difficult. As in any trauma, results of treatment will depend upon the characteristics of the client going into treatment. What was the child's vulnerability and resilience? What was the child's temperament, attachment status, neurodevelopmental activity, developmental stage, and other indicators of his or her pre-abuse functioning? One must also look at the risk and protective factors, including family functioning, emotional resources (e.g., emotional health of the nonoffending parent), and financial resources (Nurcombe, 2008; Saunders, 2012; Saywitz et al., 2000). Numerous factors will influence how well the child will respond to treatment.

It may also be difficult to determine how effective treatment is because of other reasons. Due to their underdeveloped discernment and communication abilities, children may not be the most reliable informants about initially explaining their symptoms and later describing the changes that they have made. If these changes are not observable by others, it may be difficult to tell what has been accomplished. Parents or other caregivers may be relied upon to pinpoint the initial problems, but only the child can determine if he or she feels better after treatment (King et al., 2003; Olafson & Boat, 2000; Saywitz et al., 2000).

Children do not always come to sexual abuse treatment in a straightforward manner. More often they are brought because some symptom is observed.

❧

Sawyer's acting out in day care was the precipitating event that brought his mother to bring him to a therapist. His day care provider complained that he would never sit still, was torturing her cat, and masturbating extensively. After several sessions, it was disclosed that Sawyer had been sexually abused by a babysitter. Not feeling that his expertise was with sexual abuse, the therapist transferred Sawyer's case to a female colleague. Having been abused by an older female, Sawyer was unable to relate to this therapist and sat in therapy sucking his thumb and rocking.

ஐ

It took some time before the therapist trained in sexual abuse issue was able to penetrate the child's defenses. By this time, Sawyer's symptoms had intensified.

Improvement of functioning will also be dependent upon the ability of the adults around the child to support him or her. If parents are having their own issues, marital conflict, divorce, stirring up of personal conflicts around the abuse, and so on, the child's treatment progress may be made more difficult (Nurcombe, 2008; Saunders, 2012; Saywitz et al., 2000, Crosson-Tower, 2014).

Experts now lean toward those therapies, the results of which can be measured. Saunders (2012) suggests that clinicians should look for evidence-based practice or those techniques that have been tested and found to be clinically effective.

Adolescent Treatment

Adolescents face a myriad of additional issues developmentally, and these figure significantly in their treatment needs. Because one of the developmental issues of adolescence is exploring one's own sexuality and the formulation of values around sexuality, the presence of sexual abuse can confuse the adolescent and make the normal developmental issues even more challenging (McGee & Holmes, 2012).

The brain development of traumatized children has gained attention in the last few decades. Perry (2006) explains that when trauma occurs, the brain development may be interrupted. As children age, the arrested neurodevelopment level becomes more obvious until the teen years when it becomes clear that this neurodevelopmental level does not match the chronological age of the individual. This author further suggests that the more therapists understand how sexual abuse affects the brain, the better they can tailor their treatment methods to the issues that the teen brings to therapy (see also Ziegler, 2002). Nelson-Gardell (2008) recommends a complete biopsychosocial assessment for adolescents coming into treatment. This assessment can also be challenging as teen years are the time when youth are conflicted about what they want from and how they will relate to parents (McGee & Holmes, 2012).

Even with adolescents who may have gained more independence than their child counterparts, engagement and support of caregivers will be important (McKay & Bannon, 2004; Nelson-Gardell, 2008). Thompson, Bender, Lantry, and Flynn (2007) in their study of the impact of using family therapy with abused adolescents, as a way of helping them with treatment issues as well as family and emancipation issues, supported the use of developing both family engagement and therapist alliances in helping adolescents.

Adolescents too respond well to CBT, by learning skills to change symptomatic behaviors and process the elements of their abuse. Teens in treatment need to learn how to express their feelings; develop problem solving and coping skills, recognizing the relationship between their thoughts, feelings, and actions; and make sense of the abuse experience. In addition, psycho-education on sexual abuse, healthy sexuality, and their bodies will be especially beneficial (Cohen, Mannarino, & Deblinger, 2006; McGee & Holmes, 2012; Nelson-Gardell, 2008).

Group support and therapy is also effective with teens given their natural reliance on peer experiences. Therapeutic intervention in groups allows adolescents to recognize that they are not alone and gives them an arena for risking the development of new relationships.

Careful consideration should be given to cultural background as adolescents undergo treatment. Adolescents from different cultural background may have different views of sex, and therefore, their treatment will require knowledge of their perspective. Fontes (2008) points out that immigrant teens live in two worlds—the culture of their home and that of the wider world. Parents may not be able to help them cope with the greater society, making their task more difficult. The skill of the therapist in recognizing and addressing cultural concerns or issues may also impact the success of the adolescent's therapy.

Children and Adolescents in Out-of-Home Placements

Not all sexually abused children and adolescents can remain at home. As mentioned earlier, if the nonabusing parent is not able to protect the child in the future or if the symptoms of the child's or teen's abuse or his or her behavioral acting out are beyond what the parents can handle, the child may be placed in either foster care or residential treatment. Hopefully, children and adolescents in foster care will receive treatment specifically for their sexual abuse symptoms, although it may not always occur. Residential treatment centers may be specific to sexual abuse treatment or, recognizing that many of the children coming into care have been sexually abused, integrate some type of sexual abuse-specific treatment into the program.

Crenshaw and Mordock (2004) suggest that seven basic tasks should be accomplished in the treatment of abused children in residential care. These are empowering the children; respecting their need for privacy; helping them to feel safe; developing "safety nets'" for them; building and supporting their defenses, helping them to develop basic skills; building their self-esteem; and assisting them in understanding the trauma that they have experienced.

One of the challenges for out-of-home placements is the fact that many sexually abused children and teens will act out their sexual traumas. Farmer and Pollock (2003) studied 40 young people in over 10 residential care facilities and found that two thirds demonstrated sexual behaviors whereas one third did not. These authors believe that the most significant factors in the management of sexually acting out behavior

in residential care are effective supervision and management, adequate sex education, modification of inappropriate behavior, and therapeutic attention to the underlying causes of the behaviors (see also Crosson-Tower, 2013; Johnson & Aoki, 1993).

THE TREATMENT OF FAMILIES _____

Preparation for Treatment

Only after several questions are answered can treatment begin. These questions include but may not be limited to the following:

- Does the family believe the child has been abused?
- Can the family recognize the needs of the child and put them above the needs and desires of the offender?
- Where is the offender?
- Can the child remain home with protection from his or her family against future abuse?
- If placement outside the home is necessary, where will the child reside, and what type of involvement will the family have?
- Is the eventual goal the reunification of the family?
- How committed to or motivated for treatment are the family members?

We discussed earlier the need for families to be engaged in the treatment of abused children, but family members themselves battle with emotional issues when their children have been abused and may need to confront these issues in order to be emotionally available to their children. Bolen (2007) suggests that caretaker support may be hampered by concerns over the basics such as housing and poverty and fears about their own safety, as well as psychological concerns. Nonoffending caretakers may have felt blamed by the child protection or criminal justice system, sometimes making them believe that they were also responsible for the child's being abused.

Treatment of Nonoffending Parents

Research indicates that nonoffending parents of sexually abused children suffer anxiety, guilt, sleep disorders, ambivalent feelings toward the child, tension, fatigue, and intrusive thoughts (Alaggia & Knott, 2008; Hernandez et al., 2009). Before expecting these parents to be in full support for their children, these personal and emotional conflicts and possible deficits must be addressed.

ෆ

Willa often felt she was in competition with her 12-year-old daughter Danalyn, who was well developed for her age and quite attractive. Willa had been a single mother for some years and had dated extensively. Although she never saw this as endangering her daughter, Danalyn described several occasions when her mother fell asleep, leaving her current manfriend, who was usually also drinking, alone with the girl. Several of these men sexually abused Danalyn, a fact that Willa did not initially believe. Once she became convinced that her daughter was telling the truth, Willa was overcome by guilt. She said that she dated out of loneliness, and the men were "really nice and never would have hurt my kid." Willa battled with resentment that Danalyn had "let" these men touch her and had to be helped to recognize the child's powerlessness. After she saw a videotape of Danalyn telling of her abuse, Willa's guilt intensified, and she remembered her own abuse at the hands of her stepfather. She became anxious and had difficulty sleeping. One minute she was overprotective of Danalyn; the next she was critical and rejecting. It was necessary for Willa to undergo her own long-overdue treatment for her own post-traumatic stress before she was able to provide support for her child. In the meantime, she did alter her habits in the interest of protecting Danalyn and agreed to work with the girl's therapist. ෨

Some nonoffending parents are still influenced by the perpetrator.

ෆ

Becca loved her husband, Dwight, and found it difficult that he would have abused 6-year-old Justin. But as the lengthy trial progressed, Becca recognized that her son was telling the truth, and she supported him. However, after Dwight was incarcerated, he wrote pleading letters to his wife about his innocence and asking that she take him back when he was released. Becca wavered. She did not know who her own father was and had wanted Justin to "have a daddy." She wondered if everyone had been mistaken. Maybe the boy had imagined the bedtime abuse. Becca struggled with her own loyalties even though she was determined to protect Justin from any future harm. It was some months in individual therapy that Becca was able to recognize that she was being manipulated by a crafty abuser. ෨

Bolen and Lamb (2004), in their summary of existing literature on nonoffending mothers, reported that although 25% were not supportive of their abused child and 31% were partially supportive or ambivalent, 44% of these mothers were fully supportive. Considering that these mothers often also experience marital stress, isolation, anger, embarrassment, guilt, and a resurgence of memories and conflicts when they were also traumatized as children, these numbers are even more encouraging (Alaggia, 2002; Alaggia & Knott, 2008; Joyce, 2007; Kouyoumdjian, Perry, & Hansen, 2009; Plummer, 2006).

In addition, treatment can be compromised by the attitude of the helper. Early literature on nonoffending mothers presented the picture of a mother who often colluded with the perpetrator on some level to enable the child's sexual abuse (Sgroi & Dana, 1982; Tinling, 1990). Johnson (1992a) characterizes the collusive mother as only one profile of a nonoffending mother, whereas more recent research (Bolen, 2007; Bolen & Lamb, 2004; Joyce, 1997) refutes the idea of collusion all together, citing the mother's reaction after disclosure as more germane to the case management and treatment. However, Joyce (2007) found, in a study of 15 female master's level social workers in an urban setting, there were several factors that influenced the manner in which social workers saw the nonoffending mother. Although these clinicians did not see the mothers as collusive, they did demonstrate some pessimism related to the disorganization of their clients' lives and the belief that there was little that could be done to change them completely. There was also some degree of vicarious traumatization (when a worker feels personally impacted by the client's story; see Chapter 16 for further explanation), which may have impacted the manner in which the clinicians worked with clients. Shared ethnicity between clinician and nonoffending mother intensified the former's reaction. In addition, clinicians who felt misunderstood or that they lacked control within their agencies more often bought into the construct that nonoffending mothers were victimized by forces beyond their control and therefore may not have been as effective in helping these mothers with empowerment.

Admittedly the chemistry between any client and his or her clinician is important, but given the conflicting views on the treatment of the nonoffending mother over the years, the nature of this relationship becomes especially important for effective treatment.

Treatment Issues for Nonoffending Parents

Effective treatment of nonoffending parents can be divided into the addressing of several problem areas:

- Intrapsychic issues
- Relationship with the child
- Family dynamics
- Community supports

Nonoffending parents usually come to treatment with their own *intrapsychic issues* that need to be addressed so that they can move on to supporting their children and attending to the realignment of family dynamics (Alaggia & Knott, 2008; Powell & Cheshire, 2010). So often, in the interest of seeing that the nonoffending parent can protect the child in the future, the immediate needs of the parent are expected to take a back seat. But treatment for the child will be greatly enhanced if his or her parents' needs are also addressed.

Often nonoffending parents have also been traumatized or abused as children, a fact that they may never have addressed. The abuse of their child often brings up old memories that can hamper the parents' ability to be supportive. In addition, they may feel that they have failed in their role as parents and must be helped to gain or regain confidence in their ability to parent. Research indicates that nonabusing parents suffer from a high level of distress, which may manifest itself in eating and sleeping problems, anxiety, fatigue, tension headaches, guilt, intrusive thoughts, and ambivalence. These reactions may even be present when the abuse was perpetrated by a nonfamily member (Alaggia & Knott, 2008). Thus, it will be vital to address the nonoffending parent's own needs before focusing on her or his ability to support the child.

Hernandez et al. (2009) conducted a pilot study of nonoffending parents that used a group program combining the use of evidence-based, trauma-focused CBTs and psychoeducational or supportive interventions specifically developed for these parents. These interventions differed from other interventions in that they addressed specifically the nonoffending parents' post-traumatic experience of the abuse and the potential effects on family distress and functioning. Although most family interventions focus on the child's perspective, this program looked at the nonabusing parent as the treatment target in order to address parent and child mental health issues, as well as improving family functioning in a number of areas. These researchers found this approach to be particularly helpful.

The nonabusing parent's *relationship with the child* is also a crucial piece of treatment (Bratton et al., 2012). Some of these parents may still question the child's truthfulness, especially if the perpetrator is someone with whom this parent has a relationship. In a summary of existing reviews, Bolen and Lamb (2004) found that although 44% of nonabusive mothers supported and believed their children, 25% were not supportive and 31% were ambivalent. An earlier study by Pintello and Zuravin (2001) had found that of 437 nonperpetrating mothers, close to 42% believed and protected their children, whereas a little over 27% were ambivalent and close to 31% were not able to believe their children or demonstrate a consistent protective response. The early task of therapy may be to help the mother to understand and overcome her hesitancy to believe the child.

Some parents have not sufficiently bonded to their children because of their own intrapsychic issues, issues at birth, or the complexity of family relationships. The abuse itself may also have damaged the relationship that did exist. Thus, the therapist may need to repair some of the basics of the parent-child relationship. The use of therapeutic massage was mentioned earlier. Powell and Cheshire (2010) describe the Mosaic Massage Program, a London-based program that teaches nonabusing mothers of children who have been sexually abused basic massage skills. The mothers then use massage on their children centering on the hands, feet, head, and face under supervision by trainers. The goal—which is reportedly attained—is to help with bonding, rebuild the confidence between mother and child, and reframe touch as something appropriate, nurturing, and nonabusive. These researchers feel that such techniques open new vistas for treatment in child sexual abuse.

Abused children also benefit from joint therapy with nonabusing parents to help them sort out issues about the parent's role in the abuse. Parents' own feelings of guilt may have distorted their ability to clearly communicate feelings with abused children. It will be beneficial if the child is helped to understand that the nonabusing parent (Alaggia, 2002; Alaggia & Knott, 2008)

- believes that the abuse happened;
- recognizes the seriousness of the impact on the child;
- recognizes that the perpetrator, not the child, was responsible for the abuse;
- acknowledges the child's feelings about not being protected from the abuse; and
- is willing and able to protect the child in the future.

Child sexual abuse is impacted by and impacts *family dynamics*. In intrafamilial abuse, the family climate provides fertile ground for the abuse. Abuse may reoccur unless a careful look is taken at the role that each family member has played in the abuse. It is usually necessary for the perpetrator to leave the home, at least for a specified period of time, so that he or she and the rest of the family might have time to understand and come to terms with what has transpired. Therapy for the nonabusing parent will also be centered around helping him or her sort out the complexity of roles within the family and how he or she can protect the child in the future. If the perpetrator, after his or her own therapy, is to be reunited with the family, this must be addressed and feelings worked through.

And finally, nonabusive parents need help with accessing *community supports*. If the abuse was intrafamilial, the stigma may prevent parents from exploring and reaching out to resources in the community. Even if there is a readiness, most people are not aware of what might be available for them. And they may need guidance in finding out what exists in the community. Parents whose children are abused outside the home may also be resistant to looking for community support because their inclination is often to hide what has happened. Thus, part of the therapist's role will be identifying community supports and brokering so that clients are able to access these supports.

Treatment for Siblings of Sexually Abused Children

Often the most forgotten members of a family touched by sexual abuse are the siblings of the abused child. These siblings may or may not have been abused. Often although the spotlight is on one child, careful investigation will determine that other siblings have also been abused but have not come forward. If the abuse is discovered, they too should receive treatment.

But what of the siblings who have not been abused by either the intrafamilial perpetrator or someone outside the home?

Siblings of Children Abused at Home

Siblings who grow up in the shadow of incest may also have treatment needs. As mentioned in Chapter 6, siblings who are aware on some level that a sister or brother is being abused may have a variety of reactions and thus require some type of treatment to sort out their feelings. Some of these children will act out the abuse they have observed on others, often younger siblings.

ଔ
_____

Dick at 13 knew that his father was abusing 9-year-old Ona because he had once walked in when Pop was touching her "down there." His first response was to protect his sister, but he also knew about his father's rages. The scars on his back were enough to convince him that you didn't cross Pop. Trying to figure out what to do, he began listening at the door when he knew that Ona and Pop were together. It wasn't long before he felt stimulated by what he knew was going on and began to masturbate to the sounds. Often in charge of his 3-year-old brother, Kyle, Dick began to masturbate him. Soon it became a part of his life. When he knew Pop was abusing Ona, Dick would find Kyle and talk him into being masturbated.
_____
ଔ

When Ona's abuse came to the attention of CPS, the father was removed from the home, and the mother sought treatment with her daughter. The other children, Dick and Kyle, were initially not part of treatment. And then Kyle disclosed his own abuse, bringing the whole family into treatment. Kyle was seen by a therapist for play therapy. Dick, thought to be reactive rather than a budding pedophile himself, was assigned to a group of young teens in similar situations.

Nonabused siblings are often confused by what they know is happening. If they act out this confusion as Dick did, this will be a treatment issue to determine how this pattern can be interrupted.

Baker, Tanis, and Rice (2001) suggest several reasons why they believe that siblings in familial abuse should be included in therapy. First, the presence of incest suggests that the family dynamics are dysfunctional, making it important to involve the entire family in therapy. Second, no matter what the family dynamics were before the abuse, the abuse has altered the picture, and all of those exposed to that abuse need to be involved in treatment. In addition to the contention of these authors, social agencies can attest to the frequency of seeing acting out or sexually abusive teens and adults whose history includes a child sexual abuse perpetrator within their family.

There are specific issues that many siblings bring to treatment. Ironically, there may be, as mentioned in Chapter 6, a question in the sibling's mind about why they were not "chosen" for the parental attention that often goes along with the abuse. This impacts their self-concept and should be addressed. Often, because they were not abused by the offender, the sibling's contact with him or her may continue to some degree. This may generate confusion, especially if the contact is unsupervised and the offender is allowed to tell his or her side of the story to the sibling. There are also feelings of conflicting loyalties, especially given that the sibling may be angry with the victim for what he or she perceives as having caused all the trouble that has been generated by the disclosure. The sibling must be helped to understand and process these difficult feelings about his or her family members. He or she may also experience conflicts about the necessary family realignment that will be taking place in the aftermath of the abuse.

When the child is abused by someone outside the home, the siblings are still impacted. Some parents of children abused outside the home try to shelter their other children from this information. However, siblings frequently perceive the family unrest and may fear that they are somehow responsible. Parents are encouraged to share with their other children that the abuse has happened, gearing the explanation to the level of the siblings' age. Then the siblings can be helped to deal with their fears and conflicts. There may be anger at the victim for the upheaval that surrounds reporting abuse or concerns about the shame and the stigma of being somehow tainted by sexual abuse. Siblings sometimes have fears that the sexual abuse might happen to them, especially if they are in contact with the offender or frequent the places where the abuse occurred.

ᘓ

"I could never go to the playground again," explained one sister of an abused child. "I was always sure that the man who molested my sister was there, waiting for me too, even though Dad said that he had been caught by the police." ᘔ

Unfortunately, despite the need for siblings to have an opportunity to work out their conflicts and express their feelings, it is rare that they are given the opportunity of their own therapy. One hope is that, although most siblings do not receive their own individual therapy, some agencies assign siblings to sibling support/therapy groups, where they can be helped to recognize that they are not alone and benefit from the healing achieved though interacting with others in similar situations.

Child sexual abuse impacts the whole family whether it is perpetrated within the family or not. Therefore it is crucial that all members have access to help if they need it.

THE ROLE OF OTHER PROFESSIONALS

The treatment of victims and families touched by sexual abuse is about helping them to overcome the trauma and strive to normalize their lives in the aftermath of the abuse. This does not take place in a vacuum, and reintegration into the community is an important piece. Thus, it behooves the therapist to involve other professionals within the community, especially those within natural support systems such as churches and civic groups. Clergy especially can be important allies as families try to bridge the gap between reliance on the social service system and life on their own after the abuse.

Some clinicians report difficulties with other professionals and members of the community.

ᘓ

My experience, explained one therapist, is that well-meaning people can get in the way of successful treatment. I have had several clergy, for example, who tell my clients that God will bring them through if they just pray hard enough. I am not saying that it might not help for a client to embrace a faith, but dropping out of therapy at a crucial point because of just such advice is not what I believe will help her. ᘔ

People whose inclination is to help often want very much to be involved in the lives of those who need that help. If a client is involved in a church, for example, he or she may be helped to involve the clergy person in being of support during and after therapy. Often some guidance on the part of the therapist can help the community representative to know what form this support might take (see Crosson-Tower, 2006).

Part of therapy should be helping the clients to explore what is available to them in the community and how these resources can be used.

Summary

When considering treatment in child sexual abuse, it is important to first determine who needs treatment. While children may find other ways of making sense of what has happened to them, they do need to be screened to determine if treatment would benefit them. Families of victims may also have feelings that need to be addressed. Even if needed, treatment may not take place for several reasons: insufficient resources, untrained staff, family reluctance to accept or follow through with treatment, and funding for services.

When a child is in treatment, several factors must be considered including the availability of parental support, where the child will reside, how the identity of the perpetrators impacts treatment, and whether there will be involvement with the criminal justice system. Children experience numerous feelings that are the basis for treatment. Finkelhor and Browne (1985) divided these into four problem areas: traumatic sexualization, stigmatization, betrayal, and powerlessness. Children should also be screened for post-traumatic stress disorder.

Various treatment methods are used in treating children. Perhaps some of the most successful of these are play or other expressive therapies and cognitive behavioral therapy (CBT). It is not always easy to determine the efficacy of treatment for children, and clinicians continue to look for evidence-based techniques that have been proven to be effective. Adolescents also respond well to CBT as well as or in conjunction with group therapy, which builds on the adolescent's developmental preference for peer relationships.

Family members, especially nonabusive mothers (and fathers) may also require treatment. These parents can be an important support system for their children provided their own conflicts are addressed. Parents must deal with their own intrapsychic issues, their relationship with their children, and the family dynamics. Siblings are the often forgotten family members when it comes to offering treatment for child sexual abuse. They may also be confused or conflicted about what is going on in the family and need to have these concerns and fears addressed.

Therapists may also play the role of interface with other professionals in the community on behalf of abused children and their families.

Review Questions

1. What are some barriers to treatment in child sexual abuse?

2. What are some assumptions around treatment?

3. What are the treatment issues for children who have been sexually abused?

4. What types of therapy are used with child victims?

5. How effective is treatment with children?

6. How are families prepared for treatment?

7. What is involved in the treatment of the nonoffending parent?

8. What is involved in the treatment of siblings?

CHAPTER 14

Assessment and Treatment for Adult Sexual Offenders

☙❧

Working with sexual offenders may not be the most popular line of therapeutic interventions, but I have always kept in mind that successfully treating one sexual offender may have prevented numerous young potential victims from being sexually abused. It's a thought that keeps me going—doing the work I do.

☙❧

There is much truth to the words of a therapist whose specialty is treating sexual offenders against children, but prevention of sexual abuse is actually one of the many satisfactions in working with this population. As frustrating as the work can sometimes be, the gains can be significant too.

In order to discuss the treatment of child sexual offenders, it is useful to first consider how they are assessed for treatment.

ASSESSMENT OF ADULTS WHO SEXUALLY ABUSE CHILDREN

Child sexual offenders come in contact with numerous professionals and with several systems—most commonly social services, criminal justice, and mental health. Until relatively recently, professionals within these systems—social workers, attorneys, judges, police, and therapists—had little or no training in dealing with this challenging population. Working with sexual offenders requires skill and knowledge, and for this reason, there is an increasing body of knowledge available through books, articles, and training. Those who regularly work with sex offenders must prepare themselves for this task.

Who Intervenes?

Assessment begins at the moment that sexual abuse is reported or detected. As mentioned in Chapter 11, child sexual abuse usually comes first to the attention of the police or the child protective service (CPS) agency. Some police departments have established sexual crime units (Sax, 2010), and many

CPS agencies have also created units that specialize in the investigation of child sexual abuse. This allows training to be more specialized for those who will be working with victims, offenders, and families.

Sexual abuse of children is a crime, and therefore, the case is referred to the district attorney's (DA) office usually at the onset. The last person usually interviewed is the offender as the investigators first collect information from the victim and family members that can be used as a measure by which to assess the offender's version (as he or she has the most to lose). If there is enough evidence, and/or if the child appears to be in danger, the offender will usually be arrested and possibly incarcerated pending further investigation. The DA has a good deal of discretion in determining if offenders should be charged, but the DA must also consider if there will be enough evidence to get a conviction (Staller & Vandervort, 2010). In most states, an arraignment is held immediately following arrest and an attorney can be appointed if the offender is unable to afford one. The DA's office stipulates that the offender have no contact with the child. Depending upon the laws of the state, the offender may be released on bail until the hearing or will be kept in custody until the hearing determines his or her risk of flight or reoffending. Thus, in most cases, the offender's first route will be through the criminal justice system. In situations where there is familial abuse, the victim and the family, although interviewed by the police and DA's office, may be more involved with CPS and possibly the mental health system (Flora, 2001). When the offender is not a family member, the case may not come under the jurisdiction of CPS. These are the situations when victim-witness advocates may become involved to protect the child's rights.

Once the offender has been convicted and incarcerated or mandated to receive outpatient therapy, he or she will be assessed to determine treatment needs.

Assessing Treatability, Compliance, and Risk of Recidivism

A variety of assessment tools have been developed to determine the treatment needs of sexual offenders, to monitor their compliance during treatment, and to predict their risk of offending, especially posttreatment. It should be noted that because most reported sexual offenders are men and the abundance of literature addresses the characteristics and treatment of male sexual offenders, most of the assessment tools are geared toward that population.

Beech, Fisher, and Thornton (2003) divide assessment strategies into three areas: (a) *functional analyses*, (b) *actuarial risk assessments*, and (c) *dynamic risk assessments*. *Functional analysis* looks at the offender in terms of what led up to his offense (*antecedent*), what he did and to whom and how (*behavior*), and what were the *consequences* of his offending (known as the ABC model). Offenders are not always ready to disclose all this information as denial is a chief form of defense (Blagden, Winder, Gregson, & Thorne, 2013). One framework often used with offenders is called the *decision chain* (Ward, Louden, Hudson, & Marshall, 1995) where clients are asked to talk about the choices that they made at each point along the way toward the offense. At each point, the feelings, thoughts, and attitudes of the offender are discussed to help him reveal more information. Ward, Polaschek, and Beech (2006) suggested that offenders can be classified according to the pathways they use for offending (see Chapter 3, the pathways model), depending upon the cluster of symptoms that motivate them to abuse.

Actuarial risk prediction has been gaining popularity over the last 15 years. Various tools have been developed that use the risk factors that have been identified in various research studies of offenders and measure an offender against these factors to develop a score. This score places the offender along a continuum of high to low risk of dangerousness and reoffending. Some researchers believe that this actuarial assessment is more accurate than clinical assessments in evaluating the amount of risk an offender presents and therefore assigning him the appropriate intensity of treatment (Smid, Kamphuis, Wever, & VanBeek, 2013). Many of these tools have been developed in Canada and the United Kingdom (Beech et al., 2003; Seto, 2008). An example of such an assessment developed in the United States is the Minnesota Sex Offender Screening Tool (revised) that uses a 16-item scale, covering the offender's number of convictions, his sexual offending history, where and how the sexual offense was committed, choice of victims, substance abuse, employment history, and other factors. It was developed for use with prisoners and covers a broad number of assessment factors. One criticism of actuarial assessments is that they measure probability rather than certainty of future recidivism. In addition, these static instruments may ignore other unique characteristics of the offender, and the instrument does not indicate what factors need to be addressed in treatment and how they will reduce risk (Beech et al., 2003).

Dynamic risk assessments were developed in an effort to overcome the weaknesses in actuarial risk assessments that are based on risk factors that cannot change (e.g., an offender's history). Dynamic risks are "changeable (e.g., social attitudes and beliefs about sex with children) or temporarily fluctuating (e.g., level of alcohol intoxication) factors that could, in principle, be targets of intervention" (Seto, 2008, p. 150).

These assessment tools may be used for initial evaluation but are also used for ongoing assessment to determine the rate of recidivism. The goal of assessment is to determine the path for what Laws and Ward (2011) refer to as *desistance*—or the process through which the offender can be turned away from offending.

Tools for Assessment

There are a variety of tools that are used for the assessment of sexual offenders.

Clinical Interviews

Clinical interviews involve history taking and determining the nature of the offender's sexual interests, thoughts, and behaviors especially in reference to children and if those attitudes change over time.

At the onset, history taking gives the clinician a picture of the offender and how his sexually acting out began. Typical areas that might be explored are the following (Flora et al., 2008; Laws & Ward, 2011; Prendergast, 2004; Seto, 2008):

- Age that puberty began
- Age when first sexual thoughts or feelings began
- Nature of these sexual thoughts or feelings
- Nature of current fantasies
- Age when first masturbated
- Current masturbation patterns and thoughts while doing so
- Any sexual contact with opposite sex? When, and at what age? Age of partner?
- How many partners to date? Male or female?
- Current sexual partner?
- Ever had unusual sexual fantasies? Nature of these?
- How many underage victims? Male or female? How gained access?
- Ever use pornography? Nature of this?

The interviewer may also ask questions about the offender's living situation and his relationship with other adults. The offender's support system is assessed. Does he use alcohol or drugs? How frequently? The clinician will ask about marital status, children of his own, or other topics that will give the interviewer an idea of who this offender is and whether or not he is a good candidate for treatment. Through these questions, the clinician is also assessing the offender's sexual interests and potential problems that might arise in treatment. It is quite common for offenders to lie, whether out of self-delusion/denial or self-protection, but experienced clinicians expect this. Many researchers feel that the interview lacks reliability and validity, although there is some usefulness in face-to-face evaluations (Lindeman, 2005; Seto, 2008; Smid et al., 2013).

More recently, this process of assessment has been colored by the use of several strength-based models including the risk-needs-responsivity (RNR) model, good lives model (GLM), and the integration of these models (introduced in Chapter 3 and discussed later in this chapter in reference to their use in treatment). These models look at the basic facts of the offender's life but through the lens of assessing not only the risk of the individual to reoffend but also the offender's strengths and determining what might be involved in the individual's achievement of some primary human goals (see the section "Good Lives Model").

Questionnaires and Tests

Questionnaires and tests (mentioned earlier) have been developed to assess offending behaviors, compliance with treatment, and possible risk for reoffending. These enable an offender to answer questions without having to have a face-to-face interview. Because social skills are difficult for many offenders and trust is often at a very low level, this model may allow the offender more comfort in answering difficult questions. Seto (2008) also points out that it eliminates the human error of having an interviewer forget to ask some crucial questions (see also Lindeman, 2005).

Ward and Stewart (2003) point out that it is important when evaluating sexual offenders to look at both sexual interest and deviance as well as assessing other factors such as substance abuse, antisocial attitudes, criminal violence, poor judgment, and so on. Instruments used with sex offenders measure many of the same issues that would be addressed in an interview—for example

(but not limited to), sexual history, interests and deviance, victim preference, assessment of relationship, and social functioning and attitudes—all of which may determine future risk and treatability (Beech et al., 2003; Craig, 2010; Lindeman, 2005; Proeve, 2009; Seto, 2008).

When assessing risk in offenders, most evaluators recommend the use of broad criteria that cover all possible risk factors. Beech et al. (2003) suggest that these risk factors, as identified in the research literature, fall into four broad categories: (a) *dispositional factors*, such as psychotic or antisocial personality characteristics; (b) *historical factors*, such as adverse developmental events, prior history of crime and violence, prior hospitalization, and poor treatment compliance; (c) *contextual antecedents to violence*, such as deviant social networks and lack of positive social supports; and (d) *clinical factors*, such as psychiatric diagnosis, poor level of functioning, and substance abuse (p. 339).

Laboratory Testing

The *penile plethysmograph* measures erectile response in males and has been useful in measuring arousal patterns to determine not only deviant sexual preferences but also how these may have changed over the course of treatment. This test is done in a controlled laboratory setting, during which the offender is instructed to place a gauge over the shaft of his penis while the evaluator keeps verbal contact with him from an adjoining room. The offender is given different types of both sexual and nonsexual stimuli (usually audiotapes or computer-generated images) while the gauge measures the changes in the size of his penis (Cumming & Buell, 1997; Flora et al., 2008; Seto, 2008). A printout is then generated that enables the evaluator to assess the offender's response to specific images. It might be expected that an offender who victimized young boys would become more aroused when shown such images.

Although the penile plethysmograph may be a valuable tool, some critics question its reliability in all cases. An offender's sexual arousal to some stimuli does not necessarily mean he will act on that impulse. In addition, it is possible for the offender to suppress his response. The laboratory is not the real world and may not really measure the offender's reactions to real people or situations. For example, some offenders may use alcohol to overcome their inhibitions about offending, and this would not be detectable in the laboratory. Critics also point to a lack of guidelines in the use of this tool. Due to these criticisms, the Association for the Treatment of Sex Offenders has developed standardized guidelines (Cumming & Buell, 1997). Despite these guidelines, there continues to be debate in some circles about the invasiveness in the use of this tool.

The *polygraph*, sometimes referred to as a *lie detector*, is used to measure emotional arousal through physiological changes in the body that are a response to fear (e.g., blood pressure, respiration, perspiration). Thus, when the offender lies, his fear is of detection, and his response pattern may change (Cumming & Buell, 1997; Seto, 2008). There are two types of polygraphs: the control question test and the guilty knowledge test. In the *control question test*, the offender is asked questions about his behaviors (e.g., sexual offense history, risky activities such as being alone with children) as well as questions about neutral topics. The expectation is that the offender would react more significantly to the relevant questions about his offending rather than to the control questions (Seto, 2008).

The *guilty knowledge test* asks the offender about specific details of his crime known only to the evaluators and the offender. Again, the expectation is that the offender would have a different response to the relevant questions about his offending than to the control questions (Seto, 2008). This test may be used to increase disclosures and to gather additional pertinent information.

Various types of assessments may be used in conjunction with one another, or some treatment facilities will favor one or more over others.

TREATMENT OF SEXUAL OFFENDERS AGAINST CHILDREN

Who Treats Sex Offenders?

The treatment of sexual offenders is a specialized field that requires knowledge and skill. Some prisons offer sex offender treatment either in house or through contracting with specialized agencies. These same agencies may also offer outpatient sex offender treatment. In fact, a percentage of offenders reside in their communities and have been ordered by court to receive treatment. Sex offender treatment is usually long term and should include aftercare to follow intensive treatment. Unfortunately, this aftercare does not always happen due to limited resources, both financial and in terms of therapists who are skilled in treating and doing follow-up with offenders.

Therapists who treat sexual offenders must have specialized training and be prepared to see these offenders as individuals who—despite their crimes—deserve what any client is entitled to, respect. Working with these clients can be challenging. In addition to their offending behaviors, offenders may also have a variety of other psychological problems like depression, anxiety, posttraumatic stress disorder (PTSD), drug addiction, personality disorders, and developmental delays.

Theorists suggest that therapists wanting to work with offenders should have certain qualifications (O'Connell, Leberg, & Donaldson, 1990; Flora et al., 2008):

- Therapists should have a formal education with a professional degree at the masters, doctorate, or medical degree level.
- Therapists should have clinical experience, which is the single-most important qualification for a sex offender therapist.
- Clinical experience should include work with involuntary patients.
- Therapists must be aware of the psychological impact that the sexual abuse has had on victims.

- Clinicians should be assertive and direct.
- Clinicians should be alert to manipulation by the sex offender.
- Clinicians should have the ability to question the offender about his or her sexually inappropriate behavior in a very detailed manner.
- Clinicians should have knowledge of
  - the criminal justice system,
  - the dynamics of the court system, and
  - community resources.

The "Current Practices and Emerging Trends in Sexual Abuser Management: The Safer Society 2009 North American Survey" recently looked at professionals working with sexual offenders and found that within community programs, 51% had doctorates, 85% master's degrees, and only 7.8% had bachelor's degrees, attesting to the recognition that sex offender treatment requires advanced degrees. In residential settings, 15% of staff working with offenders had doctorates, 45% had master's degrees, 25% had bachelor's degrees, and 15% had none of these degrees (McGrath, Cumming, Burchard, Zeoli, & Ellerby, 2010).

If possible, clinicians' training should be specific to working with sexual offenders and/or child sexual abuse in general. Although there is a dearth of courses and certificates in this field specifically, graduate training usually requires an internship, which could be done in a facility or an agency that treats offenders.

As new models emerge, there is a change in emphasis in the training of clinicians. Laws and Ward (2011) point out that, in the early history of treatment, clinicians who have used deficit models rather than strength-based models were expected to be in control of the treatment process at all times. This translated into confrontation and seemingly harsh attitudes that could become adversarial and power plays between clinician and client. More recently—and especially with the GLM—there is recognition that offender motivation plays a significant role in the therapeutic process. There is also increased emphasis on the fact that when offenders are encouraged to buy into their treatment, they are more likely to achieve lasting change. Recent research has attested to the fact that the basic tenets of counseling—validation, collaboration, empathy, and flexibility—are more effective in promoting change in sexual offenders than the more authoritarian techniques of the past.

As mentioned earlier, sex offender therapy is a long-term therapy that requires a realistic but hopeful view. Offenders do not improve overnight. Some never do, but it will be important to remain hopeful that something will reach them. Forging a therapeutic relationship based on hope and the encouragement of the offender's motivation is essential to successful treatment. Offenders may deny that they abused, set up road blocks, oppose therapists, resist change, and attempt to sabotage treatment, and clinicians must be prepared (Blagden et al., 2013; Flora et al., 2008; O'Connell et al., 1990; Prendergast, 2004), ever mindful of the need to find ways to encourage offender motivation.

Those who choose to treat sexual offenders should have a strong sense of self and have done their own psychological work. If a therapist has been a victim of child sexual abuse, this work may be too difficult and unwise for both the therapist and the offender. Offenders recognize when a therapist does not hold them in positive regard because of his or her own residual issues. Such work requires good personal boundaries and the ability to recognize when countertransference issues are getting in the way.

Stress is an integral part of working with sex offenders. Working with this population is not necessarily popular in the community, and the therapist must be prepared for a variety of public reactions. Sexual deviancy is unpleasant, and sometimes those who work with it may feel ostracized themselves; thus, it is important to have a good personal support system and to keep one's work in the workplace. Working with sexual offenders requires attention to detail, accuracy, and the ability to seek out additional information when needed. A therapist must learn to be objective no matter what the offender says or does (Flora et al., 2008; O'Connell et al., 1990).

In Chapter 16, we discuss what is needed to work with sexual abuse issues in general. But because sexual offenders are a difficult population, we will consider some specifics to working with them. Clinicians who have worked with sexual offenders recommend some ways of preparing oneself to work with offenders and of taking care of one's self when working with this population. These recommendations fall into three categories: acquiring knowledge and skills, attending to ethical issues, and practicing self-care.

Acquiring Knowledge and Skills

First, it is important for a therapist to have training specific to working with sexual offenders. Understanding the pathology and how it might lead to manipulation is vital. Education in sexual abuse should be followed by supervision by someone who is trained in and experienced with sexual offenders. Ongoing peer support and the availability of consultation are also necessary (Brampton, 2011; Crosson-Tower, 2006; Flora et al., 2008; Hilarski, 2008c; van Dam, 2001). At the same time, offenders are people who can change and grow and should be respected as such. Skill in developing encouraging therapeutic relationships is crucial for the work.

Attending to Ethical Issues

Each profession in counseling has a code of ethics, and knowledge of this code is important. Sexual offenders are masters at stretching ethical boundaries; the clinician must be constantly aware of his or her boundaries, both personal and professional. At the same time, the boundaries of each client must also be respected within the therapeutic relationship.

Practicing Self-Care

Practicing self-care is especially important with this population. In Chapter 16, we will discuss more fully what anyone who chooses to work with sexual abuse must do to prepare for that task. But a discussion of treating sexual offenders requires additional recommendations. First, clinicians should be aware of their own attitudes toward sex. They should develop in their own mind a set of standards that are appropriate and be aware of their own sexual boundaries and diligent about keeping them. They should assess and recognize their strengths and challenges as a clinician. If a case is beyond their capabilities, clinicians should refer it or get good supervision. Countertransference may enter into their work with offenders, and it is important to be aware when it does. Supervision, peer or individual, and/or consultation can help clinicians to monitor their own responses to client material.

Boundaries, as stated earlier, are important. It is also vital for clinicians to separate from work, taking time for their own space and leisure activities. Even during the course of a day, it is wise to take time to regroup and refocus their energies. And it is advisable to not work alone. Some sexual offenders (though not as often as offenders against children) employ intimidation as a tactic, and it is best not to be caught in a vulnerable position. Above all, clinicians should know that this can be a challenging population to treat. They should know when they are experiencing symptoms of burnout and attend to those signs (Brampton, 2011; Crosson-Tower, 2006; Flora et al., 2008; Hilarski, 2008c; van Dam, 2001).

Despite some of the challenges of treating sexual offenders, this work can be rewarding for those who have prepared themselves through training, skill acquisition, and ongoing monitoring of their own responses and stress.

Considerations for Treatment

Incarceration or Outpatient Therapy

As mentioned earlier, some offenders will be incarcerated, and some will be seen in the community, usually under court order. The inclination of the public is often to incarcerate for as long as possible, but incarceration alone does not work with offenders. In jails and prisons, they are at the bottom of the pecking order, which means that they are often beaten, humiliated, and ostracized by other offenders. Many penal facilities are forced to keep them in protective custody or away from the inmates who are not there for sexual offenses. Sexual offenders come to prison already burdened with anger, resentment, and often fear. The negative treatment at the hands of other prisoners and even correctional officers intensifies their anger and resentment. Thus, a sex offender who is incarcerated and receives no sex offender–specific treatment will return to society angrier and at greater risk for reoffending and venting his anger on his victims.

In recognition of these possibilities, most prisons now either mandate or recommend that sex offenders attend sex offender treatment arranged by the facility. Sex offenders may also be a part of other treatment programs within the prison. Some facilities will give "good time" (figurative points toward the favorable consideration of a reduced sentence or parole) if an offender attends sex offender treatment, whereas others do not.

What determines whether an offender is incarcerated or mandated to outpatient treatment? Much of this depends upon the nature of the offender's crime, his or her prior record, and the proceedings in court. Ideally the bottom line when dealing with offenders is the protection of the community, so if offenders are considered a danger, they are more likely to be sentenced and incarcerated. However, there are other variables such as plea bargaining for probation and outpatient therapy, whether the case is heard before a jury, and how the case proceeds may have an influence on where the offender resides and what type of treatment is expected. If a case is dismissed, usually for lack of sufficient evidence, an offender may receive no treatment at all. Sexual offenders rarely seek out such treatment voluntarily (Sax, 2010).

Sax (2010, adapted from p. 220) points out that there are numerous options for those who come before the court for sex offenses. The court may mandate

- jail or prison time;
- house arrest;
- community service;
- alcohol or drug treatment;
- psychotherapy and/or group treatment;
- treatment for domestic violence, parenting issues, or anger management; or
- a protective order for the perpetrator to stay away from the victim.

Any of these options might be combined with sex offender treatment.

An offender who is ordered to receive outpatient treatment will also require supervision to ensure that he or she follows through with this plan. Often this is done through probation where the offender reports regularly to a probation officer, although Cumming and Buell (1997) argue that traditional forms of supervision do not work with sexual offenders. These authors feel that it is important to use this resource in conjunction with the treatment agency's supervision and training the offender to self-monitor. And if the treatment is court mandated, the treating agency will be expected to report to the court periodically.

Once it is determined how the offender will get to therapy, the question becomes, "What types of therapies work?"

What Works

Prendergast (2004), who has worked with sexual offenders for over 40 years, explains that he has learned some valuable lessons about treating this population. First, he and other experts agree that passive, nondirective techniques do not work with sexual offenders. They require instead a combination of confrontation and supportive techniques. Further, this clinician suggests that treating homogeneous groups does not work. The passive child molester, says Prendergast, needs the confrontation often provided by a rapist to dislodge him from the comfort of his denial. Child molesters, incestuous fathers, rapists, and flashers are treated in the same group in this clinician's facility.

More recent techniques (Laws & Ward, 2011; Yates, Prescott, & Ward, 2010) de-emphasize overt confrontation in favor of reliance on the therapeutic relationship and encouragement that the offender be more fully involved with and motivated toward treatment (see the section "Good Lives Model").

Individual therapy alone does not work (see also Flora et al., 2008). Most experts today favor a combination of different modalities and techniques (to be discussed). Most would consider groups as the treatment of choice for sexual offenders, with other modalities used as support of these groups. Likewise, traditional psychotherapy does not work. Because sexual offending is such a pervasive problem, most theorists favor a holistic approach (Flora et al., 2008; Prendergast, 2004).

Not every sexual offender targeting children is a good candidate for treatment. For example, sexual sadists are not (Flora et al., 2008). The sexual offender for whom treatment is recommended has the potential for taking responsibility for his offense (although most will deny initially) and must be willing to examine his or her own attitudes, prejudices, and beliefs being open to change. Without expertise and experience in working with this population, it is often difficult to determine if the offender will benefit from treatment.

Group Versus Individual Therapy

Research has demonstrated that the treatment of choice for sexual offenders is group therapy. This is another reason why offenders should be included in programs where there are other offenders so that there is an opportunity for groups. Although individual treatment may be employed as a support of group treatment, it should not be the only type of therapy for several reasons. First, offenders can be exceptionally manipulative, and no matter how skilled a clinician, he or she has the potential for being taken in by this manipulation. On the other hand, in a group with other offenders who also manipulate, the offender is often called on his behavior by other group members. Second, offenders often want to sugarcoat their behaviors so as to please the therapist. Or they may want to shock and alter their version of what happened for maximum shock value. Again, other group members are more likely to recognize these ploys and confront these offenders (Flora et al., 2008; Prendergast, 2004).

Offenders also gain support as well as confrontation from being in a group with other offenders who have committed like crimes. The impact of this type of support may outweigh the support given by an individual therapist.

☙

"My therapists were great," explained Tony, "but being with a bunch of guys who had had similar childhood experiences to mine and who knew where I was coming from really helped me. When I tried to excuse what I had done to my daughter, they wouldn't let me get away with it. At the same time, I knew that these guys cared." ☙

The feedback that offenders get about their behavior and attitudes is also multiplied in groups. As they try to understand the deviant attitudes and behaviors of others, they may gain insight into their own. The group becomes a useful tool for confronting and understanding the nature of sexual offenses.

In addition, it is also possible for offenders to hear how others have changed and to measure their own progress against where other group members might be. Yet each member can work at his or her own capacity. And finally, because social skills are a challenge for many offenders, a group provides a safe place to develop these skills and explore social connection and intimacy (Flora et al., 2008; O'Connell et al., 1990; Prendergast, 2004; Yates et al., 2010).

Defense Mechanisms and Difficult Clients

Sexual offenders come into therapy using a variety of similar defense mechanisms. Defense mechanisms are the psyche's way of limiting the danger or damage to the mind of certain ideas or a way to minimize stress. There are three classic defense mechanisms used by sex offenders: denial (refusing to acknowledge that the abuse happened, that the act was abusive, or that he or she had any part in the abuse), projection (being convinced that the unacceptable feelings, thoughts, or desires he or she is having are actually how others are feeling), and rationalization (giving a socially acceptable explanation for an act or behavior that is negative) (Flora et al., 2008).

ᘒ _____

Alfred had sexually abused his 10-year-old daughter, Hannah, and was mandated to receive outpatient sex offender treatment. He had never admitted the abuse (denial) saying that Hannah must have dreamed what happened in her bed at night. He insisted that he was such a heavy sleeper that he was never awake at night anyway. At his wife's insistence that she had found him in their daughter's bedroom, Alfred decided that he must have been sleepwalking, and maybe Hannah was trying to wake him and get him back to bed (rationalization). At another session, he suggested that Hannah sometimes had nightmares, and he would have to go to her room to comfort her. He also insisted that he and his daughter had to "stick together" as his wife, Margot, was always out at Bingo or with friends. Obviously her needs were more important to her than his and Hannah's if she rejected them that way (projection).

_____ **ᘖ**

Although the defense mechanisms explained here are the most commonly seen, offenders use other defense mechanisms as well, including but not limited to (adapted from Flora et al., 2008, pp. 157–159)

- intellectualization (avoiding stress or emotional distress by separating emotions from thoughts; facts are used to explain things while feelings are repressed),
- anger (an emotional state, which is directed toward the self or others as a defense),
- acting out (using actions, usually negative, to resist dealing with emotions),
- passive aggression (avoiding face-to-face conflict by expressing aggression in other more subtle ways; disguising the resistance or hostility felt by seeming compliant on the surface but often acting covertly in resentment),
- repression (dismissing unpleasant or upsetting thoughts from the consciousness),
- depersonalization (detaching the self emotionally from others),
- devaluation (exaggerating negative attributes of self or others as a way of rationalizing or understanding the emotional conflict felt),
- idealization (dealing with stress by convincing the self that others are better than he or she is), and
- minimization (reducing the significance of what he or she has done or another has done to him or her).

It will be important for the therapist to have an understanding of these mechanisms through which offenders try to reduce stress and have developed ways to help them to overcome their defenses to benefit from therapy.

Some offenders will be more difficult to treat than others. And therapists have different tolerances for the difficulties that offenders present. Many sexual offenders who target children approach treatment with a *passivity* that can be challenging to the therapist. Often these clients just show up saying little and seemingly contributing nothing. In reality, their control of the group is in their silence. If treated in a mixed group of sex offenders, the rest of the group—not knowing what they are thinking—can imagine all types of insight that they are not sharing or even censure. Such feelings can be disruptive to the group, often inhibiting others' willingness to share. As a result, members will often confront the silent, passive member or can be helped to do so by a skilled group facilitator. A clear statement of expectations at the onset of the group also helps members to deal with this behavior (Flora et al., 2008).

Many clients come to treatment angry. They often express their *anger* related to having been accused of the abuse, being incarcerated, or having to attend the group at all. They may try to get into power struggles with therapists or other group members, thus deflecting their own treatment issues and sometimes getting the group off track. Setting clear contracts about what is acceptable and what is not, maintaining boundaries, avoiding power struggles, and keeping the focus on the offender's offense can help deal with this type of client (Flora et al., 2008; Prendergast, 2004).

Some offenders will be *overly compliant*, ready to admit their offense early and going overboard at professing remorse. They may be quite emotional, often monopolizing the group and playing on sympathies about how willing they are to change. These are the clients who can delude therapists into feeling successful, when in reality, this is a means that these offenders use to keep their therapy superficial and not face the issues that will be the most difficult for them. By limiting the amount of time they are given to speak, by limiting the feedback that these clients are given (they hope for positive reinforcement on how well they are doing), and by seeking to supplement therapy by such techniques as journaling, these clients may be helped to give up their defenses and use therapy effectively (Flora et al., 2008; Seto, 2008).

Sex offenders present with a variety of other problems and diagnosis that may be problematic. These, like substance abuse, PTSD, and other mental health issues, may have to be addressed by other types of therapy as well.

Treatment Methods and Outcomes

A variety of treatment modalities have been tried with sexual offenders over the last few decades. Individual and group therapy, psychotropic medications, rational emotive therapy, behavior modification, cognitive-behavioral techniques, self-help groups, and chemical or physical castration have all been implemented in various centers (Prendergast, 2004).

Cognitive-Behavioral Therapy

The "Current Practices and Emerging Trends in Sexual Abuser Management: The Safer Society 2009 North American Survey" reported that 65% of the community programs taking part in the survey used cognitive-behavioral techniques as their primary treatment method, and 92% used this modality as one of their top three theories as part of their therapeutic process. Of residential programs, almost 66% used cognitive-behavioral techniques as their primary method of treatment, and 95% as one of their top three methods (McGrath et al., 2010, pp. 41–42).

CBT (mentioned also in Chapter 13) blends two approaches. Cognitive therapy is based on the assumptions that how people think determines how they will act. To change one's behavior, it is necessary to change one's thinking patterns. Behavior therapy is based on the premise that behavior is learned and that it can be changed by a variety of conditioning methods. CBT is based on the belief that thinking (cognition), actions (behavior), and feelings (emotion) all act together. Because people's thoughts determine how they feel, the thoughts also influence how they behave. Thoughts can be changed, but often not without some work. Offenders have often grown up with distorted thoughts, which influence their offenses (Fitzgerald & Cohen, 2012; Flora et al., 2008; Laws & Ward, 2011; McGrath et al., 2010).

CBT uses various techniques to change these *thinking errors. Self-talk* refers to what people say to themselves in order to make sense of their world. Offenders have often learned negative self-talk ("I'm no good," "I don't have a choice,"

I should have," and so on). These can sometimes lead to offending to prove to themselves that they are, in fact, no good. Substituting positive self-talk helps offenders to think through what they are going to do before they act. For example, "I must or should" can be replaced by "I have a choice." *Thought stopping* refers to the ability to stop negative thoughts. Often the offender uses some word that is said out loud to remind him or her not to think a specific thought. For example, Jack used the words *Cancel! Cancel!* when he began to think that he was not as good as everyone else. *Thought switching* asks the offender to switch to a more appropriate thought when a negative one comes to mind (Flora et al., 2008; Laws & Ward, 2011). Clinicians using CBT will often use *journaling*, or have the offenders keep a journal of their thoughts and feelings to help them recognize what thoughts must be stopped or changed in order not to reoffend (Fitzgerald & Cohen, 2012).

Although this type of therapy has been particularly successful with sexual offenders, other clinicians and researchers have fine-tuned treatment, developing variations and newly designed therapies.

Relapse Prevention

One widely used treatment strategy based upon CBT is the relapse prevention model (RPM), which, until recently, was one of the most popular and widely used models with sexual offenders. Using some of the principles of CBT, this model is actually educational in nature, focusing on helping the offender to recognize his or her own pattern of abusing and learning to monitor and interrupt it himself or herself. With roots in the treatment of substance abuse, the original RPM was developed by Alan Marlatt and his colleagues, who also suggested (see Marlatt, 1985) that such treatment designed to deter relapse could also be used with sexual offenders. After some revision, Richard Laws later tailored this technique to the sex offender population and published it in his volume *Relapse Prevention*

With Sex Offenders (1989) with the warning of sorts that this technique might not be the perfect treatment for sex offenders. Despite this remark, many clinicians began to use this model as the best method to treat sex offenders (Laws, Hudson, & Ward, 2000). Certainly with a motivated offender, the idea of self-regulation can be an asset.

Relapse prevention strives to train offenders to recognize their own offense cycle, recognize the choices that they have made along that cycle, and develop strategies to intervene.

☙ —————————————————

Victor had sexually molested a 13-year-old girl in the neighborhood. He had an alcohol problem, and although he had been going to Alcoholics Anonymous (AA), he had lapsed just before his offense. After molesting the child, he was given probation with mandatory treatment, and he was expected to return to AA. Although he had kept his job as the foreman at a factory, he also had a new boss who was putting a great deal of stress on Victor about "his performance" as a supervisor. Victor's ex-wife had told him that he could no longer visit their daughter, and because the separation was not a legal one, Victor felt that he had no recourse. He had recently started living with a woman, May, but was finding her to be overly demanding, needy, and critical when he did not meet her needs.

Although Victor had fantasies in the past, both about his daughter and other young girls, this was his first offense. He had a small pornography collection, mostly downloaded pictures of young girls from the Internet. These he destroyed right after he entered treatment.

When his work was particularly stressful and May unusually demanding, he started taking his new dog for long walks. He said that this eased his stress and that he also felt better physically. ☙

—————————————————————————

Victor had made some seemingly unimportant decisions. He had opted not to discuss his stress at work with his group and nor did he consider approaching his new boss about how to improve his performance. He had chosen not to talk with his wife about supervised visits with their daughter. His decision to allow May, whom he had already realized was demanding and critical, to move in was also problematic. And his group pointed out to him that getting a dog that he knew would have to be walked regularly gave him an opportunity to return to his old behavior of watching young girls in playgrounds and parks, putting himself in high-risk situations to reoffend.

Victor's first recognition that he may lapse was when he went to an old web site on the computer where he had previously found pictures of nude young girls. Through his treatment, Victor was able to recognize his own individual cycle and how he was setting himself up to reoffend. He learned that the thinking errors that he developed in childhood—especially that he had no control over his life, he was "no good," and no one cared about him—were being perpetuated by the choices that he was making. He then developed a personal safety plan that outlined different ways of thinking about his life and alternate methods for responding to the situations in his life. For example, his belief that he was "no good" prevented him from approaching his boss, talking with his wife about their daughter, and confronting May about their problems. Once he began to value himself, he recognized that he had choices in the way that he dealt with others. He learned to recognize when his feelings of lacking control would lead him toward risky behavior and was taught some self-talk that helped to channel his needs into acceptable behaviors. Needless to say, an offender using this model needs a great deal of training, support, and motivation.

Relapse prevention works best when there are both internal (thoughts, feelings, ideas, attitudes, and behaviors that will be addressed in therapy) and external motivators (supervision within the community to ensure that the plan is followed). According to the "Current Practices and Emerging Trends in Sexual Abuser Management:

The Safer Society 2009 North American Survey," only 14.8% of community programs were using relapse prevention as their primary method in the treatment of offenders in 2008, but about 67% used it as one of their top three modalities. In residential facilities, only 13% used it as their primary method but 67% as one of the top three used (McGrath et al., 2010, pp. 41–42).

Currently, several other models have been designed that have gained popularity in the field of offender treatment: the RNR and the GLM.

Risk-Needs-Responsivity Model

The RNR model (introduced in Chapter 3) is now widely used in correctional settings. Initially, the risk of the offender to recidivate is assessed, concentrating on factors that are known to put offenders at risk for reoffending.

ः

Joel had always been impulsive and a risk taker. He grew up in an alcoholic home where both parents drank. His mother died when he was 10. His father sexually abused all of his four sisters. Joel remembers being sexually aroused as he listened to his father with one of his sisters through the thin walls of their apartment. Joel was known to the police early in his life, first for vandalism and later for stealing cars. He did some time in juvenile detention, but the fact that his father was a correctional officer who knew many of the police officers saved Joel from more stringent punishments.

"He's just a kid," his father would argue, and somehow Joel would get off. As a youth, Joel was also part of a crowd that supported his criminal behavior and made him feel like a big man because his father always got him off.

Joel began using alcohol when he was 13. Later, he would say that it was because he hated school and did not feel that he could succeed anyway. He was expelled from school after coming in several times drunk, but his father's intervention always got him back into school. At 17, he impregnated a 13-year-old local girl, and they lived with her parents until the baby was born. Tired of the child's screaming, Joel stole a car, robbed a gas station, and left town. Drifting for a bit, he finally met and moved in with a woman who had a young daughter. While the mom worked at a local restaurant, Joel cared for the child and began to sexually abuse her. When he again robbed a store with the child in the car and fled over the state line, he was apprehended and arrested for robbery, sexual abuse, and kidnapping.

━━━━━━━━━━━━━━━━━━━━━━━ ∞

Joel would be placed in a high-risk category to reoffend due to his deviant sexual interests, intimacy problems, antisocial personality pattern, procriminal attitudes and behaviors, substance abuse, emotional identification with a sexual offender (his father), poor school performance in the past, and problems with general self-regulation. In the correctional facility in which he was incarcerated, he was felt to be someone who would benefit from the RNR model of treatment. Initially, building a therapeutic relationship with Joel was difficult. Once Joel could be engaged, it was then necessary to look at the risk factors that could be modified in some way to prevent his repeat offending (criminogenic needs). The responsivity principle dictates that interventions should be delivered in a manner that takes into consideration the offender's learning style, abilities, and personality, considering how his strengths can be enhanced. For Joel, short-term goals in which he could see a definite payoff worked best. It was also discovered that he suffered from mild fetal alcohol syndrome that made learning difficult and required a concrete approach. In addition, Joel, who not only resented authority figures but also assumed that they would look the other way when he needed them to do so, had to be helped to desire change rather than expecting that he would conform because he had been ordered by the court into treatment.

Obviously one of the important components of the use of the RNR model is a thorough and competent assessment of the offender at the onset. Inappropriate treatment of an offender leads to wasted resources in what may otherwise be an effective deterrent to reoffending (Andrews & Bonta, 2010; Andrews, Bonta, & Hoge, 1990; Andrews & Dowden, 2007). Although the RNR model has been found to be especially effective in correctional settings where staff are well trained in its use, the challenge comes with using this model in the real world—settings that cannot be as easily controlled (Andrews & Bonta, 2010).

Good Lives Model

The GLM is a strength-based model that is based on the premise that offenders have similar needs and aspirations as any other nonoffending individual. The goal of this model of treatment is twofold: to reduce risk and to promote the attainment of goals (referred to in the model as *goods*) aspired to by most humans with the assumption that when an individual is able to achieve these goals and find personal fulfillment, he or she will be at less risk to reoffend. Further, proponents of the GLM postulate that people commit criminal offenses because they lack the ability to attain the fulfillment that they desire. Those factors that put offenders at risk for reoffending are the obstacles that prevent them from realizing good lives (Ward et al., 2006; Yates et al., 2010).

The primary human goals or goods for which people strive include the basic needs of living, knowledge, mastery in play and work, autonomy and independence, inner peace, friendship, a sense of belonging to a community, spirituality or meaning, happiness, and innovation or creativity. To concretize what can be abstract constructs, the GLM suggests instrumental goals and secondary goals. For example, the secondary goal of attaining knowledge might be met by the instrumental goals of accessing ways to attain that knowledge like attending classes (Yates et al., 2010).

The GLM works through helping offenders to identify their primary goods and recognize how their ways of attaining these goods have been flawed. They are then helped to examine their life plans and design and implement more functional life plans that will enable them to meet their goals. This will necessitate the development of new skills, attitudes, values, and resources that will be required to lead lives that are more satisfying and that lower their risk of reoffending (Ward et al., 2006; Yates et al., 2010).

Use of this model requires a strong therapeutic alliance between therapist and client that fosters the offender's motivation to succeed. It also necessitates a thorough assessment by clinicians trained in this model (Yates et al., 2010).

It may be too early to determine the long-term efficacy of some of the newer models of sex offender treatment, but treatment of this population has nonetheless come a long way over the last several decades.

Treatment Issues for Offenders

No matter what treatment model is used, most offenders have similar treatment issues. A majority of offenders have *difficulties with social skills*. This may have been one of the many reasons they have been unable to develop relationships that are satisfying with other adults. Many battle with *issues of anger* and have little idea of how to handle their anger appropriately.

Trust is a major stumbling block for offenders who may have felt betrayed throughout their lives. As a result, developing a therapeutic relationship with them may require some skills (Fitzgerald & Cohen, 2012; Flora et al., 2008; Laws & Ward, 2011; McGrath et al., 2010; Stinson and Becker, 2012).

For offenders who have been sexually abused, *their own sexual abuse history* may need to be processed in order to help them to resolve the issues associated with it and not reenact it with other children. Even offenders who have not been sexually abused may have had dysfunctional childhoods. Physical abuse, neglect, substance abuse, abandonment, and other types of trauma are often seen in the lives of sexual offenders,

and the residual issues need to be addressed in order for them to understand their own feelings and behaviors.

At some point in treatment, sexual offenders must *acknowledge that they have harmed others* and *take responsibility for their actions*. For some, these tasks are difficult but are essential to their healing. Some programs do this task in the form of a cost analysis that requires that the offender determine how much his offending has cost in monetary terms. Has he lost his home, his family, a job, been sent to prison, and so on? This technique brings what he has done into a very tangible framework that can be easily understood and measured (Flora et al., 2008; Stinson and Becker, 2012).

Detailing is the time when the *offender reviews the details of his crime and his sexual history*. Offenders tend to minimize, distort, lie, and rationalize, but through confrontation, they are encouraged to develop honesty to the best of their ability. The offender must also create an inventory of his relationships, affairs, and partners. Strengthening and hope are also necessary for the offender to believe that he can change. The therapist maintains a realistic but hopeful posture, giving him support when this is needed to grow (Flora et al., 2008).

An important task for sexual offenders is to *develop empathy*. Significant people have been hurt—not only the victims and the victims' family but the offenders' own family and friends as well. The offender's thinking errors often mean that he cannot recognize the degree of harm that he has caused. One therapeutic goal will be to help with that recognition. Once he reviewed the harm he has inflicted, person by person, the offender is asked to offer an *apology*, opening the door for possible *atonement*. This may be accomplished by having the offender write a letter, first to himself for what he had done and then to others whom he has hurt. These letters are usually not mailed but still serve to frame the apology in the offender's own mind (Flora et al., 2008).

There are numerous *educational components* that must also be addressed in therapy. For example, ironically many sexual offenders know little of healthy sexuality, which often prevents them from forging healthy sexual relationships with age-mates. Therefore, education in healthy sexuality is frequently included as part of sex offender treatment programs. Other education may be in social skills, vocational training, and other skills that enable the offender to gain needed resources for leading a healthier and nonoffending lifestyle.

Effective treatment must also include *preparation for termination*, which will take time. The offender has probably found some security with the therapist and his groups. Being "out on his own" is frightening. Will he be able to implement the safety plan that he has developed, or will he relapse? In being encouraged to face termination, the offender has an opportunity to review his progress and discuss his hopes and fears for the future. What supports will he have in the community? Some offenders will act out at this point in an effort to avoid termination. This must be worked through before the client is allowed to leave treatment (Flora et al., 2008; Prendergast, 2004; Stinson & Becker, 2012).

When *termination* actually happens, the offender will hopefully have some type of support group or aftercare arrangement. Unfortunately, such resources are not plentiful, and it may be up to the offender to reach out to the treating agency if he has difficulties on the outside. Prendergast (2004) comments about his own work:

> I make it a practice never to use the terms *finished*, *terminated*, and especially *cured*. My preference, when a patient is ready, is to promote him to PRN status, explaining that this status means that it is okay and desirable for the individual to maintain contact by telephone on a regular basis . . . and to stop for a visit at least annually. (p. 241)

Not all therapists would agree with such a policy, but it is crucial that the client have some type of support to fall back on.

Female Offenders in Treatment

Although I have used *he* in the previous section, female offenders may also go through similar treatment although their issues may be somewhat different. Some theorists have suggested that using the same treatment models for men and women is not appropriate due to the variation in their needs (Ford, 2006; Hayes & Carpenter, 2013; Nathan & Ward, 2002; Saradjian, 1996). Flora et al. (2008) frame some of the differences that inform variations in treatment. First, female sex offenders are more likely to have been sexually abused or have experienced significant trauma. Thus, an important part of their therapy will be addressing past trauma. Women abusers are more likely to have had a relationship with the victim and see that relationship as significant. Many male offenders see their victim as a sexual object rather than a person. Gannon, Rose, and Williams (2009) suggest that female offenders do not have sexual interest in children as many male offenders do, although this is disputed by another study (Beech et al., 2009). It will be therefore necessary, in the course of her treatment, to determine what the victim meant to the female offender and address this. Female offenders are more likely to use greater forms of control and manipulation with their victims. They are often more skilled in manipulation in general, and the therapist will need to be aware of this. They also express anger differently, internalizing rather than externalizing, necessitating variations in how they will be helped to deal with the expression of that anger.

The defense mechanisms most commonly used by female offenders differ from the primary defenses of males. Women's defense tends to be (adapted from Flora et al., 2008, pp. 159–159)

- devaluation of self—when the individual overexaggerates the negative attributes of herself as a way of understanding the conflicts she feels;
- disassociation—separating feelings from actions in the central consciousness;

- isolation—removing herself from others either physically or emotionally;
- repression—dismissing stress, negative thoughts, or conflicts from the consciousness;
- displacement—when faced with disappointment or failure by a person or thing, the individual finds another person or thing of a similar nature to replace it; and
- undoing—responding to stress or emotional conflict by making a symbolic gesture through words or behaviors to offset the unacceptable behaviors, feelings, or actions.

In addition, some authors believe that female offenders experience emotional difficulty with sex surrounded by a good deal of anxiety, avoidance, or overuse (Hislop, 2001). Thus, an important part of therapeutic intervention will be to help these women to understand their sexual issues and develop healthier attitudes toward sex. The good news is that the literature indicates that female offenders have a lower recidivism rate than male sexual offenders (Flora et al., 2008; Hayes & Carpenter, 2013).

Group therapy is also the preferred treatment model for female offenders, which may be problematic given that there are fewer female abusers in treatment and therefore fewer to form groups. Females should never be placed in a group of male sexual offenders as this would place them at risk (Flora et al., 2008; Ford, 2006).

Although the issues and the manner in which they are addressed differ between male and female offenders, the mechanics of treatment may be similar. The therapist must work with the female offender on the following (Flora et al., 2008; Ford, 2006; Saradjian, 1996):

- Her own victimization
- Taking responsibility for perpetrating child sexual abuse
- Developing an understanding of her own abuse cycle—including her beliefs, her triggers, how she targets children—recognizing the role her fantasies play in the abuse, and understanding her emotions about the abuse

- Understanding her views of and trauma around sex and developing a healthier outlook about her own body and her own sexuality
- Processing relationships and how she can forge healthy ones in the future
- Developing healthy self-esteem
- Developing a relapse prevention plan

One of the advantages of the newer models gaining popularity (e.g., the RNR model and the GLM) is that they can accommodate the variations in treatment issues that female offenders present. The fact remains that the treatment of female offenders can be challenging, especially because there is a limited body of knowledge to inform such treatment.

Special Populations of Offenders

Treating Offenders and Cultural Differences

Working with sexual offenders from different cultures necessitates that the therapist bring to the treatment relationship not only knowledge of sexual offending but also a sensitivity to cultural issues. In Chapter 5, we discussed some of the cultural attitudes that influence sexual abuse. In addition, therapists must be mindful of variations in the areas of self-concept, economic influences, spirituality and religion, and other culturally specific issues. Language barriers may also have an influence. For offenders who do not speak English well, it may be necessary to engage an interpreter. However, an interpreter is one more filter between the therapist and the client as distortions are possible in the way that ideas are translated. Further, many minorities have a cultural mistrust of therapists, especially those from a different culture. Ford and Prunier (2005) point out that with sex offenders of both African American and Latino descent, personal information, especially of a sexual nature, is not discussed outside the family, and it will be even more difficult for this client to share his or her history and sexual issues than many other clients. Guilt and shame take on an even more significant role when the client has felt stigmatized his or her whole life. The offender may have difficulty building a therapeutic alliance with the white therapist. And the therapist must be aware of his or her own attitudes and prejudices.

Thus, it is vital that agencies working with sexual offenders prepare for the treatment issues that arise when the offender is from a minority culture.

Offenders With Special Needs

The literature over the last decade had devoted comparatively little attention to offenders with disabilities (Craig, 2010). Part of the problem in assessment and treatment has been the difficulty in dealing with those involved with criminal law and corrections, a relationship that is still unsettled (Ashford, Sales, & Reid, 2001). There has been some hesitation on the part of the legal agencies to treat any type of sexual offender different from any other. And yet, addressing different needs may determine the rate of recidivism with any given offender. It has also been difficult to define special needs for the purpose of different modes of treatment. Today, special handling by the justice system comes down to attention to three specific purposes: to provide for the care and safety of prisoners, to ensure that offenders are treated fairly, and to protect society from the offenders (Ashford et al., 2001, p. 42). In working with the criminal justice system, Ashford et al. (2001) define special needs as "any changeable factors associated with disorders of cognition, thought, mood, personality, development or behavior that are linked to desired outcomes for offenders at any phase of the justice process" (p. 42). This definition strives to develop a treatment plan at the very onset that will meet the individual's specific needs, and there is a better chance that he or she will be matched with treatment facilities that can meet these needs.

Offenders with cognitive disabilities have additional treatment needs. For example, Day and Berney (2001) suggest that the offender with mental retardation tends to be young and have experienced significant psychosocial deprivation. He or she has probably exhibited a number of behavioral problems in childhood and adolescence and may have spent time in residential care. There has been little in the offender's life to enhance his or her self-esteem and provide for healthy recreational or occupational use of his or her time. The offender has greater dependency needs and requires more supervision and structure. The difficulty he or she may have had in negotiating peer relationships may have made him or her angry and resentful. The offender may require intervention that recognizes his or her cognitive level and addresses his or her specific deficits.

Recent research has determined that—given treatment programs that meet their needs—offenders with special needs demonstrate lower levels of recidivism than other offenders (Craig, 2010). The problem is that there are not enough community-based treatment programs that can tailor treatment in this way, and in prison settings, there may not be the resources to do so (Craig & Hutchinson, 2005). Advocates for this population continue to seek ways to meet the needs of these offenders. Again, there are advantages to the RNR model as well as the GLM for this population because taking into consideration the individual needs of the offender is a crucial component of these approaches.

AFTER TREATMENT _____

Offender Reentry

Offenders who are treated within a prison setting may make progress, but some believe that this progress cannot be evaluated until the offender returns to live outside the prison walls. In the past, the release of individuals from prisons has presented challenges to both prisons and communities. Fortunately, prisoner reentry has become the subject of a number of studies in an effort to find ways to improve the transition. Of the 150,000 individuals incarcerated for sexual offenses, approximately 60% of them were for sexual offending against underage people (Harrison & Beck, 2006). The increase in incarceration for sexual offenses and the fact that sentences are often for only 3 to 5 years necessitates that measures be taken to plan for sex offender reentry.

The Center for Sex Offender Management of the U.S. Department of Justice proposes that plans for reentry should begin at the onset of incarceration with all who work with the offender being trained to share ownership in the successful outcome of the offender reentering the community. Yates et al. (2010) contend that posttreatment maintenance and supervision are essential parts of the treatment of sexual offenders. Collaborations must be set up between corrections, law enforcements, and community agencies involved in mental health, social services, victim advocacy, educational and vocational services, and housing (Center for Sex Offender Management, 2007; Palmioto & MacNichol, 2010). Throughout the prison experience, prisoners should be managed with an eye toward their eventual release by the creation of programs that work toward the reduction of recidivism. This may involve fostering a rehabilitative philosophy that parallels the expectations of offenders in the community. Some experts suggest that at intake, reception, and classification, prisons should be looking at what the barriers for reentry might be for the offender and tailor his or her case management to address them. This will require a retraining of staff in many cases to adjust to a new philosophy (Center for Sex Offender Management, 2007).

In order to better facilitate reentry, several other issues should be addressed. The timing of sex offender treatment should be considered with the assumption that the closer to release that the offender participate in this type of training, the better, as this will help him or her more effectively transfer these skills to living outside. There should also be a recognition that sex offenders are not just sex offenders but often have a range of needs. Other psychosocial needs may need addressing as well as tools that will prevent them from committing other crimes (e.g., education, vocational training) because statistics indicate that when sex offenders return to prison, it is usually for nonsexual crimes (Center for Sex Offender Management, 2007). And special needs must be considered (Rutherford, Griller-Clark, & Anderson, 2001). Programs that begin to address these needs while the offender is incarcerated (e.g., RNR and GLM) provide a better basis for community reentry (Yates et al., 2010).

During the transition process, professionals in both the correctional and community settings must work closely to foster connections with community agencies and resources. Family reunification also requires special attention (see Chapter 13). Housing and employment must be brokered so that the offender can transition into a useful life (Center for Sex Offender Management, 2007). Supervision of offenders within the community must be matched with their risk for reoffending, which includes an assessment of their involvement in the process. Ongoing therapeutic services are essential with strong working alliances between therapists and offenders (Yates et al., 2010; Palmioto & MacNichol, 2010).

Each year, large numbers of sexual offenders will be released from incarceration, and their transition to community life may be fraught with challenges. Successful sex offender management and community well-being require working together to facilitate a smooth transition for the offender.

Sex Offender Registration

There has been a good deal of controversy over who needs to know when a sex offender is released from prison and takes up residence in a community. The federally mandated requirement that offenders register with authorities when they are released from an institutional setting (Jacob Wetterling Act) and the community notification when an offender moves into a community (amendment to the Wetterling Act referred to as Megan's Law) have been implemented to varying degrees from state to state. In the early days of these required notification programs, a Washington study compared 96 offenders released before the notification went into effect and 90 who were required to register. They discovered that although registration allowed offenders to be apprehended more quickly by law enforcement, having to register did not significantly change the recidivism rate for these offenders. And most of the offenses took place in the jurisdiction where they were registered, which means that sex offenders do not go elsewhere if they choose to reoffend (Schram & Milloy, 1995).

Critics of offender registration argue that there is little impact of registration on recidivism, and yet the impact on the offender's life is great. As a result of community notification, offenders who are trying to rebuild their lives may be subjected to harassment, loss of employment, loss of residence, or property damage. And fearful citizens have been known to threaten offenders with bodily harm (Beck & Travis, 2004; Levenson & Cotter, 2005; Seto, 2008).

Recidivism of Sex Offenders

Although there has been much written in the last few years about the recidivism of sexual offenders, there is a lack of consistency in how the word is used and the measures used in these studies. Some studies have measured recidivism by when the offender is again arrested. However, the literature shows that sex offenders are often arrested again for nonsexual offenses. This then cannot be considered to be recidivism for sexual abusing. Other studies look at recidivism when the offender has been reconvicted, whether a sexual crime or not—and yet conviction does not always follow arrest if sufficient evidence cannot be gleaned. And finally, some studies say that offenders have relapse when

they have committed any new sexual offense whether or not it comes to the attention of law enforcement. This again may be difficult to measure (Center for Sex Offender Management, 2001; Durkin & Digianantonio, 2007). Further, some studies group all sexual offenders together and do not always differentiate between sexual offenses against adults and against children. And all studies do not differentiate between those offenders who have undergone sex offender–specific treatment and those who have not.

Keeping the earlier discussion in mind, it is useful to look at some of the research. Langevin, Curnoe, Fedoroff, Bennett, and Peever (2004) conducted a 25-year follow-up study, specifically of child molesters, looking at those who offended outside the family as well as incestuous offenders. These researchers found that the recidivism rate for those abusing victims outside the family was 70%, whereas for incestuous abusers, the rate was 50%. On the other hand, a more recent study (Patrick & Marsh, 2009) estimated that, of the 447 offenders studied (in the state of Idaho), there was only a 13.6% recidivism rate over a 13-year period for all types of offenses and a 9.2% rate for sexual offenses. In this study, the majority of the offenders were male (98%), whereas their victims were more likely to be female (86%) (p. 127). These authors also reported that only 14.3% of these offenders received sex offender–specific treatment, whereas 36.1% had other types of treatment or training (p. 128). Ethnicity did not seem to be statistically significant.

The results of other studies tend to fall between these two sets of statistics (Bartol & Bartol, 2008; Craig, 2010; Craig, Browne, Stringer, & Beech, 2005; Hanson, 2002; Hanson, Steffy, & Gauthier, 1993), pointing to the difficulty of isolating accurate recidivism rates.

There is some consensus on the factors associated with recidivism. The first of these is *static (or historical) factors*, so named because they cannot be changed. An example of a static factor would be the victim-offender relationship. Research and clinician reports indicate that there is a higher recidivism rate among offenders who target victims outside the home, while rates of recidivism for incestuous abusers are lower (Bartol & Bartol, 2008; Center for Sex Offender Management, 2001; Craig et al., 2005; Durkin & Digianantonio, 2007; Hanson, 2002; Hanson et al., 1993). In addition, offenders who victimize females tend to have lower rates of recidivism, whereas those who victimize boys have higher rates (Bartol & Bartol, 2008; Hanson & Bussiere, 1998; Hanson et al., 1993). Other factors associated with higher recidivism are never having been married, having a previous offense, targeting younger children, and using force during the offense (Bartol & Bartol, 2008; Center for Sex Offender Management, 2001; Craig et al., 2005; Durkin & Digianantonio, 2007; Hanson, 2002; Hanson et al., 1993; Levenson & Morin, 2006).

A second set of factors is referred to as *dynamic factors* or those that clinicians believe can be changed. Offenders who demonstrate deviant sexual arousal and other pathology, continue to use cognitive distortions, have a low IQ, or continue to use pornography have a higher rate of recidivism (Bartol & Bartol, 2008; Craig et al., 2005; Durkin & Digianantonio, 2007; Hanson, 2002; Kingston, Federoff, Firestone, Curry, & Bradford, 2008; Patrick & Marsh, 2009). Sex offender–specific treatment lowers the rate of recidivism (Durkin & Digianantonio, 2007; Levenson & Morin, 2006).

Experts agree that much more research must be done on recidivism among sexual offenders using consistent measures to pinpoint what constitutes relapse. The research to date favoring treatment as a deterrent to reoffending supports the need for increased services in this area.

Summary

Treatment of sexual offenders must be based on a thorough assessment of their treatment needs. Assessment may begin with the district attorney's office determining the dangerousness of the offender and the particulars of his or her crime. Risk assessment is divided into several categories: functional analysis of risk that looks at the offending behaviors and how they occurred, the actuarial assessment that gives an idea of the offender's level of risk, and the dynamic risk assessment that looks at other factors affecting future treatment.

A variety of tools are used to assess offenders. Clinical interviews look at the offender's own story along with his or her rationalizations and thinking distortions. A variety of tests and questionnaires have also been developed that will aid in assessment. Laboratory tests such as the penile plethysmograph and polygraph can evaluate the offender's sexual arousal and truthfulness.

The treatment of offenders is a specialized field that requires special training and an interest in this population. Those involved in such treatment must have a good support system and attend to their own self-care as such work can be emotionally draining.

Offenders may be treated either on an outpatient basis or while incarcerated. Group therapy is favored over individual therapy as their peer group is often in the best position to hold offenders accountable. Offenders use a number of defense mechanisms to minimize their stress, especially denial, rationalization, and projection.

A variety of treatment methods are used with offenders. Cognitive-behavioral techniques have been found to be especially successful. Relapse prevention helps them to identify their cycle of abuse and interrupt that cycle in order not to reoffend. Newer models like the RNR model and the GLM require thorough assessment and a strong therapeutic relationship. These treatment methods then strive to build on each offender's individual needs and characteristics to reduce the risk of reoffending. Female offenders have slightly different treatment needs from their male counterparts, given the fact that their degree of pathology is often greater. In addition, treatment must be adapted to accommodate the special needs and cultural difference of some sexual offenders.

Offenders who have been incarcerated may have a difficult time with reentry into society. Adequate supervision after treatment is important to prevent recidivism, but unfortunately, such supervision is not always available.

Review Questions

1. Who intervenes with sexual offenders?

2. How are offenders assessed?

3. What are some of the tools used for assessment?

4. What are the most popular forms of laboratory testing?

5. Who treats sexual offenders, and where?

6. What are some cautions for those interested in treating offenders?

7. What works better: incarceration or outpatient therapy?

8. What are the advantages of treating offenders in groups?

9. Cite some of the primary methods of treating offenders. What seems to work the best?

10. How are female offenders treated?

11. What considerations must be made for special populations of offenders?

CHAPTER 15

Treatment for Adult Survivors

Surviving Child Sexual Abuse

Sexual abuse can leave scars that remain with a child into and sometimes throughout adulthood. These scars can be intensified by numerous factors related to the abuse or the reactions of others to the abuse.

Courtois (2010) makes the point that when the sexual abuse is intensified by the betrayal of a formerly trusted individual like a parent, the result is a greater degree of trauma. As early as 1978, Butler conceptualized what she called secondary injuries from incest, which she theorized occurred at four levels of betrayal: (a) the abuse itself and the actual betrayal by a family member; (b) the failure to respond on the part of the nonoffending parent or other family members; (c) the nonresponse by professionals such as teachers, physicians, nurses, counselors, and so on; and (d) the betrayal of self when the child denies his or her own reality and experience in order to cope with what has happened (as cited in Courtois, 2010, p. 13).

Any sexual abuse can be traumatic for a child, but studies have shown that the added dimension of betrayal intensifies this trauma. Because sexual abuse occurs in childhood, it will naturally impact the child's development toward adulthood. And given that the home is, for most children, the most significant influence on development, it stands to reason that intrafamilial abuse will create the most likelihood of trauma. Courtois (2010) summarizes the findings of numerous researchers on child sexual abuse and trauma by saying that

> the impact of incest is more serious than the impact of other forms of child sexual abuse and . . . overt incestuous contact has more serious ramifications than covert seductive behavior between family members. [italics are author's] (pp. 171–172)

A variety of factors will influence the degree of trauma to the sexually abused individual. The child's individual personality is the foundation for how the abuse is interpreted. The degree of trauma is influenced by such factors as (Briere, Kaltman, & Green, 2008; Courtois, 2010; Crosson-Tower, 2014; Davies & Frawley, 1994; Duncan, 2008; Lew, 2004; Lorentzen, Nilsen, & Traeen, 2008; Rodriquez-Srednicki & Twaite, 2006; Sanderson, 2006; Tower, 1988)

- the child's attachment to caretakers,
- the child's age at the onset of the abuse,
- how the abuse terminated,

- the degree of force,
- specifics of the abuse,
- reactions of others upon disclosure,
- the identity of the perpetrator,
- the child's relationship with other family members, and
- the degree and type of other family dysfunction and other variables.

Still, it is a myth that every adult who was abused as a child will necessarily have difficulty functioning in adulthood. Some use the survival techniques that they have developed to function quite well. For others, the memories do not cause problems until some trigger brings them to the fore, and survivors must cope with feelings that they may not have learned to cope with in childhood.

ﾣ _____

Martha suspected that her childhood had not been the best, but she remembered little of it. She did know that both parents drank a good deal, but she was determined to not make that her style and that she would leave that life behind her. She had left home at 16 and never looked back. She had no place for her parents' drunken behavior in the life she had made for herself. Her husband, Bill, was a long-distance truck driver, and although she loved him deeply, she valued their times apart. Intimacy was difficult for her, and Bill's times at home provided about as much closeness as she could handle. She didn't even mind feeling like a single mother. Nan and Billy Jr. were good kids and never gave her much trouble. She liked her job as the receptionist at a dentist's office and had worked out day care arrangements when the children got out of school. She would have said that her life was pretty near what she wanted it to be until Nan, at age 9, was molested by a neighbor. Dealing with the police and answering Bill's frantic questions as he called her from across the country sent her into acute anxiety. The anxiety attacks made her head spin, filling her sense with strange impressions of smells that frightened her. She felt as though she could not breathe, as

if there was a terrible weight on her chest. These reactions happened at work as well as at home, and her colleagues were concerned. Even Bill's assurance that he would be home as soon as he could did not help. Finally, in desperation, feeling like her well-ordered life was falling apart, Martha saw a therapist whom her employer had recommended. After several sessions, she began to remember the abuse she had suffered at the hands of her father. Her concern over her own daughter's abuse, the therapist felt, may have triggered her own memories.

ﾣ

REPRESSION, MEMORY, AND SEXUAL ABUSE _____

Sexual abuse is not always reported or addressed in childhood. Even if it is disclosed, a child may not receive the help that he or she needs to understand and cope with the abuse. When the mind cannot process trauma, that experience is often repressed—pushed far back into the unconscious. Yet repression can intensify the feelings when they finally are allowed to emerge. Repression can also be present in degrees—from submerging the recall totally to knowing what happened by deciding not to think about it.

Wherever the memory of abuse has been stored in the psyche, the memory and feelings associated with the abuse resurface and require attention for a variety of reasons or as a result of a myriad of stimuli.

Why Memories Emerge or Need to Be Addressed

Repressed memories of child sexual abuse emerge in a variety of ways. As mentioned earlier, some memories are just below the surface and are stimulated into more active recall by events or associations. Other memories have been buried deeply in the psyche and may be wrenched to the surface by some stimuli or slowly emerge over time. The stimulus that revives the memory may take a variety of forms.

The *pressures of adulthood* may bring to mind the times when there were seemingly unconquerable barriers.

ᛒ ──────────────────────

Honor had recently been promoted and was eager to take on her new role as supervisor. At the same time, she wondered if she had what it took to direct a diverse group of employees. One of her subordinates reminded her a bit of her mother, always criticizing and complaining. As a coworker, Honor had been able to ignore her, but as her supervisor, Honor was often in the position of having to address her complaints. There was another subordinate who was not pulling his weight, meaning that his peers were frequently picking up the slack. And an employee-to-employee romance had ended, and the barbs that flew between the former lovers made it clear that the parting was not amicable. Often Honor found herself wondering how she would get through the day. She began feeling out of control of her work environment. At the same time, a long-term relationship had just ended for her, and she wondered if she could have done anything more to save it.

Honor began having dreams that always centered around her feeling out of control. With the dreams were veiled images that there was something wrong or that she was somehow tainted. Images of her older brother began to emerge. Then became nightmares; she would be running from her brother in terror. He was always carrying the same knife that he would threaten to impale her with. In one dream, the knife became a penis, and what began to merge were memories of her brother's sexual abuse and the helplessness that she felt at not knowing what to do about it.

──────────────────────── ᛒ

Honor began to write about her memories in a writing group she attended. As her memories emerged in vivid detail, she recognized the need to come to terms with what had happened to her in childhood.

When the pressures of adulthood, change, and even success begin to engender similar feelings to what the survivor experienced during or after the abuse, images of or feelings about the abuse may resurface (Courtois, 2010; Crosson-Tower, 2014; Duncan, 2008; Lew, 2004; Rodriquez-Srednicki & Twaite, 2006; Tower, 1988). Even *achievements in adulthood* provide a stimulus. Some survivors begin to achieve success in their lives, and the remnant of stigma that they feel about what happened to them makes them feel unworthy. This too might bring memories to the fore.

Relationships may also be at the root of adult disclosure.

ᛒ ──────────────────────

I felt like I had finally found someone who could understand any deep dark secret that I might have in my past. Justin was so wise, so good. My comfort at being with him began to make me believe that it would be safe to tell him what my uncle did to me.

──────────────────────── ᛒ

Sometimes the survivor feels safe, often for the first time, and believes that he or she can share the fact that he or she was abused. In other situations, the survivor feels a need to test the security of the relationship. If he or she can talk about the abuse and it does not make a difference to the partner, the survivor will know that he or she is fully accepted.

ᛒ ──────────────────────

Lou kept telling me how wonderful I was. I wondered if he would feel the same way if he knew I had been abused. I thought about it for a long time and finally decided that if he could accept the abuse, I knew that he really loved me.

──────────────────────── ᛒ

Sometimes this inclination to tell one's partner about the abuse works out; but when it does not, the feelings of rejection and isolation may be intensified for the survivor.

Childhood sexual abuse is an issue of loss. The individual has lost his or her innocence, a healthy childhood, and often his or her own ability to feel good about himself or herself. As a result, *other losses* may stimulate memories of abuse, requiring that the feelings of having been abused be addressed.

☙ _____

When my partner died of AIDS, I remember crying uncontrollably for hours. How could life do this to me? I had two neglectful, alcoholic parents; a lousy childhood; and a ton of abuse at the hands of my father and brothers, and finally, I had found someone to love. And now he was gone. My feelings forced me into therapy where I finally had to confront the sexual abuse, some of which I had put so far back in my mind that I hardly remembered it. But it was there, making a mess of my self-concept and my life. _____ ❧

Sometimes the *normal events of living* will bring up issues of abuse. One survivor talked about watching his children and thinking "How could anyone ever abuse a child? And how could someone so young and innocent be expected to resist?" He began to think about his own abuse, and, suddenly recognizing that it was not his fault, he gained the courage to get help in sorting out his feelings. Parents who were abused as children often worry about their own children especially when their children reach an age at which these parents were abused. Such fears may actually bring their memories to the surface or, in dealing with these fears, force these parents to address their own residual issues (Crosson-Tower, 2014; Tower, 1988).

False Memory Controversy

During the late 1980s and 1990s, there emerged a controversy that questioned the validity of the memories of sexual abuse described by survivors. At the core of this debate was not only the concepts of repression and dissociation but also the manner in which these memories were remembered (Colangelo, 2009). Explanations for the validity of memory retrieval were based on the work of Sigmund Freud and his colleague Breuer who together first presented the concept of repression (see Chapter 1). Freud and Breuer were also influenced by the previous studies of Charcot who employed hypnosis to treat hysterical reactions. All of these theorists came to the same conclusion initially—that hysteria was caused by psychological trauma that had been hidden from the consciousness or repressed (Colangelo, 2009; Courtois, 2010; Davis, 2005; Herman, 1997; McNally, 2005).

Holmes (1990), after his review of 60 years of literature on repression, suggested that repression had three elements: (a) the selective forgetting of memories that cause pain, (b) the forgetting is not entirely voluntary, and (c) the memories are not lost altogether but stored within the consciousness. Memories can resurface if some trigger calls them up and can also have the anxiety associated with the original trauma removed if they are worked through and understood. Holmes also mentioned two types of repression described by Freud—repression proper (when the individual recognizes that a thought or memory produces anxiety and represses the thought to avoid the anxiety) and primary repression (when the anxiety-provoking material is assigned to the unconscious before the conscious mind recognizes it as stressful). However, after his laborious review, Holmes concluded that there was not sufficient controlled laboratory evidence to support the existence of repression (see also Colangelo, 2009).

What followed were years of writings that disagreed with Holmes's position, the variables used, and his study (see especially Reisner, 1998; Sivers, Schooler, & Freyd, 2002). Some critics felt that there was a plethora of evidence to support the concept of repression. Sivers et al. (2002) highlighted that the Holmes article looked at mechanisms for repression rather than the concept of memory inaccessibility and the fact that there had been a number of laboratory studies reported that supported the evidence of repression since Holmes had written his article.

Central to the controversy was the work of Elizabeth Loftus, a noted psychology professor and expert on memory. Loftus (1993, 2003) postulated that false memories could be implanted in the minds of individuals who would later believe that the memories were of events that had been a part of their experience. It was the suggestions of therapists that they had been abused, argued Loftus, that could have created erroneous memories in the minds of supposed survivors. Loftus (1993) did allow that some of the recovered memories could be accurate but not in the number that the media at the time was suggesting.

Part of the problem with recovered memories is that they usually do not emerge in a clear chronological version, but rather in bits and pieces often encoded in sense-related images (e.g., the smell of a type of soap) or dissociated thoughts (Courtois, 2010; van der Kolk & Fisler, 1995). Determining from these recovered memories what is real and what is imagined can be difficult.

The false memory controversy came to the attention of a nonresearcher when in 1990 Jennifer Freyd privately accused her parents of sexually abusing her as a child. She had apparently uncovered the memories as part of the therapy that she had entered for an unrelated matter. Jennifer's mother, Pamela, then published, under the name Jane Doe, an article in a journal that focused on the false accusations made of child abuse. The article, circulated widely, suggested that the memories of abuse by her father had been planted in Jennifer's mind in therapy. The article became the impetus for the development of the False Memory Syndrome Foundation (FMSF), founded in 1992 by Pamela Freyd and her husband, Peter. The FMSF expressed concern that such practices as hypnosis, relaxation exercises, guided imagery, drug-mediated interviews,

body memories, literal dream interpretation, and journaling used in therapy might bring up false memories in adults that they were abused as children. In addition, the FMSF asserted that false memories could be planted in the minds of adults by their therapists (Dallam, 2001; FMSF, 2010; Olio, 2004).

While a heated battle raged between those who believed that memories of child sexual abuse could be engineered through therapy and those who asserted that such memories were authentic, those treating abuse survivors sought to guard against therapeutic contamination of recovered memories. Therapists were cautioned not to jump to conclusions about abuse having occurred in a patient's life but rather to listen more carefully and address the healing that needed to be accomplished for the patient. Current texts written for therapists continue to address this issue (see Courtois, 2010).

RESIDUAL EFFECTS OF CHILD SEXUAL ABUSE

When an individual is abused as a child, he or she is not only faced with understanding and dealing with the aftereffects of the sexual abuse but also with the influence that the secrecy and effort to repress the feelings and memories have had on the individual's psyche. It is difficult to separate these treatment needs when working with an adult survivor. Although these treatment issues are all interrelated, they can be categorized for the sake of discussion. Courtois (2010) groups the aftereffects of incest into eight groups that affect intrapsychic and interpersonal functioning: (a) post-traumatic stress disorder (PTSD) and tension-reduction behaviors; (b) emotional distress and reactions; (c) self-perceptions; (d) learning problems, cognitive distortions, and misattributions; (e) physical, somatic, and medical effects; (f) sexual effects; (g) interpersonal relating and functioning; and (h) social functioning (p. 196). These groups can be further collapsed into four categories: (a) PTSD and the impairment of everyday functioning; (b) the self-concept, growth, and achievement; (c) physical, medical, and sexual issues; and (d) interpersonal relationships.

Post-Traumatic Stress Disorder and the Impairment of Everyday Functioning

PTSD has long been recognized as a result of trauma. From the assaults of war and political torture to the domestic war zone in an abusive home, survivors describe symptoms of intrusion and reexperiencing, avoidance, numbing and dissociation, and physiological hyperarousal, which have been identified and categorized into a disorder referred to as PTSD (Herman, 1997). So complex and severe have the responses of some victims of incest been that the term *complex post-traumatic stress disorder* has been coined to describe the experiences of these individuals (Courtois, 2010). And not every individual who is sexually abused either intra-familially or outside the home will develop PTSD.

For those who do develop PTSD, the symptoms can feel or be debilitating. These symptoms can be seen in three very simple category groups: reexperiencing the trauma, avoiding the trauma, and emotional arousal over the trauma.

Reexperiencing the Trauma

When the psyche experiences an assault like sexual abuse, especially if it is at the hands of someone who was previously trusted as in cases of incest, the feelings are not fully processed and will emerge again and again in disturbing ways. Sometimes, these involve intrusive thoughts that are upsetting and can debilitate (Briere et al., 2008; Courtois, 2010; Crosson-Tower, 2014; Davies & Frawley, 1994; Duncan, 2008; Lew, 2004; Lorentzen et al., 2008; Rodriquez-Srednicki & Twaite, 2006; Tower, 1988).

ℛ

I remembered my uncle's hot breath on my face, his cigar breath, and his whispered obscenities in my ear. This image would come upon me when I least expected it. The result was that I would feel cold and anxious. I would often shake and feel like I had to get away. It was like I would just fall apart. ℬ

Flashbacks refer to pictures of the traumatic event that may seem quite vivid and over which the survivor does not have control. Dissociation has been defined as involving "a vertical split of the ego that results in two or more self states that are more or less organized and independently functioning" (Davies & Frawley, 1994). In other words, certain feelings and ideas lose their relationship, usually temporarily, with other aspects of the personality or consciousness. Survivors describe episodes during their abuse when the only way to endure it is for their mind to "leave" the body.

ℛ

I felt like I was looking down on the body that was being abused. It wasn't really me at that moment. I could hear it cry, but I was outside of the experience. It is probably what got me through it. ℬ

Dissociation exists on a continuum. When you sit in a boring class or meeting and suddenly come to realize that you were out on the ski slopes instead of in that room, you have experienced a mild form of dissociation. But trauma can kick dissociative experiences into overdrive. At the far end of the dissociative continuum are those who experience *dissociative identity disorder* (formerly known as multiple personality disorder), where personality fragments take on different roles for the host individual. One entity may remember the details of the abuse while protecting the host from these memories, whereas other entities store other memories or assume other roles. Truddi

Chase, who became known through her book *When Rabbit Howls* (1990), had over 90 distinctive personalities that allowed her to survive and navigate through her life after sadistic abuse in childhood.

Some survivors reexperience their abuse through nightmares or night terrors.

ༀ

I would wake up drenched, shaking, and anxious. I knew that I had been dreaming that dream again. He was coming after me, chasing me, and I knew that if he caught me he would crush me and rape me again and again. I never knew how to avoid having the dream. Sometimes I would just lay awake at night, fearful that, if I slept, I would be assaulted by the dream! **ༀ**

Avoiding the Trauma

Survivors of child sexual abuse expend a good deal of energy, often unconsciously, trying to avoid reexperiencing the trauma that was the abuse. Many survivors describe suppressing their emotions to the point where they do now feel them (Briere, 1996b; Courtois, 2014; Tower, 1988). One survivor of childhood abuse explained,

ༀ

My only goal while I was being abused was to get through it and eventually to get out of the house. I couldn't afford to have feelings. I just wanted to survive. I guess I was pretty successful at pushing away those feelings. After a rather difficult marriage, my wife finally told me that she couldn't be with me anymore. She said that she used to think that my feelings toward her weren't strong enough to maintain a marriage. But then she realized that I had no feelings for anyone. **ༀ**

Survivors also find themselves consciously or unconsciously avoiding relationships. Abuse, especially at the hands of a loved individual, destroys trust. When an individual cannot trust or trusts little, it is difficult for him or her to enter into or maintain a relationship. Possibly feeding into these difficulties with others is the tendency of some survivors to avoid taking responsibility. Because they felt helpless and out of control during and even after the abuse, they may feel that they are unable to be responsible for their own lives.

When one has been sexually abused, there is also a tendency to want to avoid situations in which the abuse will happen again or the feelings associated with it will reemerge.

ༀ

I couldn't go back into the house where I grew up. There were too many memories of my mother's abuse of me. Once I even tried to go there, and I was overwhelmed with anxiety and couldn't even go in. Now I just avoid it altogether. **ༀ**

Briere (1996b) suggested that some survivors use what he called *tension-reduction behaviors* such as substance abuse, eating disorders, self-mutilation, continuous suicide attempts, and promiscuous sexual behaviors as ways to avoid feelings associated with the abuse.

Hyperarousal

Hyperarousal is another piece of PTSD that can also be debilitating. The survivor always feels on guard or is constantly watchful for danger. Hyperarousal may include reactions like being easily startled, becoming anxious, getting frightened or irritable in situations that seem threatening, or being awakened from sleep (Briere et al., 2008; Courtois, 2010; Crosson-Tower, 2014; Davies & Frawley, 1994; Duncan, 2008; Lew, 2004; Lorentzen et al., 2008; Rodriquez-Srednicki & Twaite, 2006; Stone, 2005; Tower, 1988).

ༀ

I would frequently be jolted from sleep. My reaction would be to jump out of bed on the alert. I couldn't have told you what had done it. It was just some fear that lurked in the back of my mind waiting to ambush me. But I knew that it had started one night after my father had raped me in my bed. ∞

PTSD may result in the survivor acting out in a variety of ways. It may come to the attention of family members and professionals before the individual is actually diagnosed and will need to be addressed therapeutically.

Everyday functioning when one is a survivor of sexual abuse can be challenging. Feeling out of control and living with the residual effects of abuse can produce a life filled with confusion, guilt, fear, anxiety, anger, rage, helplessness, shame, and humiliation (Courtois, 2010). Fears sometimes insinuate themselves into sleep, meaning that the individual not only has difficulty sleeping but may be afraid to sleep in the dark, alone, near a window, under too many covers, or in other ways that make him or her feel unsafe. No amount of reason will allay the fears. Only understanding and processing their origin will help the survivor to lessen or eliminate them. Fears may also produce symptoms that interrupt normal daily living. Dissociative reactions are ways in which the psyche tries to cope with such fears. Some people lose periods of time; others feel that they are "only half there" in certain stressful situations.

∞

My uncle used to abuse me at family gatherings. While my rather boisterous relatives—most of who had had too much to drink by that time—were partying in the living room and den, my uncle would take me into the bedroom and molest me. I remember hearing the voices and wanting to cry out. I doubt that they would have heard me, but I never could cry out anyway. I was frozen with fear. When I got older, I used to have difficulty with the noise of loud gatherings or parties. I would always flash back to being that small child being abused in the bedroom. Hearing those voices raised in fun would remind me that they weren't there for me, and I would feel frozen once again to act for myself. ∞

Self-Concept, Growth, and Achievement

The self-concept of survivors can be impaired by being sexually abused; this manifests itself in a variety of ways. Survivors may not feel good about themselves or have faith in their abilities. Some try to compensate for this by acting out, which can in turn add to the view of self as negative. Others have learned in childhood to be "good" in the fervent hope that it will stop the abuse. If the abuse is disclosed and not responded to effectively, the child may take the blame upon himself or herself and develop a view of self that is tainted, ashamed, and bad (Briere, 1996b; Courtois, 2010; Davies & Frawley, 1994). Survivors describe feelings of self-loathing that may lead them into dysfunctional lives.

There are a few survivors who bask in the feelings of power and specialness that come from being the abuser's favorite—especially in cases of father-daughter incest (Courtois, 2010). These feelings may coexist with the shame and feelings of blame that also result. The view of self becomes confused as the survivor tries to come to terms with her feelings.

When a child does not have the psychic energy required for learning, development can be impaired. Surviving child sexual abuse requires a good deal of emotional energy, which may rob the brain of the ability to excel at other developmental tasks. The brain is in survival mode so that its learning functions are hampered. Thus, it is not unusual for abused children to grow up with learning disabilities, problems with concentration (e.g., ADD or ADHD), or memory problems that follow them into adulthood (Courtois, 2010).

Physical, Medical, and Sexual Issues

Survivors of child sexual abuse often complain of distressing medical issues in later life. Headaches, gastrointestinal issues, eating disorders, fainting, seizures, and the results of actual physical injuries caused by sexual abuse can cause problems (Briere, 1996b; Courtois, 2010; Davies & Frawley, 1994; Tower, 1988). Often these physical symptoms are centered on areas that were involved in the trauma.

ᗅ _____

Serena had been seen for several years for symptoms that presented like acid reflux. When she went to bed at night, she felt as if there was acid in her throat and she could not breathe. Her physician could find nothing organically wrong with her. He treated her with a mild acid blocker, but she reported that it did not help. Finally he set her for a psychiatric evaluation. Finally she admitted to the therapist that she had been sexually abused in childhood. This consisted primarily of her stepfather's insistence that she give him oral sex. As she remembered these times, the acid feeling began again. Eventually she was able to make the connection between the abuse and the symptoms she was experiencing.

_____ ᘒ

Vomiting, nausea, and other issues related to swallowing may also be related to flashbacks from the abuse. Respiratory problems such as difficulty breathing, shortness of breath, and hyperventilation may be indicative of feeling smothered or having the pressure of an adult on top of the child at the time of the assault. Rectal infections, constipation, diarrhea, and urinary tract issues may also be related to abuse (Briere, 1996b; Davies & Frawley, 1994; Kendall-Tackett & Klest, 2009; Tower, 1988). Some ailments are specific to the area in which the abuse was localized, whereas others are more generic (Kendall-Tackett & Klest, 2009). Courtois (2010) describes a patient who

> complained of a sore index finger while emotionally processing memories of her incest experience. As the memories emerged, so did the explanation for the sore finger: As part of the abuse, this woman was forced to digitally penetrate her

father's anus. Her finger stopped hurting once the association was made. (p. 210)

A significant number of survivors of sexual abuse, especially incest, developed difficulties in sexual functioning (Lemieux & Byers, 2008; Maltz, 2012). In a sample of 272 female college students, Lemieux and Byers (2008) found that women who experienced only fondling as part of childhood abuse did not report adverse sexual outcomes, whereas women whose abuse had involved penetration or attempted penetration reported significant issues. These women (a) were more likely to be revictimized in adulthood; (b) were more likely to have engaged in casual sex, unprotected sex, or voluntary sexual abstinence; and (c) reported fewer sexual rewards, more sexual costs, and poorer self-esteem related to sexual matters. In addition, survivors of incest report that they are more likely to engage in early and promiscuous sexual behaviors yet have more difficulty with sexual arousal, response, and satisfaction (Ahmad, 2006; Courtois, 2010; Kia-Keating, Sorsoli, & Grossman, 2010; Maltz, 2012; Tower, 1988).

As children, survivors were exposed to sexuality prematurely, resulting in a feeling that some describe as being out-of-sync with peers who have not been abused. Some act out with peers or conversely withdraw from age-appropriate sexual exploration and activity. Some feel bad and believe that they have gained reputations as sexually easy. Others do act out sexually with a feeling that they might as well do what is expected of them by peers who know of the abuse. In addition, sexually abused children have been taught to barter and manipulate with sexual favors, and this can carry over into adult relationships. One survivor explained,

ᗅ _____

I always knew I could get my way with my stepfather by flirting and offering to give him a blowjob. I remember liking one boy in high school who I was sure wouldn't look at me. So I resorted to what I knew worked at home and offered to "make him feel good." I didn't think about him telling his buddies and them all coming to me too. It was a nightmare. And just because I had wanted him to like me.

ℰℴ

Male survivors may question their masculinity and, in response, need to be more sexually dominant or active (Kia-Keating et al., 2010; Lew, 2004). There may also be cultural implications for both sexes about their sexual behaviors (Fontes, 2008).

Sexual orientation or preference is often called into question when there has been sexual abuse in an individual's background. There are numerous and varied scenarios. Women who are basically heterosexual may prefer relationships with other women due to their negative experiences with male abusers. Some incest survivors may not discriminate in their choice of partners. Lesbians who were abused as children may find that their choice of women partners is supported by being abused by males. Those abused by women may have been conditioned to prefer female partners.

The majority of male survivors have been abused by another male (Courtois, 2010; Grossman, Sorsoli, & Kia-Keating, 2006; Groth, 2001; Kia-Keating et al., 2010; Lew, 2004). They may wonder why they were selected for the abuse. Does that mean they are homosexual? If they enjoyed the abuse at the hands of another male, does that mean they are homosexual? Did the abuse make them gay?

Men abused by women live in a culture where sexual indoctrination of young men by women is often cause for a wink and a laugh. As an adult, this man may have difficulties based on how he experienced the abuse and how others reacted to it if he told anyone. If he perceived the experience as abusive, he may wonder whether this in itself means that he is homosexual. Gay men may wonder if the abuse influenced their sexual preference (Courtois, 2010; Grossman et al., 2006; Kia-Keating et al., 2010; Lew, 2004).

Interpersonal Relationships

It becomes obvious as theorists try to characterize the residual effects facing adults abused as children that these all overlap. Because people are social beings, it stands to reason that trauma to the individual would affect relationships in a variety of ways. Theorists have considered the avoidance of relationships, difficulty with trust issues, and problems with openness, intimacy, responsibility, and commitment. All of these will impact the way in which survivors are able to be in relationships with others. Although most theorists feel that child sexual abuse will have a significant impact on relationships, some believe that this is not the only variable (Walker, Holman, & Busby, 2009). Nonetheless, it plays a part in the way survivors relate to others.

Survivors vary in the degree to which they are ready or able to forge relationships. Some prefer to avoid them, isolating themselves. Others proceed cautiously, always ready to retreat if it becomes too difficult. Still others dash into relationships indiscriminately without taking the time to build them thoughtfully.

For incest survivors especially, the family patterns of the past can impact the way in which they engage with others. Marital problems between their parents may have set their stage in what to expect in their intimate dealings. Fears, anger, rage, and anxiety come into the mix. Even parenting their own children becomes something that they need to do with great forethought as their own models have been faulty. Cultural variations are also important.

Survivors may bring to relationships a variety of insecurities (Walker et al., 2009). How they are able to deal with them in conjunction with others will depend on an array of variables.

Revictimization is often part of the experience of survivors, both in relationships and at the hands of acquaintances or strangers (Courtois, 2010; Lau & Kristensen, 2010; Messman-Moore & Long, 2000; Tower, 1988). There may be several reasons for this. First, being victimized as a young child causes the survivor to feel helpless and vulnerable. Such vulnerability is often preyed upon by later abusers. And the survivor may not believe that he or she can act in defense.

ᦉ _____

The abuse by my father robbed me both literally and figuratively of my ability to scream. When a boyfriend raped me in my early 20s, I felt mute. I couldn't resist, and I couldn't say "no." When a stranger attacked me years later, I curled up in a ball and hoped that I could disappear. ᦉ

Survivors also may not feel that they are worth much and perhaps feel that they deserve whatever happens to them, including additional victimization. As one survivor explained,

ᦉ _____

I figured that I was damaged when I was abused as a kid. What difference did it make if someone else did something to me later? Maybe it was just what I had coming. ᦉ

Caring about themselves sufficiently to recognize that they do not deserve to be abused is difficult for some survivors. Some individuals relate that they are afraid to say "no."

ᦉ _____

My father was a big guy, and if I said "no" to him about anything, he would beat me. I guess when he figured out that I wouldn't resist, he decided that it was okay to sexually abuse me too. ᦉ

And finally, being abused feels familiar to survivors. It has become a part of their reality. Some survivors relate that they put themselves into relationships or situations because they were familiar and the familiar seemed safe. And yet the familiarity of these situations is often that they will be abused again.

Seeking treatment may be a way for a survivor to not only cope with the debilitating or disturbing symptoms of child sexual abuse but also prevent the likelihood of multiple victimizations.

TREATMENT FOR ADULT SURVIVORS

Considerations for Treatment

Every survivor of child sexual abuse does not require the same type, length, or intensity of treatment. Treatment is also often not a one-time experience. Some survivors spend time in treatment but may return at different times in their lives for what one survivor called "my mini tune-ups." Others experience stops and starts—when they begin treatment, drop out, and later begin again. Still others require crisis therapy before they are able to or have the stability to commit to intensive therapy.

ᦉ _____

The memories of my abuse began to emerge when I was in real crisis. My house had burned, and with it, all the idealized pictures of my past. My partner of 10 years had broken up with me, and a dear friend had just died. The flashbacks that began in the midst of this were debilitating. I was sure I was going crazy and sought therapy. The therapist helped me through the crisis, but we both realized that I was not ready to sort out the abuse memories and what they meant to me. My therapist told me that I had opened a door, and when I was ready, I could return to explore what was inside. It took me 5 years, but I finally went back to her when I felt that I was in a good position to explore the nightmare that was my childhood. ᦉ

The type of therapy that a survivor needs at a given moment will depend upon several things:

- The duration and intensity of the abuse (the more traumatic the abuse the more intense may be the therapeutic needs)

- The identity of the abuser (those abused by family members or those upon whom they depended for survival may have greater therapeutic needs)
- How the abuse was handled by those who may have known about it (denial on the part of those close to the child can intensify feelings of guilt, shame, and self-blame)
- The degree of repression (when survivors expend a great deal of energy to repress the memory of the abuse, they may require more time to uncover and process it)
- The degree of stability in their lives (being in crisis requires stabilization and is not usually the time for in-depth long-term therapy to begin)

The choice of a therapist is also important. Those who have been victims of incest especially may require someone who is well trained in the field of child sexual abuse recovery. Sometimes a survivor enters therapy for symptoms, which may seem unrelated to the abuse.

CR ▬▬▬▬▬▬▬▬▬▬▬▬▬▬▬▬

Pat found herself unable to conceive a child. Her gynecologist could find nothing wrong with her physically. He referred her to a therapist who specialized in fertility issues. After some work together, the therapist believed that her issues were related to the sexual abuse that Pat had experienced as a child. Recognizing that this was not his area of expertise, he wisely referred her to a specialist who worked with survivors of childhood abuse.   **SO**

▬▬▬▬▬▬▬▬▬▬▬▬▬▬▬▬▬▬▬▬▬

Survivors of incest often experience what some clinicians refer to as complex trauma. Courtois and Ford (2009) explain complex psychological trauma as referring to experiences that

(1) involve repetitive or prolonged exposure to or experiencing of multiple traumatic stressors, most often of an interpersonal nature in a variety of milieus and roles,

(2) involve harm or abandonment by caregivers or other ostensibly responsible adults, and (3) occur at developmentally vulnerable times in the victim's life, especially over the course of childhood, and become intertwined with and incorporated within the child's biological, psychophysiological, and psychosexual development. (p. 84)

Survivors of complex trauma need treatment specific to the complexity of these issues by a therapist skilled with this population (Courtois, 2010; Herman, 2008; Moss, 2008).

Types of Therapeutic Intervention

Crisis Intervention for Acute Stress

As mentioned earlier, survivors of childhood abuse may have difficulty with self-regulation and often problem solving. Their fears about being out of control sometimes inhibit their abilities to organize their resources in the face of unexpected or upsetting events or experiences. This inhibition may throw them into crisis. Although the underlying causes of their feelings are related to the abuse and the residual effects, it will be important for a therapist to stabilize them in the face of the present crisis rather than attending to the underlying causes. Support, a listening ear, enabling them to problem-solve, and connecting them with resources within their immediate environment and the community are what is needed at this juncture.

Situations of extreme stress may throw survivors back into old patterns of coping like suicidal ideation, binging on food or alcohol, excessive sleeping, and other tension-relieving behaviors that may also need to be addressed in therapy.

Crisis intervention therapy is expected to be short term in an effort to help the individual regain some homeostasis.

Long-Term Psychotherapy

Long-term treatment is an opportunity for a survivor who has achieved some degree of stability to work on the underlying issues that prohibit optimum functioning. Courtois (2010) suggests that there are three treatment stages to long-term therapy, the first of which involves building of trust. She identifies these stages as (a) safety, building alliance, stabilization, education, and skill building; (b) addressing and processing the incest or other trauma; and (c) posttrauma life integration toward a "new kind of normal" (p. 278).

The underlying and vital component of such therapy is the therapeutic relationship between the therapist and the survivor. Trust must be created between these two individuals so that the survivor feels safe before any successful work can be undertaken. There is also a certain amount of education in that the therapist explains to the patient what will be expected of each of them. And then the survivor is taught ways of coping with the arousal states that he or she may experience as the therapy progresses. This way, he or she learns to protect himself or herself from feeling overwhelmed.

 CR ─────────────────────

My therapist spent a good deal of time helping me remember when I had felt safe during my childhood. I finally remembered that my grandmother had given me this quilt that she made for my bed. I never used it on the bed. Instead, I would curl up in it or under it, convinced that if it was over me, no one could hurt me in any way. In therapy, my therapist helped me to visualize what that felt like—that safe warm and untouchable feeling. Then we used it as I began to remember the episodes of the abuse. He would help me visualize getting under the quilt so that I could not be harmed by the frightening feelings.
─────────────────────── ℘

During the second stage of therapy, once the alliance has been built, the survivor feels safe and knows what to expect and how to cope when the feelings become too overwhelming; the therapist takes the survivor through his or her memories of the abuse, uncovering those that are hidden and understanding the patterns that emerge. The survivor learns mastery over the feelings associated with remembering and having been abused (Courtois, 2010; Herman, 2008; Kia-Keating et al., 2010; Moss, 2008).

The final stage of therapy will involve reintegration of the various aspects of the trauma experience and separating them from family patterns. The survivor then learns ways to see himself or herself differently in an effort to prepare for the future. Existing relationship may need to be understood and recrafted to be supportive and nonabusive. The survivor will also be helped to develop a relapse plan should he or she fall back into old patterns.

Long-term therapy requires great deal of commitment, patience, courage, and the willingness to work closely with the therapist, but the rewards can be significant.

Cognitive-Behavioral Techniques

Cognitive-behavioral therapy (CBT) (mentioned earlier in Chapter 14) refers to a group of techniques that have been found to be most effective with guilt, anger, anxiety, and depression—key pieces of PTSD. Although a relationship with the therapist is important, proponents of CBT say that this is only a piece of the therapy. The underlying concept is that individuals' thoughts and feelings play a fundamental role in their behavior (Craske, 2009; Follette & Ruzek, 2007). And, although it is understood that individuals cannot control every aspect of their environment, they can take control over how they interpret and deal with that environment.

The therapist who uses cognitive-behavioral techniques begins by helping the client to identify specific problematic beliefs, which, it is assumed, contribute to maladaptive behaviors that are also identified. Goals are then set with the client about how he or she can unlearn these maladaptive behaviors. The individual then takes incremental steps toward changing his or her behavior. Homework is a regular feature of CBT, allowing the client to practice what he or she has learned in therapy (Craske, 2009; Follette & Ruzek, 2007).

A recent review of cognitive-behavioral treatments identified seven categories: (a) *exposure therapy*, which exposes the patient to anxiety-inducing stimuli without the benefit of anxiety-reducing methods until he or she develops the ability to cope with them; (b) *stress-inoculation therapy*, which provides techniques for anticipatory planning and anxiety management; (c) *cognitive-processing therapy*, which challenges problematic or distorted beliefs about the traumatic experience; (d) *cognitive therapy*, which focuses on the interpretation of events as they relate to emotional states; (e) *relaxation training*, which helps the clients to reduce the anxiety engendered by the stress and trauma stimuli; (f) *dialectic behavioral therapy*, which involves the use of behavioral theory and dialectics to promote acceptance and change; and (g) *acceptance and commitment therapy*, which helps the individual to accept his or her internal experiences and commitment to making changes that are in keeping with his or her personal values (Cahill, Rothbaum, Resick, & Follette, 2008; Courtois, 2010).

In a study of 74 women with PTSD related to their childhood sexual abuse, McDonagh et al. (2005) compared the efficacy in the use of CBT compared to problem-solving therapy and found that the patients with whom CBT had been used were more likely than the other group to no longer meet the criteria for PTSD after treatment. However, they also found that the dropout for the clients receiving CBT was higher, attesting to the need for commitment and motivation with this directed type of therapy.

Expressive Therapies

Some survivors find expressive or experiential therapies useful in allowing them to access emotional material that is too difficult to get at through just talking. Fosha, Siegel, and Solomon (2009) explain their use by saying "experiential psychotherapies are designed to systematically assist people in enhancing the ability to access emotions and the psychosocial resources linked to emotions" (p. 286). Pieces of memory that are so difficult that they have been forbidden from the conscious mind or have been the fodder for dissociative experiences can be uncovered through alternative types of expression (Carey, 2006; Malchiodi, 2012).

Types of expressive therapies, albeit not an exhaustive list, include art therapy, dance movement therapy, psychodrama, sandtray therapy, play therapy, poetry and writing therapy, and journaling.

In *art and dance movement therapies*, the client is asked to express emotions or symbolize emotions or events through the use of art media or through the movement of the body. Sometimes clients are able to then talk about what they have expressed. In a study of women sexual abuse survivors who have experienced dance therapy, Mills and Daniluk (2002) found that the women gained feelings of spontaneity, freedom, intimate connection, and body reconnection as a result of their therapy.

Psychodrama and *sandtray therapies* are methods of acting out memories or emotions associated with the trauma. In sandtray therapy, the client is offered an empty tray of sand and a variety of small figures. The role of the therapist is to observe as the client chooses figures and places them on the tray in ways that mean something to him or her. The therapist may then ask questions or help the survivor to make interpretations based on the pictures that are emerging.

GR ───────────

"I felt like a little kid at first," said one survivor, "playing with all these little people and animals in sand. But I got into it pretty quickly. What happened was that I could feel some of the old emotions coming to the surface. The symbols I chose to represent the people in my family were telling. My father became scary figures that were unapproachable. My mother was so small and insignificant. When we had finished, I could see how trapped I had felt as a child, and I began to get a sense of how little control I had over the abuse that had happened to me."

ᏕᎧ

Poetry and other forms of writing have been used as forms of expression with survivors. Many therapists invite patients to keep a journal throughout therapy, which enables them to write down thoughts and feelings as they emerge and to discuss them in therapy. Writing groups or poetry groups for survivors are one type of support group that has been particularly successful.

Music, too, can have a therapeutic effect and is used in various ways in conjunction with therapy.

Although expressive therapies can be particularly effective, they should be employed by those trained in such techniques, and the timing of their use should be carefully orchestrated (see Courtois, 2010).

In addition to the earlier mentioned therapies, energy work is being used and explored as a beneficial form of therapy. Neurofeedback, massage, acupuncture, and a variety of other practices have been found to be helpful to survivors in various ways. This emerging group of complimentary therapies should not be underestimated.

Individual or Group Treatment?

Each survivor is unique and may want the opportunity for a one-to-one relationship with a therapist dealing with the client's individual issues. But the use of group treatment in conjunction with individual therapy can be especially helpful. Some survivors can tolerate talking about their issues in a group of individuals who have also experienced childhood abuse, whereas sitting with one individual therapist may be too stressful. Some survivors will enter group therapy and then realize that they could also benefit from individual sessions.

Group treatment does provide a number of advantages especially for survivors of incest and abuse by people they trusted. First, survivors can be helped to recognize that *they were not alone* in having been abused. Sometimes the details of the abuse seem so horrific to the individual that he or she cannot imagine that anyone could have experienced anything similar. Hearing the stories of other group members provides support and a sense of shared strength in their survival. Second, survivors develop a *therapeutic alliance with one another.* One person's healing is encouraged by others with a common goal for all to get better. *Telling the secret* details of the abuse *may become easier* in a group as others have also shared their details. In individual therapy, the client may feel that he or she is the only one with a secret and that makes it more difficult to talk about. As one survivor put it:

 CR

What happened to me seemed like nothing compared to the stories I heard in my group. I had trouble disclosing the intimate details with my individual therapist, but in groups, it felt like we were all in it together and could tell each other anything.

ᏕᎧ

The *group becomes the survivor's new functional family,* often filling a need that the dysfunctional family of the past did not. Learning to feel safe in this new context, the survivor learns that *there is safety in exploring feelings and beliefs* and *in risking new behaviors.* Survivors learn to challenge other's beliefs and in so doing *become more comfortable to confront their own distortions.* And finally, a group of survivors provides a place in which all *can grieve their lost childhoods* of abuse and dysfunction (Courtois, 2010; Davies

& Frawley, 1994; Llewelyn, 1997; Morgan & Cummings, 1999; Tower, 1988).

The focus of a particular survivors' group will vary. Some are open ended, taking new members at any time. Others are closed or time limited, retaining the same membership for a specified amount of time. Members are usually screened by the sponsoring agency to determine the level of group compatibility. Some clinicians suggest that incest survivors not be mixed with those from other types of abusive situations. Successful groups require the commitment of their members, and regular attendance is usually part of the group contract as is confidentiality—that what is said in the group remains in the group.

Therapy groups should be facilitated by a therapist who is skilled in group work as well as being knowledgeable about sexual abuse. The question also arises, "Should a therapist have a sexual abuse or incest history?" One survivor commented,

൙ _____

Whether my group leader has an incest history or not, I don't want to know. If she does, I may think she is damaged like I feel that I am. And will she be influenced by the way she survived and think everyone can do it? On the other hand, if she was not a victim of incest, will she understand how I'm feeling? I just don't want to know, so I never asked.

_____ ൙

Nonetheless, therapists leading groups can expect that someone in the group will ask the questions about their survival experience. The wise therapist will discern the reason for the question before answering if at all. This question often becomes some of the work that the group must do as it relates to the perceptions that survivors have of themselves. (For an excellent in-depth discussion of the use of groups and

the group process with survivors of incest, see Courtois, 2010.)

WORKING WITH THE SURVIVOR WITHIN HIS OR HER ENVIRONMENT ____

The survivor is not the only one who is impacted by his or her childhood sexual abuse. Family members and partners as well as close friends may be drawn in as the survivor discloses the abuse and tries to heal. The survivor's therapist may involve these significant others in therapy as collaterals as a way of helping the survivor.

Confronting Perpetrators and Other Family Members

Often, while in therapy, the survivor is able to recognize his or her anger at the perpetrator of the abuse and wants to confront that abuser. This may or may not be advisable. On one hand, it can help the survivor place the blame where it belongs—on the abuser. It may be an integral step for him or her toward moving on. It may be necessary to protect younger siblings, children, or grandchildren from the abuser's continuing patterns of abuse. In some situations, it opens a dialogue between the survivor and the abuser, which may even result in an apology. The latter is often the hope of the client, but is not usually the response.

One the other hand, abusers who deny or intensify their blame of the victim may feel like revictimization to the survivor. Thus, it is vital that the survivor seeks help in planning the timing of such a confrontation and the possible response this confrontation may bring. This will enable the therapist to help the client anticipate her or his reactions and may minimize any further damage a perpetrator might do (Courtois, 2010; Davies & Frawley, 1994; Llewelyn, 1997; Tower, 1988).

It may not be the perpetrator who the survivor is most interested in confronting. One therapist explained as follows:

ℭℛ ———————————————————

In the group that I facilitated for incest survivors, it was more often the nonprotecting parent that the survivors resented. The abuser, they often discounted, while they were tortured by the fact that their other parent did nothing to stop the abuse. Sometimes the nonabusing parent may not even have known that the abuse was occurring, but that was difficult for these women to believe, so consumed were they by anger and hurt.

——————————————————— **ଦ୬**

Confronting either the abuser or the nonprotecting parent need not be done in person. In therapy, survivors are often encouraged to write letters in which they express their feelings about the abuse. These letters may or may not be sent but do provide a forum for the cathartic release of emotion. Other techniques may also provide the chance to confront without facing the other person. An empty chair designated to be the abuser, for example, allows the survivor to tell that person how he or she felt and what the effects of the abuse were.

Confrontations such as these may allow the survivor to go forward in his or her therapy, once that unfinished business is taken care of.

Work With Partners and Children

Partners are often confused about the myriad of reactions they see in the survivor with whom they are involved. Husbands complain that something happens to their wives or lovers when they have sex.

ℭℛ ———————————————————

Gretchen and I were making love, and suddenly, she was screaming and crying and pushing me away from her. I was confused, hurt, angry, and had a whole range of emotions. What had I done? Even though I knew she had been abused as a child, it had never come up before. What had suddenly happened?

——————————————————— **ଦ୬**

Partners feel helpless to protect those they love from the emotions associated with having been abused (Engel, 1993). They may be threatened by the fact that survivors feel that they need therapy to sort out the relationship between their partners and themselves. Partners may want to know what has caused the survivor's distress, yet not want to know the details of the abuse. Involving a partner in therapy to some extent may help him or her provide support for the survivor as she or he heals.

Children of survivors may also have difficulty understanding what their survivor parent is experiencing. Survivors worry about their own children's victimization and may be particularly overprotective in certain situations or at certain times in their lives. The children too may benefit from consultation with the survivor's therapist.

Surviving child sexual abuse is not always an easy task, not only as a child getting through the abusive situations but as an adult dealing with the aftereffects of that abuse. Healing does not take place overnight—a fact that can be difficult for the individual who just wishes he or she could put it in the past and move on. But survivors have shown that healing is possible.

Summary

Surviving child sexual abuse may leave scars that are difficult to heal, especially if the abuser was someone the victim trusted. Betrayal intensifies trauma. Trauma is also impacted by such factors as the age of the victim, the identity of the abuser, the degree of force, the child's role in the family, and the reactions of those who first learn of the abuse.

Some survivors repress the memories of their abuse. These memories may reemerge as a result of pressures in adulthood, when the survivor feels safe, in the face of loss, and sometimes just triggered by the normal events of living.

The false memory syndrome was coined to describe the belief of some theorists that abuse reports can be influenced by the suggestion of therapists. The False Memory Syndrome Foundation was created by Pamela and Peter Freyd after their adult daughter accused her father of having sexually abused her as a child. Much controversy has surrounded the concept of false memories.

The residual effects of child sexual abuse can be divided into several categories: post-traumatic stress and the impairment of functioning; issues around self-esteem and achievement; physical, medical, or sexual problems; and problems with relationships. Post-traumatic stress resulting from trauma causes symptoms in three areas. Survivors may reexperience the trauma, feeling out of control, fearful, and even dissociating. They may want to avoid the traumatic memories by suppressing them and avoiding contact with others. Or the survivor may experience hyperarousal feeling constantly watchful for danger, which often interrupts sleep and daytime activities. Survivors may also experience problems with learning; have a poor self-concept; struggle with physical, medical, or psychiatric problems; and have difficulty forging relationships.

Treatment for adult survivors takes many forms. Crisis intervention is for acute stress, whereas many survivors will eventually seek out long-term therapy to fully understand their issues. Cognitive-behavioral therapy is also used effectively with survivors to help them to cope with everyday life. Expressive therapies such as writing, art, and dance movement have all had significant success as treatment methods. Therapy may be individual or in a group depending upon the needs of the survivor.

Review Questions

1. What is meant by repression?

2. How and why might memories of sexual abuse emerge to be addressed?

3. Explain the false memory controversy.

4. Cite some of the residual effects that plague survivors of child sexual abuse.

5. What are the symptoms of post-traumatic stress?

6. What physical, medical, and sexual effects might there be for survivors?

7. What are some considerations when survivors are beginning treatment?

8. What are the types of therapeutic intervention for survivors?

9. What are the advantages of group or individual treatment?

10. What are some advantages and disadvantages in survivors confronting offenders?

CHAPTER 16

Working With Child Sexual Abuse

ભ્ટિ૭

I thought that I was a pretty well put-together person until I got transferred to the sex abuse unit of the child protection agency where I worked. I had no idea how that work would affect me emotionally. I sought out some training at a program specializing in sex abuse and even went into therapy for a time to sort out my own issues. But in the end, I found that I really enjoyed the work. When I got my masters in social work, I specialized in child sex abuse, which meant that I had to tailor my program to meet those needs. Now, I treat sex offenders in a private practice with several other clinicians. Every day presents a new challenge, but I enjoy what I do. My best advice to anyone wanting to work in this field is to go into it with your eyes wide open, get your training, seek an advanced degree, get a handle on your own "tapes" from the past, and bolster your support system so that—after a day of dealing with sex offenders and their victims—you can go home and just chill. Do all that, and the work is really rewarding.

ભ્ટિ૭

THE INDIVIDUAL PERSPECTIVE

As this clinician recommends, one must consider carefully and prepare one's self for working with child sexual abuse. The nature of the work will bring up a variety of issues, both personal and professional, and it is important to be prepared.

Preparing for the Work

Preparing to work with child sexual abuse requires some soul searching. There are several important areas that a therapist should assess before working in the area of sexual abuse. These may be areas in which you decided that you need more work, but that too is an important realization. Assessing the following five initial interconnected areas is a place to start:

- What is your comfort in talking about sex?
- How comfortable are you with your own sexuality?
- How have you accomplished differentiation from your own family of origin?

- How secure are you in your own sense of autonomy?
- How comfortable are you with your own vulnerability?

Let us consider these in more detail.

Comfort With Talking About Sex and Your Own Sexuality

It may sound rather basic to suggest that someone wanting to go into work with sexually abused children and families must be able to talk about sex.

CR _____

I once conducted a role-play in a class where I was teaching on child sexual abuse. The class members were to simulate a situation in which a child reports to her guidance counselor that she has been sexually abused. Those playing the roles of social workers then intervene and were supposed to interview the child and the parents including the father-offender. These students were already working in the field, and this was a course to fine-tune their skills. What I found interesting was that during the entire role-play, no one ever mentioned the word sex or used any sexually explicit term for any behavior or part of the body. When I pointed this out, the class members were surprised at themselves. Some suggested that it was embarrassing, whereas others just assumed that everyone was on the same page and knew what they were talking about. **SO**

_____

The reality is that you cannot be hesitant to talk about sex when working with clients in the area of sexual abuse. That is what you are doing—investigating or treating a sexual crime. How could a physician give you a diagnosis or treat you if he or she never mentioned a part of your body to you? In addition, children, families, and offenders are often uncomfortable talking about sex. If you do not mention it, they take that as a cue that generalizations are fine with you. You cannot assume that you know what your clients are talking about. You must ask using correct terminology:

CR _____

When I first started in the sex abuse unit, I shadowed another worker who had been at the job for a while. She was a pro and told everything like it was. We were interviewing an offender who was talking circles of denial around what he had done to his little girl. Finally my colleague just said to him, "Okay, where were you when you put your penis in your daughter's mouth?" I couldn't believe it, but the guy's face turned red. Like he'd done it, but he couldn't talk about it. But he started to cry and admitted what he'd done. And he started using the correct terms too. It was like my colleague just gave him permission. **SO**

_____

Not only is it necessary to determine what actually happened but also the use of proper sexual terms gives permission to reluctant clients to give you more accurate information and may relieve their own embarrassment.

In addition, children often do not know appropriate anatomical or sexual terms. It may be necessary for you to provide them in order to investigate or treat them. When the child talks about her "pookie" and you assume that she refers to her vagina, you need to be comfortable in asking her that. Your discomfort will be quickly picked up by the child who may then not want to tell you anything.

Becoming more comfortable talking about sex may necessitate taking a course in human sexuality or discussing this with a partner or counselor.

Why does it matter whether you are comfortable with your own sexuality? Once again, your lack of comfort with your own sexual life style and experiences will readily be picked up by clients. And any discomfort that you might have with your own sexuality will make it more difficult for you to listen to some of the details that will face you everyday as you do this work. Comfort with yourself as a sexual being, comfort with sexual partners, and the ability to talk about your sexual needs with your partner will better prepare you to understand and process what you learn about clients.

Differentiation for Your Family of Origin

Differentiation is a term coined by family therapist Murray Bowen to refer to the manner in which an individual is able to differentiate himself or herself from the family that raised him or her so that he or she is an emotionally separate person—able to think, feel, and act as an individual. As an adult, you may be thinking that you are certainly able to function independently from your family. And yet, when you make a decision, do you hear the voice of your mother or father telling you what you should do? Do you feel guilty if you do not listen to that voice and act accordingly? If this is the case, you may need a bit more work on separating yourself from the influences of the past.

Differentiation of self is also related to the extent to which that person is able to distinguish between the intellectual process and the feeling process (emotions) he or she is experiencing. The question arises, "Who is running my life and what I do, my emotions or my brain?" Emotions often stem from the past and can be based on attitudes that individuals have learned in the past. Not sorting these emotions out may make one more susceptible to countertransference issues with sexually abusive clients. If a dysfunctional and abusive family, for example, stimulates unresolved memories of your own family, it may be difficult for you to work with the client daily effectively.

"I'm fine," said one worker in a sex abuse unit. "My family was nuts, but I cut them off totally and don't have anything to do with them." In fact, this individual had not even begun to process her own need to differentiate from the dysfunction of her family. Again and again she found that client issues stimulated old feelings related to her family to the degree that they interfered with her work. She finally had to find a job that did not force her to relive her unresolved family issues.

Separating from the family of origin while still maintaining healthy adult-to-adult relationships with mother, father, and siblings is not always easy and may require work over time, but it is essential to working with abusive families. In addition, studies have shown that differentiation of self is an important task for overall psychological well-being (Mandell, 2008; Murdock & Gore, 2004; Skowron, Stanley, & Shapiro, 2009).

Autonomy and Vulnerability

Comfort with your own autonomy and vulnerability are related. Autonomy in turn is related somewhat to how well you have come to terms with your past. Can you act independently without feeling guilty or second-guessing yourself? As one worker explained,

ℭ

Protective services work and especially sexual abusive situations really test your sense of autonomy. Sure, I have supervision, but when I am out in the field, there will be times when I need to make decisions that have to be made then and there. It took me awhile to learn to develop the independence to make these decisions and to trust that my training and experience would guide me. Then I had to take responsibility for the decisions that I had made. ℬ

Along with the need for autonomy comes the need to be comfortable with your own vulnerability. You may not always make right decisions. Sex offenders especially will love to trip you up. Remember that they are often intent upon taking control in any way they can. Making the worker feel foolish is one thing they may try. If you too are worried about maintaining a power position, you may sacrifice honesty and integrity to keep the power. Sex offenders, in their own feelings of powerlessness, seek to steal power from others. A social worker's power must come from within himself or herself rather than getting into a power struggle with a client. One worker commented,

ℭ

I learned a great deal from my first supervisor. I think I was kind of cocky when I came into her unit, but she didn't call me on it right away. Then I was working with this one offender who had more power issues than I did. During supervision one day, my supervisor and I were talking about a decision I had made in the case. She pointed out to me that I had made the decision to prove to the offender that I had more power. And the decision was not a good one. My first reaction was to get really defensive, and then I realized that she was right. I didn't have to prove I had power. The reality was that I did by virtue of the fact that this offender had committed a crime and I was investigating. I also had to admit that I had made a mistake and to find another way to work with him. It taught me quite a lesson.

ॐ

Mandell (2008) cautions the social worker to be aware of how he or she uses power in the client-worker relationship. Abuse places victims, families, and even perpetrators in positions where they feel vulnerable. The worker must assess his or her own vulnerability and not use his or her position of power in a negative manner.

Even though you may find yourself still working on some of these issues, you will find that the more you master them, the less likely you will be to be sabotaged by your own countertransference issues.

Countertransference in Work With Sexual Abuse

Transference and countertransference may be part of any therapy relationship. Transference describes the feelings from the client's past or present life that he or she displaces onto the therapist. Countertransference refers to the therapist displacing his or her own emotions onto the client, usually denoting emotional entanglement with the client (Courtois, 2010; Flora et al., 2008). Gartner (2001) suggested the following definition for countertransference: "all feelings and reactions to the patient, unconscious or conscious, enacted or not, reality- or fantasy-based, that originate and

are located in the therapist" (p. 234). Pearlman and Saakvitne (1995) define countertransference simply as *the therapist's own feelings about his or her own feelings or reactions* (Courtois, 2010).

Early work on countertransference identified three categories: *avoidance, attraction,* and *attack* (Courtois, 2010; Renshaw, 1982). *Avoidance* describes the therapist's desire to get away from the feelings or not see them as they really are. The therapist may be feeling dread, anxiety, anger, repugnance, or horror in light of what the client has described or done (Friedrich & Leiper, 2006). For example, Hannah, a therapist working with sexual offenders, describes,

ॐ

I was never sexually abused as a child and wonder if I could work with offenders if I had been. My father was an alcoholic but also a high school principal and kept his alcoholism pretty secret. We saw it on weekends, but I am not sure anyone outside the family knew.

One of the clients I had been treating for several months in a sex offender group had finally given up his denial and admitted that he actually did commit the sexual abuse. I felt that he was making real progress and was encouraged. Then he began talking about the fact that he had been drinking during the abuse. This never came up before. And he talked about how he would make his daughter wait on him, including bringing him a drink when he wanted one. He liked his drinks mixed a certain way, and he had taught his daughter how to mix them the way he liked. He went into great detail about this. And suddenly I began to perspire and feel uneasy. I was actually beginning to feel angry with this client. What was going on? At the same time, I felt overwhelmed by my anger and could not wait for the session to end.

Later, as my coleader and I talked about the group, he remarked about how my affect had changed toward this client. I began to have a glimmer of a memory that I took to my own therapy that week. I finally remembered that my father used to do that with me—have me make his drinks—until there was a terrible scene with my mother. She accused me of contributing to his drinking by enabling him in that manner. I began to realize that I had begun to take the blame emotionally for all that had happened to our family from then—the fights, my parent's divorce—all of it. My anger at my father for my feelings had surfaced when I heard my client talk about behaving in a similar manner as Dad did.

&

Not every feeling or memory is so deeply repressed as this therapist's was.

Attraction is about moving toward the client, feeling attracted or even aroused (Courtois, 2010; Mintzer, 1996). Offenders especially can be very engaging and often try to play on the therapist's susceptibility.

&

Gayle was a young and somewhat naïve intern who was doing her field work in a prison setting. She was offered an opportunity to sit in on an offender's therapy group. Max was a handsome older man who had sexually abused teen girls. It became obvious to two experienced therapists that Max had targeted Gayle and put on the charm. The group recognized it too and called him on it. Gayle was obviously embarrassed by the group's forthright comments about what was happening.

As the therapists and Gayle talked about the group meeting afterward, Gayle commented, "Max is such a sweet guy and so misunderstood. The other men gave him such a hard time. He was just trying to be nice to me." It was clear that Gayle's attraction to this sex offender could easily hamper any work that she might do with him unless she began to recognize what had happened.

&

Those who work with juvenile offenders often find themselves doubting that this child or youth could be as "bad" as described. This may cause them to treat the offender more like a victim while missing the importance of holding him or her accountable (Mintzer, 1996).

Attack is motivated by anger or disapproval of what has been said or done by the client. It is the therapist's aggression coming to the surface. Hannah, mentioned in the first scenario, felt angry with the sexual offender. Instead of wanting to avoid that anger, she may have become hostile to him and/or said something to convey her anger and condemnation. Such a response is more about the therapist than about the client.

Courtois (2010) points out that when working with incest, there are several areas in which therapists may experience countertransference issues. She outlines these as being *dread and horror, denial and avoidance, shame, pit, and disgust, guilt, rage and anger, and grief and mourning.*

Sexual abuse is difficult to hear about. The idea of a child being manipulated, coerced, or forced to have sex with an adult can foster feelings of *horror and dread* in the therapist who hears from the victim or perpetrators what has been done. Investigation and later therapy necessitates the recounting of details that may be upsetting and overwhelming. The fact that one family member could sexually use another or that a child is betrayed by someone he or she trusted is disturbing (Courtois, 2010; Flora, 2001). One result of these feelings may be that the worker or therapist has difficulty engaging with the client (Friedrich & Leiper, 2006). Those working with sexual abuse must be constantly monitoring their own feelings and be aware of the effects that hearing details can have on them. Having some type of support on the job to discuss their feelings is also important. Supervision often provides this processing.

Denial and avoidance are natural reactions when faced with material that is so far out of the frame of reference of most of us. It is also easy to believe adults who can tell clear stories that therapists understand rather than children who may not know the appropriate words and whose innocence can lend itself to disbelief. Offenders too can be very convincing in their denial, making the worker or therapist want to believe that nothing happened. It is natural to want to deny rather than accept that some of the disturbing details have actually happened. Some sexual abuse can be bizarre, violent, gruesome, and sadistic, and it would be easier to avoid the reality than to work with those involved. Courtois (2010) recommends to therapists working with incest survivors that they must "absolutely accept that incest can and does take place and that children are quite routinely used and exploited by their adult caretakers, including parents" (p. 449). Recognition that abuse does happen and is often difficult to hear about helps those working with it to prepare themselves.

Shame, pity, and disgust are other reactions that plague social workers and therapists in the field of sexual abuse.

"I felt tainted just listening to what my client did to that child sexually," reported one therapist. Other workers describe feeling pity for victims or family members or even for offenders. But pity does not help but rather can disempower clients when they are attempting to deal with recovery. Some workers recount that they feel disgust toward anyone who could abuse a child. Although the act may be reprehensible, there is still a person in need of help behind that act, an individual who does not benefit from the worker's feelings of disgust.

Guilt takes several forms for social workers and therapists. First, the social worker or therapist who grew up in a relatively stable family and had a happy childhood may feel guilty for that in the face of what he or she hears of the client's experiences. Guilt can prompt helpers to try to rescue clients and imply to them that they are fragile and helpless (Courtois, 2010). Clients need empowerment rather than rescue.

Guilt might be aroused when the worker feels helpless to undo what has happened to the client. One worker commented,

ᑭ ————————————————————
I kept imagining the horror that this little boy had gone through—being brutally sodomized—and I just wanted to hold him and tell him that everything would be okay. But I knew that it wouldn't be. He still had to face court and possibly foster

care, and the magic wand that I wanted to wave for him was just my fantasy. ᔐ

Guilt might also be a result of feeling "out of one's league," as one therapist explained.

ᑭ ————————————————————
I had never worked with anyone who had had such a horrendous abuse history. There was so much trauma. From sadistic abuse at the hands of his father and uncle and brothers to the abuse that he suffered when he was befriended by a parish priest. I wondered if I had the skills to help this boy and felt guilty that maybe I did not. ᔐ

Feelings of helplessness and reactions to what has been done can give rise to anger in helpers and even rage.

ᑭ ————————————————————
"The whole family angered me," recounted one helper. "I was filled with rage at what the perpetrator had done to his stepdaughter but almost angrier at the mother who stayed with him when she learned what was going on. But what surprised me the most about my reaction to this family was my anger at the victim. She kept going back for more. We placed her in foster care and she ran home, knowing that the stepfather still lived there. Intellectually I knew that she was crying for love and approval and that her home was all that she knew. But it was tough for me to understand. I knew that I had to deal with my own emotional reactions before I could be of any help to the family." ᔐ

Some workers and therapists report feeling *grief and mourning* over what has happened to a child.

ᑭ ————————————————————
"It made me so sad," said one worker, "hearing about what that little girl had to go through. It wasn't her fault that some guy had abducted and sexually abused her. And yet her parents made her feel like it was her fault because she was at the

playground. They told her she could go! And it really got to me that this had changed her whole life. I had known her before the abuse, and I found myself grieving over who she had been and what happened to her."

———————————————— ᔕᑎ

There are other reactions experienced by those working with sexual abuse. Being bombarded constantly with details of sexual abuse can make them feel that there is sexual abuse everywhere.

ᶜᴿ ————————————————

When I first started working as a social worker in the sex abuse unit, I found myself looking at every man on the street and wondering if he was a perpetrator and every child being fearful that he or she was being sexually abused. I shared my fantasies with my husband. He listened for a while and then said, "Enough! I can't stand it when you do it." It made me really think. Why was I doing that?

———————————————— ᔕᑎ

Another common reaction is often referred to as *contact victimization* (Courtois, 2010). Therapists who work closely with sexual abuse, hearing details over and over, may begin to feel victimized, and—if not dealt with—these feelings of victimization can actually lead to post-traumatic stress disorder (PTSD), which involves a variety of reactions including hypervigilance, startle responses, anxiety, nightmares, and so on.

Finally, Courtois (2010) suggests that those hearing the details of sexual abuse multiple times may experience what she refers to as *privileged voyeurism* or "an attraction to or inquisitiveness" about the abuse (p. 456). Survivors who are faced with this type of worker or therapist reaction begin to feel dehumanized and as if they are cases rather than unique individuals. Although it is the responsibility of the professional investigating or treating child sexual abuse to learn the details of the abuse, the reality is that the person being interviewed or treated is a unique individual independent of the sexual aspects of his or her experience and needs to be treated as such.

Those working with sexual abuse must be constantly monitoring his or her own counter-transference issues as these can contaminate the therapeutic relationship.

Vicarious Traumatization

One possible hazard of working with child sexual abuse on a regular basis is *vicarious traumatization*, a term coined by McCann and Pearlman (1990) when describing the trauma to therapists as a result of this exposure. This term was expanded to include others dealing with trauma, especially frontline social workers (Pryce, Shackelford, & Pryce, 2007). Although anyone working with traumatized clients might be at risk for vicarious traumatization, the most susceptible are (adapted from Courtois, 2010, pp. 361–362)

- those who treat large numbers of trauma clients, especially without sufficient professional supports, a knowledge base, or opportunities to practice self-care;
- those exposed to especially graphic stories of abuse;
- those with their own personal history that is unresolved;
- those experiencing other major life or mental health stressors, especially with a limited support system;
- those whose organizational or cultural socialization dictates that they "keep things to themselves";
- those who are not able to or choose not to use appropriate supervision;
- inexperienced workers who have not been sufficiently prepared for the work; and
- helpers or therapists who do not have an opportunity to debrief.

The symptoms of vicarious trauma parallel those of directly experienced trauma, including, but not limited to, nightmares or sleep disturbances, anxiety, withdrawal, cynicism, somatic symptoms, intrusive images, sexual difficulties, and irritability (Chouliara, Hutchinson, &

Karatzias, 2009; Courtois, 2010; Figley, 1995; McCann & Pearlman, 1990; Moulden & Firetsone, 2007; Pryce et al., 2007). Those with vicarious trauma find that relationships suffer, life can feel hopeless, and they often shut down emotionally. Unlike countertransference, which can provide therapists with important information about their clients and the relationship, vicarious trauma is about worker/therapist overload and burnout. The professional's effectiveness suffers, and clients can be impacted.

Guarding against and combating vicarious traumatization is both an individual and an agency responsibility. First, those working with sexual abuse issues should be well trained, not only in the dynamics of abuse but also in the impact that dealing with these cases has on social workers and therapists. Training should use case examples and give opportunities for new workers/therapists to react to and process what they are hearing (Courtois, 2010; Sommer, 2008). This training is especially difficult for therapists who go into private practice and choose to work with sexual abuse cases. Thus, such sensitivity training is often required at the graduate or even undergraduate college level.

Beyond careful training, skillful supervision is vital. Preparation should continue through supervision on a case-to-case basis with an opportunity to debrief after working with clients. Supervisors should be aware of countertransference issues, boundary violations, overidentification, and indications that their supervisees are overwhelmed by the material (Sommer, 2008). Any worker or therapist who is not receiving adequate supervision has a right to request it or to request a change in supervisors.

And finally, good self-care is vital for those working with sexual abuse cases. Special care should be taken to develop a healthy personal support system and participate in activities that bring relaxation and personal pleasure. Working with sexual abuse should not impact the worker's own life negatively, or he or she cannot effectively deal with clients.

WORKING WITHIN AN AGENCY

Child protection, and especially work with child sexual abuse, can be challenging and draining. Being successful and maintaining your mental health require good support and supervision within an agency that respects the difficult work that you must do. Unfortunately, even though the general public wants to know that children are protected, those who strive to do this are not always valued as professionals. And especially if you work with sexual offenders, you may not feel as though your work is respected. As a result, your support often comes from inside the agency and from colleagues from agencies doing similar work.

Agency support begins at the point that you are hired. Adequate training is the token of respect that agencies give those who are about to do the difficult tasks required by child protection. Training should be formal, both classroom (cognitive) and practice oriented (experiential and affective), and take place before you even see a client. Years ago, agencies used to do a "trial-by-fire" type of training that put the worker out into the field, and then through supervision, the worker was supposed to learn the job. Hopefully, there is no agency that currently uses this as training as it can be intimidating to the new worker and may not be beneficial for clients.

Ideally, after training, when you will be given the knowledge and skills to at least begin your job, you will be allowed to shadow another social worker. Some agencies, especially for safety reasons, favor a partner approach in which you go out on cases with another, hopefully more experienced worker. Having an opportunity to accompany a variety of different workers will also give you an idea of different styles as you begin to develop your own.

If you work in a public child protection office, you can expect that your physical environment may not be the most inviting. Typically social workers are clustered in units, and workers may all be housed within one large unit area. Ringing phones, simultaneous conversations, and confusion are the norm. You get used to it, but anyone who approaches such a work environment might initially wonder how anything gets done. The up side of such an environment is the support that can be found in a well-functioning unit.

ॡ —————

I had just gotten off the phone about a particularly difficult case. The father whom we suspected of sexually abusing his daughter was well connected. I had just been talking to a congressman who had called me on the father's behalf insisting that there was no way the father could have abused his daughter. I had been yelled at, threatened, and belittled, and after the rest of the day that I had, I was totally frazzled. After I hung up, I just sat there, trying to pull myself together.

"Rough call?" I heard the soothing, concerned voice of my colleague Jane from the next desk.

"Unbelievable!" I responded. I shared with her some of what had transpired and felt considerably better, especially after she told me of a call she had once had from the mayor. As much as I complained sometimes about the openness of our office area, I was thankful that someone had been there to cheer me up! ॷ

The availability of emotional support is crucial in a job that taxes one's emotions to the degree that child protection can. Munro (2008) comments that the "emotional dimension of practice is as crucial as the cognitive. An agency's failure to provide a work environment that offers good emotional support is most dramatically illustrated in worker burnout" (p. 135).

Another tool that the agency provides is supervision. Many agencies now use supervisors not only to process case material with their workers, teach them, and keep documentation but also to help them make decisions.

ॡ —————

Any decisions that had to be made on a particular case were supposed to be run by the supervisor. At first, I wondered if they didn't think I would know enough to make a decision, but then I realized that it was not only for the client's benefit but for mine. The decisions that we make in child protection are pretty serious ones. Should I remove a child from a home where there is abuse? Sure, the child needs to be protected, but these decisions are not easy ones. Perhaps there are other alternatives that I could consider. I learned to depend on my supervisor's input, confident that I wasn't the only one making the decision that would affect these clients' lives so dramatically. ॷ

Good supervision, as mentioned earlier, is the right of every social worker. The role of the supervisor is, in general (although agencies may differ), to (Munro, 2008)

- provide training,
- oversee correct procedure,
- process cases with the social worker,
- provide support,
- help worker monitor and process counter-transference, and
- aid the worker in building his or her personal strengths and overcoming challenges.

Supervisors should be trained and should continue to have ongoing training as needed.

Probably one of the most difficult aspects of working within an agency is that it is a bureaucracy, and bureaucracies can be cumbersome. Sometimes what workers think is best for clients seemingly cannot be accomplished within an agency setting. Nonetheless, it is important clients are better served when their worker finds creative ways to work within the system. Pitting them against the system does not benefit them or you as an employee of that system.

Whether you are employed by an agency or in private practice, working with child sexual abuse presents significant challenges. At the same time, the work can be most rewarding.

Summary

Preparing to work with child sexual abuse requires some soul searching. Have you developed comfort in talking about sex, with your own sexuality, and in your own relationship with your family of origin? And have you developed a healthy sense of autonomy that allows you to accept your own vulnerability? Maturity in these areas will help you with the inevitable countertransference issues that arise in working with clients.

Countertransference has to do with your own feelings or reactions toward your clients, and sometimes these feelings get in the way of working with clients. Such issues as attraction, anger, horror, avoidance, shame, disgust, guilt, and grief can color the way in which you interact with the victims, perpetrators, and families that you see.

Those who work regularly with traumatized people may begin to take on some of their symptoms. This is referred to as vicarious traumatization. Monitoring your own feelings, plus accessing good supervision, is vital to avoiding these feelings and preventing burnout.

Working within an agency can have its advantages and disadvantages. On one hand, there is support from coworkers and the availability of supervision. On the other hand, working conditions may not be the best. Two important tools that the agency should offer you, however, are adequate training and effective supervision. These tools are important for a successful career in working with child sexual abuse cases.

Review Questions

1. What should one consider when preparing to work in the field of child sexual abuse?

2. What role might countertransference play in working with child sexual abuse?

3. What feelings might come up while working with child sexual abuse?

4. What is meant by *vicarious traumatization*?

5. How can an agency in which you work provide support to you?

6. What is the role of supervision?

7. Why is supervision important?

CHAPTER 17

Working Toward Prevention

Child abuse prevention has a relatively long history (see Daro, 2009), but organized efforts to prevent child sexual abuse have been more recent, possibly for several reasons. First, the recognition of sexual abuse and the subsequent intervention and treatment of this form of abuse came later than those for other types of maltreatment (see Chapter 1). Unlike the prevention efforts made in the areas of physical abuse and neglect that have sought to address family issues such as the parents' awareness of child rearing and community resources, the target population for sexual abuse became the child victims, necessitating the development of new types of intervention strategies (Daro, 1994, 2009; Wurtele & Kenny, 2012). One of the concerns was how much people wanted to talk to children about sex, especially considering that many adults have difficulty discussing sex. Prevention programs in sexual abuse were first developed to be presented in schools, as this seemed to be the most appropriate way to educate children about their need for self-protection.

PREVENTION OF CHILD AND ADOLESCENT SEXUAL ABUSE

Today, every agency seeking to intervene with and treat child sexual abuse is also concerned with its initial prevention. Child sexual abuse prevention has been targeted in three areas: empowering children, raising the consciousness of communities, and prevention with potential offenders (Daro, 2009; Finkelhor, 2009; Wurtele & Kenny, 2012).

Finkelhor (2009, p. 55, see also Smallbone, Marshall, & Wortley, 2008) suggests that the risk factors for sexual abuse are well documented by research. Risk factors for children to be abused are as follows:

- Girls outnumber boys as victims.
- Risk rises with age for girls, whereas risk peaks at puberty for boys.
- Other risk factors include
  - not living with both parents and
  - living in families where there are marital discord, alcoholism, divorce, and violence.

About 25% of victims who come to the attention of law enforcement or social services for sexual abuse are abused by family members, whereas 60% are abused by someone in their social network. Histories of sexual abuse are also associated with difficulties with psychological, social, and physical well-being for children (Finkelhor, 2009).

Looking at offenders, research indicates the following (Finkelhor, 2009; Smallbone et al., 2008):

- They are more likely to be male.
- Their age can range from adolescents to older adults.
- There are two life-stage peaks for the onset of offending: adolescence (when delinquent behavior rises) and during the 30s (when there is more access to children).
- About 33% of those who offend against juveniles are juveniles themselves.

Experts on offender behavior also caution that statistics are based on those offenders who were caught, arrested, and convicted, whereas numerous offenders, especially those who are female, have never come to the attention of social service, law enforcement, or criminal justice personnel.

Having this knowledge has enabled those in the field of child sexual abuse to develop strategies to hopefully prevent the problem. What are these prevention strategies, programs, and techniques that are being used now, and how effective are they? From a variety of sources, several categories of sexual abuse prevention have emerged: offender-centered (or potential offender-centered) prevention, victim-centered (or potential victim-centered) prevention, situational prevention, and community awareness and prevention (Bowman, Scotti, & Morris, 2010; Daro, 1994, 2009; Finkelhor, 2007, 2009; Renk, Baksh, Donnelly, & Roddenbery, 2008; Saul & Audage, 2007; Smallbone et al., 2008; Waldfogel, 2009; Wurtele & Kenny, 2012).

Offender-Centered (or Potential Offender-Centered) Prevention

Offender-specific prevention is designed to keep individuals who might sexually abuse from doing so in the first place. Even if an offender abuses once, it is paramount that he or she is prevented from committing additional offenses.

Smallbone et al. (2008) suggest that there are three offender-specific prevention approaches designed to deter abuse. These authors group prevention into the categories of developmental prevention, criminal justice interventions, and treatment approaches.

Developmental Prevention and Offenders

Developmental prevention involves reducing the risk of those who might abuse a child sexually. Smallbone et al. (2008) suggest that

> [o]ne way to achieve this goal is to prevent the emergence, over the course of individual social cognitive development, of dispositions or vulnerabilities associated with CSA [child sexual abuse] offending. This approach, known as developmental prevention, involves systematic efforts to reduce the number of individuals exposed to adverse developmental circumstances, to reduce the negative impact for those who have been exposed to adverse circumstances, and to strengthen protective factors associated with responsible social and sexual conduct. (p. 65)

By looking at some of the backgrounds and characteristics of convicted offenders, it is possible to pinpoint the developmental challenges that may have led to sexual offending and to address these challenges. Programs that specialize in home visiting, early intervention, and preparation for school, such as Head Start, strive to address parental incapacity and deficits such as abuse and neglect, harsh discipline, insufficient knowledge of child rearing, and broader issues such as isolation, family dysfunction, and poverty. Many of these social issues have been found in the early lives of offenders. Other early intervention programs target the reduction of antisocial behaviors. Research has reported that families and children able to access such programs have benefited from these interventions (Smallbone et al., 2008).

Literature addressing the characteristics of offenders also indicates that men offend when they feel out of control, powerless, or helpless, in an attempt to achieve some degree of control over their circumstances. Often this seeming lack of control leads to and/or is created by a diminished self-concept. Thus, programs designed to enhance self-esteem in children and youth and to promote self-reliance and a sense of personal control can also impact appropriate sexual relationships and behavior.

A wide array of evidence also points to the coexistence of delinquent behavior with sexual offending in young offenders. Because sexual offending is both an antisocial and criminal behavior, programs that address and diminish delinquency can be beneficial (Hunter, Becker, & Lexier, 2006; Johansson-Love & Fremouw, 2009; Smallbone et al., 2008).

In addition to delinquency prevention, healthy sexual education is vital to inhibit offending behavior. DeLamater and Friedrich (2002) created a model of sexual development that is apropos to this discussion. These authors believe that sexual development is a life-long process that influences and shapes the individual relationship and ability to achieve sexual intimacy. According to their model, healthy sexual maturity has been achieved when an individual (a) has established a stable gender identity, (b) has established a healthy sexual identity, (c) can manage physical and emotional intimacy, (d) has established a healthy sexual lifestyle, and (e) can achieve sexual satisfaction. Because sexual offenders have not achieved sexual maturity and may offend in part as a way of compensating for this lacking, programs that promote sexual maturity can be seen as one method of developmental prevention.

Faulty attachment is another characteristic that is often identified in sexual offenders. The degree to which an individual has been able to bond with primary caretakers influences his or her later life in so many ways, especially in relationships including sexual development and intimacy. In addition, early attachment influences the individual's ability to develop self-restraint, emotional self-regulation, and empathy, qualities that must often be developed in sexual offender treatment. Early intervention, mentioned earlier, strives to promote healthy attachment between children and caregivers.

The transition to school and early school experiences may also influence an individual's attitudes toward others and toward himself or herself. Being isolated or scapegoated by peers or failure in the school setting can breed feelings of helplessness, poor self-esteem, and delinquent behaviors (Smallbone et. al., 2008). Thus, school-based programs that promote school adjustment and prevent delinquency can also impact future sexual offending.

And finally, Smallbone et al. (2008) suggest that sexual offenders who are often unprepared for parenthood and burdened with other personal deficits may turn to sexual abuse. Men and women with a history of insecure attachment may have trouble with intimate peer relationships, making them feel powerless and isolated. Thus, these authors suggest that efforts to assist men especially in developing secure intimate attachment with their partners may lead to improved attachment and reduce the risk of inappropriate sexual behaviors.

Through looking at the challenges to healthy development in sexual offenders, researchers can gain insight into how to prevent future offenders through developmental intervention.

Criminal Justice Interventions

Criminal justice interventions are used to prevent sexual abuse from being perpetrated again by the same offender. If, in fact, more than a third of offenders are juveniles themselves (Finkelhor, 2009), a quick response followed by appropriate intervention may well prevent further abuse by an offender. Increasing emphasis on juvenile offender programs attests to the recognition that intervention at a young age has positive results.

Finkelhor (2009) points out that even adult offenders are not as likely to reoffend, especially with adequate intervention, as the general public supposes. In fact, sexual offenders' rate of recidivism is significantly lower than that of other types of offenders. Child molesters are more likely to be educated and employed than other types of criminals, which some believe reduces the rate of recidivism.

Several different programs have been instituted over the last few years in an attempt to decrease recidivism among sexual offenders. The first of these is *offender registration*, in which a sexual offender is required to register with the state in which he or she resides. All states now keep these records on an electronic sex offender registry. The intent of this program is to promote visibility, to deter future offending, and to make apprehension easier if an offense does occur (Finkelhor, 2009; Flora, 2001; Seto, 2008).

Critics of sex offender registries argue that they hamper an offender's ability to function in the community through difficulty finding jobs, employment, and public stigma. Possibly for these reasons and others, some offenders do not register (Duwe & Donnay, 2008; Vasquez, Maddan, & Walker, 2008). Because controversy over the efficacy of offender registration continues (see Chapter 14), some experts believe that registration must be more carefully analyzed to determine if it is worthwhile (Finkelhor, 2009).

Community notification is often grouped with offender registration but is in fact a separate issue. Initially, registries were developed for law enforcement, and it was only later that policies were enacted that enabled the communities to know if there were offenders within them. In some states, law enforcement goes door to door, makes calls, or produces flyers, alerting citizens of the proximity of sexual offenders, whereas in others, the information is merely available to any citizen who asks for it. To date, there is no clear evidence as to whether or not community notification actually reduces recidivism (Finkelhor, 2009).

Because offenders must gain access to their victims, it is not uncommon for them to seek out employment or volunteer opportunities with children. For this reason, *mandatory background checks* were instituted and available to organizations wishing to use them. Criminal prosecution is recorded by states, and a record of an individual's criminal record is available to organizations like schools and youth agencies upon request (Saul & Audage, 2007). Critics of this program say that an individual may be an offender but not be criminally charged and therefore would not have a record. In addition, a negative background check may prohibit someone from being employed, despite the fact that the offense was not sexual and would pose no danger to children (Finkelhor, 2009). Although background checks are widely used by a variety of agencies and organizations, no thorough research has been done to help employers and others receiving the reports determine how to use the results (Finkelhor, 2009).

Fearful of having an offender close to schools, day care centers, and other places where children frequent, many states have now enacted ordinances restricting where offenders can live (call *residency restrictions* and sometimes referred to as Jessica's laws). Numerous states now have such restrictions. Critics of these laws argue that not only is it more difficult for offenders to find housing but the fact that they may be forced to be transient increases the likelihood of their reoffending. Some have insisted that not only do these laws unduly restrict offenders but they might also be seen as unconstitutional (Agudo, 2008), whereas the proponents of such laws believe that they are necessary to protect children. Finklehor (2009) suggests that the rationale for these laws is flawed given that most sexual abuse occurs within the family or social circle and not at the hands of strangers. He feels the need for revaluation of such statutes.

Other efforts have been made to decrease recidivism. Some states have developed policies to *lengthen sentences* for offenders and require that they serve a minimum amount of time. There has also been a movement on the part of some states to institute *civil commitment*—that is, holding offenders after they have completed their criminal time if they are deemed to be sexually dangerous. Although they may make the community feel better, it is unclear whether these steps work to reduce recidivism (Finkelhor, 2009; Seto, 2008).

There has been pressure on law enforcement by the public to more speedily *investigate and arrest* offenders who are deemed to be a danger to children sexually. No research currently exists on whether this is effective (Finkelhor, 2009; Smallbone et al., 2008). At the same time, some people have applauded the use of *mental health treatment* for offenders rather than just incarceration. Most of the studies of offender treatment outcomes have indicated that treatment does lower the recidivism rate for sexual offending (Finkelhor, 2009; Flora, 2001; Flora et al., 2008; Seto, 2008).

Although criminal justice strategies are especially popular today, Finkelhor (2009) suggests that enormous energy goes into the management of sexual offenders through these means. And yet there is little empirical research that favors one strategy over another. He believes that the justice system should concentrate on the highest risk offenders and develop tools to differentiate between high- and low-risk offenders.

Victim-Centered (or Potential Victim-Centered) Prevention

One of the earliest initiatives to prevent sexual abuse was to train or empower children to both recognize and resist such abuse (Daro, 2009; Wurtele & Kenny, 2012). The programs that evolved were designed to raise the consciousness of potential victims (primary prevention) and also to alert current victims to the fact that reporting would get them help. Raising consciousness involved helping children to identify

dangerous situations—that is, being touched inappropriately or other ways that offenders might try to engage them—and to refuse or interrupt the offender's attempts. In addition, children were instructed in how to seek help. These programs (e.g., Personal Safety Curriculum, Talking About Touching, the Child Sexual Assault Program) were taught in school settings, kindergarten through grade 12, by trained professionals or by the regular classroom teacher who had been specially trained in the program material.

What was another hoped-for additional benefit was that—in the atmosphere of openness and encouragement promoted by the classroom prevention presentations—children who were being abused were encouraged to report the abuse to trusted adults. The curricula also placed emphasis on helping those children who were already exposed to abuse not to feel at fault (Finkelhor, 2009; Smallbone et al., 2008; Wurtele & Kenny, 2012). Programs are geared to different age groups, and most are designed to be used throughout a child's school career, geared to the developmental level of the grade in which the child is being taught.

Although originally used in public school settings, these programs have been adapted by private and parochial schools, religious education programs, and youth-serving agencies. For example, after the child abuse scandal that rocked the Archdiocese of Boston, its newly formed Office for Child Advocacy, under the direction of Deacon Anthony Rizzuto, trained all of the schools and religious education departments of the many churches in the Archdiocese in abuse prevention (Crosson-Tower, 2014).

Widely used in the late 1980s and 1990s, these programs also had their critics. Parents worried that children would be exposed to sexual knowledge and language and that the concepts would be too complicated for children to learn. Still others argued that children could not be expected to nor should they have the responsibility for preventing abuse by foiling an offender's attempts. These critics suggested that being abused despite their efforts to prevent it might be of even more harm to children (Finkelhor, 2009).

These criticisms gave rise to numerous studies on the efficacy of personal safety prevention programs. It was concluded that children do in fact learn prevention concepts that are being taught. Interestingly enough, younger children learn them more effectively than their older peers (Davis & Gidycz, 2000; Finkelhor, 2007, 2009; Hebert & Tourigney, 2004). One study reported that children exposed to the classroom training programs were 7 times more likely to use protective behavior in simulated trials than children who had not had these programs (Zwi, 2007).

Addressing the concern that children would suffer from unintended consequences such as increased anxiety, researchers found that very few parents and teachers reported that children had adverse reactions. Nor were children hesitant to be touched or misinterpreted appropriate physical touching because of the programs. Children did learn appropriate terms for body parts, while the information presented to them did not appear to hamper their sexual development (Davis & Gidycz, 2000; Finkelhor, 2007, 2009; Hebert & Tourigney, 2004; Smallbone et al., 2008).

Another criticism was that children could not be successful in thwarting the attempts of a motivated sexual offender. And yet offenders come with all types of motivations and determination. Many studies of offender behavior report that if the potential victim resists, the offender will not pursue him or her (Flora et al., 2008; Groth, 2001; Seto, 2008). If any child benefits from being empowered, many feel that the programs are worth the effort. Finkelhor (2009) comments as follows:

> In addition, the goal of [this] education is not only to teach resistance behavior, but also to promote disclosure, reduce self-blame, and mobilize bystanders. Meeting such goals could justify the programs even if resistance and avoidance were in themselves difficult to achieve. (p. 65)

Situational Prevention

Situational prevention refers to the concept of targeting inappropriate behavior in prescribed settings rather than trying to change the offender. Borrowed from the situational crime prevention model, this strategy seeks to create safer environments rather than safer individuals. Settings that can be addressed through situational prevention in child sexual abuse are public places, institutional settings, and domestic locations (Smallbone et al., 2008).

Public settings that provide opportunities for offenders to have access to children tend to be playgrounds, shopping malls, public restrooms, parks, arcades, and isolated spots. Those interested in prevention must become more aware of how these places can be used by offenders. Parents and others who take care of children might be encouraged to provide better supervision. Surveillance of such areas by police and security can be increased. Passersby should be encouraged to report or intervene in a behavior between an adult and a child that concerns them. And the earlier-mentioned training of children in self-protection may also be an asset (Smallbone et al., 2008).

Institutional settings, such as child care settings, group homes, residential facilities, schools, youth organizations, and churches, are encouraged to more effectively screen employees. For example, Saul and Audage (2007) suggest that screening should include an application, personal interview, reference checks, criminal background checks, and in some cases (depending upon the agency) the assessment of an applicant's home and possibly an Internet search. Increasingly, schools, youth organizations, and even churches are developing policies and procedures to keep children safe by requiring such safeguards as having no adult be alone with a child, having windows in classrooms and office doors, allowing parents to observe classrooms at any time, and requiring criminal record checks (Crosson-Tower, 2002, 2006). Facilities are also assessed to determine how they can be made safer for children (Smallbone et al., 2008).

In homes and domestic settings, access for offenders is often easier. Thus, mothers must be educated to be more discerning about who has access to their homes and therefore their children. The location of sleeping quarters should be scrutinized. Babysitters should be carefully chosen and screened. Children should be encouraged to develop privacy rules early and abide by them (Smallbone et al., 2008).

Although there is little direct research that points to situational preventions specifically, there is evidence that these play into abuse. For example, in Finkelhor's preconditions model (see Chapter 3), it is clear that offenders take advantage of many situational factors.

Community Awareness and Prevention

Community-centered approaches to prevention promote awareness and engage the community in finding ways to protect children. These can be seen as falling into several categories: community awareness and education, policy and legislation, changing organizational practices, fostering coalitions and networks, and community prevention of offending (Daro & Dodge, 2009; Finkelhor, 2009; Lyles, Cohen, & Brown, 2009; Wurtele & Kenny, 2012).

Promoting Community Awareness and Education

Child sexual abuse is framed within the environment where it happens. Societal beliefs influence not only the commission of crimes such as abuse

but also must be addressed in order to devise prevention efforts that work. Lyles et al. (2009, pp. 4–5) suggest that there are certain environmental factors that now contribute to the sexual abuse of children. They outline these as follows:

- Advances in technology and the influence of that technology on every aspect of children's lives make it more difficult for young people to learn and achieve healthy boundaries with both peers and adults.
- Society promotes sexualized children, submissive females, and dominant males, whereas discussion of healthy sexuality is absent from the information regularly available to children in their environment.
- Consumer messages assault children, whereas the opportunities to share with caring adults such as parents and teachers are often limited and even drowned out by consumerism.
- Although these damaging norms have an impact on all communities, marginalized communities are more frequently exposed to unhealthy environments.
- A dearth of resources and support for community-based, healing, and empowering responses to child sexual abuse actually perpetuates the cycle of abuse.

These authors go on to say that there are five norms that still exist within society that contribute to sexual abuse. These are *stereotypical traditional male roles*, which can promote domination, exploitation, objectification, control, oppression, and risk-taking behaviors; *limited female roles*, where females receive subtle and overt messages that they should be controlled by others and allow themselves to be sexualized; *power*, where the value is placed on having power over others, and children are made especially vulnerable; *violence*, where aggression is not only tolerated but often accepted as a way to solve disputes with others; and *privacy*, where individual and family privacy is considered to be a right, and those who witness violence are encouraged to respect the privacy of others by not reporting it (Lyles et al., 2009,

p. 6). It is against this backdrop of held beliefs that society attempts to prevent the abuse that is often a by-product of them. Thus, people must recognize that the responsibility is not only on the shoulders of the perpetrators but also shared by the greater society that allows abuse by such underlying values.

To promote community awareness in the interest of prevention, the public must learn to *look at its beliefs and values* and to think about them in the context of abuse (Finkelhor, 2009; Renk et al., 2008). One of the teachings of the school-based personal safety curricula was that children should not be made to do things that make them uncomfortable. This is not in reference to cleaning one's room or other tasks that help the child to grow into responsible adulthood but rather in reaction to those requests that make it clear that the child's opinion does not matter. For example, should a child be compelled to kiss Great Uncle Harry if she or he does not want to do so? Historically, it has been expected that along with being "seen and not heard," children were to "do as they were told." This serves to make the adults feel powerful, whereas it may also set up children for abuse. The recognition of societal held beliefs that could put a child at risk for abuse is just one small piece of promoting community awareness.

Further, the general public must be made aware of the *specifics of child sexual abuse* and how to protect children. One parent explained:

ଔ ───────────────────────────

I took part in a community awareness program where a social worker from the local child protection agency came and talked to us about abuse prevention. He told us how perpetrators engage children and how to instruct our children to resist such ploys. For example, there is the "come and see my puppies" routine to lure a child away. We were to teach our children not to fall for that and to tell someone if a perpetrator tried it on them. The social worker also told us that the majority of perpetrators are not strangers but family members or close acquaintances like relatives or babysitters. We were given some ideas of behaviors that should concern us.

We spent a good deal of time talking about how the primary way that nonfamily members engage children is through the Internet. We came away with safety tips to help us monitor our children's Internet use and resources to access that could also help us. It was a worthwhile presentation, and I came away feeling like I was in a better position to protect my child from sexual abuse. ଔ

Some communities not only have such programs but also sponsor community groups to enhance awareness throughout the community. These efforts are designed to alleviate fear-based messages, while promoting fact-based information and tips to protect children. Neighborhoods must also be encouraged to recognize that all types of violence can be prevented if neighbors make themselves aware of each other's children and what is necessary for their protection.

One community, when informed that the school did not have the finances to purchase school-based prevention materials, raised funds so that the materials could be provided to the school and used to train their children. Promoting an interest in providing education in healthy sexual development is another area in which community groups can provide leadership.

ଔ ───────────────────────────

Our local girls and boys club had a board member who was an educator in healthy sexuality. We found funds to buy materials, and she gave the youths in the club and community a series of workshops on healthy sexuality and child rearing. We had been asking the school to provide such information in its health curriculum, but it never happened. We parents felt that teaching our children about healthy sexual relationships would also arm them with knowledge about resisting those that were unhealthy. ଔ

Communities can also help to build skills that lead children to become healthy adults. For example, literacy and English as a second language promotes feelings of enhanced self-esteem and confidence in those who benefit from these programs. Teaching conflict resolution skills and relationship building may be one solution to bullying and fosters healthier families in the future of young people. Libraries, social agencies, and church groups have often been used as springboards from which such skill-based learning is made possible.

Parenting skill classes also enable parents to feel more confident about raising their children. One parent said:

☙ ────────────────────────

The YMCA in our town held a series of classes on parenting. I didn't think I needed it, but I wanted to support its efforts. What an eye opener. I learned a great deal, including how to deal with the issues we had been having with our 15-year-old. I had just thought that her rebellion was inevitable and we'd get through it. But I learned that I had set up a power relationship that was a no-win situation. I wish all parents could have an opportunity for such classes.

────────────────────────── ❧

The community needs to be aware of how to best support and protect its children. The effort is an important one that impacts the future.

Influencing Policy and Legislation

Lyles et al. (2009) comment that "[p]olicy change is often the tipping point for norms change. Policies shape the overall environment for everyone in a community" (p. 8). They go on to suggest that when the underlying conditions that affect child abuse are altered through the changing of policies, abuse is less likely to happen. For example, in one community, the owner of a building next to a school sought to open a café on that premises. It became clear that the "café" would be predominantly a bar, and some of the parents in the community became concerned. The would-be proprietor had a similar establishment in a nearby town that was known to sell liquor to minors and was suspected of drug traffic. The community leaders joined together and were able to alter the zoning law in such a manner that the café selling liquor could not be opened in that location. The parents also felt that they had protected their children from a variety of risks.

Other ways that communities could have an impact on policies might be to work to decrease the media messages that bombard children on television or through advertising, work to encourage advertisers to eliminate or decrease the sexual or violent messages in their advertisements, and strive to require legal pornography sites to remove any messages that objectify or sexualize children (Lyles et al., 2009, pp. 9–10).

Changing Organizational Practices

Organizations provide an opportunity to reach a number of people and can play a prominent role in prevention. Workplace policies and offerings can have a significant impact on family health and child well-being. For example, the movement for industries to sponsor on-premises day care for employees enabled parents to have more contact with their children. Employers could also sponsor various types of child safety awareness programs in addition to those that support family life.

Public pressure can influence organizations and industry to promote policies in the interest of children. For example, Lyles et al. (2009) report that

> Hip-hop magazine the *Source* has announced that it will no longer run ads for pornographic movies, adult websites and escort services. So-called "booty ads" featuring scantily clad women are being banned from the *Source*'s pages and its website. Co-publisher L. Londell McMillan told

the *New York Times* that the *Source* should be able to appeal to core hip-hop fans and still be a magazine that "you wouldn't mind your kids seeing." (p. 11)

Communities that sponsor or house youth programs can insist that all such programs have policies to prevent and report child sexual abuse. Staff should be adequately trained in how to recognize and respond when abuse is reported to them (Saul & Audage, 2007).

When communities make it known that their interest is in the protection of children, organizations wishing to succeed within those communities will need to take notice. However, Wald (2009) advises that preventing child abuse "must be a *desired outcome*, but not the primary focus, of public investments in children" (p. 183). Because resources are not infinite and political trade-offs are often a necessity, Wald believes that the "largest payoff will come from a focus on promoting the positive development of all children 'at risk' of poor development, not from a focus on preventing maltreatment" (2009, p. 184).

Fostering Coalitions and Networks

History tells us again and again that it is through the strength in numbers that people can succeed against the most overwhelming problems. Joining together in the interest of children and eliminating child sexual abuse is an important component of prevention. There is no room for turf battles when the well-being of children is at stake. Partnerships must be developed across disciplines and fields in the interest of protecting children. For example, when child protection agencies join with education, child advocacy, survivor groups, and faith-based groups to tackle the problems of child well-being, more will be accomplished. Using the web to unite these agencies, linking their resources, and providing information for all those who are interested can be a powerful initiative.

On a national level, the National Coalition to Prevent Child Sexual Exploitation (see http://www.missingkids.com) strives to bring together a variety of agencies in the interest of protecting children from child sexual abuse and exploitation. In 2008, this organization developed a National Plan to Prevent the Sexual Exploitation of Children, the purpose of which is to "help assure that all children have childhoods free from sexual abuse and exploitation in both physical and digital environments and have opportunities to develop into health adults capable of having healthy relationships" (National Coalition to Prevent Child Sexual Exploitation, 2008, p. 2). Through this plan, this organization hopes to (p. 3)

- promote norms that support healthy behaviors, images, and messages;
- support environments and education that promote healthy development, relationships, and sexuality;
- collaborate with media, industry, and policy makers to develop and implement strategies to prevent child sexual exploitation; and
- reduce the commercial and individual demand for sexual exploitation of children by countering normalization.

The emphasis will be on engaging and strengthening communities, improving the response to victim reports, and, in general, promoting more awareness of the need to such action. In addition, this coalition hopes to influence the enhancement of positive social norms and organizational practices and end the demand for material that exploits children sexually. Possible efforts to decrease the demand for such media will be centered around helping people to understand what promotes sexual interest in children, advocating to reduce recidivism among offenders, reducing access to sexually exploitive materials, and advocating for public policy to address ending the demand (National Coalition to Prevent Child Sexual Exploitation, 2008). This coalition brings together many of the organizations and initiatives that have dedicated time and resources to the prevention of child sexual abuse, including (but not limited to) National Children's Advocacy Center, National Center for Missing and Exploited Children, Stop It Now!, Prevent Child Abuse America, National Alliance of Children's Trust and Prevention Funds, Association for the Treatment of Sexual Abusers, and the National Alliance to End Sexual Violence.

Lyles et al. (2009) recommends that this coalition be expanded by exploring links with groups that address other childhood issues like teen pregnancy, cyber bullying, domestic violence, and health reform in the interest of sharing resources that benefit children.

Community Prevention of Offending

In addition to justice system, school, and other community efforts, Finkelhor (2009) describes other primary prevention strategies that have been used with potential offenders. These strategies have included developing and reinforcing awareness that abusing children is wrong through the use of public advertisements and even a confidential telephone hotline for those who are tempted to sexually interact with children or have done so. There has been some success in these efforts to target offenders for prevention. Studies have indicated that some offenders will use hotlines, for example, to encourage themselves not to abuse children (Smallbone et al., 2008). The hotline established by Vermont's Stop It Now! received 657 calls in the first 4 years of its operation (between 1995 and 1999). Although only about 15% of the calls were from self-reporting abusers, over half were from community members, reporting that they suspected abuse (as reported in Smallbone et al., 2008). By contrast, Stop It Now! of the United Kingdom and Ireland received 4,013 calls between June 2002 and May 2005. Of these, 45% of the calls were from adults who were concerned about their own abusive

or potentially abusive behaviors. Of these, 37% stated that they had not as yet abused a child and wanted help refraining from doing so. Of those who identified their relationship with the victim, 69% related that the victim was a family member and 31% a friend or family acquaintance (as reported in Smallbone et al., 2008). Although these are not U.S. statistics, they do suggest that there is some efficacy to hotlines that allow offenders to call in.

Critics of hotlines and self-referral programs argue that in a culture that has distinct retributive feelings about those who abuse children, it is difficult to be able to assure offenders that they will receive help and not be punished for coming forward (Finkelhor, 2009).

Another effort has been directed toward bystanders—that is, family members, friends, colleagues of either victims or offenders—who have been trained and encouraged to be more aware of what is occurring and to intervene in order to protect the child. For example, one community member explained:

ॐ ─────────────────────

We had an agency in our town that was dedicated to the treatment of offenders. It also offered training for those who associated with offenders and the community at large to recognize the patterns of offenders as they either engage children or groom the adults around these children. I took the course and was amazed at what I learned. I learned how some offenders isolate children and ingratiate themselves with the adults in the children's lives so that they gain their trust and as a result have more access to the children. We were also educated on how and when to report sexually inappropriate behaviors toward children even if these were just suspicions on our part. As a result of having taken this course, a colleague and I were able to alert the police to a child pornography ring that was later uncovered. In my role as a teen hotline volunteer, I began to be suspicious of the comments that a teen caller was making and recognized that he had been compelled to be a part of this pornography scam. I am not sure that I would have recognized the veiled messages he was giving me had I not taken such a course.

ೞ

Prevention is a crucial piece in the effort to combat child sexual abuse. It is also the obligation of every citizen to find ways to become involved. Waldfogel (2009) contends that society is "on the threshold of an exciting new era in the provision of prevention programs" (p. 206) but cautions that researchers must keep in mind the need for ongoing research as well as learning from their past efforts in designing prevention initiatives.

Although a variety of different types of prevention have been discussed, the emphasis has shifted from preventing child sexual abuse from continuing to preventing it from happening at all (Stagner & Lansing, 2009). Thus, researchers must look especially toward building in protective factors especially in relation to the communities in which children live. Children are society's future, and it is up to everyone to protect that future for the good of all.

WHAT DOES THE FUTURE HOLD? _____

Protecting children from being sexually abused or exploited and addressing the needs of those who have been abused is a complex system that involves individuals, communities, and systems. Individuals must strive to become more aware of the dynamics of child sexual abuse and the impact that being abused has on children, as well as how they might intervene and protect children. Communities can be integrally involved in recognizing what can harm children sexually, in searching for ways to provide support and resources to those agencies and organizations that intervene in child abuse situations, and in seeking ways that they can foster prevention efforts.

The consensus among the experts is that a great deal has been accomplished over the last several decades to combat child sexual abuse, yet more evaluation is needed of the efficacy of these efforts. The school-based prevention programs have had success in not only empowering children but encouraging those who have been abused to report. But these programs should not only be fine-tuned and evaluated but be made available in *all* schools. This may require altering programs for specific settings. Youth organizations and schools must cooperate so that what children learn in school-based prevention is reinforced in other areas of their environment.

It is clear that sex offender management may require standardization and improvement in some areas. States differ as to how sex offenders are addressed through the criminal justice system and what resources are available for supervision and treatment. Additional research on what works best with offenders in the areas of treatment and prevention is also necessary. The general public and therefore policy makers may have flawed misconceptions about offenders based on fear for children. Education around offending behavior for both policy makers and others in the community is an important step toward finding what works.

Child protection agencies may need to reevaluate and improve their services. Most agencies focus on physical abuse and neglect, which represent a significant number of cases. However, attention must also be given to the unique aspects of child sexual abuse and exploitation and how these might be addressed. There must be more formalized training for social workers and other staff in child sexual abuse and offending behavior (Munro, 2008). Colleges might provide courses that could be accessed by social service organizations.

It is important for researchers in the United States to be in touch with their colleagues throughout the world. As Europe, the United Kingdom, Australia, New Zealand, and Canada battle to understand and deal with their sexual abuse programs, the new information that emerges can be a benefit to all countries.

The sexual abuse and exploitation of children and adolescents presents a significant challenge to all who have an interest in the well-being of children. Society has made great strides in the last few decades toward addressing the issues posed by such abuse. It cannot give up the fight to understand, educate, envision, mobilize resources, and take action that strives toward a day when no child will be sexually abused.

Summary

Although there has been a good deal of emphasis on the prevention of all types of child maltreatment, the prevention of child sexual abuse has been developing. Although initially, prevention was aimed at training children so that they might protect themselves from offenders, there is now a broader array of prevention initiatives.

Offender-specific prevention seeks to address offenders, preventing them from abusing at all or seeing that they do not continue to do so. Because offenders often have difficult childhoods, experts say that addressing issues that protect the healthy development of all children will help to eliminate some offenders. Promoting healthy attachment and intervening early when children have emotional difficulties and act out behaviorally or sexually may interrupt the development of an adult offender.

The criminal justice system is also creating programs and intervention to address young offenders and hopefully see that they do not go on to be adult offenders. Some believe that offender registration, community notification, and residency requirements for offenders serve to prevent future abuse. Other experts feel that more research is needed on the efficacy of such programs. Law enforcement is also encouraged to investigate sexual crimes more expediently. And some believe that lengthened sentences will deter further offending.

Victim-centered prevention continues to train children to recognize dangerous situations and share information with adults when they are concerned. Although some worry that this puts too much pressure on children, studies have shown that children are not traumatized by prevention efforts and do learn from them.

Situational prevention refers to making environments safer and not hospitable to abuse. Public settings should be better monitored, and staff in group facilities should be screened and should receive training about keeping children safe.

Community awareness and prevention addresses the need for communities to provide education for citizens about what to look out for in regard to child sexual abuse. Policies and legislation may also be directed toward the prevention of child sexual abuse. Coalitions of community members who join together in the interest of prevention can also have an impact. Although the incidence of child and adolescent sexual abuse has decreased over the last few years, there is still much work to do as society confronts the problem in the years to come.

1. What are some of the risk factors associated with sexual abuse that must be considered when designing prevention programs?

2. What is meant by offender-centered prevention?

3. Why is attention to development important when it comes to sexual offenders?

4. What are some of the criminal justice interventions that might prevent future offending? Do they work?

5. What is the approach of victim-centered prevention?

6. How effective has school-based prevention been? Is it detrimental to children?

7. What is meant by situational prevention?

8. What are the types of prevention that can be used by communities?

9. What are coalitions, and what do they do?

10. What should be done in the future to prevent child and adolescent sexual abuse?

REFERENCES

Abbott, J. S. (1994). Little Rascals Day Care case the bitter lesson, a healthy reminder. *Journal of Child Sexual Abuse, 3*(2), 125–131.

Abel, G. G., Gore, D. K., Holland, C. L., Camp, N., Becker, J., & Rathner, J. (1989). The measurement of cognitive distortions of child molesters. *Annals of Sex Research, 2*(2), 135–153.

Abel, G. G., Mittelman, M. S., & Becker, J. V. (1985). Sexual offenders: Results of assessment and recommendations for treatment. In M. H. Ben-Aron, S. J. Hucker, & C. D. Webster (Eds.), *Clinical criminology: Current concepts* (pp. 191–205). Toronto, Ontario, Canada: M&M Graphics.

Abel, G. G., & Osborn, C. (1992). The paraphilias: The extent and nature of sexually deviant and criminal behavior. *Clinical Forensic Psychiatry, 15*(3), 675–687.

Abel, G. G., Rouleau, J. L., & Cunningham-Rathner, B. A. (1986). Sexually aggressive behavior. In W. J. Curran, A. L. McGarry, & S. A. Shah (Eds.), *Forensic psychiatry and psychology* (pp. 289–314). Philadelphia, PA: Davis.

Adams, J. A. (1995). The role of medical evaluation in suspected child sexual abuse. In T. Ney (Ed.), *True and false allegations of child sexual abuse: Assessment and case management* (pp. 231–241). New York, NY: Brunner/Mazel.

Adams, J. A. (2010). Medical evaluation of suspected child sexual abuse: 2009 update. *APSAC Advisor, 22*(1), 2–7.

Agudo, S. E. (2008). Irregular passion: The unconstitutionality and inefficacy of sex offender registry laws. *Northwestern University Law Review, 102*(1), 307–341.

Ahmad, S. (2006). Adult psychosexual dysfunction as a sequela of child sexual abuse. *Sexual and Relationship Therapy, 21*(4), 405–418.

Ainsworth, M. D. S. (1969). Object relations, dependency and attachment: A theoretical review of the mother-infant relationship. *Child Development, 40*(4), 969–1025.

Alaggia, R. (2002). Balancing acts: Reconceptualizing support in maternal response to intra-familial child sexual abuse. *Clinical Social Work, 30*(1), 41–56.

Alaggia, R., & Knott, T. (2008). Treatment for the non-offending caregiver. In C. Hilarski, J. S. Woodarski, & M. D. Feit (Eds.), *Handbook of social work in child and adolescent sexual abuse* (pp. 203–227). New York, NY: Haworth.

Alexander, P.C. (1985). A system theory conceptualization of incest. *Family Process, 24,* 79–88.

Almond, L., Canter, D., & Salfati, C. G. (2006). Youth who sexually harm: A multivariate model of characteristics. *Journal of Sexual Aggression, 12*(2), 97–114.

Ambrosino, L. (1971). *Runaways.* Boston, MA: Beacon Press.

American Academy of Pediatrics. (2001). Sexuality education for children and adolescents. *Pediatrics, 108*(2), 498–502.

American Association of University Women Educational Foundation. (1993). *Hostile hallways: The AAUW survey on sexual harassment in America's schools.* Washington, DC: AAUW Educational Foundation.

American Association of University Women Educational Foundation. (2001). *Hostile hallways: The AAUW survey on sexual harassment in America's schools: Follow up study.* Washington, DC: AAUP Educational Foundation.

American Humane Association. (1981). *National Reporting Study of Child Abuse and Neglect.* Denver, CO: Author.

Anderson, C. L., & Alexander, P. C. (2005). The effects of abuse on children's development: An attachment perspective. In P. F. Talley (Ed.), *Handbook for the treatment of abused and neglected children* (pp. 3–23). New York, NY: Haworth.

Andrews, D.A., & Bonta, J. (2010). *The psychology of criminal conduct.* Newark, NJ: LexisNexis.

Andrews, D. A., Bonta, J., & Hoge, R. D. (1990). Classification of effective rehabilitation: Rediscovering psychology. *Criminal Justice and Behavior, 17*(1), 19–52.

Andrews, D. A., & Dowden, C. (2007). The risk-need-responsivity model of assessment and human service in prevention and corrections: Crime-prevention jurisprudence. *Canadian Journal of Criminology and Criminal Justice, 49*(4), 439–464.

Araji, S. K. (1997). *Sexually aggressive children: Coming to understand them.* Thousand Oaks, CA: SAGE.

Armstrong, L. (1978). *Kiss daddy goodnight: A speak-out on incest.* New York, NY: Penguin.

Ashford, J. B., Sales, B. D., & Reid, W. H. (2001). Political, legal and professional challenges to treating offenders with special needs. In J. B. Ashford, B. D. Sales, & W. H. Reid (Eds.), *Treating adult and juvenile offenders with special needs* (pp. 31–49). Washington, DC: American Psychological Association.

Association for the Treatment of Sexual Abusers (ATSA). (2001). *Practice standards and principles for the management of sexual abusers.* Beaverton, OR: Association for the Treatment of Sexual Abusers.

Atwood, J. D. (2007). When love hurts: Preadolescent girls' reports of incest. *American Journal of Family Therapy, 35*, 287–313.

Bacon, H. (2001). Attachment, trauma and child sexual abuse. In S. Richardson & H. Bacon (Eds.), *Creative responses to child sexual abuse* (pp. 44–59). London,UK: Jessica Kingsley.

Bajt, T. R., & Pope, K. S. (1989). Therapist-patient sexual intimacy involving children and adolescents. *American Psychologist, 44*, 455.

Baker, J. N., Tanis, H. J., & Rice, J. B. (2001). Including siblings in treatment of child sexual abuse. *Journal of Child Sexual Abuse, 10*(3), 1–16.

Baker, K. A., & Dwairy, M. (2003). Cultural norms versus state laws in treating incest: A suggested model for Arab families. *Child Abuse and Neglect, 27*(1), 109–123.

Baker, L. (2002). *Protecting your children from sexual predators.* New York, NY: St. Martin's Press.

Baker, L. (2011). 10 rules of Internet safety for kids. Retrieved April 30, 2012, from http://www.ivillage.com/10-rules-internet-safety-kids-0/6-a-128700

Ball, C. J., & Seghorn, T. K. (1999). Diagnosis and treatment of exhibitionism and other sexual compulsive disorders. In B. K. Schwartz (Ed.), *The sexual offender: Theoretical advances, treating special populations and legal developments* (pp. 28.1–28.16). Kingston, NJ: Civic Research Institute.

Bancroft, L., & Sullivan, J. (2002). *The batterer as parent.* Thousand Oaks, CA: SAGE.

Barbaree, H. E., Marshall, W. L., & McCormick, J. (1998). The development of deviant behavior among adolescents and its implication for prevention and treatment. *Irish Journal of Psychology, 19*(1), 1–31.

Barbaree, H. E., & Marshall, W. L. (2008). *Juvenile Sexual Offender.* New York, NY: Guilford.

Barkley, R. A. (1998). *Attention-deficit/hyperactivity disorder.* New York, NY: Guilford.

Barkley, R. A. (2002). Major life activity and health outcomes associated with attention-deficit/hyperactivity disorder. *Journal of Clinical Psychiatry, sup. 12*, 10–15.

Barnestone, W. (trans.). (1972). *Greek lyric poetry.* New York, NY: Schocken. As cited in *The best kept secret: Sexual abuse of children*, F. Rush. (1992). New York, NY: McGraw Hill.

Barry, K. (1995). *The prostitution of sexuality.* New York, NY: New York University Press.

Bartol, C. R., & Bartol, A. M. (2008). *Criminal behavior: A psychosocial approach.* Upper Saddle River, NJ: Pearson/Prentice Hall.

Bass, L., Taylor, B. A., Knudson-Martin, C., & Huenergardt, D. (2006). Making sense of abuse: Case studies of sibling incest. *Contemporary Family Therapy, 28*(1), 87–109.

Beck, V. S., & Travis, L. F. III. (2004). Sex offender notification and fear of victimization. *Journal of Criminal Justice, 32*, 455–462.

Becker, J. V. (1990). Treating adolescent sexual offenders. *Professional Psychology Research and Practice, 21*, 362–365.

Becker, J. V. (1998). What we know about the characteristics and treatment of adolescents who have committed sexual offences. *Child Maltreatment, 3*(4), 317–329.

Becker J. V., & Hunter, J. A. (1997). Understanding and treating child and adolescent sexual offenders. In T. H. Ollendick & R. J. Prinz (Eds.), *Advances in clinical child psychology* (pp. 177–197). New York, NY: Plenum Press.

Becker, J. V., & Johnson, B. R. (2001). Treating juvenile sex offenders. In J. B. Ashford, B. D. Sales, & W. H. Reid (Eds.), *Treating adult and juvenile offenders with special needs* (pp. 273- 280). Washington, DC: American Psychological Association.

Becker, M. (2005). Forbidden Washington lovers tie the knot. *New York Daily News,* (May 22), p. 13. *Professional Psychology: Research and Practice, 34*(4), 339–352.

Beech, A. R., Fisher, D. D., & Thornton, D. (2003). Risk assessment of sex offenders. *Professional Psychology: Research & Practice, 34*(4,) 339–353.

Beech, A. R., & Mann, R. E. (2002). Recent developments in the assessment and treatment of sexual offenders. In J. Mcguire (Ed.), *Offender rehabilitation and treatment: Effective programmes and policies to reduce re-offending* (pp. 259–288). Chichester, UK: John Wiley.

Beech, A. R., Parrett, N., Ward, T., & Fisher, D. (2009). Assessing female offenders' motivations and cognitions: An exploratory study. *Psychology, Crime and Law, 15*(2/3), 201–216.

Bender, L., & Blau, A. (1937). The reaction of children to sexual relations with adults. *American Journal of Orthopsychiatry, 7*, 500–518.

Berk, L. E. (2012). *Child development.* Boston, MA: Allyn and Bacon.

Berkoff, M., Zolotar, A., Makoroff, K., Thackery, J., Shapiro, R., & Runyan, D. (2008). Has this prepubescent girl been sexually abused? *JAMA, 300*(23), 2779–2792.

Berliner, L. (2011). Child sexual abuse: Definitions, prevalence and consequences. In J. E. B. Myers (Ed.), *The APSAC handbook on child maltreatment* (pp. 215–232). Thousand Oaks, CA: SAGE.

Bernet, W. (1993). False statements and differential diagnosis of abuse allegations. *Journal of the Academy of Child and Adolescent Psychiatry, 32*(5), 903–910.

Berry, J. (2000). *Lead us not into temptation: Catholic priests and the sexual abuse of children.* New York, NY: Doubleday.

Besharov, D. (1990). Lessons from the McMartin case. Retrieved June 4, 2007, from http://www .welfareacademy.org/pubs/ childwelfare/ childabuse-0290 .shtml

Blagden, N., Winder, B., Gregson, M., & Thorne, K. (2013). Working with denial in convicted sexual offenders: A qualitative analysis of treatment professionals' views and experiences and their implications for practice. *International Journal of Offender Therapy & Comparative Criminology, 57*(3), 332–356.

Blaustein, M. E., & Kinniburgh, K. M. (2010). *Treating traumatic stress in children and adolescents.* New York, NY: Guilford.

Bolen, R. M. (2007). *Child sexual abuse: Its scope and our failure.* New York, NY: Springer Verlag.

Bolen, R., & Lamb, J. L. (2004). Ambivalence of non-offending guardians after child sexual abuse disclosure. *Journal of Interpersonal Violence, 19*(2), 185–211.

Bonner, B. L., Walker, C. E., & Berliner, L. (1999). *Children with sexual behavioral problems: Assessment and treatment.* Washington, DC: Administration for Children, Youth and Families, Department of Human Services.

Boston Globe Investigative Staff. (2002). *Betrayal: The crisis in the Catholic Church.* Boston, MA: Little, Brown and Company.

Bourke, M., & Hernandez, A. (2009). The 'Butner Study' redux: A report of the incidence of hands-on child victimization by child pornography offenders. *Journal of Family Violence, 24*, 183–191.

Bowker, A., & Gray, M. (2005). The cybersex offender and children. *FBI Law Enforcement Bulletin, 74*(3), 12–17.

Bowlby, J. (1979). *The making and breaking of affectional bonds.* London, UK: Routledge.

Bowman, R. A., Scotti, J. R., & Morris, T. L. (2010). Sexual abuse prevention: A training program for developmental disabilities service providers. *Journal of Child Sexual Abuse, 19,* 119–127.

Boyer, D., & Fine, D. (1992). Sexual abuse as a factor in adolescent pregnancy and child maltreatment. *Family Planning Perspectives, 24,* 4–19.

Bradford, M. W. (2001). The neurobiology, neuropharmacology and pharmacological treatment of the paraphilias and compulsive sexual behavior. *Canadian Journal of Psychiatry, 46*(2), 26–43.

Brampton, L. (2011). *Working with sexual offenders.* Saarbrücken, Germany: Lambert Academic.

Bratton, S. C., Ceballos, P. L., Landreth, G. L., & Costos, M. B. (2012). Child-parent relationship therapy with nonoffending parents of sexually abused children. In P. Goodyear-Brown (Ed.), *Handbook of child sexual abuse* (pp. 321–339). Hoboken, NJ: John Wiley.

Bremner, J. D. (2002). *Does stress damage the brain?* New York, NY: Norton.

Briere, J. (1996a). *Trauma symptom checklist for children (TSCC).* Odessa, FL: Psychological Assessment Resources.

Briere, J. (1996b). *Therapy for adults molested as children: Beyond survival.* New York, NY: Springer.

Briere, J., Kaltman, S., & Green, B. L. (2008). Accumulated childhood trauma and symptom complexity. *Journal of Traumatic Stress, 21*(2), 223–226.

Brimer, R., & Rose, R. T. (2012, April) 'Sext' offenders and their victims. Workshop presented at the MASOC and MATSA 14th Annual Joint Conference on the Assessment, Treatment and Safe Management of Sexually Abusing Children, Adolescents, and Adults, Marlborough, MA.

Bringer, J. D., Brackenridge, C., & Johnston, L. H. (2006). Swimming coaches' perception of sexual exploitation in sport: A preliminary model of role conflict and role ambiguity. *Sport Psychologist, 20*(4), 465–479.

Brisch, K. H. (2012). *Treating attachment disorders: From theory to therapy.* New York, NY: Guilford.

Brown, S. M., & Schwartz, C. (2006). Promoting healthy sexuality in sexually abusive youth. In R. E. Longo & D. S. Prescott (Eds.), *Current perspectives: Working with sexually aggressive youth and youth with sexual behavior problems* (pp.193–214). Holyoke, MA: NEARI Press.

Bruck, M., Ceci, S., & Hembrooke, H. (1998). Reliability and credibility of young children's reports. *American Psychologist, 53*(2), 136–151.

Bruni, F., & Burkett, E. (2002). *A gospel of shame: Children, sexual abuse and the Catholic Church.* New York, NY: Perennial.

Bumby, K. M., & Hansen, D. J. (1997). Intimacy deficits, fear of intimacy, and loneliness among sexual offenders. *Criminal Justice and Behavior, 24,* 315–331.

Bunting, L. (2007). Dealing with a problem that doesn't exist? Professional responses to female perpetrated child sexual abuse. *Child Abuse Review, 16*(4), 252–267.

Burgess, A. W., Groth, A. N., Holstrom, L., & Sgroi, S. (1978). *Sexual assault of children and adolescents.* Lexington, MA: Lexington Books.

Burke, P. (2008). *Disability and impairment: Working with children and families.* London, UK: Jessica Kingsley.

Burrow-Sanchez, J. J., Call, M. E., Zheng, R., & Drew, C. J. (2011). How school counselors can help prevent online victimization. *Journal of Counseling and Development, 89* (1), 3–10.

Burton, D. L. (2000). Were adolescent sexual offenders children with sexual behavior problems? *Sexual Abuse: A Journal of Research and Treatment, 12*(1), 37–48.

Burton, D. L., & Smith-Darden, J. (2001). *North American survey of North American sexual abuser treatment models: Summary data 2000.* Brandon, VT: Safer Society Press.

Butler, S. (1978). *Conspiracy of silence: The trauma of incest.* New York, NY: Bantam Books.

Caffaro, J. V., & Conn-Caffaro, A. (1998). *Sibling abuse trauma: Assessment and intervention strategies for children, families and adults.* New York, NY: Haworth.

Cahill, S., Rothbaum, B. O., Resick, P. A., & Follette, V. M. (2008). Cognitive- Behavioral Therapy for Adults. In E. B. Foa, T. M. Keane, M. J. Freidman, & J. A. Cohen (Eds.), *Effective treatments for PTSD: Practice guidelines form the International Society for Trauma Stress Studies* (2nd ed., pp. 139–222), New York, NY: Guilford.

Calder, M. C. (2001). *Juveniles and children who sexually abuse: Frameworks for assessment.* Dorset, UK: Russell House.

Campagna, D. (1985). *Sexual exploitation of children: A resource manual.* Southwick, MA: Daniel S. Campagna.

Cantwell, H. B. (1995). Sexually aggressive children and societal response. In M. Hunter (Ed.), *Effective treatments for PTSD: Practice guidelines form the International Society for Trauma Stress Studies* (pp. 79–107). Thousand Oaks, CA: SAGE.

Carey, L. (Ed.). (2006). *Expressive and creative arts methods with trauma survivors.* New York, NY: Jessica Kingsley.

Carlson, B. E., Maciol, K., & Schneider, J. (2006). Sibling incest: Reports from forty-one survivors. *Journal of Child Sexual Abuse, 15*(4), 19–34.

Carnes, C., & LeDuc, D. (1998). *Forensic evaluation of children.* Huntsville, AL: National Children's Advocacy Center.

Carnes, P. (1992). *Don't call it love: Recovery from sexual addiction.* New York, NY: Bantam Books.

Carnes, P. (2001). *Out of the shadows: Understanding sexual addiction.* Deerfield Beach, FL: Hazelden.

Carter, B. J. (1999). *Who's to blame? Child sexual abuse and the non-offending parent.* Toronto, Ontario, Canada: University of Toronto Press.

Carter, M. M., & Matson, S. (1999). *Understanding juvenile sexual offending behavior: Emerging research, treatment approaches and management practices.* Silver Springs, MD: Center for Sex Offender Management.

Cartor, P., Cimbolic, P., & Tallon, J. (2008). Differentiating pedophilia and ephebophilia in cleric offenders. *Sexual Addiction and Compulsivity, 15,* 311–319.

Cassese, J. (Ed.). (2000). *Gay men and childhood sexual trauma: Integrating the shattered self.* New York, NY: Harrington Park Press.

Cassese, J. (2001). *Gay men and childhood sexual trauma: Integrating the shattered self.* New York, NY: Haworth.

Cattanach, A. (2008). *Play therapy with abused children,* London, UK: Jessica Kingsley.

Ceci, S. J., & Bruck, M. (1993). Suggestibility of child witnesses: A historical review and a synthesis. *Journal of the American Academy of Child and Adolescent Psychiatry, 36,* 948–970.

Cederborg, A. C., & Lamb, M. (2006). How does the legal system respond when children with learning disabilities are victimized. *Child Abuse and Neglect, 30*(5), 537–547.

Center for Sex Offender Management. (2001). *Recidivism of sex offenders.* Silver Spring, MD: Author.

Center for Sex Offender Management. (2007). *Managing the challenges of offender reentry.* Silver Spring, MD: Author.

Chalfen, R. (2009). 'It's only a picture': Sexting, 'smutty' snapshots and felony charges. *Visual Studies, 24*(3), 258–268.

Charles, G. (1995). The assessment and investigation of ritual abuse. In T. Ney (Ed.), *True and false allegations of child sexual abuse: Assessment and case management* (pp. 303–315). New York, NY: Brunner/Mazel.

Chase, T. (1990). *When rabbit howls.* New York, NY: Penguin.

Chiara, S., Wolak, J., & Finkelhor, D. (2008). The nature and dynamics of internet pornography exposure for youth. *CyberPsychology & Behavior, Vol. 11*(6), 691–693

Children's Bureau, Administration on Children, Youth and Families (2012). *Child maltreatment 2011: Reports from the states to the National Child Abuse and Neglect Data System.* Washington, DC: U.S. Department of Health and Human Services.

Chouliara, Z., Hutchinson, C., & Karatzias, T. (2009). Vicarious traumatization in practitioners who work with adult survivors of sexual violence and child sexual abuse: Literature review and directions for future research. *Counseling and Psychotherapy, 9*(1), 47–56.

Cimbolic, P., & Cartor, P. (2006). Looking at ephebophilia through the lens of cleric sexual abuse. *Sexual Addiction and Compulsivity, 13*(4), 347–359.

Cloud, J. (1998, May 4). A matter of hearts. *Seattle Times,* pp. 60–64.

Cohen, J. A., Mannarino, A., & Deblinger, E. (2006). *Treating trauma and traumatic grief in children and adolescents.* New York, NY: Guilford.

Cohen, T. (1983). The incestuous family revisited. *Social Casework, 64,* 154–161.

Colangelo, J. J. (2009). The recovered memory controversy: A representative case study. *Journal of Child Sexual Abuse, 18,* 103–121.

Colon, A. R. (2001). *A history of children: A socio-cultural survey across the millennia.* Westport, CT: Greenwood Press.

Conte, J. (2002). *Critical issues in child sexual abuse.* Thousand Oaks, CA: SAGE.

Conte, J., & Shore, D. (1982). Social work and sexual abuse. *Journal of Social Work and Human Sexuality, 1,* 1–2. New York, NY: Haworth.

Conte, J., Sorenson, E., Fogarty, L., & Dalla Rosa, J. (1991). Evaluating children's reports of sexual abuse: Results from a survey of professionals. *American Journal of Orthopsychiatry, 61*(3), 428–437.

Cook, C. (1991). *Understanding ritual abuse through the study of thirty-three ritual abuse survivors from thirteen different states.* Sacramento, CA: Ritual Abuse Project.

Cooper, A. (Ed.). (2002). *Sex and the internet.* New York, NY: Brunner-Routledge.

Cooper, A., Scherer, C., & Mathy, R. (2001). Overcoming methodological concerns in the investigations of online activities. *Cyberpsychology and Behavior, 4*(4), 437–448.

Cooper, S. W., Estes, R. J., Giardino, A. P., Kellogg, N. D., & Vieth, V. I. (2007). *Child sexual exploitation.* St. Louis, MO: G. W. Medical Publishing.

Cortoni, F., & Marshall, W. L. (2001). Sex as a coping strategy and its relationship to juvenile sexual history and intimacy in sexual offenders. *Sexual Abuse: A Journal of Research and Treatment, 13*(2), 27–43.

Corwin, D. L. (2002). An interview with Roland Summit. In J. Conte (Ed.), *Critical issues in child sexual abuse* (pp. 1–25). Thousand Oaks, CA: SAGE.

Courtois, C. A. (2010). *Healing the incest wound.* New York, NY: W. W. Norton.

Courtois, C. A., & Ford, J. D. (Eds.). (2009). *Treating complex trauma stress disorders: An evidence-based guide.* New York, NY: Guilford Press.

Cozzens, D. (2002). *Sacred silence: Denial and the crisis in the Catholic Church.* Collegeville, MD: Liturgical Press.

Craig, L. A. (2010). Controversies in assessing risk and deviancy in sex offenders with intellectual disabilities. *Psychology, Crime and Law, 16*(1–2), 75–101.

Craig, L., Browne, K. D., Stringer, I., & Beech, A. (2005). Sexual recidivism: A review of static, dynamic and actuarial predictions. *Journal of Sexual Aggression, 11,* 65–84.

Craig, L., & Hutchinson, R. B. (2005). Sexual offenders with learning disabilities: Risk, recidivism and treatment. *Journal of Sexual Aggression, 11*(3), 289–304.

Craissati, J., McClurg, G., & Browne, K. (2002). Characteristics of perpetrators of child sexual abuse who have been sexually victimized as children. *Sexual Abuse: A Journal of Research and Treatment, 14*(3), 225–239.

Craske, M. G. (2009). *Cognitive-behavioral therapy.* Washington, DC: American Psychological Association.

Creeden, K. (2005). Trauma, attachment, and neurodevelopment—implications for treating sexual behavioral problems. In B. K. Schwartz (Ed.), *The sexual offender: Issues in assessment, treatment, and supervision of adult and juvenile populations* (pp. 1.1–1.26). Kingston, NJ: Civic Research Institute.

Crenshaw, D. A., & Mordock, J. B. (2004). An ego-strengthening approach with multiply traumatized children: Special reference to the sexually abused. *Residential Treatment for Children and Youth, 21*(3), 1–18.

Cross, T., Jones, I., Walsh, W., Simone, M., & Kolko, D. (2007). Child forensic interviewing in children's advocacy centers. *Child Abuse and Neglect, 31*(10).

Crosson-Tower, C. (2002). *When children are abused.* Boston, MA: Allyn and Bacon.

Crosson-Tower, C. (2006). *A clergy guide to child abuse and neglect.* Cleveland, OH: The Pilgrim Press.

Crosson-Tower, C. (2013). *Exploring child welfare: A practice perspective.* Boston, MA: Pearson.

Crosson-Tower, C. (2014). *Understanding child abuse and neglect.* Boston, MA: Allyn and Bacon.

Crowley, P. (1989). *Not my child: A mother confronts her child's sexual abuse.* New York, NY: Doubleday.

Cumming, G., & Buell, M. (1997). *Supervision of the sex offender.* Brandon, VT: The Safer Society Press.

Cunningham, J. (1988). Contributions to the history of psychology: French historical views on the acceptability of evidence regarding child sexual abuse. *Psychological Reports, 63,* 342–353.

Curtis, R., Terry, K., Dank, M., Dombrowski, K., & Khan, B. (2008). *Commercial sexual exploitation of children in New York City.* Washington, DC: U.S. Department of Justice and New York, NY: John Jay College of Criminal Justice.

Cyr, M., Wright, J., McDuff, P., & Perron, A. (2002), Intrafamilial sexual abuse: Brother-sister incest does not differ from father-daughter incest. *Child Abuse and Neglect, 26*(9), 957–973.

Dallam, S. J. (2001). Crisis or creation: A systematic examination of 'False Memory Syndrome.' *Journal of Child Sexual Abuse, 9*(3/4), 9–36.

Daro, D. (1994). Prevention of child sexual abuse. *The Future of Children, 4*(2), 198–223.

Daro, D. (2009). The history of science and child abuse prevention. In K. A. Dodge & D. L. Coleman (Eds.), *Preventing child maltreatment: Community approaches* (pp. 9–25). New York, NY: Guilford.

Daro, D., & Dodge, K. A. (2009). Creating community responsibility for child protection: Possibilities and challenges. *The Future of Children: Preventing Child Maltreatment, 19*(2), 67–92.

Davies, D., & Faller, K. C. (2007). Interviewing children with special needs. In K. C. Faller (Ed.), *Interviewing children about sexual abuse* (pp. 152–163). New York, NY: Oxford University Press.

Davies, J. M., & Frawley, M. G. (1994). *Treating the adult survivor of child sexual abuse.* New York, NY: Basic Books.

Davin, P. A., Hislop, J. C. R., & Dunbar, T. (1999). *The female sexual offender: Three views.* Brandon, VT: Safer Society Press.

Davis, J. E. (2005). *Accounts of innocence: Sexual trauma and the self.* Chicago, IL: University of Chicago Press.

Davis, J. K., & Gidycz, C. A. (2000). Child abuse prevention programs: A meta-analysis. *Journal of Clinical and Child Psychology, 29*(2), 257–65.

Day, K., & Berney, T. (2001). Treatment and care of offenders with mental retardation. In J. B. Ashford, B. D. Sales, & W. H. Reid (Eds.),

Treating adult and juvenile offenders with special needs (pp. 199–220). Washington, DC: American Psychological Association.

Dean, R., & Thompson, R. (1997). *Teen prostitution.* Farmington Hill, MI: Gale Group.

DeBellis, M. D. (2001). Developmental traumatology: The psychobiological development of maltreated children and its implications for research, treatment, & policy. *Development and Psychopathology, 13*(3), 539–564.

Deblinger, E. D., & Heflin, A. H. (1996). *Treating sexually abused children and their non-offending parents: A cognitive behavioral approach.* Thousand Oaks, CA: SAGE.

DeLamater, J., & Friedrich, W. N. (2002). Human sexual development. *The Journal of Sex Research, 39*(1), 10–14.

Demand, N. (2004). *Birth, death and motherhood in classical Greece.* Baltimore, MD: Johns Hopkins Univ. Press.

deMause, L. (1991). The universality of incest. *The Journal of Psychohistory, 19*(2), 123–164.

Densen-Garber, J. (1980). Child prostitution and pornography: Medical, legal and societal aspects of the commercial exploitation of children. In B. Jones, L. Jenstroime, & K. MacFarlane, (Eds.), *Sexual abuse of children: Selected readings* (pp. 77–82). Washington, DC: U.S. Department of Health and Human Services.

Densen-Garber, J., & Hutchinson, S. (1978). Medical, legal and societal problems involving children—child prostitution, child pornography and drug related abuse: Recommended legislation. In S. Smith (Ed.), *The maltreatment of children* (pp. 317–50). Baltimore, MD: University Park.

DePanfilis, D., & Salus, M. K. (2003). *Child protective services: A guide for caseworkers.* Washington, DC: Children's Bureau, U.S. Department of Health and Human Services.

Dorias, M. (2009). *Don't tell: The sexual abuse of boys.* Montreal, Quebec, Canada: McGill-Queens University Press.

Dryden, W. (1991). Therapist sexual abuse: An interview with Jill Sinclair. *British Journal of Guidance and Counseling, 19*(3), 1–12.

Duncan, K. (2008). *Healing from the trauma of childhood abuse.* Westport, CT: Greenwood.

Durkheim, E. (1963). *Incest: The nature and origin of the taboo.* New York, NY: Lyle Stuart. (Original work published 1898).

Durkin, K. F., & Digianantonio, A. L. (2007). Recidivism among child molesters: A brief overview. *Mental Health Issues in the Criminal Justice System, 45*(1/2), 249–256.

Duwe, G., & Donnay, W. (2008). The impact of Megan's Law on sex offender recidivism: The Minnesota experience. *Criminology, 46*(2), 411–46.

Eberle, P., & Eberle, S. (2003). *The abuse of innocence: The McMartin Preschool trial.* Amherst, NY: Prometheus Books.

Echols, M. (1996). *Brother Tony's boys: The largest case of child prostitution in U.S. history.* Amherst, NY: Prometheus Books.

Efta-Breitbach, J., & Freeman, K. A. (2004a). Treatment of juveniles who sexually offend: An overview. In R. Geffner, K. C. Franey, T. G. Arnold, & R. Falconer (Eds.), *Identifying and treating youth who sexually offend* (125–138). New York, NY: Haworth.

Efta-Breitbach, J., & Freeman, K. A. (2004b). Recidivism and resilience in juvenile sexual offenders: An analysis of the literature. In R. Geffner, K. C. Franey, T. G. Arnold, & R. Falconer (Eds.), *Identifying and treating youth who sexually offend* (257–279). New York, NY: Haworth.

Elliot, K. N., & Carnes, C. N. (2001). Reactions of non-offending parents to the abuse of their child: A review of the literature. *Child Maltreatment, 6*(40), 314–331.

Elliot, M. (1993). *Female sexual abuse of children: The ultimate taboo.* London, UK: Longman.

Ellsworth, L. (2007). *Choosing to heal: Using reality therapy in the treatment of sexually abused children.* London, UK: Routledge.

Engel, B. (1993). *Partners in recovery.* New York, NY: Random House.

Erooga, M., & Masson, H. (Eds.). (2006). *Children and young people who sexually abuse others.* New York, NY: Routledge.

Faller, K. C. (1987). Women who sexually abuse children. *Violence and Victims, 2*(4), 236–276.

Faller, K. C. (1988a). *Child sexual abuse: An interdisciplinary manual for diagnosis, case management and treatment.* New York, NY: Columbia University Press.

Faller, K. C. (1988b). The spectrum of sexual abuse in day care: An exploratory study. *Journal of Family Violence, 3*(4), 283–298.

Faller, K. C. (1990). Sexual abuse by paternal caretakers: A comparison of abusers who are biological fathers in intact families, stepfathers and noncustodial father. In A. L. Horton, B. L. Johnson, L. M. Roundy, & D. Williams (Eds.), *The incest perpetrator* (pp. 65–73). Newbury Park, CA: SAGE.

Faller, K. C. (1991). Possible explanations for child sexual abuse in divorce. *American Journal of Orthopsychiatry, 61*(1), 86–91.

Faller, K. C. (1996). Interviewing children who may have been abused: A historical perspective and overview of controversies. *Child Maltreatment, 1*(2), 4–18.

Faller, K. C. (2003). *Understanding and assessing child sexual maltreatment.* Thousand Oaks, CA: SAGE.

Faller, K. C. (2007a). *Interviewing children about sexual abuse.* New York, NY: Oxford University Press.

Faller, K. C. (2007b). Mother-blaming in the shadow of incest: Commentary on motherhood in the shadow of incest by Rachel Lev-Weisel. *Journal of Child Sexual Abuse, 16*(1), 129–136.

Faller, K. C., Cordisco-Steele, L., & Nelson-Gardell, D. (2010). Allegations of sexual abuse of a child: What to do when a simple forensic interview isn't enough. *Journal of Child Sexual Abuse, 19*(5), 572–589.

Faller, K. C., & DeVoe, E. (1995). Allegations of sexual abuse in divorce. *Journal of Child Sexual Abuse, 4*(4), 1–25.

Faller, K. C., & Henry, J. (2000). Child sexual abuse: A case study in community collaboration. *Child Abuse and Neglect, 24*, 1215–1225.

False Memory Syndrome Foundation. (2010). Retrieved October 28, 2010, from http://en.wikipedia.org/wiki/False_Memory_Syndrome_Foundation

Farmer, E., & Pollock, S. (2003). Managing sexually abused and/or abusing children in substitute care. *Child and Family Social Work, 8*(2), 101–112.

Fasting, K., & Brackenridge, C. (2009). Coaches, sexual harassment and education. *Sport, Education and Society, 14*(1), 21–35.

Feiring, C., Taska, L., & Lewis, M. (2002). Adjustment Following Sexual Abuse Discovery: The role of shame and attributional style. *Developmental Psychology, 38*, 79–92.

Ferrara, F. F. (2002). *Childhood sexual abuse: Developmental effects across the lifespan.* Pacific Grove, CA: Brooks/Cole.

Ferrara, M. L., & McDonald, S. (1996). *Treatment of the juvenile sex offender: Neurological and psychiatric impairments.* Northvale, NJ: Jason Aronson.

Fibkins, W. L. (2006). *Innocence denied: A guide to preventing sexual abuse by teachers and coaches.* Lanham, MD: Rowman and Littlefield.

Figley, C. R. (1995). *Compassion fatigue.* London, UK: Brunner/Routledge.

Finkelhor, D. (1979). What's wrong with sex between adults and children? *American Journal of Orthopsychiatry, 49*, 692–697.

Finkelhor, D. (1984). *Child sexual abuse.* New York, NY: Free Press.

Finkelhor, D. (1986). *Sourcebook on child sexual abuse.* Beverly Hills, CA: SAGE.

Finkelhor, D. (1990). *Sexually victimized children.* New York, NY: Free Press.

Finkelhor, D. (2007). Prevention of sexual abuse through educational programs directed toward children. *Pediatrics, 120*(3), 640–645.

Finkelhor, D. (2009). Prevention and child sexual abuse. *The Future of Children: Preventing Child Maltreatment, 19*(2), 169–194.

Finkelhor, D., & Browne, A. (1985). Traumatic impact of child sexual abuse: A conceptualization. *American Journal of Orthopsychiatry, 55*, 530–541.

Finkelhor, D., Mitchell, K., & Wolak, J. (2000). *Online victimization: A report on the nation's youth.* Alexandria, VA: National Center for Missing and Exploited Children.

Finkelhor, D., Ormrod, R., & Chaffin, M. (2009). Juveniles who commit sexual offenses agaginst minors. *Juvenile Justice Bulletin.* Retrieved May 2, 2012, from https://www.ncjrs.gov/pdffiles1/ojjdp/227763.pdf

Finkelhor, D., Williams, L. M., Burns, N., & Kalinowski, M. (1988). *Nursery crimes: Sexual abuse in day care.* Newbury Park, CA: SAGE.

Firestone, P., Moulden, H. M., & Wexler, A. F. (2009). Clerics who commit sexual offenses: Offender, offense, and victim characteristics. *Journal of Child Sexual Abuse, 18*, 442–454.

Fitzgerald, M. M., & Cohen, J. (2012). Trauma-focused cognitive behavioral therapy. In P. Goodyear-Brown (Ed.), *Handbook of child sexual abuse* (pp. 199–228). Hoboken, NJ: John Wiley.

Flood, M. (2009). The harms of pornography exposure among children and young people. *Child Abuse Review, 18*, 384–400.

Flora, R. (2001). *How to work with sex offenders: A handbook for criminal justice, human service, & mental health professionals.* New York, NY: The Haworth Press.

Flora, R., Duehl, J. T., Fisher, W., Halsey, S., Keohane, M., Maberry, B. L., McCorkindale, J. A., & Parson, L. C. (2008). *Sex-offender therapy.* New York, NY: Haworth.

Flowers, R. B. (2001). *Runaway kids and teenage prostitution.* Westport, CT: Praeger.

Flowers, R. B. (2005). *The prostitution of women and girls.* Jefferson, NC: McFarland.

Flowers, R. B. (2010). *Street kids: The lives of runaway and throwaway teens.* Jefferson, NC: McFarland.

Follette, V. M., & Ruzek, J. I. (Eds.). (2007). *Cognitive behavioral therapies for trauma.* New York, NY: Guilford.

Fontes, L. A. (2008). *Child abuse and culture.* New York, NY: Guilford.

Fontes, L. A., Cruz, M., & Tabachnick, J. (2001). Views of child sexual abuse in two cultural communities: An exploratory study of African-Americans and Latinos. *Child Maltreatment, 6*, 103–117.

Fontes, L. A., & Faller, K. C. (2007). Conducting culturally competent sexual abuse interviews with children from diverse racial, cultural, and socioeconomic backgrounds. In K. C. Faller (Ed.), *Interviewing children about sexual abuse* (pp. 164–174). New York, NY: Oxford University Press.

Fontes, L. A., & Plummer, C. (2012). Cultural issues in child sexual abuse intervention and prevention. In P. Goodyear-Brown (Ed.), *Handbook of child sexual abuse* (pp. 487–508). Hoboken, NJ: John Wiley.

Ford, H. (2006). *Women who sexually abuse children.* West Sussex, UK: John Wiley.

Ford, W. C., & Prunier, W. (2005). Working with African American and Latino sex offenders. In B. K. Schwartz (Ed.), *The sex offender* (Vol. V, pp. 5.2–5.21). Kingston, NJ: Civic Research Institute.

Forward, S., & Buck, C. (1978). *Betrayal of innocence: Incest and its devastation.* New York, NY: J. P. Tarcher.

Fosha, D., Siegel, D. J., & Solomon, M. F. (2009). *The healing power of emotion: Affective neuroscience, development and clinical practice.* New York, NY: Norton.

Fox, J. R. (1980). *The red lamp of incest.* New York, NY: Dutton.

Frawley-O'Dea, M. G. (2007). *Perversion of power: Sexual abuse in the Catholic Church.* Nashville, TN: Vanderbilt University Press.

Frawley-O'Dea, M. G., & Goldner, V. (2007). *Predatory priests, silenced victims: The sexual abuse crisis and the Catholic Church.* Mahwah, NJ: The Analytic Press.

Fredrickson, R. (1992). *Repressed memories.* New York, NY: Simon and Schuster.

Freeman, N. J., & Sandler, J. C. (2008). Female and male sex offenders: A comparison of recidivism and risk factors. *Journal of Interpersonal Violence, 23*(10), 1394–1413.

Freeman-Longo, R. E., & Blanchard, G. T. (1998). *Sexual abuse in America: Epidemic of the 21st century.* Brandon, VT: Safer Society Press.

Freud, S. (1946). *Totem and taboo* (A. A. Brill, Trans.). New York, NY: Vintage. (Original work published 1913).

Frey, L. L. (2006). Girls don't do that, do they? Adolescent females who sexually abuse. In R. E. Longo & D. S. Prescott (Eds.), *Current perspectives: Working with sexually aggressive youth and youth with sexual behavior problems* (pp. 255–272). Holyoke, MA: NEARI Press.

Friedrich, F. W., Fisher, J., Broughton, D., Houston, M., & Shafran, C. (1998). Normative sexual behavior in children: A contemporary sample. *Pediatrics, 101*(4), 693–696.

Friedrich, M., & Leiper, R. (2006). Countertransference reactions in therapeutic work with incestuous sexual abuse. *Journal of Child Sexual Abuse, 15*(1), 51–68.

Friedrich, W. N. (1990). *Psychotherapy of sexually abused children and their families.* New York, NY: Norton.

Friedrich, W. N. (2002). *Psychological assessment of sexually abused children and their families.* Thousand Oaks, CA: SAGE.

Friedrich, W. N., & Reams, R. A. (1987). Course of psychological symptoms in sexually abused children. *Psychotherapy, 24*(2), 160–170.

Friedrich, W., & Sim, L. (2006). Attachment styles and sexual abuse. In R. E. Longo & D. S. Prescott (Eds.), *Current perspectives: Working with sexually aggressive youth and youth with sexual behavior problems* (pp. 369–382). Holyoke, MA: NEARI Press.

Future of Sex Education Initiative. (2012). National sexuality education standards: Core content and skills, K–12 [a special publication of the *Journal of School Health*]. Retrieved from http://www.futureofsexed.org/documents/josh-fose-standards-web.pdf

Gallagher, B. (1998). *Grappling with smoke: Iinvestigating and managing organized abuse.* London, UK: NSPCC.

Gallagher, B. (2005). New technology: Helping or harming children? *Child Abuse Review, 14,* 367–373.

Gannon, T. A., Gilchrist, E., & Wade, K. A. (2008). Intrafamilial child and adolescent sexual abuse. In C. Hilarski, J. S. Wodarski, & M. D. Feit (Eds.), *Handbook of social work in child and adolescent sexual abuse* (pp. 71–101). New York, NY: Haworth.

Gannon, T. A., Rose, M. R., & Williams, S. E. (2009). Do female child molesters implicitly associate children and sex? A preliminary investigation. *Journal of Sexual Aggression, 15*(1), 55–61.

Gannon, T., Rose, M. R., & Ward, T. (2010). Pathways to female offending: Approach or avoidance. *Psychology, Crime & Law, 16*(5), 359–380.

Garrett, L. (2010). Childhood experience of incarcerated male child sexual abuser. *Issues in Mental Health Nursing, 31,* 679–685.

Gartner, R. B. (2001). *Betrayed as boys: Psychodynamic treatment of sexually abused men.* New York, NY: Guilford.

Gaskill, R. L., & Perry, B. D. (2012). Child sexual abuse, traumatic experience, and their impact on the developing brain. In P. Goodyear-Brown (Ed.), *Handbook of child sexual abuse* (pp. 29–47), Hoboken, NJ: John Wiley.

Geltz, R. M. (1994). The Little Rascals' Day Care Center case: A prosecutor's perspective. *Journal of Child Sexual Abuse, 3*(2), 103–106.

Giaretto, H. (1982). *Integrated treatment of child sexual abuse*. Palo Alto, CA: Science and Behavior.

Gil, E., & Johnson, T. C. (1993). *Sexualized children.* Walnut Creek, CA: Launch Press.

Gilgun, J. (1990). Factors mediating the effects of childhood maltreatment. In M. Hunter (Ed.), *The sexually abused male* (Vol. 1, 177–190). Newbury Park, CA: SAGE.

Gilgun, J. F., & Connor, T. M. (1990). Isolation and the adult male perpetrator of child sexual abuse: Clinical concerns. In A. L. Horton, B. L. Johnson, L. M. Roundy, & D. Williams (Eds.), *The incest perpetrator* (pp. 74–87). Newbury Park, CA: SAGE.

Glasser, M., Kolvin, I., Campbell, D., Glasser, A., Leitch, I., & Farrelly, S. (2001). Cycle of child sexual abuse: Links between being a victim and becoming a perpetrator. *British Journal of Psychiatry, 179*, 482–494.

Goodyear-Brown, P., Fath, A., & Myers, L. (2012). Child sexual abuse: The scope of the problem. In P. Goodyear-Brown (Ed.), *Handbook of child sexual abuse* (pp. 3–28). Hoboken, NJ: John Wiley.

Green, A. (2011). *The tragic effect: The Oedipus complex in tragedy.* Cambridge, MA: Cambridge University Press.

Greenberg, J. (1992). *Oedipus and beyond: A clinical theory.* Cambridge, MA: Harvard University Press.

Greenspun, W. S. (1994). Internal and interpersonal: The family transmission of father-daughter incest. *Journal of Child Sexual Abuse, 3*(2), 1–14.

Grossman, F. K., Sorsoli, L., & Kia-Keating, M. (2006). A gale force wind: Meaning making by male survivors of childhood sexual abuse. *American Journal of Orthopsychiatry, 76*(4), 434–444.

Groth, A. N. (2001). *Men who rape.* New York, NY: Perseus.

Hall, D. K., Mathews, F., & Pearce, J. (2002). Sexual behavior problems in sexually abused children: A preliminary typology. *Child Abuse and Neglect, 26*, 289–312.

Hall, G. C. N., & Hirschman, R. (1992). Sexual aggression against children: A conceptual perspective of etiology. *Criminal Justice and Behavior, 19*, 8–23.

Hanson, R., & Harris, A. J. R. (2001). A structured approach to evaluating change among sex offenders. *Sexual Abuse: A Journal of Research and Treatment, 13*(2), 105–122.

Hanson, R. F., Lipovsky, J. A., & Saunders, B. E. (1994). Characteristics of fathers in incest families. *Journal of Interpersonal Violence, 9*(2), 155–169.

Hanson, R. K. (2000). *Risk assessment.* Beaverton, OR: Association for the Treatment of Sexual Abusers.

Hanson, R. K. (2002). Recidivism and age: Follow-up data from 4,673 sexual offenders. *Journal of Interpersonal Violence, 17*, 1046–1062.

Hanson, R. K., & Bussiere, M. T. (1998). Predicting relapse: A meta-analysis of sexual offender recidivism studies. *Journal of Consulting & Clinical Psychology, 66*(2), p348-363.

Hanson, R. K., Steffy, R. A., & Gauthier, R. (1993). Long-term recidivism of child molesters. *Journal of Consulting and Clinical Psychology, 61*, 646–652.

Hardy, M. S. (2001). Physical aggression and sexual behavior among siblings: A retrospective study. *Journal of Family Violence, 16*(3), 255–267.

Harrison, P. M., & Beck, A. J. (2006). *Prison and jail inmates at mid-year 2005.* Washington, DC: U.S. Department of Justice, Office of Justice Programs, Bureau of Justice Statistics.

Hartley, C. C. (2001). Incest offenders' perceptions of their motives to sexually offend within their past and current life context. *Journal of Interpersonal Violence, 16*(5), 459–475.

Hayes, S., & Carpenter, B. (2013). Social moralities and discursive constructions of female sexual offenders. *Sexualities, 16*(1/2), 159–179.

Hebert, M., & Tourigny, M. (2004). Child sexual abuse prevention: A review of evaluative studies and recommendations for program development. *Advances in Psychology Research, 29*, 123–155.

Hechler, D. (1988). *The battle and the backlash: The child sexual abuse war.* Lexington, MA: Lexington Books.

Hendrie, C. (1998, December 2, 9, 16). A trust betrayed: Sexual abuse by teachers. *Education Week.*

Henry, D. L. (1999). Resilience in maltreated children: Implications for special needs adoptions. *Child Welfare, 78,* 519–541.

Herman, J. (1981). *Father-daughter incest.* Cambridge, MA: Harvard University Press.

Herman, J., & Hirschman, L. (2000). *Father-daughter incest.* Cambridge, MA: Harvard University Press.

Herman, J. L. (1997). *Trauma and recovery.* New York, NY: Basic Books.

Herman, J. L. (2008). The craft and science in the treatment of traumatized people. *Journal of Trauma and Dissociation, 9*(3), 293–300.

Hernandez, A., Buble, C., Rockmore, L., McKay, M., Messam, T., Harris, M., & Hope, S. (2009). An integrated approach to treating non-offending parents affected by sexual abuse. *Social Work in Mental Health, 7*(6), 533–555.

Hewitt, S. K. (1999). *Assessing allegations of sexual abuse in preschool children.* Thousand Oaks, CA: SAGE.

Hewitt, S. (2012). Developmentally sensitive assessment methods in child sexual abuse cases. In P. Goodyear-Brown (Ed.), *Handbook of child sexual abuse* (pp. 121–142), Hoboken, NJ: John Wiley.

Hickey, E. W. (2005). *Sex crimes and paraphilia.* Englewood Cliffs, NJ: Prentice Hall.

Hidalgo, M. L. (2007). *Sexual abuse and the culture of Catholicism.* New York, NY: Haworth.

Hilarski, C. (2008a). Child and adolescent sexual abuse. In C. Hilarski, J. S. Woodarski, & M. D. Feit (Eds.), *Handbook of social work in child and adolescent sexual abuse* (pp. 29–50). New York, NY: Haworth.

Hilarski, C. (2008b). Historical overview. In C. Hilarski, J. S. Woodarski, & M. D. Feit (Eds.), *Handbook of social work in child and adolescent sexual abuse* (pp. 1–27). New York, NY: Haworth.

Hilarski, C. (2008c). The nonfamily sex offender. In C. Hilarski, J. S. Woodarski, & M. D. Feit (Eds.), *Handbook of social work in child and adolescent sexual abuse* (pp. 103–117). New York, NY: Haworth.

Hirshfeld-Becker, D. R., Masek, B., Henin, A., Blakely, L. R., Pollock-Wurman, R. A., McQuade, J., DePetrillo, L., Briesch, J., Ollendick, T. H., Rosenbaum, J. F., & Biederman, J. (2010). Cognitive behavioral therapy for 4- to 7-year-old children with anxiety disorders: A randomized clinical trial. *Journal of Consulting & Clinical Psychology, 78*(4), 498–510.

Hirshfeld-Becker, D. R., Masek, B., Henin, A., Blakely, L. R., Rettew, D. C., Dufton, L., & Biederman, J. (2008). Cognitive-behavioral intervention with young anxious children. *Harvard Review of Psychiatry, 16,* 113–125.

Hirschy, S. T., & Wilkinson, E. (2010). *Protecting our children: Understanding and preventing abuse and neglect in early childhood.* Belmont, CA: Wadsworth.

Hislop, J. (2001). *Female sexual offenders.* Ravensdale, WA: Issues Press.

Hollingsworth, J. (1986). *Unspeakable acts.* New York, NY: Congdon and Weed.

Hollingsworth, J., Glass, G., Heisler, K. W. (2007). Empathy deficits in siblings of severely scapegoated children: A conceptual model. *Journal of Emotional Abuse, 7*(4), 69–88.

Holmes, D. S. (1990). The evidence for repression: An examination of sixty years of research. In Jerome L. Singer (Ed.), *Repression and dissociation: Implications for personality theory, psychopathology, and health* (pp. 85–102). Chicago, IL: University of Chicago Press.

Hoorwitz, A. N. (1983). Guidelines for treating father-daughter incest. *Social Casework, 64,* 515–524.

Horton, C. B., & Kochurka, K. A. (1995). The assessment of children with disabilities who report sexual abuse: A special look at those most vulnerable. In T. Ney (Ed.), *True and false allegations of child sexual abuse: Assessment and case management* (pp. 275–289). New York, NY: Brunner/Mazel.

Hudson, P. S. (1991). *Ritual child abuse: Discovery, diagnosis and treatment.* Saratoga, CA: R & E Publications.

Hughes, D. R. (1998). *Kids online.* Grand Rapids, MI: Baker Book House.

Hughes, J. R. (2007). Review of medical reports on Pedophilia. *Clinical Pediatrics, 46*(8), 667–682.

Hunter, J. A. (Ed.). (2006). Understanding diversity in juvenile sexual offenders: Implications for assessment, treatment and legal management. *Current perspective: Working with sexually aggressive youth and youth with sexual behavior proboems* (pp. 63–77). Holyoke, MA: NEARI Press.

Hunter, J. A., Becker, J. V., & Lexier, L. J. (2006). The female juvenile sex offender. In H. E. Barbaree & W. L. Marshall (Eds.), *The juvenile sex offender* (pp. 148–165). New York, NY: Guilford.

Hunter, M. (1990). *The sexually abused male.* Newbury Park, CA: SAGE.

Jaffa, T., & McDermott, B. (2006). *Eating disorders in children and adolescents.* Cambridge, MA: Cambridge University Press.

James, B., & Nasjleti, M. (1983). *Treating sexually abused children and their families.* Palo Alto, CA: Consulting Psychologists.

James, B., & McKinnon, M. (1990). The 'incestuous family' revisited: A critical analysis of family therapy myths. *Journal of Marital and Family Therapy, 16*(1), 71–88.

Janoff-Bulman, R. (1992). *Shattered assumptions: Toward a new psychology of trauma.* New York, NY: Simon and Schuster.

Jenkins, P. (1998). *Moral panic: Changing concepts of the child molester in modern America.* New Haven, CT: Yale University Press.

Jenkins, P. (2001a). *Beyond tolerance: Child pornography and the internet.* New York, NY: New York University Press.

Jenkins, P. (2001b). *Pedophiles and priests: Anatomy of a contemporary crisis.* Oxford, UK: Oxford University Press.

Jennings, D., & Tharp, R. (2003, May 4–6). Betrayal of trust. *Dallas Morning News.*

Jespersen, A. F., Lalmiere, M. L., & Seto, M. C. (2009). Sexual abuse history among adult sex offenders and non-sex offenders: A meta-analysis. *Child Abuse and Neglect, 33*(3), 179–192.

Johansson-Love, J., & Fremouw, W. (2009). Female sexual offenders: A controlled comparison of offender and victim/crime characteristics. *Journal of Family Violence, 24,* 367–376.

John Jay College of Criminal Justice. (2004). *The nature and scope of the problem of sexual abuse of minors by Catholic priests and deacons in the United States.* Washington, DC: U.S. Conference of Bishops.

Johnson, B. R. (2006). Co-morbid diagnosis of sexually abusive youth. In R. E. Longo & D. S. Prescott (Eds.), *Current perspectives: Working with sexually aggressive youth and youth with sexual behavior problems* (pp. 167–192). Holyoke, MA: NEARI Press.

Johnson, J. (1992a). *Mothers of incest survivors: Another side of the story.* Bloomington, IN: Indiana University Press.

Johnson, J. J. (1992b). *Teen prostitution.* Danbury, CT: Franklin Watts.

Johnson, P. A., Owens, R. G., Dewey, M. E., & Eisenberg, M. E. (1990). Professional's attributions of censure in father-daughter incest. *Child Abuse and Neglect, 14,* 419–428.

Johnson, T. C. (1999). *Understanding your child's sexual behavior: What's natural and healthy.* Oakland, CA: New Harbinger.

Johnson, T. C. (2000). Sexualized children who molest. *Siecus Report, 29*(1), 35–39.

Johnson, T. C. (2009). *Helping children with sexual behavior problems.* San Diego, CA: Institute on Violence, Abuse and Trauma.

Johnson, T. C. (2010). *Understanding children's sexual behaviors.* San Diego, CA: Institute on Violence, Abuse and Trauma.

Johnson, T. C., & Aoki, W. T. (1993). *Sexual behaviors in latency age children in residential treatment.* New York, NY: Haworth.

Johnson, T. C., & Doonan, R. (2006). Children twelve and younger with sexual behavior problems: What we know in 2005 that we didn't know in 1985. In R. E. Longo & D. S. Prescott (Eds.), *Current perspectives: Working with sexually aggressive youth and youth with sexual behavior problems* (pp. 79–118). Holyoke, MA: NEARI Press.

Johnson, T. C., & Hooper, R. I. (2003). Boundaries and family practices: Implications for child abuse. In R. Geffner, K. C. Franey, T. Arnold, & R. Falconer (Eds.), *Identifying and treating sex offenders: Current approaches, research, & techniques* (pp. 103–125). New York, NY: Haworth.

Johnson-Reid, M. (1998). Youth violence and exposure to violence in childhood: An ecological review. *Aggression and Violent Behavior, 3*, 159–179.

Jones, D. P. (1997). Assessment of suspected child sexual abuse. In M. E. Helfer, R. S. Kempe, & R. D. Krugman (Eds.), *The battered child* (pp. 296–312). Chicago, IL: University of Chicago Press.

Jones, D. P., & McGraw, E. M. (1987). Reliable and fictitious accounts of sexual abuse to children. *Journal of Interpersonal Violence, 2*(1), 27–45.

Jones, J. H. (1997). *Alfred C. Kinsey: A public/private life.* New York, NY: W. W. Norton.

Jones, L., Cross, T., Walsh, W., & Simone, M. (2007). Do child advocacy centers improve families' experiences of child sexual abuse? *Child Abuse and Neglect, 31*(10), 1069–1085.

Jones, L. M., Mitchell, K. J., & Finkelhor, D. (2012). Trends in youth Internet victimization: Findings from three youth Internet safety surveys 2000–2010. *Journal of Adolescent Health, 50*, 179–186.

Jones, R. L., Loredo, C. M., Johnson, S. D., & McFarlane-Nathan, G. H. (1999). A paradigm for culturally relevant sexual abuser treatment: An international perspective. In A. D. Lewis (Ed.), *Cultural diversity in sexual abuser treatment* (pp. 3–44). Brandon, VT: Safer Society Press.

Joyce, P. (1997). Mothers of sexually abused children and the concept of collusion. *Journal of Child Sexual Abuse, 6*(2), 75–92.

Joyce, P. A. (2007). The production of therapy: The social process of construction of the mother of the sexually abused child. *Journal of Child Sexual Abuse, 16*(3), 1–18.

Justice, B., & Justice, R. (1979). *The broken taboo: Sex in the family.* New York, NY: Human Services Press.

Kadushin, A., & Martin, J. (1988). *Child welfare services.* New York, NY: Macmillan.

Kafka, M. P., & Hennen, J. (2003). Hypersexual desire in males: Are males with paraphilias different from males with paraphilia-related disorders? *Sexual Abuse: A Journal of Research and Treatment, 15*, 307–319.

Kamphuis, J. H., DeRuiter, C., Janssen, B., & Spiering, M. (2005). Preliminary evidence for an automatic link between sex and power among men who molest children. *Journal of Interpersonal Violence, 20*(11), 1351–1365.

Kaplan, D. L. (2010). Emotional incest and what's wrong with being special. *Cutting Edge.* Winter 2010, 4–5, 14.

Kaplan, H. I., & Sadock, B. J. (Eds.). (1998). Paraphilias and sexual disorder not otherwise specified. *Synopsis of psychiatry: Behavioral science/clinical.* (pp. 700–710). Baltimore, MD: Williams and Wilkins.

Karson, M. (2001). *Patterns of child abuse: How dysfunctional transactions are replicated in individuals, families and the child welfare system.* Binghamton, NY: Haworth Press.

Kelley, S. (1994). Abuse of children in day care centres: Characteristics and consequences. *Child Abuse Review, 3*, 15–25.

Kelley, S. J. (1990). Responsibility and management strategies in child sexual abuse: A comparison of child protective workers, nurses and police officers. *Child Welfare, 69*(1), 43–51.

Kelley, S. J., Brant, R., & Waterman, J. (1993). Sexual abuse of children in day care centers. *Child Abuse and Neglect, 17*(1), 71–89.

Kellner, L. (2013). Teenage pregnancy and parenting. In C. Crosson-Tower (Ed.), *Exploring child welfare: A practice perspective* (pp. 201–279). Boston, MA: Pearson.

Kempe, R., & Kempe, C. H. (1984). *The common secret.* New York, NY: W. H. Freeman.

Kendall, P. C., Hudson, J. L., Gosch, E., Flannery-Schroeder, E., & Suveg, C. (2008). Cognitive-behavioral therapy for anxiety disordered youth: A randomized clinical trial evaluating child and family modalities. *Journal of Consulting and Clinical Psychology, 76*, 282–297.

Kendall-Tackett, K. A., & Klest, B. (2009). Casual mechanisms and multidimensional pathways between trauma, dissociation and health. *Journal of Trauma and Dissociation, 10*(2), 129–134.

Kennedy, E. (2002). *The unhealed wound: The church, the priesthood and the question of sexuality.* New York, NY: St. Martin's.

Kia-Keating, M., Sorsoli, L., & Grossman, F. K. (2010). Relational challenges and recovery processes in male survivors of childhood sexual abuse. *Journal of Interpersonal Violence, 25*(4), 666–683.

Kingston, D. A., Federoff, P., Firestone, P. , Curry, S., & Bradford, J. M. (2008). Pornography use and sexual aggression: The impact of frequency and type of pornography use on recidivism among sexual offenders. *Aggressive Behavior, 34*(4), 341–351.

Kinnear, K. (2007). *Childhood sexual abuse.* Santa Barbara, CA: ABC-CLIO.

Kinsey, A. C., Pomeroy, W., Martin, C., & Gebhard, P. (1953). *Sexual behavior in the human female.* Philadelphia, PA: W. B. Saunders.

Kline, P. M. , McMackin, R., & Lezotte, E. (2008). The impact of the clergy abuse scandal on parish communities. *Journal of Child Sexual Abuse, 17*(3–4), 290–300.

Knight, M. O., Chew, J., & Gonzalez, E. (2005). The child welfare system: A map for the bold traveler. In P. F. Talley (Ed.), *Handbook for the treatment of the abused and neglected child* (pp. 25–37). New York, NY: Haworth.

Knoll, J. (2010). Teacher sexual misconduct: Grooming patterns and female offenders. *Journal of Child Sexual Abuse, 19,* 371–386.

Kouyoumdjian, H., Perry, A. R., & Hansen, D. J. (2009). Non-offending parent expectations of sexually abused children: Predictive factors and influence on children's recovery. *Journal of Child Sexual Abuse, 18,* 40–60.

Krane, J. (2003). *What's mother got to do with it? Protecting children from sexual abuse.* Toronto, Ontario, Canada: Toronto University Press.

Kreiger, M. J., Rosenfeld, A. A., Gordon, A., & Bennett, M. (1980). Problems in the psychotherapy of children with histories of incest. *American Journal of Psychotherapy, 34*(1), 81–88.

Kuehnle, K., & Connell, M. (2010). Child sexual abuse suspicions: Treatment considerations during investigation. *Journal of Child Sexual Abuse, 19*(5), 554–571.

Lamb, N. (1994). The Little Rascals Day Care Center case: The ingredients of two successful prosecutions. *Journal of Child Sexual Abuse, 3*(2).

Lane, S. (1991). Special offender populations. In G. D. Ryan & S. L. Lane (Eds.), *Juvenile sexual offending: Causes, consequences and correction* (pp. 299–332). Lexington, MA: Lexington Books.

Langevin, R., Curnoe, P., Fedoroff, P., Bennett, R., & Peever, C. (2004). Lifetime sex offender recidivism: A 25-year follow-up study. *Canadian Journal of Criminology and Criminal Justice, 46,* 531–552.

Langstrom, N., & Grann, M. (2000). Risk for criminal recidivism among young sex offenders. *Journal of Interpersonal Violence, 15,* 855–871.

LaRoy, D., Lamb, M., & Pipe, M. E. (2008). Repeated interviewing: A critical evaluation of the risks and potential benefits. In K. Kuehnle & M. Connell (Eds.), *Child sexual abuse: Research, evaluation and testimony for courts* (pp. 327–364). London, UK: John Wiley.

Latham, C., & Kinscherff, R. T. (2006). Legal and ethical considerations in evaluations of children with sexual behavioral problems. In R. E. Longo & D. S. Prescott (Eds.), *Current perspectives: Working with sexually aggressive youth and youth with sexual behavior problems* (pp. 215–233). Holyoke, MA: NEARI Press.

Lau, M., & Kristensen, E. (2010). Revictimization in a clinical sample of women reporting childhoos sexual abuse. *Nordic Journal of Psychiatry, 64*(1), 4–10.

Laws, D. R. (Ed.). (1989). *Relapse prevention with sex offenders.* New York, NY: Guilford.

Laws, D. R., Hudson, S. M., & Ward, T. (Eds.). (2000). *Remaking relapse prevention with sex offenders.* Thousand Oaks, CA: SAGE.

Laws, D. R., & Ward, T. (2011). *Desistance from sexual offending: Alternatives to throwing away the keys.* New York, NY: Guilford.

Leberg, E. (1997). *Understanding child molesters.* Thousand Oaks, CA: SAGE.

Lee, J. K. P., Jackson, H. J., Pattison, P., & Ward, T. (Eds.). (2002). Developmental risks for sexual offending. *Child Abuse and Neglect, 26*(1), 73–92.

Leifer, M., Kilbane, T., & Grossman, G. (2001). A three-generational study comparing the families of supportive and unsupportive mothers of sexually abused children. *Child Maltreatment, 6*(4), 353–364.

Lemieux, S. R., & Byers, E. S. (2008). The sexual well-being of women who have experienced child sexual abuse. *Psychology of Women Quarterly,* *32*(2), 126–144.

Lenhart, A. (2009). Teens and Sexting. *Pew Internet and American Life Project.* Washington, DC: Pew Research Center.

Levenson, J., & Cotter, L. P. (2005). The impact of sex offender residence restrictions: 1,000 feet from danger or one step from absurd? *Offender Therapy and Comparative Criminology, 49,* 168–178.

Levenson, J. S., & Morin, J. W. (2006). Risk assessment in child sexual abuse cases. *Child Welfare, 85,* 59–82.

Lev-Wiesel, R. (2006). Intergenerational transmission of sexual abuse? Motherhood in the shadow of incest. *Journal of Child Sexual Abuse, 15*(2), 75–101.

Levy, T. M., & Orlans, M. (1998). *Attachment, trauma and healing.* Washington, DC: CWLA Press.

Lew, M. (2004). *Victims no longer: The classic guide for men recovering from child sexual abuse.* New York, NY: HarperCollins.

Lewis, A. D. (1999). Working with culturally diverse populations. In A. D. Lewis (Ed.), *Cultural diversity in sexual abuser treatment* (pp. 45–67). Brandon, VT: Safer Society Press.

Lindblad, F., & Kaldal, A. (2005). Child witness statements about sexual abuse in day-care: Reports from a case with confessions for the suspect. *Journal of Investigative Psychology and Offender Profiling, 2,* 165–178.

Lindeman, H. (2005). Sex offender tests - SAI and SAI Juvenile. In B. K. Schwartz (Ed.), *The sex offender: Issues in assessment, treatment, and supervision of adult and juvenile populations* (pp. 7.1–7.23). Kingston, NJ: Civic Research Institute.

Linder, D. (2003). The McMartin Preschool abuse trial: A commentary. Retrieved June 4, 2006, from http://www.law2umkc.edu/faculty/projects/ftrials/mcmartin/mcmartin.html

Llewelyn, S. P. (1997). Therapeutic approaches for survivors of childhood sexual abuse: A review. *Clinical Psychology and Psychotherapy, 4*(1), 32–41.

Lloyd, R. (1976). *For love or money: Boy prostitution in America.* New York, NY: Vanguard Press.

Loftus, E. (2003). Elizabeth Loftus: Award for distinguished scientific applications of psychology. *American Psychologist, 58*(11), 864–867.

Loftus, E. F. (1993). The reality of repressed memories. *American Psychologist, 48*(5), 518–538.

Logan, C., Holcombe, E., Ryan, S., Manlove, J., & Moore, K. (2007). *Childhood sexual abuse and teen pregnancy.* Washington, DC: Child Trends and National Campaign to Prevent Teen Pregnancy.

Lorentzen, E., Nilsen, H., & Traeen, B. (2008). Will it never end? The narratives of incest victims on the termination of child sexual abuse. *Journal of Sex Research, 45*(2), 164–174.

Lothstein, L. M. (1994). Psychological theories of pedophilia and ephebophilia. In S. T. Rossetti (Ed.), *Slayer of the soul: Child sexual abuse and the Catholic Church* (pp. 20–27). Mystic, CT: Twenty-Third Publications.

Lowe, W. Jr., Pavkov, T. W., Casanova, G. M., & Wetchler, J. L. (2005). Do American ethnic cultures differ in their definitions of child sexual abuse? *American Journal of Family Therapy, 33,* 147–166.

Lowenstein, L., & Freeman, R. C. (2012). Group therapy with sexually abused children. In P. Goodyear-Brown (Ed.), *Handbook of child sexual abuse* (pp. 355–375). Hoboken, NJ: John Wiley.

Lundrigan, P. S. (2001). *Treating youth who sexually abuse: An integrated multi-component approach.* New York, NY: Haworth.

Lustig, N., Spellman, J., Dresser, S., & Murray, T. (1966). Incest. *Archives of General Psychiatry, 14,* 31–40.

Luthar, S. S. (1991). Vulnerability and resilience: A study of high-risk adolescents. *Child Development, 62,* 600–616.

Lyles, A., Cohen, L., & Brown, M. (2009). *Transforming communities to prevent child sexual abuse and exploitation: A primary prevention approach.* Oakland, CA: Prevention Institute.

Lyon, T. D. (2005). Speaking with children: Advice from investigative interviewers. In P. F. Talley (Ed.), *Handbook for the treatment of abused and neglected children* (pp. 65–81). New York, NY: Haworth.

Madonna, P., Van Scoyk, S., & Jones, D. P. H. (1991). Family interactions within incest and nonincest families. *American Journal of Psychiatry, 128*(1), 46–49.

Magid, L. Protect kids on MySpace. CBS News (2006, February 3). Retrieved August 1, 2007, from http://www.cbsnews.com/news/protect-kids-on-myspace-03-02-2006/

Malchiodi, C. A. (2012). Trauma informed art therapy and sexual abuse of children. In P. Goodyear-Brown (Ed.), *Handbook of child sexual abuse* (pp. 341–354), Hoboken, NJ: John Wiley.

Malinowski, B. (1927). *Sex and repression in savage society.* London, UK: Routledge and Kegan Paul.

Maltz, W. (2012). *The sexual healing journey: A guide for survivors of sexual abuse.* New York, NY: HarperCollins.

Mandell, D. (2008). Power, care and vulnerability: Considering use of self in child welfare work. *Journal of Social Work Practice, 22*(2), 235–248.

Mansell, S., Sobsey, D., & Moskal, R. (1998). Clinical findings among sexually abused children with and without developmental disabilities. *Mental Retardation, 36*(1), 12–22.

Marcum, C. D. (2007). Interpreting the intentions of Internet predators: An examination of online predatory behavior. *Journal of Child Sexual Abuse, 16*(4), 99–114.

Marlatt, G. A. (1985). Relapse prevention: Theoretical rationale and overview of the model. In G. A. Marlatt & G. R. Gordon (Eds.), *Relapse prevention* (pp. 3–70). New York, NY: Guilford.

Marshall, L. E., & Marshall, W. L. (2006). Sexual addiction in incarcerated sexual offenders. *Sexual Addiction and Compulsivity, 13*(4), 377–390.

Marshall, W. L. (1997). Pedophilia: Psychopathology and theory. In D. R. Laws & W. T. O'Donahue (Eds.), *Sexual deviance: Theory assessment and treatment* (pp. 152–174). New York, NY: Guilford Press.

Marshall, W. L., & Barbaree, H. E. (1990). An integrated theory of the etiology of sexual offending. In W. L. Marshall, D. R. Laws, & H. E. Barbraee (Eds.), *Handbook of sexual assault: Issues, theories and treatment of the offender* (pp. 257–275). New York, NY: Plenum.

Marshall, W. L., & Marshall, L. E. (2000). The origins of sexual offending. *Trauma, Violence and Abuse, 1,* 250–263.

Marziano, V., Ward, T., Beech, A. R., & Pattison, P. (2006). Identification of five fundamental implicit theories underlying cognitive distortions in child abusers: A preliminary study. *Psychology, Crime and Law, 12*(1), 97–105.

Masson, J. M. (1984). *The assault on truth: Freud's suppression of the Seduction Theory.* New York, NY: Farrar, Straus, and Giroux.

Matthews, R., Matthews, J., & Speltz, K. (1989). *Female sexual offenders: An exploratory study.* Orwell, VT: Safe Society Press.

Maybrey, V., & Perozzi, D. (April 1, 2010). 'Sexting': Should child pornography laws apply? ABC News/Nightline. Retrieved May 1, 2012, from http://abcnews.go.com/Nightline/phillip-alpert-sexting-teen-child-porn/story?id=10252790#.T6RM5u3K0so

Mayer, A. (1983). *Incest.* Holmes Beach, FL: Learning Publications.

Mayer, A. (1985). *Sexual abuse: Causes, consequences and treatment of incestuous and pedophilic acts.* Holmes Beach, FL: Learning Publications.

McCann, I. L., & Pearlman, L. A. (1990). *Psychological trauma and the adult survivor: Theory, therapy and transformation.* New York, NY: Brunner/Mazel.

McCarty, L. (1986). Mother-child incest: Characteristics of the offender. *Child Welfare, 65*(5), 447–458.

McDonagh, A., Freidman, M., McHugo, G., Ford, J., Sengupta, A., Mueser, K., Demment, C. C., Fournier, D., Schnurr, P. P., & Descamps, M. (2005). Randomized trial of cognitive-behavioral therapy for chronic posttraumatic stress disorder in adult female survivors of child sexual abuse. *Journal of Consulting and Clinical Psychology, 73*(3), 515–524.

McGee, S. A., & Holmes, C. C. (2012). Treatment considerations with sexually traumatized adolescents. In P. Goodyear-Brown (Ed.), *Handbook of child sexual abuse* (pp. 447–468). Hoboken, NJ: John Wiley.

McGlone, G. J. (2003). The pedophile and the pious: Towards a new understanding of sexually offending and non-offending Roman Catholic priests. In J. L. Mullings, J. W. Marquart, & D. J. Hartley (Eds.), *The victimization of children* (pp. 115–131). New York, NY: Haworth.

McGoldrick, M., & Pearce, J. K. (1981). Family therapy with Irish Americans. *Family Process, 20,* 223–44.

McGrath, R. J., Cumming, G. F., Burchard, B. L., Zeoli, S., & Ellerby, L. (2010). *Current practices and emerging trends in sexual abuser management: The Safer Society 2009 North American Survey.* Brandon, VT: Safer Society Press.

McKay, M., & Bannon, W. (2004). Engaging families in mental health services. *Child and Adolescent Psychiatric Clinics of North America, 13*, 905–921.

McLaughlin, J. F. (1998). Technophilia: A modern day paraphilia. *New Hampshire Police Association Knight Stick Magazine, 51*, 47–51.

McLaughlin, J. F. (2000). Cyber child sex offender typology. *New Hampshire Police Association Knight Stick Magazine, 55*, 39–42.

McLaughlin, J. F. (2003). Personal Correspondence, March 5, 2003.

McNally, R. J. (2005). *Remembering trauma.* Cambridge, MA: Belknap Press.

Meiselman, K. (1992). *Incest.* San Francisco, CA: Jossey-Bass.

Merchant, L., & Toth, P. (2001). *Child interview guide.* Seattle, WA: Harborview Center for Sexual Assault and Traumatic Stress.

Messman-Moore, T. L., & Long, P. J. (2000). The revictimization of child sexual abuse survivors: An examination of the adjustment of college. *Child Maltreatment, 5*(10), 18–28.

Middlebrook, D. W. (1991). *Anne Sexton.* Boston, MA: Houghton Mifflin.

Miles, V. J. (2012). *Boys of the cloth: The accidental role of church reforms in causings and curbing abuse by priests.* Lanhan, MD: Hamiliton Books.

Mills, L. J., & Daniluk, J. C. (2002). Her body speaks: The experience of dance therapy for survivors of child sexual abuse. *Journal of Counseling and Development, 80*(1), 77–84.

Miner, M. H., Siekert, G. P., & Ackland, M. A. (1997). *Evaluation: Juvenile sex offender program, Minnesota Correctional Facility-Sauk Centre.* Minneapolis, MN: University of Minnesota.

Mintzer, M. B. (1996). Understanding countertransference reactions in working with adolescent perpetrators of sexual abuse. *Bulletin of the Menninger Clinic, 60*(2), 219–229.

Mitchell, J., & Morse J. (1997). *From victim to survivor: Women survivors of female perpetrators.* New York, NY: Taylor and Francis.

Mitchell, K. J., Finkelhor, D., & Becker-Blease, K. A. (2007). Linking youth Internet and conventional problems: Findings from a clinical perspective. *Journal of Aggression, Maltreatment and Trauma, 15*(2), 39–58.

Monga, S., Young, A., & Owens, M. (2009). Evaluating a cognitive behavioral therapy group program for anxious five to seven year old children: A pilot study. *Depression and Anxiety, 26*, 243–250.

Morgan, M. (1995). *How to interview sexual abuse victims.* Thousand Oaks, CA: SAGE.

Morgan, T., & Cummings, A. L. (1999). Change experienced during group therapy by female survivors of child sexual abuse. *Journal of Counseling and Clinical Psychology, 67*(1), 28–36.

Morgenbesser, L. I. (2010). Educator sexual abuse: Introduction and overview. *Journal of Child Sexual Abuse, 19*, 367–370.

Moss, E. (2008). The place of psychodynamic psychotherapy in the integrated treatment of posttraumatic stress disorder and trauma recovery. *Psychotherapy, Theory, Research, Practice and Training, 42*, 171–179.

Moulden, H. M., & Firestone, P. (2007). Vicarious traumatization the impact on therapists who work with sexual offenders. *Trauma, Violence and Abuse, 8*(1), 67–83.

Munro, E. (2008). *Effective child protection.* Thousand Oaks, CA: SAGE.

Muram, D., & Simmons, K. (2008). Pattern recognition in pediatric and adolescent gynecology: A case for formal education. *Journal of Pediatric Adolescent Gynecology, 21*(2), 103–108.

Murdock, N. L., & Gore, P. A. Jr. (2004). Stress, coping and differentiation of self. *Contemporary Family Therapy: An International Journal, 26*(3), 319–335.

Myers, J. E. B. (1998). *Legal issues in child abuse and neglect practice.* Newbury Park, CA: SAGE.

Myers, J. E. B. (2011). A short history of child protection in America. In J. E. B. Myers (Ed.), *The APSAC handbook on child maltreatment* (pp. 3–15). Thousand Oaks, CA: SAGE.

Nathan, D. (1993). Revisiting country walk. *Forensics, 5*(1), 5–11.

Nathan, P., & Ward, T. (2002). Female sexual offenders: Clinical and demographic features. *Journal of Sexual Aggression, 8*(1), 5–21.

National Center for Missing and Exploited Children (NCMEC). (2002). *Female juvenile prostitution: Problem and response.* Alexandria, VA: National Center for Missing and Exploited Children.

National Center for the Prosecution of Child Abuse. (1997). *Child abuse and neglect statutes series* (Vol. 3). Washington, DC: National Center on Child Abuse and Neglect Clearinghouse.

National Coalition to Prevent Child Sexual Exploitation. (2008). *The national plan to prevent the sexual exploitation of children.* Retrieved January 12, 2011, from http://www.missingkids.com/en_US/documents/NCPCSE_NationalPlan.pdf

Nelson, E. B., Soutullo, C. A., DelBello, M. P., & McElroy, S. L. (2002). The psychopharmacological treatment of sex offenders. In B. K. Schwartz (Ed.), *The sex offender: Current treatment modalities and system issues* (pp. 13.1–13.30). Kingston, NJ: Civic Research Institute.

Nelson-Gardell, D. (2008). Treatment for sexually abused adolescents. In C. Hilarski, J. S. Woodarski, & M. D. Feit (Eds.), *Handbook of social work in child and adolescent sexual abuse* (pp. 171–201). New York, NY: Haworth.

Noblitt, J. R., & Perskin, P. S. (2000). *Cult and ritual abuse: It's history, anthropology, and recent discover in contemporary America.* Westport, CT: Praeger.

Noblitt, R., & Noblitt, P. P. (Eds.). (2008). *Ritual abuse in the twenty-first century: Psychological, forensic, social and political implications.* Bandon, OR: Robert D. Reed.

Noel, J. A. (2013). Court services on behalf of children. In C. Crosson-Tower (Ed.), *Exploring child welfare: A practice perspective* (pp. 231–250). Boston, MA: Pearson.

Noll, J. G. (2005). Does childhood sexual abuse set in motion a cycle of violence against women? *Journal of Interpersonal Violence, 20,* 155–162.

Nurcombe, B. (2008). Treatment for the sexually abused child. In C. Hilarski, J. S. Woodarski, & M. D. Feit (Eds.), *Handbook of social work in child and adolescent sexual abuse* (pp. 153–169). New York, NY: Haworth.

Oates, R. K., Jones, D. P. H., Denson, A., Sirotnak, A., Gary, N., & Krugman, R. (2000). Erroneous concerns about child sexual abuse. *Child Abuse and Neglect, 24*(1), 149–157.

Oates, R. K., Tebbutt, J., Swanson, H., Lynch, D. L., & O'Toole, B. I. (1998). Prior childhood sexual abuse in mothers of sexually abused children. *Child Abuse and Neglect, 22*(11), 1113–1118.

O'Connell, M. A., Leberg, E., & Donaldson, C. R. (1990). *Working with sex offenders: Guidelines for therapist selection.* Newbury Park, CA: SAGE.

Ogilvie, B. A. (2004). *Mother-daughter incest.* New York, NY: Haworth.

Olafson, E. (2002). When paradigms collide: Roland Summit and the rediscovery of child sexual abuse. In J. Conte (Ed.), *Critical issues in child sexual abuse* (pp. 71–106). Thousand Oaks, CA: SAGE.

Olafson, E., & Boat, B. W. (2000). Long-term management of the sexually abused child: Considerations and challenges. In R. M. Reece (Ed.), *The treatment of child abuse* (pp. 14–35). Baltimore, MD: Johns Hopkins.

Olafson, E., Corwin, D. L., & Summit, R. (1993). Modern history of sexual abuse: Cycles of discovery and suppression. *Child Abuse and Neglect, 17,* 7–24.

Olafson, E., & Lederman, C. (2006). The state of the debate about children's disclosure patterns of child sexual abuse. *Juvenile and Family Court Journal, 57*(1), 27–40.

Olio, K. A. (2004). The truth about False Memory Syndrome. In L. Cosgrove & P. J. Caplan (Eds.), *Bias in psychiatric diagnosis* (pp. 163–168). Northvale, NJ: Jason Aronson.

O'Neil, C., & Brown, W. (2010). *Child incest.* Tallahassee, FL: Wm. Gladden Foundation Press.

O'Reilly, G., & Carr, A. (2006). Assessment and treatment of criminogenic needs. In H. E. Barbaree & W. L. Marshall (Eds.), *The juvenile sex offender,* (pp. 189–218). New York, NY: Guilford.

Ost, S. (2002). Children at risk: Legal and societal perceptions of the potential threat that the possession of child pornography poses to society. *Journal of Law and Society, 29*(3), 436–460.

Palmioto, M., & MacNichol, S. (2010). Supervision of sex offenders: A multi-faceted and collaborative approach. *Federal Probation, 74*(2), 27–30.

Parent, S. (2011). Disclosure of sexual abuse in sports organizations: A case study. *Journal of Child Sexual Abuse, 20,* 322–337.

Parent, S., & Demers, G. (2011). Sexual abuse in sport: A model to prevent and protect. *Child Abuse Review, 20,* 120–133.

Park, F. (1996). Clergy sexual abuse. *Connecticut Sexual Assault Newsletter.* Retrieved from http://www.advocateweb.org/cease/csa.htm

Parsons, T. (1954). The incest taboo in relation to social structure and the socialization of the child. *British Journal of Sociology, 5,* 101–117.

Patrick, S., & Marsh, R. (2009). Recidivism among child sexual abusers: Initial results of a 13-year longitudinal random sample. *Journal of Child Sexual Abuse, 18,* 123–136.

Pearlman, L. A., & Saakvitne, K. W. (1995). *Trauma and the therapist: Countertransference and vicarious traumatization in psychotherapy with incest survivors.* New York, NY: Norton.

Pelto, V. L. (1981). Male incest offenders and non-offenders: A comparison of early sexual history. *Dissertation Abstracts International, 42*(3-B), 1154.

Pemberton, A. E., & Wakeling, H. C. (2009). Entitled to sex: Attitudes of sexual offenders. *Journal of Sexual Aggression, 15*(3), 289–303.

Perry, B. (2003). Sexual abuse of infants: A five-part question focusing on sexual abuse during infancy. Retrieved from http://www.childtrauma.org/CTAMATERIALS/infant_abuse.asp

Perry, B. (2006). Applying principles of neurodevelopment to clinical work with maltreated and traumatized children. In N. Webb (Ed.), *Working with traumatized youth in child welfare* (pp. 27–52). New York, NY: Guilford Press.

Perry, B. (2009). Examining child maltreatment through a nuerological lens: Clinical applications of neurosequential model of therapeutics. *Journal of Loss and Trauma, 14,* 240–255.

Peterson, J. (2004). Don't trust me with your child: Non-legal precautions when the law cannot prevent sexual exploitation in youth sports. *The Texas Review of Entertainment and Sports, 5*(2), 297–323.

Pintello, D., & Zuravin, S. (2001). Intrafamilial sexual abuse: Predictions for postdiscloure maternal belief and protective action. *Child Maltreatment, 6*(4), 344–352.

Pipe, M., Lamb, M. E., Orbach, Y., & Cederborg, A. (Eds.). (2007). *Child sexual abuse: Disclosure, delay and denial.* Mahwah, NJ: Lawrence Erlbaum.

Pithers, W. D. , Gray, A., Busconi, A., & Houchens, P. (1998). Children with sexual behavior problems: Identification of five distinct child types and related treatment considerations. *Child Maltreatment, 3*(4), 384–406.

Plante, T. (Ed.). (2004). *Sin against innocents: Sexual abuse by priests and the role of the Catholic Church.* Westport, CT: Praeger.

Plummer, C. (2006). Non-abusive mothers of sexually abused children: The role of rumination in maternal outcomes. *Journal of Child Sexual Abuse, 15*(2), 103–122.

Poole, D. A., & Lamb, M. (1998). *Investigative interviews with children.* Washington, DC: American Psychological Association.

Pope, K. S. (2001). Sex between therapists and clients. In J. Worell (Ed.), *Encyclopedia of women and gender: Sex similarities and differences and the impact of society on gender* (pp. 955–962). San Diego, CA: Academic Press.

Pope, K. S., & Vetter, V. A. (1991). Prior therapist-patient sexual involvement among patients seen by psychologists. *Psychotherapy, 28*(3), 429–438.

Powell, L., & Chesire, A. (2010). A preliminary evaluation of a massage program for children who have been sexually abused and their non-abusing mothers. *Journal of Child Sexual Abuse, 19*(2), 141–155.

Preble, J. M., & Groth, A. N. (2002). *Male victims of same-sex abuse.* Baltimore, MD: Sidran Press.

Prendergast, W. E. (2004). *Treating sex offenders.* New York, NY: Haworth.

Prescott, D. S., & Longo, R. E. (2006). Current perspectives: Working with young people who sexually abuse. In R. E. Longo & D. S. Prescott (Eds.), *Current perspectives: Working with sexually aggressive youth and youth with sexual behavior problems* (pp. 45–61). Holyoke, MA: NEARI Press.

Proeve, M. (2009). A preliminary examination of specific risk assessment for sexual offenders against children. *Journal of Child Sexual Abuse, 18,* 583–593.

Pryce, J. G., Shackelford, K. K., & Pryce, D. H. (2007). *Secondary trauma stress and the child welfare worker.* Chicago, IL: Lyceum Books.

Public Broadcasting System (O. Bikel, producer and director). (1993). *Innocence lost: The verdict.* Retrieved June 7, 2007, from http://www.pbs.org/wgbh/pages/frontline/shows/innocence/html

Quackenbush, R. E. (2003). Role theory in the assessment of sex offenders. In R. Geffner, K. C. Franey, T. G. Arnold, & R. Falconer (Eds.), *Identifying and treating sex offenders: Current approaches, research, and techniques* (pp. 77–102). New York, NY: Haworth Press.

Rabinowitz, D. (2004). *No crueler tyrannies: Accusation, false witness and other terrors of our times.* New York, NY: Simon and Schuster.

Rapee, R. M., Schniering, C. A., & Hudson, J. L. (2009). Anxiety disorders during childhood and adolescence: Origins and treatment. *Annual Review of Clinical Psychology, 5,* 311–314.

Raskin, D. C., & Steller, M. (1989). Assessing credibility of allegations of child sexual abuse: Polygraphic examinations and statement analysis. In H. Wegener, F. Losel, & J. Haisch (Eds.), *Criminal behavior and the justice system: Psychological perspectives* (pp. 290–302). New York, NY: Springer-Verlag.

Rasmussen, L. A. (2004). Differentiating youth who sexually abuse: Applying a multidimensional framework when assessing and treating subtypes. In R. Geffner, K. C. Franey, T. G. Arnold, & R. Falconer (Eds.), *Identifying and treating youth who sexually offend* (pp. 57–82). New York, NY: Haworth.

Reckling, A. E. (2004). Mother-daughter incest: When survivors become mothers. *Journal of Trauma Practice, 3*(2), 49–71.

Rediger, G. L. (2003). *Beyond the scandals.* Minneapolis, MN: Fortress.

Reidy, T. J., & Hochstadt, N. J. (1993). Attribution of blame in incest cases: A comparison of mental health professionals. *Child Abuse and Neglect, 17,* 371–381.

Reijen, L., Bulten, E., & Nijman, H. (2009). Demographic and personality characteristics of Internet child pornography downloaders in comparison to other offenders. *Journal of Child Sexual Abuse, 18*(6), 611–622.

Reisner, A. D. (1998). Repressed memories: True and false. In R. A. Baker (Ed.), *Child sexual abuse and false memory syndrome* (pp. 193–212). New York, NY: Prometheus Books.

Renk, K., Baksh, E., Donnelly, R., & Roddenbery, A., (2008). Prevention endeavors. In C. Hilarski, J. S. Woodarski, & M. D. Feit (Eds.), *Handbook of social work in child and adolescent sexual abuse* (pp. 229–251). New York, NY: Haworth.

Renshaw, D. (1982). *Incest: Understanding and treatment.* Boston, MA: Little, Brown.

Rice, M. E., & Harris, G. T. (2002). Men who molest their sexually immature daughters: Is a special explanation required? *Journal of Abnormal Psychology, 111,* 329–339.

Rich, P. (2003). *Understanding, assessing and rehabilitating juvenile sexual offenders.* Hoboken, NJ: John Wiley.

Rich, P. (2006). *Attachment and sexual offending.* West Sussex, UK: John Wiley.

Rich, P. (2009). *Juvenile sexual offenders: A comprehensive guide to risk evaluation.* Hoboken, NJ: John Wiley.

Rich, P. (2011). *Understanding, assessing and rehabilitating juvenile sexual offenders.* Hoboken, NJ: John Wiley.

Righthand, S., & Welch, C. (2004). Characteristics of youth who sexually offend. In R. Geffner, K. C. Franey, T. G. Arnold, & R. Falconer (Eds.), *Identifying and treating youth who sexually offend* (pp. 15–32). New York, NY: Haworth.

Robinson, S. (2006). Adolescent females with sexual behavior problems: What constitutes best practice. In R. E. Longo & D. S. Prescott (Eds.), *Current perspectives: Working with sexually aggressive youth and youth with sexual behavior problem* (pp. 273–324). Holyoke, MA: NEARI Press.

Rodriquez-Srednicki, O., & Twaite, J. A. (2006). *Understanding, assessing and treating adult survivors of childhood sexual abuse.* Lanham, MD: Jason Aronson.

Ronis, S. T., & Borduin, C. M. (2007). Individual, family, peer and academic characteristics of male juvenile sexual offenders. *Journal of Abnormal Child Psychology, 35,* 153–163.

Rosas, A. J. (2005). Medical diagnosis of child abuse and neglect. In P. F. Talley (Ed.), *Handbook for the treatment of the abused and neglected child* (pp. 39–62). New York, NY: Haworth.

Rosencrans, B. (1997). *The last secret: Daughters abused by mothers.* Brandon, VT: Safer Society Press.

Rossetti, S. (1996). *Tragic grace: The Catholic Church and sexual abuse.* Collegeville, MD: Liturgical Press.

Rossetti, S. (2003). *Slayer of the soul: Child sexual abuse and the Catholic Church.* New London, CT: Twenty-Third Publications.

Rothman, J. C. (2007). *Cultural competence in process and practice: Building bridges.* Upper Saddle River, NJ: Pearson.

Rush, F. (1992). *The best kept secret: Sexual abuse of children* (Rev. ed.). New York, NY: McGraw-Hill.

Rush, F. (1996). The Freudian cover-up. *Feminism and Psychology, 6*(2), 261–276.

Russell, D. (1983). The incidence and prevalence of intrafamilial and extrafamilial sexual abuse. *Child Abuse and Neglect, 7*, 133–147.

Russell, D. E. (1999). *Secret trauma: Incest in the lives of girls and women.* New York, NY: Basic Books.

Russell, D. E., & Bolen, R. M. (2000). *The epidemic of rape and child sexual abuse in the United States.* Thousand Oaks, CA: SAGE.

Rutherford, R. B., Griller-Clark, H. M., & Anderson, C. W. (2001). Treating offenders with educational disabilities. In J. B. Ashford, B. D. Sales, & W. H. Reid (Eds.), *Treating adult and juvenile offenders with special needs* (pp. 221–245). Washington, DC: American Psychological Association.

Rutter, M. (2003). Crucial paths from risk indicator to causal mechanism. In B. B. Lahey, T. E. Moffitt, & A. Caspi (Eds.), *Causes of conduct disorder and juvenile delinquency* (pp. 3–24). New York, NY: Guilford.

Ryan, G., Leversee, T., & Lane, S. (2010). *Juvenile sexual offending.* Hoboken, NJ: John Wiley.

Ryan, G. D. (1999). Treatment of sexually abusive youth: The evolving consensus. *Journal of Interpersonal Violence, 14*(4), 422–436.

Ryan, G. D., & Lane, S. L. (1997). *Juvenile sexual offending: Causes, consequences and correction.* San Francisco, CA: Jossey-Bass.

Ryan, G. D., Miyoshi, C. D., Metzner, J. L., Krugman, R. D., & Fryer, G. E. (1996). Trends in a national sample of sexually abusive youths. *Journal of the American Academy of Child and Adolescent Psychiatry, 35*(1), 17–25.

Saakvitne, K. W., Gamble, S., Pearlman, L. A., & Lev, B. T. (2000). *Risking connection: A training curriculum for working with survivors of childhood abuse.* Lutherville, MD: The Sidran Press.

Saffiotti, L. M. (2011). Sexual abuse and systematic dynmics in the church. *Human Development, 32*(1), 17–23.

Sagatun, I. J., & Edwards, L. P. (1995). *Child abuse and the legal system.* Chicago, IL: Nelson-Hall.

Salter, A. (1988). *Treating child sexual offenders and victims.* Newbury Park, CA: SAGE.

Salter, A. (1995). *Transforming trauma.* Thousand Oaks, CA: SAGE.

Sanderson, C. (2006). *Counselling adult survivors of child sexual abuse.* London, UK: Jessica Kingsley.

Saradjian, J. (1996). *Women who sexually abuse children: From research to clinical practice.* West Sussex, UK: John Wiley.

Saul, J., & Audage, N. C. (2007). *Preventing child sexual abuse within youth-serving organizations: Getting started on policies and procedures.* Atlanta, GA: Centers for Disease Control and Prevention, National Center for Injury Prevention and Control.

Saunders, B. E. (2012). Determining best practice for treating sexually victimized children. In P. Goodyear-Brown (Ed.), *Handbook of child sexual abuse* (173–197). Hoboken, NJ: John Wiley.

Saywitz, K. J., Mannarino, A., Berliner, L., & Cohen, J. A. (2000). Treatment for sexually abused children and adolescents. *American Psychologist, 55*(9), 1040–1050.

Sax, R. (2009a). *Predators and child molesters.* Amherst, NY: Prometheus.

Sax, R. (2009b). *The criminal justice system.* New York, NY: Penguin.

Sax, R. (2010). *It happens every day: Inside the world of a sex crimes DA.* New York, NY: Prometheus Books.

Scannapieco, M., & Connell-Carrick, K. (2005). *Understanding child maltreatment: An ecological and developmental perspective.* New York, NY: Oxford University Press.

Schmidt, S. R., Bonner, B. L., & Chaffin, M. (2012). Understanding and treating adolescents with illegal sexual behavior. In P. Goodyear-Brown (Ed.), *Handbook of child sexual abuse* (pp, 469–485). Hoboken, NJ: John Wiley.

Schoen, C., Davis, K., DesRoches, C., & Shekhder, A. (2004). The health of adolescent boys: Commonwealth fund survey findings. *The Commonwealth Fund Survey of the Health of Adolescent Girls*. Retrieved from http://www .cmwf.org/programs/women/boyssv271.asp

Schram, D., & Milloy, C. (1995). *Community notification: A study of offender characteristics and recidivism*. Olympia, WA: Washington State Institute for Public Policy.

Schumacher, R., & Carlson, R. (1999). Variables and risk factors associated with child abuse in daycare settings. *Child Abuse and Neglect, 23*, 891–898.

Schwartz, B. K. (1995). Theories of sex offenses. In B. K. Schwartz & H. R. Cellini (Eds.), *The sex offender: Corrections, treatment and legal practice* (pp. 2.1–2.32). Kingston, NJ: Civic Research Institute.

Seto, M. C. (2008). *Pedophilia and sexual offending against children*. Washington, DC: American Psychological Association.

Seto, M. C., & Lalumiere, L. L. (2006). Conduct problems and juvenile sexual offending. In H. E. Barbaree & W. L. Marshall (Eds.), *The juvenile sex offender* (pp. 166–188). New York, NY: Guilford.

Sexton, L. G. (2011). *Half in love: Surviving the legacy of suicide*. Berkeley, CA: Counterpoint.

Sgroi, S. (1982). *Handbook of clinical intervention in child sexual abuse*. Lexington, MA: Lexington Books.

Sgroi, S., & Dana, N. T. (1982). Individual and group treatment of mothers of incest victims. In S. Sgroi (Ed.), *Handbook of clinical intervention in child sexual abuse* (pp. 191–214). Lexington, MA: Lexington Books.

Shakeshaft, C. (2003). Educator sexual abuse. *Hofstra Horizons*, Spring, 10–13.

Shakeshaft, C. (2004). *Educator sexual misconduct: A synthesis of existing literature*. Washington, DC: U.S. Department of Education.

Shakeshaft, C., & Cohan, A. (1995). Sexual abuse of students by school personnel. *Phi Beta Kappa, 76*(7), 513–520.

Silva, R. (2004). *Posttraumatic stress disorders in children and adolescents*. New York, NY: W. W. Norton.

Silverman, W. K., Pina, A. A., & Viswesvaran, C. (2008). Evidence-based psychosocial treatments for phobic and anxiety disorders in children and adolescents. *Journal of Clinical Child and Adolescent Psychology, 37*, 105–130.

Simons, D. A., Wurtele, S., & Durham, R. (2008). Developmental experiences of child sexual abusers and rapists. *Child Abuse and Neglect, 32*(5), 549–560.

Sinason, V., Galton, G., & Leevers, D. (2008). Where are we now? Ritual abuse, diossociation, police and media. In R. Noblitt & P. P. Noblitt (Eds.), *Ritual abuse in the twenty-first century: Psychological, forensic, social and political implications* (pp. 363–380). Bandon, OR: Robert D. Reed.

Sipe, A. W. R. (1995). *Sex, priests and power: Anatomy of a crisis*. New York, NY: Brunner/Mazel.

Sipe, A. W. R. (2003). *Celibacy in crisis: A secret world revisited*. New York, NY: Brunner/Mazel.

Sivers, H., Schooler, J., & Freyd, J. J. (2002). Recovered memories. In V. S. Ramachandran (Ed.), *Encyclopedia of the human brain* (Vol 4, pp. 169–184). San Diego, CA: Academic.

Skowron, E. A., Stanley, K. L., & Shapiro, M. D. (2009). A longitudinal study on differentiation of self, interpersonal and psychological well-being in young adulthood. *Contemporary Family Therapy, 31*(1), 3–18.

Smallbone, S., Marshall, W. L., & Wortley, R. (2008). *Preventing child sexual abuse: Evidence, policy and practice*. New York, NY: Taylor & Francis.

Smallbone, S. W. (2006). Social and psychological factors in the development of delinquency and sexual deviance. In H. E. Barbaree & W. L. Marshall (Eds.), *The juvenile sex offender* (pp. 105–127). New York, NY: Guilford.

Smid, W. J., Kamphuis, J. H., Wever, E. C., & VanBeek, D. (2013) Treatment referral for sex offenders based on clinical judgment versus actuarial risk assessment: Match and analysis of mismatch. *Journal of Interpersonal Violence, 28*(11), 2273–2289.

Sommer, C. (2008). Vicarious traumatization, trauma-sensitive supervision, and counselor preparation. *Counselor Education & Supervision, 48*(1), 61–71.

Sonkin, D. J. (1998). *Wounded boys, heroic men*. Avon, MA: Adams Media.

Sperry, L. (2003). *Sex, priestly ministry, and the church*. Collegeville, MN: Liturgical Press.

Stagner, M. W., & Lansing, J. (2009). Progress toward a prevention perspective. *The Future of Children: Preventing Child Maltreatment, 19*(2), 19–36.

Staller, K. M., & Vandervort, F. E. (2010). Child sexual abuse: Legal burden and scientific methods. In K. M. Staller & K. C. Faller (Eds.), *Seeking justice in child sexual abuse* (pp. 1–32). New York, NY: Columbia University Press.

Stanton, M. (1997, July/August). U-turn down memory lane. *Columbia Journalism Review. 36*, 44.

Stein, N. D., Marshall, N., & Tropp, L. R. (1993). *Secrets in public: Sexual harassment in our schools*. Wellesley, MA: Wellesley Centers for Woman.

Steller, M., & Boychuck, T. (1992). Children as witnesses in sexual abuse cases: Investigative interview and assessment techniques. In H. Dent & R. Flin (Eds.), *Children as witnesses* (pp. 47–71). New York, NY: Wiley.

Stern, M., & Mayer, L. (1980). Family and couple interactional patterns in cases of father-daughter incest. In B. Jones, L. Janstrom, & K. MacFarlane (Eds.), *Sexual abuse in children: Selected readings* (pp. 83–86). Washington, DC: U.S. Department of Health and Human Services.

Stevens, D. J. (2001). *Inside the mind of sexual offenders*. Lincoln, NE: iUniverse.

Stinson, J. D., & Becker, J. (2012). *Treating sex offenders: An evidence-based manual*. New York, NY: Guilford.

Stone, R. D. (2005). *No secrets, no lies: How black families can heal from sexual abuse*. New York, NY: Broadway Books.

Strand, V. C. (2000). *Treating secondary victims: Intervention with the nonoffending mother in the incest family*. Thousand Oaks, CA: SAGE.

Subrahmanyam, K., Kraut, R. E., Greenfield, P. M., & Gross, E. F. (2000). The impact of home computer use on children's activities and development. *The Future of Children: Children and Computer Technology, 10*(2), Fall/Winter.

Sue, D. W., & Sue, D. (2013). *Counseling the culturally diverse*. New York, NY: Wiley.

Sullivan, J., & Beech, A. (2002). Professional perpetrators: Sex offenders who use their employment to target and sexually abuse the children with whom they work. *Child Abuse Review, 11*, 153–167.

Summit, R. C. (1983). Child abuse accommodation syndrome. *Child Abuse and Neglect, 7*, 177–193.

Summit, R. C. (1989). The centrality of victimization: Regaining the focal point of recovery for survivors of child sexual abuse. *Psychiatric Clinics of North America, 12*, 413–430.

Summit, R. C. (1994). The dark tunnels of McMartin. *Journal of Psychohistory, 21*(4), Spring, 1–14.

Tamraz, D. N. (1996). Nonoffending mothers of sexually abused children: Comparisons of opinions and research. *Journal of Child Sexual Abuse, 5*(4), 75–104.

Tattersall, C. (1999). *Drugs, runaways, and teen prostitution*. New York, NY: Rosen.

Taylor, M., & Quayle, E. (2003). *Child pornography: An Internet crime*. New York, NY: Brunner-Routledge.

Teicher, M., Andersen, S., Polcari, A., & Navalta, C. (2002). Developmental neurobiology of childhood stress and truama. *Psychiatric Clinics of North America, 25*, 397–426.

Thompson, S., Bender, K., Lantry, J., & Flynn, P. (2007). Treatment engagement: Building therapeutic alliance in home-based treatment with adolescents and their families. *Contemporary Family Therapy: An International Journal, 29*(1/2), 39–55.

Tinling, L. (1990). Perception of incest by significant others: Mothers who do not want to see. *Individual Psychology, 46*(3), 280–297.

Tower, C. (1988). *Secret scars*. New York, NY: Viking/Penguin.

Trepper, T. S., Niedner, D., Mika, L., & Barrett, M. J. (1996). Family characteristics of intact sexually abusing families: An exploratory study. *Journal of Child Sexual Abuse, 5*, 1–18.

Twardosz, S. (2010). Child maltreatment and the developing brain: A review of neuroscience perspectives. *Aggression and Violent Behavior, 15*(1), 59–68.

Ullman, S. E., & Filipas, H. H. (2005). Ethnicity and child sexual abuse experiences of female college students. *Journal of Child Sexual Abuse, 14* (3), 67–89.

United States Conference of Catholic Bishops (USCCB). (2005). *The report on the implementation of the charter of children and young people.* Washington, DC: United States Conference of Catholic Bishops.

U.S. Department of Justice. (2004). Bureau of Justice statistics. Retrieved July 2, 2007, from http://www.ojp.usdoj/gov/bjs

Valliere, V. N. (1997). Relationship between alcohol use, alcohol expectancies, and sexual offenses in convicted offenders. In B. K. Schwartz & H. R. Cellini (Eds.), *The sex offender: New insights, treatment innovations and legal developments* (pp. 3.1–3.14). Kingston, NJ: Civic Research Institute.

van Dam, C. (2001). *Identifying child molesters: Preventing child sexual abuse by recognizing the patterns of offenders.* New York, NY: Haworth.

van Dam C. (2006). *The socially skilled child molester.* New York, NY: Haworth.

van der Kolk, B. A., & Fisler, R. (1995). Dissociation and the fragmentary nature of traumatic memories: Overview and exploratory study. *Journal of Trauma and Stress, 8*(4), 505–525.

van Eys, P., & Truss, A. (2012). Comprehensive and therapeutic assessment of child sexual abuse. In P. Goodyear-Brown (Ed.), *Handbook of child sexual abuse* (pp. 143–170). Hoboken, NJ: John Wiley.

Vandiver, D. M., & Kercher, G. (2004). Offender and victim characteristics of registered female sexual offenders in Texas: A proposed typology of female sexual offenders. *Sexual Abuse: A Journal of Research and Treatment, 16*(2), 121–137.

Vandiver, D. M., & Teske, R. (2006). Juvenile female and male sex offenders. *International Journal of Therapy and Comparative Criminology, 50,* 148–165.

Vasquez, B. E., Maddan, S., & Walker, J. T. (2008). The incidence of sex offender registration and notification laws in the United States. *Crime and Delinquency, 54*(2), 175–92.

Verstraete, B. (2004). New pedagogy on ancient pederasty. *Gay and Lesbian Review, 11*(3), 13–14.

Vizard, E. (2013). Practitioner review: The victims and juvenile perpetrators of child sexual abuse-assessment and intervention. *Journal of Child Psychology and Psychiatry, 54*(5), 503–515.

Wald, M. S. (2009). Preventing maltreatment or promoting positive development—where should a community focus its resources: A policy perspective. In K. A. Dodge & D. L. Coleman (Eds.), *Preventing child maltreatment: Community approaches* (pp. 182–195). New York, NY: Guilford.

Waldfogel, J. (2009). Prevention and the child protection system. *The Future of Children: Preventing Child Maltreatment, 19*(2), 195–210.

Walker, E., Holman, T., & Busby, D. (2009). Childhood sexual abuse, other childhood factors, and pathways to survivor's adult relationship quality. *Journal of Family Violence, 24*(6), 397–406.

Walker, N. (Ed.). (2002). Prostituted teens: More than a runaway problem. *Michigan Family Impact Seminars,* Briefing Report 2002–2. East Lansing, MI: Institute for Children, Youth and Families, Michigan State University.

Walker, S., Sanci, L., & Temple-Smith, M. (2011). Sexting and young people: Experts' views. *Youth Studies Australia, 30*(4), 8–16.

Walsh, W. A., Jones, L. M., Cross, T. P., & Lippert, T. (2010). Prosecuting child sexual abuse. *Crime and Delinquency, 56*(3), 436–454.

Ward, E. (1985). *Father-daughter rape.* New York, NY: Grove Press.

Ward, T., & Keenan, T. (1999). Child molester's implicit theories. *Journal of Interpersonal Violence, 14*(8), 821–838.

Ward, T., Louden, K., Hudson, S., & Marshall, W. L. (1995). A descriptive model of the offense chain in child molesters. *Journal of Interpersonal Violence, 10,* 453–473.

Ward, T., & Maruna, S. (2007). Rehabilitation beyond the risk-paradigm. In T. Newburn (Series Ed.), *Key ideas in criminology series.* London, UK: Routledge.

Ward, T., Melser, J., & Yates, P. M. (2007). Reconstructing the Risk-Need-Responsivity model: A theoretical elaboration and evaluation. *Aggression and Violent Behavior, 12*(2), 208–228.

Ward, T., Polaschek, D. L. L., & Beech, A. R. (2006). *Theories of sexual offending.* West Sussex, UK: John Wiley.

Ward, T., & Siegert, R. J. (2002). Toward a comprehensive theory of child sexual abuse:

A theory knitting perspective. *Psychology, Crime and Law, 9,* 319–351.

Ward, T., & Stewart, C. (2003). The relationship between human needs and criminogenic needs. *Psychology, Crime and Law, 9,* 219–224.

Waterman, J., Kelley, S. J., Oliveri, M. K., & McCord, J. (1993). *Behind the playground walls: Sexual abuse in preschools.* New York, NY: Guilford.

Weisberg, K. (1985). *Children of the night.* Lexington, MA: Lexington Books.

Weiss, R., & Samenow, C. P. (2010). Smart phones, social networking, sexting and problematic sexual behaviors—a call for research. *Sexual Addiction and Compulsivity, 17,* 241–246.

Wells, M., Finkelhor, D., Wolak, J., & Mitchell, K. J. (2007). Defining child pornography: Law enforcement dilemmas in investigations of internet child pornography possession. *Police Practice and Research, 8*(3), 269–282.

Westerlund, E. (1986). Freud on sexual trauma: An historical review of seduction and betrayal. *Psychology of Women Quarterly, 10,* 297–310.

Whetsell-Mitchell, J. (1995). *Rape of the innocent: Understanding and preventing child sexual abuse.* Washington, DC: Accelerated Development.

White, L. A. (1948). The definition and prohibition of incest. *American Anthropologist, 50,* 416–435.

Wieckowski, E., Hartsoe, P., Mayer, A., & Shortz, J. (1998). Deviant sexual behavior in children and young adolescents: Frequency and patterns. *Sexual Abuse: A Journal of Research and Treatment, 10*(4), 293–304.

Wiehe, V. R. (1997). *Sibling abuse: Hidden physical, emotional and sexual trauma.* Thousand Oaks, CA: SAGE.

Wiehe, V. R. (2002). *Sibling abuse.* Springfield, VT: Bonneville.

Wiehe, V. R., & Herring, T. (1991). *Perilous rivalry: When siblings become abusive.* Lexington, MA: Lexington Books.

Williams, L. M., & Finkelhor, D. (1992). *The characteristics of incestuous fathers: Final report.* Washington, DC: Clearinghouse on Child Abuse and Neglect Information.

Wilson, R. F. (2004). Recognizing the threat posed by an incestuous parent to the victim's siblings: Part

I, appraising the risk. *Journal of Child and Family Studies, 13,* 142–162.

Wishnietsky, D. H. (1991). Reported and unreported teacher-student sexual harassment. *Journal of Educational Research, 84*(3), 164–169.

Wolak, J. (2007). *Pediatrics,* February, *119,* 247–257.

Wolak, J., & Finkelhor, D. (2011). Sexting: A typology. Crimes Against Children Research Center. Retrieved May 5, 2012, from http://unh.edu/ccrc/pdf/CV231_Sexting%20Typology%20Bulletin_4–6-11_revised.pdf

Wolak, J., Finkelhor, D., & Mitchell, K. J. (2008). Is talking online to unknown people always risky? Distinguishing online interaction styles in a national sample of youth internet users. *CyberPsychology & Behavior, 11*(3), 340–343.

Wolak, J., Finkelhor, D., & Mitchell, K. J. (2012). Trends in arrests for child pornography possession: The third national juvenile online victimization study. Retrieved May 5, 2012, from http://unh.edu/ccrc/pdf/CV269_Child%20Porn%20Possession%20Bulletin_4–13–12.pdf

Wolak, J., Finkelhor, D., Mitchell, K. J., & Ybarra, M. L. (2008). Online 'predators' and their victims. *American Psychologist, 63*(2), 111–128.

Woody, D. (2003). Infancy and toddlerhood. In E. Hutchinson (Ed.), *Dimensions of human behavior* (pp. 113–158). Thousand Oaks, CA: SAGE.

Worling, J. R., & Langstrom, N. (2006). Risk of sexual recidivism in adolescents who sexually offend. In H. E. Barbaree & W. L. Marshall (Eds.), *The juvenile sex offender* (219–247). New York, NY: Guilford.

Wright, R. C., & Schneider, S. L. (1997). Deviant sexual fantasies as motivated self-deception. In B. K. Schwartz & H. R. Celleni (Eds.), *The sexual offender* (Vol. II, pp. 8.1–8.14). Kingston, NJ: Civic Research Institute.

Wurtele, S. K., & Kenny, M. C. (2012). Preventing childhood sexual abuse: An ecological approach. In P. Goodyear-Brown (Ed.), *Handbook of child sexual abuse* (pp. 531–565). Hoboken, NJ: John Wiley.

Wyatt, G. E. (1985). The sexual abuse of Afro-American and White-American women in childhood. *Child Abuse and Neglect, 9,* 507–519.

Wyre, R. (2000). Paedophile characteristics and patterns of behavior. In C. Itzen (Ed.), *Home truths about child sexual abuse: Influencing policy and practice* (pp. 49–69). London, UK: Routledge.

Yates, P. M., Prescott, D., & Ward, T. (2010). *Applying the good lives and self-regulation models to sex offender treatment.* Brandon, VT: Safer Society.

Zankman, S., & Bonomo, J. (2004). Working with parents to reduce juvenile sex offender recidivism. In R. Geffner, K. C. Franey, T. G. Arnold, & R. Falconer (Eds.), *Identifying and treating youth who sexually offend* (pp. 139–156). New York, NY: Haworth.

Zeanah, C. H. (2009). The importance of early experiences: Clinical, research, and policy perspectives. *Journal of Trauma and Loss, 14*(4), 266–279.

Ziegler, D. (2002). *Traumatic experience and the brain.* Phoenix, AZ: Acacia.

Zwi, K. J. (2007). School-based education programs for the prevention of child sexual abuse. *Cochrane Database for Systematic Reviews, 2,* 1–44.

INDEX

female abusers, 156–157
legal/ethical issues in working
    with, 157
maltreatment as precursor to
    abusing, 150–151, 155, 156, 161
molesters, 148–149
recidivism risk for, 161–162
relapse prevention planning, 161
relationship development and,
    152–153, 156, 161–162
sexualized behaviors *vs.* sexual abuse,
    147–149
sexual knowledge and experience,
    155–156
sexually aggressive child, 143–144,
    150, 151
sexually reactive child, 147–148, 150
social isolation and, 161–162
social skills and, 151, 152, 153, 154,
    155, 160
treatment follow-up, 162
treatment issues, 147, 156, 157–162
understanding, 149–157
working with, 162–163

Kadushin, A., 104
Kafka, M. P., 94
Kaldal, A., 172
Kalinowski, M., 169, 172
Karson, M., 19
Keenan, T., 49
Kelley, S. J., 172
Kelly, Betsy, 170–171
Kelly, Bob, 170–171
Kempe, C. H., 12, 104
Kempe, R., 104
Kempe Center, 201
Kennedy, E., 182
Kercher, G., 55–56
Kinnear, K., 21, 167
Kinscherff, R. T., 157
Kinsey, A., 11–12
*Kiss Daddy Goodnight: A Speak-Out on
    Incest* (Armstrong), 12
Kissing, as sexual abuse, 27, 28 (table),
    31, 32
Klismaphilia, 59
Krane, J., 45

Lamb, J. L., 241, 243
Landreth, G. L., 237
Langevin, R., 266

Lantry, J., 239
Latham, C., 157
Law, B., 179
Law enforcement
    AMBER alerts and, 198–199
    assessment of sexually abused child
      by, 213, 214, 215, 220–221
    child/juvenile prostitution and, 135
    Internet-initiated sex crimes and,
      125, 127, 132
    joint investigations by, 205–206,
      213–214
    mandated reporting and, 199
    registration of sex offenders and,
      265–266, 302
    See also Courts, involvement in child
      sexual abuse
Laws, D. R., 53–54, 249, 252
Learning difficulties
    as indicator for sexual abuse, 77
    of adult sexual abusers, 260
    of adult sexual abuse survivors, 276
    of juvenile sexual abusers, 153, 155
    of sexually abused children, 71,
      77, 273
Leberg, E., 31
LeTourneau, M. K., 167
Lev-Wiesel, R., 113
Lewis, A. D., 200
Lewis, H., 107–108
Leyva, T., 14
Lindblad, F., 172
Little Rascals Day Care Center, 170–171
Lloyd, R., 133
Loftus, E., 16, 273
Lolita complex, 59
Longo, R. E., 147
Loredo, C. M., 199
Lowe, W. Jr., 24
Lundrigan, P. S., 159, 162
Lyles, A., 305, 307–308, 309
Lyon, T. D., 220

Magid, L., 126–127
Malinowski, B., 6, 7, 103
Mandated reporting, 199
Mandatory background check, 302
Mandell, D., 292
Manufacturer pornographers, 129
Marlatt, G. A., 53, 258
Marriage, in ancient world, 4
Marshall, L. E., 87–88

Marshall, W. L., 50, 87–88, 94
Martin, C., 11
Martin, J., 104
Masochism, sexual, 58
Massage therapy, 238, 283
Masson, J. M., 9, 10
Masturbation
    as indicative of sexual abuse, 71, 76
    chronic, by offender, 93
    during normal sexual development,
      66 (table), 67 (table), 69
    fantasies and, 59
    grooming of child and, 32–34
Matthews, F., 150
Matthews, J., 55
Matthews, R., 55, 99
Mayer, A., 155
Mayer, L., 110
McCann, I. L., 295
McCarty, L., 54
McCord, J., 172
McDonagh, A., 282
McDonald, S., 153
McFarlane-Nathan, G. H., 199
McLaughlin, J. F., 129–130, 132
McMartin preschool case, 15, 169–170,
    173–174
Medical examinations, 217–218
Medical professionals, role in
    intervention, 206
Medical symptoms, 37
Megan's Law, 266
Meiselman, K., 6, 12
Memories
    addressing repressed, 270–272
    false memory controversy and,
      272–273
Mental health treatment, 303
Michaels, K., 170
Michelangelo, 5
Middlebrook, D. W., 116
Miles, V. J., 180
Minnesota Sex Offender Screening
    Tool (revised), 249
Mitchell, K. J., 14, 127
Models. *See* Theories of child sexual
    abuse
Money, J., 59
Mordock, J. B., 240
Mosaic Massage Program, 243
Mother-daughter incest, 116–117
Mother-son incest, 117–118

Multifactorial theories, 49–51
  integrated theory, 50
  pathways model, 50–51, 52 (figure)
  preconditions model, 48, 49–50
  quadripartite theory, 50
Multiple personality disorder. See
  Dissociative identity disorder
Munro, E., 297
Murdock, N. L., 7
Music therapy, 283
Myth(s)
  child sexual abuse, 24–25
  false memory, 16

NAMBLA (North American Man-Boy
  Love Association), 18, 123
Name recognition, 34
Nathan, D., 171
National Center for Missing and
  Exploited Children, 137, 139
National Center on Child Abuse and
  Neglect, 12, 149
National Child Abuse and Neglect Data
  System (NCANDS), 25
National Children's Advocacy Center
  (NCAC), 216
National Coalition to Prevent Child
  Sexual Exploitation, 308
National Conference of Catholic
  Bishops (NCCB), 178–179
National Juvenile Online Victimization
  Study (N-JOV), 127
National Plan to Prevent the Sexual
  Exploitation of Children, 308
NCAC (National Children's Advocacy
  Center), 216
NCANDS (National Child Abuse and
  Neglect Data System), 25
NCCB (National Conference of
  Catholic Bishops), 178–179
Necrophilia, 59
Neglect, 12, 50, 97, 119, 151, 155, 199,
  207, 310
Nelson-Gardell, D., 216, 239
Nepiophilia, 59
Neurofeedback, 283
N-JOV (National Juvenile Online
  Victimization Study), 127
Noblitt, J. R., 221
Noncontact/indirect sexual abuse
  components of, 22, 26–27, 28 (table)
  exhibitionism, 22, 26–27, 58, 145

exposure to pornography, 27, 28
  (table)
grooming and, 31
sexual comments, 26, 28 (table)
voyeurism, 27, 28 (table)
Nonfamilial sexual abuse, 26
Nonoffending parents
  ambivalent, 241, 243
  bond with child, importance to
    healing, 233, 243
  community support for, 243
  father-daughter incest and, 113–114
  intrapsychic issues and, 242
  nonsupportive, 223, 241, 243
  responsibility theories on, 45–46
  shame and, 108
  supportive, 223, 241, 243
  traumatized/abused, 242
  treatment of, 241–243
Normal sexual exploration, 147
North American Man-Boy Love
  Association (NAMBLA), 18, 123

Obscene phone calls, 26
Obsessive-compulsive behavior, 77
Oedipus complex, 8–9
Offender/potential offender-centered
  prevention, 300–303
Offender(s), 83–101
  basic inadequate personality of,
    84–85
  brain development and role of
    attachment in, 86–88
  cognitive distortions theory and,
    48–49, 51, 53
  defense mechanisms used by,
    256–257, 262–263
  development and sexual offending,
    85–88
  early theories on, 46–49
  empathy and, 53, 88, 261, 301
  fixated, 46, 184, 209
  hebophilia, 94, 261
  physical appearance of, 24–25
  preconditions model and, 48
  preferential, 130, 209
  progression of pathology of, 88–90
  regressed, 46–47, 184
  sexual addiction theory and, 47–48
  sexually abused, 261
  statistics on, 300
  typology of pedophilia and, 46–47

See also Offender(s), female;
  Offender(s), male
Offender(s), female
  adolescents and, 98
  characteristics of, 96–99
  defense mechanisms used by,
    262–263
  other types of women offenders, 99
  research needs, 99
  sexually abused, 262
  theory on, 54–57
  treatment for, 262–263
  women initially coerced by men, 99
  young children and, 97–98
Offender(s), male
  characteristics of, 90–96, 301
  fantasy and offending, 94–95
  relationship issues and, 95–96
  self-esteem/social competence issues,
    91–92
  sexual experiences of, 92–94
  substance use and, 96
Office of Juvenile Justice and
  Delinquency Prevention, 132
Oliveri, M. K., 172
One-way mirror, use in child interview,
  215–216
Online Victimization (Finkelhor,
  Mitchell, & Wolak), 14
Oppositional defiant disorder, 154
Oral sexual contact
  cunnilingus, 28 (table), 32, 33
  defining, 28 (table)
  fellatio, 28 (table), 32, 33, 198
Ost, S., 124, 125
Overcompensation, by offender, 91

PAN (Pedophile Alert Network), 123
Paraphilias, 58–59, 93
Parent-child interaction model, 214
Parentified child, 111
Parents. See Nonoffending parents
Partialism, 59
Pathways model, 50–51, 52 (figure)
Pearce, J., 150
Pearlman, L. A., 295
Pederasty, 5, 59
Pedophile Alert Network (PAN), 123
Pedophile Information Exchange
  (PIE), 123
Pedophilia
  as paraphilia, 58, 59

distorted thinking and, 95
ephebophilia *vs.*, 184
inclusion in diagnostic indexes, 25
typology of, 46–47
Peer relationships. *See* Relationships
Peever, C., 266
Penile penetration, 29 (table), 33–34
Penile plethysmograph, 250–251
Perry, B., 239
Perskin, P. S., 221
Personality disorders, 139, 162, 251, 274–275
Personal safety prevention programs, 304–305
Persuasion techniques, 30
Pew Research Center, 128
Phases of child sexual abuse, 27–39
    disclosure phase, 37–38
    engagement phase, 27, 29–35
    sexual interaction and secrecy phase, 35–36
    suppression phase, 38–39
Physical abuse
    as precursor to sexual abuse of child, 151
    child prostitutes and, 137
    during childhood of offender, 86, 113, 261
    early research on, 12
    of juvenile sexual abusers, 151, 154, 155, 156
Physical force strategy, 30–31, 34
Physical indicators of sexual abuse, 75–76, 77, 198
PIE (Pedophile Information Exchange), 123
Pithers, W. D., 149–150, 152
Plea bargain, 225, 226
Plummer, C., 114
Poe, E. A., 4
Poetry therapy, 282–283
Polaschek, D. L. L., 248
Pollock, S., 240
Polygraph (lie detector test), 251
Pomeroy, W., 11
Pope, K., 175
Pornography, child, 123–133
    arrests for possession of, 130
    as precursor to sexual offending, 94
    chatter pornographer, 129–130
    collector pornographer, 129
    dabbler pornographer, 130

day care centers and, 172
effect of Internet sexuality on children and youth, 130–131
Internet use by youth and, 125–128, 132–133
intervention into, 131–132
legislation on, 14–15
lure of cybersex for adults, 128–130
manufacturer pornographer, 129
miscellaneous offender, 130
on Internet, 94
preferential offender, 130
problem with, 123–125
teens and sexting, 127–128
traveler pornographer, 129
types of pedophilic pornographers, 129–130
Pornography, effects of exposure to
    on child, 27, 28 (table), 125
    on juvenile, 155
    See also Pornography, child
Porter, J., 14, 179
Possessive-passive pattern of father-daughter incest, 110
Post-traumatic stress disorder (PTSD)
    cognitive behavioral therapy and, 282
    contact victimization as cause of, 295
    hyperarousal and, 275–276
    impairment of everyday functioning and, 274–276
    overview of, 80
    screening sexually abused child for, 236–237
    sexting and, 128
    sexually reactive child and, 148
    symptom categories for, 236–237
Powell, L., 238, 243
Powerlessness, of victims of sexual abuse, 79–80
Preble, J. M., 30
Preconditions model, 48, 49–50
Preferential offender, 130, 209
Pregnancy, 33, 37–38, 198, 217
Prendergast, W. E., 84–85, 89, 93, 254–255
Preschool-age children, sexual abuse of, 70–71
Prescott, D. S., 147
Prevention, community awareness and, 305–310
    changing organizational practices, 307–308

community prevention of offending, 309–310
fostering coalitions and networks, 308–309
influencing policy and legislation, 307
promoting awareness and education, 305–307
Prevention, of child and adolescent sexual abuse
    criminal justice interventions, 301–303
    developmental prevention approach, 300–301
    future of, 310–311
    offender/potential offender-centered prevention, 300–303
    situational prevention, 304–305
    victim/potential victim-centered prevention, 303–304
Privacy, 305
Privileged voyeurism, 295
Probate court, 223
Promiscuity
    adult sexual abuse survivors and, 275, 277
    behavioral disorders and, 154
    female sexual offenders and, 156
    sexually abused juveniles and, 72, 78
    sexually explicit material on Internet and, 131
Prosecutor. *See* District attorney (DA)/ prosecutor
Prostitution, child and juvenile, 133–139
    boys in prostitution, 133, 138–139
    definition of, 134–136
    drug use and, 136
    exiting prostitution, 139
    girls in prostitution, 133, 136–138
    HIV/AIDS and, 139
    homeless prostitutes, 136, 137
    incidence of, 134–136
    in Victorian era, 5
    law enforcement encounters, 135
    parent/caretaker role in, 136
    pimps and, 135, 137–138, 139
    runaways and, 133–134, 136, 137, 139
    sexually transmitted diseases and, 139
    throwaways and, 134, 136, 139
Protective factors, 69–70

Sexual assault, criminal justice definition of, 208–209

Sexual behaviors, types of defined, 28 (table)–29 (table)

Sexual comments, as abuse, 26, 28 (table)

Sexual confusion, of sons abused by fathers, 116

Sexual development, healthy, 65, 66 (table)–67 (table). *See also* Child development, effects of sexual abuse on

Sexual education, 156, 301

Sexual exploitation, criminal justice definition of, 209

Sexual Exploitation of Children Act (1977), 14–15

Sexual exploration, normal, 147

Sexual identity
  of daughters abused by mothers, 117
  of sons abused by fathers, 116

Sexual interaction and secrecy phase, 35–36

Sexually aggressive child, 143–144, 150, 151

Sexually reactive child, 147–148

Sexually transmitted diseases (STDs), 139, 198, 209, 217

Sexual molestation, criminal justice definition of, 209

Sexual orientation/preference, adult sexual abuse survivors and, 278

Sexual predator, female, 55

Sexual scripts, 51, 52 (figure)

Sgroi, S., 77, 107, 197, 220, 234

Shafran, C., 106

Shakeshaft, C., 166

Shame
  adult sexual offender and, 92, 203
  adult survivors of sexual abuse and, 276
  as indicator of abuse, 71
  clerical sexual abusers and, 184, 186
  cultural implications of, 30, 107–108
  family members of sexual abuse victim and, 204, 205
  fixated offender and, 46
  interfamilial abuse and, 108, 115, 117, 120, 293
  nonoffending parents and, 108
  regressed offender and, 47
  sexting and, 128

sexually abused child and, 71, 107–108, 202, 245

Shortz, J., 155

Shota complex, 59

Siblings, sexual abuse by, 118–120
  older brother-younger sister, 119–120
  older sister-younger brother, 120
  same-sex siblings, 120

Siblings of sexually abused child, 115, 205
  treatment for, 244–245

Siegert, R. J., 50–51

Simons, D. A., 86

Single-factor theories: 51–53
  cognitive distortions theory, 48–49, 51, 53

Sipe, A. W. R., 14, 182

Situational molester, 209

Situational prevention, 304–305

Sivers, H., 272–273

Slaves, abuse of female children of, 4

Smallbone, S., 300, 301

Smith-Darden, J., 159

SNAP (Survivors Network of those Abused by Priests), 178

Social competence, 87, 88, 91–92

Social skills
  adult sexual abusers and, 46, 48, 51, 85, 94, 250, 261
  cybersex and, 128
  intrafamilial abusers and, 112, 119
  juvenile prostitutes and, 137
  juvenile sexual abusers and, 151, 152, 153, 154, 155, 160

Social workers/therapists, 289–298
  autonomy and vulnerability of, 291–292
  comfort with talking about sex/own sexuality, 290
  countertransference and, 175, 252, 253, 291, 292–295, 296, 297
  differentiation of self from family of origin and, 291
  empathy and, 252
  individual perspective on, 289–298
  preparing for work, 289–292
  vicarious traumatization and, 295–296
  working within agency, 296–297

Socioeconomic class
  incidence of sexual abuse and, 25

of female prostitutes, 136–137

Sodomy, 5, 14, 148, 208

Special needs
  treatment of offenders with, 264
  vulnerability of child with, 25

Speltz, K., 55

Sperry, L., 182

Spirituality, cultural differences in, 200–201

STDs (sexually transmitted diseases), 139, 198, 209, 217

Steller, M., 220

Stepfathers, 112–113

Stereotypical gender roles, 305

Stern, M., 110

Stewart, C., 250

Stigmatization, of sexually abused victim, 79, 109, 116, 234, 235, 264

Streetwalkers, 136

Stress-inoculation therapy, 282

Substance abuse
  by adult sexual abuse survivors, 275
  by juvenile sexual abusers, 156
  child/juvenile prostitution and, 134, 136, 139
  influence on offending, 96

Suicide/suicide ideation
  abuse by teachers and, 167
  adult sexual abuse survivors and, 275
  as ultimate control, 77
  child/juvenile prostitutes and, 139
  juvenile sexual abusers and, 156
  offenders and, 203
  sexting and, 128

Sullivan, J., 173

Summer of '42 (film), 23

Summer of '42 Syndrome, 23

Summit, R. C., 9–10, 13, 44, 169

Suppression phase, 38–39

Survivors Network of those Abused by Priests (SNAP), 178

Symptoms and indicators of child sexual abuse, 75–77
  behavioral indicators, 76–77
  physical indicators, 75–76, 198

Systems theory, on father-daughter incest, 43–44

Talking cure, 8

Tamraz, D. N., 46

Tanis, H. J., 244

Tardieu, A., 7, 8

Dr. Cynthia Crosson-Tower is a national expert on child abuse and neglect and the author of numerous books and publications including *Understanding Child Abuse and Neglect, Exploring Child Welfare: A Practice Perspective, When Children Are Abused: An Educator's Guide to Intervention, Secret Scars: A Guide for Survivors of Child Sexual Abuse, Homeless Students, A Clergy Guide to Child Abuse and Neglect,* and *How Schools Can Combat Child Abuse and Neglect.* In addition, she has authored several monographs including *Designing and Implementing a School Reporting Protocol: A How-to-Manual for Massachusetts Teachers* for the Children's Trust Fund in Boston and *An Educator's Guide to School Reporting Protocol for Catholic Schools.*

Dr. Crosson-Tower is a Professor Emerita at Fitchburg State University where she taught for 24 years and also founded and served as the Director of the Child Protection Institute there. She also served on the subcommittee to develop protocol for the Cardinal's Commission of the Archdiocese of Boston as part of the church's effort to address the sexual abuse crisis. She later consulted to the Archdiocese as part of the Implementation and Oversight Committee of the Archdiocese's Office of Child Advocacy.

Dr. Crosson-Tower serves on the Board of Directors for NEADS/Dogs for Deaf and Disabled Americans and created the Trauma Assistance Dog Program (TAD) of the Canines for Combat Veterans Program. TAD, for which she now serves as psychiatric consultant, places specially trained service dogs with veterans with post-traumatic stress disorder.

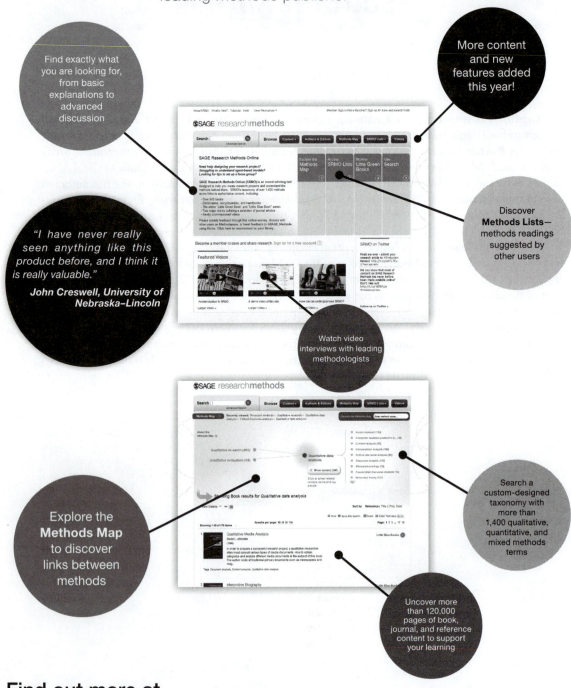